Comprehensive
Perioperative Nursing Review

The Jones and Bartlett Series in Nursing

Adult Emergency Nursing Procedures, Proehl

Basic Steps in Planning Nursing Research, Third Edition, Brink/Wood

Bloodborne Pathogens, National Safety Council

Bone Marrow Transplantation, Whedon

Breastfeeding and Human Lactation, Riordan/Auerbach

Study Guide for Breastfeeding and Human Lactation, Auerbach/Riordan

Cancer Chemotherapy: A Nursing Process Approach, Barton Burke, et al.

Cancer Nursing: Principles and Practice, Third Edition, Groenwald, et al.

Chemotherapy Care Plans, Barton Burke, et al.

Children's Nutrition, Lifshitz, et al.

Chronic Illness: Impact and Intervention, Second Edition, Lubkin

Comprehensive Cancer Nursing Review, Groenwald, et al.

A Comprehensive Curriculum for Trauma Nursing, Bayley/Turcke

Desk Reference for Critical Care Nursing, Wright/Shelton

Drugs and Protocols Common to Prehospital and Emergency Care, Cummings

Emergency Care of Children, Thompson

Essential Medical Terminology, Stanfield

Essentials of Oxygenation, Ahrens/Rutherford

Family Life: Process and Practice, Janosik/Green

Handbook of Oncology Nursing, Johnson/Gross

Health Assessment in Nursing Practice, Third Edition, Grimes/Burns

Health and Wellness, Fourth Edition, Edlin/Golanty

Healthy Children 2000, U.S. Department of Health and Human Services

Healthy People 2000, U.S. Department of Health & Human Services

Human Development: A Life-Span Approach, Fourth Edition, Freiberg

Introductory Management and Leadership for Clinical Nurses, Swansburg

Intravenous Therapy, Nentwich

Introduction to the Health Professions, Stanfield

Introduction to Human Disease, Third Edition, Crowley

Journal of Perinatal Education, ASPO/Lamaze

Management and Leadership for Nurse Managers, Swansburg

Management of Spinal Cord Injury, Second Edition, Zejdlik

Math for Health Professionals, Third Edition, Whisler

Medical Terminology, Stanfield

Memory Bank for Chemotherapy, Second Edition, Preston/Wilfinger

Memory Bank for Critical Care: EKGs and Cardiac Drugs, Second Edition, Ervin

Memory Bank for Hemodynamic Monitoring: The Pulmonary Artery Catheter, Second Edition, Ervin/Long

Memory Bank for Intravenous Therapy, Second Edition, Weinstein

Memory Bank for Medications, Second Edition, Kostin/Sieloff

Mental Health and Psychiatric Nursing: A Caring Approach, Davies/Janosik

The Nation's Health, Third Edition, Lee/Estes

Nursing and the Disabled: Across the Lifespan, Fraley

Nursing Assessment and Diagnosis, Second Edition, Bellack/Edlund

Nursing Diagnosis Care Plans for Diagnosis-Related Groups, Neal/Paquette/Mirch

Nursing Pharmacology, Second Edition, Wallace/Wardell

Nursing Research: A Quantitative and Qualitative Approach, Roberts/Burke

Nursing Research with Basic Statistical Applications, Dempsey/Dempsey

Nutrition and Diet Therapy: Self-Instructional Modules, Second Edition, Stanfield

Oncology Nursing in the Ambulatory Setting, Buchsel/Yarbro

Oncology Nursing Drug Reference, Wilkes, et al.

Oncology Nursing Homecare Handbook, Barton Burke

Oncology Nursing Society's Instruments for Clinical Nursing Research, Frank-Stromborg

Pediatric Emergency Nursing Procedures, Bernardo/Bove

Perioperative Nursing: Principles and Practice, Fairchild

Perioperative Nursing Review, Fairchild et al. *Perioperative Patient Care, Second Edition*, Kneedler/Dodge

Policy Manual for Bloodborne Pathogens, Wetle

A Practical Guide to Breastfeeding, Riordan

Psychiatric Nursing Diagnosis Care Plans for DSM-III-R, Paquette, et al.

Ready Reference for Critical Care, Strawn/Stewart

Understanding/Responding, Second Edition, Long

Women's Health: A Global Perspective, McElmurry/Norr

Comprehensive Perioperative Nursing Review

Susan S. Fairchild, MSN, RN, CNOR, CNS
Assistant Professor of Nursing
Barry University School of Nursing
Miami Shores, Florida

with contributions by

Dr. Shirley Belock, RN, Ed.D., JD, ARNP, C.S.
Professor and Associate Dean
School of Nursing
Florida International University
Miami, Florida

Linda A. Engdahl, MSN, CNOR
Perioperative Clinical Nurse Specialist
Abbott-Northwestern Hospital
Minneapolis, Minnesota

Carmen Gusek Hall, RN, BS, C, CNOR
Perioperative Clinical Education Specialist
Abbott-Northwestern Hospital
Minneapolis, Minnesota

Dr. Kathleen Blais, RN, Ed.D
Director, School of Nursing
Broward Program
Florida International University
Miami, Florida

Dr. Alfredo Ferrari, MD, PA
Department of Anesthesia
Imperial Point Medical Center
Ft. Lauderdale, Florida

Vicki A. Moss, RN, MS, DNSc(c), CNOR
Associate Professor of Nursing
Viterbo College
La Crosse, Wisconsin

Sandra L. Sword, RN, MSHA, CNOR
Director, Surgical Services
Our Lady of the Lakes Medical Center
Baton Rouge, Louisiana

JONES AND BARTLETT PUBLISHERS
Boston   London

Editorial, Sales and Customer Service Offices

Jones and Bartlett Publishers
One Exeter Plaza
Boston, MA 02116

Jones and Bartlett Publishers International
P.O. Box 1498
London W6 7RS
England

ISBN 0-86720-644-6

The selection and dosage of drugs presented in this book are in accord with standards accepted at the time of publication. The authors and publisher have made every effort to provide accurate information. However, research, clinical practice, and government regulations often change the accepted standard in this field. Before administering any drug, the reader is advised to check the manufacturer's product information sheet for the most up-to-date recommendations on dosage, precautions, and contra-indications. This is especially important in the case of drugs that are new or seldom used.

Printed in the United States of America
97 96 95 94 93 10 9 8 7 6 5 4 3 2 1

Contents

Preface

This **Comprehensive Perioperative Nursing Review** guide can be used effectively by nurses preparing for the CNOR examination, by students taking a course in Perioperative Nursing, by teachers preparing for course lectures and discussions, and by others wishing to review or test their knowledge of the subject.

Because Study Outlines in this guide derive from Susan S. Fairchild's text, *PERIOPERATIVE NURSING: Principles and Practice,* users of that text (both teachers and students) may also find this guide a valuable adjunct to the Fairchild text in classes for which it has been adopted. In addition, Chapter 14 of the Fairchild text, which offers a monograph of major surgical procedures and their perioperative nursing implications, can be used to supplement the coverage of this guide.

Each chapter in the guide contains three sections: a **Study Outline**, a set of **Practice Questions**, and **Answer Explanations** for the Practice Questions.

Study Outlines are presented in a highly structured, understandable, and concise format. Key terms, definitions, concepts, and skills are boldfaced for emphasis. Tables and figures are used where appropriate. Throughout, the perioperative nursing implications of surgical practice and the principles of patient care management--information a perioperative nurse will need to know in practice, in class, and on the CNOR examination--have been highlighted.

Practice Questions derive from the outlines and test the user's mastery of information presented in them. The format of these questions is similar to that of the CNOR exam, and items range from simple and factual to challenging and applied. Complementing these questions is the CNOR-type Comprehensive Practice Examination described below.

Answer Explanations serve two important functions: (1) they provide the number of the correct answer to each Practice Question; and (2) they repeat and reinforce information covered in the Study Outlines. These explanations should help clarify points the reader may have overlooked or misunderstood in an outline, especially many important distinctions between closely related terms or concepts.

Practice questions and answers may be used without first reading the outlines, of course. This fact may have special relevance to users who are pressed for time and who wish to spot check their content knowledge in preparation for the CNOR test or a course examination.

In addition to these chapter elements, a **Comprehensive Practice Examination** of 150 board-type test questions has been provided at the end of the guide. The items on this examination, in general, test the perioperative nurse's ability to apply facts and ideas to actual patient care. Many are focused on a specific surgical case or perioperative nursing problem. Like the chapter Practice Questions, answer explanations are given for all examination questions; unlike the chapter items, however, chapter references are also given for most answers. Users of this guide are encouraged to take the examination in a simulated test mode: as if it represented an actual CNOR examination. This means finding a quiet room and allowing approximately 3 hours to complete the exam. (Note, however, that the exam was not prepared under AORN auspices, and results on this exam do not promise similar results on an actual CNOR test. In addition, the CNOR exam contains 200 items and is taken over a four-hour period.)

Purchasers of this guide are encouraged to purchase as well the National Certification Board's own **CNOR Study Guide**, as the two guides complement each other well. Whereas this guide provides a structured and factual overview of perioperative nursing, with supporting test items, the CNOR guide emphasizes perioperative nursing tasks, activities, and case studies, as well as information specific to taking the CNOR exam. Together, the two guides cover most of what a candidate will want to know before entering the exam room.

Please write to the publisher at the following address if you have any comments about the guide or any suggestions for improving its value to perioperative nurses:

Jones and Bartlett Publishers
One Exeter Plaza
Boston, MA 02116

1 Introduction to Perioperative Nursing

STUDY OUTLINE

I. THE BEGINNINGS OF PERIOPERATIVE NURSING

1. Surgery has been described as a planned alteration of the human body designed to (1) arrest, (2) alleviate, or (3) eradicate some pathologic process. This does not adequately define the surgical experience, however, since it does not address the biosocial or psychologic aspects of patient care. **Nursing intervention** has made this definition complete, since as a specialty perioperative nursing has become an important, vital factor in the success of the planned surgical intervention.

2. Perioperative nursing is a natural outgrowth of operating room (O.R.) nursing as it was practiced in early years. But unlike its predecessor, perioperative nursing practice involves caring for the surgical patient during all three phases of surgical intervention.

3. Perioperative nursing is **patient-centered rather than task-oriented**, combining both the physiologic and psychosocial aspects of nursing, which ultimately benefits both the patient and the nurse.

A. THE TEAM CONCEPT IS ESTABLISHED

1. Operating room nursing is the oldest nursing specialty on record. It was a Scottish surgeon, Dr. Joseph Bell, who began to recognize the importance of specialized training for the nurses assisting in the O.R., and thus began the specialty of operating room nursing. However, it was not until the early 1900s that hospital-based nursing programs added a surgery component to their generic curricula, providing students an opportunity to spend 3 to 4 months in the operating room as part of their initial clinical experience.

2. In 1894, at the request of Dr. Hunter Robb, a surgeon at Johns Hopkins, the "Team Concept" for surgical procedures was first introduced as a means for providing quality patient care in the surgical suite.

3. The team consisted of a **senior nurse** in the scrub role, a **junior nurse or student** to assist with dispensing sterile supplies to the surgical field, and a **physician assistant**, usually an intern, trained to assist the attending surgeon, depending on the type of procedure being performed. The senior nurse, who was more experienced in procedures and tasks, became the **scrub or instrument nurse**, while the junior nurse/student performed all other duties required within the procedure room (**circulating nurse**).

4. This team concept remained in effect until 1910, when the American Nurses Association (A.N.A.) wrote a paper describing the need for the senior nurse to function in the circulating role, since the duties required a "more experienced nurse in patient care and aseptic technique." In this paper, the A.N.A. also said the role of the scrub nurse required less experience, since the duties were technically oriented and somewhat mechanical, and did not require any vast nursing experience in surgery. To this day, the role of the circulating nurse is delegated to the profes-

sional registered nurse (R.N.), while the role of the scrub nurse is performed by either an R.N. or a surgical technician.

5. In 1919, the National League for Nursing-Education Committee, who wrote and approved nursing school curricula, established the O.R. rotation as a "worthwhile clinical area" and included in their standard curricula a section on O.R. technique, consisting of 10 hours of theory, 20 hours of bacteriology and surgical diseases, and a 2 to 3 month rotation in surgery, depending on the student/hospital needs.

6. Formal training of the student nurse for surgery did not exist, however, since most of the clinical training was performed by the operating room supervisor, with most of the concepts passed on to the student based on previous practices. By 1933, the National League for Nursing (N.L.N.) had outlined a master curriculum plan for advanced courses in O.R. theory and technique, which served as a model for training O.R. nurses during the next decade.

B. 1940 TO 1960: THE WAR YEARS AND THEIR AFTERMATH

1. World War II was a turning point for operating room nursing and for hospitals in general. With nurses leaving the hospitals and joining the Armed Forces, an acute shortage of nurses was felt, especially in critical areas such as surgery.

2. Since the war had recruited most of the experienced nurses, leaving operating rooms with inadequate personnel for both the scrub and circulating roles, a new member of the O.R. team was created: the **surgical technician**, who was instructed to assist in surgical procedures through an on-the-job training program. Today these technicians, although now classroom trained, continue to function in their original role, with slight expansion depending on the needs of the institution.

3. Since many nursing positions had been filled with nonnursing personnel during the war years, and since the shortage of patient-care nurses still existed, the shift from general practitioners to specialists began to emerge in an attempt to capture lost professional positions within the hospital and operating rooms. Nurses in surgery began to see their roles as leaders, supervisors, and teachers and as professional nurses who accepted the responsibility for all nursing activities performed in the procedure room. By the late 1940s, O.R. nurses managed not only the care of the patient during surgical intervention, but also became managers and administrators of surgical departments, while the role of scrub nurse transferred to the surgical technician.

4. The changes that had started during the immediate post-war years were beginning to affect the future of O.R. nursing, in both the professional and educational arenas. Since surgical technicians could perform the routine duties of the scrub nurse, under the supervision of an R.N., the need to train nurses for the O.R. became the lowest priority of the N.L.N. Consequently, the O.R. rotation was phased out, until by 1949 the O.R. rotation was eliminated from the nursing curriculum and was maintained only by those schools that were hospital-based and/or by instructors who believed it would be beneficial. Even then, it was only for observational purposes; O.R. nursing was no longer a mandatory subject or area of clinical practice.

C. THE EMERGENCE OF OPERATING ROOM NURSING AS A SPECIALTY

1. In January 1949, while the number of nurses specifically trained for surgery was being reduced and as their new role in surgery was emerging, many O.R. nurses believed that it was time to create an organization for their specialty designed to exchange knowledge and ideas. To this end, 17 operating room supervisors from New York City met to establish such an organization, to be called the **Association of Operating Room Nurses (A.O.R.N.)**, which would eventually stimulate O.R. nurses around the country to form similar groups; to share knowledge; to motivate experienced O.R. nurses to teach the neophyte; and to promote and benefit professional operating room nursing to a level of specialization.

2. Because the parent organization, American Nurses Association (A.N.A.), was unwilling to support or offer suggestions for this group, it became apparent that to create an organization that would benefit the operating room nurse, some independent alternatives had to be found. By 1950, through the work of this group, 26 chapters had been formed around the country. In

1956, just 5 short years later, the A.O.R.N. was ready to become a separate professional organization, dedicated to improving professional nursing care in the operating room.

3. In 1957, following an unsuccessful meeting with the A.N.A. Board of Directors, it was decided that the A.O.R.N. should draft a separate charter, making it an independent professional nursing organization with its own national officers and Board of Directors. This decision eventually led to the incorporation of A.O.R.N. the following year, with the national membership of 3200 operating room nurses.

4. Concerned for the future of operating room nurses, and realizing they were about to face their greatest challenge, the A.O.R.N. began to attempt to change the overall perspective of operating room nursing, from the task-oriented profession it had been to a patient-centered profession, and, with input from the A.N.A., the association created the original *Standards of Practice: O.R.* as a basis for sage and effective clinical practice.

5. As the professional operating room nurses' activities expanded, further clarification of the role was needed, and in 1976, a proposal to define further the role of nurses in the operating room was approved by the A.O.R.N. Board of Directors. Two years later (1978), via the efforts of a task force selected by the members, the term **perioperative** was first used to describe the role of the professional nurse during the three phases of surgical intervention: **preoperative, intraoperative,** and **postoperative.**

II.   PERIOPERATIVE NURSING PRACTICE

A.   THE PERIOPERATIVE NURSE'S ROLE

1. In 1978 the first description of perioperative nursing practice was presented to the A.O.R.N. members at the 25th National A.O.R.N. Congress, stating: *The R.N. specializing in Perioperative Nursing practice performs nursing activities in the preoperative, intraoperative, and postoperative phases of the patients' surgical experience.*

2. In addition to the newly defined role, the Nursing Practice Committee of the A.O.R.N. was charged with the responsibility of reviewing and revising the original standards to reflect the new dimension of the perioperative nurses' role. It is these standards that govern and guide the nurse when rendering patient care during the perioperative period.

3. In 1982, the standards were revised as requested, and the definition of perioperative nursing practice was expanded to its current content, stating that perioperative nursing practice begins at an entry level based on clinical expertise and continues on to an advanced level of practice, recognized today as **Certification in Perioperative Nursing Practice (CNOR).**

4. In 1984 and 1985, the Nursing Practice Committee of the A.O.R.N. redefined perioperative nursing practice to reflect more accurately the scope of nursing practice in the operating room: *The registered nurse specializing in perioperative nursing practice performs nursing activities in the preoperative, intraoperative, and postoperative phases of the patient's surgical experience. Registered nurses enter perioperative nursing practice at a beginning level depending on their expertise and competency to practice. As they gain knowledge and skills, they progress on a continuum to an advanced level of practice.*

5. Based on the *Standards and Recommended Practices for Perioperative Nursing--A.O.R.N.*, the operating room nurse provides a continuity of care throughout the perioperative period, using scientific and behavioral practices with the eventual goal of meeting the individual needs of the patient undergoing surgical intervention. This process is dynamic and continuous, and requires constant reevaluation of individual nursing practice in the operating room.

6. Perioperative nursing represents a multifaceted challenge to today's operating room nurse. In this role, the nurse has an opportunity to:
   a. **Prepare the patient and family for surgery.**
   b. **Provide comfort and support to patient and family.**
   c. **Use sound nursing judgment and problem-solving techniques to assure a safe and effective surgical experience.**

7. **Whether scrubbing, circulating, or supervising other team members, the perioperative nurse is always aware of the total environment, as well as the patient's reaction to the environment and**

the care given during all three phases of surgical intervention. The perioperative nurse is knowledgeable about aseptic technique, patient safety, legal aspects of nursing, and the management of nursing activities associated with the specific surgical procedure being performed.

8. Perioperative nursing is unique: it provides a specialty service during the perioperative period that stresses the need for continuity of care and respect for the individuality of the patient's needs.

B. THE PERIOPERATIVE NURSE'S DUTIES AND RESPONSIBILITIES

1. The perioperative nurse is responsible and accountable for the major nursing activities occurring in the surgical suite. These include but are not limited to the following:

   a. Assessing of the patient's physiologic and psychologic status before, during, and after surgery.

   b. Identifying priorities and implementing care based on sound nursing judgment and individual patient needs.

   c. Functioning as a role model of a professional perioperative nurse for students and colleagues.

   d. Functioning as a patient advocate by protecting the patient from incompetent, unethical, or illegal practices during the perioperative period.

   e. Coordinating all activities associated with the implementation of nursing care by other members of the health-care team.

   f. Demonstrating a thorough knowledge of aseptic principles and techniques to maintain a safe and therapeutic surgical environment.

   g. Directing or assisting with the care and handling of all supplies, equipment, and instruments, to ensure their economic and efficient function for the patient and personnel under both normal and hazardous conditions.

   h. Performing as a scrub or circulating nurse as needed, based on knowledge and expertise for a specific procedure.

   i. Participating in continuing education programs directed toward personal and professional growth and development.

   j. Participating in professional organizational and research activities that support and enhance perioperative nursing practice.

III. PROFESSIONALISM AND PERIOPERATIVE NURSING

Nursing is an independent, autonomous, self-regulating profession with the primary function that of helping each person attain the highest possible level of general health...
--M. Schlotfeldt, 1973

1. In 1978, perioperative nursing took on a different look because of a reevaluation of professional nursing practice in the operating room and the practice of nursing in general. Society continued to depict nurses as dependent individuals, even though great strides had been accomplished to change that image.

2. Toward this effort, nursing as a profession moved from an occupation to a profession, which is distinguished by cognitive, normative, and evaluative dimensions. As part of this change, nursing has defined the characteristics and behaviors that are necessary for a profession, including the entry level requirements for nursing education in a university setting. Increased higher education has become a prerequisite for many nurses, including those wishing to practice perioperative nursing.

3. The model of this practice could be likened to a "wheel," in which the "hub" is the basis for professional perioperative nursing practice and each of the "spokes" is a component of that practice, depicting additional, related attributes and characteristics that are inherent to the practice of perioperative nursing, including the nurse's role as caregiver and patient advocate.

IV. THE PRESENT: A NEW CHAPTER

1. In 1985, the Joint Commission for Accreditation of Healthcare Organizations (J.C.A.H.O.), in their accreditation manual, required hospitals to establish a mechanism to assure that quality

patient care was being performed in accordance with the standards of practice currently in force for all nursing areas.

2. In response to this, the A.O.R.N. developed a credentialing model which was used by the J.C.A.H.O. as a basis for nursing practice in the surgical unit, and in 1987 a new chapter was added to the manual, entitled "Surgery and Anesthesia Services," addressing most of the key issues presented by the A.O.R.N. This chapter was intended to serve as a guideline for acceptable, minimal levels of practice, but each operating room and each perioperative nurse is ultimately responsible for assuring quality patient care, the central core of all nursing practice.

3. These basic competency statements were not confined to the hospitalized patient, but to any patient, in any setting, who was about to undergo surgical intervention and/or invasive procedures, including freestanding ambulatory surgical facilities.

4. Additionally, the J.C.A.H.O. issued a separate manual for ambulatory care facilities in 1984, and it too reflects current recommendations for safe, therapeutic nursing intervention for the surgical patient.

PRACTICE QUESTIONS

1. **Perioperative nursing differs in scope from operating room (O.R.) nursing in that it:**

    1. *involves caring for the surgical patient during all three phases of surgical intervention.*

    2. *incorporates the concept of nursing intervention into the surgical experience.*

    3. *delegates the role of the circulating nurse to the professional registered nurse (R.N.), while the role of scrub nurse is performed by either an R.N. or a surgical technician.*

    4. *requires the nurse to manage not only the care of the patient during surgical intervention, but also the surgical department.*

2. **The role of the circulating nurse in an O.R. team is typically performed by a:**

    1. *surgical technician.*

    2. *scrub nurse.*

    3. *registered nurse (R.N.).*

    4. *student nurse.*

3. **Which of the following statements *most* accurately summarizes the status of O.R. nursing during and immediately after World War II?**

    1. *Since O.R. nurses could perform many of the routine duties of surgical technicians, the need to train nurses for the O.R. became an increasingly high priority.*

    2. *The role of the O.R. nurse began to change from the patient-centered profession it had been to a task-oriented profession.*

    3. *By 1949, largely because of the emergence of the surgical technician, O.R. nursing was no longer a mandatory subject in the nursing curriculum.*

    4. *By the late 1940s, the role of the O.R. nurse had shifted from that of manager and administer of surgical departments to manager of patient care during surgical intervention.*

4. **Which of the following statements *most* accurately summarizes the status of the Association of Operating Room Nurses (A.O.R.N.)?**

   1. *It is one of many divisions of the American Nurses Association (A.N.A.) and operates under the charter of that organization.*

   2. *It is an independent professional nursing organization with its own national officers and Board of Directors.*

   3. *It operates in close cooperation with the American Medical Association to set general standards of practice for operating room nursing.*

   4. *It is one of three competing national organizations whose principal function is to improve nursing care in the operating room.*

5. **The overall perspective of operating room nursing began to change in 1957, under the auspices of the newly formed A.O.R.N. Which of the following statements *most* accurately summarizes this change?**

   1. *O.R. nursing became more clearly focused on the intraoperative phase of surgical intervention.*

   2. *O.R. nursing became a more patient-centered and less task-oriented profession.*

   3. *O.R. nursing became less reliant on scientific and behavioral practices to meet the individual needs of patients undergoing surgical intervention.*

   4. *O.R. nursing became less reliant on standards of practice and more reliant on standards of outcome in patient care.*

6. **Which of the following is NOT essential to a valid definition of perioperative nursing?**

   1. *Continuity of care throughout the perioperative period.*

   2. *Commitment to one plan that applies throughout the three phases of surgical intervention.*

   3. *Use of scientific and behavioral practices to meet patient needs.*

   4. *Respect for the individuality of the patient's needs.*

7. **Included among the major responsibilities of the perioperative nurse are all of the following EXCEPT:**

   1. *participation in educational and research activities that support perioperative nursing practice.*

   2. *patient safety, including knowledge of aseptic technique.*

   3. *legal and patient advocacy aspects of perioperative nursing.*

   4. *coordination of all operating room activities related to surgical intervention.*

8. **Nursing is now defined as a profession rather than an occupation. One important aspect of this definition is:**

   1. *increased higher education as a prerequisite for many nurses.*

   2. *society's recognition of nurses as caregivers.*

   3. *accreditation of the A.O.R.N. by the American Nurses Association.*

   4. *adoption of the* <u>Standards of Practice: O.R.</u> *by most hospitals and clinics.*

ANSWER EXPLANATIONS

1. **The answer is 1.** Perioperative nursing is a natural outgrowth of operating room (O.R.) nursing as it was practiced in early years. But unlike its predecessor, perioperative nursing practice involves caring for the surgical patient during all three phases of surgical intervention: preoperative, intraoperative, and postoperative.

2. **The answer is 3.** Initially, in the late 19th century, the O.R. team consisted of senior nurse in the scrub role, a junior nurse or student to assist with dispensing sterile supplies to the surgical field, and a physician assistant, usually an intern, trained to assist the attending surgeon. The senior nurse, who was more experienced in procedures and tasks, became the scrub or instrument nurse, while the junior nurse/student performed all other duties required within the procedure room (circulating nurse). As the team concept evolved, however, the senior nurse began to function in the circulating role, since the duties required a more experienced nurse in patient care and aseptic technique. The scrub nurse required less experience, since the duties were technically oriented and somewhat mechanical, and did not require any vast nursing experience in surgery. Today, the role of the circulating nurse is delegated to the professional registered nurse (R.N.), while the role of the scrub nurse is performed by either an R.N. or a surgical technician.

3. **The answer is 3.** During the war the role of the surgical technician was created to compensate for the shortage of experienced nurses. Since surgical technicians could perform the routine duties of the scrub nurse, under the supervision of an R.N., the need to train nurses for the O.R. became the lowest priority of the National League for Nursing (N.L.N.), whose curriculum model had been in use since the 1930s. Consequently, the O.R. rotation was phased out, until by 1949 the O.R. rotation was eliminated from the nursing curriculum and was maintained only by those schools that were hospital-based and/or by instructors who believed it would be beneficial. Even then, it was only for observational purposes; O.R. nursing was no longer a mandatory subject or area of clinical practice.

4. **The answer is 2.** In 1957, following an unsuccessful meeting with the A.N.A. Board of Directors, it was decided that the fledgling A.O.R.N. should draft a separate charter, making it an independent professional nursing organization with its own national officers and Board of Directors. This decision eventually led to the incorporation of A.O.R.N. the following year, with the national membership of 3200 operating room nurses.

5. **The answer is 2.** Following its incorporation in 1958, the A.O.R.N., concerned for the future of operating room nurses and realizing they were about to face their greatest challenge, began to change the overall perspective of operating room nursing from the task-oriented profession it had been to a patient-centered profession. With input from the A.N.A., the association created the original *Standards of Care: O.R.* as a basis for effective clinical practice.

6. **The answer is 2.** Based on the *Standards and Recommended Practices for Perioperative Nursing--A.O.R.N.*, the operating room nurse provides a continuity of care throughout the perioperative period, using scientific and behavioral practices with the eventual goal of meeting the individual needs of the patient undergoing

surgical intervention. This process is dynamic and continuous, and requires constant reevaluation of individual nursing practice in the operating room.

7. **The answer is 4.** The perioperative nurse is knowledgeable about aseptic technique, patient safety, legal aspects of nursing, and the management of **nursing activities** (but not all O.R. activities) associated with the specific surgical procedure being performed. Specific responsibilities include but are not limited to: assessing the patient's physiologic and psychologic status before, during, and after surgery; functioning as a patient advocate by protecting the patient from incompetent, unethical, or illegal practices during the perioperative period; coordinating all activities associated with the implementation of nursing care by other members of the health-care team; demonstrating a thorough knowledge of aseptic principles and techniques to maintain a safe and therapeutic surgical environment; directing or assisting with the care and handling of all supplies, equipment, and instruments, to ensure their economic and efficient function for the patient and personnel under both normal and hazardous conditions; performing as a scrub or circulating nurse as needed, based on knowledge and expertise for a specific procedure; participating in continuing education programs directed toward personal and professional growth and development; and participating in professional organizational and research activities that support and enhance perioperative nursing practice.

8. **The answer is 1.** Nursing as a profession moved from an occupation to a profession, which is distinguished by cognitive, normative, and evaluative dimensions. As part of this change, nursing has defined the characteristics and behaviors that are necessary for a profession, including the entry level requirements for nursing education in a university setting. Increased higher education has become a prerequisite for many nurses, including those wishing to practice perioperative nursing.

2 The Surgical Setting: Environment and Organization

STUDY OUTLINE

I. **INTRODUCTION**

    1. The modern surgical suite serves four fundamental purposes, and the activities that occur in this area have one common goal: to provide a safe therapeutic environment for the patient undergoing surgical intervention. These purposes are described as:
        a. **To obtain geographic isolation within the hospital, protected from unauthorized persons.**
        b. **To obtain bacteriologic isolation through specific practices, attire, delivery, and disposal systems,** in order to prevent cross-contamination from other areas of the hospital.
        c. **To centralize equipment and supplies,** providing immediate access to specific items needed for surgery without leaving the protected area.
        d. **To centralize specialty personnel,** since modern surgery requires the combined efforts of many groups to perform a variety of specialized tasks.
    2. These four fundamental functions permit surgery to be performed in an isolated, restricted, yet flexible environment, dedicated to the safety of the surgical patient and the personnel working within the suite.

II. **DEMOGRAPHICS OF THE SURGICAL SUITE**

    1. The surgical suite consists of specific areas in which selected tasks are performed. These are the **procedure rooms (operating rooms), storage areas (sterile and nonsterile),** and **ancillary support areas,** such as the preoperative holding/admission area, the postanesthesia care unit (recovery room), and satellite pathology labs within the suite.
    2. **The overall floor plan of a surgical suite is divided into three areas, or zones, which are directly or indirectly involved with the operative procedure, equipment, supplies, or personnel.** For descriptive purposes, the zones represent the type of activities, dress code, or restrictions for that zone, and each person working within the suite must abide by the policies and procedures related to the zone.

A. THE THREE-ZONE CONCEPT

    1. **The unrestricted area**
        a. **The unrestricted area provides an entrance and exit from the surgical suite for personnel, equipment, and patients.** Depending on the physical design of the surgical suite, the **holding/admission area** and the **postanesthesia care unit** may be found in this zone, along with dressing rooms, lounges, offices, and receiving/storage areas for supplies to be used within the surgical suite.
        b. Street clothes are permitted in this area, and the area provides access to communication with personnel within the suite and with personnel and patient's families outside the suite.

2. **The semirestricted area**
   a. **The semirestricted area provides access to the procedure rooms and peripheral support areas within the surgical suite.** Personnel entering this area must be in proper operating-room attire, and traffic control must be designed to prevent violation of this area by unauthorized personnel or persons improperly attired for this zone.
   b. Peripheral support areas consist of storage areas for clean and sterile supplies; a sterilization, processing, and distribution area for instruments and nondisposable equipment; and corridors leading to procedure rooms and substerile utility areas.
3. **The restricted area**
   a. **The restricted area includes the procedure room where surgery is performed and adjacent substerile areas where the scrub sinks and autoclaves are located.** Additional storage for immediate use by the adjacent procedure rooms is also found in the substerile areas, such as blanket/solution warmers, solutions, and so on.
   b. Personnel working in this area must be in proper operating-room attire, including a mask since this area requires maximum protection from possible contamination.
4. **In addition to these three zones, a central administration area, located in any of the three areas, acts as the coordinator for all activities performed within the suite.** This area, commonly referred to as the **nursing core desk** or **surgery desk**, provides continuity, coordination, and communication within the surgical suite.

III. SURGICAL SUITE DESIGN CONCEPTS

1. The design and size of the surgical suite is usually determined by the functions and needs of the institution and the community it serves (e.g., a small rural hospital versus a large metropolitan hospital).
2. A rule of thumb used when planning a surgical suite is based on a formula that recommends that the number of procedure rooms should equal 5 percent of the total number of surgical beds. Additional considerations could include:
   a. Types of surgery being performed.
   b. Type of hospital (teaching, county, private).
   c. Emergency department services provided.
   d. Number of surgeries being performed and the hours in which the service is provided.

A. TRAFFIC PATTERNS: CONTROLLING THE ENVIRONMENT

1. The surgical suite design must conform to the three-zone concept discussed earlier, yet must be able to support the services' needs through established traffic patterns.
2. **Regardless of the design or age of the hospital, specific traffic patterns for personnel, patients, and supplies and equipment must be established to maintain an aseptic environment and provide the services needed to perform safe and effective surgery.**
3. According to the guidelines recommended by the A.O.R.N. for traffic patterns in the surgical suite:
   a. All personnel entering the surgical suite should follow a well-delineated traffic pattern.
   b. Movement of patients, supplies and/or equipment should be along the most direct route that prevents cross-contamination and/or undue exposure by either space or time.
4. **Traffic flow within the surgical suite is based on the principles of asepsis and infection control. In general, traffic flows both in and out of the surgical suite, depending upon the surgical suite design, but within a specific area the flow must be established according to principles that maintain an aseptic environment.**
5. **Ideally, each pattern is unidirectional; that is, the flow of traffic is from entry to exit and from clean to dirty.** However, this concept is ideal, and flexibility, based on acceptable principles, is required to achieve the ultimate goal: *the prevention of cross-contamination from one area to another.*

6. Before entering the surgical suite, visible signs should be posted restricting the area of authorized personnel only, thus reducing the number of persons within the actual suite to those who are directly involved with the activities occurring within the suite.

7. Once inside the suite, traffic patterns should prevent the mixing of clean, sterile, and dirty by maintaining the institution's policies involving patients, supplies, and equipment and personnel.

8. Patients usually enter the suite through the unrestricted area, that is, the holding area, and will wait in that area while preoperative activities are performed, such as the preoperative assessment, the shave prep if ordered, starting preoperative intravenous infusions, and so on.

9. Before entering the semirestricted area, the patient's hair should be covered by a cap, then transported through this area to the restricted area of the suite. Since the patient does not wear a mask in the procedure room, the sterile set-up should be well away from both the head of the table and the entrance to the room, since respiratory droplets, which could lead to contamination of the sterile set-up, travel less than 10 feet, even with forced exhalation.

10. After surgery, the patient will again travel through the semirestricted area to the postanesthesia care unit (PACU), which in some institutions is considered both semirestricted and unrestricted, depending upon its proximity to outside hallways within the institution.

11. If the suite is designed with an inner core/outer core layout, the patient should never be moved through the inner core.

B. SUPPLIES AND EQUIPMENT

1. **Supplies and equipment entering or moving within the surgical suite should also follow a designated traffic pattern. Separation of clean and dirty items is essential to maintain the aseptic environment, just as clean and sterile items must be separated.**

2. Items should be removed from corrugated paper boxes and outside shipping cartons before they enter the surgical suite, since they can be a source for dust and possible vermin, and because the containers have been handled and transported by common carriers working outside the protected area.

3. Equipment coming from outside the area should be damp-dusted with the recommended germinal solution before entering into the semirestricted area of the suite. If clean or sterile supplies are coming from another area (central service), they should be transported to the suite on covered carts; the cover is removed prior to entry into the semirestricted areas.

4. Soiled instruments and items used during a surgical procedure that require reprocessing must leave the procedure room covered or contained in some manner to prevent cross-contamination during transport to the designated area. Soiled items and instruments should never be left next to clean or sterile items for any length of time, and should be decontaminated immediately upon arrival into the decontamination area.

5. Items such as linen and trash should be double-bagged for proper containment, sealed and tied, and taken to a designated area for pick-up and disposal by appropriate personnel.

6. **Most important in the prevention and control of infection is the practice of good handwashing technique by all members of the surgical staff, both between cases and before reentry into the suite from an outside area.** This practice serves to protect both the person and the people working outside the surgical suite.

IV. ENVIRONMENTAL SAFETY

1. **Environment safety is the responsibility of all personnel, and with on-going safety programs and diligent observation and detection methods, the surgical suite can remain a safe environment for both patients and staff.**

2. Five important considerations concerning the internal environment of the surgical suite directly relate to patient safety and infection control:
   a. The size of the procedure room.
   b. Temperature and humidity control.
   c. Ventilation and air exchange systems.

     d.   Electrical safety.
     e.   Communication systems.

A. SIZE OF THE PROCEDURE ROOM

1. The standard procedure room is usually rectangular or square in shape, and should be 20 x 20 x 10 (or similar dimensions) that provide a minimum floor space of 360 square feet, exclusive of fixed cabinets and built-in shelves. The design of the suite should allow for two to four procedure rooms to share a substerile area and scrub facilities, depending on the actual floor plan.
2. Procedure rooms requiring more equipment (e.g., for open heart surgery, neurosurgery, orthopedic surgery) or less equipment (e.g., for endoscopy) will require correspondingly more or less space.
3. Each procedure room should have at minimum the following equipment to ensure maximum efficiency and safety for both patient and staff:
    a. Communication system, internal and external.
    b. Oxygen and vacuum outlets.
    c. Mechanical ventilation assistance equipment.
    d. Respiratory and cardiac monitoring equipment.
    e. X-ray film illumination boxes.
    f. Cardiac defibrillator with synchronization capability (adequate number to service the suite).
    g. High-efficiency particulate air filters.
    h. Adequate room lighting.
    i. Emergency lighting system (battery-powered).
    j. Entry and exit from substerile area for personnel.

B. TEMPERATURE AND HUMIDITY CONTROL

1. **Since most pathogenic bacteria grow best in temperatures close to 98.6° (37° C), the temperature in a procedure room should be maintained between 68°F and 75°F (20°C to 24°C), with humidity levels kept between 50 and 55 percent at all times.** Controlling the internal temperature and humidity at this constant level greatly reduces the chance of growth of microorganisms or the production of static electricity, thus providing a safe environment for both patient and staff.
2. **One exception to this temperature guideline involves preparation for pediatric surgery, which requires that the room be as warm as possible, at least 10 to 15 minutes before the arrival of the patient, since children rapidly lose body heat.**

C. VENTILATION AND AIR EXCHANGE SYSTEMS

1. Airborne contamination can occur in a procedure room; therefore, an effective ventilation and filtration system is one that minimizes this threat to patients and staff.
2. Current recommendations for designing a new procedure room state that the air exchange in each procedure room should be at least 25 air exchanges every hour, and that five of these exchanges should be fresh air.
3. Each procedure room should be maintained with positive pressure, which forces the old air out of the room and prevents the air from surrounding areas from entering into the procedure room. To maintain this positive pressure and reduce the risk of airborne contamination, the doors to the procedure rooms should *always* remain closed.
4. The anesthesia machine should contain an effective scavenging system to rid the air of escaped gases, thus eliminating the exposure of personnel and patient to a low concentration of vapors trapped in the room.
5. If hazardous solutions or materials are required during surgery, a separate evacuation system must be used to eliminate possible exposure to that material or waste product.

D. ELECTRICAL SAFETY

1. **The three most common hazards associated with electricity are fire, burns, and electric shock. The risk of each of these potentially dangerous situations can be greatly reduced by following recommended practices during the preparation, performance, and termination of a surgical procedure.**

2. Faulty wiring, excessive use of extension cords, poorly maintained equipment, and a lack of current safety measures are just some of the hazardous factors that must be constantly checked for by all members of the staff whether they are directly or indirectly involved with patient care activities.

3. All electrical equipment, new or used, should be routinely checked by qualified personnel and certified as safe to use according to national, state, and local safety codes. Equipment that fails to function at 100 percent efficiency should be taken out of service immediately, reported, and removed for repair or replacement as required.

E. COMMUNICATION SYSTEMS, INTERNAL AND EXTERNAL

1. Since each procedure room becomes a separate entity within the suite during the surgical procedure, an effective, reliable means of communication must be established to maintain a safe environment. The system chosen should be capable of separating routine calls from those requiring immediate attention or assistance.

2. In addition, the nursing core desk should have a direct communication link to each procedure room and ancillary area within the suite. Intercoms, telephones, or both provide a means of communication within and outside the suite, and all personnel should be taught how to use the system effectively and efficiently.

V. INFECTION CONTROL: AN OVERVIEW

A. OPERATING ROOM ATTIRE

1. **All personnel entering the semirestricted area of the surgical suite should be in proper O.R. attire.**

2. Operating room attire is an important factor in controlling the potential spread of infection to the surgical patient and to the population outside the protected area. By restricting the clothing worn within the suite, the first barrier to infection has been established, and it is an essential component for the maintenance of an aseptic environment.

3. **The scrub suit**
    a. In accordance with the A.O.R.N. recommended guidelines, the scrub suite should be made of a lint-free, flame-resistant fabric that meets or exceeds the National Fire Prevention Association (N.F.P.A.) standards for proper fabric construction.
    b. The scrub suit top should have short sleeves, and be tucked into the pants to prevent accidental contamination during movement within the restricted area. If scrub dresses are worn, the use of panty hose is required to prevent bacterial shedding from uncovered legs. When donning the scrub attire, care should be taken to avoid contacting the floor with the pants or bottom of the dress.
    c. Scrub attire should be changed daily or when it becomes soiled or wet.
    d. Scrub suits or dresses can be either cloth or paper fabric, as long as the fabric meets the minimum standards as previously stated.
    e. Name tags and protective eye wear are included as part of the proper operating room attire, and circulating nurses and anesthesia personnel should wear jackets to prevent shedding from bare arms.
    f. Jackets should be closed to prevent excess air movement, and removed prior to performing any aseptic procedure, for example, the surgical skin prep, thus avoiding possible contamination of the sterile field.

4. Headgear
   a. **All possible head and facial hair, including sideburns and neckline, should be covered before entering the semirestricted area.**
   b. The scrub cap or hood must be clean and lint-free, and made of a fabric that meets or exceeds the N.F.P.A. standards. The headgear should be donned before the scrub attire to prevent fallout from the hair collecting on the scrub attire. The headgear should be discarded before leaving the surgical suite, and a new one applied prior to reentry into the semirestricted area.

5. Shoe covers
   a. **Shoe covers should be worn by all personnel entering the semirestricted area of the suite.**
   b. Shoes worn during the surgical procedure have a chance of becoming soiled by solutions, blood, and organic debris, and it is extremely difficult to clean contaminated shoes properly. Therefore, shoe cover, or "booties," should be worn over shoes by all personnel whether they are directly or indirectly involved with patient care areas, and changed as needed to prevent tracking of contaminates throughout the suite. Shoe covers should be removed before leaving the suite, and new ones applied prior to reentry into the semirestricted area.

6. Surgical masks
   a. **Since large numbers of potentially pathogenic microorganisms reside in the respiratory tract, a high-filtration mask, covering both the nose and mouth, should be worn at all times while in the procedure rooms or substerile and scrub areas.**
   b. Guidelines for the proper use of masks
      (1) Masks must be changed between each procedure, if it becomes moist or wet, or both.
      (2) While wearing a mask, conversation should be kept to a minimum to prevent moisture build-up.
      (3) Masks should be removed by the strings and properly discarded before leaving the procedure room.
      (4) Masks are *never* worn outside the surgical suite.
      (5) Masks are either *on* or *off*. They should not be left dangling around the neck or placed in a pocket for future use.
      (6) Masks should fit snugly around the nose and chin, and tied securely to prevent accidental slipping during a procedure.

7. **Surgical attire should be worn only within the surgical suite, but if it becomes necessary to leave the suite in O.R. attire, a cover gown must be worn over the scrub attire to protect the front of the suit or dress.** Changing the scrub attire upon reentry into the surgical suite is governed by the institution's policies and procedures for operating room attire.

8. **Wearing jewelry, such as rings, watches, and necklaces, is not recommended since they can harbor bacteria. Earrings should be small (i.e., stud earrings) and must be totally contained within the cap or hood.**

9. **In addition, the Occupational Safety and Health Administration (O.S.H.A.) requires that all members of the staff use protective eye wear if the individual does not use corrective glasses.** Contact lenses do not provide adequate protection for the eyes; therefore, protective eye wear is required for those individuals, including anesthesia personnel.

B. ENVIRONMENTAL SANITATION

1. **Patients should be provided with a safe, clean environment, free from dust and debris.**
2. **Effective environmental sanitation programs must be established to reduce the possibility of cross-contamination, which may lead to surgical wound infections, as well as the protection of personnel within and without the surgical suite. The basis for such a program is the concept of universal precautions, which states that *all patients should be considered potentially contaminated* and therefore treated exactly alike regardless of the procedure being performed.**
3. Although the environment cannot be sterilized, appropriate cleaning and disinfection procedures can reduce the possibility of transmitting pathogens, thus maintaining an aseptic environment. Environmental sanitation practices are performed by all members of the staff who are present

in the suite before, during, and after a surgical procedure, and require constant observation to maintain a safe, therapeutic environment.

4. Careful attention is given to the preparation of a procedure room by the surgical team, and the principles of contain and control become of primary importance to all personnel associated with the surgical procedure. Methods used to accomplish this goal should include:
    a. Containment in clear plastic bags of soiled sponges during the procedure.
    b. Double-bagging all soiled linen and disposable items before their removal at the conclusion of the procedure.
    c. Immediate cleaning with an effective disinfectant solution of spills and debris from floors and walls.
    d. Removing soiled shoe covers before leaving the procedure room, thus eliminating the "tracking" effect within the suite.

5. **In addition to these general recommendations, specific procedures should be used before and after each surgery and before the first case of the day. These are referred to as preliminary, interim, and terminal cleaning procedures.** In addition, a weekly and/or monthly cleaning program should be established by environmental services personnel.
    a. **Preliminary cleaning**
        (1) **Proper preparation of the procedure room before the first case is essential to an effective surgical outcome.** It is the responsibility of the scrub and circulating nurses to see that everything is ready prior to the acceptance of a patient.
        (2) To avoid unnecessary clutter, furniture and equipment not expressly required for the procedure should be removed. Before bringing in the selected surgical supplies for the case, horizontal surfaces should be damp-dusted with a hospital-approved disinfectant solution. Damp-dusting reduces viable microbial contamination from air and other sources by 90 to 99 percent. Adequate containers, properly lined, should be available and placed well away from the sterile field to avoid possible contamination during the set-up phase.
        (3) During the procedure, all efforts must be made to contain and confine the contaminated items. If an instrument falls to the floor, and requires immediate sterilization, the item should be washed first to reduce the number of contaminated microorganisms on the instrument.
        (4) At the conclusion of the case, gross soil and debris should be removed from the instruments if necessary, and the tray covered and taken to the appropriate area for decontamination and reprocessing.
        (5) If a case cart system is used, all reusable items and equipment are placed inside the cart. The cart is closed and taken to the decontamination area. The cart should be emptied and then washed with disinfectant solution or cleaned in an automatic steam cart washer system before it is restocked with items for the next procedure.
    b. **Interim cleaning**
        (1) **After the surgical procedure, all items that have come in contact with the patient or sterile field should be considered contaminated.** Interim cleaning of the procedure room is performed at the end of each case, using an established protocol. Wet vacuuming is the method of choice for cleaning the floors since it is more effective than manual cleaning methods. If the wet-mop method is used, the mop head and disinfectant solution *must* be changed after each case and properly disposed of according to hospital policy.
        (2) **Adequate time must be allowed for proper disinfection and set-up of the procedure room.** Environmental services personnel, working within the suite to assist the surgical team, must be thoroughly knowledgeable about aseptic technique and proper methods used during the interim cleaning process, and should be supervised during the procedure to ensure maximum efficiency. With a well-coordinated team effort, turnover time between procedures can be accomplished in an average of 15 to 20 minutes.
    c. **Terminal cleaning**
        (1) **At the conclusions of the day's schedule, each procedure room, scrub/utility area, corridors, furnishings and equipment should be terminally cleaned.**

(2) All furniture is thoroughly cleaned with an appropriate disinfectant. Casters and wheels should be cleaned, and debris, such as suture strands, removed. Horizontal surfaces should be cleaned; ceiling and wall fixtures and tracks are cleaned on all surfaces. Floors are flooded after the furniture has been removed, and a thorough wet-vacuuming is performed along with spot removal from the walls as needed. Once the floor is dry, the furniture is replaced and clean linen is placed on the O.R. table.

(3) The cabinets in the room should be restocked with sterile supplies, with the cleaning personnel being careful to rotate the stock of "in-hospital" sterilized items to reduce the risk of using "outdated" sterile supplies. Avoidance of overstocking shelves will assist in easy retrieval of the items when needed.

d. **Weekly and/or monthly cleaning**

(1) **In addition to the routine daily cleaning procedures, a weekly and/or monthly cleaning program, set up with environmental services personnel, should be established in the surgical suite.** It should include thorough cleaning of ceilings, walls, floors, air-conditioning grills, sterilizers, and solution dispensers. Kick buckets should be washed and sterilized, and the cleaning equipment routinely used should be disassembled and disinfected.

VI. ORGANIZATIONAL STRUCTURE: THE TEAM CONCEPT

1. Surgery is a complex field that requires a coordinated, well-directed team effort. There are three basic objectives of surgical patient care, and each team member plays a vital role in achieving these objectives:

   a. **The delivery of a physiologically and psychologically prepared patient for the planned surgical experience.**

   b. **The safe, efficient, and therapeutic alleviation of the patient's problem based on sound scientific knowledge and proficiency in technique.**

   c. **The careful guidance of the patient's immediate postoperative care in order to minimize the possibility of future problems or complications.**

2. These objectives are partially met in the clinical unit during the preoperative phase, and in the postanesthesia care unit (PACU) immediately following surgery. But it is during the intraoperative phase that the surgical team provides much of the care necessary to meet the stated objectives of surgical patient care successfully.

3. The surgical team, usually consisting of the **surgeon,** his or her **assistant,** the **scrub nurse/ technician,** the **circulating nurse,** and the **anesthesiologist/anesthesia clinician** (nurse anesthetist), must coordinate their efforts if the surgical experience is to be successful and therapeutic. Although each team member has specific duties and responsibilities, one member cannot function efficiently without the assistance and support of the others.

VII. THE DEPARTMENT OF SURGERY

A. ADMINISTRATIVE STRUCTURE

1. The **Operating Room Supervisor/Nurse Manager** is responsible for the clinical aspects of the surgical suite in addition to its day-to-day management, including the delegation, planning, staffing, and directing of nursing activities occurring in the area.

2. Additional nursing management personnel include, but are not limited to:

   a. Head nurse.

   b. Assistant head nurses (specialty coordinators).

   c. Clinical nurse specialist (education/management).

   d. Team leaders.

3. The position titles and responsibilities will vary with each institution and hospital, depending on its size and organizational structure, but the goal is the same: **to render quality patient care during all three phases of surgical intervention.**

B. ADMINISTRATIVE PRACTICES

1. Two sets of A.O.R.N. administrative standards--the *Standards and Recommended Practices for Perioperative Nursing Practice* and the *Standards of Administrative Practices: O.R.*--are intended to serve as guidelines for the development of a successful program that will provide efficiency while promoting professional perioperative nursing care through research, education, and effective management skills.

2. The former set of standards consists of the following:
    a. A philosophy, purpose and objectives shall be formulated to guide operating room services.
    b. An organizational plan for the operating room shall be developed and communicated.
    c. A registered nurse shall be authorized with administrative accountability and responsibility for the operating room services.
    d. The registered nurse administrator shall be accountable and responsible for developing mechanisms that assure optimal patient care.
    e. The operating room management team shall develop and manage the budget for operating room services.
    f. The operating room service shall have written standards of nursing practice.
    g. The operating room services shall have written policies and procedures that serve as operational guidelines.
    h. The operating room management team shall be responsible for establishing staffing requirements, selecting personnel, and planning for appropriate utilization of human resources.
    i. Staff development program shall be provided for operating room personnel.
    j. A safe operating room environment shall be established, controlled and consistently monitored.
    k. The operating room management team shall promote the discovery and integration of new knowledge by encouraging development and use of nursing research.
    l. The operating room staff shall maintain appropriate documentation related to OR activities.
    m. The operating room management team shall recognize a professional responsibility to promote, provide and participate in a learning environment for students in health care disciplines.
    n. There shall be a quality assurance program for operating room services.

VIII. FUNCTIONS OF THE SURGICAL TEAM

1. **The surgeon**
    a. A physician who has specialized in the practice of surgery. Major responsibilities include, but are not limited to:
        (1) Performance of the operative procedure according to the needs of the patient.
        (2) The primary decision maker regarding surgical technique to use during the procedure (instruments, sutures, etc.).
        (3) May assist with positioning and prepping the patient or may delegate this task to other members of the team.
2. **The first assistant to the surgeon**
    a. May be a resident, intern, physicians' assistant, or a perioperative nurse.
    b. Assists with retracting, hemostasis, suturing, and any other tasks requested by the surgeon to facilitate speed while maintaining quality during the procedure.
3. **The anesthesiologist**
    a. A physician who specializes in the administration and monitoring of anesthesia while maintaining the overall well-being of the patient.
4. **The nurse anesthetist (anesthesia clinician)**
    a. The nurse anesthetist or anesthesia clinician is an advanced registered nurse practitioner who after additional training and certification in anesthesia (the Certified Registered Nurse Anesthetist [C.R.N.A.]) may administer and monitor the anesthesia using the anesthesiologist as a consultant if necessary.

5. **The scrub assistant**
   a. May be either a nurse or surgical technician.
   b. Responsible for assisting the surgeon and assistant with instrumentation, set-ups, suture presentation, sponges, etc., while maintaining the sterility of the surgical field through aseptic practices.
   c. Key elements for successful implementation of this role is based on knowledge of anatomy and the sequence of the surgical procedure, to facilitate and anticipate the needs of the surgeon and the assistant.
6. **The circulating nurse**
   a. Must be a registered nurse who, after additional education and training, is specialized in perioperative nursing practice.
   b. Responsible and accountable for all activities occurring during a surgical procedure, including equipment, supplies, and the environment during a surgical procedure, and managing the flow of information to and from the surgical team members scrubbed at the field.
   c. Patient advocate, teacher, research consumer, leader, and role model.
   d. May be responsible for monitoring the patient during local procedures if a second perioperative nurse is not available.
7. **Paraprofessional/ancillary positions**
   a. In addition to the above team members, the ancillary staff personnel play a vital role in the day-to-day functioning of the surgical suite. These positions include, but are not limited to:
      (1) Sterilization, processing and distribution (S.P.D.) technicians (instrument room aides).
      (2) Orderlies/nursing assistants.
      (3) Environmental services personnel.
      (4) Clerical personnel.
   b. Although these positions are not directly involved with surgery itself, they are invaluable in preparing and maintaining supplies, equipment, and the environment and in generally assisting the nursing staff before, during, and after the surgical procedure.

IX. NURSING MANAGEMENT

A. A CONCEPTUAL OVERVIEW

1. **Management, or supervision, can be described as the process of getting work done with and by others proficiently and within given constraints, such as budget or available human resources.**
2. In surgery, as in any other area of nursing practice, all nurses are leaders and managers of patient care to some degree; either in an appointed role or in one the individual has assumed.

B. ROLE DEFINITIONS

1. **Leadership**
   a. **Leadership is the effective use of skills that can influence or motivate others to perform to their fullest potential.**
   b. The leadership process influences the actions of a person or group to attain stated desired goals. It is dependent upon effective interpersonal skills, mutual respect, and mutually satisfying action and/or results for both the leader and the follower.
   c. Leadership can occur in two distinct forms:
      (1) **Informal leadership,** in which a person or team member is chosen by a group, but who is not specifically designated and who lacks formal authority, yet still influences group decision-making processes.
      (2) **Formal leadership,** in which a person who is by virtue of education and preparation appointed to the position and is given official authority to act and make decisions in the name of the organization or department.

2. **Management**
   a. **Management, or supervision, is described as the ability to get things done, making use of human, technical, and physical resources, while providing guidance and directing people toward the organization's goals.**
   b. The management process consists of accomplishing organizational objectives through four distinct, yet integrated, functions: (1) planning, (2) organizing, (3) directing, and (4) controlling human, physical, and technical resources.
   c. Management is a series of inputs and outputs; inputs occur through the use of human, physical, and technical resources, while outputs are the realization of specific goals.
   d. Leadership is usually a prerequisite to effective management: management requires a more global responsibility, while leadership is recognized as the "change-factor", assisting management in achieving stated goals.

C. **LEADERSHIP AND MANAGEMENT: SIMILARITIES AND DIFFERENCES**

   1. Although similar, leadership and management are different, not only in their official status but also in their overall effect.
      a. The leader, whether formal or informal, can command power and authority only as long as there are followers, and may or may not have the ability to be an effective manager. The perioperative nurse, by virtue of his or her educational preparation, is the natural "leader" within the surgical environment, and therefore must project a positive role model for others to follow.
      b. Managers, on the other hand, have the power and authority to command action from individuals, owing to their position within the organization, but they may or may not be effective leaders if they lack the ability to achieve their goals due to a weak interrelationship with the group.
      c. To be successful, one has to blend qualities of both the leader and the manager, so that the followers continue to be influenced by them, by choice. This concept is applicable not only in business, but can be applied to perioperative nursing practice.
      d. While leadership is an art, management is a science, deriving its basis from educational preparation consisting of sociologic and technical skills. Each can enhance the other in daily practice.
   2. Sullivan and Decker (1985) describe management as having six basic yet essential responsibilities:
      a. **Planning:** Short- and long-term objectives and goals for a specific area or group of people within that area that are designed to complement the institution's philosophy and meet the needs of the individuals working within the department.
      b. **Staffing:** To select the appropriate staff members to meet the goals and objectives stated, and to place them in appropriate positions so that implementation is effective.
      c. **Organizing:** The effective use of human and material resources to achieve maximum efficiency to accomplish the stated goals and objectives.
      d. **Directing:** Involves leadership and motivation so that the selected personnel can accomplish the institutional/department objectives.
      e. **Controlling:** Relies on the use of criteria or standards of performance and the corrective actions needed when personnel deviate from the acceptable standards, policies, or regulations of the institution and/or department.
      f. **Decision-making:** Relies on the ability to identify problems and search for alternative solutions to correct the problem.

D. **FACTORS AFFECTING THE NURSE MANAGER**

   1. Six common factors can ultimately affect the nurse managers' effectiveness:
      a. **Institutional structure**
         (1) Authority and power (where and how much)
         (2) Centralization versus decentralization concepts

        (3) Recruitment and selection system

        (4) Reward system/clinical ladders

   b. Social structure

        (1) Role conflicts

        (2) Organizational climate

        (3) Philosophy

   c. Staffing

        (1) Group process/cohesiveness

        (2) Motivation

        (3) Change factors

   d. Tasks/technology

        (1) Personnel requirements

        (2) Work environment

        (3) Educational support

   e. Organizational objectives

        (1) Realistic

        (2) Dynamic

        (3) Participation in research

   f. Environmental factors

        (1) Economic climate

        (2) Legal restraints

        (3) Physical layout and design

2. The transition from a clinical role to a managerial role calls for learning and practicing a new set of skills. Nurses are not prepared for management during their initial educational preparation, so they must learn the necessary skills for effective leadership/management roles as they pursue higher education.

3. In the day-to-day practice of nursing, perioperative nurses are required to use management skills as they provide quality patient care during the surgical experience. This type of management is based on decision-making processes, which can determine the right approach to manage safely and effectively the patient and the environment.

E. MANAGEMENT AND LEADERSHIP STYLES

1. There are many theories and styles of management, some that are effective and others that may not always be successful, depending on their application.

   a. A new manager and/or leader should be familiar with the essential elements of each style, and decide which style is comfortable and yet still produce the best results.

   b. Experienced managers need to reassess their own management styles occasionally to evaluate the effectiveness of their current management practices and/or modify the style as needed. Such reassessment is necessary to accomplish the overall goals and objectives of the department and/or the organization.

2. According to Douglas (1988), there are four management styles, each with its own individual strengths and weaknesses.

   a. Authoritarian/autocratic style

        (1) Managers who use the authoritarian style make all decisions *alone*, never involving others in the process. This usually results in lack of group support or respect for the position of the manager. Such managers usually exhibit a low opinion of the workers, and feel that they (the worker) must be controlled to accomplish requested tasks.

        (2) Many situations require this style of management owing to the nature of the task required or requested, but it should not be the only style used if the manager is seeking to establish a cohesive, satisfied group.

   b. Democratic/consultative style

        (1) The democratic style is also known as **participative management**, and emphasizes team work, open communication, and group dynamics.

(2) By using this style, the leader or manager becomes people-oriented rather than task-oriented. There is a mutual responsiveness to meeting group goals, and the manager/leader serves as a consultant when decisions affecting the group need to be made.

   c. **Permissive style**

     (1) Also known as **laissez-faire managers**, permissive managers usually have no established goals, and do not lead. They *assume* that the staff is self-motivated and that the job will be done with or without direction or control

     (2) This is directly opposite to the autocratic style of management, and can be highly effective, but only when used with motivated professional groups. It is rarely successful when the institution, or top management, believes in a highly structured, controlled management style.

   d. **Multicratic style**

     (1) In the multicratic management style, the positive aspects of the traditional styles just mentioned are combined to produce a flexible approach to management.

     (2) Since operating room nursing is a team effort, the perioperative nurse manager and/or leaders need to have an understanding of group dynamics, develop effective communication skills and interpersonal relationships, and be able to apply this knowledge to develop a supportive climate that fosters group cohesiveness and positive change.

X. ROLE ASSESSMENT

A. A MANAGER'S PERCEPTION

1. Management should be thought of as building relationships with people, since management is people-oriented, whether it involves encouraging growth of key personnel or managing patient care. It is people working *with* people for the good of the organization and/or the improvement of nursing practice and patient care standards.

2. Many times, just the mere presence of a person suggests that they are a manager, possibly by the way they communicate, act, or react with and to people. They possess a quality known as **charisma**; such people usually accomplish what they need to with the help of other people.

B. DESIRED CHARACTERISTICS IN A MANAGER

1. Many successful managers possess certain characteristics that enable them to be effective, including:

   a. Being able to make decisions.

   b. Being able to praise honestly and sincerely.

   c. Being able to think independently.

   d. Looking at the global picture before making decisions.

   e. Listening and hearing what people are saying.

   f. Delegating and allowing those delegated to do the job and grow at the same time.

   g. Being self-motivated, dynamic, and willing to take constructive criticism, in order to grow.

2. A manager is there to facilitate learning and growth for the staff and ultimately for the organization. For the process to be successful, however, open lines of communication and an open-door policy must be in force. If the manager is inaccessible or unapproachable, the group cohesiveness will break down, which can result only in failure to accomplish the goals that were originally established by the organization and/or staff.

C. THE DICHOTOMY OF MANAGEMENT

1. Although nurses routinely make management-type decisions involving the quality of patient care, not everyone is management (administrative) material, and here lies the dichotomy: *All nurses manage patient care, but not all nurses should be managers.* There is absolutely nothing wrong with this, since nursing, as a profession, requires a *team* effort of both clinicians and managers to deliver effectively quality patient care.

2. Although theories and styles can and should be learned, the individual must decide which aspect of nursing accomplishes his or her individual goals and objectives, and being the best clinician in a specific area or setting is just as important as being a successful manager.

D. IMPACTS OF COST-EFFECTIVE MANAGEMENT ON EDUCATION

1. **The educator or clinical nurse specialist is an important component of the management team, and is essential in maintaining quality patient care in a rapidly changing and highly technical environment.** In institutions that promote education, management will be more successful and efficient. If not, it is the manager's job to promote education by stressing its contribution to the organization and the staff.
2. Unfortunately, when budget cuts are requested, the first or second position to be eliminated is the educator, since that position is not usually perceived as being directly involved with patient care, nor does it generate revenue for the department. However, this assumption is what can cause the majority of unforeseen problems, for without education, a direct link to cost-effective and proficient management is in jeopardy, especially in surgery.
3. It is the successful manager who recognizes the need for continuing quality education, since through this process the staff not only knows what to do, but more importantly, how to do it effectively and safely. A dynamic education program in surgery can save the department and organization unnecessary expenses in the areas of:
    a. Recruitment and retention of staff.
    b. Efficiently managing highly technical equipment.
    c. Producing patient and physician satisfaction.
    d. Maintaining an awareness of new technologies and maintenance of quality patient care as required by accrediting bodies.
    e. Promoting enhancement of professionalism through an on-going learning process, whether self-motivated or directed through formalized educational programs.

PRACTICE QUESTIONS

1. **The modern surgical suite serves several important functions, with the overall purpose of providing a safe therapeutic environment for the patient undergoing surgical intervention. Which of the following is NOT one of these functions?**

    1. *To obtain geographic isolation within the hospital, protected from unauthorized persons.*

    2. *To obtain bacteriologic isolation through specific practices, attire, delivery, and disposal systems, in order to prevent cross-contamination from other areas of the hospital.*

    3. *To decentralize equipment and supplies, in order to reduce the risk that contamination will be spread by means of a single contaminated source.*

    4. *To centralize specialty personnel, since modern surgery requires the combined efforts of many groups to perform a variety of specialized tasks.*

2. **A nurse enters the admission room of the surgical suite without proper operating-room attire. Which of the following policies is *most* likely to apply in this case?**

    1. *Street clothes are permitted in this area.*

    2. *Traffic control in this area must be designed to prevent violation of this area by persons improperly attired for this zone.*

    3. *All personnel entering this area must be in proper operating-room attire; masks are optional.*

    4. *All personnel entering this area must be in proper operating-room attire, including masks.*

3. **Which of the following factors is LEAST likely to influence the design and size of the surgical suite?**

    1. *The types of surgery being performed.*

    2. *The type of hospital in which surgery is being performed.*

    3. *The number of surgeries being performed.*

    4. *The number of surgical zones in the suite.*

4. **The flow of traffic within the surgical suite is designed to meet which ultimate objective?**

    1. *Optimal ease of entry and exit by surgical personnel.*

    2. *Allowing the patient to be moved to the inner core of the surgical suite without passing through the outer core.*

    3. *Prevention of cross-contamination from one area of the surgical suite to another.*

    4. *Segregation of the patient from all surgical equipment and supplies.*

5. **Preoperative activities, including preoperative assessment, shave prep, and starting preoperative intravenous infusions, typically take place in which of the following areas of the surgical suite?**

    1. *Unrestricted area.*

    2. *Semirestricted area.*

    3. *Restricted area.*

    4. *Either the semirestricted or restricted area, depending on the type of hospital.*

6. **The *most* important means of prevention and control of infection in the surgical suite is:**

    1. *germicidal damp-dusting of all surgical equipment entering the semirestricted area of the suite.*

    2. *good handwashing technique by all members of the surgical staff.*

    3. *separation of clean and dirty items in the surgical suite.*

    4. *covering or containing all soiled instruments and items used during a surgical procedure to prevent cross-contamination during transportation.*

7. **The ideal temperature and humidity ranges for the surgical procedure room are, respectively:**

    1. *temperature, 68-75°; humidity, 50-55 percent.*

    2. *temperature, 82-86°; humidity, 75-80 percent.*

3. *temperature, 58-65°; humidity, 25-40 percent.*

4. *temperature, 78-82°; humidity, 10-15 percent.*

8. **Which of the following is essential to an effective ventilation and filtration system in the surgical procedure room?**

    1. *Moderate temperature and low humidity.*

    2. *A single system that handles both normal airborne contamination and hazardous airborne materials.*

    3. *Doors in an open position to allow for maximum air exchange.*

    4. *Maintenance of positive air pressure.*

9. **Maintenance of an aseptic environment in the surgical suite is accomplished by means of several measures involving the scrub suit. Which of the following is NOT one of these measures?**

    1. *Scrub attire should be changed if it becomes soiled or wet.*

    2. *The scrub suit top should be tucked into the pants.*

    3. *Jackets should be donned prior to performing any aseptic procedure.*

    4. *Name tags and protective eye wear should be worn.*

10. **Which of the following standards of practice governs the use of headgear within the surgical suite?**

    1. *Headgear should not be discarded or changed prior to reentry into semirestricted area.*

    2. *Headgear should be donned before the scrub attire to prevent fallout from the hair collecting on the scrub attire.*

    3. *To prevent moistening of the mask, beards should not be covered by headgear.*

    4. *All possible head and facial hair, including sideburns and neckline, should be covered after leaving the semirestricted area.*

11. **Under which of the following conditions should a surgical mask *always* be changed between procedures?**

    1. *If the mask slipped during the procedure.*

    2. *If hazardous materials have been released into the procedure room during the procedure.*

    3. *If the mask becomes moist or wet.*

    4. *If conversation has taken place during the procedure.*

12. **The concept of universal precautions, applied to the surgical suite environment, states that:**

    1. *traffic flow in the surgical suite should always be unidirectional.*

    2. *all patients should be considered potentially contaminated.*

3. *the patient's personal safety must be maintained at all costs.*

4. *specific sanitation procedures should be used before and after all surgical cases.*

13. **Among the surgical suite cleaning procedures that should be followed before the first case of the day are all of the following EXCEPT:**

    1. *Furniture and equipment not expressly required for the procedure should be removed.*

    2. *Before bringing in the surgical supplies for the case, horizontal surfaces should be damp-dusted with a hospital-approved disinfectant solution.*

    3. *Properly-lined containers should be placed within the sterile field to avoid contamination during the procedure.*

    4. *At the conclusion of the case, gross soil and debris should be removed from the instruments if necessary.*

14. **Which of the following pairs, all relating to environmental sanitation of the surgical suite, is IMPROPERLY matched?**

    1. *Preliminary cleaning: containment and confinement of contaminated items during the procedure.*

    2. *Interim cleaning: wet vacuuming of floors following the conclusion of each case.*

    3. *Terminal cleaning: washing and sterilizing walls and ceilings at the end of each day.*

    4. *Weekly/monthly cleaning: disassembling and disinfecting equipment routinely used in procedures.*

15. **The day-to-day management of the surgical suite, including the delegation, planning, staffing, and directing of nursing activities, is a primary responsibility of the:**

    1. *head nurse.*

    2. *clinical nurse specialist.*

    3. *surgeon.*

    4. *O.R. supervisor/nurse manager.*

16. **As a member of the surgical team, a perioperative nurse might occupy any of the following roles EXCEPT that of:**

    1. *first assistant to the surgeon.*

    2. *circulating nurse.*

    3. *scrub assistant.*

    4. *anesthesiologist.*

17. **In helping the O.R. supervisor achieve his or her stated management goals, a scrub nurse is *most* likely to be exercising:**

    1. *the management function of directing.*

    2. *informal leadership.*

3. *the management function of controlling.*

4. *formal leadership.*

18. **As an O.R. supervisor, you rely principally on a management style that emphasizes team work, open communication, and group dynamics. Your style of management is known as the:**

1. *authoritarian/autocratic style.*

2. *democratic/consultative style.*

3. *permissive style.*

4. *multicratic style.*

19. **Which of the following statements *best* summarizes the role of the perioperative nurse in the management of the operating room?**

1. *All perioperative nurses manage patient care and therefore function as both clinicians and administrators.*

2. *The perioperative nurse is primarily a clinician and therefore should not be expected to manage.*

3. *All perioperative nurses manage patient care, but not all should be managers (administrators).*

4. *The perioperative nurse is primarily a manager and therefore should not be expected to be a clinician.*

20. **According to this guide, the key to cost-effective, proficient patient-care management in surgery is:**

1. *research.*

2. *leadership.*

3. *money.*

4. *education.*

ANSWER EXPLANATIONS

1. **The answer is 3.** In addition to the functions stated in 1, 2, and 4, the surgical suite allows equipment and supplies to be centralized. This provides immediate access to specific items needed for surgery without leaving the protected area. These four fundamental functions permit surgery to be performed in an isolated, restricted, yet flexible environment, dedicated to the safety of the surgical patient and the personnel working within the suite.

2. **The answer is 1.** Depending on the physical design of the surgical suite, the admission area and the postanesthesia care unit may be found in the **unrestricted area (zone)** of the suite, along with dressing rooms, lounges, offices, and receiving/storage areas for supplies to be used within the surgical suite. In the three-zone concept of the surgical suite, the unrestricted area provides an entrance and exit from the suite for personnel, equipment, and patients. For descriptive purposes, the zones represent the type of activities, dress code, or restrictions for that zone, and each person working within the suite must abide by the policies and procedures related to the zone. Street clothes are permitted in the unrestricted zone, and the area provides access to communication with personnel and patient's families outside the suite.

3. **The answer is 4.** The design and size of the surgical suite is usually determined by the functions and needs of the institution and the community it serves (e.g., a small rural hospital versus a large metropolitan hospital). A rule of thumb used when planning a surgical suite is based on a formula that recommends that the number of procedure rooms should equal 5 percent of the total number of surgical beds. Additional considerations include the types of surgery being performed, the type of hospital (teaching, county, private), emergency department services provided, and the number of surgeries being performed and the hours in which the service is provided.

4. **The answer is 3.** Traffic flow within the surgical suite is based on the principles of asepsis and infection control. In general, traffic flows both in and out of the surgical suite, depending upon the surgical suite design, but within a specific area the flow must be established according to principles that maintain an aseptic environment. Ideally, each pattern is unidirectional; that is, the flow of traffic is from entry to exit and from clean to dirty. However, this concept is ideal, and flexibility, based on acceptable principles, is required to achieve the ultimate goal: the prevention of cross-contamination from one area to another.

5. **The answer is 1.** Patients usually enter the suite through the unrestricted (holding) area, and will wait in that area while preoperative activities are performed, such as the preoperative assessment, the shave prep if ordered, starting preoperative intravenous infusions, and so on.

6. **The answer is 2.** Most important in the prevention and control of infection is the practice of good handwashing technique by all members of the surgical staff, both between cases and before reentry into the suite from an outside area. This practice serves to protect both the person and the people working outside the surgical suite. The other practices listed (1, 3, and 4) are also important and contribute to the maintenance of an aseptic surgical suite environment.

7. **The answer is 1.** Since most pathogenic bacteria grow best in temperatures close to 98.6°F (37°C), the temperature in a procedure room should be maintained between 68°F and 75°F (20°C to 24°C), with humidity levels kept between 50 and 55 percent at all times. Controlling the internal temperature and humidity at this constant level greatly reduces the chance of growth of microorganisms or the production of static electricity, thus providing a safe environment for both patient and staff. One exception to this temperature guideline involves preparation for pediatric surgery, which requires that the room be as warm as possible, at least 10 to 15 minutes before the arrival of the patient, since children rapidly lose body heat.

8. **The answer is 4.** Airborne contamination can occur in a procedure room; therefore, an effective ventilation and filtration system is one that minimizes this threat to patients and staff. Each procedure room should be maintained with positive pressure, which forces the old air out of the room and prevents the air from surrounding areas from entering into the procedure room. To maintain this positive pressure and reduce the risk of airborne contamination, the doors to the procedure rooms should always remain closed. If hazardous solutions or materials are required during surgery, a separate evacuation system must be used to eliminate possible exposure to that material or waste product.

9. **The answer is 3.** Jackets should be closed to prevent excess air movement, and **removed prior to performing any aseptic procedure,** for example, the surgical skin prep, thus avoiding possible contamination of the sterile field. The scrub suit top should have short sleeves, and be tucked into the pants to prevent accidental contamination during movement within the restricted area. If scrub dresses are worn, the use of panty hose is required to prevent bacterial shedding from uncovered legs. When donning the scrub attire, care should be taken to avoid contacting the floor with the pants or bottom of the dress. Scrub attire should be changed daily or when it becomes soiled or wet. Name tags and protective eye wear are included as part of the proper operating room attire, and circulating nurses and anesthesia personnel should wear jackets to prevent shedding from bare arms.

10. **The answer is 2.** Head and facial hair should be covered **before** entering the semirestricted area. Headgear should be discarded before leaving the surgical suite, and a new one applied prior to reentry into the semirestricted area.

11. **The answer is 3.** Since large numbers of potentially pathogenic microorganisms reside in the respiratory tract, a high-filtration mask, covering both the nose and mouth, should be worn at all times while in the procedure rooms or substerile and scrub areas. Guidelines for the proper use of masks include: (1) masks must be changed between each procedure, if they become moist or wet, or both; (2) while wearing a mask, conversation should be kept to a minimum to prevent moisture build-up; (3) masks should be removed by the strings and properly discarded before leaving the procedure room; (4) masks are never worn outside the surgical suite; (5) masks are either on or off; they should not be left dangling around the neck or placed in a pocket for future use; and (6) masks should fit snugly around the nose and chin, and tied securely to prevent accidental slipping during a procedure.

12. **The answer is 2.** Effective environmental sanitation programs must be established to reduce the possibility of cross-contamination, which may lead to surgical wound infections, as well as the protection of personnel within and without the surgical suite. The basis for such a program is the concept of universal precautions, which states that all patients should be considered potentially contaminated and therefore treated exactly alike regardless of the procedure being performed.

13. **The answer is 3.** Although the surgical suite environment cannot be sterilized, appropriate cleaning and disinfection procedures can reduce the possibility of transmitting pathogens, thus maintaining an aseptic environment. Methods used to accomplish this goal should include: (1) containment in clear plastic bags of soiled sponges during the procedure; (2) double-bagging all soiled linen and disposable items before their removal at the conclusion of the procedure; (3) immediate cleaning with an effective disinfectant solution of spills and debris from floors and walls; (4) removing soiled shoe covers before leaving the procedure room, thus eliminating the "tracking" effect within the suite. In addition to these general recommendations, specific procedures should be used before and after each surgery and before the first case of the day. Preliminary cleaning measures include removing furniture and equipment not expressly required for the procedure; damp-dusting all horizontal surfaces with a hospital-approved disinfectant solution; and placing lined containers **well away from the sterile field to avoid possible contamination during the set-up phase.**

14. **The answer is 3.** Thorough cleaning of walls, ceilings, floors, air-conditioning grills, sterilizers, and solution dispensers is part of a weekly and/or monthly cleaning program and typically is not done at the conclusion of the day's schedule, when each procedure room, scrub/utility area, corridors, furnishings and equipment is terminally cleaned. With terminal cleaning, all furniture is thoroughly cleaned with an appropriate disinfectant. Casters and wheels are cleaned, and debris, such as suture strands, removed. Horizontal surfaces are cleaned; ceiling and wall fixtures and tracks are cleaned on all surfaces. Floors are flooded after the furniture has been removed, and a thorough wet-vacuuming is performed along with spot removal from the walls as needed. Once the floor is dry, the furniture is replaced and clean linen is placed on the O.R. table.

15. **The answer is 4.** The Operating Room Supervisor/Nurse Manager is responsible for the clinical aspects of the surgical suite in addition to its day-to-day management, including the delegation, planning, staffing, and directing of nursing activities occurring in the area.

16. **The answer is 4.** The **anesthesiologist** is a physician who specializes in the administration and monitoring of anesthesia while maintaining the overall well-being of the patient. The **first assistant to the surgeon** may be a resident, intern, physicians' assistant, or perioperative nurse, and assists with retracting, hemostasis, suturing, and any other tasks requested by the surgeon. The **scrub nurse** may be either a nurse or surgical technician and is responsible for assisting the surgeon and assistant with instrumentation, set-ups, suture presentation, sponges, etc., while maintaining the sterility of the surgical field through aseptic practices. The **circulating nurse** must be a registered nurse who, after additional education and training, is specialized in perioperative nursing practice. The circulating nurse is responsible and accountable for all activities occurring during a surgical procedure, including equipment, supplies, and the environment during a surgical procedure, and managing the flow of information to and from the surgical team members scrubbed at the field.

17. **The answer is 2.** In surgery, as in any other area of nursing practice, all nurses are leaders and managers of patient care to some degree; either in an appointed role or in one the individual has assumed.

Leadership is the effective use of skills that can influence or motivate others to perform to their fullest potential. The leadership process influences the actions of a person or group to attain stated desired goals. It is dependent upon effective interpersonal skills, mutual respect, and mutually satisfying action and/or results for both the leader and the follower. Leadership can occur in two distinct forms: (1) informal leadership, in which a person or team member is chosen by a group, but who is not specifically designated and who lacks formal authority, yet still influences group decision-making processes; and (2) formal leadership, in which a person who is by virtue of education and preparation appointed to the position and is given official authority to act and make decisions in the name of the organization or department.

18. **The answer is 2.** According to Douglas (1988), there are four management styles, each with its own individual strengths and weaknesses. Managers who use the **authoritarian** style make all decisions alone, never involving others in the process. This usually results in lack of group support or respect for the position of the manager. Such managers usually exhibit a low opinion of the workers, and feel that they (the worker) must be controlled to accomplish requested tasks. The **democratic/consultative** style, also known as participative management, emphasizes team work, open communication, and group dynamics. By using this style, the leader or manager becomes people-oriented rather than task-oriented. There is a mutual responsiveness to meeting group goals, and the manager/leader serves as a consultant when decisions affecting the group need to be made. **Permissive** managers usually have no established goals, and do not lead. They assume that the staff is self-motivated and that the job will be done with or without direction or control. In the **multicratic** management style, the positive aspects of the traditional styles just mentioned are combined to produce a flexible approach to management.

19. **The answer is 3.** Although nurses routinely make management-type decisions involving the quality of patient care, not everyone is management (administrative) material. Therein here lies the dichotomy: All nurses manage patient care, but not all nurses should be managers. There is absolutely nothing wrong with this, since nursing, as a profession, requires a team effort of both clinicians and managers to deliver effective patient care. Although theories and styles can and should be learned, the individual must decide which aspect of nursing accomplishes his or her individual goals and objectives, and being the best clinician in a specific area or setting is just as important as being a successful manager.

20. **The answer is 4.** Without education, a direct link to cost-effective and proficient patient-care management is in jeopardy, especially in surgery. In institutions that promote education, management will be more successful and efficient. If not, it is the manager's job to promote education by stressing its contribution to the organization and the staff. It is the successful manager who recognizes the need for continuing quality education, since through this process the staff not only knows what to do, but more importantly, how to do it effectively and safely.

3 Standards for Perioperative Nursing Practice

STUDY OUTLINE

I. DEVELOPMENT OF NATIONAL STANDARDS

1. **For nursing professionals to determine competency levels of performance, the profession must first establish, maintain, and improve where possible the standards of care, and these standards must serve as the minimum levels of acceptable performance by the professional and/or the organization.** As a professional body, nursing must guarantee the quality of its service to the public, and these standards are a commitment and an assurance that the highest quality of care will be provided to all patients in all health care settings, as guaranteed by the Patient's Bill of Rights (American Hospital Association, 1985).

2. To evaluate the quality of care provided, the nursing profession has established **Standards of Practice** through the American Nurses Association (A.N.A.), the professional body for all professional nurses in the country, and these standards serve as a guideline for peer evaluation, employee assessment, and self-evaluation of nursing practice according to the latest theories and technologic advances associated with the practice of professional nursing.

3. Since perioperative nursing is referred to as *the practice of professional nursing in the operating room*, it too needs standards that state the minimum performance competencies required for the implementation of quality patient care during the perioperative period.

II. WHAT IS A STANDARD?

1. **A standard is described as a criterion used by general agreement to denote an acceptable level of practice or established form. Nursing practice standards are descriptive statements that reflect the nature of current nursing practice, current knowledge, and current quality of patient care. As such, they are a means for establishing accountability of nursing care rendered by the professional nurse.**

2. Broad in scope, and relevant to today's technology, standards provide for the uniformity of perioperative nursing practice on a national level, and are modified or revised continually to accommodate changes in theory, skill, or knowledge of nursing practice during the perioperative period.

3. Because a standard is considered the minimum level of performance required, they must be achievable to meet competency levels.

4. Standard are derived from four acceptable sources:
   a. **Opinion:** of knowledgeable professionals
   b. **Authority:** national organizations/agencies
   c. **Research:** concurrent and descriptive
   d. **Theory:** scientific basis

A. **TYPES OF STANDARDS**

1. The nursing profession has three types of standards:
    a. **Structural standards**: These provide the framework for the system in which nursing care is delivered. Examples include the Joint Commission for Accreditation of Healthcare Organizations (J.C.A.H.O.), A.N.A., and A.O.R.N. Administrative Standards.
    b. **Process standards**: These are nursing-oriented and describe the activities and behaviors designed to achieve patient-centered goals. Examples include the A.N.A. Standards and Perioperative Nursing Standards, both based on the nursing process, which describe the correlation between the nursing process activities and the quality of patient care rendered.
    c. **Outcome standards**: These standards focus on what has happened to the patient as a direct result of nursing intervention. Examples include oncology outcome standards and patient outcome standards: perioperative nursing.

B. **WHY DO WE NEED STANDARDS?**

1. Five major reasons define why standards are an important aspect of professional nursing practice:
    a. **Communications**: Communications provide for sharing a common language with nursing professionals, which can cross barriers between specialties.
    b. **Research**: The standards provide a framework for further investigation, so that current practices are no longer based on intuition or "word-of-mouth" but are derived from theory developed by authorities within the nursing profession.
    c. **Legal implications**: The nursing profession must be self regulating to maintain credibility as a profession. The courts use the professional standards as a yard stick to determine whether hospitals and health care professionals have provided quality patient care according to nationally acceptable standards.
    d. **Quality assurance**: Standards can be used as the criteria for quality assurance studies, to assess the current levels of practice rendered by the healthcare team, services provided by the organization or both.
    e. **Professional accountability**: Standard set guidelines for nursing practice, providing a uniform basis for collecting and reviewing individual and departmental performance in conjunction with an established quality assurance program and/or performance appraisal system.
2. All these reasons are related to quality patient care, and any measurement must be based on the acceptable Standards of Practice.

C. **STANDARDS FOR PERIOPERATIVE NURSING PRACTICE**

1. These standards, originally written in 1975, establish a basic model with which to measure the quality of perioperative nursing practice. Today, they have a new name and a new format, but the goal and purpose are the same: *To provide quality patient care to those undergoing surgical intervention.*
2. By establishing these standards, the profession puts its obligation to quality patient care into daily practice. Through the Association of Operating Room Nurses (A.O.R.N.), the professional body for perioperative nursing practice, the standards have created a tool with which to measure how the profession in general and individuals in particular are performing compared with acceptable levels of practice expected by their colleagues, society, and the patient entrusted to their care.

D. **STANDARDS AND IMPLEMENTATION OF PRACTICE**

1. The *Standards for Perioperative Nursing Practice* are based on the nursing process framework, and reflect the specific performance expected while rendering nursing care during the perioperative period. The following table demonstrates how the standards, the phases of perioperative nursing, and the nursing process are interrelated.

Perioperative Phase	Standards	Nursing Process
	I	Assessment
Preoperative	II	Nursing Diagnosis
	III and IV	Planning
Intraoperative	V	Implementation
Postoperative	VI and VII	Evaluation and Reassessment

III. STANDARDS OF PERIOPERATIVE NURSING PRACTICE (1992)

A. STANDARD I

1. **The collection of data about the health status of the individual is systematic and continuous. The data are recorded, retrievable, and communicated to appropriate persons.**
2. The primary goal of this standard is to obtain, systematically, as much information about the patient as possible through:
   a. Chart reviews.
   b. Patient interview and observation.
   c. Physical assessment.
   d. Conferences with other health-care providers involved with the patient.
   e. Interviews with patient's family or significant others.
3. **Assessment factors**
   a. Health data should include:
      (1) Current medical diagnosis and therapy.
      (2) The individual's participation and expectations of proposed intervention.
      (3) Previous responses to illness, hospitalization, and surgery.
      (4) Psychosocial information as it relates to the individual's habits and social and work roles.
      (5) Understanding of the surgical procedure and signed informed consent.
      (6) Psychologic behaviors, such as anxiety, coping, and so on.
   b. Health data are collected by appropriate methods.
   c. Health data collection is complete.
4. When the nurse has satisfied these criterion or assessment factors, the data collection expected by Standard I is complete.

B. STANDARD II

1. **Nursing diagnoses are derived form health status data.**
2. A **nursing diagnosis** is a concise statement that identifies clinical judgment about an individual, family, or community response to actual or potential healthcare problems and/or life processes. Nursing diagnoses provide the basis for selecting nursing interventions that will achieve outcomes for which the nurse is accountable. The information is derived from the nursing assessment data collected, and forms the basis for the plan of care created for that patient.

3. The term **diagnosis** is defined as a concise technical description of facts to determine the cause, nature, or manifestation of a condition, situation, or problem, and the decision or opinion resulting from such an examination and analysis of data.
4. The goal of a nursing diagnosis is management of the nursing care problems; it is a major component of the nursing process.
5. **Assessment factors**
   a. The nursing diagnosis is based on identifiable data determined by continual analysis and interpretation of the data.
   b. Health status deviations are determined by comparing the identified data with established norms and/or the patient's previous condition.
   c. Nursing diagnosis is consistent with current scientific theory.

C. STANDARD III

1. **The plan of nursing care includes goals derived from the nursing diagnosis.**
2. Goals are statements of expected patient outcomes: what the nurse wants to observe, hear, or see as a direct result of nursing intervention.
3. Goals should be brief and concisely stated in measurable terms. Each goal should include specific criteria for measuring the success or failure of the intervention.
4. In many instances, the tendency is to focus on the nurse's goals rather than on the patient's. Goals should always be related to the patient and the planned nursing intervention.
5. **Assessment factors**
   a. Goals are derived from the nursing diagnoses statements, and are prioritized according to the individual needs of the patient.
   b. Goals are stated in measurable terms of observable outcomes.
   c. Goals are formulated through input from the patient, family, and health-care providers.
   d. Goals are realistic, determined by the patient's present and potential physical capabilities and behavioral patterns.
   e. Goals are obtainable through available human and material resources.
   f. Goals are achievable within an identified time.

D. STANDARD IV

1. **The plan for nursing care prescribes nursing actions to achieve the goals.**
2. Developing a plan of care is an intellectual process requiring the perioperative nurse to have knowledge and skills specific to patient care in surgery.
3. The department should have a care plan form consistent with other nursing service areas, or the perioperative plan of care should be incorporated into the generic care plan used throughout the hospital and be documented in writing somewhere in the patient's record or on the nursing care plan form.
4. **Assessment factors**
   a. The care plan includes setting priorities for appropriate actions.
   b. The plan includes a logical sequence of events and actions to attain the stated goals.
   c. The plan is based on current scientific knowledge.
   d. The plan incorporates available and appropriate human and material resources.
   e. The plan is realistic and can be implemented.
   f. The plan is developed with and communicated to the patient and other appropriate personnel and family.
   g. The plan specifies what nursing actions are performed and when, where, and by whom.
   h. The plan reflects preoperative assessment.
   i. The plan includes, but is not limited to:
      (1) Preoperative teaching.
      (2) Verification of all documents.
      (3) Adherence to principles of asepsis, positioning safety, monitoring, psychologic and physiologic support, communication methods, and documentation of nursing activities performed.

E. STANDARD V

1. **The plan for nursing care is implemented.**
2. As the perioperative nurse begins to implement the care plan, he or she draws on intellectual skills involving decision making, observation, judgment, critical thinking, and interpersonal relationships, in addition to manual dexterity, technical skill performance, and the application of nursing knowledge.
3. While the plan is being implemented, additional data are being collected, and the original goals are being revised as necessary.
4. It is during this phase that documentation of all nursing activities performed becomes especially important, both legally and professionally, since such documentation will serve as a communication tool for the nurses resuming postoperative care of the patient.
5. **Assessment factors**
   a. Nursing actions are consistent with the care plan and provide continuity during all three phases of surgical intervention.
   b. Nursing actions are performed with safety, skill, and efficiency, and reflect the individualism of the patient.
   c. Nursing activities are documented on appropriate forms.

F. STANDARD VI

1. **The nursing care plan is evaluated.**
2. The term evaluation refers to the appraisal of the quality of care and the results of nursing intervention.
3. Actual measurements of goal attainment can be a formal or informal process. Notations on the care plan, describing achievements of developing an evaluation tool such as a postoperative interview sheet, are methods that can be used to determine to what extent the patient outcome goals have been met.
4. **Assessment factors**
   a. Current data about the individual is recorded and used to measure progress toward the goals.
   b. All parties involved assist in the evaluation process, including the patient and family.

G. STANDARD VII

1. **Reassessment of the individual; reconsideration of the nursing diagnosis; resetting of goals and modification and implementation of the nursing care plan are a continual process.**
2. As the perioperative nurse cares for the patient, new information is continually being gathered that affects the original goals and care plan. Based on this new information, or patient problems, the perioperative nurse must reexamine the original goals and determine whether they are still pertinent, realistic, and achievable.
3. When the goals have been restated, the care plan must be modified and followed through with appropriate nursing actions. The cycle begins again, and will continue until the patient no longer requires nursing intervention.
4. **Assessment factors**
   a. Reassessment is directed by achievement of goals, new data, or both.
   b. The care plan is modified to meet changes in the condition or needs of the patient.
5. If the perioperative nurse can incorporate the Standards of Perioperative Nursing Practice into daily activities, he or she will have met all the expected professional obligations, resulting in a higher caliber of patient care during the perioperative period. The extent to which the perioperative standards can be implemented depends on the individual's commitment to quality patient care.

IV. OUTCOME STANDARDS FOR PERIOPERATIVE NURSING

1. Originally drafted in 1984, outcome standards with the goal to provide nurses practicing in the operating room with guidelines for providing the highest quality of patient care have not changed as a result of the complexity of today's perioperative nursing practice.
2. Used as a tool to measure the extent to which quality patient care has been achieved, the following standards can assist the perioperative nurse during the Evaluation and Reassessment Phases of the process:
   a. The patient demonstrates knowledge of the physiologic and psychologic responses to surgical intervention.
   b. The patient is free from infection.
   c. The patient's skin integrity is maintained.
   d. The patient is free from injury related to positioning, extraneous objects, or chemical, physical, and electrical hazards.
   e. The patient's fluid and electrolyte balance is maintained.
   f. The patient participates in the rehabilitation process.

V. COMPETENCY STATEMENTS

1. **Competency is described as the ability to practice a skill with safety and efficiency, and usually is a result of continual application of knowledge and skill.**
2. During the initial phase of exploration into the perioperative nurse's role, the nurse is in the **entry** level of practice, acquiring new skills and knowledge relating to patient care during the perioperative period. This phase usually lasts 6 months, and its completion is based on the nurse's ability to safely function independently as a perioperative nurse.
3. The next level, beginning at 6 months and continuing for approximately 2 years, is referred to as the **competency phase** of practice. It is characterized by an increase in knowledge and skills that reflect the total aspect of perioperative nursing practice.
4. To assist the nurse in determining whether this level has been achieved, the A.O.R.N. has researched and developed the Competency Statements for Perioperative Nursing Practice, applicable to nurses working in surgery for 6 months or longer.
5. Using the nursing process format and the Standards of Perioperative Nursing Practice as the framework, the competency statements can be directly correlated with current technology and implementation of patient care activities. The statements are written in measurable terms, clearly redefining the need for qualified registered nurses performing specialized tasks for the patient undergoing surgical intervention.
6. Additionally, the perioperative nurse can use the competency statements as a self-assessment tool and as a study guide for the Certification Examination in Perioperative Nursing Practice (C.N.O.R.).
7. **Phases of competency**
   a. **Assessment phase**
      (1) Competency to assess the physiologic health status of the patient.
      (2) Competency to assess the psychosocial health status of the patient, family, or both.
      (3) Competency to formulate nursing diagnoses based on health status data.
   b. **Planning phase**
      (4) Competency to establish patient goals based on the nursing diagnoses.
      (5) Competency to develop a care plan that prescribes nursing actions to achieve patient goals.
   c. **Implementation phase**
      (6) Competency to implement nursing actions in transferring the patient according to prescribed plan.
      (7) Competency to participate in patient/family teaching.
      (8) Competency to create and maintain a sterile field.
      (9) Competency to provide proper equipment and supplies based on patient/team needs.
      (10) Competency to perform sponge, sharp, and instrument counts at proper intervals.

(11) Competency to administer drugs and solutions as prescribed.
(12) Competency to physiologically monitor patients during surgery.
(13) Competency to monitor and control the environment.
(14) Competency to respect patient's rights.
d. **Evaluation phase**
(15) Competency to perform nursing actions that demonstrate accountability.
(16) Competency to evaluate patient outcomes.
(17) Competency to measure effectiveness of nursing care.
(18) Competency to continually reassess all components of patient care based on new data.
8. By continually using the standards of practice, outcome standards, and competency statements as a guide, the perioperative nurse practicing in today's operating rooms can assure the delivery of quality patient care during all three phases of surgical intervention.

PRACTICE QUESTIONS

1. **One of the primary functions of Standards of Practice in nursing is to:**

   1. *establish accountability of nursing care rendered by the professional nurse.*

   2. *provide a tool for assessing the psychologic health status of the patient.*

   3. *define the organizational structure of groups such as the American Nurses Association (A.N.A.).*

   4. *state the highest level of performance competencies required for the implementation of quality patient care.*

2. **Standards of nursing derive from all of the following acceptable sources EXCEPT:**

   1. *the opinions of knowledgeable professionals.*

   2. *concurrent and descriptive research.*

   3. *the authority of national organizations and agencies.*

   4. *specific A.N.A. competency statements.*

3. **Standards such as the A.N.A. Standards and Perioperative Nursing Standards that are nursing-oriented and describe the activities and behaviors designed to achieve patient-centered goals are called:**

   1. *structural standards.*

   2. *process standards.*

   3. *outcome standards.*

   4. *intervention standards.*

4. **Standards are an important aspect of professional nursing practice for several reasons. Which of the following is NOT one of these reasons?**

   1. *Standards provide a framework for further investigation through research.*

   2. *Standards can be used by courts to determine whether hospitals and health care professionals have provided quality patient care.*

3. *Standards serve as the basis for the nursing process, and as such determine the type of care provided by nurses.*

4. *Standards can be used as the criteria for quality assurance studies of current levels of practice and services.*

5. **The stage of the nursing process that applies most directly to the intraoperative phase of perioperative patient care management is:**

   1. *nursing diagnosis.*

   2. *planning.*

   3. *implementation.*

   4. *evaluation.*

6. **The basis for the plan of care created for a patient is the:**

   1. *expected outcome.*

   2. *health status report.*

   3. *set of goals derived from the preoperative assessment.*

   4. *nursing diagnosis.*

7. ***Mrs. F. is free from injury related to positioning.* Does this statement illustrate a properly stated goal?**

   1. *Yes, because it focuses on a nursing rather than a patient outcome.*

   2. *Yes, because it is a statement of an expected patient outcome.*

   3. *No, because it s not stated in measurable terms.*

   4. *No, because it is not related to nursing intervention.*

8. **A properly formed care plan incorporates which of the following?**

   1. *Nursing actions to achieve the goals derived from diagnosis.*

   2. *A clear and specific list of competency statements based on expected patient outcomes.*

   3. *Actual measurements of goal attainment, done either formally or informally.*

   4. *Specific outcomes based on the 1984 Outcome Standards for Perioperative Nursing.*

9. **Documentation becomes important during the implementation phase of the nursing care plan. This is because documentation:**

   1. *contains specific recommendations for resetting of goals and modification of the nursing care plan.*

   2. *incorporates consent forms and other legal documents completed by the patient.*

   3. *is specific to postoperative nursing activities.*

   4. *provides continuity for the nurses resuming postoperative care of the patient.*

10. **The appraisal of the quality of nursing care and the results of nursing intervention is known as:**

    1. *reassessment.*

    2. *evaluation.*

    3. *implementation.*

    4. *assessment.*

11. **All of the following are major reasons that nursing care plans are frequently modified EXCEPT:**

    1. *New information is gathered that affects the original goals of the care plan.*

    2. *Goals stated in the original plan are met.*

    3. *Nursing intervention ends with implementation.*

    4. *The condition or needs of the patient change.*

12. **An example of an outcome statement used during evaluation and reassessment to measure the extent to which quality patient care has been achieved is:**

    1. *The patient previously was operated on for cancer.*

    2. *The patient's pulse is rapid and irregular.*

    3. *The patient will be released within 24 hours.*

    4. *The patient's skin integrity is maintained.*

13. **A perioperative nurse has acquired the ability to formulate a nursing diagnosis based on a patient's health status data. This nurse has achieved competency in one important aspect of which phase of the nursing process?**

    1. *Assessment.*

    2. *Implementation.*

    3. *Planning.*

    4. *Evaluation.*

14. **In achieving competency in all nursing activities related to the implementation phase of the nursing process, a perioperative nurse is competent to do all of the following EXCEPT:**

    1. *to administer drugs and solutions as prescribed.*

    2. *to evaluate patient outcomes.*

    3. *to participate in patient/family teaching.*

    4. *to create and maintain a sterile field.*

ANSWER EXPLANATIONS

1. **The answer is 1.** A standard is described as a criterion used by general agreement to denote an acceptable (i.e., minimum) level of practice or established form. Nursing practice standards are descriptive statements that reflect the nature of current nursing practice, current knowledge, and current quality of patient care. As such, they are a means for establishing accountability of nursing care rendered by the professional nurse. Broad in scope, and relevant to today's technology, standards provide for the uniformity of perioperative nursing practice on a national level, and are modified or revised continually to accommodate changes in theory, skill, or knowledge of nursing practice during the perioperative period.

2. **The answer is 4.** A fourth acceptable source of standards of nursing is theory, which provides a scientific basis for establishing nursing standards.

3. **The answer is 2.** The nursing profession has three types of standards. **Structural standards** provide the framework for the system in which nursing care is delivered. Examples include the Joint Commission for Accreditation of Healthcare Organizations (J.C.A.H.O.), A.N.A., and A.O.R.N. Administrative Standards. **Process standards** are nursing-oriented and describe the activities and behaviors designed to achieve patient-centered goals. Examples include the A.N.A. Standards and Perioperative Nursing Standards, both based on the nursing process, which describe the correlation between the nursing process activities and the quality of patient care rendered. **Outcome standards** focus on what has happened to the patient as a direct result of nursing intervention. Examples include oncology outcome standards and patient outcome standards: perioperative nursing.

4. **The answer is 3.** In addition, standards provide a common language among nursing professionals in different specialties, and they set guidelines for nursing practice, providing a uniform basis for collecting and reviewing individual and departmental performance in conjunction with an established quality assurance program and/or performance appraisal system. All these reasons are related to quality patient care, and any measurement must be based on the acceptable Standards of Practice. Standards of practice are based on the nursing process, not vice versa.

5. **The answer is 3.** Nursing diagnosis and planning occur principally during the preoperative phase; evaluation and reassessment principally during the postoperative phase. The plan for nursing care is implemented during the intraoperative phase (Standard V). As the perioperative nurse begins to implement the care plan, he or she draws on intellectual skills involving decision making, observation, judgment, critical thinking, and interpersonal relationships, in addition to manual dexterity, technical skill performance, and the application of nursing knowledge. While the plan is being implemented, additional data are being collected, and the original goals are being revised as necessary.

6. **The answer is 4.** A nursing diagnosis is a concise statement that identifies clinical judgment about an individual, family, or community response to actual or potential healthcare problems and/or life processes. Nursing diagnoses provide the basis for selecting nursing interventions that will achieve outcomes for which the nurse is accountable. The information is derived from the nursing assessment data collected, and forms the basis for the plan of care created for that patient.

7. **The answer is 2.** The goal stated in this question satisfies these various criteria: Goals are statements of expected patient outcomes--what the nurse wants to observe, hear, or see as a direct result of nursing intervention. Goals should be brief and concisely stated in measurable terms. Each goal should include specific criteria for measuring the success or failure of the intervention. Goals should always be related to the patient and the planned nursing intervention.

8. **The answer is 1.** The plan for nursing care prescribes nursing actions to achieve the goals derived from nursing diagnosis. Assessment factors relating to care plans include the following: (1) the care plan includes setting priorities for appropriate actions; (2) the plan includes a logical sequence of events and actions to attain the stated goals; (3) the plan is based on current scientific knowledge; (4) the plan incorporates available and appropriate human and material resources; (5) the plan is realistic and can be implemented;

(6) the plan is developed with and communicated to the patient and other appropriate personnel and family; (7) the plan specifies what nursing actions are performed and when, where, and by whom; (8) the plan reflects preoperative assessment; and (9) the plan includes, but is not limited to: preoperative teaching; verification of all documents; and adherence to principles of asepsis, positioning safety, monitoring, psychologic and physiologic support, communication methods, and documentation of nursing activities performed.

9.   **The answer is 4.** It is during the implementation phase of the nursing process that documentation of all nursing activities performed becomes especially important, both legally and professionally, since such documentation will serve as a communication tool for the nurses resuming postoperative care of the patient. Documentation provides a continuous picture of the status of the patient to all persons providing care. Accurate documentation also may protect the nurse and institution from lawsuits.

10. **The answer is 2.** The term evaluation refers to the appraisal of the quality of care and the results of nursing intervention. Actual measurements of goal attainment can be a formal or informal process. Notations on the care plan, describing achievements of developing an evaluation tool such as a postoperative interview sheet, are methods that can be used to determine to what extent the patient outcome goals have been met. During this phase of the nursing process, current data about the individual is recorded and used to measure progress toward the goals. All parties involved assist in the evaluation process, including the patient and family.

11. **The answer is 3.** As the perioperative nurse cares for the patient, new information is continually being gathered that affects the original goals and care plan. Based on this new information, or patient problems, the perioperative nurse must reexamine the original goals and determine whether they are still pertinent, realistic, and achievable. Reassessment is directed by achievement of goals, new data, or both, and the care plan is modified to meet changes in the condition or needs of the patient. When the goals have been restated, the care plan must be modified and followed through with appropriate nursing actions. The cycle begins again, and will continue until the patient no longer requires nursing intervention.

12. **The answer is 4.** Outcome standards provide nurses practicing in the operating room with guidelines for providing the highest quality of patient care. Used as a tool to measure the extent to which quality patient care has been achieved, the following standards can assist the perioperative nurse during the Evaluation and Reassessment phases of the process: (1) the patient demonstrates knowledge of the physiologic and psychologic responses to surgical intervention; (2) the patient is free from infection; (3) the patient's skin integrity is maintained; (4) the patient is free from injury related to positioning, extraneous objects, or chemical, physical, and electrical hazards; (5) the patient's fluid and electrolyte balance is maintained; and (6) the patient participates in the rehabilitation process.

13. **The answer is 1.** Using the nursing process format and the A.O.R.N.'s Standards of Perioperative Nursing Practice as the framework, competency statements can be directly correlated with current technology and implementation of patient care activities. The statements are written in measurable terms, clearly redefining the need for qualified registered nurses performing specialized tasks for the patient undergoing surgical intervention. Competency in the assessment phase consists of competency to assess the physiologic health status of the patient; competency to assess the psychosocial health status of the patient, family, or both; and competency to formulate nursing diagnoses based on health status data.

14. **The answer is 2.** Competency during the implementation phase of the nursing process requires competency to perform all of the following activities: implement nursing actions in transferring the patient according to a prescribed plan; participate in patient/family teaching; create and maintain a sterile field; provide proper equipment and supplies based on patient/team needs; perform sponge, sharp, and instrument counts at proper intervals; administer drugs and solutions as prescribed; physiologically monitor patients during surgery; monitor and control the environment; and respect patient's rights. Competency to evaluate patient outcomes relates to the evaluation phase.

4 Anesthesia and Perioperative Nursing Implications

STUDY OUTLINE

I. HISTORICAL OVERVIEW OF ANESTHESIA

A. ANESTHESIA IN ANCIENT CULTURES

1. **Anesthesia is based on changes produced due to chemical substances, and relies on psychodynamics, toxicology, and pharmaceutical chemistry as it relates to the human body.**
2. Most of the methods of anesthesia used during its early years were associated with mysticism or religious rites, and with potions and topical agents containing anesthetizing plant substances. Examples include **mandrake root** (used by the ancient Hebrews and Greeks among others) and the **opium poppy** (used by the ancient Greeks and others). **Wine** was also frequently used to help deaden pain.
3. The gastrointestinal tract remained the only avenue for anesthesia until the inhalation of vapors became an alternative approach and the intravenous method for administering drugs became a reality.

B. DEVELOPMENT OF MODERN ANESTHESIA

1. Three methods began to emerge during the Middle Ages, although they were not widely practiced for fear of reprisals from the church and the medical community. These methods involved the use of **inhalation** (e.g., ether), **intravenous administration** (e.g., injection of opiate solution), and **regional application** (e.g., cocaine applied topically, as by the Incas).
2. The use of surgery for other than superficial problems (e.g., fractures, amputations) proceeded slowly, largely due to a **lack of effective pain control** during the procedure and to the ever-present **risk of infection.** Anesthesia reduced the former, while improved surgical hygiene reduced the latter.
3. By 1831 three basic inhalation agents--**ether, nitrous oxide,** and **chloroform**--had been discovered, but no successful medical application of their pain-relieving properties had yet been made. In 1846, W.T.G. Morton finally showed the worth of nitrous oxide during a tooth extraction. From that point on, great strides were made in the use of anesthesia for a variety of surgical, obstetric, and diagnostic procedures.
4. Today, anesthesiology is a mature specialty, with certification administered by the American Board of Anesthesiology. Its limits have not yet been clearly defined, however.

II. PHASES OF ANESTHESIA PRACTICE

1. **Anesthesia consists of making the patient insensitive to pain in a specific area of the body or the body as a whole. Its objectives are to (1) produce analgesia, (2) produce amnesia, (3) induce muscle relaxation, and (4) provide control of the autonomic nervous system reflexes to the brain and the stress of surgery.**

2. Anesthesia can be related to three phases of surgical intervention: **preoperative, intraoperative, and postoperative management.**

III. PREOPERATIVE PHASE

1. **The preoperative phase revolves around the assessment and preparation of the surgical patient.**

A. PREPARATION FOR ANESTHESIA

1. **All patients receiving anesthesia, regardless of type, should undergo an evaluation and assessment by an anesthesiologist prior to the administration of anesthesia. Past and present medical history should be reviewed with attention focused on prior surgical experiences and the physiologic alterations induced by disease.**
2. The ability to tolerate the adverse effects of anesthesia depends largely on the normality of respiration and circulation and the homeostatic functions of the liver, kidneys, and endocrine and central nervous systems.
3. A **formal evaluation program** should be established, consisting of an interview, a systems review, and a record of important data that can be used later as a guide for an individualized anesthesia program that meets the needs of the patient.
4. Any special diagnostic procedures and tests should be carried out as soon as possible so that the results are on the chart prior to surgery. This allows a comprehensive assessment of the patient's physical status to be performed.
5. The patient should then be told of the plan for anesthesia, including the methods proposed, so that the patient can make an intelligent decision. At that point, an **informed consent** should be signed and witnessed. Most institutions insist on both an **anesthesia summary** and a **signed anesthesia consent permit** before anesthesia can be administered.

B. AMERICAN SOCIETY OF ANESTHESIOLOGY CLASSIFICATION SYSTEM

1. For the purpose of providing appropriate anesthesia, a classification of the patient's physical status was adapted by the American Society of Anesthesiology in 1963, and is used to determine the risk factors based on the current health status of the patient. Included in this evaluation are the **presence of coexisting diseases** and **type of surgery (emergency or elective) being performed.**
2. As part of the preoperative evaluation, the anesthesiologist will place the patient into one of the following classifications, according to the physiologic description of the patient:

Classification: Class 1
Description:
The patient has no organic, physiologic, biochemical, or psychiatric disturbances. The pathologic process for which the operation is to be performed is localized and does not entail a systematic disturbance.
Examples: include, but are not limited to:
hernia repairs, uterine fibroids, dysmenorrhea.

Classification: Class 2
Description:
Mild-to-moderate systemic disturbance caused either by the condition to be treated surgically or by another pathophysiologic process. The extremes of age (neonate or adult between 80 and 90 years old) may be added to this classification, even though no discernible systemic disease is present. Extreme obesity and chronic bronchitis may be included in this category.
Examples: include, but are not limited to:
nonlimiting or slightly limiting organic heart disease, mild diabetes, essential hypertension, anemia.

Classification: Class 3
  Description:
> Severe systemic disturbance/disease from whatever cause even though it may not be possible to define the degree or disability with finality.

  Examples: include, but are not limited to:
> severely limiting organic heart disease, severe diabetes with vascular complications, moderate to severe pulmonary insufficiency, angina or old myocardial infarction (M.I.).

Classification: Class 4
  Description:
> Severe systemic disorders that are already life-threatening, not always correctable by surgery or operation planned.

  Examples: include, but are not limited to:
> marked signs of cardiac insufficiency, persistent (unstable) angina, active myocarditis, advanced pulmonary, hepatic, renal, or endocrine insufficiency.

Classification: Class 5
  Description:
> The moribund patient who has little chance of survival but is submitted to surgery in desperation. The patient may require surgery as a resuscitative measure, with little or no anesthesia.

  Examples: include, but are not limited to:
> leaking or ruptured abdominal aortic aneurysm, cerebral trauma with increasing intracranial pressure, comatose patient requiring a tracheostomy, massive pulmonary embolism.

Classification: Class 6 (1990)
  Description:
> A patient declared legally dead according to state statutes and definition, whose organs are being removed for donor preparation.

Status: E (Emergency)
  Description:
> Any patient in one of the classes previously listed who is operated on as an emergency. The letter E is placed beside the numerical class, reflecting that this patient is considered a poor risk and/or is in poor physical condition, with no evaluation performed owing to the acuity of the situation (for example: 1E; 2E).

3. **Perioperative nursing implication:** As part of the perioperative nursing assessment, this classification system can serve as a guide to assist the nurse in anticipating unusual events that may occur as a result of anesthesia and/or the surgical procedure.
4. **Preoperative medications**
   a. Preoperative medications are given to:
      (1) Reduce preoperative anxiety.
      (2) Decrease secretions in the mouth and respiratory tract.
      (3) Reduce reflux irritability.
      (4) Relieve pain.
      (5) Lower the body's metabolism so that less analgesic agent is required.
   b. **Selection of preoperative medications**
      (1) The selection is made by the anesthesiologist, based on the preoperative assessment of the patient. The assessment includes the patient's physical and emotional status, age, weight, past medical history (including medication history), and demands of the proposed surgical procedure.
      (2) The anesthesiologist tries to avoid causing disturbances in the cardiorespiratory system, while providing physical and emotional support and comfort.

    c.   **Pharmacologic agents and physiologic effects:** Which of the four types of preoperative medications chosen depends on the physical and psychologic needs of the patient. These agents include:

        (1) Sedative-hypnotics: to promote relaxation and rest, and to stabilize the blood pressure and pulse.

        (2) Anticholinergics: as drying agents to decrease secretions of mucus in the mouth.

        (3) Narcotics: to promote relaxation and enhance the effect of the anesthetics, and to control pain.

        (4) Antianxiety/antiemetics: to produce relaxation and reduce anxiety and nausea.

    d.   See **Appendix A** for a description of specific agents of each type, including their desired and adverse effects.

C. NURSING IMPLICATIONS: PREOPERATIVE MEDICATIONS

1. Most patients expect the preoperative shot they receive to "put them out." Therefore, they may arrive in the preoperative holding area anxious because they are still awake, thinking the medication is not working properly. **Both proper education of the patient and an attitude of caring by the nurse will help reduce anxiety. This in turn will assist in the administration of the actual anesthetic agents used during surgery.**

2. If a preoperative I.M. injection is not given in the unit following the initiation of an intravenous line, the medication may be given via I.V. push while the patient is in the holding area.

3. When planning nursing intervention for the surgical patient, the responses to the preoperative medication should be considered and the patient continually monitored for possible adverse side effects. **Signs and symptoms of adverse reactions include vomiting, hypotension, cardiac changes, and unexpected changes in sensorium.** All responses should be reported immediately to the anesthesiologist for intervention and correction as necessary.

IV. INTRAOPERATIVE PHASE

1. **The focus of the intraoperative phase is to produce anesthesia.** Agents used to abolish the sensation of pain, achieve muscle relaxation, produce amnesia, and control the autonomic system include:

    a.   **Inhalation agents:** gases or volatile liquids that produce general anesthesia.

    b.   **Intravenous agents:** agents that produce anesthesia in large doses through sedative-hypnotic analgesic action.

    c.   **Local anesthetics:** agents that block nerve conduction in a specific area.

A. ANESTHESIA METHODS AND TECHNIQUES

1. Anesthesia methods fall into two general categories: **general** and **regional.**

2. **General anesthesia** is described as a state of complete loss of consciousness as a direct result of anesthesia agents with conservation of the regulative (A.N.S.) functions.

3. **Regional anesthesia** is described as causing insensibility to pain owing to the interruption of sensory nerve conduction via a nerve block, field block, or by topical application to skin or mucous membrane.

B. METHODS OF GENERAL ANESTHESIA

1. There are two methods used, either alone or together, to induce general anesthesia: **inhalation anesthesia** and **intravenous anesthesia.**

    a.   **Inhalation anesthesia** involves the administration of gases into the systemic circulation through the alveolar membranes of the lungs, with diffusion to the pulmonary circulation and finally to the brain.

    b.   **Intravenous anesthesia** involves the administration of agents as a bolus or continuous drip infusion directly into the systemic circulation for rapid effects. It is used primarily as an

induction agent, for relaxation, analgesia, and/or sleep, and as the sole anesthetic agent under spinal techniques.

2. **Balanced anesthesia** describes anesthesia methods that combine a muscle relaxant, a barbiturate, a narcotic, and an inhalation agent (nitrous oxide). When combined, these agents produce a state similar to that produced by a general anesthesia agent.

C. PHASES OF GENERAL ANESTHESIA AND NURSING ACTIVITIES

1. General anesthesia is accomplished in phases, with each phase requiring specific nursing activities.

Phase 1. Preinduction Phase
a. **Scope:** Begins when the patient enters the procedure room and is placed on the operating table, and ends prior to the induction of anesthesia.
b. **Nursing activities:** Nursing actions revolve around the safety and comfort of the patient, and include proper positioning of the patient on the table, padding of the pressure points, and applying the safety strap over the patient's legs. The perioperative nurse must be available to assist anesthesia personnel as needed, and to provide emotional support to the patient during the preliminary preparations. Additionally, the nurse must be sure that the anesthesiologist's suction is readily available and in proper working condition prior to the start of this phase.

Phase 2. Induction/Intubation
a. **Scope:** Begins with the introduction of anesthetic agents, and ends with the successful intubation and stabilization of the patient.
b. **Nursing activities:** This phase is considered to be the most dangerous for the patient; therefore, all precautions must be taken to ensure the patient's safety.
   (1) The atmosphere must be calm and quiet; devoid of any extraneous noise that could result in uncontrolled patient movement or reflexes during the intubation period. The perioperative nurse should remain beside the patient, assisting anesthesia personnel with the induction/intubation procedure, including the performance of the Sellick maneuver (cricoid pressure) as needed, while all other activities and movement has been stopped.
   (2) It is only after successful intubation and stabilization, and with permission of anesthesia personnel, that the patient can be repositioned as necessary and the surgical prep can be performed. If a radio is on in the procedure room, the volume should be turned down as hearing is acute during this phase.
   (3) *At no time during the induction phase should the circulating nurse leave the room,* since she or he may be the only person available to assist anesthesia personnel should a complication arise.

Phase 3. Maintenance
a. **Scope:** Begins when stabilization has been accomplished and ends prior to the start of the reversal process, toward the end of the surgical procedure.
b. **Nursing activities:** Perioperative nursing activities may differ in each institution during this phase, but usually consist of monitoring urinary output and blood loss; arranging for various lab tests as requested; and obtaining additional drugs, solutions, and/or supplies. By remaining alert to any unforseen events, and assisting anesthesia personnel during the procedure as necessary, the team will be able to maintain a safe, therapeutic environment.
   (1) **It is important to remember that you, as the circulating nurse, are the only nonscrubbed member of the team who can assist anesthesia personnel if an emergent situation arises, so if you must leave the room to get urgent supplies, notify anesthesia personnel you are leaving, and return as quickly as possible.**
   (2) *Never leave the room for an extended period of time without another nurse to replace you while you are gone.*

Phase 4. Reversal/Extubation

a. **Scope:** Begins during the closure of the operative wound and ends immediately prior to transporting the patient to the postanesthesia care unit or designated postanesthesia area.

b. **Nursing activities:** As with Phase 2, the extubation phase is a dangerous time for the patient, since physiologic changes could trigger unexpected events, such as laryngospasm; vomiting, slow spontaneous respirations, or uncontrolled reflex movement.

    (1) Some patients can emerge from anesthesia with wild, uncontrolled movements that could cause harm if not handled gently, while others emerge smoothly, without difficulty. **The perioperative nurse must constantly be aware of the patient's status and be prepared to assist anesthesia personnel to prevent unnecessary injury.**

    (2) If special equipment is needed during the immediate postanesthesia period, arrangement should be made by the perioperative nurse prior to transport, and the recovery room nurses alerted to these special needs.

    (3) Additionally, the perioperative nurse should always accompany the patient with anesthesia personnel to the postanesthesia care unit (PACU), since the perioperative nursing role has not ended until the patient is transferred to another professional nurse and a report of nursing activities during the intraoperative phase has been given to the nurse who will continue the patient's postoperative care.

D. **STAGES OF GENERAL ANESTHESIA: CLASSIC CHARACTERISTICS AND NURSING IMPLICATIONS**

1. According to Guedel (1920), unpremedicated inhalation anesthesia has four classic stages. These are most easily observed with ether.

Stage I. Relaxation (Amnesia/Analgesia)

a. **Scope:** From the beginning of anesthesia to the loss of consciousness. Pain sensation is not completely lost, but reaction to pain has been altered.

b. **Patient reaction/biologic response**
    (1) Feelings of drowsiness and dizziness
    (2) Hearing becomes exaggerated
    (3) May appear inebriated
    (4) Pain sensation is decreased

c. **Nursing implications**
    (1) Close the O.R. doors to reduce extraneous noises.
    (2) Confirm proper positioning, including all safety factors.
    (3) Verify anesthesia suction is available and working correctly.
    (4) Reduce talking, unnecessary movement, and noise to only what is absolutely necessary.
    (5) Remain at the head of the O.R. table; assist the anesthesia clinician, and provide the patient with emotional support.

Stage II. Delirium/Excitement

a. **Scope:** From the loss of consciousness to the onset of respiratory apnea and loss of lid reflexes.

b. **Patient reaction/biologic response**
    (1) Irregular respirations
    (2) Loss of consciousness
    (3) Loss of lid reflexes
    (4) Increased muscle tone and involuntary motor response
    (5) Sensitive to external stimuli (can be startled)

c. Considered an extremely dangerous stage that could result in laryngospasms, vomiting, aspiration, arrhythmias, and myoclonic movement.
NOTE: Short-acting barbiturates expedite time related to Stages I and II.

d. **Nursing implications**
    (1) Avoid any type of extraneous stimulation.

(2) Lightly restrain extremities to avoid injury.

(3) Remain at the head of the table to assist anesthesia personnel as needed (e.g., cricoid pressure, etc.).

(4) Remain alert for any emergency situations that could arise.

Stage III. Surgical Anesthesia

a. **Scope:** From the regular pattern of respirations to the total paralysis of intercostal muscles and cessation of voluntary respirations. This stage can be further divided into four planes, ranging from light anesthesia through excessively deep anesthesia:

Plane 1. Light Anesthesia
- Loss of lid reflexes; pupils are smaller.
- Patterns of normal breathing visible.
- Vomiting/gag reflex gradually disappearing.
- Respiratory rate and depth may increase.
- eye movement may still be present.

Plane 2. Medium Anesthesia (surgery could begin)
- Respirations are more regular, but tidal volume has decreased.
- Loss of eye movement; pupils in midline, concentrically fixed.
- Vocal cord reflex (which could result in laryngospasms) begins to disappear.
- Decreased muscle tone as anesthesia deepens.

Plane 3. Deep Surgical Anesthesia
- Begins with decreased intercostal muscle movement.
- Only diaphragmatic respirations remain.
- Increased muscle relaxation.

NOTE: These stages will be seen in reverse order during the emergence or reversal stage.

Plane 4. Deeper Anesthesia (Danger)
- Begins with intercostal paralysis and progresses to complete cessation of spontaneous respirations.
- If allowed to go deeper, circulatory system failure is imminent.
- Pupils no longer react to light.

b. **Nursing implications**

(1) Be available to assist anesthesia personnel as necessary.

(2) Validate with anesthesia appropriate time to reposition and prep.

(3) Recheck patient positioning and reaffirm safety precautions.

Stage IV. Danger (Premortem)

a. **Scope:** From the time of cessation of respirations to failure of the circulation, caused by high levels of anesthesia in the C.N.S. Accidentally reached; not desirable.

b. **Patient reaction/biologic response**

(1) Medullary paralysis; cardiac/respiratory collapse.

(2) Pupils fixed and dilated.

(3) Pulse rapid and thready.

(4) Respirations ceases, coma develops.

(5) Circulatory and respiratory arrest.

c. **Nursing implications**

(1) Be prepared to assist in emergency resuscitation measures (C.P.R.).

(2) Obtain emergency cart and defibrillator.

(3) Remain in the room at all times.

(4) Document all events and therapies as they occur.

V. INHALATION ANESTHESIA

A. SEQUENCE FOR INHALATION ANESTHESIA

1. The patient is usually given oxygen via a mask prior to the administration of the anesthesia agent.
2. A barbiturate and/or muscle relaxant is administered to relax the patient.
3. The clinician hyperventilates with oxygen and inserts the endotracheal/nasotracheal tube. The tube is attached to the breathing circuit and the maintenance stage is begun.
4. Upon completion of the surgical procedure, and prior to extubation, the clinician hyperventilates with 100 percent oxygen, then removes the tube and continues administering oxygen with the mask until the patient is stable for transport with no signs of respiratory obstruction.

B. TYPES OF INHALATION AGENTS

1. Inhalation agents are of two types: **gaseous and volatile.**
2. **Gaseous agents** include **nitrous oxide,** a colorless, odorless, nonexplosive gas usually used in combination with other agents and oxygen. High-concentration nitrous oxide (N_2O) can produce hypoxia; its use therefore requires caution.
3. **Volatile agents** are liquids that are easily vaporized and produce anesthesia when inhaled. Included in this category are ether, trichloroethylene, chloroform, halothane, enflurane, methoxyflurane, and isoflurane. The first three agents are rarely used today.
4. See Appendix A for a description of specific inhalation agents, including characteristics, risks, and contraindications.

C. INHALATION ANESTHESIA SAFETY MEASURES

1. A **chemical absorber** is used during the administration of any inhalant agents to scavenge waste anesthetics (CO_2) and avoid unnecessary exposure to health-care professionals. The absorber must be monitored and changed as needed.
2. In addition, disposable breathing circuits, masks, endotracheal (or nasotracheal) tubes, and reservoir bags are used to prevent cross-contamination or unwarranted mixtures of agents.

VI. INTRAVENOUS ANESTHESIA

A. GENERAL CATEGORIES OF INTRAVENOUS AGENTS

1. **Intravenous medications** are frequently used to supplement inhalation agents, and thus provide a safe, reversible state of anesthesia. These drugs are metabolized and excreted by the kidneys.
2. Intravenous agents can be administered by bolus dose or by continuous drip infusion, depending on the effect desired.
3. Three categories of intravenous drugs are associated with general anesthesia:
   a. **Barbiturates:** act directly in the C.N.S., producing an effect ranging from the mild sedation to sleep. Included are Pentothal, Brevital, and Surital.
   b. **Narcotics:** render the patient pain-free and, in some cases, produce a euphoric state. Included are Demerol, morphine sulfate, Sublimaze, Alfenta, and Sufenta.
   c. **Muscle relaxants:** provide total relaxation of skeletal muscles, resulting in reduced tissue trauma (this cannot be accomplished by other intravenous agents). Included are depolarizing relaxants such as succinylcholine (Anectine and Quelicin) and nondepolarizing agents such as curare, Pavulon, Flaxedil, Norcuron, Tracrium, and Diprivan.
4. In addition, tranquilizers (Valium, Versed, Inapsine), neuroleptanalgesics, and phencyclidines are used to supplement the inhalation technique.
5. Some agents, such as narcotics, can be totally reversed (antagonized), while others can only be partially reversed. This factor may influence the choice of intravenous agent used.

B. BARBITURATES

1. See **Appendix A** for a description of specific barbiturates, including characteristics, risks, and contraindications.

C. NARCOTIC ANALGESICS

1. **Narcotics can be used both as a preoperative medication and as an adjunct therapy during local, regional, or general anesthesia.**
2. The respiratory and cardiovascular depressive effects of narcotics are well known, and these agents are most often given by bolus injection. They can be given via infusion drip, however, under certain conditions or procedures such as open-heart surgery.
3. Because all narcotic analgesics are derived from basically the same substance or synthetic derivatives, their basic characteristics are very similar:
    a. They produce potent analgesia.
    b. They are fast-acting, with prolonged analgesic effect.
    c. They are reversible with a narcotic antagonist (naloxone).
    d. They may produce nausea and vomiting.
    e. They must be administered slowly to avoid severe cardiopulmonary depression.
    f. There are, however, some differences that should be mentioned.
4. See **Appendix A** for a description of specific narcotics, including characteristics, risks, contraindications, and reversal agents.

D. MUSCLE RELAXANTS

1. **Neuromuscular relaxants are used to provide muscle relaxation during surgery and/or to facilitate the passage of an endotracheal tube.** These agents work on the striated muscles of the body by blocking the impulses that occur at the motor end-plate, where the nerve fiber connects with the muscle fiber.
2. Muscle relaxants are divided into two groups: **depolarizing** and **nondepolarizing**, based on their specific actions and properties.
3. **Depolarizing muscle relaxants**
    a. Depolarizing muscle relaxants mimic acetylcholine by reacting with the motor-end plate receptors to cause prolonged depolarization. Thus, the muscle remains relaxed, and repolarization is very slow. Onset of action is rapid (within 1 minute), with a short duration (3 to 5 minutes).
    b. Depolarizing muscle relaxants can be very useful in the treatment of profound laryngospasm; in reversing frozen chest syndrome, or assisting respiratory management with insertion of an endotracheal tube, both inside and outside the surgical area.
    c. Although they have excellent therapeutic properties, special problems do exist with these agents:
        (1) Mycin interaction (Neomycin, Streptomycin) tends to prolong the action of neuromuscular blocking agents.
        (2) Hypothermic states increase the duration of action.
        (3) Bradycardia due to neostigmine/atropine reversal techniques is not uncommon.
        (4) Depolarizing agents cannot be lessened (reversed); therefore, they must be used cautiously.
    d. See **Appendix A** for a description of specific agents, including characteristics, risks, contraindications, and reversal agents.
4. **Nondepolarizing muscle relaxants**
    a. Nondepolarizing agents occupy acetylcholine receptor sites and block the depolarizing action at the neuromuscular junction. Because they do not cause depolarization, they are referred to as **competitive neuromuscular blocking agents.**
    b. Induction is slower and emergence is of longer duration (45-60 minutes) than with depolarizing agents. Administration is by bolus injection, and can be reversed by neostigmine,

atropine, physostigmine, pyridostigmine, or edrophonium by allowing the acetylcholine to accumulate at the neuromuscular junction.

c. See **Appendix A** for a description of specific agents, including characteristics, risks, contraindications, and reversal agents.

5. **Safety considerations**
   a. **The safe use of neuromuscular blocking agents requires the establishment of an effective airway, either by oral airway and mask, or by endotracheal intubation, along with controlled, monitored ventilation.**
   b. For anesthesia to be safe, the anesthesiologist/C.R.N.A. must carefully monitor the patient's physiologic status and be prepared to correct any adverse effects caused by the agent(s) being used. Muscle relaxation can be evaluated by using a nerve stimulator placed between the ulnar nerve at the elbow or wrist, which can determine the presence or absence of contractions or diminished strength of the hand muscles.
   c. In addition to evaluating the muscle relaxation, the saturation of oxygen within the cells can be monitored with a **pulse oximeter**, and because of its accuracy, is now considered the standard of care for all patients receiving anesthesia or I.V. sedation via narcotic analgesia, not only in surgery but in the immediate postoperative recovery areas.

VII. MONITORING OF INTRAVASCULAR HOMEOSTASIS DURING ANESTHESIA

1. **Surgical procedures impose a variety of stressors on the patient, both psychologically and physiologically. Among those that require constant monitoring are body fluids, electrolytes, and acid-base disturbances.**
2. Most patients facing elective operative procedures have oral intake withheld during the 8 to 12 hours preceding surgery, resulting in unreplaced solute and water loss. In view of this preoperative loss, the monitoring and restoration of normal fluid balance becomes the primary concern of the anesthesia clinician, since this deficit can ultimately affect all body systems and directly or indirectly affect the outcome of the surgical procedure.
3. Although the ultimate management of fluids and electrolytes and acid-base balance is part of the total anesthesia care, the perioperative nurse should have a working knowledge of the disturbances and how to prevent/correct them. By carefully assessing the patient, the perioperative nurse can anticipate potential problems and therefore be of greater assistance to the anesthesiologist during the intraoperative period.
   a. **Preoperative assessment**
      (1) Collection of data regarding:
      • Nutritional status
      • G.I., renal, cardiovascular, and respiratory systems
      • General health
      • Current medications
      (2) Review of laboratory values, including C.B.C., electrolyte profiles, hematology studies, and A.B.G. report.
      (3) Assessment of psychologic status, coping mechanisms, support systems, and current therapies/treatments.
   b. **Intraoperative phase:** Specific factors affecting the fluid, electrolyte, and acid-base balances include:
      (1) I.V. fluid administration of nonelectrolyte/electrolyte solutions.
      (2) General anesthetic agents, which can alter respiratory status and can predispose to cardiac arrhythmias related to retention of CO_2 and potassium loss.
4. **Monitoring intraoperative homeostatic status**
   a. The following recommendations may help to prevent complications from hemodynamic disturbances:
      (1) Accurate measurement of blood loss and urinary output during the procedure.
      (2) Hemodynamic monitoring for long or complicated cases, especially those involved with the cardiorespiratory systems.

(3) Periodic measurement of intravascular status: Hct and Hgb; C.B.C.; A.B.C; chemistry profiles.

(4) Continuous temperature monitoring; use of pulse oximeter (measurement of O_2 saturation at tissue levels).

(5) Proper positioning with supportive aids padding bony prominences; providing adequate support devices; maintaining near proper alignment.

(6) Preoperative education to reduce stress levels.

b. The perioperative nurse has an important role in performing functions that can assist the anesthesiologist in maintaining fluid, electrolyte, and acid-base balance; therefore, he or she should be able to:

(1) Recognize imbalances and interventions needed to correct the disturbances.

(2) Anticipate changes due to external and internal stressors and plan accordingly.

(3) Accurately record patient's hemodynamic status (I & O; fluid/blood loss; amount of irrigation; etc.).

(4) Reduce stress through preoperative teaching programs and ongoing intraoperative supportive measures.

(5) Collaborate with anesthesia personnel by anticipating specific needs for the planned surgical procedure, and work as a team to provide quality patient care.

VIII.   HEMODYNAMIC MONITORING DURING ANESTHESIA

1. **Hemodynamic monitoring is used primarily to (1) evaluate left and right ventricular function, (2) assess fluid volume status, and (3) evaluate cardiovascular therapies. Changes in hemodynamic measurements always precede changes in the patient's clinical status, and early detection using hemodynamic monitoring can prevent critical conditions from developing.**

2. Hemodynamic monitoring can be performed by noninvasive techniques, such as noninvasive blood pressure monitoring, measurement of intake and output, and so on, or by an invasive technique through the insertion of a catheter that measures values of hemodynamic status.

3. Although most patients may not need the invasive monitoring technique, the perioperative nurse must be aware of normal values and be able to recognize any abnormal values being presented by the patient during the perioperative period.

4. **Nursing implications**

a. Although hemodynamic monitoring is usually the responsibility of the anesthesia clinician, the perioperative nurse should be aware of normal cardiac function and be able to recognize hemodynamic changes that accompany the physiologic stress associated with a disease state and/or surgical intervention, to anticipate possible complications.

b. As with any therapy, invasive hemodynamic monitoring has definite advantages and disadvantages. Some of the advantages include:

(1) Early recognition of cardiogenic shock or disturbances in the fluid volume status.

(2) Provision of accurate measurements of cardiac function for otherwise unstable patients or those undergoing extensive surgery.

(3) Ability to detect minute changes in the physiologic status of the patient.

(4) Provision of information as to the patient's response to drugs.

c. Disadvantages might include:

(1) Risk of complications, such as bleeding, infection, vascular damage, or possibility of an embolism.

(2) Need for proficiency in insertion techniques to prevent trauma and to monitor and interpret values.

(3) Patient anxiety regarding the invasive technique and family anxiety seeing the multiple lines postoperatively without adequate explanation.

5. **Troubleshooting possible monitoring problems**

a. The perioperative nurse can assist in deciphering possible problems by understanding how the equipment functions.

Problem	Dampened arterial wave form resulting in abnormally low pressure readings.
Causes	Catheter obstruction or clot at distal tip; air and/or leak in transducer and/or tubing.
Actions	Flush line with heparinized saline; check all connectors; recalibrate and check monitor settings; confirm appropriate transducer level.
Problem	Arterial pressure tracing more than 20 mm Hg higher than cuff pressure.
Causes	Catheter kinked or positioned against arterial wall; transducer not calibrated or zeroed correctly.
Actions	Check for kinks in tubing; reposition and splint arm/hand if needed; recalibrate and rezero.
Problem	Pulmonary catheter will not "wedge" when balloon is inflated.
Causes	Catheter has migrated out of position; insufficient air in balloon; balloon has ruptured.
Actions	Assess location with X-ray/fluoroscopy and reposition; deflate and reinflate balloon slowly, if air placed in balloon is not recoverable, or if no resistance to inflation, catheter may require replacement.

    b. Hemodynamic monitoring offers a valuable tool for assessing and managing cardiac performance during the intraoperative period, and the perioperative nurse should be prepared to assist the physician during the insertion procedure in addition to recognizing the physiologic changes that may result through the use of invasive monitoring techniques.

IX. COMPLICATIONS OF GENERAL ANESTHESIA: MALIGNANT HYPERTHERMIA SYNDROME

1. **The most common severe complications of general anesthesia are aspiration pneumonia, failure to ventilate adequately, and malignant hyperthermia syndrome (M.H.S.).**
2. **M.H.S. is a potentially fatal hypermetabolic, genetically transmitted syndrome that appears without warning or preexisting symptoms.** It may be induced by inhalation agents, particularly halothane, and by injection of the depolarizing muscle relaxant succinylcholine (Anectine). It has also been seen occasionally in the emergency department following severe trauma or shock producing elevated stress levels.
3. **Etiologic considerations**
   a. M.H.S. is a dominantly inherited trait, but it remains dormant until one of the triggering agents or circumstances is activated. It is most often associated with circumstances producing anxiety, stress, or trauma, or in persons who pursue strenuous exercise on a routine basis.
   b. Physiologically, the patient apparently has a defect in the reticuloendothelial system of the muscle cell, allowing the anesthetic to trigger a sudden rise of calcium within the muscle cell. This increased calcium then sets off a series of biochemical reactions that lead to an increased metabolic rate, transforming the energy of the contracted muscle into heat **(hyperthermia).**
   c. Malignant hyperthermia syndrome, if untreated or not treated fast enough, has a 50 to 80 percent mortality rate, but this has improved through education about immediate treatment and the ability to prescreen with a muscle biopsy individuals with familial histories or previous complications with anesthesia.
4. **Signs and symptoms**
   a. **The most consistent early symptom is sudden and unexplained tachycardia, followed by tachypnea and occasionally spontaneous respirations.**
   b. Other signs and symptoms include unstable blood pressure; arrhythmias; dark blood at the surgical field; cyanosis and mottling of the skin; profuse sweating; fasciculations and/or rigidity; metabolic/respiratory acidosis; elevation of serum potassium and creatine phosphokinase, and a sudden rise in temperature (1° F every 15 minutes) to as high as 108° F or more.

5. **Emergency treatment**
   a. Each institution should have its own written protocol for treating a malignant hyperthermia crisis, which should include the following actions:
      (1) Stop the surgery and anesthesia immediately.
      (2) Change the anesthesia breathing circuits, and hyperventilate with 100 percent oxygen.
      (3) Administer Dantrium (dantrolene sodium) I.V., starting with 1 mg/kg up to a maximum cumulative dose of 10 mg/kg via rapid infusion; if arrhythmias are present, follow standard protocol.
      (4) Initiate cooling:
         • Iced saline solution (not Ringer's lactate) I.V.
         • Surface cooling via hypothermia blanket or ice packs.
         • If necessary, extracorporeal perfusion (femoral to femoral) may be needed to reduce fever, then warm until normothermia is regained.
      (5) Monitor all hemodynamic indicators: urinary output, arterial pressure, central venous pressure and arterial blood gas readings; maintain urinary output of at least 2 mL/kg per hour with Mannitol and/or Lasix (furosemide) if needed.
      (6) Once the patient is stable, transfer him or her to the I.C.U. for 24 to 48 hours of observation, follow-up monitoring, and postcrisis treatment.

6. **General nursing considerations**
   a. Although an M.H.S. crisis is uncommon, each surgical suite should have an emergency M.H.S. crisis cart available, stocked with the necessary drugs, supplies, and solutions according to the written protocol created by the department of anesthesia.
   b. A sheet with specific assignments should be kept on the cart, and each person or group of persons in the suite should be familiar with the standard operating procedure during a crisis.
   c. If preoperative evaluations reveal an unusual anesthesia history, all precautions should be taken prior to the start of the procedure, including the availability of iced saline solutions; Dantrium (unmixed), and additional drugs and supplies as directed by protocol.
   d. During the crisis, additional R.N.'s will be needed to assist with the preparation of the drugs and solutions, since 36 vials or more of Dantrium may have to be reconstituted, depending on the weight of the patient.

7. **Postcrisis follow-up**
   a. Although 80 percent of M.H.S. crises occur in surgery, the ·patient should be closely monitored for the next 72 hours, since the mortality rate from latent crisis is still high. Fast, comprehensive nursing actions, coupled with a **team effort**, can be the factor that prevents M.H.S. from becoming a life-threatening situation.
   b. A comprehensive scenario of all events should be documented as part of the patient's record, and the attending physician (if not the surgeon) should be informed, to continue follow-up therapy.

X. REGIONAL ANESTHESIA: TECHNIQUES AND AGENTS

1. **Regional anesthesia is defined as a temporary interruption of the transmission of nerve impulses to and from a specific area or region.** When using this technique, the patient does not lose consciousness, but motor function may be affected, depending on the extent of the anesthetized field, the level of injection, and the penetration capabilities of the agent.
2. Regional anesthesia has several advantages, including:
   a. Less systemic disturbance to body function than occurs with general anesthesia.
   b. The infeasibility of general anesthesia owing to recent ingestion of food.
   c. The presence of cardiac and/or pulmonary dysfunctions.
   d. Appropriateness when surgery is superficial and an anesthesiologist is not available.

A. **REGIONAL ANESTHESIA TECHNIQUES**

1. Several techniques are used with regional anesthesia, and the choice depends on the type and duration of surgery; the preference of the anesthesiologist and surgeon; and the patient's preference when feasible.
   a. **Topical anesthesia:** the anesthetic agent is applied directly to the skin and mucous membranes, which readily absorb the agent; therefore, it acts rapidly.
   b. **Local anesthesia (infiltration):** used for minor and superficial procedures in which the agent is injected into a specific area. If an anesthesiologist is present during the procedure, the technique is referred to as **local with M.A.C. (monitored anesthesia care).**
   c. **Nerve block:** a technique in which the anesthetic agent is injected into and around a nerve or a nerve group that supplies sensation to a small area of the body. Major blocks involve multiple nerves or a **plexus,** while minor blocks involve a single nerve.
   d. **Intravenous block (Bier block):** involves the intravenous injection of a local agent and the use of an occlusion tourniquet. The occlusion tourniquet prevents infiltration of the circulating agent beyond the extremity, thus preventing absorption into the general circulation. Bier blocks are used most often for procedures involving the arm, wrist, and hand.

B. **SPINAL AND EPIDURAL ANESTHESIA**

1. **Spinal anesthesia techniques**
   a. **Spinal anesthesia is created when the anesthetic agent is injected into the circulating cerebrospinal fluid (C.S.F.) contained in the arachnoid/subarachnoid space of the spinal cord.** The injection is performed through one of the interspaces between lumbar disk 2 (L_2) and the sacrum (S_1); the level of anesthesia depends mainly on the amount of the anesthetic injected, the position of the patient, and the level of the interspace used for the spinal.
   b. Spinal anesthesia can be divided into three levels: **low, mid, and high spinals.**
      (1) **Low spinals (saddle or caudal blocks)** are primarily used for surgeries involving the perineal or rectal areas.
      (2) **Mid spinals (below the level of the umbilicus--T_{10})** can be used for hernia repairs or appendectomies.
      (3) **High spinal (reaches the nipple line--T_4)** can be used for surgeries such as cesarean sections.
   c. Spinal anesthesia produces excellent analgesia and relaxation for abdominal and pelvic procedures, and is administered, most commonly, via a one-time bolus injection through a small-gauge needle, to prevent creating a large hole in the spinal cord. The most common position for spinal anesthesia is sitting or lateral decubitus (knee to chest) with the back curled outward.
   d. The level of anesthesia depends on the following factors:
      (1) Dose and concentration of agent used.
      (2) Volume of agent used.
      (3) Specific gravity of the solution.
      (4) C.S.F. pressure.
      (5) Positioning of the patient during and immediately after the injection.
2. **Epidural (peridural) anesthesia technique**
   a. **Epidural anesthesia, commonly associated with obstetric surgery, involves the injection of an anesthetic agent into the epidural space, the area outside the dura mater, but inside the spinal column.** Epidural anesthesia can be administered via bolus injection or through a small, thin catheter, and can be used for anorectal, vaginal, and perineal procedures.
   b. Patient positioning for epidural anesthesia is similar to spinal positioning. When a catheter is used, it must be securely taped to avoid migration of the catheter.
   c. Because the anesthetic agent does not enter the spinal cord, greater quantities of the agent must be used with the epidural technique.

3. **Possible complications and corrective actions**
   a. **Hypotension:** The most common adverse effect of spinal/epidural anesthesia is hypotension due to the anesthetic agent and vasodilation that can occur peripherally, reducing the venous blood return to the heart. Treatment consists of supportive vasopressors that increase the circulatory volume, the administration of oxygen, and fluid overloading before the block is administered.
   b. **Total spinal anesthesia:** Another, more critical adverse effect is a condition referred to as **total spinal**, which occurs when the anesthetic level is too high, depressing the respiratory and cardiac systems. Treatment involves respiratory assistance and cardiovascular support. This condition reverses itself, however, as the agent is absorbed and detoxifies within the body.
   c. **Nausea and vomiting:** Nausea and vomiting are not uncommon during the injection sequence. They may be due to the agent, hypotension, abrupt position change, apprehension, or all of these factors. Treatment consists of administration of oxygen and antiemetics.
   d. **Urinary retention:** Urinary retention is caused by an anesthetic-induced decrease in bladder tone; it may occur intraoperatively and postoperatively. Treatment is to monitor urinary output, increase fluid volume, and administer appropriate diuretics according to severity.
   e. **Paralysis and/or muscle weakness in legs or feet:** Peripheral paralysis is caused by a decrease in neuromuscular sensation, sometimes to a dangerous level. It is very rare, occurring in only 1 of 1000 to 2000 blocks. Treatment consists of careful and continuous assessment of the patient and immediately reporting any untoward reactions to the anesthesiologist for corrective action.
   f. **Postspinal headache:** A postspinal headache is due to intraspinal C.S.F. pressure changes or leaks in the dura or epidural space. Cerebrospinal fluid pressure causes stress on the nerves between the cranium and the brain. Postspinal headaches, not seen with epidural techniques, can occur immediately or 24 to 48 hours after injection; the treatment usually consists of bedrest, increased fluid intake, sedation, and, in severe cases, a blood patch graft to seal the hole (5-10 mL of the patient's blood via an epidural injection).
   g. **Backache:** Tenderness at the level of the block may last for a few weeks after spinal anesthesia. Epidural anesthesia has fewer adverse effects than spinal anesthesia, but occasionally urinary retention, pruritus, nausea, respiratory depression, and pronounced orthostatic hypotensive episodes can occur.
4. **Perioperative nursing management**
   a. Specific nursing activities that may prevent complications in patients receiving spinal or epidural anesthesia include:
      (1) Assisting anesthesia personnel in obtaining and maintaining optimum positioning during and after injection. Since the sensory system has been compromised, protection of all areas of lost sensation from pressure or improper body alignment is essential.
      (2) Moving the patient slowly when changing his or her position.
      (3) Maintaining sterile technique during the procedure.
      (4) Assessing the security of the catheter by anchoring it to prevent its possible migration.
      (5) Reporting any return of feelings expressed by the patient.
   b. The success of spinal and epidural anesthesia techniques requires patient cooperation. Providing emotional support and reassurance during the procedure, answering questions, and remaining close to the patient will in most instances reduce the patient's anxiety level and produce a successful result.

C. REGIONAL ANESTHESIA AGENTS

1. Regional anesthetic agents fall into two primary groups, **amides** and **esters,** based on their chemical composition and actions.
   a. **Amides** are organic substances that are primarily metabolized in the liver and excreted in the urine. Examples of amides include Marcaine, Corbocaine, and Duranest.
   b. **Ester** derivatives are metabolized rapidly and almost completely by blood cholinesterase. The remaining drug is then metabolized by the liver and excreted in the urine. Examples of

esters include Nesacaine, Metycaine, novocain, Pontocaine, and cocaine (the first local anesthetic agent).

    c. Only a few of these agents are used routinely during regional anesthesia, and the choice largely depends on the type of regional technique to be used and the choice of the anesthesiologist or surgeon based on the surgical procedure and its anticipated length.

2. Local anesthetics block depolarization by interfering with sodium-potassium exchange across the nerve cell membrane, preventing generation and conduction of the nerve impulses.

3. **Epinephrine additive**

    a. Most commercially prepared regional agents come both plain and with **epinephrine.** Epinephrine serves two purposes:

        (1) It produces vasoconstriction, thus aiding in the control in bleeding.

        (2) It potentiates the agent, giving it more strength and increasing the drug's time of action.

    b. Epinephrine may cause local irritation and dermatitis, tachycardia, palpitations, restlessness, or feelings of anxiety. In large doses, signs of overdose include convulsions, severe hypotension, respiratory depression, and anaphylactic reactions.

    c. Absorption varies according to dose, site of injection, and vasodilation produced by the drug. Epinephrine combined with a local anesthetic decreases absorption.

XI. MONITORING THE PATIENT RECEIVING LOCAL ANESTHESIA

1. In many instances, anesthesia personnel may not be present during a procedure involving local anesthesia, and the monitoring responsibilities fall to the perioperative nurse assigned to the case.

2. **Effective monitoring of the local anesthesia patient requires that the perioperative nurse have a working knowledge of the local agents and their potential adverse effects; basic cardiac monitoring skills; I.V. therapy management; and a general knowledge of drug interactions and administration of agents being used for I.V. sedation and/or relaxation.**

A. RECOMMENDED PRACTICES

1. According to A.O.R.N., the following recommended practices are considered the minimum standards of care for the patient undergoing surgery with local anesthesia:

    a. Each patient should be monitored for a reaction to drugs and for physiologic and behavioral changes.

    b. The perioperative nurse should have a working knowledge of the function and use of monitoring equipment and be able to interpret the data obtained.

    c. Documentation on the patient record during the administration of local anesthesia should reflect evidence of continued assessment, planning, implementation, and evaluation of patient care.

    d. Policies and procedures on monitoring the patient receiving local anesthesia should be written, reviewed annually, and be readily available within the practice setting.

B. ESTABLISHING STANDARDS OF PATIENT CARE

1. The establishment of standardized protocols for the management of local anesthesia procedures ensures quality nursing care for the patient and provides the necessary legal guidelines for the perioperative nurse, according to hospital and department approval and the Nurse Practice Act governing that practice.

2. **In general, greater preparation is needed for the surgical patient who is receiving local anesthesia than one receiving general anesthesia.** In addition to the preparation of instruments required for the case, the perioperative nurse must:

    a. Meet the psychologic and physiologic needs before, during, and after the procedure.

    b. Apply sound nursing judgment based on a knowledge of the biophysical sciences.

    c. Perform accurate assessment techniques in addition to precise documentation of the patient's responses and the care provided.

3. **Protocols should be written to define ongoing care and precise management of nursing interventions and to provide concrete direction for all staff involved with a specific aspect of care.** Protocols for management of the patient receiving local anesthesia, therefore, should include:
   a. Patient selection criteria.
   b. Extent and responsibility for monitoring.
   c. Method of recording patient data.
   d. Frequency of documentation of physiologic data obtained.
   e. Medications that may be administered by the perioperative nurse.
   f. Discharge criteria.

4. **Local infiltration or "field block," can be used for a wide variety of cases ranging from oral surgery to furnishing a field block surrounding a hernia or the incision and drainage of an abscess.** In this technique, the subcutaneous branches of the appropriate sensory nerves are anesthetized by the injection of a local anesthetic agent. When the agents are combined with epinephrine, the effect of the agent is prolonged, in addition to aiding in the control of bleeding due to vasoconstriction.

5. In addition to the local agent administered at the field, the patient may also receive an I.V. sedative to minimize the fear and anxiety associated with being "awake" during the procedure, in addition to minimizing the discomfort that may occur from the procedure.

6. To provide a safe environment for the patient, the perioperative nurse must be knowledgeable about how these agents work together, or alone, and be prepared to counteract their adverse effects in a safe and effective manner.

7. Most local anesthetics begin to act in less than 15 minutes after application or infiltration, but the duration of their action varies with each agent. The dosage and choice of agent will vary according to the **procedure**, the **level of anesthesia needed, tissue vascularity, patient responses,** and **surgeon's preference,** but the nurse monitoring the patient should be aware of these variables to render safe care.

C. PHYSIOLOGIC MONITORING DURING LOCAL ANESTHESIA

1. **Physiologic monitoring during local anesthesia consists of the continual observation of the patient's vital signs, including blood pressure (B/P), pulse (rate and rhythm), and respiratory rate; oxygen saturation; skin condition and color; and any changes in the patient's physical or behavioral status.** The patient must be constantly monitored during the procedure, and documentation of this monitoring must be specific as to frequency and methods used.

2. **Effective physiologic monitoring cannot be performed without baseline information to use as a guide; therefore, the nurse should obtain, through interview and observation, all pertinent data regarding the patient's past or present medical history, including allergies; history of hypertension; physical limitations (which could affect positioning), and emotional status.**

3. An I.V. line should be started preoperatively, or be readily available, according to hospital policy, and the information recorded on the appropriate form.

4. Upon entry into the operating room, and following the positioning of the patient on the operating room table, the perioperative nurse should apply the electrocardiograph leads and blood pressure cuff, explaining the procedure to the patient to relieve the "fear of the unknown." Initial baseline data should be recorded, which will serve as a reference point throughout the procedure. Additionally, oxygen via nasal cannula may be started, and a pulse oximeter should be used to monitor oxygen saturation levels.

5. Emergency equipment and medications should be in the room or be available for immediate use, according to established protocols.

6. Assessment and recording of the physiologic status should continue at least every 5 to 15 minutes during the procedure, depending on hospital protocol, and before and after each dose of medication. Any significant changes, either in vital signs, cardiac rhythm or sensorium should be reported to the surgeon immediately for appropriate corrective action.

7. Documentation of the physiologic status should flow throughout the record, with special notations of when medications are administered and the amount given. This critical documentation should

reflect the patient's responses to the drugs, and can serve as a reference in the event that complications develop during the procedure.

D. CONSCIOUS INTRAVENOUS SEDATION

1. Although the incision area has been desensitized, the patient who is awake frequently experiences anxiety, which can be treated with I.V. sedatives. These agents usually fall into two major categories: **narcotic analgesics** and **tranquilizers.** They may be administered separately or together, depending on the desired effect, and are administered, according to protocol, by the perioperative nurse.

2. **Tranquilizers cannot be easily reversed, so careful administration and frequent monitoring must be followed.** Narcotics, on the other hand, can be reversed with naloxone (Narcan), but the patient still requires continual observation, since the I.V. route allows the agent to enter the bloodstream quickly and can therefore do more harm in a shorter period of time.

3. Since I.V. sedation plays a major role in providing comfort to the patient receiving local anesthesia, each operating room should have a specific written protocol detailing which drugs can be administered by the perioperative nurse, the administrative techniques, including dilution factors, frequency, and emergency measures to be taken should a problem arise.

4. As with any medication administered to a patient, the nurse administering the drug should be aware of its pharmacologic properties, recommended dosages, side effects, and reversal agents associated with each drug. A reference chart or I.V. Sedation Monograph should be available so that precise and safe administration can be used throughout the procedure.

XII. ADDITIONAL NURSING MANAGEMENT RECOMMENDATIONS FOR LOCAL ANESTHESIA

1. **In addition to physiologic monitoring, the establishment and maintenance of I.V. solutions, and medication administration, the perioperative nurse is responsible for the assessment, planning, implementation, and evaluation of nursing care throughout the perioperative period, including the environmental management and psychologic support.**

2. **Creating a therapeutic environment**
   a. The atmosphere of the procedure room plays an important part in contributing to the patient's comfort during a local procedure. Maintaining a natural environment, talking to the patient, and allowing the patient to express his or her feelings and needs should be encouraged, since levels of pain tolerance are somewhat higher when concentration is shifted to other areas.
   b. It is equally important that a nonprofessional, carefree environment should be avoided, to maintain the patient's confidence in not only the surgeon, but also the nursing team. Careful planning and consideration, coupled with sound nursing judgment are the best guidelines for creating and maintaining a safe, therapeutic environment.

3. **Providing patient comfort**
   a. Many times the patient undergoing local anesthesia will be on the operating room table for several hours. By providing physical comfort during the procedure, anxiety and pain levels can be reduced, resulting in the need for less medication through a few simple comfort measures.
      (1) A **flotation mattress** should be placed on the operating table, to provide padding for bony areas of the back and hips.
      (2) The patient should be positioned in **proper body alignment,** with the elimination of ridges caused by sheets or gowns.
      (3) **Extremity pads** should be used on elbows and knees, especially if the patient is to be in the supine position.
      (4) **Small pillows** should be placed under the lower back and, if it does interfere with the patient's airway, under the head.
      (5) **Warm blankets** should be used to reduce the chill factor, since these patients will be more acutely aware of temperature drop than patients totally anesthetized.

    b. An explanation to the patient about limitations in movement during the procedure is recommended. The patient should be informed that a slight shift in position is permissible as long as the surgeon approves and the change does not interfere with the surgery or the positioning of the sterile drapes.

    c. If the patient requires oxygen administration during the procedure, a brief explanation of the nasal cannula and its purpose is in order, since the patient may interpret this therapy as a sign of an impending problem.

4. Controlling extraneous noise and traffic

    a. For all local cases, a sign posted on the O.R. door stating "This Patient is Awake" or something similar should be used, and the staff should be cautioned to avoid extraneous noise outside the room.

    b. Because the patient is awake, use of the intercom should be restricted, and if pathology is needed for a diagnostic examination of tissue specimens, a notation on the requisition stating that the patient is awake can eliminate any misinterpretation of the information heard by the patient.

    c. Staff permitting, two nurses should be assigned to local cases; one to serve in the circulating capacity and one to provide the monitoring and nursing care activities required to make the surgical experience as pleasant as possible.

XIII. DOCUMENTING PERIOPERATIVE NURSING CARE DURING LOCAL ANESTHESIA

1. **Documentation is the legal responsibility of the perioperative nurse.** Documentation during a local anesthesia case not only requires the nurse to record the surgical aspects of the case (e.g., intraoperative nurses record), but also requires that the monitoring of physiologic and psychologic status, and the appropriate nursing care and patient responses to that care, be accurately described.

2. In some institutions, the use of a **narrative nurses note** serves as the local anesthesia record, in addition to the operative record required for all operative procedures. In other hospitals, a **local anesthesia record** has been created for the documentation of this information, and like the narrative note, is used in addition to the operative record. This record, then, becomes a substitute for the anesthesia record.

XIV. POSTPROCEDURAL FOLLOW-UP AFTER LOCAL ANESTHESIA

1. **The preoperative interview offers the perioperative nurse the opportunity to individualize the care planned for the patient undergoing surgical intervention; the effectiveness of this care is evaluated during the postoperative phase of surgical intervention.**

2. Unlike general anesthesia patients, who are transported to the postanesthesia care unit for immediate monitoring and assessment, the local anesthesia patient usually returns to the designated postprocedural area (Ambulatory Surgery Unit or Patient Care Unit) for follow-up monitoring, which must continue to maintain the patient's safety.

3. **The main objective of postoperative care is to facilitate the rapid, safe, and comfortable recovery of the patient's normal functions.** Therefore, a safe rule of practice dictates that patients receiving I.V. sedation be returned to the PACU for a minimal period of time before being transferred to the designated postoperative area. If the patient received only the local agent, without I.V. sedation, transfer to the PACU area may not be necessary, depending on the policies of the hospital and the postoperative condition of the patient.

4. In either situation, the perioperative nurse's responsibility for patient care does not end in surgery, but continues until an accurate report of the patient's status has been given and documented to provide continuity of care.

5. For patients who are returning home the same day as surgery, the perioperative nurse should accompany the patient to the Ambulatory Care Unit, where a verbal report can be given to the nurse assigned to the patient, and the patient can relax and recover from the surgical procedure prior to returning home. Additionally, any postoperative instructions can be given to both the patient and family, with explanations as necessary.

PRACTICE QUESTIONS

1. **Which of the following is NOT one of the major goals of anesthesia?**

   1. *To produce analgesia.*

   2. *To reduce inflammation.*

   3. *To produce amnesia.*

   4. *To induce muscle relaxation.*

2. **A patient's ability to tolerate anesthesia depends largely on two factors: the normality of respiration and circulation and the:**

   1. *homeostatic functions of the patient's liver, kidneys, and endocrine and central nervous systems.*

   2. *patient's tolerance levels for metabolites that build up during a surgical procedure involving anesthesia.*

   3. *patient's psychologic status.*

   4. *interactions between the drugs used in anesthesia and those administered to the patient for his/her disease.*

3. **Prior to a patient's undergoing anesthesia, the anesthesia team should follow all of the following procedures EXCEPT:**

   1. *Establish a formal evaluation program that can be used later us a guide for an anesthesia program that meets the patient's needs.*

   2. *Carry out any special diagnostic procedure and test needed to provide a comprehensive assessment of the patient's physical status.*

   3. *Tell the patient the plan for anesthesia so that the patient can make an intelligent decision.*

   4. *Administer any preoperative agents required to abolish pain and/or relax muscles, at least 2 hours prior to the procedure.*

4. **The American Society of Anesthesiology's Classification System is used prior to a patient's receiving anesthesia in order to:**

   1. *determine the risk factors of anesthesia based on the current health status of the patient.*

   2. *educate the patient as to the actual anesthetic agents to be used during surgery, and their effects.*

   3. *identify specific postoperative measures that must be followed to avoid complications from anesthesic agents to be administered.*

   4. *classify the likely physiologic effects of anesthesia on the patient's body systems into one of eight A.S.A. categories.*

5. **A patient admitted for open-heart surgery has a history of mild diabetes and is overweight. As part of the preoperative evaluation of this patient, the anesthesiologist *most* likely will place the patient into which A.S.A. Classification System class?**

    1. *Class 1.*

    2. *Class 2.*

    3. *Class 3.*

    4. *Class 4.*

6. **A patient admitted to Emergency with marked signs of cardiac insufficiency is rushed into surgery before an evaluation can be performed. The anesthesiologist *most* likely will place this patient into which A.S.A. class?**

    1. *Class 2E.*

    2. *Class 3.*

    3. *Class 4E.*

    4. *Class 5.*

7. **The anesthesiologist's *primary* objective in the selection of preoperative medications to use with a patient is to:**

    1. *prepare the patient physically and psychologically for the effects of the specific anesthetic agents to be used.*

    2. *avoid combining agents that will interact to the detriment of the patient's physiologic status.*

    3. *avoid causing disturbances in the patient's cardiovascular system, while providing physical and emotional support and comfort.*

    4. *anticipate unusual events that may occur as a result of anesthesia and/or the surgical procedure.*

8. **The term *balanced anesthesia* refers to anesthesia methods that combine:**

    1. *a general and a regional anesthesia to reduce sensation while minimizing systemic side effects.*

    2. *two or more inhalation agents that together work more effectively than would any single agent alone.*

    3. *anesthetic agents with other, non-anesthetic medications required to treat the patient's physical condition.*

    4. *intravenous induction agents with an inhalation agent to simulate the effects of a general anesthesia agent.*

9. **In the administration of general anesthesia, performance of the surgical prep and the repositioning of the patient prior to surgery should take place:**

    1. *when the patient enters the procedure room and is placed on the operating table, and prior to intubation.*

    2. *in the holding area prior to bringing the patient into the operating room for induction.*

3. *only when stabilization has been accomplished and prior to the start of the reversal process.*

4. *during induction, after successful intubation and stabilization.*

10. **The perioperative nurse's responsibilities during the reversal/extubation phase of general anesthesia include all of the following EXCEPT:**

    1. *to make arrangements if special equipment is needed during the immediate postanesthesia period.*

    2. *to accompany the patient with anesthesia personnel to the postanesthesia care unit (PACU).*

    3. *to be aware of the patient's status and be prepared to assist anesthesia personnel to prevent unnecessary injury.*

    4. *to remain in the postanesthesia care unit (PACU) until the patient has emerged fully.*

11. **Among the following nursing activities, the one that would be *most* appropriate during the relaxation stage of general anesthesia is:**

    1. *validating with anesthesia the appropriate time to reposition and prep.*

    2. *closing the O.R. doors to reduce extraneous noises.*

    3. *lightly restraining the extremities to avoid injury.*

    4. *obtaining the emergency cart and defibrillator.*

12. **The following are all signs that a patient is in Stage 3 of general anesthesia, Surgical Anesthesia, EXCEPT:**

    1. *loss of eye movement.*

    2. *decreased intercostal muscle movement.*

    3. *appearance of the vocal cord reflex.*

    4. *decreased muscle tone.*

13. **One sign of Stage IV of Surgical Anesthesia is if:**

    1. *pulse is rapid and thready.*

    2. *reflexes (e.g., vomit/gag reflex) disappear.*

    3. *eye movement ceases.*

    4. *intercostal muscle movement decreases.*

14. **The sequence for inhalation anesthesia consists of all of the following measures EXCEPT:**

    1. *The patient is given oxygen via a mask following the administration of the anesthesia agent.*

    2. *A barbiturate and/or muscle relaxant is administered to relax the patient.*

3. *The clinician hyperventilates with oxygen and inserts the endotracheal tube/nasotracheal tube.*

4. *Upon completion of the surgical procedure, and prior to extubation, the clinician hyperventilates with 100 percent oxygen.*

15. **Of the following intravenous drugs, the only one capable of providing total relaxation of skeletal muscles, resulting in reduced tissue trauma, is:**

    1. *Pentothal.*

    2. *Demerol.*

    3. *Pavulon.*

    4. *Valium.*

16. **In administering a narcotic analgesic, either preoperatively or as an adjunct therapy during analgesia, one must remember that narcotic agents:**

    1. *cannot be reversed and therefore must be used with caution.*

    2. *are slow-acting and therefore must be administered at least 90 minutes before general anesthesia.*

    3. *must be administered slowly to avoid severe cardiopulmonary depression.*

    4. *interact with mycin (e.g., Neomycin) to prolong the narcotic effect of the agent.*

17. **An essential factor in the safe use of neuromuscular blocking agents in general anesthesia is:**

    1. *careful monitoring of blood loss and urinary output to detect any signs of kidney failure.*

    2. *recognizing that both induction and emergence are very rapid with nondepolarizing relaxants.*

    3. *careful monitoring of changes in CO_2 and potassium levels related to cardiac arrhythmias.*

    4. *the establishment of an effective airway along with controlled, monitored ventilation.*

18. **The *primary* concern of the anesthesia clinician during anesthesia is the:**

    1. *monitoring and restoration of normal fluid balance.*

    2. *establishment of an effective airway, along with controlled, monitored ventilation.*

    3. *evaluation of left and right ventricular function.*

    4. *possible induction of malignant hyperthermia syndrome by narcotic agents.*

19. **Among the measures that may help to prevent complications from hemodynamic disturbances during anesthesia are all of the following EXCEPT:**

    1. *accurate measurement of blood loss and urinary output during the procedure.*

    2. *hemodynamic monitoring for long or complicated cases.*

3. *the use of a flotation mattress or extremity pads to reduce discomfort.*

4. *continuous temperature monitoring and the use of a pulse oximeter.*

20. **Hemodynamic monitoring during anesthesia is used primarily for all of the following EXCEPT:**

    1. *to assess fluid volume status.*

    2. *to evaluate cardiovascular therapies.*

    3. *to evaluate left and right ventricular function.*

    4. *to prevent malignant hyperthermia syndrome.*

21. **While participating in the hemodynamic monitoring of a patient under general anesthesia, a perioperative nurse notices that an arterial pressure tracing is more than 20 mm Hg higher than cuff pressure. The nurse's correct reaction is to notify the anesthesia clinician that the:**

    1. *patient is undergoing cardiogenic shock.*

    2. *monitor transducer may be leaking.*

    3. *catheter tubing may be kinked.*

    4. *monitor balloon has ruptured.*

22. **The most common severe complications of general anesthesia include each of the following EXCEPT:**

    1. *malignant hyperthermia syndrome (M.H.S.).*

    2. *aspiration pneumonia.*

    3. *failure to ventilate adequately.*

    4. *adverse drug interactions.*

23. **Which of the following statements about malignant hyperthermia syndrome (M.H.S.) is correct?**

    1. *It is genetically transmitted.*

    2. *It is rarely fatal, even if untreated.*

    3. *It rarely appears without warning or preexisting symptoms.*

    4. *It cannot be induced by inhalation agents.*

24. **Which of the following would be the LEAST appropriate action to take in the emergency treatment of malignant hyperthermia syndrome (M.H.S.)?**

    1. *Increase anesthesia and proceed quickly with surgery.*

    2. *Change the anesthesia breathing circuits, and hyperventilate with 100 percent oxygen.*

3. *Administer Dantrium I.V., starting with 1 mg/kg up to a maximum cumulative dose of 10 mg/kg via rapid infusion.*

4. *Initiate cooling, using iced saline I.V. and surface cooling via hyperthermia blanket or ice packs.*

25. **An intravenous (Bier) block differs from a nerve block in that it involves:**

    1. *injection of anesthesia into a specific area.*

    2. *infiltration of anesthesia.*

    3. *procedures involving the trunk of the body.*

    4. *intravenous injection of a local agent.*

26. **Epidural anesthesia is being used in a patient admitted for an anorectal procedure. The most common position for administration of this type of anesthesia is:**

    1. *sitting or knee to chest with the back curled outward.*

    2. *supine with head lower than the feet.*

    3. *supine with buttocks near lower break in the table.*

    4. *prone with patient's arms rotated to the padded armboards.*

27. **During spinal/epidural anesthesia, the nurse should be alert to all of the following potential adverse effects of anesthesia EXCEPT:**

    1. *hypotension and vasodilation that can occur peripherally, reducing the venous blood return to the heart.*

    2. *total spinal anesthesia, with depression of the respiratory and cardiac systems.*

    3. *sudden and unexplained tachycardia, followed by tachypnea and occasionally spontaneous respirations.*

    4. *urinary retention caused by an anesthesia-induced decrease in bladder tone.*

28. **Epinephrine may be added to commercially prepared regional anesthetic agents, both to aid in the control of bleeding and to:**

    1. *reduce the inflammatory effects of regional agents.*

    2. *give agents more strength and increase their time of action.*

    3. *minimize the patient's fear and anxiety associated with being "awake" during the procedure.*

    4. *reduce the risks of severe hypotension and respiratory depression.*

29. **Effective monitoring of the local anesthesia patient requires the perioperative nurse to exercise several important skills. Of the following skills, the one LEAST likely to apply to the nurse is:**

    1. *a working knowledge of the local agents and their potential side effects.*

    2. *basic cardiac monitoring skills.*

3. *I.V. therapy management skills.*

4. *hemodynamic monitoring skills.*

30. **Perioperative nursing protocols covering the management of the patient receiving local anesthesia typically would include all of the following EXCEPT:**

    1. *the criteria to be used by the nurse in planning the procedure.*

    2. *the medications that may be administered by the nurse.*

    3. *the extent and responsibility for monitoring by the nurse.*

    4. *the frequency of documentation of physiologic data obtained throughout the procedure.*

31. **A patient undergoing a surgical procedure involving local anesthesia is wheeled into the operating room and positioned on the operating room table. The perioperative nurse's next responsibility is to:**

    1. *assess and record the patient's physiologic status.*

    2. *apply the electrocardiograph leads and blood pressure cuff.*

    3. *note on the patient's chart the medications to be administered and the amounts to be given.*

    4. *start oxygen via nasal cannula and start the pulse oximeter.*

32. **In addition to physiologic monitoring, I.V. maintenance, and medication administration, the perioperative nurse is responsible for a variety of other activities throughout the perioperative period. Included among these responsibilities are all of the following EXCEPT:**

    1. *creating a therapeutic environment for the patient (e.g., reducing patient anxiety).*

    2. *providing patient comfort (e.g., positioning the patient in proper body alignment).*

    3. *controlling extraneous noise and traffic (e.g., posting a "Patient is Awake" sign outside the patient's room).*

    4. *documenting the surgical and nursing aspects of the case (e.g., preparing a narrative nurses note).*

33. **Postoperatively, the surgical patient undergoing local anesthesia usually is:**

    1. *transported to the postanesthesia care unit for monitoring and assessment.*

    2. *returned to his/her room for monitoring by floor nurses.*

    3. *released without further monitoring or assessment unless complications are anticipated.*

    4. *returned to the designated postprocedural area for follow-up monitoring.*

ANSWER EXPLANATIONS

1. **The answer is 2.** Anesthesia consists of making the patient insensitive to pain in a specific area of the body or the body as a whole. Its objectives are to (1) produce analgesia, (2) produce amnesia, (3) induce muscle relaxation, and (4) provide control of the autonomic nervous system reflexes to the brain and the stress of surgery.

2. **The answer is 1.** The ability to tolerate the adverse effects of anesthesia depends largely on the normality of respiration and circulation and the homeostatic functions of the liver, kidneys, and endocrine and central nervous systems. All patients receiving anesthesia, regardless of type, should undergo an evaluation and assessment by an anesthesiologist prior to the administration of anesthesia. Past and present medical history should be reviewed with attention focused on prior surgical experiences and the physiologic alterations induced by disease.

3. **The answer is 4.** During the preparation stage for anesthesia, a formal evaluation program should be established, consisting of an interview, a systems review, and a record of important data that can be used later as a guide for an individualized anesthesia program that meets the needs of the patient. Any special diagnostic procedures and tests should be carried out as soon as possible so that the results are on the chart prior to surgery. This allows a comprehensive assessment of the patient's physical status to be performed. The patient should then be told of the plan for anesthesia, including the methods proposed, so that the patient can make an intelligent decision. At that point, an informed consent should be signed and witnessed. Most institutions insist on both an anesthesia summary and a signed anesthesia consent permit before anesthesia can be administered.

4. **The answer is 1.** For the purpose of providing appropriate anesthesia, a classification of the patient's physical status was adapted by the American Society of Anesthesiology in 1963, and is used to determine the risk factors based on the current health status of the patient. Included in this evaluation are the presence of coexisting diseases and type of surgery (emergency or elective) being performed. As part of the preoperative evaluation, the anesthesiologist will place the patient into one of the six classifications, according to the physiologic description of the patient. Each class (1 through 6) considers the presence of coexisting diseases and the type of surgery (emergency or elective) being performed. With any patient in one of these six classes who is operated on as an emergency, the letter E is placed beside the numerical class, reflecting that this patient is considered a poor risk and/or is in poor physical condition, with no evaluation performed owing to the acuity of the situation (for example: 1E; 2E).

5. **The answer is 2.** Class 2 in the A.S.A.'s Classification System covers mild-to-moderate systemic disturbances caused either by the condition to be treated surgically or by another pathophysiologic process. The extremes of age (neonate or adult between 80 and 90 years old) may be added to this classification, even though no discernible systemic disease is present. Extreme obesity and chronic bronchitis may be included in this category. Examples include, but are not limited to: nonlimiting or slightly limiting organic heart disease, mild diabetes, essential hypertension, anemia.

6. **The answer is 3.** Class 4 covers severe systemic disorders that are already life-threatening and are not always correctable by surgery or operation planned. Examples include, but are not limited to: marked signs of cardiac insufficiency, persistent (unstable) angina, active myocarditis, advanced pulmonary, hepatic, renal, or endocrine insufficiency. The letter E is placed beside the numerical class, reflecting that this patient is considered a poor risk and/or is in poor physical condition, with no evaluation performed owing to the acuity of the situation.

7. **The answer is 3.** The selection of preoperative medications is made by the anesthesiologist, based on the preoperative assessment of the patient. The assessment includes the patient's physical and emotional status, age, weight, past medical history (including medication history), and demands of the proposed surgical procedure. The anesthesiologist tries to avoid causing disturbances in the cardiorespiratory system, while providing physical and emotional support and comfort. Which of the four types of preoperative medications chosen depends on the physical and psychologic needs of the patient. These agents include: (1) sedative-hypnotics, to promote relaxation and rest and to stabilize the blood pressure and pulse; (2) anticholinergics, as drying agents to decrease secretions of mucus in the mouth; (3) narcotics, to promote relaxation and enhance the effect of the anesthetics, and to control pain; and (4) antianxiety/antiemetics, to produce relaxation and reduce anxiety and nausea.

8. **The answer is 4.** Balanced anesthesia describes anesthesia methods that combine a muscle relaxant, a barbiturate, a narcotic, and an inhalation agent (nitrous oxide). When combined, these agents produce a state similar to that produced by a general anesthesia agent.

9. **The answer is 4.** The induction/intubation phase of general anesthesia begins with the introduction of anesthetic agents, and ends with the successful intubation and stabilization of the patient. This phase is considered to be the most dangerous for the patient; therefore, all precautions must be taken to ensure the patient's safety. It is only after successful intubation and stabilization, and with permission of anesthesia personnel, that the patient can be repositioned as necessary and the surgical prep can be performed. At no time during the induction phase should the circulating nurse leave the room, since she or he may be the only person available to assist anesthesia personnel should a complication arise.

10. **The answer is 4.** The reversal/extubation phase of general anesthesia begins during the closure of the operative wound and ends immediately prior to transporting the patient to the postanesthesia care unit or designated postanesthesia area. As with Phase 2, the extubation phase is a dangerous time for the patient, since physiologic changes could trigger unexpected events, such as laryngospasm, vomiting, slow spontaneous respirations, or uncontrolled reflex movement. Some patients can emerge from anesthesia with wild, uncontrolled movements that could cause harm if not handled gently, while others emerge smoothly, without difficulty. In addition to the activities in choices 1, 2, and 3, the perioperative nurse should prepare a report of nursing activities during the intraoperative phase and give the report to the nurse who will continue the patient's postoperative care.

11. **The answer is 2.** The relaxation (amnesia/analgesia) stage of general anesthesia runs from the beginning of anesthesia to the loss of consciousness. Pain sensation is not completely lost, but reaction to pain has been altered. The patient has feelings of drowsiness and dizziness and may appear inebriated; hearing becomes exaggerated; and pain sensation is decreased. The nurse should close the O.R. doors to reduce extraneous noises; confirm proper positioning, including all safety factors; verify that anesthesia suction is available and working correctly; reduce talking, unnecessary movement, and noise to only what is absolutely necessary; and remain at the head of the O.R. table to assist the anesthesia clinician and provide the patient with emotional support.

12. **The answer is 3.** The vocal cord reflex (which could result in laryngospasms) begins to disappear, not to appear. The stage of Surgical Anesthesia ranges from the regular pattern of respirations to the total paralysis of intercostal muscles and cessation of voluntary respirations. This stage can be further divided into four planes, ranging from light anesthesia through excessively deep anesthesia. During this stage muscle tone and various reflexes diminish, eye movement ceases, and, in deep surgical anesthesia, only diaphragmatic respiration remains.

13. **The answer is 1.** Stage IV, the Danger (Premortem) stage of Surgical Anesthesia, runs from the time of cessation of respirations to failure of the circulation, caused by high levels of anesthesia in the C.N.S. It is accidentally reached and is not desirable. The patient's biologic responses include: medullary paralysis, cardiac/respiratory collapse; pupils fixed and dilated; pulse rapid and thready; respirations cease, coma develops; circulatory and respiratory arrest. Should these signs appear, the nurse should be prepared to assist in emergency resuscitation measures (C.P.R.); obtain the emergency cart and defibrillator; remain in the room at all times; and document all events and therapies as they occur.

14. **The answer is 1.** The patient is given oxygen **before** rather than after administration of the anesthesia agent. Upon completion of the surgical procedure, and prior to extubation, the clinician hyperventilates with 100 percent oxygen, then removes the tube and continues administering oxygen with the mask until the patient is stable for transport with no signs of respiratory obstructions.

15. **The answer is 3.** Intravenous medications, administered by bolus dose or continuous drip infusion, are frequently used to supplement inhalation agents, and thus provide a safe, reversible state of anesthesia. Three categories of intravenous drugs are associated with general anesthesia: (1) **Barbiturates** act directly in the C.N.S., producing an effect ranging from the mild sedation to sleep; included are Pentothal, Brevital,

and Surital. (2) **Narcotics** render the patient pain-free and, in some cases, produce a euphoric state; included are Demerol, morphine sulfate, Sublimaze, Alfenta, and Sufenta. (3) **Muscle relaxants** provide total relaxation of skeletal muscles, resulting in reduced tissue trauma (this cannot be accomplished by other intravenous agents); included are depolarizing relaxants such as succinylcholine (Anectine and Quelicin) and nondepolarizing agents such as curare, Pavulon, Flaxedil, Norcuron, Tracrium, and Diprivan. In addition, **tranquilizers** (Valium, Versed, Inapsine), neuroleptanalgesics, and phencyclidines are used to supplement the inhalation technique. Some agents, such as narcotics, can be totally reversed (antagonized), while others can only be partially reversed. This factor may influence the choice of intravenous agent used.

16. **The answer is 3.** The respiratory and cardiovascular depressive effects of narcotics are well known, and these agents are most often given by bolus injection. They can be given via infusion drip, however, under certain conditions or procedures such as open-heart surgery. Because all narcotic analgesics are derived from basically the same substance or synthetic derivatives, their basic characteristics are very similar: they produce potent analgesia; they are fast-acting, with prolonged analgesic effect; they are reversible with a narcotic antagonist (naloxone); they may produce nausea and vomiting; and they must be administered slowly to avoid severe cardiopulmonary depression.

17. **The answer is 4.** The safe use of neuromuscular blocking agents requires the establishment of an effective airway, either by oral airway and mask, or by endotracheal intubation, along with controlled, monitored ventilation. For anesthesia to be safe, the anesthesiologist/C.R.N.A. must carefully monitor the patient's physiologic status and be prepared to correct any adverse effects caused by the agent(s) being used. Muscle relaxation can be evaluated by using a nerve stimulator placed between the ulnar nerve at the elbow or wrist, which can determine the presence or absence of contractions or diminished strength of the hand muscles. In addition to evaluating the muscle relaxation, the saturation of oxygen within the cells can be monitored with a pulse oximeter, and because of its accuracy, is now considered the standard of care for all patients receiving anesthesia or I.V. sedation via narcotic analgesia, not only in surgery but in the immediate postoperative recovery areas.

18. **The answer is 1.** Surgical procedures impose a variety of stressors on the patient, both psychologically and physiologically. Among those that require constant monitoring are body fluids, electrolytes, and acid-base disturbances. Most patients facing elective operative procedures have oral intake withheld during the 8 to 12 hours preceding surgery, resulting in unreplaced solute and water loss. In view of this preoperative loss, the monitoring and restoration of normal fluid balance becomes the primary concern of the anesthesia clinician, since this deficit can ultimately affect all body systems and directly or indirectly affect the outcome of the surgical procedure.

19. **The answer is 3.** Although the ultimate management of fluids and electrolytes and acid-base balance is part of the total anesthesia care, the perioperative nurse should have a working knowledge of the disturbances and how to prevent/correct them. By carefully assessing the patient, the perioperative nurse can anticipate potential problems and therefore be of greater assistance to the anesthesiologist during the intraoperative period. The following recommendations may help to prevent complications from hemodynamic disturbances: (1) accurate measurement of blood loss and urinary output during the procedure; (2) hemodynamic monitoring for long or complicated cases, especially those involved with the cardiorespiratory systems; (3) periodic measurement of intravascular status: Hct and Hgb; C.B.C.; A.B.C; chemistry profiles; (4) continuous temperature monitoring; use of pulse oximeter (measurement of O_2 saturation at tissue levels); (5) proper positioning with supportive aids padding bony prominences; providing adequate support devices; maintaining near proper alignment; and (6) preoperative education to reduce stress levels.

20. **The answer is 4.** Hemodynamic monitoring is used primarily to (1) evaluate left and right ventricular function, (2) assess fluid volume status, and (3) evaluate cardiovascular therapies. Changes in hemodynamic measurements always precede changes in the patient's clinical status, and early detection using hemodynamic monitoring can prevent critical conditions from developing. Hemodynamic monitoring can be performed by noninvasive techniques, such as noninvasive blood pressure monitoring, measurement of intake and output, and so on, or by an invasive technique through the insertion of a catheter that measures values of hemodynamic status.

21. **The answer is 3.** The perioperative nurse can assist in deciphering possible problems that occur in invasive hemodynamic monitoring by understanding how the equipment functions. In this situation, with arterial pressure tracing more than 20 mm Hg higher than cuff pressure, the catheter may be kinked or positioned against an arterial wall, or the monitor transducer may not be calibrated or zeroed correctly. The proper response is to check for kinks in the tubing; reposition and splint arm/hand if needed; and recalibrate and rezero the transducer.

22. **The answer is 4.** The most common severe complications of general anesthesia are aspiration pneumonia, failure to ventilate adequately, and malignant hyperthermia syndrome (M.H.S.).

23. **The answer is 2.** M.H.S. is a potentially fatal hypermetabolic, genetically transmitted syndrome that appears without warning or preexisting symptoms. It may be induced by inhalation agents, particularly halothane, and by injection of the depolarizing muscle relaxant succinylcholine (Anectine). It has also been seen occasionally in the emergency department following severe trauma or shock producing elevated stress levels.

24. **The answer is 1.** Surgery and anesthesia should be stopped immediately. Additional measures for treating an M.H.S. emergency include: (1) following standard protocols if arryhthmias are present; (2) if necessary, reducing fever via extracorpeal perfusion (femoral to femoral), then warming until normothermia is regained; (3) monitoring all hemodynamic indicators (e.g., urinary output); (4) maintaining urinary output of at least 2 mL/kg per hour with Mannitol and/or Lasix (furosemide) if needed; and (5) once the patient is stable, transferring him or her to the I.C.U. for 24 to 48 hours of observation, follow-up monitoring, and postcrisis treatment.

25. **The answer is 4.** An intravenous block (Bier block) involves the intravenous injection of a local agent and the use of an occlusion tourniquet. The occlusion tourniquet prevents infiltration of the circulating agent beyond the extremity, thus preventing absorption into the general circulation. Bier blocks are used most often for procedures involving the arm, wrist, and hand.

26. **The answer is 1.** Epidural anesthesia, commonly associated with obstetric surgery, involves the injection of an anesthetic agent into the epidural space, the area outside the dura mater, but inside the spinal column. Epidural anesthesia can be administered via bolus injection or through a small, thin catheter, and can be used for anorectal, vaginal, and perineal procedures. Patient positioning for epidural anesthesia is similar to spinal positioning, in which the patient is sitting or in a lateral decubitus (knee to chest) position with the back curled outward. When a catheter is used, it must be securely taped to avoid migration of the catheter.

27. **The answer is 3.** The most common adverse effects of spinal/epidural anesthesia are: (1) **hypotension** due to the anesthetic agent and vasodilation that can occur peripherally, reducing the venous blood return to the heart; treatment consists of supportive vasopressors that increase the circulatory volume, the administration of oxygen, and fluid overloading before the block is administered; (2) **total spinal anesthesia**, which occurs when the anesthetic level is too high, depressing the respiratory and cardiac systems; treatment involves respiratory assistance and cardiovascular support; (3) **nausea and vomiting** due to the agent, hypotension, abrupt position change, apprehension, or all of these factors; treatment consists of administration of oxygen and antiemetics; (4) **urinary retention** caused by an anesthetic-induced decrease in bladder tone; treatment is to monitor urinary output, increase fluid volume, and administer appropriate diuretics according to severity; (5) rarely, **paralysis and/or muscle weakness in legs or feet** caused by a decrease in neuromuscular sensation, sometimes to a dangerous level; treatment consists of careful and continuous assessment of the patient and immediately reporting any untoward reactions to the anesthesiologist for corrective action; (6) **postspinal headache** due to intraspinal C.S.F. pressure changes or leaks in the dura or epidural space; treatment usually consists of bedrest, increased fluid intake, sedation, and, in severe cases, a blood patch graft to seal the hole (5-10 mL of the patient's blood via an epidural injection); and (7) **tenderness at the level of the block (backache)**, which may last for a few weeks after spinal anesthesia. Sudden tachycardia is an early symptom of M.H.S.

28. **The answer is 2.** Most commercially prepared regional agents come both plain and with epinephrine. Epinephrine serves two purposes: (1) it produces vasoconstriction, thus aiding in the control of bleeding; and (2) it potentiates the agent, giving it more strength and increasing the drug's time of action. Epinephrine may cause local irritation and dermatitis, tachycardia, palpitations, restlessness, or feelings of anxiety. In large doses, signs of overdose include convulsions, severe hypotension, respiratory depression, and anaphylactic reactions. Absorption varies according to dose, site of injection, and vasodilation produced by the drug. Epinephrine combined with a local anesthetic decreases absorption.

29. **The answer is 4.** In many instances, anesthesia personnel may not be present during a procedure involving local anesthesia, and the monitoring responsibilities fall to the perioperative nurse assigned to the case. Effective monitoring of the local anesthesia patient requires that the perioperative nurse have a working knowledge of the local agents and their potential adverse effects; basic cardiac monitoring skills; I.V. therapy management; and a general knowledge of drug interactions and administration of agents being used for I.V. sedation and/or relaxation. Hemodynamic monitoring is usually the responsibility of the anesthesia clinician, although the nurse should be able to recognize hemodynamic changes that accompany a disease state and/or surgical procedure, and to anticipate possible complications.

30. **The answer is 1.** In general, greater preparation is needed for the surgical patient who is receiving local anesthesia than one receiving general anesthesia. Protocols should be written to define ongoing care and precise management of nursing interventions and to provide concrete direction for all staff involved with a specific aspect of care. Protocols for management of the patient receiving local anesthesia, therefore, should include: patient selection criteria; extent and responsibility for monitoring; method of recording patient data; frequency of documentation of physiologic data obtained; medications that may be administered by the perioperative nurse; and discharge criteria.

31. **The answer is 2.** Upon entry into the operating room, and following the positioning of the patient on the operating room table, the perioperative nurse should apply the electrocardiograph leads and blood pressure cuff, explaining the procedure to the patient to relieve the "fear of the unknown." Initial baseline data should be recorded, which will serve as a reference point throughout the procedure. Additionally, oxygen via nasal cannula may be started, and a pulse oximeter should be used to monitor oxygen saturation levels. Emergency equipment and medications should be in the room or be available for immediate use, according to established protocols. Assessment and recording of the physiologic status should continue at least every 5 to 15 minutes during the procedure, depending on hospital protocol, and before and after each dose of medication. Any significant changes, either in vital signs, cardiac rhythm or sensorium should be reported to the surgeon immediately for appropriate corrective action. Documentation of the physiologic status should flow throughout the record, with special notations of when medications are administered and the amount given. This critical documentation should reflect the patient's responses to the drugs, and can serve as a reference in the event that complications develop during the procedure.

32. **All of the answers are correct.** In addition to physiologic monitoring, the establishment and maintenance of I.V. solutions, and medication administration, the perioperative nurse is responsible for the assessment, planning, implementation, and evaluation of nursing care throughout the perioperative period, including the environmental management and psychologic support. This includes creating a therapeutic environment, providing patient comfort, controlling extraneous noise and traffic, and documenting the procedure. Documentation is the legal responsibility of the perioperative nurse. Documentation during a local anesthesia case not only requires the nurse to record the surgical aspects of the case (e.g., intraoperative nurses record), but also requires that the monitoring of physiologic and psychologic status, and the appropriate nursing care and patient responses to that care, be accurately described. In some institutions, the use of a narrative nurses note serves as the local anesthesia record, in addition to the operative record required for all operative procedures. In other hospitals, a local anesthesia record has been created for the documentation of this information, and like the narrative note, is used in addition to the operative record. This record, then, becomes a substitute for the anesthesia record.

33. **The answer is 4.** Unlike general anesthesia patients, who are transported to the postanesthesia care unit for immediate monitoring and assessment, the local anesthesia patient usually returns to the designated postprocedural area (Ambulatory Surgery Unit or Patient Care Unit) for follow-up monitoring, which must

continue to maintain the patient's safety. However, the main objective of postoperative care is to facilitate the rapid, safe, and comfortable recovery of the patient's normal functions. Therefore, a safe rule of practice dictates that patients receiving I.V. sedation be returned to the PACU for a minimal period of time before being transferred to the designated postoperative area. If the patient received only the local agent, without I.V. sedation, transfer to the PACU area may not be necessary, depending on the policies of the hospital and the postoperative condition of the patient. In either situation, the perioperative nurse's responsibility for patient care does not end in surgery, but continues until an accurate report of the patient's status has been given and documented to provide continuity of care.

5 Operating Room Theory and Techniques: Infection Control and Asepsis

STUDY OUTLINE

I. **THE INFECTIOUS PROCESS**

    A. **HOST-MICROBE INTERACTION**

1. The mere presence of microorganisms in or on the body does not signify disease. Many microorganisms inhabit the body surface and lumen of the intestinal tract as resident flora, never causing disease or harm to the host. But when a microorganism is allowed to invade tissues and multiply, it can become capable of causing infection or disease and stimulating a host response.
2. The infection may or may not be accompanied by overt symptoms of the disease. A local infection, for example, is usually restricted to a specific anatomic site, causing only an inflammatory response to that site. A systemic or generalized infection can occur as the result of microorganisms and their products spreading throughout the body.
3. An initial infection, caused by one kind of microorganism is called a **primary infection**, while the **secondary infection** usually involves a second microorganism entering the system and can result in a more toxic form of infection, making it harder to arrest or destroy.
4. When a tissue becomes damaged, either by injury or disease, the initial stage of **acute inflammation** occurs, causing vascular and cellular changes. This acute inflammation will persist as long as the tissue damage occurs. Bacteria are the most common cause of injury to the surgical patient; therefore, every effort must be made to prevent this injurious substance from entering the surgical wound.

    B. **SOURCES OF INFECTION**

1. Infections caused by microorganisms that are considered part of the normal resident flora are said to be **endogenous**. An endogenous infection occurs when the normal balance between the organism and the human host is upset owing to impaired defenses, or when the organism is introduced into a part of the body where it does not normally occur, for example, *Escherichia coli* from the intestinal tract into the urinary tract.
2. Infections caused by microorganisms that are not part of the normal resident flora are said to be **exogenous**. These infections are usually acquired through personnel or hospital environments, and are referred to as **nosocomial infections** caused by opportunistic pathogens. Exogenous infectious agents can be transmitted by a variety of causes, either directly or indirectly.
3. **Most nosocomial infections occurring during the postoperative period (endogenous or exogenous) appear to result from contamination acquired in the operating room,** not only because the patient is compromised by illness, but also because the natural defense system, mainly the skin and mucous membranes, has been violated.

C. TRANSMISSION OF INFECTION

1. Two methods of contact can result in contamination and postoperative wound infection in the surgical patient:
    a. **Direct contact:** close association between an infected person and a susceptible host through blood, sputum, or mucous membrane.
    b. **Indirect contact:** contact between a susceptible person and infectious material derived from an infectious host or contaminated source, such as skin, air, instruments, or dust particles.

D. ENTRY OF MICROORGANISMS

1. To gain entry into the body, microorganisms must penetrate natural barriers, such as the skin, the mucous membranes lining the respiratory, gastrointestinal, and urologic tracts, or the conjunctivae. These barriers constitute the body's first line of defense against microbial invasion. When these barriers are intact, the microorganisms establish themselves on the body's surface and wait to gain entry.
2. If the surgical patient is compromised before surgery, either by treatments or diagnostic procedures performed during the preoperative phase, the intraoperative phase can pose the greatest hazard to the patient, since the skin and mucous membranes are no longer intact or the system has been weakened.
3. Once pathogenic microorganisms have entered the body, they may establish a local infection at the site of entry or may disseminate throughout the body and establish themselves at sites remote from the site of entry.
4. Whether or not the invading microorganisms establish an infection at the site of entry or at another location depends on the **growth requirements of the organism,** the **local tissue environment,** the **strength of the host,** and the **ability of the microorganism to overcome the host defenses.**

E. THE IMMUNE RESPONSE

1. Resistance to infection involves the ability of the immune system to not only recognize a substance as foreign to the body (e.g., non-self), but also to initiate mechanisms to destroy and eliminate the substance.
2. The exact mechanism by which the immune system distinguishes between pathogenic and nonpathogenic invaders and non-self is not understood. It appears that exposure of the immune system to circulating and tissue substances during fetal development results in a state of immunologic tolerance to these substances. In other words, the body recognizes these substances as *self* and does not normally initiate an immune response against them.

F. THE INFLAMMATORY-REPARATIVE RESPONSE

1. **Inflammation** is the local response of tissue to damage, whether by injury or pathogenic microorganisms. Many agents can cause tissue damage, which starts an inflammatory reaction. This response proceeds through several stages, until the tissue has been healed. These stages are commonly described as the **acute inflammation, demolition,** and **restoration stages.**
2. Clinical signs and symptoms of this process consist of redness, swelling, warmth, pain, and limitation of movement, and are present immediately following any invasive procedure in which the natural defense system has been compromised.

II. INFECTION CONTROL: PRINCIPLES AND NURSING IMPLICATIONS

1. According to the A.O.R.N.'s Patient Outcome Standards, protecting the patient from infection is a primary goal. Therefore, it becomes the responsibility of all persons rendering care to the patient during the perioperative period.

2. Since the majority of infections can be acquired in the operating room, most preventive measures should be directed toward three primary areas: (1) the preparation of the surgical patient, (2) technical and aseptic practice of the surgical team, and (3) the maintenance of the surgical environment.

A. PREOPERATIVE PREPARATION OF THE PATIENT

1. **Measures aimed at preventing microbial contamination of the wound begin before the operation, by treating active infections and improving the general health of the patient to reduce the risk of postoperative infections.**
2. Other preoperative measures include:
   a. Keeping the preoperative stay as short as possible.
   b. Avoiding hair removal, or, if necessary, removing the hair with clippers or depilatories rather than a razor.
   c. Proper antimicrobial preparation of the skin, which may include a shower using an antimicrobial agent (e.g., Betadine) the night before and the morning of the surgery, in addition to the surgical skin preparation performed immediately before the start of the procedure.

B. INTRAOPERATIVE ASEPTIC TECHNIQUE

1. **Contamination from the surgical team is another potential source of infection, usually related to direct contact from hands or from shedding skin or mucous membranes.**
2. The use of a **surgical hand scrub** with an effective antimicrobial agent prior to the application of sterile gloves should assist in retarding bacterial growth, and corrective action should be taken immediately if this barrier is compromised in any way before or during the surgical procedure.
3. **According to recent studies conducted by the Centers for Disease Control (C.D.C.), the most important factor in preventing wound infections is operative technique.** Poor technique can result in the contamination of the operative wound, causing an extension of the anesthesia time, and unnecessary injury to surrounding tissue, which can result in necrosis and delayed healing. Any of these conditions can result in postoperative wound infections, since the patient's natural defense system has been compromised.

C. MAINTENANCE OF THE SURGICAL ENVIRONMENT

1. **Air is also a potential source of microorganisms that can contaminate the surgical wound.** Air inside the operating room is often contaminated with microorganisms that can be attached to airborne particles (dust, lint, respiratory droplets) that could be potential pathogens.
2. **A large number of airborne particles are directly related to the number of persons in the operating (procedure) room, and/or to the O.R. doors remaining open and personnel talking near or in the procedure room.** Failure to adhere to proper O.R. attire in the semirestricted and restricted areas of the suite may also account for potential problems, and must be addressed through rigid adherence to policies and procedures for all persons entering these areas.
3. **Movement or activity in the O.R. can be decreased by keeping the procedure room doors closed and by limiting the number of persons in the procedure room and adjacent corridors.** This can be accomplished through the implementation of strict traffic control procedures and policies, as suggested by the *A.O.R.N. Recommended Practices for Traffic Control.*
4. In the modern, well managed surgical suite, the risk of infection related to the physical environment is not as great as the human factor. This does not, however, reduce the need for constant vigilance on the part of all personnel, since the environment must be maintained to render safe, aseptic patient care.

D. **PRINCIPLES OF UNIVERSAL PRECAUTIONS**

1. **While there are several means of transferring pathogenic microorganisms during the perioperative period, exposure to blood and body fluids presents the greatest threat to personnel working in the surgical suite.**

2. In 1987, in response to the needs of persons working in "high-risk" areas, the C.D.C. established the Universal Precautions concept for health-care workers, designed to protect personnel from unknown exposure from the patient or the environment. Through the implementation of the Universal Precautions, the need for isolation of specific cases and the special cleaning procedures associated with these cases is no longer applicable. *All procedures and/or patients are potentially contaminated*; therefore, they are treated alike.

3. The C.D.C. stated that "since medical history and examination cannot identify all patients who are potentially infected with blood-borne pathogens, specific precautions should be used with ALL patients, thereby reducing the risk of possible exposure to its minimum." Accordingly, the C.D.C. recommended that health-care workers could reduce the risk of contamination and exposure by adhering to the following guidelines:

   a. **All health-care workers should routinely use appropriate barrier protection to prevent skin and mucous membrane exposure when contact with blood or other body fluids of ANY patient is anticipated. Gloves, masks, and protective eye wear or face shields should be worn during all surgical procedures and when handling soiled supplies or instruments during or after a procedure to prevent exposure of mucous membranes.**

   b. **Hands and other skin surfaces should be washed immediately and thoroughly if contaminated with blood or other body fluids.** Although gloves are worn by all personnel during a surgical procedure, handwashing after the removal of gloves should become a routine practice for both scrub and nonsterile personnel working in a procedure room.

   c. **Health-care workers should take all necessary precautions to protect against injuries caused by needles, scalpels, and other sharp instruments or devices during procedures; when cleaning used instruments; and when handling sharp instruments after a procedure.**

      (1) Needles should never be recapped or bent after use. Suture needles and sharps should be contained in a puncture-resistant container, and sealed for proper disposal according to recommended practices and established protocols. Sharp instruments should be placed in a tray in such a way that their points are not exposed, to avoid injury to persons working with the trays.

      (2) During the procedure, care must be taken when handling suture needles to ensure that no one receives an injury by placing the needle on a needle holder and passing it with the point down.

   d. **Health-care workers who have exudate lesions or weeping dermatitis should refrain from all direct patient care and from handling patient care equipment until the condition resolves.** Minor breaks in the skin, especially on the hands of the scrub nurse, should restrict scrubbing activities until the break has healed. Circulating nurses should wear sterile gloves if a skin lesion is present, and should cover the lesion with a protective covering when working in a procedure room.

4. **Additionally, the C.D.C. recommends that aspirated or drainage material never be allowed to come in contact with the health-care worker, either during the aspiration process or following the procedure.** Therefore, use of an efficient suctioning system is imperative during surgery, with extreme caution used during its disposition following the procedure.

5. **When dealing with soiled sponges, towels, or disposable supplies, the principle of *Contain and Control* must be used by all personnel both during and after the procedure.**

E. **EPIDEMIOLOGIC MONITORING PROGRAM**

1. Through a surveillance technique initiated by the C.D.C. that monitors postoperative infections, the surgeon and the nurse-epidemiologist can monitor those patients who are more likely to develop postoperative infections and those who, owing to the nature of their surgery, should be least likely.

2. This technique establishes a criteria for monitoring the surgical infection rates and taking appropriate steps to reduce the incidence of these infections. This system is referred to as the **C.D.C. Classification of Surgical Wounds** and is used throughout the country as a quality assurance measure for all surgical patients.

F. **CENTERS FOR DISEASE CONTROL CLASSIFICATION OF SURGICAL WOUNDS**

1. Surgical wound infections are divided into two types:
   a. Those confined to the incisional wound.
   b. Those involving structures adjacent to the wound that were entered or exposed during the surgical procedure.
2. To track infections involving the surgical patient, and to learn how they may have occurred or how to prevent their recurrence, the C.D.C. established a classification system for surgical wounds based on the risk factor of possible postoperative infections occurring due to the nature of the surgical procedure. The following descriptions can assist in classifying a wound, and are used throughout the country to describe a specific type of surgical procedure and its risk factor.
3. **Class I: Clean wounds**
   a. **Definition:** Uninfected operative wounds in which no inflammation is encountered, and the respiratory, alimentary, genital, or uninfected urinary tracts are not entered. Additionally, clean wounds are elective surgery, with primary closure and, if necessary, drained with a closed drainage device. Operational incisional wounds that follow nonpenetrating (blunt) trauma should be included in this class, if all other criteria have been met.
   b. **Risk factor:** 1 to 5 percent risk of postoperative infection.
   c. **Examples:** include, but are not limited to, eye surgery, hernia repairs, breast surgery, neurosurgery (nontraumatic), cardiac or peripheral vascular surgeries.
4. **Class II: Clean-contaminated wounds**
   a. **Definition:** Operative wounds in which the respiratory, alimentary, genital or urinary tract is entered under controlled conditions and without unusual contamination. Specifically, operations involving the biliary tract, appendix, vagina, and oropharynx are included provided there is no evidence of infection or no major break in aseptic technique is encountered.
   b. **Risk factor:** 3 to 11 percent risk of postoperative infection.
   c. **Examples:** include, but are not to, gastrectomy, cholecystectomy (without spillage), elective appendectomy, cysto or cysto-TUR (negative urine cultures), total abdominal hysterectomy (TAH), dilation and curettage, "C" sections and tonsillectomy (noninfected at time of surgery).
5. **Class III: Contaminated wounds**
   a. **Definition:** Surgery that involves open, fresh, traumatic wounds, or with major breaks in sterile technique or with gross spillage from the G.I. tract, and incisions in which acute, nonpurulent inflammation is encountered.
   b. **Risk factor:** 10 to 17 percent risk of postoperative infection.
   c. **Examples:** include, but are not limited to, rectal surgery, laparotomy (significant spillage), traumatic wounds (e.g., gunshot, stab wounds [non-perforation of visceral]) or acute inflammation of any organ without frank pus present (e.g., acute appendicitis or cholecystitis, compound fractures.)
6. **Class IV: Dirty (infected) wounds**
   a. **Definition:** Old traumatic wounds with retained devitalized tissue, and wounds that involve existing clinical infection or perforated viscera and/or delayed primary closure wounds. This classification suggests an infectious process was present prior to surgery.
   b. **Risk factor:** greater than 27 percent risk of postoperative infection.
   c. **Examples:** include, but are not limited to, debridement, incision and drainage, total evisceration, perforated viscera, amputations, or positive preoperative blood cultures.
7. It is important to remember, when deciding what classification the surgical procedure belongs in, that coexisting diseases do not influence the classification, only preexisting infectious processes that may be present at the time or surgery.

8. Placing a surgical procedure in its proper category is an important responsibility of the perioperative nurse, since it will help the epidemiology department and the surgeons effectively monitor and care for the postoperative patient.

G. MANAGING THE POSTOPERATIVE PATIENT

1. **In the postoperative period, the risk of wound infection can be reduced by proper techniques when handling the wound, proper and frequent handwashing, and by the use of closed wound-drainage systems when indicated.**
2. If a drain is used, having it enter through adjacent, separate stab wound rather than the incision will, according to some physicians, lessen the chance of infection, since the incision site is not directly involved.
3. **When changing a dressing, strict aseptic technique must be used by all personnel working with the postoperative patient, including proper handwashing before and after the procedure.** This will reduce the risks of contamination during the critical stages of wound healing and cross-contamination from or to other patients.
4. **A patient's intrinsic susceptibility to infection is also an important factor in determining the risk of postoperative wound infections.** Patients with preexisting diseases or conditions pose a greater risk than those who begin the surgical experience in optimal health. If the patient has a preexisting disease, postponement of elective surgery and/or the initiation of corrective treatment may help reduce the potential risk factors, thus protecting the surgical patient from infection.
5. The following cites the C.D.C.'s recommendations for preventing surgical wound infections, encompassing all three phases of surgical intervention:

C.D.C. Recommendations for Prevention of Surgical Wound Infections.

Preoperative Phase
1. Medical treatment of active infections including the prophylactic administration of antibiotics as recommended by established protocols.
2. Reducing preoperative hospital stay (same-day surgery).
3. Avoiding hair removal or removal when necessary by the use of clippers or depilatories rather than a razor.
4. Antimicrobial bath/shower the evening prior to surgery and the morning of surgery.
5. Preoperative hand scrub using acceptable antimicrobial solution and technique.

Intraoperative Phase
1. Strict adherence to aseptic technique.
2. Proper surgical skin preparation.
3. Usage of effective barrier materials to establish the sterile field.
4. Proper environmental control within the surgical suite.
5. Proper O.R. attire in the semirestricted and the restricted areas of the surgical suite.
6. Proper operative techniques; that is , preventing possible contamination or perforation; prolonged operative time; and careful tissue handling.
7. Classification and documentation of all surgical procedures/patients.

Postoperative Phase
1. Aseptic dressing changes.
2. Proper handwashing between patients/treatments.
3. Discontinuance of antibiotic therapy unless the condition merits treatment.
4. Protection of patients from other infected patients or personnel.
5. Routine postoperative surveillance of all surgical patients.
6. Quality assurance programs and periodic audits of patient care, including preventive measures for preventing wound infections.

By following the recommendations given, all members of the health-care team involved with the surgical patient during the perioperative period can strive toward the optimal patient outcome: an infection-free surgical experience.

Source: Modified from Centers for Disease Control (1987) *Guidelines for Prevention of Surgical Wound Infections.*

III. WOUND HEALING

A. PHYSIOLOGY OF WOUND HEALING

1. The medical definition of wound healing is described as a "process which restores the structure and function of injured or diseased tissue." This process includes four aspects: (1) blood clotting, (2) tissue mending, (3) scarring, and (4) bone healing. The body is extremely efficient in its ability to recover from trauma. In fact, a surgical wound begins to heal as soon as the surgeon makes the initial incision.
2. The acute inflammatory response, discussed earlier in the chapter, occurs immediately after tissue damage and begins its cycle as the smaller blood vessels in the area of injury constrict, followed by vasoconstriction, thereby supplying the injured site with nutrients needed to accomplish the healing process. In the pathogenic context, the lost or destroyed tissue is replaced by living tissue and the healing process begins.

B. TYPES OF WOUNDS

1. There are two types of wounds. The first involve possible tissue loss and are known as **open wounds,** while the second are those without tissue loss, known as **closed wounds.** The loss or destruction of tissue can occur in several ways:
   a. By traumatic excision (accidental or surgical).
   b. By chemical or physical agents (burns, ischemia).
   c. By severe inflammation resulting in tissue necrosis.
2. Replacement of lost tissue can be accomplished by repair or regeneration. **Repair** is the replacement of lost tissue with granulation tissue that matures to form a fibrous connective tissue scar. Although it does not restore function, it fills the anatomic defect and restores tissue integrity. **Regeneration** is the replacement of lost tissue with tissue of the same type, through multiplication of undamaged cells that replace those that were damaged. When regeneration occurs, normal function is usually restored. If both restoration and repair occur, the basic framework of the tissue will survive, producing a tissue mass that will be completely restored.

C. METHODS OF SURGICAL WOUND HEALING

1. The **open wound** heals in three distinct ways, depending on the variables present during the healing cycle.
   a. **Primary union (first intention):** First intention wound healing occurs with incised or sutured wounds with no tissue loss, or minimum tissue loss without "dead space." This is the *ideal* wound, since no contamination has occurred, and it results in a cosmetic effect similar to the normal skin surface. The edges are approximated, resulting in a "hairline scar."
   b. **Granulation (second intention):** Granulation occurs when wounds experience tissue loss, preventing the approximation of edges and thereby forcing the wound to heal with granulation tissue, which is finally covered by epithelial cells. The cause may be infection or necrosis of tissue, and it produces a wider and deeper scar.
   c. **Delayed primary closure (third intention):** Third intention healing uses a combination of first and second intention healing, and occurs when a wound is left open to heal. After 4 to 6 days, the granulation tissue covers the surface of the wound, at which time it is sutured closed (delayed closure). This procedure is used when there is a high risk of infection or

the need for drainage, but because the wound must be left open, this technique can result in additional complications during the postoperative period.

D. FACTORS INFLUENCING NORMAL WOUND HEALING

1. The general health status of an individual, as well as local factors and intraoperative considerations, can influence the process of wound healing.
2. **General factors**
    a. **Nutrition**
       (1) Nutrition is an important factor in the total healing process. **Protein** deficiencies impair the formation of granulation tissue and collagen, which can decrease wound strength. Sufficient amounts of **amino acids** necessary for wound healing are usually available from a well-balanced diet and from mobilization and breakdown of tissue protein.
       (2) **Vitamin C** (ascorbic acid) is necessary for the formation of collagen, and deficiencies can add to the delay of wound healing and decrease strength. Adequate **calcium** and **vitamin D** are necessary for the healing of fractures, since vitamin D is required for calcification of bone.
    b. **Cell oxygenation:** Adequate oxygen is critical for wound healing. Anemia would be expected to interfere with wound healing because it impairs oxygen transport in the blood.
    c. **Age:** Age can influence wound healing, since it is generally believed that healing is better and faster in the young than in the elderly. Impaired healing in the elderly is most often associated with inadequate circulation due to atherosclerosis, or the presence of coexisting diseases.
    d. **Chemical imbalances**
       (1) Fluid and electrolyte imbalances can delay wound healing since these components and the ultimate affect of the acid-base status of the patient will delay the effectiveness of the lag phase.
       (2) Drugs, such as steroids, chemotherapeutic agents, and abused substances, including alcohol and tobacco, can affect the production of collagen and protein synthesis, directly affecting the total healing process.
    e. **General physical condition**
       (1) Patients with preexisting or coexisting diseases are more prone to wound infections due to a compromise in the body's immune response.
       (2) Specific diseases, such as uremia, uncontrolled diabetes, malignancies, respiratory dysfunction, or the effects of radiation therapy make the wound more vulnerable to disruption and/or infection, resulting in an abnormal healing process.
       (3) Smoking has an impact on wound healing, since it can reduce the amount of functional hemoglobin by 10 to 15 percent. The result is a prolonged or abnormal healing process.
       (4) Obese patients are also at risk, since fatty tissue is relatively avascular and is therefore prone to microbial contamination and general weakening.
2. **Local factors**
    a. **Adequate circulation:** An adequate blood supply is probably the most critical factor in wound healing. Oxygen and nutrients are brought to the injured site via the circulatory system. Therefore, anything that impairs blood flow to the area will interfere with the healing process.
    b. **Inflammation**
       (1) Although healing begins shortly after injury, while the acute inflammatory phase is in progress, repair or regeneration cannot be completed until the acute inflammation subsides and debris is removed from the wound.
       (2) Any factor that incites inflammation, such as the presence of infection or foreign bodies, will delay healing. Sutures, for example, must be chosen carefully and handled with precision, because they are foreign substances. Too many sutures or one that is not absorbing properly can interfere with healing. Some sutures can form keloids, stones, or other disruptive factors.

   c. **Hemorrhage:** Excessive bleeding into the wound not only stimulates inflammation but requires repair before healing can begin. Both inflammation and hemorrhage can delay the healing process, posing additional risks to the patient.
   d. **Immobilization:** In the treatment of fractures, immobilization of the wound is crucial. It may also promote healing of soft tissue wounds, especially if they are large or deep, since movement may separate the wound edges and disrupt the fragile granulation tissue, which can cause excessive bleeding.
   e. **Stress:** Stress, which in some instances produces a chemical imbalance, can be a major factor in the wound healing process. Acute stress apparently does not interfere with wound healing, but chronic stress may retard healing and decrease wound strength.
3. **Intraoperative factors**
   a. **Improper tissue handling:** Rough handling of tissue can damage the fibers and delay the healing process. Tissue should be handled with minimal trauma to preserve whatever is naturally available to assist in the healing process.
   b. **Previous surgery:** Previous surgery that produced scar tissue or adhesions can slow down the healing process, since circulation may not be adequate in that area. Following a lysis of adhesions, the wound may be weak, resulting in a delay of the healing process.
   c. **Suturing and wound closure materials**
      (1) Too many sutures or the wrong type for a specific area can interfere with the healing process. Patients may react adversely to suture material, which can set up an inflammatory response due largely to irritation to tissue, similar to when the body tries to reject foreign bodies as a defense mechanism. Synthetic monofilament suture material causes less reaction than braided suture material, and have proven to be less reactive than those made of natural substances. Surgical gut and nonabsorbable sutures, especially those made of silk or cotton, are often associated with inflammation or irritation, resulting in a delayed healing process. For this reason, if an infection is present at the time of surgery, the surgeon will request a synthetic suture rather than one made from natural fibers.
      (2) Recently, the use of internal staples has become a popular replacement for sutures, since they are generally nonreactive, thus minimizing the risk of irritation. Additionally, they can aid in the reduction of operative time, and possibly decrease the extensive handling of tissues.
4. **Exogenous factors:** Maintaining an aseptic environment is paramount in preventing exogenous contamination of the surgical wound. The perioperative nurse must ensure the sterility of the instruments and supplies and proper preparation of the surgical site, and monitor all activities and personnel involved with the procedure to maintain a safe, therapeutic environment.

E. **COMPLICATIONS OF WOUND HEALING**

1. **Even with the best techniques and precise nursing care during the perioperative period, some patients may experience complications involving the surgical wound.**
2. **The greatest concern during the first 2 to 5 postoperative days is wound disruption causing either dehiscence or evisceration.** Additionally, incisional hernias, fistulas and sinuses, and keloids are complications that may be encountered during the postoperative period.
3. **Wound dehiscence or evisceration**
   a. **Wound dehiscence** is the partial or total separation of the wound. It occurs most often during the lag phase of the healing process, while the wound is still in a delicate condition.
   b. Total dehiscence, usually involving an abdominal incision, results in **evisceration**, or protrusion of the viscera through the incisional line. **When this occurs, a true surgical emergency exists, requiring immediate action by the nurse caring for the patient.**
4. **Incisional hernias**
   a. **Incisional hernias** result from incomplete wound dehiscence in which the skin remains intact. Incisional hernias can occur as late as 2 to 3 months postoperatively, and occur most frequently in lower abdominal incisions. Incisional hernias can lead to bowel obstructions, which must be surgically corrected.

5. **Fistulas and sinuses**
   a. **Fistulas** and **sinuses** usually occur during the second phase of normal healing (fibroplasia phase). A **fistula** is a tract between two epithelium-lined surfaces, open at both ends. This type of complication is usually associated with head and neck, bowel, or genitourinary surgery, and results in drainage that is not expected from the anatomic area.
   b. A **sinus**, on the other hand, is open at only one end, producing an abnormal sinus tract. This usually requires drainage and closure, but only after the inflammation has subsided.
6. **Keloids**
   a. Changes in the metabolism of collagen during the healing process may result in the development of **keloid scars**, producing a dense fibrous tissue around the outside of the original incision. These scars can be revised; however, the condition can reappear with each new incision or manipulation of the incisional site.

F. **MONITORING POSTOPERATIVE SURGICAL WOUND INFECTIONS**

1. **Many factors can influence the acquisition of a postsurgical wound infection, but basically the acquisition of an infection requires the interaction of three potential causes:**
   a. **The patient's intrinsic resistance (susceptibility of the host).**
   b. **A source of the microorganisms (environmental or personnel).**
   c. **A means of transmission (entry into the system).**
2. Some of these causes may include air, various hospital personnel (carriers), equipment, food, heating/cooling systems, and other patients, in addition to the sources discussed earlier in this chapter.
3. While all hospital areas pose some degree of risk to the patient of acquiring an infection, surgical patients are the highest risk population within the institution, and therefore require constant monitoring to avoid possible complications.
4. Surgical wound infections are the second most frequent cause of nosocomial infections and are an important reason for the increase of morbidity, mortality, and increasing hospital-stay costs.

IV. **ASEPTIC TECHNIQUES: PRINCIPLES AND PRACTICES**

A. **SURGICAL CONSCIENCE**

1. As members of the health-care team, physicians, nurses, and paraprofessionals are entrusted with the safety and welfare of those who come to them for help or assistance. **As a patient advocate, the perioperative nurse has, as one of his or her most important functions, the responsibility of monitoring and maintaining an aseptic environment during the perioperative period, thus preventing harm from befalling the patient. Surgical conscience is that concept which allows for no compromise in the principles of aseptic technique, since anything less could increase the potential risk of infection, resulting in harm to the patient.**
2. **Developing a surgical conscience**
   a. A surgical conscience builds on the principles of asepsis, and is an act of mental discipline. It involves the assessment and regulation of one's own practice, with particular attention to deviations from acceptable, safe practices, especially during the intraoperative phase of surgical intervention.
   b. **Surgical conscience does not apply only to the surgical team, but to all those directly involved with patient care.** It demands the recognition of improper practices observed during surgery by any member of the health care team, and the ability to report one's own breaks in technique, so that corrective action may be taken, even if the person is not being observed. Additionally, surgical conscience involves the ability to set aside personal preferences and prejudices in order to provide optimum patient care.
   c. Through continual vigilance and evaluation of the patient, environment, personnel, and equipment, we can reduce the possibility of complications that could rise out of complacency or lack of professional consideration for others. When fully developed, surgical conscience can become a blend of integrity, honesty, and self-confidence, since it recognizes the human

trait of being fallible, requiring an alertness to wrongdoings and correcting them before another person is harmed. When rapport and mutual respect are established among the members of the health-care team, corrections will become constructive, but it takes time for respect of knowledge and practice to reach this level.

    d. To fully comprehend the concept of surgical conscience, ask yourself the following questions prior to the start of each procedure:

        (1) Is this the best set-up for this procedure?

        (2) Do I have everything that is logically necessary under existing conditions?

        (3) Do I understand what is required of me and how I can be of greatest assistance?

        (4) Have I done all I can do to provide a safe, therapeutic environment for my patient?

        (5) If I were the patient, what would I want the team/nurse to do for me to help reduce my fears and anxieties?

    e. The key words involving surgical practice are **caring, discipline, vigilance, honesty,** and **integrity.** Surgical conscience, simply stated, *is doing unto others as you would have others do unto you.* Florence Nightingale once summarized this concept by stating that "the nurse must keep a high sense of duty in her own mind, must aim at perfection and must be consistent always in herself."

B. DEFINITION OF ASEPTIC TECHNIQUE

1. **The basis for all infection-free surgery is founded on the principles of basic aseptic technique. Every attempt must be made to prevent the invasion of microorganisms into the surgical wound during the perioperative period.**

2. Two methods which, if practiced with precise accuracy, can prevent serious complications to the already compromised surgical patient are **aseptic technique** and **sterile technique.** Although they sound similar, they are very different in practice.

    a. **Aseptic technique** is a group of procedures that prevent contamination of microorganisms through the knowledge and principles of contain and control.

    b. **Sterile technique,** on the other hand, comprises methods by which contamination of an item is prevented by maintaining the sterility of the item/area involved with a procedure.

    c. Different in implementation, yet linked in their concepts of preventing contamination, these principles have a vital role in protecting the patient from an unwarranted postoperative infection.

3. Aseptic technique is based on the premise that most infections are introduced into the body from outside (exogenous) sources. To avoid infection, it is necessary to ensure that any procedure performed on the body is done in such a way as to introduce no bacteria.

4. **To protect the patient further, prior to handling sterile supplies the surgical team members must use appropriate measures to reduce the possibility of infection, including proper attire, the removal of existing resident flora on their hands and arms by performing a surgical hand scrub, and the application of sterile gown and gloves.**

4. A surgical procedure must be done under sterile conditions; that is, all microorganisms, including spores, have been eliminated. **Therefore, all instruments and supplies used during the procedure must be sterile.**

5. The principles of aseptic technique are no less important, however, when performing a procedure that does not require the strictness of the operating room environment. For example, sepsis introduced through a venous cut-down, can be just as detrimental to the patient as an infection introduced at the operating table.

C. BASIC PRINCIPLES OF ASEPTIC TECHNIQUE

1. **Aseptic technique** can be implemented in many different ways, and understanding of the basic principles remains an important aspect of safe perioperative nursing practice. Until empirical research demonstrates that any technique is not effective, the basic principles should remain in force and should be practiced by all members of the health-care team.

2. **Eight principles of aseptic technique**
   a. All items used within a sterile field must be sterile.
   b. A sterile barrier that has been permeated must be considered contaminated.
   c. The edges of a sterile wrapper or container are considered unsterile once the package is opened.
   d. Gowns are considered sterile in front, from shoulder to table level, and the sleeves to 2 inches above the elbow.
   e. Tables are sterile at table level only.
   f. Sterile persons and items touch only sterile areas; unsterile persons and items touch only unsterile areas.
   g. Movement within or around a sterile field must not contaminate the field.
   h. All items and areas of doubtful sterility are considered contaminated.

D. **RECOMMENDED PRACTICES FOR BASIC ASEPTIC TECHNIQUE**

1. As a means of preventing infection during any invasive procedure, the A.O.R.N. established the following recommended practices for basic aseptic technique as a guide for anyone who is present during the procedure, either directly or indirectly involved with patient care. These recommendations are based on the knowledge of epidemiology and microbiology and can be applied to any area where invasive procedures are being performed.

2. **Recommended Practice I**
   a. **Scrubbed persons should wear sterile gowns and gloves.**
   b. The surgical team is divided into two groups: those who are working directly at the surgical field (sterile team), and those who are working around the sterile field (unsterile team).
   c. All sterile team members perform a surgical scrub before entering the procedure room, to remove gross dirt from their hands and arms prior to applying their sterile gown and gloves.
   d. Since the scrubbed team members receive sterile equipment from the circulator (nonsterile member), and since sterile can only touch sterile, a bacterial barrier is needed between the circulator and the sterile item. That bacterial barrier is the sterile gown and gloves.
   e. To maintain the sterile fields, parameters of sterility for the gown have been established:
      (1) The gown is considered sterile in front from chest to the level of the sterile field.
      (2) The sleeves are considered sterile from 2 inches above the elbow to the stockinette cuff, and therefore the cuff must be covered, at all times, by sterile gloves.
   f. The areas not considered sterile, for various monitoring reasons, include the neckline, shoulders, areas under the arms, and the back of the gown.
   g. To preserve the sterility of the gloved hands, they should be kept within the sterile boundary of the gown, and since the axillary region is not sterile, the arms should never be crossed with hands positioned into the axilla.
   h. Should either of these barriers be compromised, they must be discarded, and a new gown, gloves or both applied, depending on the nature of the break in technique.

3. **Recommended Practice II**
   a. **Sterile drapes should be used to establish a sterile field.**
   b. Contamination of equipment and personnel is prevented by the placement of a bacterial barrier or sterile drape over an item located within the boundary of the sterile field.
   c. During surgery, the patient, once covered with the bacterial barrier, becomes the center of the sterile field, and since specific pieces of furniture must be used to accommodate surgical instruments and supplies, those surfaces must be covered with a bacterial barrier prior to assembly and use by sterile members of the team.
   d. Once the sterile field has been established, nonsterile persons must never reach over the draped areas, since this constitutes contamination of that area, requiring immediate corrective action to recreate the sterility of that item or field.
   e. The parameter for the sterile field is easily maintained, since only the top of the draped table and/or the patient is considered sterile. Anything below this level is unsterile, and must be treated as such by members of the sterile team.

   f. To properly drape an unsterile surface with sterile drapes, the following practice should be observed:
     (1) Sterile persons drape an unsterile surface first toward themselves, protecting their gown and gloves at all times.
     (2) When a nonsterile person drapes an area they do so away from themselves first, then towards them, avoiding reaching over a sterile field.
   g. If the drapes become permeated or moist, they must be considered contaminated, and corrective action must be initiated to cover the area in question or to change the drapes.

4. **Recommended Practice III**
   a. **All items used within a sterile field should be sterile. Under NO circumstances can sterile and unsterile items or areas be mixed, since one contaminates the other.**
   b. Some items used during surgery come presterilized from the manufacturer, such as drapes, sponges, gowns, and gloves, while others, such as instruments and trays, are sterilized in the hospital, either in the central processing area or in the operating room. Before opening or dispensing these items for sterile use, the integrity of the packaging and the assurance of sterility must be confirmed by the persons dispensing the item. This can be accomplished through:
     (1) Checking the outer wrapper/package to make sure there are no tears or holes.
     (2) Confirming the items' sterility has not been compromised by either time or handling.
     (3) Inspecting to see that the items have gone through the proper sterilization process as evidenced by the indicators on the outside of the package.
     (4) Realization that if sterility is in doubt, the item is considered contaminated and cannot be used.
   c. According to recent recommendations, the maintenance of package sterility is event-related, not time-related. Therefore, the item's sterility is dependent on the type of packaging material and its handling and storage conditions.

5. **Recommended Practice IV**
   a. **All items introduced into a sterile field should be dispensed by methods that maintain sterility of the item and integrity of the sterile field.**
   b. The edges of a sterile container or wrapper cannot be considered sterile once the container or wrapper has been opened. When opening a sterile item, a margin of safety must always be used--that is, the hands of the unsterile person should be covered or protected from accidental contact with either the field or the scrubbed person during the transfer procedure.
   c. When working with irrigation solution or fluid contained in a pour bottle, careful attention must be used to avoid "splash-back," and once the solution has been poured, the container cannot be recapped for future use, since its contents can no longer be considered sterile. The solution must be completely used or the remaining fluid discarded.
   d. When retrieving a sterile item from the autoclave, the circulating nurse cannot touch the item, and must present the item, maintaining its sterility, to the scrub nurse so that he or she can transfer it to the sterile field without contamination. This can usually be accomplished by the use of a **flash pan** with a handle for retrieving items requiring emergency sterilization for immediate use.

6. **Recommended Practice V**
   a. **A sterile field should be constantly monitored and maintained.**
   b. The sterility of the supplies used during a surgical procedure is affected by the length of time the items have not been used and/or exposed to the environment. Since contamination can accidentally occur by any member of the team, the sterile field should be created as close to the time of the procedure as possible, and once created, be constantly monitored. Under no circumstances should a sterile field be covered for use at a later time, since covering and removal of the cover can cause contamination of the field.
   c. To monitor the field and maintain its integrity, the field should be in constant view. Therefore, nurses should never turn their back on a sterile field.
   d. Air currents can become a source of contamination; thus, movement within or around a sterile field should be minimal to avoid contamination of the field.

e. Sterile persons (in gown and gloves) should not wander in and out of the sterile area while in sterile attire, since the gown is considered contaminated below waist level. Nor should sterile persons sit while in sterile attire, unless the entire procedures is performed in a sitting position, or leave the procedure room/sterile area in gown and gloves (either during or after the procedure). All these actions constitute a break in technique, and must be avoided in order to protect the patient and maintain an aseptic environment.

7. **Additional recommendations**
   a. In addition to the five recommended practices for creating and maintaining a sterile field, additional methods can be used to protect and maintain an aseptic environment. These include:
      (1) Preventing contamination of a bacterial barrier (e.g., air, moisture, or dust) by eliminating or reducing the potential source of contamination.
      (2) Restricting talking in the room to a minimum.
      (3) Not letting unsterile persons walk between two sterile fields (set-ups).
      (4) Having unsterile persons move from unsterile to unsterile areas, maintaining a safe distance from the sterile field.
      (5) Having sterile persons, when changing positions, pass sterile to sterile (face to face) or unsterile to unsterile (back to back).
      (6) Keeping the O.R. doors shut during a procedure.
      (7) Monitoring for breaks in technique, and if they occur, taking immediate and appropriate steps to correct the resulting contamination.
   b. These recommended practices provide guidelines for aseptic practices in the operating room, but can also be applied to all nursing activities requiring the use of aseptic technique.
   c. Individual hospital policies and procedures, based on these principles, will reflect variations in physical environment or clinical situations that will determine the degree to which these recommended practices can be applied.
   d. These recommended practices describe optimal levels of achievable technical and aseptic practices, and although this book does not list all the possible implementations, adherence to these principles can help create a safe and infection-free environment for both patients and staff.

E. PREPARATION OF THE SURGICAL TEAM

1. **Sterile implies the destruction and/or removal of all microorganisms from an object or surface, including spores.** For this definition to be accurate, specific preparative procedures for both the team and the equipment must be completed prior to the start of the procedure.
2. Unlike inanimate objects, the skin cannot be sterilized. **Preparation of the surgical team requires a surgical hand scrub and the donning of sterile gown and gloves.**
3. **The surgical hand scrub**
   a. **Even though the surgical team's hands must be covered by sterile gloves, it is mandatory, for several reasons, that a surgical hand scrub be performed according to acceptable technique prior to the beginning of each procedure.** For example, hands may carry pathogenic bacteria acquired from other sources within the environment, or gloves may become punctured or torn during the procedure, exposing the patient and the team to microbial contamination.
   b. The goals of the surgical scrub include: (1) mechanical removal of soil and transient microbes from the hands and forearms, (2) chemical reduction of the resident microbial count to as low a level as possible, and (3) reduction of the potential rapid rebound growth of microbes.
   c. **Recommended practices for surgical scrub**
      (1) All personnel should meet specific requirements prior to beginning the surgical scrub.
      (2) The antimicrobial soap or detergent should be effective.
      (3) The procedure used to accomplish the surgical scrub should be the same for all personnel.
      (4) An anatomic time scrub or counted-brush-stroke method should be used for all surgical scrubs.

    d. **Principles of the surgical scrub**

        (1) The surgical scrub is performed after proper preparation by the person performing the scrub.

        (2) Skin and nails should be kept clean and in good condition. Fingernails should be short (not reaching beyond the finger tips), and polish free. Artificial nails are not recommended because of their potential for harboring of bacteria and fungal development under the nails. Jewelry, including watches, rings, and bracelets, should not be worn. Hands should be inspected for breaks in the skin, which could become an entry for microbial contamination.

        (3) A clean scrub suit, a cap covering all hair, including facial hair, and a high filtration mask are required by all personnel prior to performing the scrub procedure.

    e. **Antimicrobial agents**

        (1) Both the **iodophors** and **chlorhexidine gluconates** are common agents used for the surgical scrub procedure. They are prepared in combination with detergent to give a cleaning action along with the antibacterial action.

        (2) Disposable, presterilized scrub brushes, impregnated with one or the other of these agents, are available in most operating rooms, and the choice is an independent decision, based on personal preference and/or sensitivity to the agent.

    f. **Length of scrub:** According to the latest information, a 5-minute surgical scrub of the hands and forearms is adequate for removal of gross dirt and oils from the skin, as long as mechanical friction combined with an antimicrobial agent are present.

  4. **Establishing bacterial barriers**

    a. **Before scrubbed personnel can touch sterile supplies or the sterile field, they must put on sterile gowns and gloves to prevent microbial contamination on hands or clothing from being transferred to the sterile field and/or the patient's wound.**

    b. Types of materials used as a bacterial barrier in gowns and drapes may be an important link in the prevention of wound infection. Therefore, the specifications for this material, whether disposable or nondisposable, must meet the recommended criteria established by A.O.R.N. to preserve an aseptic environment during a surgical or invasive procedure or any type:

        (1) Surgical gowns and drapes should be made of material that establishes a barrier to minimize the passage of microorganisms between nonsterile and sterile areas.

        (2) Gowns and drapes should be made of materials that are safe and comfortable for use in the operating room environment.

    c. **Principles**

        (1) Materials should be resistant to penetration by either blood or other liquids used at the sterile field. The stockinette cuff is the most contaminated portion of the gown, since is absorbs moisture from the skin more rapidly than the gown fabric, and therefore must be covered at all times with sterile gloves.

        (2) Materials should meet or exceed recommendations from the National Fire Protection Agency for flame retardation, and be as lint free as possible.

        (3) In some instances, due to the nature of the surgical procedure, extra protection gowns may be required. An additional layer of resistant material is added to the front and sleeves of the gown to add protection against penetration when copious amounts of fluids or contaminates are present.

  5. **Gowning and gloving**

    a. **Moisture remaining on the skin after the scrub procedure must be dried with a sterile towel before donning sterile gown and gloves.** Therefore, the hand drying process is part of the gowning procedure.

    b. **To preserve the sterility of the sterile field, the gowning and gloving procedure should be performed from a separate surface, away from the sterile field, to prevent accidental contamination of the field during the process.**

    c. **Sterile gloves**
       (1) Gloves come presterilized and sized from the manufacturer.
       (2) During the packaging of sterile gloves, provisions must be made for the scrubbed person to touch only the inner side of the glove cuff when donning the gloves.
       (3) When opening the package, if a wide cuff is not available, discard the gloves and request another pair to avoid possible contamination during the gloving procedure.
       (4) Sterile gloves can be applied using one of two methods: the **open method** or the **closed method**. The **closed-glove method** should be used any time the nurse is initially applying sterile gown and gloves, while the **open-glove method** should be used when the nurse is gloving another team member or changing a glove during a procedure (self or team member), or when a sterile scrub or gown is not required (aseptic procedures).
       (5) The **scrub person**, responsible for establishing and organizing the sterile field, is responsible for gowning and gloving themselves with assistance from the circulating nurse (unassisted gowning and gloving), while the rest of the sterile team members will be assisted by the scrub person (assisted gowning and gloving).

PRACTICE QUESTIONS

1. **Injury to the surgical patient is *most* commonly caused by:**

   1. *poor patient positioning.*

   2. *bacterial infection.*

   3. *improper anesthesia technique.*

   4. *poor surgical technique.*

2. **During surgery for colon cancer on Mr. B., *E. coli* bacteria normally found in the intestinal tract are introduced into and infect his urinary tract. Such an infection is known as a(n):**

   1. *exogenous infection.*

   2. *localized infection.*

   3. *nosocomial exogenous infection.*

   4. *nosocomial endogenous infection.*

3. **In the case above, Mr. B.'s infection was due principally to his intestinal tract having been violated during surgery. The other factor that is *likely* to have contributed to the patient's urinary tract infection was:**

   1. *poor surgical or nursing technique.*

   2. *the high toxicity of exogenous E. coli bacteria.*

   3. *the patient's weakened physical condition.*

   4. *contamination of surgical equipment.*

4. **Contamination and postoperative wound infection can occur in a surgical patient if there is contact between the patient and infectious material derived from an infectious host or contaminated source, such as skin, air, instruments. This type of contact is called:**

    1. *reparative.*

    2. *indirect.*

    3. *associative.*

    4. *dehiscence.*

5. **A common response by the body following any invasive procedure in which the natural defense system has been compromised is:**

    1. *inflammation.*

    2. *necrosis.*

    3. *pathogenicity.*

    4. *dehiscence.*

6. **Measures to prevent infection in the operating room are directed at three primary areas. Which of the following is NOT one of these areas?**

    1. *The preparation of the surgical patient.*

    2. *The technical and aseptic practices of the surgical team.*

    3. *The maintenance of the surgical environment.*

    4. *The sterility of all operating room equipment.*

7. **Contamination from the surgical team is a potential source of infection during the intraoperative period and usually relates to:**

    1. *improper sterilization of surgical instruments or supplies.*

    2. *contamination of air inside the operating room.*

    3. *direct contact from hands or from shedding skin or mucous membranes.*

    4. *improper aseptic preparation of the skin immediately before the surgical scrub.*

8. **According to recent studies conducted by the Centers for Disease Control (C.D.C.), the *most* important factor in preventing wound infections is:**

    1. *patient skin preparation.*

    2. *the condition of the patient.*

    3. *the nature of the surgery.*

    4. *operative technique.*

9. **Air is a potential source of microorganisms that can contaminate the surgical wound. Among the measures that can be taken to reduce air contamination in the procedure room are all of the following EXCEPT:**

    1. *keeping doors to the procedure room partly open for maximum air exchange.*

    2. *limiting conversation by personnel near or in the procedure room.*

    3. *limiting the number of persons in the procedure room.*

    4. *wearing proper O.R. attire in the restricted and semirestricted areas of the surgical suite.*

10. **The greatest threat to personnel working in the operating room is from:**

    1. *exposure to contaminated air.*

    2. *exposure to pathogens endogenous to the operating room.*

    3. *accidental injury from surgical instruments and equipment.*

    4. *exposure to infected blood and body fluids.*

11. **Among the C.D.C. recommendations for implementing the principles of Universal Precautions are all of the following EXCEPT:**

    1. *Gloves, masks, and protective eye wear or face shields should be worn during all surgical procedures and when handling soiled supplies or instruments during or after a procedure.*

    2. *Hands and other skin surfaces should be washed immediately and thoroughly if contaminated with blood or other body fluids.*

    3. *Needles should be carefully recapped or bent after use.*

    4. *Minor breaks in the skin, especially on the hands of the scrub nurse, should restrict scrubbing activities until the break has healed.*

12. **The C.D.C.'s Classification of Surgical Wounds system is intended to:**

    1. *categorize surgical wounds based on coexisting diseases and according to origin, diagnosis, and treatment.*

    2. *elaborate on the C.D.C.'s principles of Universal Precautions by establishing guidelines for treating infections should they occur.*

    3. *suggest emergency criteria for dealing with infections inside the procedure room.*

    4. *monitor postoperative infections and suggest steps to take to reduce these infections.*

13. **Which of the following pairings between a C.D.C. class of surgical wound and a surgical procedure associated with this class of wound is NOT accurate?**

    1. *Class I (clean wound): tonsillectomy.*

    2. *Class II (clean-contaminated wound): elective appendectomy.*

   3. *Class III (contaminated wound): compound leg fracture.*

   4. *Class IV (dirty or infected wound): amputation.*

14. A gunshot wound typically would be categorized as a:

   1. *clean wound (C.D.C. Class I).*

   2. *clean-contaminated wound (C.D.C. Class II).*

   3. *contaminated wound (C.D.C. Class III).*

   4. *dirty or infected wound (C.D.C. Class IV).*

15. A patient's wound is being drained postoperatively. One approach suggested by some physicians and the C.D.C. for lessening the chance of infection is to:

   1. *enter the wound through an adjacent, separate stab wound.*

   2. *wash the wound daily with an antimicrobial disinfectant agent.*

   3. *remove the drain within the first 6 hours following surgery if there is no evidence of inflammation.*

   4. *remove the drain immediately following surgery if there is no evidence of inflammation.*

16. Wounds that occur without tissue loss are known as:

   1. *primary wounds.*

   2. *closed wounds.*

   3. *secondary wounds.*

   4. *open wounds.*

17. In a wound that is healing, replacement of lost tissue that occurs without restoration of function by the new tissue is known as:

   1. *delayed healing.*

   2. *regeneration.*

   3. *repair.*

   4. *primary closure.*

18. In a patient whose wound has a high risk of infection or must be drained, wound closure occurs by:

   1. *primary union (first intention).*

   2. *granulation (second intention).*

   3. *delayed primary closure (third intention).*

   4. *regenerative closure (fourth intention).*

19. **Which of the following pairings between (a) factors that influence normal wound healing and (b) examples of such factors, is INCORRECT?**

    1. *general factors: cell oxygenation, age, and chemical imbalances in the patient.*

    2. *local factors: inflammation, hemorrhage, and immobilization.*

    3. *intraoperative factors: improper tissue handlings and suturing and wound closure materials.*

    4. *exogenous factors: stress, nutrition, and previous surgeries.*

20. **The greatest concern with wound healing during the first 2 to 5 postoperative days is:**

    1. *wound disruption causing either dehiscence or evisceration.*

    2. *fistulas and sinuses resulting in drainage not expected from the anatomic area.*

    3. *keloid scars producing a dense fibrous tissue around the outside of the original incision.*

    4. *incisional hernias leading to bowel obstructions.*

21. **During the postoperative period following Mr. L.'s neck surgery, a tract, open at both ends, develops between two epithelium lined surfaces, resulting in drainage that is not expected from the anatomic area. This type of wound healing complication is known as a:**

    1. *incisional hernia.*

    2. *sinus.*

    3. *fistula.*

    4. *keloid scar.*

22. **Which of the following is NOT one of the primary factors that influence the acquisition of a postsurgical wound infection?**

    1. *The methods used to screen for microorganisms.*

    2. *A means of transmission of microorganisms into the wound.*

    3. *A source of microorganisms (environmental or personnel).*

    4. *The patient's intrinsic resistance.*

23. **Which of the following statements does NOT apply to the concept of surgical conscience?**

    1. *This concept allows no compromise in the principles of aseptic technique.*

    2. *This concept applies principally to the surgical team rather than to others involved in patient care.*

    3. *This concept is based on the Golden Rule: Do unto others as you would have others do unto you.*

    4. *This concept involves the ability to set aside personal preferences and prejudices to provide optimum patient care.*

24. **The group of procedures that prevent contamination of microorganisms through the knowledge and principles of *contain and control* are known as:**

    1. *aseptic technique.*

    2. *disinfection.*

    3. *sterile technique.*

    4. *the surgical conscience.*

25. **Included among the basic principles of aseptic technique that should be practiced by all members of the health-care team are all of the following EXCEPT:**

    1. *Gowns are considered sterile front and back, from shoulder to knees, and the sleeves to 2 inches below the elbow.*

    2. *Tables are sterile at table level only.*

    3. *The edges of a sterile wrapper or container are considered unsterile once the package is opened.*

    4. *Sterile persons and items touch only sterile areas; unsterile persons and items touch only unsterile areas.*

26. **The sterile gown and gloves serve primarily as a bacterial barrier between:**

    1. *the circulator and all sterile items.*

    2. *the scrub nurse and all unsterile items.*

    3. *the scrub nurse and the surgeon and surgeon's assistant.*

    4. *sterile areas of the body and unsterile areas of the body.*

27. **During a surgical procedure the circulating nurse reaches over but does not touch the sterile drape covering a stand located within the sterile field. Which of the following measures should be taken?**

    1. *The area of the drape in question should be covered to correct contamination of that area.*

    2. *The sterile drape should be considered contaminated and should be replaced.*

    3. *No corrective action is necessary because the drape was not touched.*

    4. *No corrective action is necessary because the circulating nurse is gowned and gloved and therefore is assumed to be sterile.*

28. **Sterility of an unopened item that has been prepackaged (e.g., drapes, sponges, etc.) is related most closely to the:**

    1. *length of time since the item was packaged.*

    2. *manufacturer and its manufacturing methods.*

    3. *type of prepackaged item.*

    4. *integrity of the packaging material and handling and storage of the package.*

29. **A bottle of sterile irrigation solution is used during a surgical procedure. What should be done with any solution remaining in the bottle following the procedure?**

    1. *It should be combined with any other sterile irrigation solution used in the procedure, and the bottle should be recapped for future use.*

    2. *It should be kept separate from any other irrigation solution used in the procedure, and the bottle should be recapped for future use.*

    3. *It should be kept separate from any other irrigation solution used in the procedure, then resterilized and bottled for future use.*

    4. *It should be discarded.*

30. **Among the guidelines for maintaining and monitoring a sterile field are all of the following EXCEPT:**

    1. *The sterile field should be created as close to the time of the procedure as possible.*

    2. *Under no circumstances should a sterile field be covered for use at a later time.*

    3. *If possible, the sterile team should sit when not directly involved in the procedure and stand as needed.*

    4. *The field should be in constant view; therefore, members of the sterile team should never turn their back on a sterile field.*

31. **The *primary* purpose of the surgical hand scrub is to:**

    1. *sterilize hands prior to gloving.*

    2. *remove dirt and debris from hands prior to gloving.*

    3. *reduce the transient and resident microbial count on hands to as low a level as possible prior to gloving.*

    4. *provide sterility in the event surgical gloves are torn or punctured during the surgical procedure.*

32. **Among the established guidelines for an effective surgical hand scrub are all of the following EXCEPT:**

    1. *The surgical scrub is performed after proper preparation by the person performing the scrub.*

    2. *Jewelry, including watches, rings, and bracelets, should be sterilized prior to the scrub.*

    3. *Hands should be inspected for breaks in the skin.*

    4. *A 5-minute surgical scrub of the hands and forearms is adequate for removal of gross dirt and oils from the skin, as long as mechanical friction combined with an antimicrobial agent are present.*

33. **One of the essential features of surgical gowns and drapes that helps them maintain a sterile barrier is that:**

    1. *they are generally sterilized just prior to use.*

    2. *their stockinette cuffs do not absorb moisture from the skin.*

3. *they are impregnated with antimicrobial agents.*

4. *they are relatively resistant to penetration by blood or other liquids used at the sterile field.*

34. **An important principle in effective gowning and gloving is that:**

    1. *donning of sterile gloves and gown should be performed within the sterile field.*

    2. *hands should be dried prior to donning sterile gloves and gowns.*

    3. *the stockinette cuffs of the gown should be kept outside the sterile gloves.*

    4. *towels should not be used on hands prior to donning sterile gloves and gown.*

35. **Under which of the following circumstances should the** *closed-glove method* **of donning sterile gloves be used?**

    1. *When a sterile scrub or gown is not required (aseptic procedures).*

    2. *When another team member is being gloved.*

    3. *When a glove is being changed during a procedure.*

    4. *When gloves are being donned initially by the scrub person.*

ANSWER EXPLANATIONS

1. **The answer is 2.** Bacteria are the most common cause of injury to the surgical patient; therefore, every effort must be made to prevent this injurious substance from entering the surgical wound. Infection by bacteria or other microorganisms may or may not be accompanied by overt symptoms of the disease. A local infection, for example, is usually restricted to a specific anatomic site, causing only an inflammatory response to that site. A systemic or generalized infection can occur as the result of microorganisms and their products spreading throughout the body. An initial infection, caused by one kind of microorganism is called a primary infection, while the secondary infection usually involves a second microorganism entering the system and can result in a more toxic form of infection, making it harder to arrest or destroy.

2. **The answer is 4.** Infections caused by microorganisms that are considered part of the normal resident flora are said to be **endogenous.** An endogenous infection occurs when the normal balance between the organism and the human host is upset owing to impaired defenses, or when the organism is introduced into a part of the body where it does not normally occur, for example, *Escherichia coli* from the intestinal tract into the urinary tract. Infections caused by microorganisms that are *not* part of the normal resident flora are said to be **exogenous.** These infections are usually acquired through personnel or hospital environments, and are referred to as nosocomial infections caused by opportunistic pathogens. Exogenous infectious agents can be transmitted by a variety of causes, either directly or indirectly.

3. **The answer is 3.** Most nosocomial infections occurring during the postoperative period (endogenous or exogenous) appear to result from contamination acquired in the operating room, not only because the patient is compromised by illness, but also because the natural defense system, mainly the skin and mucous membranes, has been violated. To gain entry into the body, microorganisms must penetrate natural barriers, such as the skin, the mucous membranes lining, the respiratory, gastrointestinal, and urologic tracts, or the conjunctivae. These barriers constitute the body's first line of defense against microbial invasion.

4. **The answer is 2.** Two methods of contact can result in contamination and postoperative wound infection in the surgical patient. **Direct contact** involves close association between an infected person and a susceptible host through blood, sputum, or mucous membrane. **Indirect contact** involves contact between a susceptible

person and infectious material derived from an infectious host or contaminated source, such as skin, air, instruments, or dust particles. Once pathogenic microorganisms have entered the body, they may establish a local infection at the site of entry or may disseminate throughout the body and establish themselves at sites remote from the site of entry. Whether or not the invading microorganisms establish an infection at the site of entry or at another location depends on the growth requirements of the organism, the local tissue environment, the strength of the host, and the ability of the microorganism to overcome the host defenses.

5. **The answer is 1.** Inflammation is the local response of tissue to damage, whether by injury or pathogenic microorganisms. Many agents can cause tissue damage, which starts an inflammatory reaction. This response proceeds through several stages, until the tissue has been healed. These stages are commonly described as the acute inflammation, demolition, and restoration stages. Clinical signs and symptoms of this process consist of redness, swelling, warmth, pain, and limitation of movement, and are present immediately following any invasive procedure in which the natural defense system has been compromised.

6. **The answer is 4.** Since the majority of infections can be acquired in the operating room, most preventive measures should be directed toward three primary areas: (1) the preparation of the surgical patient, (2) technical and aseptic practices of the surgical team, and (3) the maintenance of the surgical environment. (Not all operating room equipment need be sterile, however.) Measures aimed at preventing microbial contamination of the wound begin before the operation, by treating active infections and improving the general health of the patient to reduce the risk of postoperative infections. Other preoperative measures include keeping the preoperative stay as short as possible; avoiding hair removal, or, if necessary, removing the hair with clippers or depilatories rather than a razor; and proper antimicrobial preparation of the skin, which may include a shower using an antimicrobial agent (e.g. Betadine) the night before and the morning of the surgery, in addition to the surgical skin preparation performed immediately before the start of the procedure.

7. **The answer is 3.** Contamination from the surgical team is another potential source of infection, usually related to direct contact from hands or from shedding skin or mucous membranes. The use of a surgical hand scrub with an effective antimicrobial agent prior to the application of sterile gloves should assist in retarding bacterial growth, and corrective action should be taken immediately if this barrier is compromised in any way before or during the surgical procedure.

8. **The answer is 4.** Poor operative technique can result in the contamination of the operative wound, causing an extension of the anesthesia time and unnecessary injury to surrounding tissue, which can result in necrosis and delayed healing. Any of these conditions can result in postoperative wound infections, since the patient's natural defense system has been compromised. The other factors listed are also important in the prevention of infection.

9. **The answer is 1.** Movement or activity in the O.R. can be decreased by keeping the procedure room doors closed and by limiting the number of persons in the procedure room and adjacent corridors. Air inside the operating room is often contaminated with microorganisms that can be attached to airborne particles (dust, lint, respiratory droplets) that could be potential pathogens. A large number of airborne particles are directly related to the number of persons in the operating (procedure) room, and/or to the O.R. doors remaining open and personnel talking near or in the procedure room. Failure to adhere to proper O.R. attire in the semirestricted and restricted areas of the suite may also account for potential problems, and must be addressed through rigid adherence to policies and procedures for all persons entering these areas.

10. **The answer is 4.** While there are several means of transferring pathogenic microorganisms during the perioperative period, exposure to blood and body fluids presents the greatest threat to personnel working in the surgical suite. The C.D.C., in 1987, established the Universal Precautions concept, designed to protect personnel from unknown exposure from the patient or the environment. The concept states that "since medical history and examination cannot identify all patients who are potentially infected with blood-borne pathogens, specific precautions should be used with ALL patients, thereby reducing the risk of possible exposure to its minimum." Through the implementation of the Universal Precautions, the need for isolation

of specific cases and the special cleaning procedures associated with these cases is no longer applicable: *All procedures and/or patients are potentially contaminated*; therefore, they are treated alike.

11. **The answer is 3.** Needles should never be recapped or bent after use. Suture needles and sharps should be contained in a puncture-resistant container, and sealed for proper disposal according to recommended practices and established protocols. Additional C.D.C. recommendations include: (1) handwashing after the removal of gloves should become a routine practice for both scrub and nonsterile personnel working in a procedure room; (2) health-care workers should take all necessary precautions to protect against injuries caused by needles, scalpels, and other sharp instruments or devices during procedures, when cleaning used instruments, and when handling sharp instruments after a procedure; sharp instruments should be placed in a tray in such a way that their points are not exposed, to avoid injury to persons working with the trays; during the procedure, care must be taken when handling suture needles to ensure that no one receives an injury by placing the needle on a needle holder and passing it with the point down; (3) health-care workers who have exudate lesions or weeping dermatitis should refrain from all direct patient care and from handling patient care equipment until the condition resolves; circulating nurses should wear sterile gloves if a skin lesion is present, and should cover the lesion with a protective covering when working in a procedure room; (4) aspirated or drainage material should never be allowed to come in contact with the health-care worker, either during the aspiration process or following the procedure; and (5) when dealing with soiled sponges, towels, or disposable supplies, the principle of Contain and Control must be used by all personnel both during and after the procedure.

12. **The answer is 4.** Through the C.D.C.'s Classification of Surgical Wounds system, the surgeon and the nurse-epidemiologist can monitor those patients who are more likely to develop postoperative infections and those who, owing to the nature of their surgery, should be least likely. This technique establishes a criteria for monitoring the surgical infection rates and taking appropriate steps to reduce the incidence of these infections. The system is used throughout the country as a quality assurance measure for all surgical patients. It is important to remember, in deciding what classification the surgical procedure belongs in, that the C.D.C. system determines the possible risk of postoperative infections related to the nature or type of surgery being performed. Neither coexisting nor preexisting conditions, except for Class IV, should influence the classification.

13. **The answer is 1.** A tonsillectomy involves a clean-contaminated wound in the C.D.C. system (class 3). Clean wounds (Class 1) are uninfected operative wounds in which no inflammation is encountered, and the respiratory, alimentary, genital, or uninfected urinary tracts are not entered. Additionally, clean wounds are elective surgery, with primary closure and, if necessary, drained with a closed drainage device. Operational incisional wounds that follow nonpenetrating (blunt) trauma should be included in this class, if all other criteria have been met. Risk factor: 1 to 5 percent risk of postoperative infection. Examples: include, but are not limited to, eye surgery, hernia repairs, breast surgery, neurosurgery (nontraumatic), cardiac or peripheral vascular surgeries. Clean-contaminated wounds (Class 3) are operative wounds in which the respiratory, alimentary, genital or urinary tract is entered under controlled conditions and without unusual contamination. Specifically, operations involving the biliary tract, appendix, vagina, and oropharynx are included provided there is no evidence of infection or no major break in aseptic technique is encountered. Risk factor: 3 to 11 percent risk of postoperative infection. Examples: include, but are not to, gastrectomy, cholecystectomy (without spillage), elective appendectomy, cysto or cysto-TUR (negative urine cultures), total abdominal hysterectomy (TAH), dilation and curettage, "C" sections and tonsillectomy (noninfected at time of surgery).

14. **The answer is 3.** Contaminated wounds are open, fresh, traumatic wounds, or wounds with major breaks in sterile technique or with gross spillage from the G.I. tract, and incisions in which acute, nonpurulent inflammation is encountered. Risk factor: 10 to 17 percent risk of postoperative infection. Examples: include, but are not limited to, rectal surgery, laparotomy (significant spillage), traumatic wounds (e.g., gunshot, stab wounds *non-perforation of visceral*) or acute inflammation of any organ without frank pus present (e.g., acute appendicitis or cholecystitis, compound fractures.

15. **The answer is 1.** In the postoperative period, the risk of wound infection can be reduced by proper techniques when handling the wound, proper and frequent handwashing, and by the use of closed wound-drainage systems when indicated. If a drain is used, having it enter through an adjacent, separate stab wound rather than the incision will, according to some physicians, lessen the chance of infection, since the incision site is not directly involved.

16. **The answer is 2.** There are two types of wounds. The first involve possible tissue loss and are known as open wounds, while the second are those without tissue loss, known as closed wounds. The loss or destruction of tissue can occur in several ways: by traumatic excision (accidental or surgical); by chemical or physical agents (burns, ischemia); or by severe inflammation resulting in tissue necrosis.

17. **The answer is 3.** Replacement of loss tissue in an open wound can be accomplished by repair or regeneration. Repair is the replacement of lost tissue with granulation tissue that matures to form a fibrous connective tissue scar. Although it does not restore function, it fills the anatomic defect and restores tissue integrity. Regeneration is the replacement of lost tissue with tissue of the same type, through multiplication of undamaged cells that replace those that were damaged. When regeneration occurs, normal function is usually restored. If both restoration and repair occur, the basic framework of the tissue will survive, producing a tissue mass that will be completely restored.

18. **The answer is 3.** The open wound heals in three distinct ways, depending on the variables present during the healing cycle. **Primary union (first intention wound healing)** occurs with incised or sutured wounds with no tissue loss, or minimum tissue loss without "dead space." This is the ideal wound, since no contamination has occurred, and it results in a cosmetic effect similar to the normal skin surface. The edges are approximated, resulting in a "hairline scar." **Granulation (second intention wound healing)** occurs when wounds experience tissue loss, preventing the approximation of edges and thereby forcing the wound to heal with granulation tissue, which is finally covered by epithelial cells. The cause may be infection or necrosis of tissue, and it produces a wider and deeper scar. **Delayed primary closure (third intention wound healing)** uses a combination of first and second intention healing, and occurs when a wound is left open to heal. After 4 to 6 days, the granulation tissue covers the surface of the wound, at which time it is sutured closed (delayed closure). This procedure is used when there is a high risk of infection or the need for drainage, but because the wound must be left open, this technique can result in additional complications during the postoperative period.

19. **The answer is 4.** All of the factors listed in choice 4 are **endogenous** (intrinsic to the patient) and not exogenous factors. Stress is a local factor; nutrition is a general factor; and the previous surgeries is an intraoperative factor affecting wound healing. Exogenous factors include the sterility of the instruments and supplies, proper preparation of the incision site, and all other factors that relate to the maintenance of a safe, therapeutic environment by the perioperative nurse and other personnel involved with the procedure.

20. **The answer is 1.** Even with the best techniques and precise nursing care during the perioperative period, some patients may experience complications involving the surgical wound. The greatest concern during the first 2 to 5 postoperative days is wound disruption causing either dehiscence or evisceration. Wound dehiscence is the partial or total separation of the wound. It occurs most often during the lag phase of the healing process, while the wound is still in a delicate condition. Total dehiscence, usually involving an abdominal incision, results in evisceration, or protrusion of the viscera through the incisional line. When this occurs, a true surgical emergency exists, requiring immediate action by the nurse caring for the patient. Additionally, incisional hernias, fistulas and sinuses, and keloid scars are complications that may be encountered during the postoperative period.

21. **The answer is 3.** Fistulas and sinuses usually occur during the second phase of normal wound healing (fibroplasia phase). A fistula is a tract between two epithelium-lined surfaces, open at both ends. This type of complication is usually associated with head and neck, bowel, or genitourinary surgery, and results in drainage that is not expected from the anatomic area. A sinus, on the other hand, is open at only one end, producing an abnormal sinus tract. This usually requires drainage and closure, but only after the inflammation has subsided. Incisional hernias result from incomplete wound dehiscence in which the skin

remains intact. They can occur as late as 2 to 3 months postoperatively, and occur most frequently in lower abdominal incisions. Incisional hernias can lead to bowel obstructions, which must be surgically corrected. Changes in the metabolism of collagen during the healing process may result in the development of keloid scars, producing a dense fibrous tissue around the outside of the original incision. These scars can be revised; however, the condition can reappear with each new incision or manipulation of the incisional site.

22. **The answer is 1.** Many factors can influence the acquisition of a postsurgical wound infection, but basically the acquisition of an infection requires the interaction of three potential causes: (1) the patient's intrinsic resistance (susceptibility of the host); (2) a source of the microorganisms (environmental or personnel); and (3) a means of transmission (entry into the system). Some of the causes may include air, various hospital personnel (carriers), equipment, food, heating/cooling systems, and other patients, in addition to the sources discussed earlier in this chapter. While all hospital areas pose some degree of risk to the patient of acquiring an infection, surgical patients are the highest risk population within the institution, and therefore require constant monitoring to avoid possible complications.

23. **The answer is 2.** Surgical conscience is that concept which allows for no compromise in the principles of aseptic technique, since anything less could increase the potential risk of infection, resulting in harm to the patient. A surgical conscience builds on the principles of asepsis, and is an act of mental discipline. It involves the assessment and regulation of one's own practice, with particular attention to deviations from acceptable, safe practices, especially during the intraoperative phase of surgical intervention. Surgical conscience does not apply to the surgical team, but to all those directly involved with patient care. It demands the recognition of improper practices observed during surgery by any member of the health care team, and the ability to report one's own breaks in technique, so that corrective action may be taken, even if the person is not being observed. Additionally, surgical conscience involves the ability to set aside personal preferences and prejudices in order to provide optimum patient care.

24. **The answer is 1.** Two methods which, if practiced with precise accuracy, can prevent serious complications to the already compromised surgical patient are aseptic technique and sterile technique. Aseptic technique is a group of procedures that prevent contamination of microorganisms through the knowledge and principles of contain and control. It is based on the premise that most infections are introduced into the body from outside (exogenous) sources. To avoid infection, it is necessary to ensure that any procedure performed on the body is done in such a way as to introduce no bacteria. To protect the patient, prior to handling sterile supplies the surgical team members must use appropriate measures to reduce the possibility of infection, including proper attire, the removal of existing resident flora on their hands and arms by performing a surgical hand scrub, and the application of sterile gown and gloves. Sterile technique, on the other hand, comprises methods by which contamination of an item is prevented by maintaining the sterility of the item/area involved with a procedure.

25. **The answer is 1.** Aseptic technique can be implemented in many different ways, and understanding the following five basic principles, along with those in choices 2, 3, and 4, remains an important aspect of safe perioperative nursing practice. Until empirical research demonstrates that any technique is not effective, these basic principles should remain in force and should be practiced by all members of the health-care team: (1) all items used within a sterile field must be sterile; (2) a sterile barrier that has been permeated must be considered contaminated; (3) gowns are considered sterile in front, from shoulder to table level, and the sleeves to 2 inches above the elbow; (4) movement within or around a sterile field must not contaminate the field; and (5) all items and areas of doubtful sterility are considered contaminated.

26. **The answer is 1.** The surgical team is divided into two groups: those who are working directly at the surgical field (sterile team), and those who are working around the sterile field (unsterile team). All sterile team members perform a surgical scrub before entering the procedure room, to remove gross dirt from their hands and arms prior to applying their sterile gown and gloves. Since the scrubbed team members receive sterile equipment from the circulator (nonsterile member), and since sterile can only touch sterile, a bacterial barrier is needed between the circulator and the sterile item. That bacterial barrier is the sterile gown and gloves.

27. **The answer is 2.** Contamination of equipment and personnel is prevented by the placement of a bacterial barrier or sterile drape over an item located within the boundary of the sterile field. During surgery, the patient, once covered with the bacterial barrier, becomes the center of the sterile field, and since specific pieces of furniture must be used to accommodate surgical instruments and supplies, those surfaces must be covered with a bacterial barrier prior to assembly and use by sterile members of the team. Once the sterile field has been established, nonsterile persons (including the circulator) must never reach over the draped areas, since this constitutes contamination of that area, requiring immediate corrective action to recreate the sterility of that item or field.

28. **The answer is 4.** Some items used during surgery come presterilized from the manufacturer, such as drapes, sponges, gowns, and gloves. Before opening or dispensing these items for sterile use, the integrity of the packaging and the assurance of sterility must be confirmed by the persons dispensing the item. This can be accomplished through: (1) checking the outer wrapper/package to make sure there are not tears or holes; (2) confirming the items' sterility has not been compromised by either time or handling; (3) inspecting to see that the items have gone through the proper sterilization process as evidenced by the indicators on the outside of the package; and (4) realizing that if sterility is in doubt, the item is considered contaminated and cannot be used. According to recent recommendations, the maintenance of package sterility is *event*-related, not *time*-related. Therefore, the item's sterility is dependent on the type of packaging material and its handling and storage conditions.

29. **The answer is 4.** All items introduced into a sterile field should be dispensed by methods that maintain sterility of the item and integrity of the sterile field. When working with irrigation solution or fluid contained in a pour bottle, careful attention must be used to avoid "splash-back," and once the solution has been poured, the container cannot be recapped for future use, since its contents can no longer be considered sterile. The solution must be completely used or the remaining fluid discarded.

30. **The answer is 3.** The sterility of the supplies used during a surgical procedure is affected by the length of time the items have not been used and/or exposed to the environment, and by environmental conditions within the sterile area of the procedure room. Sterile persons (in gown and gloves) should not wander in and out of the sterile area while in sterile attire, since the gown is considered contaminated below waist level. Nor should sterile persons sit while in sterile attire, unless the entire procedures is performed in a sitting position, or leave the procedure room/sterile area in gown and gloves (either during or after the procedure). All these actions constitute a break in technique, and must be avoided in order to protect the patient and maintain an aseptic environment.

31. **The answer is 3.** Unlike inanimate objects, the skin cannot be sterilized. Preparation of the surgical team therefore requires a surgical hand scrub and the donning of sterile gown and gloves. Even though the surgical team's hands must be covered by sterile gloves, it is mandatory, for several reasons, that a surgical hand scrub be performed according to acceptable technique prior to the beginning of each procedure. For example, hands may carry pathogenic bacteria acquired from other sources within the environment, or gloves may become punctured or torn during the procedure, exposing the patient and the team to microbial contamination. The goals of the surgical scrub include: (1) mechanical removal of soil and transient microbes from the hands and forearms; (2) chemical reduction of the resident microbial count to as low a level as possible; and (3) reduction of the potential rapid rebound growth of microbes. The principal general goal is therefore to reduce the microbial count on hands prior to gloving.

32. **The answer is 2.** Jewelry should not be worn by members of the sterile team. Additional principles of the surgical scrub include: (1) skin and nails should be kept clean and in good condition; (2) fingernails should be short (not reaching beyond the finger tips), and polish free; (3) artificial nails are not recommended because of their potential for harboring bacterial and fungal development under the nails; and (4) a clean scrub suit, a cap covering facial hair, and a high filtration mask are required by all personnel prior to performing the scrub procedure. Both the iodophors and chlorohexidine gluconates are common agents used for the surgical scrub procedure. They are prepared in combination with detergent to give a cleaning action along with the antibacterial action. Disposable, presterilized scrub brushes, impregnated with one or the

other of these agents, are available in most operating rooms, and the choice is an independent decision, based on personal preference and/or sensitivity to the agent.

33. **The answer is 4.** Surgical gowns and drapes should be made of material that establishes a barrier to minimize the passage of microorganisms between nonsterile and sterile areas. Materials should be resistant to penetration by either blood or other liquids used at the sterile field. The stockinette cuff is the most contaminated portion of the gown, since it absorbs moisture from the skin more rapidly than the gown fabric, and therefore must be covered at all times with sterile gloves. Materials should meet or exceed recommendations from the National Fire Protection Agency for flame retardation, and be as lint free as possible. In some instances, due to the nature of the surgical procedure, extra protection gowns may be required. An additional layer of resistant material is added to the front and sleeves of the gown to add protection against penetration when copious amounts of fluids or contaminates are present.

34. **The answer is 2.** Moisture remaining on the skin after the scrub procedure must be dried with a sterile towel before donning sterile gown and gloves. Therefore, the hand drying process is part of the gowning procedure. To preserve the sterility of the sterile field, the gowning and gloving procedure should be performed from a separate surface, away from the sterile field, to prevent accidental contamination of the field during the process. Stockinette cuffs on the gown must be kept covered at all times with sterile gloves.

35. **The answer is 4.** Sterile gloves can be applied using one of two methods: the open method or the closed method. The closed-glove method should be used any time the nurse is initially applying sterile gown and gloves, while the open-glove method should be used when gloving another team member or changing a glove during a procedure (self or team member), or when a sterile scrub or gown is not required (aseptic procedures). The scrub person, responsible for establishing and organizing the sterile field, is responsible for gowning and gloving himself or herself with assistance from the circulating nurse (unassisted gowning and gloving), while the rest of the sterile team members will be assisted by the scrub person (assisted gowning and gloving). During the packaging of sterile gloves, provisions must be made for the scrubbed person to touch only the inner side of the glove cuff when donning the gloves.

6 Operating Room Theory and Techniques: Preparation of Surgical Supplies

STUDY OUTLINE

I. **METHODS OF ASSURING ADEQUATE PROCESSING**

1. Instruments, supplies, and other equipment used during surgery must be made ready according to acceptable practices, through a group of processes known as **decontamination, sterilization, and disinfection.** Therefore, it is vitally important that all personnel know how to execute these tasks correctly and be able to distinguish the process of sterilization from other processes that approach sterility but do not achieve it.

2. Medical and surgical equipment and supplies are categorized into three groups based on the potential risk of infection associated with their use. These categories dictate the type of processing required for the specific item.

3. **Category I: Critical items**
    a. **Critical items are instruments or objects that are introduced directly into the bloodstream or into any normally sterile area or cavity of the body.** Examples include, but are not limited to, surgical instruments and devices, specialty trays and sets, irrigation solutions, catheters, tubes and drains, intravenous solutions, internal defibrillator paddles, and implantable devices.
    b. **Process:** Critical items must be **sterilized** by either steam, chemical, or physical methods.

4. **Category II: Semicritical items**
    a. **Semicritical items contact intact mucous membranes, may or may not penetrate body surfaces.** Examples include, but are not limited to, cystoscopes, flexible and/or rigid, endoscopes, thermometers, endotracheal tubes, anesthesia rebreathing circuits, and respiratory therapy equipment.
    b. **Process:** Sterilization is preferred, although **disinfection** is acceptable, but only when using a high-level disinfectant solution.

5. **Category III: Noncritical items**
    a. **Noncritical items are those that either do not ordinarily touch the patient or contact *only* intact skin.** Examples include such items as bedpans, crutches, E.C.G. electrodes and lead wires, blood pressure cuffs (automatic or manual), external defibrillator paddles, and grounding pads for the electrosurgical unit.
    b. **Process:** These items require only a thorough cleaning and possible **decontamination** depending on their use, since microbial entry is rare with intact skin.
    c. Regardless of the process used, the item must be clean prior to beginning the process, since effectiveness is directly correlated to the amount of bioburden on the object at the time of processing.

102

II.   THE DECONTAMINATION PROCESS

A.   PRINCIPLES OF DECONTAMINATION

1.   **Decontamination is the first step toward reducing the potential hazards associated with direct contact with blood, fluids, or tissues on contaminated instruments. It refers to a process by which the contaminates are removed, either by hand cleaning or mechanical methods, using specific solutions capable of rendering the blood and debris harmless and removing it from the surface of an object or instrument.**
2.   The decontamination process begins in the operating room, following completion of the surgical procedure.
3.   All instruments used during the procedure should be inspected for gross dirt and debris, and cleaned with water and/or scrub brush soaked with an antimicrobial solution. These instruments, along with the others exposed to the procedure, are then placed in a proper receptacle for transference to the decontamination room. It is important to note that during the transfer process, the contaminated instruments should be contained in the protective barrier.
4.   If a **case cart** system is used, the initial cleaning should still be performed, and the instruments returned to their respective carts for transport to the designated decontamination area.
5.   Once the instruments and other nondisposable items used at the field arrive in the decontamination area, the second step in the process begins, which involves the thorough cleaning of the instruments and initial sterilization prior to assembly of the tray.

B.   METHODS OF DECONTAMINATION

1.   The most common methods of mechanical cleaning are the **ultrasonic washer, washer-sterilizer,** and the new **washer-decontaminator.**
2.   **Ultrasonic washer**
     a.   The ultrasonic cleaning process removes blood and debris left on the instrument by a process known as **cavitation,** which occurs when sound waves are passed through water, creating within it cavities ranging in size from submicroscopic to very large. These bubbles expand until they implode, which generates minute vacuum areas on the instruments which are responsible for the actual cleaning process. The small particles float to the top, while the larger particles settle on the bottom of the tank and are eventually flushed away.
     b.   The particles will remain in suspension as long as the water and detergent are *fresh.* It is for this reason that the water must be changed if the ultrasonic cleaner is used for the *initial* cleaning process.
3.   **Washer-sterilizer**
     a.   When the **washer-sterilizer** is used, the soiled instruments are cleaned by mechanical agitation in a bath containing a detergent, rinsed, and then sterilized for 3 minutes. Washer-sterilizers of this type are very advantageous, since they reduce the bioburden, may save labor costs, and conserve time all in one process. However, it must have a cold cycle or the items must be washed by hand first.
4.   **Washer-decontaminator**
     a.   The newest method for decontaminating instruments is the **washer-decontaminator,** which removes excess amounts of dried debris from the instruments, eliminating the hand-cleaning phase of the decontamination process.
     b.   The numerous water jets and the increased pH of the detergent allow for thorough cleaning of even grossly soiled instruments, which is followed by a neutralizing rinse to restore the pH to its neutral state. Since the agitation of the water is minimal, it cleans without tossing the instruments around in the tray, thereby reducing the risk of damage to even delicate instruments.
     c.   There is no steam injected into the chamber; however, if steam is available, it can be used to speed up heating the water.

d. The washer-contaminator cleans instruments so thoroughly that it not only eliminates the need for hand cleaning, but can also replace the ultrasonic washer, which is a definite cost-effective factor in today's practice setting.

5. Regardless of which mechanical process is used, the decontamination phase is critical to the sterilization process, since without proper cleaning, the sterilization process cannot effectively reduce the potential hazards associated with contaminated instruments.

III. THE STERILIZATION PROCESS

A. PRINCIPLES OF STERILIZATION

1. **To sterilize means to render an item totally free of all living microorganisms, including spores, through one of three processes: (1) steam sterilization (2) chemical sterilization or (3) physical sterilization.** Each method has its own characteristics and requires specific parameters for effective completion of the process.

2. Additionally, the process must be continuously monitored to ensure that all procedural parameters and specifications have been met, assuring the sterility and traceability of the item as well as the proper functioning of the equipment.

3. **Steam sterilization**
   a. Steam alone is incapable of sterilizing an item. However, when steam is placed under pressure, its temperature rises, and the moist heat produced destroys the protein within the cell, rendering it harmless. It is, therefore, the relationship between temperature, pressure, and time of exposure that becomes the crucial factor in destroying microbes, and it is these principles that are used in the operation of the team sterilizer.
   b. **Steam under pressure is the most common and economical method of sterilization for heat-tolerable items used in the O.R. and elsewhere in the hospital.**

4. **Chemical sterilization**
   a. Not all equipment or instruments can withstand the extremes of temperature and pressure required during the steam sterilization process. An alternative method, but one just as effective, must therefore be used for these instruments and equipment.
   b. **Chemical sterilization uses a gas known as *ethylene oxide (E.T.O.)* to accomplish this process.** This gas is capable of penetrating most known substances, a criteria necessary for effective sterilization, since it works as an alkylating agent.
   c. Ethylene oxide by itself is extremely flammable and toxic, but mixing it with carbon dioxide or fluorinated hydrocarbons renders it nonflammable for hospital use. However, it still remains toxic to body tissues, which necessitates complete aeration of the sterilized item prior to its use.
   d. Ethylene oxide is expensive and requires longer to complete the sterilization process (up to 20 hours). Therefore, it should be used only when absolutely necessary, and with advanced planning in order to ensure that the item being sterilized and aerated is available when needed.

5. **Physical sterilization**
   a. In today's practice setting, most of the items used at the sterile field are available as prepackaged sterile items from the manufacturer. The sterilization process used for these items is **ionizing radiation (cobalt 60)**, and thereby falls into the category of physical sterilization.
   b. Most of these items are disposable and meant for single-use only, since resterilization may change or deteriorate the item's composition, and possibly make it a hazard to the patient.
   c. Physical sterilization is cost prohibitive for a hospital; therefore this process is always associated with commercially prepared items, and the sterility of the item is guaranteed until the package is opened or the integrity of the package has been compromised.

B. STERILIZATION EQUIPMENT

1. **Steam sterilizers**
   a. Sterilizers designed to use steam under pressure are referred to as **autoclaves** and are generally manufactured to perform this task by one of three methods: (1) **gravity displacement,** (2) **prevacuum,** or (3) **high-speed pressure.**
   b. Regardless of the autoclave used for the process, the components of the sterilizer are basically the same. The metal casing, housing the elements, contains a jacket around the chamber where the items are placed. A control panel, housing gauges that show the specific cycle, is in view above the door. The unit has a hinged door that must be locked during the cycle and, depending on the model, the unit may have a second door as a pass-through for contaminated items. A graph or computerized read-out is also part of the control panel, recording the sterilization process, and is preset according to specifications by the manufacturer.
   c. Most steam sterilizers can be run for 3 to 60 minutes, depending on the type of sterilizer and the temperature being used to sterilize the item(s).
   d. **Gravity displacement sterilizer**
      (1) **The gravity displacement sterilizer** uses the principle that air is heavier than steam. It has an inner chamber where the goods are sterilized and an outer heated jacket that ejects steam into the chamber.
      (2) When the sterilizer is activated, pressurized steam enters the top of the inner chamber from the jacket, and exerts pressure on the air inside the chamber, displacing the air downward to the bottom of the chamber where it is released through a temperature-sensitive valve.
      (3) When the valve closes, the pressure inside the jacket chamber increases, raising the temperature to the required level. At this point, the timing of the sterilization cycle begins.
      (4) **Operating temperature and length of cycle:** The length of cycle depends on the temperature reached inside the jacket. Most gravity displacement sterilizers work in a range from 250°F (121°C) to 254°F (123°C) at 15 to 17 pounds per square inch (p.s.i.), and take anywhere from 15 minutes for a conventional pack to 55 minutes for sterilization of fluids. NOTE: The higher the temperature, the shorter the cycle duration required.
   e. **Prevacuum (high-vac) sterilizer**
      (1) The automatic **prevacuum, high temperature sterilizer** has generally replaced the gravity displacement method, since it does not rely on gravity to remove the air from the chamber. Instead, the air is removed by a venturi valve that uses water movement to create the vacuum, which simultaneously draws the air out while steam is injected into the chamber, replacing the air. This mechanism reduces the time necessary to accomplish the sterilization cycle to as little as 20 minutes, but the time varies with the size of the sterilizer, the adequacy of the steam, and the supply of water.
      (2) This sterilizer, if efficient in preventing air pockets, has a greater penetrating ability than the gravity displacement type.
      (3) Because it relies on prevacuum to begin the timing cycle, a test to ensure its proper prevacuum capabilities must be performed at the beginning of each day. One such test is called a **Bowie-Dick test,** and is performed using a test pack of prewashed surgical towels with a commercially prepared monitoring sheet placed between the towel packs. A commercially prepared Bowie-Dick test pack that meets the current recommended standards is also available.
      (4) If a hospital-prepared pack is used, it should be wrapped and labeled "test-pack." It is placed on the center of the rack, over the steam drain, in an empty chamber. Upon completion of the cycle, the paper is removed and observed for a uniform color change, indicating a satisfactory test result. It does not, however, measure the efficacy of the sterilization process, only the efficient workings of the vacuum established during the process.

(5) **Operating temperature and length of cycle**
   (a) The recommended exposure time for prevacuum steam sterilizers is four minutes, at temperatures ranging from 270°F (132°C) to 274°F (134°C).
   (b) This sterilizer, like the gravity displacement sterilizer, is used primarily for wrapped goods. Faulty packaging and overloading or incorrect placement of objects may interfere with air removal, thus negating the sterilization process.
   (c) Prevacuum sterilizers can handle more items to be sterilized within the specified period of time than do gravity displacement sterilizers.

f. **High speed (flash) sterilizer**
   (1) The **high-speed** or **flash sterilizer** is a smaller version of the gravity displacement sterilizer, and is used exclusively for emergency sterilization of unwrapped items that may have been contaminated during a surgical procedure.
   (2) Items should be placed on a wire-mesh tray, or "flash pan," after cleaning, and are sterilized for a shorter cycle at a high temperature.
   (3) The flash cycle bypasses the drying phase and fast exhaust upon completion of the cycle, thereby greatly reducing the length of the process.
   (4) Because the items are unwrapped and do not have a marker indicating their exposure to the process, as do wrapped items (external indicator tape), a "flash indicator strip" is placed in the tray with the items being flashed to show that the item(s) were exposed to the sterilization process. Each indicator should be marked with the name of the patient or case, date, time, and autoclave number used. These indicators should be maintained with other sterilization records that demonstrate the efficiency of the equipment being used.
   (5) **Operating temperature and length of cycle:** The flash sterilizer is adjusted to operate at 270°F (132°C). Exposure begins when the temperature reaches 270°F, and can be set for a 3-minute or a 10-minute cycle, depending on the amount of instruments being flashed and their composition. For example, air-powered drills or a full tray of instruments would require more time for adequate exposure to the steam (10 minutes) than would two or three clamps placed in a flash pan (3 minutes).

2. **Chemical (gas) sterilizers**
a. **Gas sterilization,** using E.T.O. gas, is dependent upon (1) the concentration of the gas being used, (2) the temperature inside the chamber, (3) the humidity level, and (4) the exposure time.
b. In general, E.T.O. gas concentrations range between 450 and 800 mg/L of chamber space, and operate at temperatures ranging from 86°F to 140°F (60°C), with at least 50 percent humidity, but not less than 30 percent in order to hydrate the items during the process. (A relative humidity of 40-80 percent is recommended during the sterilization cycle.)
c. Ethylene oxide sterilizers can be permanent or portable, depending on the needs of the area it serves. The chambers can be automatically or manually operated, and range in size from 16 x 16 x 29 in. to very large units that will accommodate several patient mattresses.
d. The timing of the cycle varies; it usually takes 2 to 5 hours for the sterilization cycle to be completed. However, the process does not end here. The items must be aerated before returning the item for patient use.
e. **Aeration of gas-sterilized items**
   (1) Ethylene glycol, a toxic carcinogen, is formed by a reaction of E.T.O. gas with water or moisture. Additionally, ethylene chlorhydrin can form when a chloride ion is present in combination with E.T.O. (i.e., PVC plastic). **If either of these substances are left on the item, it could cause immeasurable harm to the patient, including destruction of red blood cells, as well as to the staff working with the item.**
   (2) Because of its peculiar properties and possible toxic effects, the sterilizer must be vented to the outside. Therefore, most E.T.O. sterilizers are located in the central processing area of the hospital, unlike the steam sterilizers, which can be located both inside and outside the O.R. suite.
   (3) All loads must be aerated for a specified period of time. Personnel working with E.T.O. must be specifically trained to execute this process effectively, yet safely, following

acceptable standards established by the Occupational Health and Safety Administration (O.S.H.A.) and the Association for the Advancement of Medical Instrumentation (A.A.M.I.) These recommendations concern the handling, removal, and aeration process for gas sterilization.

    f. Preparing items for ethylene oxide sterilization

        (1) Items to be sterilized by E.T.O. require special preparation before being exposed to the gas sterilent. All items must be cleaned and *completely* dried, as water may unite with E.T.O. to form ethylene glycol, which is not eliminated by aeration and may result in toxic reactions in patients and personnel.

        (2) Lumens of tubings, needles, and so on should be air dried and open at both ends to avoid accumulation of gas inside the item. Packaging material should be specific for E.T.O. sterilization and aeration, or indicated that both processes, steam and gas, are acceptable for that item.

C. RECOMMENDED PRACTICES FOR STERILIZATION

    1. Recommended Practice I

        a. **All items to be sterilized should be prepared to reduce the bioburden. Bioburden** relates to the number of actual or suspected microorganisms, of whatever type, found on a specific article at the same time.

        b. To ensure that the item has been properly sterilized, all gross dirt, blood, and tissue debris must be removed before the item can undergo the sterilization process. This can be accomplished through use of proper decontamination procedures, discussed earlier in this chapter.

    2. Recommended Practice II

        a. **All articles to be sterilized should be arranged so all surfaces will be directly exposed to the sterilizing agent for the prescribed time and temperature.** Preparing instrument trays and equipment properly is just as important as the sterilization cycle itself, since proper preparation ensures exposure to all facets and areas of the item.

        b. Instruments that have joints (box locks) or rachets should be opened to allow the agent to penetrate all surfaces. The use of instrument racks or pegs is well suited for this purpose, and should be used whenever possible.

        c. Instrument sets should be contained in perforated or wire mesh bottom trays, and the total weight of the tray (metal mass) should not exceed 16 or 17 pounds (other written weight recommendations from the manufacturer should be followed).

        d. When preparing basin sets, they should be **nested** with an absorbent towel separating the metal surfaces to prevent contact and moisture build-up.

        e. If a rigid container system is used, the filter papers must be discarded after each use, and new ones inserted, to ensure proper filtration and protection of items inside the tray.

        f. Instruments should not be strung or arranged on a **closed** loop, since the sterilizing agent cannot penetrate hollow items that are closed at one end. Heavier instruments should be at the bottom of the tray, with lighter or delicate instruments on top.

    3. Recommended Practice III

        a. **All wrapped articles to be sterilized should be packaged in materials that meet the criteria given in the A.O.R.N.** *Recommended Practices for In-Hospital Packaging Materials.*

        b. Materials should allow for the penetration of the sterilizing agent and be compatible with the process to be used. Packaging materials can include reusable and single-use fabrics, peel-back pouches, and rigid container systems.

        c. The rigid container systems require no additional wrappers, but must designate the process to be used on the outside of the container.

        d. Since the sterility of an item is event-related, the packaging material should be strong enough to maintain its integrity following the sterilization process and to protect the item from contamination.

  e. When using the disposable fabric, the wrapper must be of double-thickness, equaling a minimum of 280-thread count per layer, and each layer should be wrapped sequentially, making the item easy to dispense to the sterile field without compromise to sterility.

4. **Recommended Practice IV**

  a. **Chemical indicators, also known as sterilization process indicators, should be used to indicate that items have been exposed to a sterilization process.**

  b. Before the item is wrapped for a sterilization cycle, a chemical indicator corresponding to the sterilization process is placed inside the tray, item, or package, and stamped with a load indicator label itemizing the load number, sterilizer number, expiration/sterilization date, and the person preparing the item.

  c. The item is then wrapped using either the envelope style or square method, and taped with the appropriate pressure tape for the process. The pressure tape serves as the outside indicator for the package, and signifies that the item has been exposed to one or more specific physical conditions during the cycle.

  d. **A load indicator label** is also placed on the outside tape (as on the inside indicator), and a description of the item is noted for easy identification when needed.

  e. When a peel-back package is used, one indicator with a load indicator seal is placed on the inside of the package, while the outer package is heat-sealed to prevent the package from opening. An external chemical indicator strip should be clearly visible on every package prepared for sterilization.

  f. It is important to note that chemical indicators do not guarantee that the item is sterile, only that the process is complete.

5. **Recommended Practice V**

  a. **The efficacy of the sterilizing process should be monitored at regular intervals with reliable biological indicators.**

  b. It is necessary to have a reliable, inexpensive method of checking the effectiveness of the sterilization process. This is accomplished through the use of **biological indicators**, commercially prepared according to the U.S. Pharmacopeia minimum performance criteria, and used according to the manufacturer's recommendations. As each sterilization method is different, so too are the biologic substances used to test the sterilization cycle.

  c. **Spores used to test the process**

    (1) A highly resistant, nonpathogenic, spore forming bacteria, contained in a glass ampule or on an impregnated strip, is placed in a test pack in the sterilizer load. When the cycle is completed, the spore and a control ampule (one not exposed to sterilization) are incubated either in the hospital laboratory or in the department, or mailed to an independent laboratory for analysis.

    (2) *Bacillus stearothemophilus* is used with a steam sterilizer and *B. subtilis* is used with a gas sterilizer. When using a closed system (ampule), the incubation period is 24 to 48 hours for 93 percent accuracy, and up to 7 days for 99.9 percent accuracy. Written protocols should follow the manufacturer's instructions and should coincide with infection control procedures within the institution.

    (3) Within the last year, an additional method of biologic testing, specifically designed for the flash sterilizer (Rapid ATTEST Readout) confirms a biologic readout in 1 hour, thus assuring the sterility of those articles to be flash-sterilized throughout the day.

  d. **Frequency of spore testing**

    (1) The frequency for testing is based on the following recommendations:

      (a) **Steam sterilizer:** at least weekly, preferably daily, and as necessary should steam pressure be lost or interrupted, or following down-time due to repairs.

      (b) **Gas sterilizer:** every load, and as needed, as stated above.

      (c) **Implantable objects:** regardless of the method used for sterilization, a biologic indicator should accompany each load, and these objects should not be used until the incubation period is completed, revealing destruction of the spores.

    (2) It is further recommended that since sources may vary regarding the frequency testing recommendations for biologic monitoring, the perioperative nurse should refer to the

institutional policy governing the biologic testing interval in order to ensure compliance within that specific institution.

 e. **Recommended procedure for positive spore test**
  (1) **In the event of a positive spore test occurring with either the gas or steam sterilizers, immediate action must be taken to prevent harm to the patient.**
  (2) Institutional policies and procedures dictating acceptable protocols should be well known by all personnel involved with the sterilization process, and should include the following recommendations:
   (a) Review all records (graphs, charts, chemical indicators) for that day.
   (b) The suspect sterilizer should be taken out of service immediately until a qualified person can perform an operational inspection of the sterilizer.
   (c) The items processed by that sterilizer need not be recalled, except implantables, but the surgeon and the Epidemiology Department should be notified, in order to provide closer monitoring of patients on the O.R. schedule for that day.
   (d) If sterilizer malfunction is discovered, all available items from the suspect sterilizer should be recalled, and an incident report filed with the Risk Management Department noting that an unusual occurrence has taken place.
   (e) Once the malfunction has been corrected, another biologic indicator test must be performed before the sterilizer is placed back into service; if this test is negative, the suspect sterilizer may be placed back into full service.
   (f) Items sterilized by the suspect sterilizer must be stripped, rewrapped, and relabeled for resterilization.
  (3) Biologic indicators are the only methods that indicate that a kill has taken place during the sterilization process. An accurate record of all the test results must be maintained, using an appropriate record-keeping system, according to J.C.A.H.O. requirements.

6. **Recommended Practice VI**
 a. **Saturated steam under pressure should be used for sterilization of heat- and moisture-stable items. Steam sterilizers should be used according to manufacturer's written instructions.**
 b. Like any piece of equipment, the steam sterilizer needs routine preventive maintenance and cleaning. A thorough cleaning removes scales and concealed organisms that may be present, affecting the sterilization process.
 c. Trisodium phosphorate solution should be used to keep the drains open and should be used at least weekly.
 d. A list of items that can be routinely steam sterilized should be available within the process area, and new items added according to the manufacturer's recommendations for the specific procedures.

7. **Recommended Practice VII**
 a. **Ethylene oxide sterilizers should be used for processing heat- and moisture-sensitive items. Ethylene oxide sterilization and aerators should be used and vented according to manufacturer's written instructions.**
 b. Like the steam sterilizer, routine preventive maintenance and cleaning is an important part of assuring reliability of the sterilization process.
 c. Items requiring E.T.O. sterilization should be listed and available within the process area and updated as necessary.
 d. Adequate time must be provided for the sterilization and aeration cycle; therefore, careful planning of the use of the item is essential, since once the cycle has started, it cannot, for *any reason*, be interrupted to retrieve an item, even from the aeration chamber.
 e. Ethylene oxide sterilizers and aeration designs and venting guidelines should be available within the process area for the specific unit being used, and O.S.H.A. and the manufacturer's recommendations for additional requirements should be obtained and kept with the official safety officer with the institution, including monitoring the personnel and the sterilization area.

8. **Recommended Practice VIII**
   a. **Every package should be imprinted or labeled with a load control number that indicates the sterilizer used, the cycle or load number, the date of sterilization, and an expiration date.**
   b. To avoid confusion, the **sterilization date** should be recorded according to the *Julian* calendar date (day 1-365) and the expiration date (if required) according to the *Gregorian* calendar date (month/day/year). The notation "Sterile until contaminated and/or opened" can be used as an expiration date according to J.C.A.H.O. recommendations.
   c. The **lot control number** should be placed both inside and outside the package for visibility both in a sterile area and in the storage area for sterile supplies and instruments.
9. **Recommended Practice IX**
   a. **Sterilized articles should be carefully handled, and only as necessary. They should be stored in a well-ventilated, limited access area with controlled temperature and humidity.** Repeated handling of sterilized items forces air in and out of the wrapper, which could shorten the shelf life of the item.
   b. **Loading the sterilizer**
      (1) Because sterilization depends upon the direct contact of the sterilizing agent with all surfaces of goods, the sterilizer must be loaded so that the sterilizing agent will penetrate through each package. This is best accomplished by placing packs, trays, and basins on their sides.
      (2) For a gravity displacement sterilizer, wire mesh or perforated metal shelves should be used to separate layers of packages. For the best result, the following loading guidelines should be followed:
         (a) **Flat packages:** placed on edge so that flat surfaces are vertical.
         (b) **Large packages:** should be placed in only one layer on the cart (nothing on top of it), and packages should not be touching each other.
         (c) **Small packages:** if placed on top of one another they should be in a criss-cross position.
         (d) **Basins or solid containers:** placed on their sides to allow air to flow out of them and prevent water accumulation. Basins and packs should be placed on the bottom shelves when a mixed-size load is prepared.
         (e) **Rigid container systems:** can lie flat and be stacked according to the manufacturer's recommendations.
      (3) When using a prevacuum sterilizer, follow the manufacturer's recommended guidelines for loading, since the principle of operation is slightly different, although the concept is the same; to prevent air from being trapped in the sterilizer.
   c. **Unloading the sterilizer**
      (1) Once the cycle is complete, the sterilizer door should be *cracked* open to allow steam to escape, then opened completely. The wrapped packages should be removed from the sterilizer and left untouched to cool for 15 to 60 minutes.
      (2) Time can be saved when the wire shelves can be placed on a transfer carriage and then rolled into the sterilizer and removed in the same manner, avoiding the actual handling of the packages prior to total cooling.
      (3) Packages should be left to cool, at a room temperature of 68° to 75°F (20°-24°C), for a minimum of 1 hour.
      (4) If packages are still warm, they should not be transferred to a solid metal shelf as they may sweat. This would cause condensation and result in a wet pack that can no longer be considered sterile.
   d. **Storage of sterile items**
      (1) When storing sterilized items, a method for routine rotation of stock should be used to avoid using outdated supplies or instruments. Older supplies should be used first and new supplies placed behind them (F.I.F.O: First In First Out).
      (2) In accordance with J.C.A.H.O. recommendations, cabinets used for storing sterile items should have doors that are closed at all times and are situated 8 in. above the floor, 18 in. from the ceiling, and 2 in. from an outside wall.

(3) Additionally, the storage area should be shielded from extreme changes in temperatures, be maintained as dust-free as possible, and should not be used to cross over between two areas of the operating room suite.

e. **Shelf life**

(1) **Shelf life** is described as the length of time a wrapped sterile package remains sterile while in storage. Items in continual use are dated at the time they are prepared, indicating the time interval for safe use. For infrequently used items, however, another system is available. By applying a sealed plastic cover over the wrapper, an **indefinite shelf life** can exist, as long as the integrity of the package is not compromised in any manner.

(2) Sterility is *event-related*, not *time-related*, and contamination occurs only when the contents have been exposed via tears or perforations in the protective wrapper. This principle also governs commercially prepared items, and is why an expiration date does not usually appear on a package, simply the manufacturer's assurance that the contents are "guaranteed sterile until package is opened or compromised."

(3) Recently, at the request of different organizations, manufacturers have been asked to include indicators, inside commercially prepared packages to further guarantee the creation of a truly "sterile field." This indicator should appear on "custom packs," drapes, gowns, and so on.

10. **Recommended Practice X**

a. **Performance records for all sterilizers should be maintained for each cycle and retained for the period of time indicated by institutional policy and/or the state's statutes of limitation.**

b. Most sterilizers are equipped with an automatic or microcomputer time-temperature control and/or a graphic recorder for recording operational data. For both, the time-temperature is recorded for a 24-hour period, noting each time the sterilizer was used, for what duration (timing of cycle), and what temperature was reached and maintained during the cycle.

c. These records should be collected at a prescribed, routine time each day (prior to the first run of the sterilizer), and a new record started for the next 24 hours. The information should be maintained in individual envelopes within the O.R., and should be used as a reference base should the sterilization process be questioned.

d. Institutional policies describing the collection and storage of these records should be explicit and standardized throughout the institution wherever a sterilizer is located.

e. The performance record book should include the following data:

(1) Sterilizer number

(2) Cycle number

(3) Contents of each load

(4) Time-temperature graphs per sterilizer

(5) Results of biologic tests performed on each sterilizer

(6) Any additional testing performed on the sterilizer and the results (Bowie-Dick, etc.)

11. **Recommended Practice XI**

a. **Flash sterilization should be used for emergency sterilization of clean, unwrapped instruments and porous items only.** Since speed works against the sterilization process and reduces the margin of safety, flash sterilization should *not* be the routine method for steam sterilization.

b. The unwrapped method may be used in emergency situations for individual items (e.g., dropped instruments). Complete sets of trays of instruments should not be sterilized in this manner unless all of the following conditions are present:

(1) Need is urgent.

(2) The physical layout ensures direct delivery of a tray to the O.R.

(3) Transfer procedures ensure the sterility of the item (e.g., retrieval by scrubbed person with cover protecting the instrument[s]).

(4) Items have been properly decontaminated before the sterilization cycle is initiated.

c. **Specialty instruments/devices**

(1) Sterilization of specialty instruments, such as drills, perforators, and power batteries, may require different exposure times with the flash method. In all instances, follow the

manufacturer's written recommendations for time and temperature using the unwrapped method.

(2) **Under no circumstances should implantable devices be flash sterilized.**

12. **Recommended Practice XII**
   a. **Preventive maintenance of all sterilizers should be performed by qualified personnel, according to individual policy on a scheduled basis, using the sterilizer manufacturers' service manual as a reference.**
   b. Routine maintenance is an effective method for preserving the life of the sterilizer, and should include daily cleaning of the gasket door and the strainers located in the opening of the discharge line, and weekly cleaning of the inside of the chamber.
   c. Time-temperature graphs and charting devices should be recalibrated after each maintenance check or any repairs performed on the sterilizer and/or at least every 6 months, whichever comes first.
   d. In accordance with J.C.A.H.O. recommendations, a maintenance log should be maintained within the surgical suite, and accurate entries be kept for all service visits and the results of the visit.

IV. THE DISINFECTION PROCESS

A. PRINCIPLES OF DISINFECTION

1. **Disinfection in the operating room has two major purposes:**
   a. **To kill pathogenic microorganisms on inanimate surfaces and objects that cannot be sterilized.**
   b. **To prevent or arrest growth of microorganisms on body surfaces through the application of an antiseptic solution.**
2. The disinfection process requires the use of an agent that can destroy infection-producing organisms. **Disinfectants** are liquid chemical compounds that destroy microbes by either physical or chemical means. These agents are used on inanimate objects such as furniture, floors, walls, equipment, and some heat-sensitive items such as fiberoptic scopes and lenses.
3. Disinfectants are identified as **bacteriostatic,** which act by inhibiting growth, or as a **bactericidal**, which will kill bacteria (sporicides, virusides, fungicides).
4. For a disinfectant to affect microorganisms, it must act on some vital part of the cell. Some alter the cytoplasmic membrane, some react directly with certain enzymes, the nucleus, or the cell wall, while others are effective against specific types of microbes and not others.
5. Of some 8000 disinfectants available in the United States, most have both advantages and disadvantages. A good disinfectant is one that is noncorrosive, readily available, relatively pleasant smelling, nonirritating to breathe, and effective on most microorganisms, in addition to being economical.
6. Solutions used to disinfect walls and furniture are not interchangeable with solutions used to disinfect instruments. Therefore, the perioperative nurse must be able to distinguish between the two in order to provide maximum protection for the patient.

B. TYPES (LEVELS) OF DISINFECTANTS

1. Disinfectants are usually available in three levels or strengths, depending on their ability to affect specific types of microbes. Like sterilization, the larger the number of organisms contaminating the object, the longer it takes for the disinfectant to destroy them or render them harmless to the body.

2. **High-level disinfectant**
   a. **Description**: High-level disinfectants can kill spores, bacteria, and viruses if contact time is sufficient. The terms **germicide** and **bactericide** may be used synonymously. However, the tubercle bacillus has a waxy envelope that makes it comparatively resistant to disinfectants, as are some other forms of vegetative bacteria. The solution should be labeled as **tuberculocidal** if it has this capability.
   b. For spores, however, only an extended exposure time can render an object sterile (10 hours or more depending on the agent), and then only when using a high-level disinfectant.
   c. An example of a high-level disinfectant is 2 percent activated glutaraldehyde aqueous solution.
3. **Intermediate-level disinfectant**
   a. **Description:** Intermediate-level disinfectants kill the more resistant bacteria and viruses. Some may be capable of exhibiting sporicidal action, but these must be labeled as such by the manufacturer.
   b. Alcohol (70-95 percent ethyl or isopropyl) and some quaternary ammonium compounds are examples of intermediate-level disinfectants.
4. **Low-level disinfectant**
   a. **Description:** Low-level disinfectants kill only less-resistant bacteria and viruses. They are usually used for housekeeping purposes, and should not be used to disinfect objects for direct patient care. Neither intermediate- nor low-level disinfectants have sporicidal capabilities under normal conditions.
   b. Examples include mercurial compounds and phenolic compounds.
5. **According to A.O.R.N.'s *Recommended Practices for Disinfection*, a high-level disinfectant should be used if an item is to be disinfected rather than sterilized.**

C. **IMPLICATIONS FOR PERIOPERATIVE NURSING PRACTICE**

1. All items to be chemically disinfected should be thoroughly cleaned, rinsed, and dried prior to beginning the process.
2. Chemical disinfectants must contact all surfaces of the item (including lumens and channels) for the process to be effective.
3. The disinfection process should be performed prior to storage and immediately prior to use.
4. Following the recommended immersion time, the item should be aseptically removed, rinsed with copious amounts of sterile water, and dried in such a manner as to reduce the risk of contamination.
5. Immersion time for the item should follow the manufacturer's recommendations and should be reinforced by policy or protocol for all items, regardless of the area, if the same disinfectant solution is used.
6. Gloves and protective eye wear should be worn by persons working directly with the solution, avoiding contact with skin or mucous membranes, since contact irritation can occur.
7. An expiration date, as recommended by the manufacturer, should be highly visible on all containers of the solution currently in use.
8. The agent should be registered with the E.P.A. and should be compatible with the type of item to be disinfected.
9. Parameters for chemical disinfection include:
   a. Time of exposure.
   b. Concentration of the solution.
   c. The amount and type of organic debris.
   d. The temperature (an increase in temperature will accelerate the rate of the chemical reaction).
10. Disinfectant solutions should be covered following reconstituting to avoid noxious odors or fumes, and should remain covered when not in use.

PRACTICE QUESTIONS

1. **Based on their potential for infection, items such as thermometers, cystoscopes, and anesthesia breathing circuits that contact mucous membranes, and that may nor may not penetrate body surfaces, are regarded as:**

   1. *noncritical items, and require decontamination only.*

   2. *semicritical items, and may be either sterilized or disinfected with a high-level disinfectant solution.*

   3. *critical items, and must be sterilized by either steam, chemical, or physical methods.*

   4. *either critical or semicritical items, depending on location of use, and should be processed accordingly.*

2. **The first step toward reducing the potential hazards associated with direct contact with blood, fluids, or tissues on contaminated instruments is:**

   1. *sterilization.*

   2. *decontamination.*

   3. *disinfection.*

   4. *cavitation.*

3. **One advantage of the washer-decontaminator over older methods for decontaminating instruments (e.g., the ultrasonic washer) is that:**

   1. *the need for hand cleaning of excess dried debris is eliminated.*

   2. *instruments are both decontaminated and sterilized.*

   3. *small particles float to the top, while larger particles settle on the bottom of the tank.*

   4. *the injection of steam into the chamber reduces cleaning time.*

4. **Rendering an item totally free of all living microorganisms, including spores, is known as:**

   1. *decontamination.*

   2. *disinfection.*

   3. *cavitation.*

   4. *sterilization.*

5. **Under what circumstances is the chemical sterilization of equipment or instruments preferred to their steam sterilization?**

   1. *When such items are meant for single-use only.*

   2. *When such items are heat- or pressure-sensitive.*

   3. *When cost is a major factor in the choice of sterilizing equipment.*

   4. *When the sterility of items must be guaranteed.*

6. **A nurse wishes to sterilize some wrapped goods in a prevacuum steam sterilizer. To assure complete sterilization, how long should the goods be left it in the sterilizer?**

   1. *Between 30 seconds and one minute.*

   2. *Four minutes.*

   3. *Ten minutes.*

   4. *Thirty minutes.*

7. **An unwrapped item being used in a surgical procedure is accidentally contaminated. In order to sterilize this item as rapidly as possible for later use in the procedure, the nurse should use a:**

   1. *gravity displacement steam sterilizer.*

   2. *prevacuum (high-vac) steam sterilizer.*

   3. *high speed (flash) steam sterilizer.*

   4. *gas (E.T.O) sterilizer.*

8. **An essential precaution in the use of gas (ethylene oxide) sterilizers is:**

   1. *aerating sterilized items before they are returned for patient use.*

   2. *checking the integrity of items following sterilization, since gas sterilization may change an item's composition.*

   3. *testing the sterilizer daily with a Bowie-Dick or other test to ensure its proper functioning.*

   4. *placing the sterilizer inside or close to the O.R. to avoid contamination during the transport of items.*

9. **In order to ensure that the surfaces of all items to be sterilized will be directly exposed to the sterilizing agent for the prescribed time and temperature, each of the following measures should be taken EXCEPT:**

   1. *Instruments that have joints (box locks) should be opened to allow the agent to penetrate all surfaces.*

   2. *Basin sets should be nested with an absorbing towel separating the metal surfaces to prevent contact and moisture build-up.*

   3. *Instrument sets should be contained in perforated or wire mesh bottom trays.*

   4. *Heavier instruments should be placed at the top of the tray, with lighter instruments below.*

10. **Chemical indicators (sterilization process indicators) are used in the sterilization of items in order to demonstrate that:**

   1. *items are sterile.*

   2. *items are free of ethylene oxide contamination.*

3. *the sterilization process is complete.*

4. *packaging material maintained its integrity following sterilization.*

11. **The only way to be certain that items that have gone through a sterilization process are completely free of microbes is to use:**

    1. *sterilization process indicators.*

    2. *a combination of steam and pressure in the sterilization process.*

    3. *biological indicators (spores).*

    4. *a combination of high-pressure steam and ethylene oxide in the sterilization process.*

12. **The number "6" and the words "Sterile until contaminated and/or opened" appear on a package that has been sterilized. This information indicates that the package:**

    1. *was sterilized in June of that year and will remain sterile unless torn or opened.*

    2. *was one of six packages that were sterilized in a load, and will remain sterile unless torn or opened.*

    3. *was sterilized on January 6 of that year and will remain sterile unless torn or opened.*

    4. *has a guaranteed shelf life of six months unless torn or opened sooner.*

13. **All of the following practices help maintain the sterility of items EXCEPT:**

    1. *handling sterilized items carefully and only as necessary.*

    2. *using sterile supplies on a Last In First Out (L.I.F.O.) basis.*

    3. *relying on flash sterilization for emergency sterilization of cleaned, unwrapped instruments and porous items only.*

    4. *placing packs, trays, and basins on their sides in the sterilizer for maximum penetration by the sterilizing agent.*

14. **The flash sterilization of unwrapped items is NOT recommended under which of the following circumstances?**

    1. *The need is urgent.*

    2. *Items have been properly decontaminated before the sterilization cycle is initiated.*

    3. *The physical layout ensures direct delivery of a tray to the O.R.*

    4. *Implantable devices must be sterilized.*

15. **Disinfection is used in the operating room for all of the following EXCEPT:**

    1. *implantable devices.*

    2. *inanimate surfaces (e.g., table tops).*

3. *objects that cannot be sterilized.*

4. *body surfaces.*

16. **Which of the following is true of the disinfection process?**

1. *Disinfection and sterilization are synonymous; the former applies to inanimate surfaces (e.g., walls), the latter to equipment and supplies.*

2. *Solutions used to disinfect walls and furniture are not interchangeable with solutions used to disinfect instruments.*

3. *Both high-level and intermediate-level disinfectants are effective against spores and the tubercle bacillus.*

4. *Low-level disinfectants are used both for housekeeping purposes and to disinfect objects for direct patient care.*

17. **All of the following are perioperative nursing implications of the use of disinfectants EXCEPT:**

1. *The disinfection process should be performed prior to storage and immediately prior to use.*

2. *Gloves and protective eye wear should be worn by persons working directly with the solution, avoiding contact with skin or mucous membranes.*

3. *All items to be chemically disinfected should be thoroughly cleaned, rinsed, and dried prior to beginning the process.*

4. *Lumens and channels of items should not come in contact with the disinfectant, to reduce the risk of toxic contamination.*

ANSWER EXPLANATIONS

1. **The answer is 2.** Medical and surgical equipment and supplies are categorized into three groups based on the potential risk of infection associated with their use. These categories dictate the type of processing required for the specific item. **Critical items** are instruments or objects that are introduced directly into the bloodstream or into any normally sterile area or cavity of the body. Examples include, but are not limited to, surgical instruments and devices, specialty trays and sets, irrigation solutions, catheters, tubes and drains, intravenous solutions, internal defibrillator paddles, and implantable devices. Critical items must be sterilized by either steam, chemical, or physical methods. **Semicritical items** contact intact mucous membranes and may or may not penetrate body surfaces. Examples include, but are not limited to, cystoscopes, flexible and/or rigid, endoscopes, thermometers, endotracheal tubes, anesthesia rebreathing circuits, and respiratory therapy equipment. Sterilization is preferred for these items, although disinfection is acceptable, but only when using a high-level disinfectant solution. **Noncritical items** are those that either do not ordinarily touch the patient or contact only intact skin. Examples include such items as bedpans, crutches, E.C.G. electrodes and lead wires, blood pressure cuffs (automatic or manual), external defibrillator paddles, and grounding pads for the electrosurgical unit. These items require only a thorough cleaning and possible decontamination depending on their use, since microbial entry is rare with intact skin. Regardless of the process used, the item must be clean prior to beginning the process, since effectiveness is directly correlated to the amount of bioburden on the object at the time of processing.

2. **The answer is 2.** Decontamination refers to a process by which the contaminants are removed, either by hand cleaning or mechanical methods, using specific solutions capable of rendering the blood and debris harmless and removing it from the surface of an object or instrument. The decontamination process begins in the operating room, following completion of the surgical procedure.

3. **The answer is 1.** The newest method for decontaminating instruments is the washer-decontaminator, which removes excess amounts of dried debris from the instruments, eliminating the hand-cleaning phase of the decontamination process. The numerous water jets and the increased pH of the detergent allow for thorough cleaning of even grossly soiled instruments, which is followed by a neutralizing rinse to restore the pH to its neutral state. Since the agitation of the water is minimal, it cleans without tossing the instruments around in the tray, thereby reducing the risk of damage to even delicate instruments. The washer-contaminator cleans instruments so thoroughly that it not only eliminates the need for hand cleaning, but can also replace the ultrasonic washer, which is a definite cost-effective factor in today's practice setting.

4. **The answer is 4.** To sterilize means to render an item totally free of all living microorganisms, including spores, through one of three processes: (1) steam sterilization, (2) chemical sterilization, or (3) physical sterilization. Each method has its own characteristics and requires specific parameters for effective completion of the process. Additionally, the process must be continuously monitored to ensure that all procedural parameters and specifications have been met, assuring the sterility and traceability of the item as well as the proper functioning of the equipment.

5. **The answer is 2.** Steam under pressure is the most common and economical method of sterilization for heat-tolerable items used in the O.R. and elsewhere in the hospital. Not all equipment or instruments can withstand the extremes of temperature and pressure required during the steam sterilization process, however. An alternative method, but one just as effective, is chemical sterilization, which uses a gas known as ethylene oxide (E.T.O.) to accomplish this process. This gas is capable of penetrating most known substances, a criteria necessary for effective sterilization, since it works as an alkylating agent. Ethylene oxide is expensive and requires longer to complete the sterilization process (up to 20 hours). Therefore, it should be used only when absolutely necessary, and with advanced planning in order to ensure that the item being sterilized and aerated is available when needed.

6. **The answer is 2.** The recommended exposure time for prevacuum steam sterilizers is four minutes, at temperatures ranging from 270°F (132°C) to 274°F (134°C). This sterilizer, like the gravity displacement sterilizer, is used primarily for wrapped goods. Faulty packaging and overloading or incorrect placement of objects may interfere with air removal, thus negating the sterilization process. Prevacuum sterilizers can handle more items to be sterilized within the specified period of time than can gravity displacement sterilizers.

7. **The answer is 3.** The high-speed or flash sterilizer is a smaller version of the gravity displacement sterilizer, and is used exclusively for emergency sterilization of unwrapped items that may have been contaminated during a surgical procedure. Items should be placed on a wire-mesh tray, or "flash pan," after cleaning, and are sterilized for a shorter cycle at a high temperature. The flash cycle bypasses the drying phase and fast exhaust upon completion of the cycle, thereby greatly reducing the length of the process. Because the items are unwrapped and do not have a marker indicating their exposure to the process, as do wrapped items (external indicator tape), a "flash indicator strip" is placed in the tray with the items being flashed to show that the item(s) were exposed to the sterilization process. Each indicator should be marked with the name of the patient or case, date, time, and autoclave number used. These indicators should be maintained with other sterilization records that demonstrate the efficiency of the equipment being used.

8. **The answer is 1.** Ethylene glycol, a toxic carcinogen, is formed by a reaction of E.T.O. gas with water or moisture. Additionally, ethylene chlorhydrin can form when a chloride ion is present in combination with E.T.O. (i.e., PVC plastic). If either of these substances are left on the item, it could cause immeasurable harm to the patient, including destruction of red blood cells, as well as to the staff working with the item. Because of its peculiar properties and possible toxic effects, the sterilizer must be vented to the outside. Therefore, most E.T.O. sterilizers are located in the central processing area of the hospital, unlike the steam sterilizers, which can be located both inside and outside the O.R. suite. All loads must be aerated for a specified period of time. Items to be sterilized by E.T.O. require special preparation before being exposed to the gas sterilent. All items must be cleaned and completely dried, as water may unite with E.T.O. to form ethylene glycol, which is not eliminated by aeration and may result in toxic reactions in patients and personnel. Lumens of tubings, needles, and so on should be air dried and open at both ends to avoid

accumulation of gas inside the item. Packaging material should be specific for E.T.O. sterilization and aeration, or indicated that both processes, steam and gas, are acceptable for that item.

9. **The answer is 4.** Preparing instrument trays and equipment properly is just as important as the sterilization cycle itself, since proper preparation ensures exposure to all facets and areas of the item. Instruments that have joints (box locks) or rachets should be opened to allow the agent to penetrate all surfaces. The use of instrument racks or pegs is well suited for this purpose, and should be used whenever possible. Instrument sets should be contained in perforated or wire mesh bottom trays, and the total weight of the tray (metal mass) should not exceed 16 or 17 pounds (other written weight recommendations from the manufacturer should be followed). When preparing basin sets, they should be nested with an absorbent towel separating the metal surfaces to prevent contact and moisture build-up. If a rigid container system is used, the filter papers must be discarded after each use, and new ones inserted, to ensure proper filtration and protection of items inside the tray. Instruments should not be strung or arranged on a closed loop, since the sterilizing agent cannot penetrate hollow items that are closed at one end. Heavier instruments should be at the bottom of the tray, with lighter or delicate instruments on top.

10. **The answer is 3.** Chemical indicators, also known as sterilization process indicators, are used to indicate that items have been exposed to a sterilization process. (It does not guarantee that items are sterile, however. The efficacy of the sterilizing process should be monitored at regular intervals with reliable biological indicators.) Before the item is wrapped for a sterilization cycle, a chemical indicator corresponding to the sterilization process is placed inside the tray, item, or package, and stamped with a load indicator label itemizing the load number, sterilizer number, expiration/sterilization date, and the person preparing the item. The item is then wrapped using either the envelope style or square method, and taped with the appropriate pressure tape for the process. The pressure tape serves as the outside indicator for the package, and signifies that the item has been exposed to one or more specific physical conditions during the cycle. A load indicator label is also placed on the outside tape (as on the inside indicator), and a description of the item is noted for easy identification when needed.

11. **The answer is 3.** Biologic indicators are the only methods that indicate that a kill has taken place during the sterilization process. A highly resistant, nonpathogenic, spore forming bacteria, contained in a glass ampule or on an impregnated strip, is placed in a test pack in the sterilizer load. When the cycle is completed, the spore and a control ampule (one not exposed to sterilization) are incubated either in the hospital laboratory or in the department, or mailed to an independent laboratory for analysis. In the event of a positive spore test occurring with either the gas or steam sterilizers, immediate action must be taken to prevent harm to the patient. If sterilizer malfunction is discovered, all available items from the suspect sterilizer should be recalled, and an incident report filed with the Risk Management Department noting that an unusual occurrence has taken place. Once the malfunction has been corrected, another biologic indicator test must be performed before the sterilizer is placed back into service; if this test is negative, the suspect sterilizer may be placed back into full service. Items sterilized by the suspect sterilizer must be stripped, rewrapped, and relabeled for resterilization.

12. **The answer is 3.** Every package should be imprinted or labeled with a load control number that indicates the sterilizer used, the cycle or load number, the date of sterilization, and an expiration date. To avoid confusion, the sterilization date should be recorded according to the Julian calendar date (day 1-365; day 6 = January 6) and the expiration date (if required) according to the Gregorian calendar date (month/day/year). The notation "Sterile until contaminated and/or opened" can be used as an expiration date according to J.C.A.H.O. recommendations. The lot control number should be placed both inside and outside the package for visibility both in a sterile area and in the storage area for sterile supplies and instruments. Sterility is event-related, not time-related, and contamination occurs only when the contents have been exposed via tears or perforations in the protective wrapper. This principle also governs commercially prepared items, and is why an expiration date does not usually appear on a package, simply the manufacturer's assurance that the contents are "guaranteed sterile until package is opened or compromised."

13. **The answer is 2.** Some recommended practices for maintaining sterility include: (1) articles should be carefully handled, and only as necessary; they should be stored in a well-ventilated, dust-free, limited access

area with controlled temperature and humidity; (2) because sterilization depends upon the direct contact of the sterilizing agent with all surfaces of goods, the sterilizer must be loaded so that the sterilizing agent will penetrate through each package; this is best accomplished by placing packs, trays, and basins on their sides; (3) when storing sterilized items, a method for routine rotation of stock should be used to avoid using outdated supplies or instruments; older supplies should be used first and new supplies placed behind them (F.I.F.O: First In First Out); (4) flash sterilization should be used for emergency sterilization of clean, unwrapped instruments and porous items only; since speed works against the sterilization process and reduces the margin of safety, flash sterilization should not be the routine method for steam sterilization; (5) performance records for all sterilizers should be maintained for each cycle and retained for the period of time indicated by institutional policy and/or the state's statutes of limitation; and (6) preventive maintenance of all sterilizers should be performed by qualified personnel, according to individual policy on a scheduled basis, using the sterilizer manufacturers' service manual as a reference.

14. **The answer is 4.** Flash sterilization of unwrapped items may be used in emergency situations for individual items (e.g., dropped instruments). Complete sets of trays of instruments should not be sterilized in this manner unless all of the following conditions are present: (1) the need is urgent; (2) the physical layout ensures direct delivery of a tray to the O.R.; (3) transfer procedures ensure the sterility of the item (e.g., retrieval by scrubbed person with cover protecting the instrument[s]); and (4) items have been properly decontaminated before the sterilization cycle is initiated. Under no circumstances should implantable devices be flash sterilized.

15. **The answer is 1.** Disinfection in the operating room has two major purposes: (1) to kill pathogenic microorganisms on inanimate surfaces and objects that cannot be sterilized; and (2) to prevent or arrest growth of microorganisms on body surfaces through the application of an antiseptic solution. The disinfection process requires the use of an agent that can destroy infection-producing organisms. Disinfectants are liquid chemical compounds that destroy microbes by either physical or chemical means. These agents are used on inanimate objects such as furniture, floors, walls, equipment, and some heat-sensitive items such as fiberoptic scopes and lenses. According to A.O.R.N.'s Recommended Practices for Disinfection, a high-level disinfectant should be used if an item is to be disinfected rather than sterilized.

16. **The answer is 2.** Sterilization and disinfection are not synonymous (see items #1 and 4 above), although high-level disinfectants can be used to sterilize semicritical items if exposure time is long enough. Solutions used to disinfect walls and furniture are not interchangeable with solutions used to disinfect instruments. Therefore, the perioperative nurse must be able to distinguish between the two in order to provide maximum protection for the patient. Intermediate-level disinfectants kill the more resistant bacteria and viruses. Some may be capable of exhibiting sporicidal action, but these must be labeled as such by the manufacturer. Low-level disinfectants kill only less-resistant bacteria and viruses. They are usually used for housekeeping purposes, and should not be used to disinfect objects for direct patient care. Neither intermediate- nor low-level disinfectants have sporicidal capabilities under normal conditions.

17. **The answer is 4.** Chemical disinfectants must contact all surfaces of the item (including lumens and channels) for the process to be effective. Other perioperative nursing implications include: (1) following the recommended immersion time, the item should be aseptically removed, rinsed with copious amounts of sterile water, and dried in such a manner as to reduce the risk of contamination; (2) immersion time for the item should follow the manufacturer's recommendations and should be reinforced by policy or protocol for all items, regardless of the area, if the same disinfectant solution is used; (3) an expiration date, as recommended by the manufacturer, should be highly visible on all containers of the solution currently in use; (4) the agent should be registered with the E.P.A. and should be compatible with the type of item to be disinfected; and (5) disinfectant solutions should be covered following reconstituting to avoid noxious odors or fumes, and should remain covered when not in use.

7 Foundations of Surgery: Sutures, Needles, and Instruments

STUDY OUTLINE

I. HEMOSTASIS AND WOUND CLOSURE MATERIALS

1. **The primary purpose of all wound-closure material is to hold tissues together until healing is completed; this purpose is applicable to both internal and external structures.** The judicious choice of wound-closure materials and the application of good surgical technique can make the difference between a smooth and complicated recovery.

2. **Hemostasis, on the other hand, is the arrest, control, or reduction of bleeding, which can assist in the wound-healing process.** Hemostasis can be accomplished by the natural clotting of blood; by the use of artificial means, such as cautery, sutures, clamps, staples, and so on; by chemical methods, using specially treated materials impregnated with a hemostatic substance; or by a combination of all three techniques. Hemostasis during a surgical procedure is essential to prevent hemorrhage, allow for visualization of the surgical field, and promote wound healing.

II. METHODS OF HEMOSTASIS

1. Blood clotting is a normal defense mechanism whereby the soluble blood protein (fibrinogen) is changed into a soluble protein (fibrin). When the natural mechanism is interrupted, and clotting does not occur, some artificial method if hemostasis must be employed. This can be accomplished by either (1) **mechanical methods** or (2) **chemical methods**.

A. MECHANICAL METHODS

1. **Instruments:** Clamping the end of a bleeding vessel with a hemostat is the most common method of achieving hemostasis. The bleeder can then be ligated or sutured to accomplish the stoppage of blood flow.

2. **Heat:** Heat, in the form of electrocautery, sears the blood, allowing dilation of the vessel, which stimulates the platelets and tissues to liberate more natural hemostatic agents (thromboplastin).

3. **Bone wax:** Bone wax is refined beeswax that is used to control bleeding in bone marrow. Pieces of bone wax are rolled into small balls and handed to the surgeon for direct application on the bone.

4. **Ligating clips:** Small clips made of titanium, stainless steel, or synthetic material are used to ligate arteries, veins, or nerves. The clip comes in various sizes with a corresponding applicator, which, when applied, stays permanently on the vessel, stopping the flow of blood from the area.

5. **Ligature:** A ligature, commonly called a **tie**, is a strand of material that is tied around a blood vessel to occlude the lumen and prevent bleeding. Large, pulsating vessels may require a **transfixion** suture.

B. CHEMICAL METHODS

1. **Absorbable gelatin sponges:** Available in either powder or compressed pad foam, gelatin sponges (Gelfoam) are absorbable hemostatic agents. When placed on the area, fibrin is deposited on the pad, and the pad swells, forming a substantial clot. The sponge may be used either dry or soaked in a hemostatic agent (thrombin or epinephrine) for a greater hemostatic effect.

2. **Collagen sponge:** Hemostatic sponges of collagen origin (Colostat, Superstat, Helostat) are applied to oozing or bleeding sites. Sponges dissolve as hemostasis occurs, and residual sponges, left in the wound, will eventually be absorbed.

3. **Microfibrillar collagen:** Microfibrillar collagen hemostat (Avitine) is an off-white "fluffy" material prepared from purified bovine collagen used as a topical hemostatic agent. It achieves hemostasis by adhering to platelets and forming thrombi with the interstices of the collagen. It functions as a hemostatic when applied directly to the source of bleeding, including bone and friable tissue or from around a vascular anastomosis. Since it adheres to wet gloves and instruments, it should be presented on a dry, smooth forcep, followed by applying pressure over the site with a dry sponge.

4. **Oxidized cellulose**
   a. Oxidized cellulose (Oxycel, Surgicel) is a specially treated gauze that is placed directly over the bleeding area. As it absorbs the blood, it swells to seven or eight times its normal size and forms coagulum.
   b. The hemostatic effect of oxidized cellulose is created when it is dry; therefore, it should not be moistened with water or saline prior to use.
   c. Oxidized cellulose may be left in the wound, as it is absorbed in 7 to 14 days with minimal tissue reaction, except when applied to areas such as the spinal cord, optic nerve and its chiasm, or bone.

5. **Thrombostat (thrombin, U.S.P.)**
   a. Thrombin is an enzyme extracted from dried beef blood, and is used as a topical hemostatic agent. It accelerates coagulation of blood and controls capillary bleeding. Thrombin is available as a powder, which is reconstituted with its own diluent, and can be sprayed on the surface or used in conjunction with an absorbable gelatin sponge. The sponge is immersed in the thrombin and presented to the surgeon with a clean forcep after excess solution has been squeezed from the sponge. Depending on the manufacturer, thrombin may or may not need refrigeration.
   b. *Thrombin must never be injected or allowed to enter large vessels, as extensive intravascular clotting may occur.*

6. **Styptic**
   a. One category of styptics includes chemicals that cause a blood vessel to constrict. Examples of this include **epinephrine, tannic acid**, and **silver nitrate**.
   b. **Epinephrine** (1:1000) may be added to local anesthetic agents to decrease the amount of bleeding or may be used to soak gelatin sponges prior to application.
   c. **Tannic acid** is a powder used on the mucous membranes of the nose and throat to control capillary bleeding, as is **silver nitrate**, which when mixed with silver chloride solution and molded into pencils (sticks), creates a topical hemostatic agent.

C. ADDITIONAL METHODS OF HEMOSTASIS

1. In addition to the mechanical and chemical methods used to control bleeding, several other means of hemostasis are available during the intraoperative period, including the use of **tourniquets, digital compression, cryosurgery** (extreme cold), **hypothermia technique, photocoagulation** (used in ophthalmology), the **heated scalpel** (hot knife), which is used to cut and coagulate small vessels, and the **laser**, which has coagulation capabilities.

2. **Hypotension,** induced and controlled by anesthesia, is another method that can reduce the amount of blood loss and provide a dry field. It is frequently used in orthopedic, vascular surgery, and neurosurgery. When compatible blood is not available or blood transfusions are against the

patient's religious beliefs, and the autologous method, using the cell saver, is not available for direct transfusion of the patient's own blood, induced hypertension may be used.

III. SUTURES

A. WHAT IS A SUTURE?

1. **A suture is a thread, wire, or other material used in the operation of stitching parts of the body together; to suture is to unite by stitching (sewing).**
2. Suturing materials can be used in many different ways, such as **ligating** a bleeding vessel, **suturing** internal structures, or **closing** the skin of a wound. The "ideal" material used for these purposes would have certain characteristics, including:
   a. Versatility that would permit its use in any operation, the only variable being its size as determined by its strength.
   b. Ease of handling, both comfortable and natural to the surgeon.
   c. Minimal tissue reaction and inability to create favorable conditions for either infection and/or rejection.
   d. A high tensile (breakage) strength, even in small-caliber suture; the knot should not fray or break off while in place.
   e. A material that is easy to thread and sterilize, and that does not shrink in the tissue.
   f. A material that is nonelectrolytic, noncapillary, nonallergenic, and noncarcinogenic in its make-up.
   g. A material that absorbs with minimal tissue reaction once it has served its purpose.
3. Technically, the ideal suture has not yet been manufactured, and so today there are over 10 different suture materials to choose from, and over 25 different types of suture for a variety of surgical needs, with more being discovered and manufactured each year.

B. TENSILE STRENGTH, DIAMETER, AND LENGTH

1. The term **tensile strength** was first described by the United States Pharmacopeia (U.S.P.), and refers to the knot-pull strength of the suture rather than the straight-pull strength. Minimum knot-pull strengths are specified for each size, and as the suture diameter decreases, so too does the tensile strength.
2. **Suture diameter or size** identifies the size of the strand, which ranges from a heavy size 7 to a very fine size 11-0. The diameter of the suture strand usually determines its effective usage in addition to its size. A basic rule for remembering suture sizes is based on the premise that *Size 0* is smaller than *Size 1* and the more 0's added the smaller and more fragile the suture.
3. The **length** of the suture is standardized to two sizes: **standard length**--54 or 60 inches, and **precut length**--17, 18, or 24 inches. Both of these lengths are available for sutures with or without needles, and the choice of length is usually determined by the suturing technique being used by the surgeon--for example, ligating or tying, interrupted or continuous stitching, and by the depth of the wound.

C. SUTURE PACKAGING AND IDENTIFICATION

1. **Suture packaging has made identification of the contents easy to distinguish.** Sutures are supplied sterile from the manufacturer in a double envelope package. The inner package contains the sterile suture, and its sterility is ensured as long as the package has not been opened. The outer package usually is a see-through peel package, or a solid D&G, designed to permit delivery of the suture to the sterile field.
2. To reduce the confusion associated with the various suture materials, each major category of suture material is color coded, and this coding is standard through the industry, regardless of the manufacturer. This is the first step in suture package recognition. (See **Table 7.1** for color codes.)
3. In addition to identifying the type of material, the suture package and its shipping box are marked with the trade name, generic name, catalog number, size, length, color of the strands,

number of sutures per package, description of the needle, whether the suture is braided or monofilament, coating material (if used), classification, date manufactured, expiration date, and compliance with the U.S.P. standards.

4. Sutures are supplied in boxes containing 1 to 3 dozen packages of suture, and additional information about the suture is printed on each box.

D. SUTURE CLASSIFICATION

1. **Surgical sutures as defined by the U.S.P. are divided into two major classifications based on their reactions with body tissue: (1) absorbable and (2) nonabsorbable.**
2. **Absorbable sutures**
   a. **Description:** capable of being absorbed by living mammalian tissue, yet may be treated to modify resistance to absorption; source is both natural and synthetic.
   b. **Tissue interaction:** absorbable sutures are digested by body enzymes by first losing their strength, then gradually disappearing from the tissue.
3. **Nonabsorbable sutures**
   a. **Description:** materials not affected by enzyme activity or absorption in living tissues, and are from natural and synthetic sources.
   b. **Tissue interaction:** nonabsorbable sutures become encapsulated in fibrous tissue during the healing process and remain embedded in body tissue unless they are surgically removed.
   c. Nonabsorbable sutures are further divided and classified as follows:
      (1) **Class 1**--silk or synthetic fibers or monofilament, twisted, or braided construction.
      (2) **Class 2**--cotton or linen fibers or coated natural or synthetic fibers. The coating forms a thickness, yet does not contribute to its strength.
4. **Monofilament suture** is a is a single strand that is noncapillary (resistant to fluids soaking into the suture); it is designated by the U.S.P. as Type B.
5. **Multifilament suture,** on the other hand, is multiple strands of suture held together by a process of twisting, braiding, or spinning the materials. All multifilament sutures have a certain capacity to absorb body fluids (capillarity), which elicits a higher degree of tissue reaction, and are classified by the U.S.P. as Type A.

E. CHOOSING APPROPRIATE SUTURE MATERIAL

1. **Absorbable suture materials**
   a. **Absorbable suture materials are primarily used on fast-healing tissue.** They come from both natural and synthetic sources.
      (1) Natural sources of absorbable sutures include **surgical, chromic,** and **plain gut,** and **collagen.** Their use is contraindicated when extended or prolonged approximation is required.
      (2) Synthetic sources include **polymers,** either dyed, or undyed, and are absorbed by a slow hydrolysis process in the presence of tissue fluids. The tensile strength of synthetic absorbable sutures exceeds that of surgical gut, and it can be used in the presence of infection since absorption time and loss of tensile strength are not affected by the proteolytic enzymes in the gastrointestinal tract. Examples include: **polyglycolic acid (Dexon), polydioxanome (PDS),** and **polyglactin 910 (Vicryl).**
   b. See Table 7.1 for a description of the types and uses of absorbable suture material.
2. **Nonabsorbable suture materials**
   a. **Nonabsorbable suture materials are primarily used with tissues that heal slower owing to their location, tissue type, or general healing factors.**
   b. Like absorbable sutures, the suture materials come from both natural and synthetic sources.
      (1) Natural sources include **silk and cotton.** Their use is contraindicated in the presence of infection or contamination and in the biliary and urinary tracts (can precipitate stone formation). In addition, they should not be used if long-term support is vital since they lose substantial strength 90 to 120 days after implantation.

(2) Advances in suture manufacturing have resulted in a decreased usage of natural substances and an increase in synthetic substances adaptable for suturing material. Examples of these substances include **nylon; polyester; polyethylene; polypropylene,** and **surgical steel/wire.**

c. See **Table 7.1** for a description of the types and uses of nonabsorbable suture material.

F. ASEPTIC TRANSFER OF SUTURES

1. To transfer the suture package to the sterile field, the suture must be opened and dispensed using aseptic technique. Two techniques are considered appropriate:

   a. **Method I--Retrieval by scrub person:** Holding the packet flaps between extended thumbs, the circulating nurse rolls his or her hands outward to peel the outer packet apart. The end of the sterile inner packet is then exposed and is offered to the scrub person, who grasps the inner packet with either gloved fingers or a sterile instrument.

   b. **Method II--"Flipping" suture packet:** The "flipping" procedure should be used only during the initial set-up of the sterile field, when scrub person has not yet donned sterile gown and gloves. Standing a safe distance from the sterile instrument table or designated receptacle, the circulator rolls the flaps of the outer package backwards, and projects (flips) the inner package onto the sterile surface, being careful not to reach over the sterile field.

IV. SURGICAL NEEDLES

1. Surgical needles are made of a steel alloy with a high carbon content. Surgical needles are precision-made instruments, and must be handled gently in order to achieve maximum effectiveness.

2. At one time, in surgical history, re-usable eyed needles were used exclusively and were available in many shapes and sizes, and required sterilization prior to each use, and in specific instances, are still being used.

3. Today, many of these needles have been replaced by either a **needle-suture combination** prepared by the manufacturer (**atraumatic**) or are available as a disposable, presterilized **free needle**, requiring the user to thread the suture strand to the needle, and both are available in a variety of shapes, sizes and points.

A. COMPONENTS OF SURGICAL NEEDLES

1. All surgical needles have three basic sections: the **point,** the **body,** or **shaft,** and the **eye.**

2. The body or shaft determines the shape of the needle, either straight or curved. Needle points range from a **taper** (noncutting) to a **cutting** (one side or both have a cutting edge) to a **blunt** tip (neither cuts nor pierces). The eye of the needle is where the suture strand is attached or threaded, and may be round, oblong, or square.

B. CLASSIFICATIONS OF SURGICAL NEEDLES

1. Needles are classified according to their **shape,** the **type of point,** the **shaft,** and the **eye.** See **Table 7.2** for the major types of surgical needles, their appearance, and their general uses.

2. **Shape**

   a. Needles come straight or curved. The amount of curvature of the needle or lack of it determines its type and can dictate its primary use. The deeper the tissue, the greater the need for sharper curve.

   b. Full curved needles are used with a needle holder, while the straight needle is held in the hand. Straight needles are generally reserved for superficial surfaces, including skin.

3. **Points and shafts**

   a. The delicacy of the tissue determines which point is most suitable to use. There are three basic needle points, with variations of each: **taper, cutting,** and **blunt point.** See **Table 7.3** for a glossary of needle points.

Table 7.1 COMMONLY USED SUTURE MATERIAL

Suture	Type	Color	Raw Material	Interaction	Frequent Uses
Surgical Gut	Plain	Yellowish-tan Blue (Dyed)	Collagen derived from healthy mammals	Absorbed relatively quickly by body tissues	Ligate superficial vessels; suture subcutaneous and other tissues that heal rapidly, may be used in presence of infection. Ophthalmology.
	Chromic	Brown Blue (Dyed)	Collagen derived from healthy mammals; treated to resist digestion by body tissues	Absorbed more slowly by body tissues due to chemical treatment	Fascia and peritoneum for support; most versatile of all materials for use in practically all tissues; may be used in presence of infection. Ophthalmology.
Coated VICRYL (Polyglactin 910)	Braided	Violet (Undyed)	Copolymer of lactide and glycolide coated with polyglactin 370 and calcium stearate	Absorbed by slow hydrolysis in tissues	Ligate or suture tissues where an absorbable suture is desirable except where approximation under stress is required.
Surgical Silk	Braided	Black White	Natural protein fiber spun by silkworm	Very slowly absorbed; remains encapsulated in body tissues	Most body tissues for ligating and suturing. Ophthalmology and plastic surgery.
Surgical Cotton	Twisted	White, blue, pink	Natural cotton fibers	Nonabsorbable; remains encapsulated in body tissues	Most body tissues for ligating and suturing.
Surgical Steel	Monofilament or multifilament	Silver-colored	An alloy of iron	Nonabsorbable; remains encapsulated in body tissues	General and skin closure; retention; tendon repair; orthopedic and neurosurgery.
ETHILON Nylon	Monofilament	Green	Polyamide polymer	Nonabsorbable; remains encapsulated in body tissues	Skin closure; retention, plastic surgery; ophthalmology, microsurgery.
NUROLON Nylon	Braided	Black	Polyamide polymer	Nonabsorbable; remains encapsulated in body tissues	Most body tissues for ligating and suturing; general closure; neurosurgery.
MERSILENE Polyester Fiber	Braided	Green, white	Synthetic material made from chemicals	Nonabsorbable; remains encapsulated in body tissues	Cardiovascular and plastic surgery.
ETHIBOND Polyester Fiber	Braided	Green, white	Polyester fiber material treated with polybutilate	Nonabsorbable; remains encapsulated in body tissues	Abdominal closure; cardiovascular and plastic surgery.
PROLENE Polypropylene	Monofilament	Clear, blue	Polymer of propylene	Nonabsorbable; remains encapsulated in body tissues	General, plastic, and cardiovascular surgery.

Source: Modified from Wound Closure Manual, Ethicon, Inc., 1985.

Table 7.2 SURGICAL NEEDLES

Types and Appearance	General Uses	Examples
Needle Points		
Blunt	Spongy tissues that are easily penetrated and/or torn	Liver; kidney
Taper	Delicate to substantial tissues that are easily penetrated and torn	Intestines; subcutaneous; muscle/fascia; veins; nonarteriosclerotic arteries
Cutting-Spear	Tissues that are tough to penetrate	Skin; sclera; tendons; arteriosclerotic arteries
Cutting-Trocar	Extremely tough tissues to penetrate and pass through	Cartilage; cervix (uteri)
Needle Shafts		
Straight	Where suturing can be done in a flat or shallow depth	Skin; any anastomosis in which the tissues may be elevated to the top level of the wound
Circle, 3/8	Shallow depths	Essentially the same as straight and skin
Circle, 1/2	General purpose, usually in wounds of some depth	The interior of any wound
Circle, 5/8	Deepest, smallest maneuvering-room wounds	Any interior of any seep, small wound, where exposure is difficult—vaginal hysterectomy; hemorrhoidectomy
Circle, 1/4	Same as 1/2 circle	
Needle Eyes		
Round (Threaded)	Gross general purpose, where tissue trauma is not a factor	Muscle/fascia approximation; subcutaneous; suture-ligatures
French (Threaded)	Delicate tissues; precursor to swaged; infrequent today	Similar to swaged, 1/2 circle taper point
Atraumatic (swaged)	Where least tissue trauma is desired	Fine/delicate anastomoses anywhere in the body; GI, ducts, cavity linings, etc; plastic repairs

   b. **Taper point:** Taper points are used on delicate tissues that are easily penetrated. These areas include the peritoneum, the heart of the intestines. A taper-point needle is designed so that the shaft gradually tapers to a sharp point, which results in a very small hole in the tissue.

   c. **Cutting point:** A cutting-point needle is designed with a razor-sharp tip and is used for tissue such as skin or tendons. There are three types of cutting needles: **taper cut** (used for tough, fibrous tissue), **conventional,** and **reverse cutting.** Generally, the tougher the tissue, the greater the need for a cutting-type shaft.

   d. **Blunt point:** Blunt-tip needles have a rounded end and are used in friable tissue, such as liver or kidney, when neither piercing nor cutting is appropriate.

  4. **The eye of the needle**

   a. The **eye,** or **head,** of the of the needle is designed to cause minimal trauma to the tissue.

   b. There are three types of eyed needles, each a variation of the other:

    (1) **Atraumatic or swaged needles:** These consist of one or two needles attached to the suture strand at the factory, eliminating the need for threading. This causes the least amount of tissue trauma, since the suture and needle are a continuous unit in which the needle size and suture diameter are matched as closely as possible. A modification of the permanently swaged suture, the **control release suture** (or "pop-off") allows for faster interrupted suturing.

    (2) **Eyed needles:** The needle must be threaded with the suture strand, thus making it necessary to pull two strands of suture through the tissue, creating larger hole and possibly more tissue trauma.

Table 7.3 GLOSSARY OF NEEDLE POINTS

Needle Point and Body Shape	Specific Application
Conventional Cutting	Ligament Nasal cavity Oral cavity Pharynx Skin Tendon
Reverse Cutting	Fascia Ligament Nasal cavity Oral mucosa Skin Tendon sheath
MICRO-POINT. Reverse Cutting Needle	Eye
Precision Point Cutting	Plastic or cosmetic procedures Skin
Side-cutting Spatulated	Eye, primary application Microsurgical procedures Reconstructive ophthalmic procedures
TAPERCUT. Surgical Needle	Bronchus — Perichondrium Calcified tissue — Periosteum Fascia — Pharynx Ligament — Tendon Nasal cavity — Trachea Oral cavity — Uterus Ovary — Vessels, sclerotic
Taper	Aponeurosis — Nerve Biliary tract — Peritoneum Dura — Pleura Fascia — Subcutaneous fat Gastrointestinal tract — Urogenital tract Muscle — Vessels Myocardium
Blunt	Blunt dissection through friable tissue Kidney Liver Spleen Uterine cervix for ligating incompetent cervix

Figure 7.1 PREPARING AND HANDLING LIGATURES

1. Continuous ties on plastic disk-type reel

a. Tear open foil packet containing appropriate material on reel.

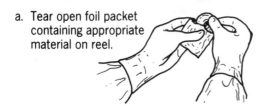

b. Hand to surgeon as needed, being certain end of ligating material is free for grasping.

2a. Single-strand ties-labyrinth pack

a. Tear open foil packets of appropriate material.

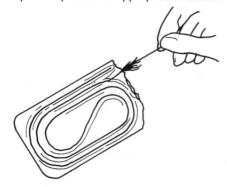

b. Remove nonabsorbable pre-cut length one strand at a time from the Labyrinth packet when the surgeon is ready to use it.

2b. Single strand–pre-cut

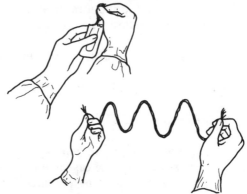

a. Extract pre-cut strands of Sutupak sterile sutures, either absorbable or nonabsorbable. Straighten surgical gut with gentle pull.

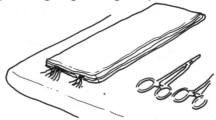

b. Place packets or strands in "suture book" with ends extended far enough for rapid extraction.

Presentation technique

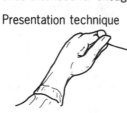

c. Hold single strand taut for easy grasping by surgeon.

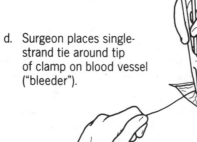

d. Surgeon places single-strand tie around tip of clamp on blood vessel ("bleeder").

> (3) **Spring or French eyed needles:** The needle has a slip from the inside of the eye to the end of the needle, where the suture is secured through the spring.

   c.   Both the eyed needle and the French eye are classified as **free needles.** Although they have been partially replaced by the control-released suture, some surgeons may still prefer them for specific uses or as a type of suture not available in the preattached format.

5.   **Free needles:** These come in the same size and shape, but have been named to differentiate them from those attached at the factory. Included are the Keith, Milner, Ferguson, Mayo, surgeon's regular, Trocar, and French eye needles.

V.   WORKING WITH SUTURES AND NEEDLES

A.   PREPARING SUTURES

1.   **Advanced preparation is the key to a smooth surgical procedure, and preparation of sutures used during the case is an important component of this phase.**

2.   **Sutures should be prepared in their order of use, but certain preliminary preparations are necessary to ensure sterility and prevent prolonged exposure, unnecessary handling, and excess waste.** See **Figure 7.1** for illustration of techniques for preparing and handling ligatures.

3.   Sutures will first be used to ligate or tie off bleeding vessels; therefore, sutures without needles (ligatures) should be prepared first.

4.   The use of suture materials in dry packages requires no special preparation, but those contained in solution must be opened carefully to avoid contamination of the field from the liquid contents. Sutures that need to be straightened for easy handling should be prepared first, and placed in a "suture book," created from a sterile towel, and leaving the ends extended to reduce time and wasted motion. Remember, chromic, plain, nylon, and prolene sutures require only slight straightening, which is accomplished by grasping the two ends, using the thumb and forefinger, and pulling gently.

5.   When using a multiple-suture packet the packet should be torn open along the dotted line and the sutures nudged forward from the package so that individual strands can be obtained as needed. The design on the labyrinth package allows for single-strand selection without disturbing the other strands in the package.

6.   Suture ligatures may be handed as a free tie, placed in the open hand of the surgeon, or placed on the end of an instrument for a deep tie. When a dispensing reel is used, both the free end and the spool are passed to the surgeon simultaneously.

7.   If the ligatures are pre-cut strands, no further preparation is required. However, if ligatures are available only in the standard length, the scrub person may have to cut the strands for ease of handling. To prepare the individual ligatures, the strand is folded in equal parts and held between the fingers, and the strand is divided into desired lengths--approximately 12 to 15 inches for superficial ties and 24 to 30 inches for deep ties.

B.   HANDLING EYED NEEDLES AND SUTURES

1.   **Preparing a suture-needle combination:** The scrub person grasps the exposed needle with fingertips or a needle holder and gently pulls the strand to remove it from the package, or if not immediately used, can leave the needle holder on the needle with the suture in the package for easy identification when the suture is requested.

2.   **Mounting the needle:** The curved needle is mounted on a needle holder. In mounting the needle, it should be placed nearest the eye, about one third of the total length of the shaft away from the eye end. When swaged needles are mounted, it is important that the needle holder not be clamped directly over the swage itself, since this weakens the area and can cause the suture to detach unexpectedly from the needle.

3.   **Threading the needle:** The suture may be threaded through the eye from either side of the curve. The suture strand is drawn through the eye about one third of its length. Both ends of the suture may be drawn between the jaws of the needle holder (or only one end depending on the surgeon preference), and the instrument is passed to the surgeon.

4. **Passing the needle holder**
   a. When mounting the needle on a needle holder, it should be positioned so that the surgeon does not have to reposition it for suturing. The outside curve of the needle should be aimed downward, with the point aimed for the ceiling, in the direction of the surgeon's chin or thumb.
   b. The instrument is passed handle first, tip pointed toward the surgeon's opposite thumb, while the scrub person gently holds onto the loose end to avoid contact with the surgeon's palm as the instrument is transferred. Suture needles must be passed on a one-to-one basis, and the previous needle retrieved before passing another. To avoid delay, two needles should be mounted so that as one is returned, another is ready to use.
   c. When passing a straight needle, the tip is covered by the scrub person's hand, and the swaged portion of the needle is handed to the surgeon.

C. **USING MULTIPLE-NEEDLE PACKS**

   1. If more than one needle is contained in the package, all needles should be seen and counted by the scrub and circulator prior to use.
   2. Multiple-strand needles can be placed in a towel fold, similar to multistrand ligatures, with needles exposed on top for ease of handling.

D. **MAINTAINING A SUTURE INVENTORY**

   1. After the suture has been used, the needle, on the needle holder, is returned to the scrub person, who places it into the needle counter for future confirmation of the needle count. *To avoid loss, needles must never be allowed to lay loose on the field.*
   2. **Maintaining a running, silent count of all needles used is the responsibility of the scrub person.** Therefore, empty suture packets must stay on the sterile field until the final needle count is confirmed in case there is a misplaced needle.

VI. **METHODS OF SUTURING**

A. **COMMON STITCHES**

   1. There are two basic methods of suturing, and various ways to use the two techniques. The suture is either **running**, using a single continuous suture, or it is **interrupted**, placed separately and tied separately. The running suture saves time, but if the suture breaks during the healing process, the wound could open along the entire length of the incision.
   2. **Retention** or **stay sutures** provide a secondary suture line. These sutures, placed at a distance from the primary suture line, relieve undue pressure and help to remove dead space. They are placed in the wound in such a way that they include most if not all of the layers of the wound. This technique is used to close long vertical abdominal wounds and lacerated or infected wounds.

B. **ALTERNATIVE METHODS TO SUTURING**

   1. **Skin clips, surgical strips (tape), ligation clips, and internal and external staples are alternatives to conventional suturing materials, and have several applications in today's surgical practice setting.** The advantages of these methods include **time saved under anesthesia and close approximation of wound edges,** promoting greater and faster healing with less tissue loss or reaction. The use of these methods, however, requires additional education of both the surgeon and the surgical team to achieve maximum efficiency when using these alternative methods.
   2. **External devices**
      a. **Surgical strips (tapes):** made of a reinforced, micropore surgical tape that is adhesive on one side. They are used to approximate skin edges following a subcuticular closure or superficial lacerations in conjunction with skin sutures, permitting the skin sutures to be removed 36

to 48 hours postoperatively. They can be used for any type of surgery, but are most often associated with plastic and pediatric surgery, since they leave no mark on the skin.

b. **Skin clips:** made of noncorroding metal, and may be used for skin closure, with or without sutures. Skin clips can be steam sterilized, or be disposable, and can be applied in the presence of infection or drainage and applied quickly using a specific application instrument. Because they are bulky and uncomfortable post-operatively, they have been replaced by the disposable skin staples.

c. **Skin staples**
   (1) **Skin staples are the fastest method of skin closure and have a low level of tissue reactivity.**
   (2) The edges of both cuticular and subcuticular layers must be everted (aligned with the edges slightly raised), and the stapler is positioned over the line of the incision so that a staple will be placed evenly on each side.
   (3) Skin staples must be removed, usually 5 to 7 days postoperatively, and a staple extractor is used for this purpose. Because the skin flattens as it heals, staples provide an excellent cosmetic result if they have been properly placed lightly over the incision.

3. **Internal devices**
   a. **Ligation clips:** used for hemostasis or to ligate nerves and ducts. The clips come preloaded or are placed on a special applicator, placed around the vessel or structure, and the handle is squeezed so the jaws of the applicator are closed with the clip secured around the structure.
   b. **Surgical staples**
      (1) Included in most surgical suite inventory lists are a group of mechanical stapling devices for internal ligation and division, resection, and anastomosis, skin and fascia closure.
      (2) **Advantages of internal stapling**
         (a) The mechanical application of the stapling instrument significantly reduces tissue manipulation and handling, thus reducing surgical and anesthesia time and permitting a more natural wound healing process to occur in a shorter period of time.
         (b) The staple produces an airtight, leakproof closure and can be safely used in many types of tissue.
         (c) The staples are essentially nonreactive; therefore, the occurrence of tissue reaction or infection is reduced, permitting an anastomosis created with staples to function sooner than one created with manual technique.
      (3) **Disadvantages of surgical stapling**
         (a) Although the positives outweigh the negatives, the reusable and disposable instruments are expensive and are not always reliable, due mainly to the user's unfamiliarity with the operation of the instrument.
         (b) The surgeon and the assistants (scrub person) should received instructions outside the operating room regarding the proper use and function of the instrument, since inappropriately placed staples are much more difficult to correct than manually placed sutures.
         (c) The nursing personnel must know how to assemble, disassemble, and sterilize the reusable instruments, since improper cleaning and assembly could cause misfiring, rendering the instrument useless.

VII. SURGICAL INSTRUMENTATION: TOOLS OF THE TRADE

1. Operating room personnel are responsible for the use, handling, and care of hundreds of surgical instruments each day. This activity requires a basic knowledge of how these instruments are manufactured, maintained, and properly used in order to prolong their usefulness. Surgical instruments are expensive and represent a major investment for every institution, regardless of its size, type, or the number of procedures performed each day.

A. USAGE OF SURGICAL INSTRUMENTS

1. A surgical instrument--any surgical instrument--is designed to do one of the following tasks:
   a. **To cut/incise/dissect:** Cutting instruments, frequently called "sharps," include knives, scalpels, blades, and scissors of all types.
   b. **To retract:** Such instruments include handheld and self-retaining retractors, skin hooks, and tenacula, all designed to hold tissues or organs away from the incision to provide better visualization.
   c. **To grasp or hold:** This category includes clamps and forceps used to hold or grasp tissue and/or structures, and are designed with either serrations or projecting teeth, depending on the specific need and type of tissue being held.
   d. **To suture:** Besides needle holders designed to accommodate very heavy to very light suture material, this category includes instruments used to apply wound clips, hemostatic/aneurysm clips, and stainless steel wire suture.
   e. **To dilate, probe, cannulate, or drain:** These instruments occupy a miscellaneous category, since they perform multiple tasks: they include suction tips, syringes, gall duct probes, trocars, cannulas for drainage of blood or fluids from an area, catheters, tubes, and drains, even to shunt blood flow around an operative site.

B. THE BASIC INSTRUMENT SET

1. Persons who use surgical instruments must know and recognize the names, uses, and care of the instruments used for a variety of surgical procedures. A **basic** or **foundation tray** is the starting point for becoming familiar with these instruments, since all instrument trays are similar except for size, shape, or amounts of specific instruments in the tray. Using the five basic categories of instruments, we can create or modify any instrument tray.
2. Since general surgery is considered a "foundation" specialty, the **major tray** or **laparotomy tray** has been designated as the foundation instrument tray for any operating room.

C. CLASSIFICATION OF SURGICAL INSTRUMENTS

1. **Category I: Cutting/dissecting instruments**
   a. **Sharps,** as they are called, are exactly what their name implies, and the usable part of the instrument has a sharp or cutting edge.
   b. **Scissors:** designed in short, long, medium, and heavy; may be blunt or sharp with straight or curved tips (cutting edge). Examples: straight Mayo (suture scissors); curved Mayo (tough tissue); short Metzenbaum (superficial delicate tissue); long Metzenbaum (deep delicate tissue).
   c. **Scalpels/blades:** the oldest of all the instruments; handles are suited to attachment of corresponding disposable blades. Examples: #4 handle/20 blade (skin knife; deep puncture wounds); #3L handle/10, 11, 15 blade (deep; abdomen).
2. **Category II: Holding/grasping instruments**
   a. **Clamps** and **forceps** are part of this category, and are designed for specific uses, including hemostasis and assisting with suturing or holding tissue. Forceps are mostly used in pairs.
      (1) **Holding clamp/forcep:** serrated jaw.
      (2) **Grasping clamp/forcep:** projected tooth/teeth.
   b. **Examples:** Mosquito hemostat (plastic and pediatric surgery); Crile hemostat (abdominal); Kelly hemostat and Pean clamp (heavier abdominal); Babcock and Allis clamps (intestinal, delicate structures); Kohler clamp (tough fibrous tissue); and tissue forceps (grasping or holding).
3. **Category III: Retracting instruments**
   a. **Retractors** are used to hold tissue away from the operative site. Retractors are either **self-retaining** via a bridge or metal bar keeping the edges apart, or **hand-held,** requiring a team member to retract using the instrument. Hand-held retractors are primarily used in pairs.

    b. **Examples of hand-held retractors:** Army-Navy, Parker, and Eastman (superficial abdominal); Richardsons and Deavers (organ retraction); mallable (abdomen); and skin hooks and Senn retractors (superficial, plastic surgery).

    c. **Examples of self-retaining retractors:** Balfour (abdominal); O'Sullivan-O'Connor (Gyn, pelvic); and Weitlander, Gelpi, and mastoid (small-to-medium structures).

4. Category IV: Suturing instruments

    a. Suturing instruments consist of **needle holders**, ranging in size and shape from a long standard to extremely delicate tips. Since they must grasp metal rather than soft tissue, they are subject to greater damage. For maximum usage, needle holders must retain a firm grip on the needle. Needle holders may have a ratchet similar to a hemostat or they may be a spring action and lock type.

    b. **Examples:** Mayo-Hegar (general surgery); Webster (plastic and pediatric surgery); Castroviejo (extremely delicate tissue; eyes); Heany and Rogers (Gyn, hysterectomy); and needle-nose (surgical steel).

5. Category V: Miscellaneous instruments

    a. The miscellaneous category contains instruments that do not fit into any other category by virtue of their function. These include **towel clips, rings forceps, suction tips, probes, groves, trocars,** and so on.

    b. **Examples of suction tips:** Yankauer (tonsils); Pool (thick or heavy fluids); Frazier/Anthony (small delicate areas).

D. CARE AND HANDLING OF SURGICAL INSTRUMENTS

1. Instruments must be handled gently. Bouncing, dropping, and setting heavy equipment on top of the delicate instruments should be avoided. At the end of a procedure, they must be handled individually and not thrown together in a tangled heap. Sharps and delicate instruments should be set aside and individually cleaned, then the tips protected with either an individual tip protector or a holding pouch.

2. Each instrument should be inspected before and after cleaning to spot chips, breaks, cracks, or imperfections. Forceps, clamps, and other hinged instruments should be inspected for alignment of jaws and teeth and for stiffness. Edges of scissors should be tested for sharpness. To cut effectively, they must be filed smoothly, and maintained sharp by careful observation and usage. It is further recommended that all instruments be periodically lubricated in special instrument "milk," which contains silicone, following the cleaning process to preserve their ease of use and prevent sticking of box locks and/or ratchets.

3. In addition, some basic guidelines for proper use and handling include:

    a. Know the names and proper use of each instrument.

    b. Constantly observe the sterile field for loose instruments. Remove used instruments promptly to original location for easy retrieval.

    c. Keep instruments clean during procedure by periodically cleaning instruments using a damp cloth (towel or lap sponge)

    d. Protect the edges of sharp instruments during and after procedure. Remove all blades and needles to a designated sharps container, and close the lid for further protection.

E. STANDARDIZED INSTRUMENTS SETS

1. **Standard basic instrument sets,** containing the minimum number and types of instruments, will facilitate an instrument count. A basic instrument set should include instruments needed to open and close the incision along with instruments needed to complete the surgical procedure.

2. A **kardex** or **pictorial reference book** for each tray, with the vendor's name, amounts of specific instruments and the cost, and any cross referencing information will assist personnel in preparing the instrument trays. The kardex book should be routinely updated as instruments are added or deleted from the tray. A **count sheet** specific to the tray should also be part of this reference book.

3. By grouping the instruments within the reference book according to service and/or by the specialty tray or set, a complex process can become an ongoing learning experience for those responsible for using and assembling the instrument trays.

4. Proper selection of additional instruments is based on information obtained during the preoperative assessment and includes the age and size of the patient, the selected surgical approach, the anatomy, the possible pathologic condition, and the surgeon's preference.

PRACTICE QUESTIONS

1. **In what way principally is hemostasis related to wound healing?**

   1. *Hemostasis provides a physiologic basis for the biochemical events that occur in wound healing.*

   2. *Hemostasis refers to the actual mechanism by which wounds are healed.*

   3. *Hemostasis is the arrest, control, or reduction of bleeding, which can assist wound healing.*

   4. *Hemostasis refers to the means by which tissues are held together until healing is completed.*

2. **Hemostasis can be achieved mechanically by a variety of methods. Which of the following is NOT one of these mechanical methods?**

   1. *Thrombostat.*

   2. *Bone wax.*

   3. *Heat.*

   4. *Ligature.*

3. **Most chemical methods of hemostasis (e.g., collagen sponge, oxidized cellulose) work by:**

   1. *causing blood vessels to constrict.*

   2. *searing the blood and allowing dilation of the vessels.*

   3. *holding tissues together until healing is completed.*

   4. *accelerating blood coagulation.*

4. **In using hemostatic agents such as microfibrillar collagen or oxidized cellulose, the nurse should be aware that these substances:**

   1. *should not be moistened prior to use.*

   2. *should not be left in the wound, since they are not absorbable.*

   3. *are highly perishable and should be refrigerated prior to use.*

   4. *must not be injected or allowed to enter large vessels, as extensive intravascular clotting may occur.*

5. **Which of the following sutures is the smallest and most fragile?**

    1. *Size 3 suture.*

    2. *Size 3-0 suture.*

    3. *Size 7 suture.*

    4. *Size 7-0 suture.*

6. **The suture material being used in a surgical procedure is brown. On the basis of its color alone, the nurse knows that the suture is:**

    1. *chromic gut, the most versatile of suture materials.*

    2. *surgical silk, often used in ophthalmologic and plastic surgery.*

    3. *plain gut, and therefore nonabsorbable.*

    4. *monofilament nylon, and therefore absorbable.*

7. **An example of a synthetic, nonabsorbable suture material is:**

    1. *polyglycolic acid (Dexon).*

    2. *nylon (e.g., Ethilon).*

    3. *polyglactin 910 (Vicryl).*

    4. *chromic gut.*

8. **The "flipping" method of transferring the suture package to the sterile field is properly used under what circumstances?**

    1. *Anytime during the surgical procedure when suture material is needed.*

    2. *Only when the suture package comes in a single rather than a double envelope.*

    3. *Only during the initial set-up of the sterile field, before the scrub nurse has donned a sterile gown and gloves.*

    4. *Only when the contents of the suture package is not properly identified or the identification is impossible to read.*

9. **A taper cut (as opposed to taper point) needle is *best* suited for which of the following types of tissues?**

    1. *For friable tissue, such as liver or kidney.*

    2. *For tough, fibrous tissue.*

    3. *For delicate tissues that are easily penetrated.*

    4. *For any type of tissue, regardless of delicacy.*

10. **One advantage of the control-release suture (or "pop-off") over other swaged needles is:**

    1. *minimization of trauma to tissue.*

    2. *precise matching of needle size and suture diameter.*

    3. *faster interrupted suturing.*

    4. *the presence of a slip from the inside of the eye to the end of the needle.*

11. **Guidelines for the perioperative nurse working with sutures and needles include all of the following EXCEPT:**

    1. *Sutures with needles should be prepared first.*

    2. *Sutures that need to be straightened for easy handling should be prepared before those that do not need straightening.*

    3. *Suture ligatures may be handed as a free tie, placed in the open hand of the surgeon, or placed on the end of an instrument for a deep tie.*

    4. *If the ligatures are pre-cut strands, no further preparation is required.*

12. **Guidelines for the perioperative nurse handling eyed needles and sutures during a surgical procedure include all of the following EXCEPT:**

    1. *In mounting a curved needle, place the needle holder about one-third down from the eye end of the needle.*

    2. *When mounting a swaged needle, be sure not to clamp the needle holder directly over the swage itself.*

    3. *When mounting the needle on a needle holder, position it with the inside curve of the needle aimed downward, with the point aimed toward the floor.*

    4. *When passing a straight needle, cover the tip with the hand and pass the swaged end to the surgeon.*

13. **In maintaining a suture inventory, which of the following procedures should be followed?**

    1. *If more than one needle is contained in a package, all needles should be seen and counted by the scrub nurse only prior to use.*

    2. *A running, silent count of all needles is maintained by the circulating nurse.*

    3. *Empty suture packets must stay on the sterile field until the final needle count is taken and confirmed.*

    4. *After the suture has been used, the needle should be removed from the needle holder and returned to the scrub person.*

14. **Skin clips, surgical strips (tape), ligation clips, and internal and external staples are alternatives to conventional suturing materials, and have several applications in today's surgical practice setting. One advantage of these methods is:**

    1. *overall greater reliability.*

    2. *reduced cost.*

3. *ease of use--little training required.*

4. *time saved under anesthesia.*

15. **Surgical strips and external surgical staples are more often used than other devices for:**

    1. *ligation of nerves and ducts.*

    2. *resection of tissue.*

    3. *plastic surgery.*

    4. *anastomosis closure.*

16. **Ligation clips are commonly used for:**

    1. *external suturing.*

    2. *hemostasis.*

    3. *plastic surgery.*

    4. *anastomosis closure.*

17. **Which of the following is NOT part of the proper care and handling of surgical instruments?**

    1. *Each instrument should be inspected weekly to spot chips, breaks, cracks, or imperfections.*

    2. *Sharps and delicate instruments should be set aside and individually cleaned, then the tips protected with either an individual tip protector or a holding pouch.*

    3. *The edges of sharp instruments should be protected during and after procedures.*

    4. *Forceps, clamps, and other hinged instruments should be inspected for alignment of jaws and teeth and for stiffness.*

18. **A kardex or pictorial reference book is used to:**

    1. *help nurses cross reference surgical procedures to the type of anesthesia to be used.*

    2. *document all needles, sutures, and other supplies used during a surgical procedure.*

    3. *track any instruments that are added to or deleted from the instrument tray.*

    4. *record all measures used to clean or lubricate instruments in the standard basic instrument set.*

ANSWER EXPLANATIONS

1. **The answer is 3.** Hemostasis is the arrest, control, or reduction of bleeding, which can assist in the wound-healing process. Hemostasis can be accomplished by the natural clotting of blood; by the use of artificial means, such as cautery, sutures, clamps, staples, and so on; by chemical methods, using specially treated materials impregnated with a hemostatic substance; or by a combination of all three techniques. Hemostasis during a surgical procedure is essential to prevent hemorrhage, allow for visualization of the surgical field, and promote wound healing.

2. **The answer is 1.** Thrombostat (Thrombin, U.S.P.) is used as a chemical hemostatic agent. Mechanical methods of hemostasis include: (1) **instruments**: clamping the end of a bleeding vessel with a hemostat is the most common method of achieving hemostasis; the bleeder can then be ligated or sutured to accomplish the stoppage of blood flow; (2) **heat**, in the form of electrocautery, sears the blood, allowing dilation of the vessel, which stimulates the platelets and tissues to liberate more natural hemostatic agents (thromboplastin); (3) **bone wax** is refined beeswax that is used to control bleeding in bone marrow; pieces of bone wax are rolled into small balls and handed to the surgeon for direct application on the bone; (4) **ligating clips**--small clips made of titanium, stainless steel, or synthetic material--are used to ligate arteries, veins, or nerves; the clip comes in various sizes with a corresponding applicator, which, when applied, stays permanently on the vessel, stopping the flow of blood from the area; and (5) a **ligature**, commonly called a tie, is a strand of material that is tied around a blood vessel to occlude the lumen and prevent bleeding.

3. **The answer is 4.** Most chemical hemostatic agents assist in the blood-clotting process, either by forming a clot (gelatin and collagen sponges) or in some way accelerating the process of clot formation (coagulation). Included in this latter category are microfibrillar collagen, oxidized cellulose, and thrombostat. Styptics, on the other hand, such as epinephrine, tannic acid, and silver nitrate, cause blood vessels to constrict, thus arresting or reducing bleeding.

4. **The answer is 1. Microfibrillar collagen** hemostat (Avitine) is an off-white "fluffy" material prepared from purified bovine collagen used as a topical hemostatic agent. It achieves hemostasis by adhering to platelets and forming thrombi with the interstices of the collagen. It functions as a hemostatic when applied directly to the source of bleeding, including bone and friable tissue or from around a vascular anastomosis. Since it adheres to wet gloves and instruments, it should be presented on a dry, smooth forcep, followed by applying pressure over the site with a dry sponge. **Oxidized cellulose** (Oxycel, Surgicel) is a specially treated gauze that is placed directly over the bleeding area. As it absorbs the blood, it swells to seven or eight times its normal size and forms coagulum. The hemostatic effect of oxidized cellulose is created when it is dry; therefore, it too should not be moistened with water or saline prior to use. Oxidized cellulose may be left in the wound, as it is absorbed in 7 to 14 days with minimal tissue reaction, except when applied to areas such as the spinal cord, optic nerve and its chiasm, or bone.

5. **The answer is 4.** Suture diameter or size identifies the size of the strand, which ranges from a heavy size 7 to a very fine size 11-0. The diameter of the suture strand usually determines its effective usage in addition to its size. A basic rule for remembering suture sizes is based on the premise that Size 0 is smaller than Size 1 and the more 0's added the smaller and more fragile the suture.

6. **The answer is 1.** To reduce the confusion associated with the various suture materials, each major category of suture material is color coded, and this coding is standard through the industry, regardless of the manufacturer. This is the first step in suture package recognition. (See Table 7.1 for color codes.) Absorbable suture materials, such as chromic and plain gut, are primarily used on fast-healing tissue and come from both natural and synthetic sources. Their use is contraindicated when extended or prolonged approximation is required. Absorbable sutures are digested by body enzymes by first losing their strength, then gradually disappearing from the tissue. Synthetic sources include polymers, either dyed, or undyed, and are absorbed by a slow hydrolysis process in the presence of tissue fluids. The tensile strength of synthetic absorbable sutures exceeds that of surgical gut, and it can be used in the presence of infection since absorption time and loss of tensile strength are not affected by the proteolytic enzymes in the gastrointestinal tract.

7. **The answer is 2.** Nonabsorbable sutures become encapsulated in fibrous tissue during the healing process and remain embedded in body tissue unless they are surgically removed. They are primarily used with tissues that heal slower owing to their location, tissue type, or general healing factors. Like absorbable sutures, the suture materials come from both natural and synthetic sources. Natural sources include silk and cotton; they should not be used if long-term support is vital since they lose substantial strength 90 to 120 days after implantation. Advances in suture manufacturing have resulted in a decreased usage of natural substances and an increase in synthetic substances adaptable for suturing material. Examples of these substances include nylon, polyester, polyethylene, polypropylene, and surgical steel/wire.

8. **The answer is 3.** The "flipping" procedure should be used only during the initial set-up of the sterile field, when the scrub person has not yet donned sterile gown and gloves. Standing a safe distance from the sterile instrument table or designated receptacle, the circulator rolls the flaps of the outer package backwards, and projects (flips) the inner package onto the sterile surface, being careful not to reach over the sterile field.

9. **The answer is 2.** The delicacy of the tissue determines which needle point--taper, cutting, or blunt--is most suitable to use. (See Table 7.3 for a glossary of needle points.) Taper points are used on delicate tissues that are easily penetrated. These areas include the peritoneum, the heart of the intestines. A taper-point needle is designed so that the shaft gradually tapers to a sharp point, which results in a very small hole in the tissue. A cutting-point needle is designed with a razor-sharp tip and is used for tissue such as skin or tendons. There are three types of cutting needles: **taper cut** (used for tough, fibrous tissue), conventional, and reverse cutting. Generally, the tougher the tissue, the greater the need for a cutting-type shaft. Blunt-tip needles have a rounded end and are used in friable tissue, such as liver or kidney, when neither piercing nor cutting is appropriate.

10. **The answer is 3.** The eye, or head, of the of the needle is designed to cause minimal trauma to the tissue. Atraumatic or swaged needles consist of one or two needles attached to the suture strand at the factory, eliminating the need for threading. This causes the least amount of tissue trauma, since the suture and needle are a continuous unit in which the needle size and suture diameter are matched as closely as possible. A modification of the permanently swaged suture, the control release suture (or "pop-off") allows for faster interrupted suturing. The needle and suture begin as one unit; however, they may be separated by means of a light pull on the needle, allowing the surgeon to tie without a needle remaining on the end of the suture.

11. **The answer is 1.** Sutures should be prepared in their order of use, but certain preliminary preparations are necessary to ensure sterility and prevent prolonged exposure, unnecessary handling, and excess waste. Some guidelines include: (1) sutures will first be used to ligate or tie off bleeding vessels; therefore, sutures without needles (ligatures) should be prepared first; (2) the use of suture materials in dry packages requires no special preparation, but those contained in solution must be opened carefully to avoid contamination of the field from the liquid contents; (3) sutures that need to be straightened for easy handling should be prepared first, and placed in a "suture book," created from a sterile towel, and leaving the ends extended to reduce time and wasted motion; (4) when using a multiple-suture packet the packet should be torn open along the dotted line and the sutures nudged forward from the package so that individual strands can be obtained as needed; (5) suture ligatures may be handed as a free tie, placed in the open hand of the surgeon, or placed on the end of an instrument for a deep tie; when a dispensing reel is used, both the free end and the spool are passed to the surgeon simultaneously; and (6) if the ligatures are pre-cut strands, no further preparation is required; however, if ligatures are available only in the standard length, the scrub person may have to cut the strands for ease of handling.

12. **The answer is 3.** Some guidelines for handling eyed needles and sutures include: (1) the curved needle is mounted on a needle holder; in mounting the needle, it should be placed nearest the eye, about one third of the total length of the shaft away from the eye end; when swaged needles are mounted, it is important that the needle holder not be clamped directly over the swage itself, since this weakens the area and can cause the suture to detach unexpectedly from the needle; (2) the suture may be threaded through the eye from either side of the curve; the suture strand is drawn through the eye about one third of its length; both ends of the suture may be drawn between the jaws of the needle holder (or only one end depending on the surgeon preference), and the instrument is passed to the surgeon; (3) when mounting the needle on a needle holder, it should be positioned so that the surgeon does not have to reposition it for suturing; the outside curve of the needle should be aimed downward, with the point aimed for the ceiling, in the direction of the surgeon's chin or thumb; (4) the instrument is passed handle first, tip pointed toward the surgeon's opposite thumb, while the scrub person gently holds onto the loose end to avoid contact with the surgeon's palm as the instrument is transferred; suture needles must be passed on a one-to-one basis, and the previous needle retrieved before passing another; to avoid delay, two needles should be mounted so that as one is returned, another is ready to use; and (5) when passing a straight needle, the tip is covered by the scrub person's hand, and the swaged portion of the needle is handed to the surgeon.

13. **The answer is 3.** If more than one needle is contained in the package, all needles should be seen and counted by the scrub person *and circulator* prior to use. After the suture has been used, the needle, on the needle holder, is returned to the scrub person, who places it into the needle counter for future confirmation of the needle count. To avoid loss, needles must never be allowed to lay loose on the field. Maintaining a running, silent count of all needles used is the responsibility of the scrub person. Therefore, empty suture packets must stay on the sterile field until the final needle count is confirmed in case there is a misplaced needle.

14. **The answer is 4.** The advantages of these methods include time saved under anesthesia and close approximation of wound edges, promoting greater and faster healing with less tissue loss or reaction. With surgical staples used internally, for example, the mechanical application of the stapling instrument significantly reduces tissue manipulation and handling, thus reducing surgical and anesthesia time and permitting a more natural wound healing process to occur in a shorter period of time. In addition, the staple produces an airtight, leakproof closure and can be safely used in many types of tissue. Finally, the staples are essentially nonreactive; therefore, the occurrence of tissue reaction or infection is reduced, permitting an anastomosis created with staples to function sooner than one created with manual technique. The use of these alternative methods, however, requires additional education of both the surgeon and the surgical team to achieve maximum efficiency.

15. **The answer is 3.** Surgical strips (tapes) are made of a reinforced, micropore surgical tape that is adhesive on one side. They are used to approximate skin edges following a subcuticular closure or superficial lacerations in conjunction with skin sutures, permitting the skin sutures to be removed 36 to 48 hours postoperatively. They can be used for any type of surgery, but are most often associated with plastic and pediatric surgery, since they leave no mark on the skin. Skin staples are the fastest method of skin closure and have a low level of tissue reactivity. The edges of both cuticular and subcuticular layers must be everted (aligned with the edges slightly raised), and the stapler is positioned over the line of the incision so that a staple will be placed evenly on each side. Skin staples must be removed, usually 5 to 7 days postoperatively, and a staple extractor is used for this purpose. Because the skin flattens as it heals, staples provide an excellent cosmetic result if they have been properly placed lightly over the incision.

16. **The answer is 2.** Ligation clips are used for hemostasis or to ligate nerves and ducts. The clips come preloaded or are placed on a special applicator, placed around the vessel or structure, and the handle is squeezed so the jaws of the applicator are closed with the clip secured around the structure.

17. **The answer is 1.** Instruments should be inspected before and after cleaning, not weekly. In addition, (1) all blades and needles should be removed and placed in a designated sharps container, and the lid closed for further protection; (2) instruments must be handled gently; bouncing, dropping, and setting heavy equipment on top of the delicate instruments should be avoided; at the end of a procedure, they must be handled individually and not thrown together in a tangled heap; (3) edges of scissors should be tested for sharpness; to cut effectively, they must be filed smoothly, and maintained sharp by careful observation; it is further recommended that all instruments be periodically lubricated in special instrument "milk," which contains silicone, following the cleaning process to preserve their ease of use and prevent sticking of box locks and/or ratchets; and (4) nurses should know the names and proper use of each instrument, should constantly observe the sterile field for loose instruments, should remove used instruments promptly to original location for easy retrieval, and should keep instruments clean during procedure by periodically cleaning instruments using a damp cloth (towel or lap sponge).

18. **The answer is 3.** A kardex or pictorial reference book for each tray, with the vendor's name, amounts of specific instruments and the cost, and any cross referencing information will assist personnel in preparing the instrument trays. The kardex book should be routinely updated as instruments are added or deleted from the tray. A count sheet specific to the tray should also be part of this reference book. By grouping the instruments within the reference book according to service and/or by the specialty tray or set, a complex process can become an ongoing learning experience for those responsible for using and assembling the instrument trays.

8 Foundations of Surgery: Procedural Supplies and Equipment

STUDY OUTLINE

I. PREPARING FOR A SURGICAL PROCEDURE

1. The scrub and circulator receive their daily case assignments from the surgical schedule board and begin to prepare the procedure room for the upcoming procedures. Part of this preparation includes the selection and assembly of supplies and equipment needed for each case, both sterile and nonsterile, by using a preference card or computer print-out.

2. Prior to starting any case, however, the perioperative nurse must "assemble mentally." This process begins long before the nurse enters the procedure room, regardless of the role being performed. Some of the questions to ask during this preparation period include knowledge of:
   a. The anatomy involved.
   b. The proposed incision site and surgical approach.
   c. The physiologic status of the patient.
   d. The preferred supplies and equipment requested and how to use them safely and effectively.

3. Four factors will determine the perioperative nurse's success in becoming a proficient member of the surgical team. These factors must be considered as listed, in correct sequential order, to avoid omission in the preparation for a surgical procedure.
   a. **Surgical approach**
      (1) How will the anatomic area involved be exposed?
      (2) How will the patient be positioned to provide maximum exposure?
      (3) Where is the incision site; what area needs to be prepped; are there any allergies that would prevent the use of routine prep solutions?
   b. **Surgical procedure**
      (1) What is the sequential order of the procedure?
      (2) When are the counts to be performed?
      (3) What additional supplies might be requested?
      (4) How should the specimens, if any, be prepared?
   c. **Surgical complications**
      (1) What unforseen difficulty might arise during surgery that may require additional supplies or equipment?
      (2) What is your role during an emergency situation, and how can you best meet the needs of the patient and team during this time?
   d. **Surgical closure**
      (1) What type of dressings will be used for the procedure?
      (2) What are the special needs of the patient during the immediate postoperative period?

4. It is practically impossible to anticipate every single aspect of every procedure and possible deviations from the routine, but what the nurse must do is be alert and totally aware of what is happening from the moment planning begins for the procedure until the patient has been safely transported to the designated postoperative area. At that time, and not before, the nurse's responsibility for that patient ends, as other professionals assume the care of the patient.

II. PLANNING INTRAOPERATIVE PATIENT CARE

1. **Perioperative nursing practice is based on the *Nursing Process* format, and the third phase of that process is identified as the *planning phase*.**
2. Quality assurance requires evidence that a specific care plan for each patient has been proposed and implemented during the intraoperative phase, and in order to be in compliance, the following prerequisites of knowledge and skill are needed:
   a. Knowledge and assessment of the patient's individual needs related to pathophysiology, the surgical procedure, and the surgeon's preferences.
   b. Knowledge of surgical supplies and instrumentation needed, and cost-effective methods for selection and assembly of these items.
   c. Knowledge of those items considered "standard" for all surgical procedures, including sterile and nonsterile supplies.
   d. Knowledge of appropriate procedure room preparation, including acquisition, usage, and placement of furniture and special equipment needed for the procedure.
   e. Knowledge and management of available resources, both material and personnel.
3. By planning perioperative patient care using these broad concepts, the perioperative nurse can establish and maintain a therapeutic environment, one that is safe for both the patient and the staff.

III. THE STERILE FIELD

1. **The sterile field, and its usage, is composed of three distinct phases: (1) creation of the sterile field, (2) maintenance of the sterile field, and (3) termination of the sterile field.**
2. The implementation of intraoperative nursing activities is directly related to the organization and coordination of sterile supplies, instruments, equipment, and health-care team members, and is based on priority setting and an on-going assessment of the surgical environment.

A. PRELIMINARY PREPARATION

1. **The first step in creating a suitable environment is related to the preparation of the procedure room, including the physical layout of furniture and equipment and the placement of supplies in a convenient location, since wasted motion is not only time-consuming but also can add to physical and mental fatigue.**
2. Preliminary preparation of the room is done before each patient enters the room, and is a team effort by both the circulating nurse and the scrub person. To be effective, it must be a cooperative effort that can also include assistance from aides, orderlies, and environmental services personnel.
3. The following is a checklist for preparing the procedure room:

   Step 1. Damp dusting/arranging furniture
   a. Damp dust all flat surfaces and all portable or mounted equipment (PRN).
   b. Position the operating room table under the overhead light fixture.
   c. Arrange the furniture needed for the specific procedure (e.g., instrument table, Mayo stand, and ring stands).

B. FURNITURE AND EQUIPMENT

1. Some of the more common pieces of furniture and equipment found in a procedure room include:
   a. **The operating room table**
      (1) The operating table is an expensive, sometimes complex yet essential piece of furniture that is used for all surgical procedures. There are several types of operating tables, some for general usage, others specifically designed for surgical specialties, such as urology, orthopedics, or cataract surgery.

(2) The table is fully adjustable in all directions to create the positions needed for various surgical procedures, and all personnel should be totally familiar with its operation and its corresponding accessories. The table should be positioned directly under the overhead light fixture, and once in position, should be locked for patient and staff safety.

b. **Instrument (back) table**

(1) Once it is draped with a bacterial barrier, the instrument table provides a set-up area for sterile supplies to be used during the procedure. The table is made of a noncorrosive metal, and has a top and bottom shelf. The bottom shelf can be used for storage of extra supplies not immediately needed. The table is on wheels, and can be positioned wherever necessary to provide maximum efficiency during the procedure.

(2) Once draped, the instrument table should be at least 18 inches away from walls and cabinets, away from linen hampers, doors, garbage receptacles, anesthesia equipment, and paths to traffic.

c. **Ring stand:** The ring stand is round or square, and is used to hold basin sets and/or instrument trays. The ring stand, once draped, should be placed close to the instrument table, since it will become part of the sterile field during surgery.

d. **Mayo stand:** The Mayo stand is used to hold instruments that will be used frequently during the procedure. It is draped with a bacterial barrier, and then placed directly over, but not in contact with, the patient once the patient drapes have been applied. It is adjustable in height, and is totally portable, since it moves on wheels. During the set-up period, the stand should remain close to the other furniture to avoid possible contamination or accidental bumping of the stand.

Step 2. Placement of packs and supplies
   a. Put sterile drape packs on the instrument table.
   b. Place wrapped sterile basin set into one of the ring stands.
   c. Put the wrapped sterile instrument tray on top of the other ring stand.
   d. Place the scrubs' gown and gloves on the Mayo stand.

2. **Additional furniture and equipment**
   a. The use of **kick buckets** (a bucket on wheels) is restricted to soiled sponges during surgery. It is lined with a disposable liner which can be removed and exchanged as required during the procedure without jeopardizing the sterility of the surgical field.
   b. All other trash should be placed in a larger trash receptacle. However, once the procedure has started, no trash may leave the room.
   c. In addition, anesthesia machines, electrosurgical units (E.S.U.), suction canisters/tubing, I.V. poles, linen receptacles for nondisposable linen, and adjustable stools (rolling or permanent) are usually found in a procedure room.
3. **All furniture and equipment should be in their proper position before opening and creating the sterile field to avoid possible contamination of the field during moving activities.**

Step 3. Collection of remaining items
   a. Collect additional instruments and supplies according to procedural need, including drugs and special items (specialty cart).
   b. Collect positioning devices, positional aids, and special equipment, such as the E.S.U., laser, microscope, and so on.
   c. Choose the proper suture and amounts for the procedure according to the surgeon's preference.
   d. Collect the irrigation fluids and prep solutions needed.
   e. To avoid time loss, all supplies and equipment should be gathered at one time and re-checked for accuracy by the scrub and circulating nurses.

IV. **STANDARD AND ACCESSORY SUPPLIES**

1. **Surgical supplies can be divided into two major categories: sterile supplies and nonsterile supplies.** Each category can then be subdivided into those items that are considered essential, or **standard supplies,** and those that are not required for every case, or **accessory supplies.**
2. To select the proper packs, drapes, and supplies for a surgical procedure, it is necessary to follow some general guidelines:
    a. Determine the required supplies based on the anatomy and proposed procedure.
    b. Use the Physician's Preference Card to select the specialty/accessory items needed for the procedure.
    c. Carefully select the proper amount of supplies, to be cost-effective, following a logical sequential order of selection.

A. **STERILE PACKS AND DRAPES**

1. Many different types of **packs** and **drapes** are available today designed for specific surgical procedures. Packs are the primary supply needed to create a sterile field. In some institutions, the use of a **customized pack,** one that contains specific items needed according to institutional preference, has been created, thus eliminating the need for obtaining additional items.
2. The packs and drape sheets are made of disposable, fluid-resistant material, which acts as a bacterial barrier against microbial infiltration. At the end of the procedure, all disposable items are discarded, reducing the possibility of cross-contamination with another patient and the surgical environment.
3. **Sterile packs**
    a. Three primary packs are commonly associated with surgical procedures: a **laparotomy pack,** a **basic pack (table drape),** and a **specialty pack.** The surgical team member choosing the appropriate pack, should be familiar with its contents in order to avoid "pulling" extra supplies, which could be wasted. Each pack has a list of contents conveniently printed on the reverse side of the pack.
    b. **Laparotomy pack**
        (1) **General usage:** flat body surfaces with a vertical fenestration (hole) in the patient drape sheet. Appropriate for general abdominal, pelvic, and spinal surgery, or any instance when a vertical incision line is used.
        (2) **Contents** (depending on manufacturer)
            *   Overwrap/table cover
            *   Absorbent towels
            *   Utility towels (small)
            *   Plastic Mayo stand cover
            *   Laparotomy sheet with fenestration
            *   Disposable gowns and absorbent hand towels
            *   Ray-Tec X-ray-detectable sponges
    c. **Basic pack (table drape)**
        (1) **General usage:** to create a "customized" pack for special procedures that require a specific fenestrated sheet or draping of an additional instrument table, or use when a fenestrated sheet is not required.
        (2) **Contents:** same as a laparotomy pack, minus the fenestrated sheet and sponges; usually only contains one surgical gown.
    d. **Specialty packs:** These include packs for specific surgical procedures, e.g., GYN pack, laparoscopy pack, etc. Each specialty pack usually contains a fenestrated sheet and additional items needed for the procedure.
4. **Sterile drape sheets**
    a. **Sterile drape sheets** come in various sizes and forms, with or without fenestrations, and are usually used in conjunction with either a basic pack or as an added bacterial barrier for specific draping needs.

b. Some examples include **transverse lap sheet, split sheet, pediatric lap sheet, thyroid sheet, craniotomy incise sheet, eye/ear sheet, plastic adherent incise sheet** (Vi-Drape) (plain or impregnated with iodine), and **stockinette cuffs** to cover extremities such as toes, fingers, or hands, in addition to three quarters and one half table drape sheets for patient drape or table cover, to name just a few.

C. BASIN SETS

1. **Basin sets are available in either a reusable or disposable format, and contain the "pots and pans" needed for surgery.** Three types of basin sets are usually found in the surgical suite; they may be used interchangeably or for a specific purpose. The contents will vary depending on the needs of the institution, and can be "customized" like the custom packs mentioned earlier.

2. **Major basin set**
   a. **General usage:** for procedures requiring large supplies of instruments, sponges, and so on (general, vascular, ortho).
   b. **Contents** (per institutional preference)
      (1) Large round basins (1-2)
      (2) Round basins (T & A basin) (2-3)
      (3) Kidney basin (emesis basin) (1)
      (4) Prep cups/medicine glasses (2)
      (5) Graduated pitcher (optional)

3. **Minor basin set**
   a. **General usage:** procedures not requiring extra basins or graduated pitcher, such as hernia repairs, peripheral vascular procedures, and plastic surgery.
   b. **Contents** (per institutional preference)
      (1) Large basin (1)
      (2) Round basin (1-2)
      (3) Medicine glasses (2)

4. **Single or hand basin**
   a. **General usage:** to clean instruments.

   NOTE: A single basin should not be used as a "splash" basin, since contamination from this basin, when used to clean gloves during surgery, can cause contamination of the sterile field.

C. SURGICAL SPONGES

1. **Surgical sponges are manufactured in a variety of shapes and sizes and serve three general purposes:**
   a. **To absorb fluid and blood.**
   b. **For blunt dissection of delicate tissue.**
   c. **To protect tissue from injury.**

2. Only those sponges with an X-ray-detectable feature should be used at the sterile field once an incision has been made, and all sponges must be counted at proper intervals during the surgical procedure, according to acceptable protocol by both the scrub and circulating nurse.

3. Surgical sponges are available in specific numerical increments, depending on the type of sponge being used, and all increments are standardized, regardless of the manufacturer.

4. **Common surgical sponges**
   a. **Ray-Tec (4 x 4):** prepackaged in increments of 10 per box; used in all procedures; Ray-Tec should be removed from the surgical field once any deep cavity has been entered, unless it is folded and used on a "sponge stick" for blunt dissection purposes.
   b. **Laparotomy sponge (18 x 18 "lap sponge"):** prepackaged in increments of 5 per package; used during major surgery or for absorbing fluid in large areas.
   c. **Small laps (tapes) (4 x 18):** packaged in increments of 5 per package; used in smaller areas when large sponges may not be applicable or advisable due to the nature of the incision, or in place of the Ray-Tec sponge.

      d. **Cottonoids (neuro patties):** prepackaged in increments of 10 per package and available in a variety of sizes ranging from 1/4 x 1/4 to 3 x 3 inches; each patty has a string attached that is left outside the wound during its use; made of a soft, lint-free material so they will not injure or scratch delicate tissue/structures; used predominantly in neurosurgery and spinal procedures.

      e. **Dissecting sponges:** available in many different sizes and shapes, dissecting sponges are used to absorb blood in very small areas or "push" away delicate tissue; have a variety of names that may change from hospital to surgeon to manufacturer; examples include Cherry, Penut, Pushers, Kittners; prepackaged in increments of 5, dissecting sponges should always be mounted on a clamp, and may be used wet or dry.

      f. **Tonsil/dental sponges**

          (1) **Tonsil sponges** are round, gauze sponges with a thread attached that is kept outside the mouth during surgery. Prepackaged in increments of 5, they are used for tonsillectomies.

          (2) **Dental sponges** (rolls) are tubular in shape, and are non-X-ray detectable. They are used for packing the mouth during teeth extractions. Although they are not X-ray detectable, they must be counted as any other sponge. Packaged either in-hospital or prepackaged, and usually in increments of 5 or 10.

      g. Depending on physician preference, surgical sponges may be wet (soaked in saline) or dry.

E. ADDITIONAL STANDARD AND ACCESSORY STERILE SUPPLIES

    1. **Irrigation solutions:** sterile water and saline are available in 500 or 1000 mL "pour bottles"; saline is always used on back table for irrigation; sterile water is poured into the large round basin for instrument cleaning, since salt water will corrode the instruments, resulting in rust stains.

    2. **Gowns, gloves** (surgeon and assistants).

    3. **Prep tray:** preassembled wet (with solution) or dry.

    4. **Sterile towels:** packaged 4 to 5 per package; can be linen or a disposable linen fabric, prepackaged and sterilized by the manufacturer or hospital created.

    5. **Suction tips/tubings:** metal or disposable tips.

    6. **Sterile accessory supplies** are those items not required for every procedure, or specifically requested by the surgeon. These include such items as:

      a. Cautery devices

          (1) Monopolar pencils/tips

          (2) Bipolar forceps

      b. Syringes: irrigation/hypodermic

      c. Needle counter (sharps container)

      d. Sutures/needles (specific to surgeon request)

      e. Catheters/tubes/drains

      f. Dressing supplies: non-Ray-Tec 4 x 4's; ABD's; Telfa

F. NONSTERILE SUPPLIES AND EQUIPMENT

    1. In addition to the furniture and equipment mentioned earlier in this unit, other **nonsterile supplies** must be selected for each case, and these supplies either complement or assist in the usage of sterile supplies. For example, one cannot use an electrocautery unit without a grounding pad, nor apply a dressing without tape.

    2. Positioning devices, special table pads, suction canisters, connecting tubings, and medications to be administered at the sterile field--all these items are needed during the procedure and must be a part of the initial preparation phase, in order to avoid leaving the room to collect them during the procedure.

V. THE PHYSICIAN'S PREFERENCE CARD

    1. **For every surgical procedure performed in the operating room by a specific surgeon, a corresponding reference list of all supplies and equipment used for the procedure, in addition**

to the supplies and equipment requested by the surgeon, should be created, and should be readily available wherever the cases are assembled, be it the operating room or in the instance of case cart assembly, in the central processing area. This card or computerized listing is referred to as a **Physician's Preference Card**, and can serve multiple purposes, including maintaining a inventory/charging list for a specific procedure by a specific surgeon for a specific patient.

2. It is vitally important that all information remains current and that any changes that occur during the procedure are noted and communicated to the staff and personnel responsible for assembling and using the supplies, thereby avoiding delays in the procedure owing to improper selection.

3. Not all supplies and equipment are specified on this reference list, but by knowing and understanding the standard and accessory supplies needed for the procedure, the surgical team can effectively prepare the procedure room for the planned surgical procedure.

VI. PHASE I: CREATING A STERILE FIELD

1. **Once the equipment and supplies have been gathered and placed on their respective surfaces, and the procedure room has been properly prepared, the surgical team can begin the task of creating the sterile field through a process of organized steps and procedures.**

A. OPENING STERILE SUPPLIES

1. Before any sterile supplies are opened, the integrity of each package must be checked. Packages not meeting acceptable criteria should be placed aside, since they cannot be considered sterile, and new ones chosen.

2. Each package must be opened under strict aseptic technique, thereby guaranteeing the sterility of the sterile field. The following steps can serve as a guideline for opening sterile supplies in preparation for a surgical procedure:
   a. Remove the tape from a C.S.R. wrapped package and check the indicator tape to be certain the item has been properly exposed to the sterilization process.
   b. Open the linen pack on the instrument table so that the inside of the wrapper becomes the sterile table cover.
   c. Open sponges, gowns, gloves, drape sheets, and towels on the back table. Open blades on the right corner of the table.
   d. Open basin sets and the instruments tray on ring stands. If sequentially wrapped, both layers are opened.
   e. Place small items and extra instruments in the basin or in the instrument tray. Maintain object in inner wrapper.
   f. Open scrub gown and gloves on the Mayo stand.

B. DELINEATION OF THE SCRUB AND CIRCULATOR ROLES

1. **Although all surgical procedures require a cooperative effort, from the time the surgical scrub begins until the operation is finished and the dressings are applied, there is a definite line of demarcation between the duties and responsibilities of the scrub person and the circulating nurse that neither may cross.** (See Table 8.1 for a delineation of duties.)

2. The **circulating nurse** performs those functions associated with the management of the room before, during, and after the procedure, while the **scrub person** (nurse or technician) performs all tasks related to the creation and maintenance of the sterile field before and during surgery, in addition to the care of the instruments when surgery is completed.

C. STANDARDIZED BASIC SET-UP

1. Each institution may have its own "standard set-up" for the instrument table and Mayo stand. The need for a standard set-up is evident for two basic reasons:
   a. Decreasing the actual set-up time.
   b. Ease of transition during relief of scrub personnel.

Table 8.1 COMPARATIVE DIVISION OF DUTIES

Scrub Nurse/Technician	Circulating Nurse
A. PREOPERATIVE	
1. Checks the card file for surgeon's special needs/requests.	**1.** Assists in assembling needed supplies.
2. Opens sterile supplies.	**2.** Opens sterile supplies.
3. Scrubs, gowns, and gloves and sets up sterile field. Obtains instruments from flash autoclave if necessary. Checks for proper functioning of instruments/equipment.	**3.** Assists scrub in gowning.
	4. Performs and records counts.
	5. Admits patient to surgical suite.
4. Performs counts with circulator.	
B. PREINCISIONAL	
1. Completes the final preparation of sterile field.	**1.** Transports patient to procedure room.
2. Assists surgeon with gowning/gloving.	**2.** Assists with the positioning of the patient.
3. Assists surgeon with draping and passes off suction/cautery lines.	**3.** Assists anesthesia during induction.
	4. Performs skin prep.
	5. Assists with drapes; connects suction and cautery.
C. DURING THE PROCEDURE	
1. Maintains orderly sterile field.	**1.** Maintains orderly procedure room.
2. Anticipates the surgeon's needs (supplies/equipment).	**2.** Anticipates needs of surgical team.
3. Maintains internal count of sponges, needles, and instruments.	**3.** Maintains record of supplies added.
4. Verifies tissue specimen with surgeon, and passes off to circulator.	**4.** Receives specimen and labels it correctly.
	5. Maintains charges and O.R. records.
	6. Continually monitors aseptic technique and patient needs.
D. CLOSING PHASE	
1. Counts with circulator at proper intervals.	**1.** Counts with scrub at proper intervals.
2. Organizes closing suture and dressings.	**2.** Finalizes records and charges.
3. Begins clean-up of used instruments.	**3.** Begins clean-up of procedure room.
4. Applies sterile dressings.	**4.** Applies tape.
5. Prepares for terminal cleaning of instruments and nondisposable supplies.	**5.** Assists anesthesia in preparing patient for transfer to P.A.C.U.
6. Reports to charge nurse for next assignment.	**6.** Takes patient to P.A.C.U. with anesthesia and reports significant information to P.A.C.U. nurse.
	7. Disposes of specimen and records.
	8. Reports to charge nurse for next assignment.

2. As a member of the surgical team, it is the perioperative nurse's responsibility to know and use the proper set-up as directed by the *Surgical Policy and Procedure Manual* at the nurse's respective institution.

3. **Draping the surgical patient:** To isolate the surgical wound from bacterial contamination, the patient must be covered with sterile drapes so that only the incisional site is exposed. The actual draping procedure is usually performed by the surgeon, with assistance from either the scrub person or the assistant.

VII. PHASE II: MAINTAINING THE STERILE FIELD

1. **According to the principles of basic aseptic technique mentioned earlier, a sterile field, once established, must be constantly monitored and maintained. This monitoring process is the responsibility of every member of the surgical team, and each must watch for events that may compromise the sterility of the field, and take appropriate corrective action.**

2. Once the patient is placed on the operating table, prepped and draped, he or she becomes the center of the sterile field, and *all movement and activities in and around the field must be performed without compromise to that field.*

3. All sterile supplies and equipment should be grouped around the patient, and must be kept in view at all times by both the sterile and nonsterile members of the team.

4. Sterile items should be presented to the scrub person or placed securely on the sterile field without reaching over the field, which would cause immediate contamination. Sharp or heavy objects should be opened on a separate surface to avoid injury or possible contamination of the object during transfer.

5. Some materials appear resistant to moisture, but should liquid be spilled, creating **strike-through**, the area must be reinforced with a sterile towel or drape since strike-through of fluids constitutes contamination of that sterile surface.

6. As always, if the sterility of an item, be it a towel, instrument, or needle, is in doubt it must be considered contaminated, removed from the field, and replaced by another sterile item.

7. Unsterile equipment, furniture, and personnel should remain a safe distance from the sterile field (at least 12 inches) to avoid accidental contact with the field. Unsterile personnel should approach the field facing it and never walk between two sterile fields.

8. *Sterile supplies should never be opened and then covered or left unguarded during the preliminary phase of the sterile field's creation.* Chances for contamination of an unguarded sterile field are numerous, and without direct observation, there is no way to ensure sterility.

9. For additional guidelines, review Chapter 5 in this guide. These principles and practices should become part of your everyday activities, since the safety of the patient rests solely on the ability to maintain the sterile field during the surgical procedure, in addition to maintaining an aseptic environment.

VIII.   PHASE III: TERMINATION OF THE STERILE FIELD

1. **It is important to terminate the sterile field in a safe and logical manner, and at the proper time.**

2. Until the patient has been prepared for transfer to the postoperative area, the environment must be maintained in an aseptic manner, in case an unforeseen emergency occurs that necessitates immediate action. Therefore, all members of the surgical team should keep their masks in place during this transition period.

3. After the last stitch is in place, and the area cleaned, the sterile dressing is applied by the scrub nurse and held in place while the drape sheets are removed with assistance from the circulator, rolling the drape sheet inside out toward the foot of the table. The scrub nurse, with the equipment, should then step back to a position away from the operating table, where the actual termination procedure will take place.

4. The criteria for disassembling the sterile set up calls for the *patient to have left the room,* but this is not realistic, since room turnover time is usually limited to 15 minutes maximum after a procedure is over (and may be longer for complicated procedures with excessive equipment).

5. The next best approach is to begin the clean-up process during the closing phase of the procedure, leaving the Mayo stand intact until the very end. This would still allow for the use of sterile equipment should an emergency situation arise necessitating reentry into the wound.

6. *All instruments, whether used or not, are considered contaminated and must be decontaminated according to acceptable protocol.* However, instruments that have been used during the procedure should be hand cleaned using a basin of sterile water and a lap sponge or brush prior to terminal decontamination. This action provides safety for those persons handling the instruments during the cleaning phase.

7. Prior to disposing of drape material, it should be checked for instruments, since they may be still attached to the drapes during the dismantling phase. Disposable linen and cloth items are then placed in their respective bags for disposal. Gloves must be worn during this process, even by the circulating nurse, since blood and fluids may still be present on the drape sheet. All sharps, including cautery tips, blades, and hypodermic needles should be placed in a container (a needle-counter box can serve this purpose) and disposed of according to acceptable protocol.

8. To avoid any unsightly transfer of instruments to the decontamination area, the tray(s) should be covered. The last step is the removal of the scrub's gown, gloves and mask.

9. Environmental services begins the interim cleaning process by removing the trash and linen from the room, followed by cleaning the floor and all surfaces according to institutional procedure.

10. *Protecting the patient and personnel from harm* is the responsibility of everyone, and by practicing the principles of basic aseptic technique, effectively monitoring the environment, and selecting, organizing, and safely utilizing the supplies and equipment used during surgery the surgical experience can become a rewarding experience for both the patient and the surgical team.

PRACTICE QUESTIONS

1. **As a perioperative nurse preparing for a surgical procedure, you first "assemble mentally" for the case by reviewing in your mind several important aspects of the case. Which of the following would be the LEAST important factor to review?**

   1. *The proposed incision site and surgical approach.*

   2. *The current status of the operating room.*

   3. *The anatomy involved in the procedure.*

   4. *The physiologic status of the patient.*

2. **In preparing for a surgical procedure, a perioperative nurse *first* considers those factors related to:**

   1. *the surgical procedure itself (e.g., counts, supplies, specimens).*

   2. *surgical complications (e.g., possible emergencies).*

   3. *the surgical approach (e.g., positioning, incision site).*

   4. *surgical closure (e.g., dressings).*

3. **To avoid omission in the preparation for a surgical procedure, the perioperative nurse should consider which of the following factors before the others?**

   1. *How should the specimens, if any, be prepared?*

   2. *What type of dressings will be used for the procedure?*

   3. *What unforeseen difficulty might arise during surgery that may require additional supplies or equipment?*

   4. *When are the counts to be performed?*

4. **The perioperative nurse's *first* step in creating a suitable environment for surgery is:**

   1. *preparing the procedure room.*

   2. *creating a sterile field.*

   3. *preparing the patient for surgery.*

   4. *assisting in anesthesia.*

5. **Instruments that will be used frequently during a surgical procedure are placed on the:**

    1. *ring stand.*

    2. *instrument table.*

    3. *operating table stand.*

    4. *Mayo stand.*

6. **Guidelines for the placement of packs and supplies in the operating room include all of the following EXCEPT:**

    1. *Place the sterile drape pack on the instrument table.*

    2. *Place the wrapped sterile basin set into one of the ring stands.*

    3. *Place the wrapped sterile instrument tray on top of the same ring stand as that holding the basin set.*

    4. *Place the scrubs' gown and gloves on the Mayo stand.*

7. **Use of kick buckets is restricted to:**

    1. *sponges soiled during surgery.*

    2. *soiled sponges and contaminated debris from the procedure.*

    3. *all trash in the operating room, contaminated or not.*

    4. *all contaminated trash in the operating room.*

8. **In selecting the proper packs, drapes, and supplies for a surgical procedure, the nurse should follow each of these guidelines EXCEPT:**

    1. *Determine the required supplies based on the anatomy and proposed procedure.*

    2. *Use the Physician's Preference Card to select the specialty/accessory items needed for the procedure.*

    3. *Carefully select the proper amount of supplies, to be cost-effective, following a logical sequential order of selection.*

    4. *Separate all supplies into two categories--standard and accessory--and place standard supplies into a sterile pack.*

9. **The *primary* supply needed to create a sterile field is the:**

    1. *sterile drape.*

    2. *covered ring stand.*

    3. *sterile pack.*

    4. *covered Mayo stand.*

10. **The appropriate sterile pack to use with a patient undergoing a gastrectomy is a(n):**

   1. *laparotomy pack.*

   2. *basic pack (table drape).*

   3. *specialty pack.*

   4. *extremity pack.*

11. **One common situation in which a basic pack (table drape) is used instead of a laparotomy pack is:**

   1. *when a fenestrated sheet is not required (e.g., some ear procedures).*

   2. *when a sterile drape sheet is not required (e.g., some specialty procedures).*

   3. *for many general abdominal and spinal procedures.*

   4. *when a vertical incision line is being used (e.g., a cystostomy).*

12. **For procedures such as hernia repairs and peripheral vascular surgery, the appropriate basin set is the:**

   1. *single or hand basin.*

   2. *"splash" basin.*

   3. *minor basin set.*

   4. *major basin set.*

13. **Which of the following is NOT one of the common uses of surgical sponges?**

   1. *To provide a bacterial barrier.*

   2. *To protect tissue from injury.*

   3. *For blunt dissection of delicate tissue.*

   4. *To absorb fluid and blood.*

14. **Perioperative nursing guidelines for the use of surgical sponges include all of the following EXCEPT:**

   1. *Once an incision has been made, use only those sponges with an X-ray-detectable feature at the sterile field.*

   2. *Count all sponges at proper intervals during the surgical procedure, according to acceptable protocol by both the scrub and circulating nurse.*

   3. *Always dampen sponges with saline solution prior to use.*

   4. *Always remove Ray-Tec sponges from the surgical field once any deep cavity has been entered, unless the sponge is folded and used on a "sponge stick."*

15. **The type of sponge that is *most* appropriate for use in neurosurgery and spinal procedures is the:**

    1. *laparotomy sponge.*

    2. *dissecting sponge.*

    3. *small lap sponge (tape).*

    4. *cottonoid.*

16. **Which of the following is regarded as a sterile *accessory* (not standard) surgical supply?**

    1. *Suction tips/tubings.*

    2. *Syringes.*

    3. *Irrigation solutions.*

    4. *Gowns and gloves.*

17. **Which of the following are normally considered *nonsterile* surgical supplies?**

    1. *Prep trays.*

    2. *Medications administered at the sterile field.*

    3. *Catheters, tubes, and drains.*

    4. *Dressing supplies.*

18. **One of the major functions of a Physician's Preference Card is to:**

    1. *create and maintain an infection-free surgical environment.*

    2. *identify specific preoperative diagnostic tests that will be or have been performed on a patient.*

    3. *provide an inventory of supplies and equipment specific to the procedure, surgeon, and patient.*

    4. *suggest general surgical approaches and procedures that might be used to treat the patient's condition.*

19. **Perioperative nursing guidelines for the opening of sterile supplies include all of the following EXCEPT:**

    1. *Open sponges, gowns, gloves, drape sheets, and towels on the instrument (back) table.*

    2. *Open scrub gown and gloves on the right corner of the back table.*

    3. *Open basin sets and the instrument tray on ring stands.*

    4. *Place small items and extra instruments in the basin or in the instrument tray.*

20. **Creating and maintaining the sterile field before and during surgery is the *principal* job of the:**

    1. *scrub person (nurse or technician).*

    2. *entire surgical team.*

   3. *circulating nurse.*

   4. *scrub person and circulating nurse.*

21. **The actual draping of a surgical patient is usually performed by the:**

   1. *scrub person, with assistance from the circulating nurse or the assistant to the surgeon.*

   2. *circulating nurse, with assistance from the scrub person or assistant to the surgeon.*

   3. *surgeon, with assistance from the scrub person or the assistant to the surgeon.*

   4. *assistant to the surgeon, with assistance from the scrub person or circulating nurse.*

22. **Perioperative nursing guidelines during the phase of a surgical procedure in which the sterile field is being monitored and maintained include all of the following EXCEPT:**

   1. *Never open sterile supplies and then leave them covered or unguarded during the preliminary phase of the sterile field's creation.*

   2. *Group all sterile supplies and equipment away from the patient, preferably on the instrument (back) table.*

   3. *Present sterile items to the scrub nurse or place them on the sterile field without reaching over the field.*

   4. *Keep all unsterile equipment, etc., a safe distance from the sterile field to avoid accidental contact with the field.*

23. **Perioperative nursing guidelines during the phase of a surgical procedure in which the sterile field is being terminated include all of the following EXCEPT:**

   1. *All members of the surgical team should keep their masks on during this period.*

   2. *All instruments, whether used or not, are considered contaminated and must be decontaminated according to acceptable protocol.*

   3. *Disassembling the sterile set must not be done until after the patient has left the operating room.*

   4. *Removal of the scrub's gown, gloves, and mask should be performed last.*

24. **Additional perioperative nursing guidelines during the phase of a surgical procedure in which the sterile field is being terminated include all of the following EXCEPT:**

   1. *After the last stitch is in place, and the area cleaned, the sterile dressing is applied by the circulating nurse and held in place while the drape sheets are removed by the scrub nurse.*

   2. *After the drape sheet has been removed, the scrub nurse, with the equipment, should step back to a position away from the operating table, where the actual termination procedure will take place.*

   3. *Instruments that have been used during the procedure should be hand cleaned using a basin of sterile water and a lap sponge or brush prior to terminal decontamination.*

   4. *All sharps, including cautery tips, blades, and hypodermic needles should be placed in a container (a needle-counter box can serve this purpose) and disposed of according to acceptable protocol.*

ANSWER EXPLANATIONS

1. **The answer is 2.** The process of "assembling mentally" begins long before the nurse enters the procedure room, regardless of the role being performed. Some of the questions to ask during this preparation period include knowledge of: the anatomy involved; the proposed incision site and surgical approach; the physiologic status of the patient; and the preferred supplies and equipment requested and how to use them safely and effectively.

2. **The answer is 3.** Four factors will determine the perioperative nurse's success in becoming a proficient member of the surgical team: surgical approach, surgical procedure, surgical complications, and surgical closure. These factors must be considered in correct sequential order, to avoid omission in the preparation for a surgical procedure. The first factor, surgical approach, includes questions such as: (1) how will the anatomic area involved be exposed? (2) how will the patient be positioned to provide maximum exposure? (3) where is the incision site; what area needs to be prepped; are there any allergies that would prevent the use of routine prep solutions?

3. **The answer is 4.** Both 1 and 4 are aspects of surgical procedure that the nurse should consider following an evaluation of the surgical approach (see Question 1). Consideration of counts, however, precedes that of the preparation of specimens. Choice 2 relates to surgical closure (the final factor to be considered in preparing for a surgical procedure); choice 3 relates to surgical complications (the third factor, following surgical procedure).

4. **The answer is 1.** The sterile field, and its usage, is composed of three distinct phases: (1) creation of the sterile field, (2) maintenance of the sterile field, and (3) termination of the sterile field. The first step in creating a suitable environment is related to the preparation of the procedure room, including the physical layout of furniture and equipment and the placement of supplies in a convenient location. Preliminary preparation of the room is done before each patient enters the room, and is a team effort by both the circulating nurse and the scrub person. Specific measures include: (1) damp dusting all flat surfaces and all portable or mounted equipment (PRN); (2) positioning the operating room table under the overhead light fixture; and (3) arranging the furniture needed for the specific procedure (e.g., instrument table, Mayo stand, and ring stands).

5. **The answer is 4.** The Mayo stand holds instruments that will be used frequently during the procedure. It is draped with a bacterial barrier, and then placed directly over, but not in contact with, the patient once the patient drapes have been applied. It is adjustable in height, and is totally portable, since it moves on wheels. During the set-up period, the stand should remain close to the other furniture to avoid possible contamination or accidental bumping of the stand. The instrument (back) table, once draped, provides a set-up area for sterile supplies to be used during the procedure, while the ring stand, once draped, is used to hold basin sets and/or instrument trays. It should be placed close to the instrument table, since it will become part of the sterile field during surgery.

6. **The answer is 3.** The wrapped sterile instrument tray should be placed on top of the other ring stand, not the one into which the sterile basin set was placed.

7. **The answer is 1.** The use of kick buckets (a bucket on wheels) is restricted to soiled sponges during surgery. It is lined with a disposable liner which can be removed and exchanged as required during the procedure without jeopardizing the sterility of the surgical field. All other trash should be placed in a larger trash receptacle. However, once the procedure has started, no trash may leave the room.

8. **The answer is 4.** Standard and accessory supplies are not separated, and are not necessarily placed into sterile packs.

9. **The answer is 3.** Packs are the primary supply needed to create a sterile field. Both packs and drape sheets are made of disposable, fluid-resistant material, which acts as a bacterial barrier against microbial infiltration. At the end of the procedure, all disposable items are discarded, reducing the possibility of

cross-contamination with another patient and the surgical environment. Three primary packs are commonly associated with surgical procedures: a laparotomy pack, a basic pack (table drape), and a specialty pack. Each pack has a list of contents conveniently printed on the reverse side of the pack. In some institutions, the use of a customized pack, one that contains specific items needed according to institutional preference, has been created, thus eliminating the need for obtaining additional items.

10. **The answer is 1.** A laparotomy pack is used on flat body surfaces with a vertical fenestration (hole) in the patient drape sheet. It is appropriate for general abdominal, pelvic, and spinal surgery, or any instance when a vertical incision line is used. Contents of a laparotomy pack (depending on manufacturer) include an overwrap/table cover, absorbent towels, utility towels (small), plastic Mayo stand cover, laparotomy sheet with fenestration, disposable gowns and absorbent hand towels, and Ray-Tec X-ray-detectable sponges.

11. **The answer is 1.** A basic pack (table drape) is used to create a "customized" pack for special procedures that require a specific fenestrated sheet or draping of an additional instrument table, or when a fenestrated sheet is not required. Its contents are the same as a laparotomy pack, minus the fenestrated sheet and sponges and usually with only one surgical gown. Sterile drape sheets, which come in various sizes and forms, with or without fenestrations, are usually used in conjunction with either a basic pack or as an added bacterial barrier for specific draping needs.

12. **The answer is 3.** Basin sets are available in either a reusable or disposable format, and contain the "pots and pans" needed for surgery. Three types of basin sets are usually found in the surgical suite; they may be used interchangeably or for a specific purpose. The contents will vary depending on the needs of the institution, and can be "customized" like custom packs. A minor basin set is used for procedures not requiring extra basins or graduated pitcher, such as hernia repairs, peripheral vascular procedures, and plastic surgery. It includes a large basin (1), round basin (1-2), and medicine glasses (2). A major basin set is used for procedures requiring large supplies of instruments, sponges, and so on (general, vascular, ortho). A single or hand basin is used to clean instruments.

13. **The answer is 1.** Surgical sponges are manufactured in a variety of shapes and sizes and serve three general purposes: to absorb fluid and blood; for blunt dissection of delicate tissue; and to protect tissue from injury.

14. **The answer is 3.** Depending on physician preference, surgical sponges--including Ray-Tec, laparotomy, small lap, cottonoid, dissecting, and tonsil/dental sponges--may be used wet (soaked in saline) or dry.

15. **The answer is 4.** Cottonoids (neuro patties), prepackaged in increments of 10 per package and available in a variety of sizes ranging from 1/4 x 1/4 to 3 x 3 inches, are used predominantly in neurosurgery and spinal procedures. Each patty has a string attached that is left outside the wound during its use. Patties are made of a soft, lint-free material so they will not injure or scratch delicate tissue/structures. Laparotomy sponges are used during major surgery or for absorbing fluid in large areas; small laps (tapes) are used in smaller areas when large sponges may not be applicable or advisable due to the nature of the incision, or in place of the Ray-Tec sponge; dissecting sponges are used to absorb blood in very small areas or "push" away delicate tissue.

16. **The answer is 2.** Sterile accessory supplies are those items not required for every procedure, or specifically requested by the surgeon. These include such items as cautery devices, monopolar pencils/tips, bipolar forceps, irrigation and hypodermicsyringes, needle counter (sharps container), sutures/needles (specific to surgeon request), catheters/tubes/drains, and dressing supplies (non-Ray-Tec 4 x 4's; ABD's; Telfa).

17. **The answer is 2.** In addition to the furniture and equipment mentioned earlier in this chapter, other nonsterile supplies are needed during the procedure and must be a part of the initial preparation phase, in order to avoid leaving the room to collect them during the procedure. Included among nonsterile supplies are positioning devices, special table pads, suction canisters, connecting tubings, and medications to be administered at the sterile field. These supplies either complement or assist in the usage of sterile supplies.

18. **The answer is 3.** For every surgical procedure performed in the operating room by a specific surgeon, a corresponding reference list of all supplies and equipment used for the procedure, in addition to the

supplies and equipment requested by the surgeon, should be created, and should be readily available wherever the cases are assembled, be it the operating room or in the instance of case cart assembly, in the central processing area. This card or computerized listing is referred to as a Physician's Preference Card, and can serve multiple purposes, including maintaining a inventory/charging list for a specific procedure by a specific surgeon for a specific patient. It is vitally important that all information remains current and that any changes that occur during the procedure are noted and communicated to the staff and personnel responsible for assembling and using the supplies, thereby avoiding delays in the procedure owing to improper selection. Not all supplies and equipment are specified on this reference list, but by knowing and understanding the standard and accessory supplies needed for the procedure, the surgical team can effectively prepare the procedure room for the planned surgical procedure.

19. **The answer is 2.** Before any sterile supplies are opened, the integrity of each package must be checked. Packages not meeting acceptable criteria should be placed aside, since they cannot be considered sterile, and new ones chosen. Each package must be opened under strict aseptic technique, thereby guaranteeing the sterility of the sterile field. Guidelines for opening sterile supplies in preparation for a surgical procedure include: (1) remove the tape from a C.S.R. wrapped package and check the indicator tape to be certain the item has been properly exposed to the sterilization process; (2) open the linen pack on the instrument table so that the inside of the wrapper becomes the sterile table cover; (3) open sponges, gowns, gloves, drape sheets, and towels on the back table; open blades on the right corner of the table; (4) open basin sets and the instruments tray on ring stands; if sequentially wrapped, both layers are opened; (5) place small items and extra instruments in the basin or in the instrument tray; maintain object in inner wrapper; and (6) open scrub gown and gloves on the Mayo stand.

20. **The answer is 1.** Although all surgical procedures require a cooperative effort, from the time the surgical scrub begins until the operation is finished and the dressings are applied, there is a definite line of demarcation between the duties and responsibilities of the scrub person and the circulating nurse that neither may cross. The circulating nurse performs those functions associated with the management of the room before, during, and after the procedure, while the scrub person (nurse or technician) performs all tasks related to the creation and maintenance of the sterile field before and during surgery, in addition to the care of the instruments when surgery is completed.

21. **The answer is 3.** To isolate the surgical wound from bacterial contamination, the patient must be covered with sterile drapes so that only the incisional site is exposed. The actual draping procedure is usually performed by the surgeon, with assistance from either the scrub person or the assistant to the surgeon.

22. **The answer is 2.** Once the patient is placed on the operating table, prepped and draped, he or she becomes the center of the sterile field, and all movement and activities in and around the field must be performed without compromise to that field. All sterile supplies and equipment should be grouped *around the patient*, and must be kept in view at all times by both the sterile and nonsterile members of the team. In addition to this guideline and to those in choices 1, 3, and 4, (1) sharp or heavy objects should be opened on a separate surface to avoid injury or possible contamination of the object during transfer; (2) should liquid be spilled, creating strike-through, the area must be reinforced with a sterile towel or drape since strike-through of fluids constitutes contamination of that sterile surface; (3) as always, if the sterility of an item, be it a towel, instrument, or needle, is in doubt it must be considered contaminated, removed from the field, and replaced by another sterile item; and (4) unsterile personnel should approach the field facing it and never walk between two sterile fields.

23. **The answer is 3.** It is important to terminate the sterile field in a safe and logical manner, and at the proper time. Until the patient has been prepared for transfer to the postoperative area, the environment must be maintained in an aseptic manner, in case an unforeseen emergency occurs that necessitates immediate action. Therefore, all members of the surgical team should keep their masks in place during this transition period. The criteria for disassembling the sterile set up calls for the patient to have left the room, but this is not realistic, since room turnover time is usually limited to 15 minutes maximum after a procedure is over (and may be longer for complicated procedures with excessive equipment). The next best approach is to begin the clean-up process during the closing phase of the procedure, leaving the Mayo

stand intact until the very end. This would still allow for the use of sterile equipment should an emergency situation arise necessitating reentry into the wound.

24. **The answer is 1.** Sterile dressing is applied by the scrub nurse and not the circulator; drapes are removed by the scrub nurse with assistance from the circulator. The drape sheet is removed inside out toward the foot of the table. Additional perioperative nursing guidelines include: (1) prior to disposing of drape material, it should be checked for instruments, since they may be still attached to the drapes during the dismantling phase; (2) disposable linen and cloth items should be placed in their respective bags for disposal; gloves must be worn during this process, even by the circulating nurse, since blood and fluids may still be present on the drape sheet; and (3) to avoid any unsightly transfer of instruments to the decontamination area, the tray(s) should be covered. Following these procedures, environmental services begins the interim cleaning process by removing the trash and linen from the room, followed by cleaning the floor and all surfaces according to institutional procedure.

9 The Perioperative Nursing Process

STUDY OUTLINE

I. INTRODUCTION

1. The *Nursing Process* offers the nurse a system for planning and providing patient care. Its goal is to identify the patient's actual or potential problems, to develop a plan to mediate the identified problems, to provide specific nursing actions or interventions, to resolve problems, and to evaluate continually the patient's response to care so that appropriate changes can be made in the plan to ensure an effective outcome. Hence, the nursing process is a dynamic and cyclical activity, continually changing in response to the patient's status.

2. The perioperative nurse uses the nursing process to plan and provide care during the three stages of surgical intervention: **preoperative**, **intraoperative**, and **postoperative**.

3. According to the scope of perioperative nursing practice as described by A.O.R.N.:
    a. The **preoperative phase** begins when the patient and physician make the decision for surgery and ends when the patient is transferred to the operating table.
    b. The **intraoperative phase** begins when the patient is transferred to the operating table and ends when the patient is transferred to the postanesthesia recovery area.
    c. The **postoperative phase** is the time from admission to the postanesthesia recovery area until the patient has recovered from the surgical event. The postoperative period includes time for resolution of the complications of surgery.

4. While the three stages of the perioperative experience are easily defined, the nursing process provides a care plan that includes the patient's needs in each stage and crosses all three stages. Once the patient has made the decision to have surgery, it is essential for the nurse to determine the current or actual and potential problems in **all three stages of the perioperative period**. After identifying patient problems, the perioperative nurse implements appropriate interventions to prevent untoward outcomes. The nursing process is an interactive process which, to be effective, requires the active participation of the patient.

II. STANDARDS OF PRACTICE AND THE NURSING PROCESS

1. The Association of Operating Room Nurses (A.O.R.N.) has developed (1975) and reaffirmed (1990) the *Standards of Perioperative Nursing Practice* to ensure that guidelines are available for delivering quality patient care during the perioperative period. The *Standards* are stated as:

    I. The collection of data about the health status of the individual is systematic and continuous. The data are retrievable and communicated to appropriate persons.
    II. Nursing diagnoses are derived from health status data.
    III. The plan of nursing care includes goals derived from the nursing diagnoses.
    IV. The plan of nursing care provides nursing actions to achieve the goals.
    V. The plan for nursing care is implemented.
    VI. The plan for nursing care is evaluated.

VII. Reassessment of the individual, reconsideration of nursing diagnoses, resetting of goals, and modification and implementation of the nursing care plan are a continuous process.

2. In assisting the patient as he or she prepares for surgery, the surgical unit nurse may develop an **initial care plan**, often in consultation with the perioperative nurse or the nurses who will care for the patient following surgery. The perioperative nurse relies on information provided by the floor nurse to continue the plan of care during surgery. The recovery nurse relies on information provided by the floor nurse and the perioperative nurse to provide care during the immediate postoperative period.

3. As the patient returns to the surgical unit to recover, the floor nurse will review the notes of the perioperative nurse and recovery room nurse to plan for the postsurgical care of the patient so that continuity of care continues.

III. ASSESSMENT

1. **Assessment is the first stage of the Nursing Process. It involves collection and validation of information about the patient.** While assessment is identified as the first stage, the nurse continues to assess the patient in all stages of the nursing process as he or she determines the appropriateness of decisions about the nursing diagnoses, plan, and interventions. Evaluation, in fact, becomes a reassessment of patient responses to the nursing care plan and the basis for future patient care planning.

A. COLLECTION OF DATA

1. The information gathered about the patient is called **data**. It is further broken down into **subjective data** and **objective data**.
    a. **Subjective data** is that which only the patient can experience--that is, it is not readily observable to the nurse or other caregivers. Examples of subjective data are pain, nausea, and itching. Another term for subjective data is **symptoms**. The perioperative nurse may collect subjective data from the patient when taking admission or health history (e.g., in the outpatient setting).
    b. **Objective data** is data that is observable or measurable by the caregiver. Examples of objective data include vital signs, observations made during the physical examination, and the results of laboratory or diagnostic studies. Another term used for objective data is **signs**.

2. Standard I states that the collection of data is systematic and continuous, and should be communicated to appropriate persons. Criteria used for meeting this standard should include such data as **current medical history, physiologic and psychologic status, understanding and perception of the planned surgical event**, and **previous medical and surgical history**.

3. For the surgical patient, assessment may begin before admission. Information about the past health history of the patient may be obtained in the physician's office and forwarded to the hospital, or in the case of outpatient surgery be sent to the ambulatory surgical unit.

4. **In many hospitals, perioperative nurses visit the prospective surgical patient to conduct a preoperative assessment and interview.** No matter how minor the surgical procedure, a thorough health history is essential and should be available to operating room staff at all times during the patient's surgical experience. Information about allergies, preexisting medical problems (e.g., heart conditions, hypertension, diabetes, blood dyscrasias and coagulation problems, chronic respiratory or renal problems), medications that the patient is currently taking, previous surgical experiences, and previous responses to anesthesia may have great significance for the present perioperative plan.

5. **In addition to previous health information, patient feelings and concerns about the proposed surgery may have an impact on the outcome.** Fear, anxiety, and depression can affect the patient's ability to cooperate with the proposed care plan.

B. PREOPERATIVE PATIENT ASSESSMENT

1. **Prior to surgery the patient must be assessed both physiologically and psychologically. Parameters of physiologic assessment should include the physical examination and review of the current diagnostic studies and laboratory values that will be used as baseline data.**

2. **Physical examination**
   a. The **physical examination** is a valuable part of the patient assessment. Baseline data regarding vital signs, cardiopulmonary function, bowel function, urinary function, nutritional status, and physical limitations are all important in developing the care plan for the perioperative experience.
   b. **Laboratory and diagnostic studies** help to validate the information obtained through the nursing history and physical examination. Most hospitals require specific diagnostic studies to determine the patient's ability to tolerate the surgical procedure. Additionally, the studies serve as a baseline for comparing laboratory and diagnostic findings obtained during and after surgery. Some of these studies include hemoglobin and hematocrit levels, blood typing, complete blood counts, coagulation studies, urinalysis, chest X-ray, and electrocardiogram.

3. **Baseline assessment components**
   a. **Vital signs**
      (1) Baseline vital signs including temperature, pulse, respirations, and blood pressure should be obtained. In addition to the pulse rate, the quality of the pulse and any irregularity in the pulse should be noted. In addition to the respiratory rate, the lungs should be assessed to determine the extent of preoperative lung expansion, breath sounds, and any difficulty the patient has with ventilation, deep breathing, or coughing.
      (2) The blood pressure should be taken on several occasions prior to surgery to establish an accurate baseline for the intraoperative and postoperative phases. Obtaining one blood pressure reading on a patient who is anxious may provide an inaccurate determination of hypertension.
   b. **Hemoglobin and hematocrit:** The hemoglobin (Hgb.) and hematocrit (Hct.) are obtained prior to surgery to determine the blood's ability to carry oxygen. A low hemoglobin or hematocrit may be reason to delay an elective procedure.
   c. **White blood cell count:** The white blood cell (W.B.C.) count is obtained to identify any preexisting infectious process. An elevated W.B.C. count may also be reason to delay or cancel elective surgery.
   d. **Blood typing and cross-matching (screening):** The patient's blood is typed and cross-matched in the event that replacement blood is required. If indicated, the patient's own blood can be filtered and returned to him or her in surgery via the **cell saver**. Patients may elect to bank their own blood for **autotransfusion** when there is sufficient time before an elective procedure.
   e. **Serum electrolytes:** Electrolyte studies (Na, K, Cl, Ca, Mg) are done preoperatively to determine any actual or potential imbalances. The three studies most often reviewed during the preoperative assessment are **potassium, sodium,** and **calcium.** These electrolytes are soon lost after an incision is made. A deficit state of electrolytes could produce potential intraoperative and postoperative complications.
   f. **Urinalysis:** A routine urinalysis is done to identify a urinary tract infection, and to determine whether glucose is present in the urine.
   g. **Chest x-ray**
      (1) The chest X-ray identifies lung pathology and the patient's postoperative ability perform deep breathing exercises. The physician and nurse may plan the postoperative respiratory support equipment and treatment according to the chest x-ray findings. Additionally, the chest x-ray shows heart size and location, an important factor in assessing cardiac function.
      (2) **Pulmonary function studies (arterial blood gases [A.B.G.'s])** may be ordered for a patient who has significant lung disease. This study is an important factor in the intraoperative management of anesthesia and the postoperative management of the patient.

     h. **Electrocardiogram**

        (1) The ECG is routinely done preoperatively to detect any cardiac disease that may affect the patient either intraoperatively or postoperatively. Patients with cardiac disease are at greater risk for problems during surgery than are noncardiac patients. Cardiac conditions that are relative contraindications to elective surgery include **recent angina pectoris, unstable angina, severe aorta stenosis, uncontrolled hypertension,** and a **myocardial infarction** within the past 6 months.

     i. Additional studies may be done preoperatively according to the specific procedure planned (e.g., C.T. scan, cardiac catheterization, arteriogram, and diagnostic X-rays). The results of all studies should be available on the patient's record when he or she goes to the operating suite. Often the surgeon will request the diagnostic X-rays be sent to the suite to be used as a reference during the procedure.

     j. **Psychologic assessment:** The patient's understanding of and response to the proposed surgical procedure needs to be assessed. Most patients will experience some degree of anxiety when undergoing surgery; therefore, the nurse must not only identify the reasons for the anxiety or fear, but also determine the support systems and coping mechanisms the patient has for dealing with these feelings. In some cases, anxiety may be incapacitating to the point of placing the patient at risk. In such situations, surgery may be postponed until the patient is better able to cope.

    4. As all information obtained during the preoperative assessment will be used in planning for care during the preoperative, intraoperative, and postoperative phases of patient care, it is essential that it be transmitted completely and accurately to all potential caregivers. To facilitate communication of the preoperative assessment findings, many hospitals use a separate **preoperative assessment form** or combine it with a **perioperative assessment form,** reflecting all three phases of surgical intervention.

C. INTRAOPERATIVE PATIENT ASSESSMENT

    1. **The assessment of the patient continues into the intraoperative phase, and is usually associated with admission to the surgical suite.**

    2. Initial assessment in the surgical suite will determine the patient's preparedness for surgery, and primarily consists of the following observations:
- Identification/verification
- Confirmation of consents and permits for surgery and anesthesia
- History and physical report by the physician(s)
- Laboratory and diagnostic testing results
- Status of parenteral fluid administration
- Urinary output
- Responses to preoperative medications
- Emotional status of the patient

    3. In the procedure room, assessment continues in order to compare the patient's status with preoperative parameters and expected postoperative outcome. Ongoing assessment during the surgical procedure will routinely include **vital signs, blood loss, skin color,** and **drainage.** Additionally, prior to final suturing, all sponges, instruments, and sharps will be counted as the perioperative nurse assesses the final outcome of the surgical procedure.

    4. Prior to discharge from the procedure, the perioperative nurse, along with the anesthesiologist/anesthesia clinician, will assess the patient's wound dressing, respiratory status, drainage tubes for patency, collection chambers for amounts, status of parenteral infusion lines, and general readiness to be transferred to the postanesthesia area.

D. POSTOPERATIVE PATIENT ASSESSMENT

    1. **In the immediate postoperative area--usually the postanesthesia care unit (P.A.C.U.)--the initial assessment should include vital signs, color, activity level, and neurologic status using the Aldrette Recovery Scoring System.** Subsequently, additional parameters of patient function will

be assessed throughout the immediate postoperative period, including levels of consciousness, dressings and drainage, pain levels, parenteral infusion, patient safety, and any specific assessments directly related to the type of procedure that was performed.

2. Prior to discharge from the P.A.C.U., the patient is again assessed using the Aldrette Scoring System, and using a preestablished criteria for discharge. Discharge from P.A.C.U. *requires a physician's order*, which is usually given after he or she has reviewed the Aldrette score and assessed the patient.

3. Assessments conducted and care provided in the postanesthesia care unit are documented to ensure adequate communication to the floor nurse.

4. The P.A.C.U. nurse will usually accompany the patient to the floor to give a verbal report, and the assessment continues as the floor nurse, using the same parameters as the P.A.C.U. nurse, continues to monitor the patient's progress through the next phase of the surgical experience.

IV. DIAGNOSIS

A. NATURE OF NURSING DIAGNOSES

1. Standard II for perioperative nursing practices relates to the creation of *Nursing Diagnoses* which are derived from information accumulated during the assessment activities. These statements reflect current problems that may or may not be specifically identified; they are communicated to other members of the health-care team to maintain continuity of care.

2. **The nursing diagnosis is the judgment or conclusion of the patient's health problem(s) made after reviewing all assessment data.** Nursing diagnoses may represent *actual* or *potential* problems.
   a. **Actual problems** are ones the patient currently exhibits during assessment.
   b. **Potential problems** are those that the patient is not presently experiencing, but may develop if appropriate interventions are not implemented. Examples of potential problems for the surgical patient in the intraoperative phase are the risk for skin breakdown during prolonged procedures, or the risk of trauma from a fall if transport cart siderails and safety belts are not used for a confused, unconscious, or sedated patient.

3. **Nursing versus medical diagnoses**
   a. Nursing diagnoses are different from medical diagnoses in that medical diagnoses identify specific disease processes, while nursing diagnoses identify the patient's responses to a disease, injury, or situation.
   b. Other differences are that nursing diagnoses focus on the *patient* not the disease, and that they change as the patient's condition changes, while medical diagnoses usually remain the same during the course of treatment.

4. **Prioritizing diagnoses**
   a. A patient may have many nursing diagnoses, actual or potential, at any one time. Nursing diagnoses are prioritized by their relative importance for being resolved. For example, a nursing diagnosis of *Alteration in gas exchange* would normally take priority over a nursing diagnosis of *Knowledge deficit*, since gas exchange problems can be life-threatening.
   b. New nursing diagnoses are added and prioritized as the patient's health status changes. As new ones are identified, old ones that have been resolved are deleted, thus providing accurate and current data regarding potential or actual problems during the continuing process.
   c. Nursing diagnoses guide and direct independent nursing activities. They may be an expression of a patient's physiologic, psychologic, social, developmental, or cultural needs.

5. **A nursing diagnosis not only is a statement of the problem, but includes the causative factor.** Manifesting data that support the diagnostic statement may also be included. An example of an appropriately worded nursing diagnosis for the perioperative patient is *Pain related to surgical incision*. Manifestations of the nursing diagnosis may include verbal expression, increased pulse, and increased respirations.

B. **STAGES OF DIAGNOSIS**

1. **Preoperative nursing diagnoses**
   a. **Several nursing diagnoses may be identified during the preoperative phase.** They may also occur during the other phases of the perioperative period, and because the statements are not specific to any given patient, they could be actual or potential, depending upon the individual patient's situation. Included among these diagnoses are the following:
      (1) Anxiety
         • Potential, related to unfamiliar environment
         • Related to impending surgery and/or diagnosis
         • Potential alteration in body image
      (2) Activity intolerance
      (3) Decisional conflict related to surgical choices
      (4) Anticipatory grieving related to possible changes in body image
      (5) Sleep pattern disturbance related to anxiety
      (6) Potential for injury-trauma
         • Related to sedation
         • Skin integrity related to positioning
      (7) Knowledge deficit related to:
         • Sequence of events; perioperative period
         • Surgical procedure
         • Effective techniques for deep breathing, coughing, turning, and ambulation
   b. Additional preoperative nursing diagnoses are related to the specific physical disease or injury process requiring surgical intervention. An example of such a nursing diagnosis might be *Gas exchange, impaired, related to cancer of the lung*. Coexisting medical problems may necessitate additional nursing diagnoses.

2. **Intraoperative nursing diagnoses**
   a. **General factors that may guide the nurse's thinking about the intraoperative patient's nursing diagnoses include the specific procedure being performed, the type of anesthesia being used (i.e., local, general, regional), and the patient's general preoperative health status.** The following are some common nursing diagnoses appropriate for the intraoperative patient:
      (1) Hypothermia
      (2) Potential for injury-trauma
         • Neuromuscular damage related to improper positioning
         • Burns related to chemical or electrical hazards
         • Nosocomial infection
         • Potential for retainment of foreign objects
         • Physical hazards
      (3) Impaired skin integrity related to:
         • Surgical incision
         • Immobility
         • Improper positioning
      (4) Fluid and electrolyte balance; deficit or excess
      (5) Impaired gas exchange related to general anesthesia
      (6) Potential for alteration in tissue perfusion
         • Decreased peripheral circulation
         • Related to interruption of flow by outside constricting factors
      (7) Potential for alteration in cardiac output
         • Decreased cardiac output related to improper positioning and/or anesthesia
   b. Additionally, more specific nursing diagnoses may be required depending upon the patient's status or the specific surgical procedure.

3. **Postoperative nursing diagnoses**
   a. **Most potential postoperative patient problems can be identified preoperatively and appropriate interventions planned.** Other postoperative patient problems may evolve related

to complications of surgery. Some of the common postoperative nursing diagnoses associated with the immediate postoperative phase are:
(1) Potential for ineffective airway clearance related to decreased level of consciousness
(2) Potential for infection
- Related to poor incision healing
- Related to inadequate lung expansion
- Related to impaired mobility
(3) Alteration in comfort related to surgical incision
(4) Body image disturbance related to surgery
(5) Potential for injury related to sedation
(6) Potential impaired gas exchange related to incision pain
(7) Potential for ineffective participation in rehabilitation process

b. Early recognition of potential problems and early intervention can provide the patient with a smooth postoperative course and swift recovery. Nursing diagnoses therefore are the judgment statements that reflect the patient problems as identified by the assessment data. They then become the foundation upon which to develop a plan for patient care and specific nursing interventions.

c. Regardless of their format, nursing diagnoses must be documented to enhance communication between health-care providers.

V. PLANNING

1. **Planning is the third stage of the Nursing Process, and involves cooperation between the nurse, the patient's support systems, and other health-care providers involved in the patient's care. Planning involves the establishment of specific goals and/or outcome criteria for the individual patient.**

2. Some important points to remember about patient outcome criteria are:
   a. Patient outcome goals are patient-focused; that is, they state clearly what the patient will be able to do.
   b. Patient outcomes are the observable and measurable physiologic and psychologic responses to planned nursing interventions.
   c. Outcome criteria include an expected time of accomplishment or completion.

A. OUTCOME STANDARDS

1. The A.O.R.N. identifies six patient outcome standards for perioperative nursing (1983), which have been derived from Standard III of the *Standards of Practice*, and state: *The plan of nursing care includes goals derived from the nursing diagnosis*. These goals or outcome standards focus on potential high-incidence problem areas of the surgical patient, including **knowledge of the response to surgical intervention, freedom from infection and harm, maintenance of skin integrity and fluid and electrolyte balance,** and **participation in the rehabilitation process.**

2. Each of these outcome standards have specific criteria to assist the perioperative nurse in determining whether the standards have been met, but it is the individual nurse's responsibility to adapt, modify, and add outcome criteria that are appropriate to the individual patient's situation.

B. DOCUMENTING THE CARE PLAN

1. **Most institutions still require a patient care plan to be completed for each patient.** These care plans serve as a guide for managing and directing patient care. The Joint Commission for Health Care Organizations (J.C.A.H.O.) currently requires written, goal-directed care plans to indicate that quality patient care, according to acceptable standards, has been administered to all patients.

2. Patient care plans should contain the following elements:
   a. What nursing actions are to be performed.
   b. How the nursing actions are to be performed.

      c. When the nursing actions are to be performed.
      d. Where the nursing actions are to be performed.
      e. Who is to perform these actions.

VI. IMPLEMENTATION AND INTERVENTION

A. TYPES OF INTERVENTIONS

1. **During implementation, the nurse continues to assess the patient and the responses to surgical/medical intervention and surgical nursing care. Implementation includes all the nursing interventions directed toward resolving the patient's nursing diagnoses.**
2. **Nursing interventions are those activities carried out by the nurse to assist the patient to achieve the outcome criteria.** Nursing interventions may be **independent, interdependent** (collaborative), or **dependent** and are written in the form of **protocols.**
3. Included among nursing interventions for the perioperative patient are promotion of physical and psychologic comfort, support of cardiopulmonary function, promotion of safety, promotion of skin integrity, support of elimination functions, maintenance of fluid and electrolyte balance, promotion of nutrition, personal hygiene care, functional rehabilitation, and education of the patient, family, and significant others who are part of the patient's support system.
4. **Independent nursing interventions** are activities the perioperative nurse institutes based on her or his own judgment; that is, a physician's order is not needed (e.g., conducting counts at specified intervals during the procedure).
5. **Interdependent** or **collaborative nursing interventions** are activities performed jointly with another health-care provider (e.g., physician) or instituted after a decision made by the nurse with another health-care provider (e.g., blood administration directed by the anesthesiologist, or positioning the patient with the surgeon).
6. **Dependent nursing interventions** are those that require physician direction either in the form of a written order, direct supervision, or standard protocols. Implementation includes all the nursing interventions that are directed toward resolving the patient's nursing diagnoses (e.g., specific instruments requested by the surgeon for a selected case or the use of specific medications).

B. CHARACTERISTICS OF NURSING INTERVENTIONS

1. **Preoperative interventions: Preoperative interventions are primarily directed toward the patient for the proposed surgical intervention.** They include:
   a. Patient and family education.
   b. Patient preparation, including care of preexisting health problems.
   c. Family/significant other preparation.
2. **Intraoperative interventions**
   a. **Interventions during the intraoperative phase are generally directed toward providing a safe environment and protecting the patient from injury.** As all members of the surgical team are present, the patient care provided is generally of a collaborative nature, with each member assuming responsibility for predetermined activities including:
       (1) Performance in the scrub person's role.
       (2) Performance in the circulating nurse's role.
       (3) Management of personnel, materials, and environment.
   b. Although the responsibilities of the scrub and circulating nurses may seem to be a series of tasks, it is important to remember that they are interventions aimed at maintaining the goals of patient safety, keeping the patient free from harm and infection, and assuring optimal recovery.
3. **Postoperative interventions**
   a. **Postoperative interventions are directed toward preventing infection, promoting optimal healing, and preventing complications, both during the *immediate* and *intermediate* phases of recovery.** Some of the activities related to this phase include:

      (1) Monitoring and evaluating the patient's status.

      (2) Managing patient care, including pain, fluid status, cardiopulmonary status, and positioning.

      (3) Assessing nutritional status and needs.

      (4) Providing rehabilitation, counseling, and emotional support.

    b. The specific interventions for every surgical patient are too numerous to list here, and so the reader is referred to the subsequent chapters in this guide and to Chapter 14 of Susan Fairchild's text, *Perioperative Nursing*, in addition to medical-surgical or standard care plan books to obtain more information about nursing interventions for specific surgical procedures.

VII. EVALUATION

1. **Evaluation is the last stage of the Nursing Process, and it becomes the basis for modifications to the overall care plan. It is the time for comparing the patient's postintervention status with the expected outcomes or outcome criteria, which includes communication and documentation for the patient, other health-care personnel, and significant others.**

2. Written communication of patient achievement will be done by the nurse, either in the patient's record and/or the patient care plan. It is the nurse's judgment whether communication to the patient and significant others be done verbally or in writing, and will also be dependent on the individual institutional policies. Depending upon the patient's status, the nurse makes judgments about the resolution or modification of existing nursing diagnoses and the addition of new nursing diagnoses.

3. Standard VII states that: *Reassessment of the individual, reconsideration of nursing diagnoses, resetting of goals and modification and implementation of the nursing care plan are a continuous process.* Hence evaluation can be viewed as the last step as well as the first step in on-going care planning. The criteria used to achieve this standard are based on observation of patient responses and the perception of the patient and significant others of the quality of patient care administered during the perioperative period.

4. **Evaluation must be conducted in an organized way, looking first at each nursing diagnosis, the prescribed patient outcomes, and the patient's level of accomplishment for each expected outcome.** For example, if the patient outcome is that he or she will be free of infection, the nurse would look at whether or not he or she has any infectious problems or complications associated with an infection. If the wound is clean, but the patient has developed a postoperative pneumonia, the nurse would maintain the existing care plan relative to the incision, and develop a more aggressive plan of care with specific interventions to resolve the postoperative pneumonia.

VIII. PATIENT CARE PLANS FOR THE PERIOPERATIVE PERIOD

A. NATURE OF CARE PLANS

1. **A plan of care could be described as a portrait of a patient's surgical experience, and describes the nursing interventions the patient needs to accomplish the stated outcome goals.**

2. There are a number of proposed formats for care plans, ranging from individual documents in kardex form to those incorporated into the operative record, but they have one common factor: they must be flexible and be individualized to meet the specific needs of the patient.

3. The process of developing a care plan that meets the needs of the individual and institutional criteria has become an on-going process, one that is still evolving. The care plan should be integrated with the *A.O.R.N. Patient Outcome Standards*, however, and contain certain key elements:

    a. The plan should reflect coordination with the overall plan of medical care.

    b. The plan should include actions that will ensure maximum physical and emotional safety and security for the patient during the intraoperative period.

    c. The plan should be based on both scientific knowledge and patient information derived during the preoperative assessment, and be therapeutically effective.

    d. The plan should reflect the immediate health and emotional needs of the patient having surgery and should include long-term planning in order to help the patient achieve or maintain optimum health status.

    e. The plan should include patient-family preparation in the rehabilitation process, including self-care and discharge planning.

    f. The plan should reflect and/or include outcome goals revised to meet the individual patient needs.

B. CREATING STANDARDIZED CARE PLANS

1. Although an individualized care plan must be developed, the format, or *style* of the care plan has never been specified, only that the components reflect the nursing process: assessment, implementation, and evaluation.

2. **Standards of care: The Marker model**

    a. Throughout this chapter we have referred to the *A.O.R.N. Standards of Practice* as the basis for implementing perioperative nursing care. For perioperative nursing, the **standards of practice form the basis for acceptable or recommended nursing practice during the three phases of surgical intervention.**

    b. **Standards of care**, however, are different. According to Marker, *Standards of Care* **define the level of practice that directly relates to the quality of care a patient receives.** They are developed through a *systematic* approach, which uses a hierarchical structure to define and delineate nursing practice, referred to as the *Marker Model for Standard Development* (1988).

    c. In this model, Marker refers to three types of nursing standards: **Structure, Process** and **Outcome.** In order to use the model effectively, nurses must be aware of how these standards impact their practice of nursing. Therefore, a brief description of each standard will be presented.

        (1) **Structure standards:** Structure standards form the basis for all activity within a given institution. They describe how the system operates and the mechanisms needed to operate that system; for example, standards applicable to the Department of Nursing within the hospital, or how a specific nursing unit operates within the department.

        (2) **Process standards:** In contrast, process standards define the actions or behaviors used to provide care to the patient, and the criteria for performing that care effectively, safely, and proficiently. Examples include the Position Description of the R.N., Procedures Used for Nursing Care, and Standard Care Plans that reflect the planning and management of the nursing care provided.

        (3) **Outcome standards:** Outcome standards are the end result of nursing intervention, and are expressed either as what the nurse should accomplish (nursing goals) or what the patient should be able to do (patient outcomes). Examples include patient outcomes and nursing goals related to patient teaching or the planning of patient care.

    d. *Standards of Care*, then, according to the Marker model, are the highest level of Process Standards, since they represent a written plan of care developed to assist the nurse in providing effective nursing care.

    e. Standards of care can be created in two different styles, depending on the type of patient and/or the area involved with the care of the patient. For patients requiring hospitalization for 48 hours or longer, the Marker model recommends the use of a *Standard Care Plan (S.C.P.)*, which provides for periodic evaluation of the patient's progress and the care given to accomplish the patient outcome goals listed. However, since some areas are a transitional area, where patients are only in the area for a short period of time (less than 48 hours), the Marker model recommends the use of the *Standard Care Statement (S.C.S.)* as a means for describing the nursing care provided.

C. **DOCUMENTING THE CARE PLAN**

1. Regardless of the style (Standard Care Plans or Standard Care Statements), care plans should be **preprinted, individualized, and used for the duration of the patient's stay,** although the Standard Care Plan will be reviewed and revised as needed.

2. By standardizing and differentiating the variety of activities performed by the perioperative nurse for the benefit of quality patient care, a systematic approach can individualize a plan of care, using the *Standards of Practice.* In addition to the accurate documentation on the intraoperative record, the care plan creates a comprehensive picture of how the patient's care was planned and executed during the perioperative period, and the patient's response to that intervention.

3. Other types of care plans can be used, in addition to the Marker model, that will accomplish the same goal, though not in the same way. For example, a care plan could be designed around a specific procedure, position, patient outcome, or a specific nursing diagnosis, using a generic concept for design, and modifying the plan as needed to fit the individual patient. In some institutions, the care plan is incorporated into the intraoperative record (Perioperative Nursing Record); this too is acceptable to J.C.A.H.O. as long as it shows that the plan of care was achieved.

4. The specific type of care plan designed should enable the perioperative nurse to plan the patient's care effectively, using the Nursing Process format for generic terminology and the *Perioperative Standards of Practice, Patient Outcome Standards,* and *Competency Statements* as a basis for the implementation and evaluation of the plan.

5. The patient care plan, if not incorporated into the perioperative nursing record, should be referred to on the intraoperative nurse's notes, since most "care plans" are not part of the patient's permanent record. For example:

Standard Care Plan Followed?
Yes [ ]   No [ ]   **If no, list exceptions:**

6. By combining the appropriate model for patient care planning with precise documentation, routine nursing care activities are identified and a foundation for nursing action can be evaluated.

PRACTICE QUESTIONS

1. **According to the scope of perioperative nursing practice as described by A.O.R.N., the preoperative phase begins when the:**

    1. *patient is admitted for assessment and diagnosis.*

    2. *plan for perioperative nursing care is submitted.*

    3. *patient makes the decision for surgery.*

    4. *patient is transferred to the operating table.*

2. **Using the A.O.R.N.'s definition, the perioperative nurse's role ends with the conclusion of the postoperative phase of surgery, which is when the patient:**

    1. *leaves the procedure room.*

    2. *is admitted to the postanesthesia recovery area.*

    3. *is released from the surgical unit.*

    4. *has recovered from the surgical event.*

3. **Which of the following statements about patient assessment during the perioperative period is correct?**

   1. *It ends when the patient is transferred to the operating table.*

   2. *It includes goals derived from the nursing diagnoses.*

   3. *It is the judgment of the patient's health problem(s) made after reviewing all health-status data.*

   4. *It continues throughout the perioperative period.*

4. **A patient admitted for surgery reports pain in the abdominal area. This type of information is most accurately called:**

   1. *subjective data.*

   2. *symptom validation.*

   3. *psychologic assessment.*

   4. *a baseline assessment component.*

5. **In conducting a preoperative assessment and interview, a perioperative nurse requests information about the past health history of the patient. Which of the following would usually NOT be part of this health history?**

   1. *A list of medications the patient is currently taking.*

   2. *Information about preexisting medical problems (e.g., diabetes, allergies, etc.).*

   3. *Previous responses to anesthesia.*

   4. *Objective data, including baseline assessment components.*

6. **An important function of laboratory and diagnostic studies done on patients prior to surgery is to:**

   1. *validate the information obtained through the nursing history and physical examination.*

   2. *generate a list of specific symptoms that may guide the surgeon in choosing a surgical approach.*

   3. *establish a baseline of subjective data that can be used to compare with the patient's status throughout the perioperative period.*

   4. *serve as the basis for a patient care plan prepared by the perioperative nurse.*

7. **Which of the following pairings between a laboratory or diagnostic study and one function of this study as a preoperative assessment tool is NOT correct?**

   1. *Pulmonary function studies: to assist in the intraoperative management of anesthesia.*

   2. *White blood cell count: to identify preexisting infection.*

   3. *Urinalysis: to determine the presence of potassium, sodium, and calcium in the urine.*

   4. *Electrocardiogram: to detect any cardiac disease that may affect the patient.*

8. **The nurse's preoperative psychologic assessment of the patient can be essential in helping to:**

   1. *determine the coping mechanisms the patient has for his or her feelings of anxiety.*

   2. *categorize subjective data reported by the patient in the health history.*

   3. *provide a physiologic baseline for the patient throughout the perioperative period.*

   4. *support the results of laboratory and diagnostic studies done on the patient.*

9. **Prior to discharge from the procedure room, the perioperative nurse, along with the anesthesiologist/ anesthesia clinician, will assess several aspects of the patient's physical status. Included are all of the following EXCEPT:**

   1. *drainage tubes for patency.*

   2. *collection chambers for amounts.*

   3. *hemoglobin for O_2 concentration.*

   4. *wound dressing.*

10. **Nursing and medical diagnoses differ in several respects. One of these differences is that nursing diagnoses:**

    1. *identify specific disease processes.*

    2. *change as the patient's condition changes.*

    3. *generally focus on actual rather than potential problems.*

    4. *are communicated to other members of the surgical staff.*

11. **Which of the following nursing diagnoses would probably assume the *highest* priority?**

    1. *Potential for injury-trauma related to sedation.*

    2. *Fluid and electrolyte deficit.*

    3. *Alteration in comfort related to surgical incision.*

    4. *Impaired skin integrity due to immobility.*

12. **"A nursing diagnosis not only is a statement of the problem, but includes the *causative factor*." Which of the following illustrates a causative factor in a nursing diagnosis?**

    1. *Verbal expression of pain.*

    2. *Ineffective airway clearance.*

    3. *Impaired skin integrity.*

    4. *Electrolyte deficit or excess.*

13. Several nursing diagnoses relating to a patient's psychologic status may be identified during the preoperative phase of surgery. Which of the following would NOT fall clearly into this category?

    1. *Decisional conflict related to surgical choices.*

    2. *Anxiety related to potential alteration in body image.*

    3. *Activity intolerance.*

    4. *Knowledge deficit related to surgical procedure.*

14. Among the *general* factors that may guide the nurse's thinking about nursing diagnoses during the intraoperative period are all of the following EXCEPT:

    1. the specific procedure being performed.

    2. *the type of anesthesia being used.*

    3. *the patient's general preoperative health status.*

    4. *the patient's tolerance of inactivity.*

15. An example of a common postoperative nursing diagnosis associated with the immediate postoperative phase is:

    1. *Impaired skin integrity related to improper positioning.*

    2. *Potential for impaired gas exchange related to inadequate lung expansion.*

    3. *Potential for retainment of foreign objects.*

    4. *Potential for burns related to chemical or electrical hazards.*

16. Which of the following statements about patient outcome criteria is correct?

    1. *Patient outcome statements are nursing-focused; they state what the nurse expects the outcomes to be.*

    2. *Patient outcome criteria have no set time limits; they may require more or less time to meet depending on criteria for completion.*

    3. *Not all patient outcomes are observable or measurable; some can only be implied.*

    4. *Patient outcome statements are derived from nursing diagnoses; they focus on potential high-incidence problem areas.*

17. *The patient will demonstrate recovery without infection.* This statement is best defined as a(n):

    1. *outcome standard.*

    2. *nursing intervention.*

    3. *nursing diagnosis.*

    4. *care plan.*

18. *Assess IV fluid, rate and site, prior to and following procedure.* **This statement is best defined as a(n):**

    1. *outcome standard.*

    2. *nursing intervention.*

    3. *nursing diagnosis.*

    4. *potential care problem.*

19. *Perform sponge, needle, and instrument count prior to, during, and after procedure per policy.* **This statement is best defined a(n):**

    1. *independent nursing intervention.*

    2. *interdependent nursing intervention.*

    3. *dependent nursing intervention.*

    4. *collaborative nursing intervention.*

20. **Interventions during the intraoperative phase are generally directed toward:**

    1. *evaluating the patient's psychologic condition.*

    2. *providing rehabilitation, counseling, and emotional support.*

    3. *protecting the patient from injury.*

    4. *assessing nutritional status and need.*

21. **Evaluation takes into account three important and closely related features of the patient care plan. Which of the following is NOT one of these features?**

    1. *The specified nursing diagnoses.*

    2. *The prescribed patient outcomes.*

    3. *The appropriate intraoperative nursing interventions.*

    4. *The patient's level of accomplishment for each expected outcome.*

22. **An appropriate and effective nursing care plan includes several elements. Which of the following is NOT one of these elements?**

    1. *The plan should reflect the immediate health and emotional needs of the patient having surgery.*

    2. *The plan should include patient-family preparation in the rehabilitation process, including self-care and discharge planning.*

    3. *The plan should reflect and/or include outcome goals revised to meet the individual patient needs.*

    4. *The plan should focus on the nursing care of the patient and remain separate from the surgeon's medical plan.*

23. Perioperative *standards of care* differ from *standards of practice*, although the two are closely related during the three stages of surgical intervention. One way they differ is that:

    1. *standards of care form the basis for acceptable nursing practice during surgical intervention.*

    2. *standards of practice define the actions or behaviors used to provide care to the patient, and the criteria for performing that care effectively, safely, and proficiently.*

    3. *standards of care define the level of practice that directly relates to the quality of care a patient receives.*

    4. *standards of practice are the end result of nursing intervention, and are expressed either as what the nurse should accomplish (nursing goals) or what the patient should be able to do (patient outcomes).*

ANSWER EXPLANATIONS

1. **The answer is 3.** The preoperative stage begins when the patient and physician make the decision for surgery and ends when the patient is transferred to the operating table.

2. **The answer is 4.** Once the patient has made the decision to have surgery, the nurse should determine the current or actual and potential problems in all three stages of the perioperative period. After identifying patient problems, the perioperative nurse implements appropriate interventions to prevent untoward outcomes. The intraoperative phase begins when the patient is transferred to the operating table and ends when the patient is transferred to the postanesthesia recovery area. The postoperative phase is the time from admission to the postanesthesia recovery area *until the patient has recovered from the surgical event*. The postoperative period includes time for resolution of the complications of surgery. While the three stages of the perioperative experience are easily defined, the nursing process provides a care plan that includes the patient's needs in each stage and crosses all three stages.

3. **The answer is 4.** Assessment is the first stage of the Nursing Process. It involves collection and validation of information about the patient. While assessment is identified as the first stage, the nurse continues to assess the patient in all stages of the nursing process as he or she determines the appropriateness of decisions about the nursing diagnoses, plan, and interventions. Evaluation, in fact, becomes a reassessment of patient responses to the nursing care plan and the basis for future patient care planning.

4. **The answer is 1.** The information gathered about the patient is called data. **Subjective data** is that which only the patient can experience--that is, it is not readily observable to the nurse or other caregivers. Examples of subjective data are pain, nausea, and itching. Another term for subjective data is symptoms. The perioperative nurse may collect subjective data from the patient when taking admission or health history (e.g., in the outpatient setting). **Objective data** is data that is observable or measurable by the caregiver. Examples of objective data include vital signs, observations made during the physical examination, and the results of laboratory or diagnostic studies. Another term used for objective data is signs.

5. **The answer is 4.** In many hospitals, perioperative nurses visit the prospective surgical patient to conduct a preoperative assessment and interview. No matter how minor the surgical procedure, a thorough health history is essential and should be available to operating room staff at all times during the patient's surgical experience. Information about allergies, preexisting medical problems (e.g., heart conditions, hypertension, diabetes, blood dyscrasias and coagulation problems, chronic respiratory or renal problems), medications that the patient is currently taking, previous surgical experiences, and previous responses to anesthesia may have great significance for the present perioperative plan. In addition to previous health information, patient feelings and concerns about the proposed surgery may have an impact on the outcome. Fear, anxiety, and depression can affect the patient's ability to cooperate with the proposed care plan.

6. **The answer is 1.** Prior to surgery the patient must be assessed both physiologically and psychologically. Parameters of physiologic assessment include the physical examination and review of the current diagnostic

studies and laboratory values that will be used as objective baseline data. Laboratory and diagnostic studies help to validate the information obtained through the nursing history and physical examination. Most hospitals require specific diagnostic studies to determine the patient's ability to tolerate the surgical procedure. Additionally, the studies serve as a baseline for comparing laboratory and diagnostic findings obtained during and after surgery. Some of these studies include hemoglobin and hematocrit levels, blood typing, complete blood counts, coagulation studies, urinalysis, chest X-ray, and electrocardiogram.

7. **The answer is 3.** A routine urinalysis is done to identify a urinary tract infection, and to determine whether glucose is present in the urine. In addition to the studies in choices 1, 2, and 4: (1) the hemoglobin (Hgb.) and hematocrit (Hct.) are obtained prior to surgery to determine the blood's ability to carry oxygen; a low hemoglobin or hematocrit may be reason to delay an elective procedure; (2) the patient's blood is typed and cross-matched in the event that replacement blood is required; (3) serum electrolyte studies (especially Na, K, and Ca) are done preoperatively to determine any actual or potential imbalances; these electrolytes are soon lost after an incision is made, and a deficit state of electrolytes could produce potential intraoperative and postoperative complications; (4) the chest X-ray identifies lung pathology and the patient's postoperative ability to perform deep breathing exercises; the physician and nurse may plan the postoperative respiratory support equipment and treatment according to the chest x-ray findings; additionally, the chest x-ray shows heart size and location, an important factor in assessing cardiac function. Additional studies may be done preoperatively according to the specific procedure planned (e.g., C.T. scan, cardiac catheterization, arteriogram, and diagnostic X-rays).

8. **The answer is 1.** The patient's understanding of and response to the proposed surgical procedure needs to be assessed. Most patients will experience some degree of anxiety when undergoing surgery; therefore, the nurse must not only identify the reasons for the anxiety or fear, but also determine the support systems and coping mechanisms the patient has for dealing with these feelings. In some cases, anxiety may be incapacitating to the point of placing the patient at risk. In such situations, surgery may be postponed until the patient is better able to cope.

9. **The answer is 3.** In the procedure room, assessment continues in order to compare the patient's status with preoperative parameters and expected postoperative outcome. Ongoing assessment during the surgical procedure will routinely include vital signs, blood loss, skin color, and drainage. Additionally, prior to final suturing, all sponges, instruments, and sharps will be counted as the perioperative nurse assesses the final outcome of the surgical procedure. Prior to discharge from the procedure, the perioperative nurse, along with the anesthesiologist/anesthesia clinician, will assess the patient's wound dressing, respiratory status, drainage tubes for patency, collection chambers for amounts, status of parenteral infusion lines, and general readiness to be transferred to the postanesthesia area.

10. **The answer is 2.** The nursing diagnosis is the judgment or conclusion of the patient's health problem(s) made after reviewing all assessment data, and may represent actual or potential problems. Nursing diagnoses are different from medical diagnoses in that medical diagnoses identify specific disease processes, while nursing diagnoses identify the patient's responses to a disease, injury, or situation. Other differences are that nursing diagnoses focus on the patient not the disease, and that they change as the patient's condition changes, while medical diagnoses usually remain the same during the course of treatment.

11. **The answer is 2.** A patient may have many nursing diagnoses, actual or potential, at any one time. Nursing diagnoses are prioritized by their relative importance for being resolved. For example, a nursing diagnosis of Fluid and electrolyte deficit would normally take priority over the other three diagnoses listed, including Potential for injury-trauma related to sedation, since fluid and electrolyte deficits can be immediately life-threatening. New nursing diagnoses are added and prioritized as the patient's health status changes. As new ones are identified, old ones that have been resolved are deleted, thus providing accurate and current data regarding potential or actual problems during the continuing process.

12. **The answer is 1.** Manifesting, or causative, data that support a diagnostic statement may also be included in the diagnosis. An example of an appropriately worded nursing diagnosis for the perioperative patient is Pain related to surgical incision. Manifestations of the nursing diagnosis may include verbal expression,

increased pulse, and increased respirations, e.g., *Verbal expression of pain related to surgical incision*. The other three choices all are properly worded diagnoses without causative factors listed. Causative data could be added to choice 1 as follows: Repeated coughing indicating ineffective airway clearance.

13. **The answer is 4.** Knowledge deficit is not clearly part of a patient's psychologic status. Other nursing diagnoses related to psychologic status might include: anxiety potential related to unfamiliar environment or impending surgery and/or diagnosis; anticipatory grieving related to possible changes in body image; and sleep pattern disturbance related to anxiety. These and other psychologic and physiologic nursing diagnoses may also occur during the other phases of the perioperative period, and because the statements are not specific to any given patient, they could be actual or potential, depending upon the individual patient's situation.

14. **The answer is 4.** General factors that may guide the nurse's thinking about the intraoperative patient's nursing diagnoses include the specific procedure being performed, the type of anesthesia being used (i.e., local, general, regional), and the patient's general preoperative health status. The following are some common nursing diagnoses appropriate for the intraoperative patient: hypothermia; injury-trauma (e.g., from physical hazards); impaired skin integrity (e.g., from immobility); fluid and electrolyte imbalance; impaired gas exchange; alteration in tissue perfusion; and alteration in cardiac output. Note that most of these diagnoses relate to potential rather than actual problems. Additionally, more specific nursing diagnoses may be required depending upon the patient's status or the specific surgical procedure.

15. **The answer is 2.** The other diagnoses listed are more likely to be associated with the intraoperative phase. Most potential postoperative patient problems can be identified preoperatively and appropriate interventions planned. Other postoperative patient problems may evolve related to complications of surgery. Some of the common postoperative nursing diagnoses associated with the immediate postoperative phase are: (1) potential for ineffective airway clearance related to decreased level of consciousness; (2) potential for infection related to poor incision healing, inadequate lung expansion, or impaired mobility; (3) alteration in comfort related to surgical incision; (4) body image disturbance related to surgery; (5) potential for injury related to sedation; (6) potential impaired gas exchange related to incision pain; and (7) potential for ineffective participation in rehabilitation process. Early recognition of potential problems and early intervention can provide the patient with a smooth postoperative course and swift recovery.

16. **The answer is 4.** The plan of nursing care includes goals derived from the nursing diagnosis. These goals or **outcome standards** focus on potential high-incidence problem areas of the surgical patient, including knowledge of the response to surgical intervention, freedom from infection and harm, maintenance of skin integrity and fluid and electrolyte balance, and participation in the rehabilitation process. Each of these outcome standards have specific criteria to assist the perioperative nurse in determining whether the standards have been met, but it is the individual nurse's responsibility to adapt, modify, and add outcome criteria that are appropriate to the individual patient's situation. Some important points to remember about patient outcome criteria are: (1) patient outcome goals are patient-focused; that is, they state clearly what the patient will be able to do; (2) patient outcomes are the observable and measurable physiologic and psychologic responses to planned nursing interventions; and (3) outcome criteria include an expected time of accomplishment or completion.

17. **The answer is 1.** See answer #16 above.

18. **The answer is 2.** Nursing interventions are those activities carried out by the nurse to assist the patient to achieve the outcome criteria. Nursing interventions may be independent, interdependent (collaborative), or dependent and are written in the form of protocols. Included among nursing interventions for the perioperative patient are promotion of physical and psychologic comfort; support of cardiopulmonary function; promotion of safety; promotion of skin integrity; support of elimination functions; maintenance of fluid and electrolyte balance (choice 2); promotion of nutrition; personal hygiene care; functional rehabilitation; and education of the patient, family, and significant others who are part of the patient's support system.

19. **The answer is 1.** Independent nursing interventions are activities the perioperative nurse institutes based on her or his own judgment; that is, a physician's order is not needed (e.g., conducting counts at specified intervals during the procedure), even though collaboration with another nurse may be involved. Interdependent or collaborative nursing interventions are activities performed jointly with another health-care provider (e.g., physician) or instituted after a decision made by the nurse with another health-care provider (e.g., blood administration directed by the anesthesiologist, or positioning the patient with the surgeon). Dependent nursing interventions are those that require physician direction either in the form of a written order, direct supervision, or standard protocols. Implementation includes all the nursing interventions that are directed toward resolving the patient's nursing diagnoses (e.g., specific instruments requested by the surgeon for a selected case or the use of specific medications).

20. **The answer is 3.** Interventions during the intraoperative phase are generally directed toward providing a safe environment and protecting the patient from injury. As all members of the surgical team are present, the patient care provided is generally of a collaborative nature, with each member assuming responsibility for predetermined activities. Preoperative interventions are primarily directed toward the patient for the proposed surgical intervention. They include patient and family education; patient preparation, including care of preexisting health problems; and family/significant other preparation. Postoperative interventions are directed toward preventing infection, promoting optimal healing, and preventing complications, both during the immediate and intermediate phases of recovery. Some of the activities related to this phase include monitoring and evaluating the patient's status; managing patient care, including pain, fluid status, cardiopulmonary status, and positioning; assessing nutritional status and needs; and providing rehabilitation, counseling, and emotional support.

21. **The answer is 3.** Evaluation provides the basis for modifications to the overall care plan. It is the time for comparing the patient's postintervention status with the expected outcomes or outcome criteria, which includes communication and documentation for the patient, other health-care personnel, and significant others. Evaluation must be conducted in an organized way, looking first at each nursing diagnosis, the prescribed patient outcomes, and the patient's level of accomplishment for each expected outcome. For example, if the patient outcome is that he or she will be free of infection, the nurse would look at whether or not he or she has any infectious problems or complications associated with an infection. If the wound is clean, but the patient has developed a postoperative pneumonia, the nurse would maintain the existing care plan relative to the incision, and develop a more aggressive plan of care with specific interventions to resolve the postoperative pneumonia.

22. **The answer is 4.** A plan of care could be described as a portrait of a patient's surgical experience, and describes the nursing interventions the patient needs to accomplish the stated outcome goals. The plan should reflect coordination with the overall plan of medical care. It should also: (1) include actions that will ensure maximum physical and emotional safety and security for the patient during the intraoperative period; (2) be based on both scientific knowledge and patient information derived during the preoperative assessment, and be therapeutically effective; and (3) include long-term planning in order to help the patient achieve or maintain optimum health status.

23. **The answer is 3.** For perioperative nursing, the standards of practice form the basis for acceptable or recommended nursing practice during the three phases of surgical intervention. Standards of care, however, are different. According to Marker, standards of care define the level of practice that directly relates to the quality of care a patient receives. According to the Marker model, standards of care define the actions or behaviors used to provide care to the patient, and the criteria for performing that care effectively, safely, and proficiently; they represent a written plan of care developed to assist the nurse in providing effective nursing care. They also define the end result of nursing intervention, and are expressed either as what the nurse should accomplish (nursing goals) or what the patient should be able to do (patient outcomes). Examples include patient outcomes and nursing goals related to patient teaching or the planning of patient care.

10 Preoperative Patient Care Management

STUDY OUTLINE

I. **THE PERIOPERATIVE NURSE'S ROLE: MANAGING PATIENT CARE**

1. During the early days of surgery, the nurse's role was primarily that of an assistant to the surgeon. It included such activities as maintaining an aseptic environment, passing instruments, and other general nonnursing tasks, with little direct contact or involvement with the patient either before, during, or after surgery.

2. **Today, the perioperative nurse practices his or her specialty during all three phases of surgical intervention in an expanded role: that of (1) caregiver, (2) patient advocate, (3) leader, (4) research consumer and (5) teacher.** The combination of these roles results in effective management of patient care during the perioperative period.

   a. As the primary **caregiver** during the intraoperative phase, the perioperative nurse uses acquired knowledge and skills related to the surgical experience, which encompass the management of supplies, equipment, and personnel, in addition to providing psychologic support to the patient, family, and significant others.

   b. As a **patient advocate**, the perioperative nurse assures a safe, therapeutic environment by maintaining the standards of practice associated with nursing care during the perioperative period. As the primary manager of patient care, the nurse's role encompasses patient safety, comfort, and an acute awareness of the surroundings. In no other setting is this role of a patient advocate more challenging, since the patient relies on the surgical team to meet physiologic as well as psychosocial needs. The perioperative nurse must ensure that the informed consent, given by the patient, has not been violated, since the surgical patient may be unable to take action on his or her own behalf, and relies on others for protection from harm.

   c. As a **leader**, the perioperative nurse projects a positive role model to other members of the health-care team by remaining current in all areas of clinical practice. By focusing on the professional role of the perioperative nurse, and motivating others, the perioperative nurse can assist others to grow and develop their professional skills.

   d. As a **research consumer**, the perioperative nurse is seeking to expand his or her knowledge relating to practice and materials (products). This knowledge is based on scientific investigation and research, in order to eliminate outdated methods, equipment, and traditions while maintaining a cost-effective work setting.

   e. And finally, as a **teacher**, the perioperative nurse is involved with the education of not only the patient and family, but also colleagues, students, and society in general, in the hope of elevating the conceptual role of a "technical nurse" to a "patient-oriented" nurse involved with all aspects of care during the perioperative period.

3. Nursing, regardless of the area, is an *art* and a *science* and must be cultivated and learned as any other specialized practice that involves people. Each nurse has a responsibility to seek out new information and perfect his or her practice in order to manage patient care safely and effectively during the perioperative period.

II.   NURSING ACTIVITIES IN THE PERIOPERATIVE ROLE: A SUMMARY

Preoperative Phase
   Assessment
      Preoperative assessment (home/ASF/E.D.)
         • Initiates initial preoperative assessment
         • Plans teaching methods appropriate to patient's needs
         • Involves family in interview
      Surgical unit
         • Completes preoperative assessment
         • Coordinates preoperative activities and teaching program
         • Develops a care plan
   Planning
      Surgical suite/holding area
         • Preoperative interview
         • Review chart
         • Admission protocol and procedures
Intraoperative phase
   Implementation
         • Transfers patient to procedure room
         • Provides emotional support
         • Positions and preps patient
         • Performs counts and documents patient care administered
         • Manages environment and patient-care activities
Postoperative phase
   Evaluation
         • Communicates intraoperative information
         • Immediate postoperative assessment (PACU; ASF)
         • Evaluates effectiveness of nursing care in the O.R.
         • Assists with discharge planning
   Reassessment
         • Discharge planning and interview
         • Patient unit/postoperative visit
         • ASF/home (follow-up)

III.   PREOPERATIVE ASSESSMENT

1. **The preoperative phase of surgical intervention begins with the patient's decision to have surgery, and ends with the transfer of the patient to the operating table.**

2. **The physiologic preparation of the patient should be continuously intermeshed with the psychologic preparation.** Preoperative preparation often consists of explanations and teaching about the sequence of events that are about to take place. The patient, family, and significant others should be assisted in gaining accurate information that will lead to a successful conclusion of a possibly traumatic experience. The perioperative nurse must take an active part in this process in order to assure quality and continuity of patient care throughout the patient's surgical experience.

A.   PSYCHOSOCIAL ASSESSMENT

1. Perioperative nursing practice is patient-oriented--not environment-oriented, physician-oriented, or task-oriented. Perioperative nursing practice believes in the patient as a *whole person* with a broad spectrum of needs, and so the **nursing activities must be geared to meet the patient's psychosocial needs as well as immediate physical needs.**

2. The term **psychosocial** involves the social and psychologic aspects of the patient's behavior, such as coping mechanisms, anxiety levels, self-image, personality, cultural influences, and support

systems that can affect the patient during this period. By being observant, an active listener and empathic with his or her responses, the perioperative nurse can have a vital role in the activities designed to help the patient adjust to the proposed surgical therapy.

3. Most patients view surgery in several ways: as (1) an aggressive act directed against them, since it involves cutting into and possible removal of a body part; (2) a radical invasion of privacy; (3) a reduction or total loss of control; and (4) the subduing of their individuality. All of these can combine to produce fear, resentment, hostility, or apathy, depending on the patient's ability to adapt to stress. On the positive side, however, patients may view surgery as an act of faith, projected as a feeling of trust in the surgeon and the perioperative nurse, and in their judgment.

4. **As part of the total care of the patient, the perioperative nurse must understand these feeling and attempt to reduce the anxiety level through teaching, communication, and the establishment of a therapeutic nurse-patient relationship.** Patients usually wish to cooperate, but stress will alter behavior patterns in most instances. Nursing care based on the individualized needs of the patient is critical to a patient's acceptance or rejection of the planned surgical procedure.

B. THE THEORY OF HUMAN NEEDS

1. A. H. Maslow, when describing a **hierarchy of human needs**, emphasized that the accomplishment of self-actualization is a motivating factor in the healthy individual, but it cannot be attained until the basic needs of survival and security have been met. From the moment a patient steps into a hospital, for whatever reason, we begin a systematic process of breaking down the individuality of the person and subsequently reducing his or her ability to think or act alone.

2. **Maslow's theory is based on the concept of wants (needs) developing on five levels, the lowest being physiologic or biologic requirements and the highest being self-fulfillment and creativity.** As the lower needs are gradually being satisfied, the higher needs gradually emerge. To satisfy these needs, humans expend energy (motivation). Once a need has been fairly well satisfied, it no longer acts as a motivator and efforts are then directed toward satisfying the need of the next level. Maslow focused his attention on the positive aspects of human behavior, such as happiness, contentment, and satisfaction as individuals strive toward their accomplishments. What then is the effect of illness, and specifically the surgical experience on the attainment of these different levels?

3. **Physical needs**
    a. **Biologic needs** focus on life-sustaining necessities, such as food, water, oxygen, sleep, and warmth. In illness, the patient and family become acutely aware of these needs, and respond accordingly when any are threatened. **These needs must be met to achieve the next level of completeness, but should not become the total focus of patient care.**
    b. Surgical intervention, at some stage of the perioperative period, adversely affects all or some of these needs, creating an anxious state that requires supportive measures from all who are in contact with the patient and family during this period.

4. **Psychosocial needs**
    a. **Safety and security**
       (1) **Safety and security focus on the feelings of being safe in a nonthreatening environment, one which is familiar and comfortable, and void of harmful substances or actions.**
       (2) In illness, this safety and security is replaced by the fear of the unknown, since the patient is surrounded by unfamiliarity in both the environment and the persons designated to care for him or her during the illness. Additionally, the patient may fear a loss of a body part or even death related to their illness. **Therefore the nursing care should establish a protective, caring environment, and provide reassurance, comfort, and spiritual well being during the hospitalization, especially during the perioperative period.**
    b. **Social acceptance**
       (1) **Social acceptance, or belonging, having an association with others, feeling affection or receiving love, friendship, and the creation of trust, are all an important aspect of this stage. It is paramount, then, that patients and their families receive an empathic and understanding response to their feelings and attitudes, whether negative or positive.**

(2) If the patient cannot trust those who are providing the care, it may result in cancellation of surgery, or high anxiety levels that require more medication to calm the patient, which can adversely affect the physiologic status of the individual both intraoperatively and postoperatively.

c. **Self-esteem**
   (1) **To feel good about oneself and to have confidence in one's own abilities leads to productivity, rational decision-making processes, and knowledgeable choices.**
   (2) Confidentiality needs to be respected, since behavior patterns may change and could become an embarrassment if known. The radical invasion of privacy leads to feelings of low self-esteem, loss of control, and decreased decision-making capabilities. To many patients, this alone is reason for panic, since adults, young and old, pride themselves on their ability to function as independent individuals. Patients may be concerned with a potential change in body image related to the surgery, and how this image could ultimately affect their lifestyle. Patients may fear rejection by loved ones should the change be perceived as cosmetically unpleasant, such as a colostomy or removal of a breast.
   (3) **Support systems must be activated as soon as possible to help the patient and family adjust to these feelings and/or impending changes in their lifestyle.** The perioperative nurse is important in activating support systems during the preoperative assessment and interview of the patient, family, and significant others.

d. **Self-actualization**
   (1) **The final step on Maslow's hierarchical ladder focuses on being creative, self-motivated, and capable of reaching ones fullest potential, and is the ultimate motivator for the healthy individual.** By allowing the patient to participate actively in health-care decisions, and providing patient education and rehabilitation programs, the goal of striving toward a normal existence can be reached. Effective and therapeutic nurse-patient relationships, created from the beginning, help the patient and family adjust and eventually achieve the optimum state of health.
   (2) By respecting the patient's individual rights and being a patient advocate, the perioperative nurse can assist the patient in feeling a sense of worth and importance, which can ultimately move the patient toward self-actualization and eventual accomplishment of his or her desired goals.

C. PREOPERATIVE TEACHING CONCEPTS

1. **A perioperative teaching program can provide the necessary means to assure quality and continuity of care during the perioperative period.**
2. If the surgeon and anesthesiologist have supplied adequate information during their portion of the preoperative interview, the patient is now ready to become involved in an individualized preoperative teaching program. To make the program meaningful, the nurse must continue to assess the patient's current level of knowledge. Assisting the patient in gaining additional knowledge assures the patient's awareness of the treatment he or she is about to receive.
3. **Sharing information and answering the patient's and family's questions concerning the scheduled surgical procedure should be incorporated with the explanations from both the surgeon and the anesthesiologist.** By doing so, the anxiety associated with the surgical procedure can be greatly reduced.
4. **A preoperative teaching program should include a general orientation to the surgical experience and instructions in anticipated postoperative activities.** Research has revealed that surgical patients who received preoperative and postoperative teaching are less anxious, more willing to participate in their own care, comply with prescribed medical regimens, and have fewer complications, thus shortening the hospitalization period.
5. Each program, though individualized, has certain key elements regardless of the type of surgery or patient status (inpatient or ambulatory patient). The perioperative nurse should be aware of these elements in order to create a comprehensive preoperative teaching program. These elements should include, but not be limited to, the following items:

    a. Information regarding the sequence of events
    b. Dietary restrictions
    c. Preoperative shave (if applicable)
    d. Preoperative medications
    e. Postoperative activities
        (1) Limitations
        (2) Pain management
    f. Family orientation
        (1) Location of surgical waiting room
    g. Self-care goals and discharge planning
        (1) Follow-up visits
        (2) Resumption of preoperative activities, medications, lifestyle, and so on
6. **In addition to these elements, the program should contain a teaching/learning component.** To facilitate recovery, the patient should be taught techniques for specific postoperative exercises, assisted ambulation, and any other postoperative activities recommended by the surgeon. The patient should be shown the proper techniques, and asked to return the demonstration with the nurse supervising the activity in order to offer any suggestions or answer any questions during the program. In this way the patient, without stress and/or pain, becomes an active participant, not just a passive observer.
7. **Preoperative teaching, including the activities conducted and performed by the patient, should be documented on the patient's record as a means of communication to other nurses and health-care members who may care for the patient during the perioperative period.** Documentation of preoperative teaching is especially important if the circulating nurse assigned to the case was not available to provide the preoperative preparation and teaching.

IV. PREOPERATIVE PLANNING

1. Based on the assessment made, the planning and goal-setting phase of patient care begins. The planning stage consists of three components:
    a. **Individual needs of the patient**
        (1) Transportation needs
        (2) Emotional support
        (3) Moving and lifting concerns
        (4) Special procedure required prior to incision, e.g., insertion of Foley catheter; positional aides; alternate prepping solutions; area and/or shave prep
    b. **Unforeseen possible complications**
        (1) Based on medical condition and diagnosis
        (2) Lab data; nurse's notes; anesthesia evaluation
        (3) Equipment and supplies anticipated
    c. **Actions/activities to be performed**
        (1) Based on assessment needs
        (2) Goal-directed; patient-oriented
        (3) Specialty equipment, e.g., O.R. table; E.S.U.; laser, microscope, monitoring devices, etc.
        (4) Surgical team needs
2. Perioperative nurses, as the professional nursing member of the surgical team, have a responsibility to *plan* as well as *give* care. If the planned and performed nursing activities are not documented, it could be assumed legally that the care did not take place. The nurse who creates this plan carries it out by communicating it to other members of the health-care team, thus ensuring the continuity of patient care after the perioperative period.
3. Although the creation of this care plan does not ensure that quality of care will be provided, it does reflect a reliable source of information for all health-care team members, and can serve as a tool for monitoring and evaluating the quality of care that the patient has received.

V. ADMITTING THE PATIENT TO SURGERY

A. ADMISSION PROCEDURES

1. **The information obtained by the perioperative nurse during the preoperative assessment, such as appropriate transport methods or unusual patient problems (e.g., impaired mobility, alterations in sensory motor perception or emotional status, and any individual patient requests), should be conveyed to the individuals responsible for preparing and transporting the patient to the surgical suite.**

2. Depending on institutional policies, a nurse may or may not accompany the patient to the holding area or preoperative area, where a report should be given to the appropriate nursing personnel as the transfer of care is accomplished.

3. **The admission procedure begins with an introduction by the holding area nurse and a series of questions to verify data on the chart, and ends when the patient has been cleared by holding area personnel and the patient is transferred to the procedure room.**

4. The institutional/operating room policy and procedure manual should contain the protocol for admitting a patient to the surgical suite. This process should include the following elements:
   a. **Verification of patient's identification:** verbally (if feasible); chart review and I.D. bracelet.
   b. **Verification of completion of appropriate forms:** history and physical; results from diagnostic studies; consent forms; preoperative assessment/teaching.
   c. **Review of related nursing procedures performed:** nursing notes; status of physical and emotional states; vital signs.
   d. **Verification of physician's orders relating to:** elimination; medication; nutrition; I.V. therapy; special procedures.
   e. **Safety and comfort measures needed during the perioperative period.**
   f. **Patient's response to preoperative medication:** physiologic monitoring; emotional status; pain control; observation of the patient.

5. A **preoperative check sheet** can assist in the documentation of this information, since it identifies, according to hospital policy, the information required on all presurgical patients. This form is completed by the surgical unit nurse, and should be started the evening before (or within a specific time for ambulatory patients). Additionally, the preoperative checklist should be completed and signed off prior to the arrival of the patient in the holding area, and is reverified by the holding area nurse and circulating nurse for completeness prior to entry into the procedure room.

B. NURSING ACTIVITIES DURING THE ADMISSION PROCESS

1. **Identification and verification:** Proper patient identification is one of the most important safety measures that can be taken by the professional nurse receiving the patient in the holding area. This identification should include verification of the patient, surgeon, surgical procedure, and type of anesthesia.

2. **Review of record**
   a. **The patient's record usually gives a total picture of the patient and completes the identification process.** Key elements include review of the patient's admission record (face sheet); allergies; results of laboratory tests; history and physical examination; preoperative medications given; and specific preoperative orders, either by the surgeon or the anesthesiologist.
   b. **Pertinent laboratory data**
      (1) **Certain laboratory values are critical to the success of the proposed surgical procedure.** The nurse caring for the patient should be aware of the results of these tests and their normal values according to institutional criteria.
      (2) Any deviations should be reported to the anesthesiologist and/or surgeon, since abnormal or unsafe levels could necessitate postponement of the procedure until the patient is in better physical condition.

(3) In addition to the laboratory values and diagnostic tests used to determine the physiologic status of the patient, **preoperative vital signs** can be used as an excellent indicator of potential problems that could occur during the intraoperative period. See **Table 10.1** below for a physiologic status review and implications.

(4) The nurse should review these findings and report any concerns to the appropriate persons for immediate intervention.

3. **Preoperative interview**
   a. **After the nurse reviews the patient's record, he or she is ready to begin the interview process.**
   b. The nurse should address the patient by proper name and title (where applicable), introduce herself or himself to the patient, and give a brief explanation of what will transpire during this phase. **The nurse should provide individual attention to the patient, and if the family is present, include them in the interviewing process.**
   c. **Special circumstances that the nurse must be aware of during the interview process should be reviewed prior to beginning the interview.** For example, elderly patients having difficulty with memory or cognitive acuity, extremely anxious patients, depressed patients, those with hearing or vision impairments, patients with a language barrier, or children with or without their parents may have difficulties with communication.
   d. **After establishing a rapport with the patient and/or family members present, the nurse should assess the patient's understanding of the surgical procedure, using the Preoperative Teaching Assessment tool as a guide to meet the needs and concerns of the patient.**
   e. If problems or concerns have not been adequately addressed, the surgeon and/or anesthesiologist should be notified immediately for further explanation and/or clarification of concepts for the patient.

4. **Consent forms**
   a. **All nurses involved with patient care should be aware of the state laws that govern the consent forms regarding the legal age requirement, mental competency of a patient, special surgical requirements, and appropriate signatures.**
   b. **Nurses must also be aware of the institution's policies pertaining to consents.** Attaining an informed consent is the responsibility of the operating surgeon. An explanation should contain information regarding the proposed surgical procedure, the possible risks involved, expected benefits, available alternatives, and so on.

5. **Related nursing procedures**
   a. **During the admission process, the patient may have an I.V. inserted, a surgical shave prep performed, or a cast bivalved or removed. The perioperative nurse should provide support for the patient by explaining all the procedures and why they are necessary.** The noise in the area should be kept to a minimum, privacy maintained, and the patient never left unattended.
   b. **Preoperative preparation of the skin**
      (1) Bacteria found on the skin are numerous, and generally are divided into **transient** and **resident flora**. Transient microbes are easy to remove with soap and water, while the resident flora adhere to epithelial cells and extend downward toward the glands and hair follicles.
      (2) Because the skin cannot be sterilized, it must be properly prepared in order to reduce the microbial count to as low as possible, thereby reducing the risk of infection.
      (3) **Preoperative skin preparation done on the unit and/or in the holding area consists of two steps:**
         (a) **A shower/bath the night before with an antimicrobial agent, and**
         (b) **The possible removal of hair directly involved with the proposed incision site.**
      (4) Removal of hair from the operative site is not necessary for all surgical procedures or for all patients.
      (5) **The ideal methods to remove unwanted hair are either by depilatory or by clipping the hair using disposable clippers.** Either of these methods eliminates the possibility of cutting or scratching the skin caused by shaving, which may create an opening for microbial contamination of the surgical wound.

Table 10.1 PHYSIOLOGIC STATUS REVIEW AND IMPLICATIONS

Vital Sign	Abnormal Finding	Possible Indication	Possible Postoperative Complication
Temperature	Fever (above 101° F [38.3° C] in an adult)	Infection; dehydration (when accompanied by decreased skin turgor)	Systemic infection; wound infection; dehiscence/evisceration; fluid imbalance; shock
Pulse	Tachycardia (above 100 beats per minute)	Pain; fever; dehydration; anemia; hypoxia; shock	Poor tissue perfusion; vascular collapse; cardiac arrhythmias; renal failure; anesthetic complications
	Bradycardia (below 60 beats per minute)	Drug effects (e.g., digitalis); spinal injury; head injury	Spinal shock; increased intracranial pressure (also for tachycardia)
Respiration	Tachypnea (above 24 breaths per minute)	Atelectasis; pneumonia; pain or anxiety; pleurisy; infection; renal failure	Tissue hypoxia; anesthetic complications; pneumonia; atelectasis
	Bradypnea (below 10 breaths per minute)	Brain lesion; respiratory center depression	See tachypnea
Blood pressure	Hypotension (below 90 mm Hg systolic)	Shock; myocardial infarction; hemorrhage; spinal injury	Poor tissue perfusion; renal failure; vasodilation; shock
	Hypertension (above 140 mm Hg systolic and/or 90 mm Hg diastolic)	Anxiety or pain; renal disease; coronary artery disease	Stroke; hemorrhage; myocardial infarction

(6) Using A.O.R.N.'s recommendations as a guide, the removal of hair should be performed not more than 2 hours prior to the surgical procedure, and should be performed by qualified personnel instructed in the proper procedure regardless of what method is used, and in an area that can afford privacy. Ideally, the holding area should be equipped to perform this task.

(7) If the shave method is the *only* choice available, the wet shave method is *mandatory* as it facilitates hair removal, minimizes skin trauma, and prevents dry hair and debris from becoming airborne.

(8) If a depilatory is used, a "patch-test" should be performed first to identify a possible reaction. If no adverse effects are visible, the agent is applied following the manufacturer's instructions for application and removal.

(9) A manual containing the procedural steps and diagrams of proposed prep areas should be available within the practice setting and referred to as necessary prior to beginning the skin prep.

PRACTICE QUESTIONS

1. **The professional roles of the perioperative nurse include all of the following EXCEPT:**

   1. *that of caregiver, which encompasses the management of surgical supplies, equipment, and personnel.*

   2. *that of therapist, which encompasses the psychologic treatment of the patient, family, and significant others.*

   3. *that of patient advocate, which encompasses patient safety, comfort, and an awareness of the surroundings.*

   4. *that of teacher, which encompasses the education of the patient, family, colleagues, students, and society in general.*

2. **An important aspect of the perioperative nurse's psychologic preparation of the patient consists of:**

   1. *planning for unforeseen complications based on the patient's medical condition and diagnosis.*

   2. *teaching the patient about the sequence of events that is about to take place.*

   3. *arranging for specialty equipment, e.g., E.S.U., laser, microscope, etc.*

   4. *meeting the individual needs of the patient by addressing moving and lifting concerns.*

3. **Which of the following would NOT be included among the psychosocial aspects of surgical patient care?**

   1. *The patient's coping mechanisms.*

   2. *The patient's anxiety levels.*

   3. *The patient's self-image.*

   4. *The patient's dietary restrictions.*

4. **Patients often view surgery with fear, anxiety, resentment, or apathy. On the positive side, however, patients may view surgery as a(n):**

   1. *act of the faith in the surgical team.*

   2. *subduing of their individuality.*

   3. *means of gaining independence from Maslow's hierarchy of human needs.*

   4. *reduction in their control of the environment.*

5. **An important application of Maslow's theory of human needs to perioperative nursing is the idea that:**

   1. *meeting the physical needs of the patient should be the total focus of patient care.*

   2. *sharing information and answering the patient's questions about the procedure are essential to meeting the patient's needs.*

3. *once a need has been satisfied, it can begin to function as a motivator toward meeting the needs of the next level.*

4. *by meeting a patient's physical needs, the nurse can help the patient satisfy higher needs, including self-actualization.*

6. **One of the *best* ways the perioperative nurse can help meet a patient's needs for self-esteem and self-actualization is by:**

1. *helping to activate support systems during the preoperative assessment of the patient, family, and significant others.*

2. *sharing the patient's anxieties and fears about a loss of self-esteem with others in the family and on the surgical team.*

3. *nurturing in the patent a sense of dependence on the nurse and on other members of the surgical team.*

4. *discouraging the patient from talking about feelings of possible rejection by loved ones should surgery produce changes perceived as cosmetically unpleasant.*

7. **Self-actualization, the final stage in Maslow's hierarchy of needs, can be fostered in the patient by:**

1. *nurturing in the patent a sense of dependence on the nurse and on other members of the surgical team.*

2. *focusing totally on meeting the physical needs of the patient.*

3. *allowing the patient to participate actively in health-care decisions.*

4. *sharing the patient's anxieties and fears about a loss of self-esteem with others in the family and on the surgical team.*

8. **A perioperative teaching program can provide the necessary means to assure quality and continuity of care for the patient during the perioperative period. Essential aspects of such a perioperative teaching program include all of the following EXCEPT:**

1. *a general orientation to the surgical experience and instructions in anticipated postoperative activities.*

2. *a teaching/learning component that emphasizes techniques for specific postoperative activities recommended by the surgeon.*

3. *documentation of all teaching activities on the patient's record.*

4. *a nursing care plan that places patient education first among various perioperative nursing activities.*

9. **The preoperative planning stage in patient care management consists of three basic components, each with specific associated activities. Which of the following is NOT one of these components?**

1. *Planning for the individual needs of the patient: transportation, emotional support, etc.*

2. *Planning for preoperative assessment: health history, etc.*

3. *Planning for unforeseen possible complications.*

4. *Planning for the actions and activities that will need to be performed: specialty equipment, etc.*

10. **The admissions procedure for a surgical case begins when the:**

    1. *patient and surgeon agree mutually that surgery is required.*

    2. *patient has been cleared by holding area personnel and is transferred to the procedure room.*

    3. *patient is introduced into the holding area and data on the chart are verified.*

    4. *preoperative checklist is completed and is signed off by the surgical unit nurse.*

11. **Following identification and verification of the patient in the holding area, the nurse's responsibilities include three important activities during the admission process. Which of the following is NOT one of these activities?**

    1. *Preparation of a preoperative checklist: safety and comfort measures, etc.*

    2. *A review of the record: admissions record, laboratory data, preoperative vital signs, etc.*

    3. *A preoperative interview: patient and family, if present.*

    4. *Related nursing procedures: I.V. insertion, skin prep, etc.*

12. **While reviewing pertinent laboratory data on a patient during the admissions process, the nurse notices that the patient's hematocrit is abnormal. The nurse should:**

    1. *ignore the deviation, since it will appear elsewhere on the patient record.*

    2. *report this deviation to the anesthesiologist and/or surgeon.*

    3. *order a new hematocrit to be taken in order to determine if the procedure should be delayed or canceled.*

    4. *immediately cancel the procedure.*

13. **A nurse's preoperative interview of the patient should include all of the following elements EXCEPT:**

    1. *establishing a rapport with the patient and those family members present.*

    2. *addressing any special circumstances that may apply to the patient, e.g., extreme anxiety, poor memory.*

    3. *assessing the patient's understanding of the surgical procedure.*

    4. *attaining a signed informed consent form and any other required signed document from the patient.*

14. **Preoperative skin preparation consists of two stages: a shower/bath the night before with an antimicrobial agent, and the:**

    1. *possible removal of hair directly involved with the proposed incision site.*

    2. *sealing off of external stomas from the operative site with a detergent-soaked sponge.*

    3. *washing of eyes with cotton balls and a nonirritating solution.*

    4. *preparation of the incision area with an antimicrobial scrub solution.*

ANSWER EXPLANATIONS

1. **The answer is 2.** The perioperative nurse practices his or her specialty during all three phases of surgical intervention and in multiple roles: that of (1) caregiver, (2) patient advocate, (3) leader, (4) research consumer and (5) teacher. The combination of these roles results in effective management of patient care during the perioperative period. As a leader, the perioperative nurse projects a positive role model to other members of the health-care team by remaining current in all areas of clinical practice. As a research consumer, the perioperative nurse is seeking to expand his or her knowledge relating to practice and materials (products). Providing psychologic support for the patient, family, and significant others is an important function of the perioperative nurse; treatment, however, is the role of a therapist.

2. **The answer is 2.** The physiologic preparation of the patient should be continuously intermeshed with the psychologic preparation. Preoperative preparation often consists of explanations and teaching about the sequence of events that are about to take place. The patient, family, and significant others should be assisted in gaining accurate information that will lead to a successful conclusion of a possibly traumatic experience. The perioperative nurse must take an active part in this process in order to assure quality and continuity of patient care throughout the patient's surgical experience. The other planning aspects refer more accurately to the physiologic preparation of the patient, mostly during the intraoperative phase.

3. **The answer is 4.** The term psychosocial involves the social and psychologic aspects of the patient's behavior, such as coping mechanisms, anxiety levels, self-image, personality, cultural influences, and support systems that can affect the patient during this period. By being observant, an active listener and empathic with his or her responses, the perioperative nurse can have a vital role in the activities designed to help the patient adjust to the proposed surgical therapy.

4. **The answer is 1.** Most patients view surgery in several ways: as (1) an aggressive act directed against them, since it involves cutting into and possible removal of a body part; (2) a radical invasion of privacy; (3) a reduction or total loss of control; and (4) the subduing of their individuality. All of these can combine to produce fear, resentment, hostility, or apathy, depending on the patient's ability to adapt to stress. On the positive side, however, patients may view surgery as an act of faith, projected as a feeling of trust in the surgeon and the perioperative nurse, and in their judgment. As part of the total care of the patient, the perioperative nurse must understand these feeling and attempt to reduce the anxiety level through teaching, communication, and the establishment of a therapeutic nurse-patient relationship.

5. **The answer is 4.** Maslow's theory is based on the concept of wants (needs) developing on five levels, the lowest being physiologic or biologic requirements and the highest being self-fulfillment and creativity. As the lower needs are gradually being satisfied, the higher needs gradually emerge. To satisfy these needs, humans expend energy (motivation). Biologic (physical) needs focus on life-sustaining necessities, such as food, water, oxygen, sleep, and warmth. In illness, the patient and family become acutely aware of these needs, and respond accordingly when any are threatened. These needs must be met to achieve the next level of completeness, but should not become the total focus of patient care.

6. **The answer is 1.** In helping to meet the patient's psychosocial needs, the nurse should address the patient's need for self-esteem--to feel good about oneself and to have confidence in one's own abilities leads to productivity, rational decision-making processes, and knowledgeable choices. Confidentiality needs to be respected, since behavior patterns may change and could become an embarrassment if known. The radical invasion of privacy leads to feelings of low self-esteem, loss of control, and decreased decision-making capabilities. Patients may be concerned with a potential change in body image related to the surgery, and how this image could ultimately affect their lifestyle. Patients may fear rejection by loved ones should the change be perceived as cosmetically unpleasant, such as a colostomy or removal of a breast. Support systems must be activated as soon as possible to help the patient and family adjust to these feelings and/or impending changes in their lifestyle.

7. **The answer is 3.** The final step on Maslow's hierarchical ladder focuses on being creative, self-motivated, and capable of reaching ones fullest potential, and is the ultimate motivator for the healthy individual. By

allowing the patient to participate actively in health-care decisions, and providing patient education and rehabilitation programs, the goal of striving toward a normal existence can be reached. Effective and therapeutic nurse-patient relationships, created from the beginning, help the patient and family adjust and eventually achieve the optimum state of health. By respecting the patient's individual rights and being a patient advocate, the perioperative nurse can assist the patient in feeling a sense of worth and importance, which can ultimately move the patient toward self-actualization and eventual accomplishment of his or her desired goals.

8. **The answer is 4.** A perioperative teaching program, though individualized, has certain key elements regardless of the type of surgery or patient status (inpatient or ambulatory patient). (1) A preoperative teaching program should include a general orientation to the surgical experience and instructions in anticipated postoperative activities. Research has revealed that surgical patients who received preoperative and postoperative teaching are less anxious, more willing to participate in their own care, comply with prescribed medical regimens, and have fewer complications, thus shortening the hospitalization period. Sharing information and answering the patient's and family's questions concerning the scheduled surgical procedure should be incorporated with the explanations from both the surgeon and the anesthesiologist. (2) The program should contain a teaching/learning component. To facilitate recovery, the patient should be taught techniques for specific postoperative exercises, assisted ambulation, and any other postoperative activities recommended by the surgeon. (3) Preoperative teaching, including the activities conducted and performed by the patient, should be documented on the patient's record as a means of communication to other nurses and health-care members who may care for the patient during the perioperative period. Documentation of preoperative teaching is especially important if the circulating nurse assigned to the case was not available to provide the preoperative preparation and teaching.

9. **The answer is 2.** Preoperative assessment serves as the basis of preoperative planning; it is a separate stage in the Nursing Process. Based on the assessment made, the planning and goal-setting phase of patient care begins, including the establishment of goals that will direct desired client outcomes. The planning stage consists of three components: (1) the individual needs of the patient (transportation needs; emotional support; moving and lifting concerns; special procedures required prior to incision, e.g., insertion of Foley catheter, positional aides, alternate prepping solutions; area and/or shave prep); (2) unforeseen possible complications (based on medical condition and diagnosis, lab data, nurse's notes, and anesthesia evaluation; equipment and supplies anticipated); and (3) actions/activities to be performed (based on assessment needs and goal-directed and patient-oriented; specialty equipment, e.g., O.R. table; E.S.U.; laser, microscope, monitoring devices, etc.; surgical team needs).

10. **The answer is 3.** The admission procedure begins with an introduction by the holding area nurse and a series of questions to verify data on the chart, and ends when the patient has been cleared by holding area personnel and the patient is transferred to the procedure room. The institutional/operating room policy and procedure manual should contain the protocol for admitting a patient to the surgical suite. This process should include the following elements: (1) verification of patient's identification; (2) verification of completion of appropriate forms; (3) review of related nursing procedures performed; (4) verification of physician's orders relating to: elimination; medication; nutrition; I.V. therapy; special procedures; (5) safety and comfort measures needed during the perioperative period; and (6) patient's response to preoperative medication.

11. **The answer is 1.** The preoperative checklist, which identifies the information required on all presurgical patients, is completed by the surgical unit nurse or (in ambulatory surgery) the admissions nurse, and signed off prior to the arrival of the patient in the holding area, and is reverified by the holding area nurse and circulating nurse for completeness prior to entry into the procedure room. The other activities are all part of the admission process that follows identification and verification of the patient in the holding area. In addition, nurses must also be aware of the institution's policies pertaining to consent forms. Attaining an informed consent is the responsibility of the operating surgeon. An explanation should contain information regarding the proposed surgical procedure, the possible risks involved, expected benefits, available alternatives, and so on.

12. **The answer is 2.** Certain laboratory values are critical to the success of the proposed surgical procedure. The nurse caring for the patient should be aware of the results of these tests and their normal values according to institutional criteria. Any deviations should be reported to the anesthesiologist and/or surgeon, since abnormal or unsafe levels could necessitate postponement of the procedure until the patient is in better physical condition. In addition to the laboratory values and diagnostic tests used to determine the physiologic status of the patient, preoperative vital signs can be used as an excellent indicator of potential problems that could occur during the intraoperative period.

13. **The answer is 4.** The preoperative interview should not begin until after the consent for surgery has been signed and witnessed. After the nurse reviews the patient's record, he or she is ready to begin the interview process. The nurse should address the patient by proper name and title (where applicable), introduce herself or himself to the patient, and give a brief explanation of what will transpire during this phase. The nurse should provide individual attention to the patient, and if the family is present, include them in the interviewing process. Special circumstances that the nurse must be aware of during the interview process should be reviewed prior to beginning the interview. For example, elderly patients having difficulty with memory or cognitive acuity, extremely anxious patients, depressed patients, those with hearing or vision impairments, patients with a language barrier, or children with or without their parents may have difficulties with communication. After establishing a rapport with the patient and/or family members present, the nurse should assess the patient's understanding of the surgical procedure, using the Preoperative Teaching Assessment tool as a guide to meet the needs and concerns of the patient. If problems or concerns have not been adequately addressed, the surgeon and/or anesthesiologist should be notified immediately for further explanation and/or clarification of concepts for the patient.

14. **The answer is 1.** The other measures are done intraoperatively, if at all. Removal of hair from the operative site is not necessary for all surgical procedures or for all patients. The ideal methods to remove unwanted hair are either by depilatory or by clipping the hair using disposable clippers. Either of these methods eliminates the possibility of cutting or scratching the skin caused by shaving, which may create an opening for microbial contamination of the surgical wound. The removal of hair should be performed not more than 2 hours prior to the surgical procedure, and should be performed by qualified personnel instructed in the proper procedure regardless of what method is used, and in an area that can afford privacy. If the shave method is the only choice available, the wet shave method is mandatory as it facilitates hair removal, minimizes skin trauma, and prevents dry hair and debris from becoming airborne. If a depilatory is used, a "patch-test" should be performed first to identify a possible reaction. If no adverse effects are visible, the agent is applied following the manufacturer's instructions for application and removal.

11 Intraoperative Patient Care Management: Transporting, Positioning, Preparing

STUDY OUTLINE

1. **The intraoperative phase begins with the transference of the patient to the procedure room, and ends with the admission of the patient to the designated postanesthesia area.**

I. PERIOPERATIVE NURSING ACTIVITIES

1. Perioperative nursing practice has one continuous goal: *to provide a standard of excellence in the care of the patient before, during, and after surgery.*
2. **As the only nonscrubbed member of the surgical team, besides anesthesia personnel, the circulating nurse represents the coordinating link between the scrub team and all other departments and personnel associated with the surgical patient and the procedure.**
3. The circulating nurse, by virtue of her professional educational preparation and specialized skill, is responsible for managing patient care activities in the procedure room during surgery, so his or her duties begin long before the patient arrives in the procedure room and continues until the final dispensation of the patient, operating room records, and specimens is completed.
4. The following list depicts some of the activities performed by the circulating nurse prior to induction and upon conclusion of the procedure:
   a. Assisting and preparing the procedure room.
   b. Supervising the transporting, moving, and lifting of the patient.
   c. Assisting anesthesia as requested during induction and reversal of anesthesia.
   d. Positioning the patient for surgery.
   e. Performing the surgical skin prep.
   f. Conducting and maintaining accurate records of counts.
   g. Maintaining accurate documentation of nursing activities during the procedure.
   h. Dispensing supplies and medications to the surgical field.
   i. Maintaining an aseptic and safe environment.
   j. Estimating fluid and blood loss.
   k. Handling special equipment, specimens, etc.
   l. Communicating special postoperative needs to appropriate persons at the conclusion of the case.

II. TRANSPORTING, MOVING, AND LIFTING THE PATIENT

1. **When the preoperative admission procedures have been completed, and the operating room is prepared for the surgical procedure, the patient is transported to the designated procedure room.**
2. The process of transporting the patient to the procedure room is often viewed by the nurse as a chore, and is usually delegated to the aide or orderly assigned to the surgical suite. It is not unusual for this transition time to be neglected by nursing personnel, yet the patient may be vulnerable, helpless, and extremely anxious during this time, and may need the support of a perioperative nurse.

3. **Of primary importance during this time is patient safety,** and the following guidelines can aid in maintaining a safe, nonthreatening transition for the patient:
   a. Transport the patient only after the preadmission procedure has been completed.
   b. Maintain the side rails in an up position during transport.
   c. Assure that upper extremities are well within the framework of the stretcher.
   d. Move the patient in a smooth, nonjerking motion, traveling feet first.
   e. Prior to moving the patient to the operating table, position the stretcher by the side of the operating table, lower the side rail nearest the operating table, lock the stretcher, and lower the other side rail. If the patient is alert, caution him or her to move slowly to the table, and provide assistance as necessary. If the patient is sedated, use a **roller** to assist in the moving process.
   f. When transporting a child in a crib, raise all side rails of the crib to their highest point to prevent the child from crawling over the top.
   g. Never leave a patient on the operating table without immediate supervision present.
4. Since safety is a primary concern, assigned transporter's duties and manipulation in and out of a procedure room should be part of an orientation program designed specifically for the surgical environment. This orientation program may include principles of aseptic technique, transportation, moving and lifting awake and anesthetized patients, and assisting with patient positioning in the procedure room.
5. If the patient has special tubes, machines, and so on, a nurse should accompany the patient to the procedure room if the circulator is unable to assist in the transport process, and assist with moving the patient in order to manage the special equipment.
6. When the patient is finally on the operating table, the nurse applies the safety strap with a brief explanation of its purpose, and remains with the patient as anesthesia prepares for induction. The perioperative nurse is responsible and accountable for all nursing care, procedures, and actions performed for or with the patient. The patient and the anesthesia induction become the priorities during this phase of the surgical experience.

III. POSITIONING THE PATIENT

1. **Patient positioning is a facet of patient-care management that is as important to the surgical outcome as adequate preoperative preparation and safe administration of anesthesia.** It requires knowledge of anatomy and physiology, and requires skill in using the various positioning equipment and accessories.
2. **The patient is positioned** *after* **induction and then only when the anesthesia clinician believes the patient is stable and can be moved safely.**
3. The following guidelines should be used when moving and repositioning any patient who has been anesthetized or whose protective reflexes have been impaired:
   a. Before moving the patient, always ask permission from the anesthesia clinician, who will ultimately be responsible for the patient's head and lines.
   b. Obtain enough help to move the patient smoothly and safely.
   c. Be gentle when manipulating joints into desired position. Abducting a limb to an angle greater than 90 degrees may cause injury to the extremity.
   d. Support all joints and extremities during the move, since they will be vulnerable to injury.
   e. Respect the patient's dignity by avoiding any unnecessary exposure during the positioning.
   f. Maintain proper body alignment, regardless of the position required for the procedure.
   g. Move the patient slowly and deliberately, maintaining a total awareness of physiologic impairment that can occur related to positioning.
   h. Protect from tension I.V. lines, catheters, and breathing circuits.
   i. Provide padding for all bony prominences.
   j. Protect yourself by using proper body mechanics during the move.
   k. Have available all necessary accessories for positioning the patient in the room before the move is initiated.
   l. Once in position, secure the patient with a safety strap, avoiding occlusion or pressure over an area. The safety strap should be placed on top of the blanket (sheet) covering the patient. If an electrocautery unit is to be used, place the ground pad in proper position at this time.

A. POSITIONING: A TEAM CONCEPT

1. **The responsibility for safely positioning the surgical patient involves the entire surgical team.** The surgeon determines the position for optimal exposure of the surgical site, while the anesthesiologist, being concerned with airway maintenance, vascular access, and cardiovascular stability, will either agree or make an alternative suggestion, trying to accommodate the surgeon while assuring physiologic stability for the patient.
2. **The perioperative nurse, aware of this decision, coordinates the activities related to positioning, such as preparation of the positioning aids and equipment.**
3. The related patient information, which will aid in safely positioning a patient, can be obtained from the Preoperative Assessment tool, and from there a plan of action can be formulated and executed using the principles of safe moving and lifting techniques.

B. PLANNING CONSIDERATIONS

Five factors should be considered when planning the position of a patient for surgery:

1. **Anatomy involved with the procedure**
   a. Knowledge of the area in relation to:
      (1) Organs, site of disease/tumor
      (2) Right or left-sided extremity
      (3) Area to be grafted or repaired
2. **Surgical approach and/or surgeon's preference**
   a. Area must be easily accessible and provide maximum exposure to expedite surgery
3. **Patient comfort**
   a. Support for head and extremities
   b. Proper body alignment
   c. Avoidance of pressure points by adequate padding
   d. Avoidance of overexposure
      (1) Maintaining privacy
      (2) Avoiding hypothermic complications
   e. Proposed length of surgery
4. **Patient and staff safety**
   a. Proper use of safety strap
   b. Proper use and placement of positioning devices
   c. Moving and lifting using proper body mechanics and adequate personnel
   d. Protecting neuromuscular and skeletal structures
   e. Proper placement of electrosurgical ground pad
   f. Knowledge of own physical limitations
5. **Respiratory and circulatory freedom**
   a. **Respiratory**
      (1) Relief of chest from external pressure
      (2) Maintenance of adequate airway
   b. **Circulatory**
      (1) Avoidance of pressure on extremities that could decrease venous blood flow
      (2) Avoidance of hyperextension of arms without proper support
      (3) Avoidance of crossed ankles or legs in supine position

C. GENERAL PHYSIOLOGIC EFFECTS OF PATIENT POSITIONING

1. **Patient positioning influences the cardiovascular, respiratory, and neurologic systems, and coupled with the effects of anesthesia, can become a potential danger for all surgical patients.**
2. **Respiratory system**
   a. A change in position alters the pulmonary capillary blood flow volume, thereby affecting the amount of blood available for oxygenation.

b. The inspired air in the lungs may be redistributed, affecting the available air needed to oxygenate blood.

c. Lung tissue compliance is decreased, which reduces the amount of air that can be taken in for rapid exchange.

d. Expansion of the lungs is limited, either by mechanical restriction of the ribs or a reduced ability of the diaphragm to force the abdominal contents downward.

3. **Cardiovascular system**
   a. Anesthesia (general or regional) causes the peripheral blood vessels to dilate.
   b. Hypotension can occur related to positioning effects.
   c. Pooling can occur in dependent areas, caused by dilated vascular beds.
   d. The amount of blood returned to the heart and lungs can be reduced, affecting oxygenation and redistribution of oxygenated blood.
   e. Usually, pressure and/or obstruction of a vessel causes the greatest amount of damage to the cardiovascular system.

4. **Neurologic system**
   a. Most of the problems related to positioning are seen during the postoperative phase.
   b. Peripheral and superficial nerves are vulnerable to damage from mechanical pressure.
   c. The majority of the problems are related to pressure, obstruction, and stretching due to faulty positioning, and are most commonly associated with nerve injury.
   d. Motor/sensory nerve loss can happen within minutes of improper positioning and tissue damage can have a long-term effect.

D. SURGICAL POSITIONS AND RELATED PHYSIOLOGIC EFFECTS

1. **There are eight common positions that can be adapted and used for most surgical procedures, and all are variations of two basic positions: supine and prone. These positions are: supine, prone, Trendelenburg, reverse Trendelenburg, lithotomy, sitting (modified Fowler), Kraske (jackknife), and lateral recumbent.**

2. **Supine (dorsal recumbent): The most common and most natural position.**
   a. **Procedures:** Abdominal, extremity, vascular, chest, neck, facial, ear, breast surgery.
   b. **Positioning techniques**
      (1) Patient lies flat on back with arms either extended on arm boards or placed along side of body.
      (2) Small padding is placed under patient's head and neck and under knees.
      (3) Vulnerable pressure points should be padded, e.g., heels, elbows, sacrum.
      (4) If procedure will be longer than 1 hour or patient is particularly vulnerable to pressure, egg crate or flotation mattress should be used.
      (5) Safety straps applied 2 in. above knees.
      (6) If head is turned to one side, doughnut or special head rest should be used to protect superficial facial nerves and blood vessels.
      (7) Eyes should be protected by using eye patch, and ointment to prevent drying.
   c. **Physiologic effects**
      (1) **Cardiovascular system**
         (a) Decrease of mean arterial pressure, heart rate.
         (b) Increase in cardiac output and stroke volume.
         (c) Decrease in diastolic blood pressure.
         (d) Potential for venous pooling in lower extremities.
      (2) **Respiratory system**
         (a) Compromised respiratory function.
         (b) Decrease in vital capacity.
         (c) Decrease in diaphragmatic excursion.
         (d) More even distribution of ventilation from apex to base of lung.

3. **Prone**
   a. **Procedures:** surgeries involving posterior surface of body, e.g., spine, neck, buttocks, lower extremities.

    b. **Positioning techniques**
      (1) Induction of anesthesia is performed in supine position either on patient's bed or operating table. Once asleep, patient is "log rolled" onto stomach.
      (2) Chest rolls or bolsters are placed on operating table prior to positioning, lengthwise on both sides.
      (3) Foam head rest or doughnut; head turned to side or facing downward.
      (4) Patient's arms are rotated to the padded armboards that face head, bringing them through their normal range of motion, elbows bent.
      (5) Padding for knees and pillow for lower extremities to prevent toes from touching mattress.
      (6) Safety strap applied 2 in. below knees.
    c. **Physiologic effects**
      (1) **Cardiovascular system**
        (a) Few cardiovascular problems if positioned correctly.
        (b) Pressure on inferior vena cava and femoral veins, which can reduce venous return resulting in a decrease in blood pressure if improperly positioned.
        (c) If head turned to one side, pressure on carotid sinuses can cause hypotension and arrhythmias.
      (2) **Respiratory system**
        (a) Most vulnerable to respiratory problems.
        (b) Body weight against abdominal wall limits diaphragmatic movement, resulting in increased airway pressure with difficulty in ventilation; limits tidal volume.

4. Trendelenburg
    a. **Procedures:** lower abdomen, pelvic organs, when there is a need to tilt abdominal viscera away from the pelvic area.
    b. **Positioning techniques**
      (1) Patient is supine with head lower than feet.
      (2) Shoulder braces should not be used as they may cause damage to brachial plexus. If needed, they should be well padded and placed over acromial process of the scapula.
      (3) When patient is returned to supine position, care must be taken to move leg section slowly, then the entire table to level position.
      (4) Modification of this position can be used for hypovolemic shock.
      (5) Extremity position and safety strap are the same as for supine position.
    c. **Physiologic effects**
      (1) **Cardiovascular system**
        (a) Blood pools in upper torso, increasing blood pressure.
        (b) Can produce drop in blood pressure when returned to supine position.
        (c) Neck veins engorged (good for C.V.P./Swan line insertion).
        (d) Cyanosis; increased vascular load to heart from lower extremities.
      (2) **Respiratory system**
        (a) Decrease in lung volume resulting in respiratory embarrassment.
        (b) Interference with respiratory exchanges.
        (c) May precipitate pulmonary congestion and edema.
        (d) Decrease in diaphragmatic expansion (abdominal contents pushed up).

5. Reverse Trendelenburg
    a. **Procedures:** upper abdominal, head and neck, facial surgery.
    b. **Positioning technique**
      (1) Patient is supine with head higher than feet.
      (2) Small pillow under neck and knees.
      (3) Well-padded footboard should be used to prevent slippage to the foot of the table.
      (4) Antiembolic hose should be used if position is to be maintained for an extended period of time.
      (5) Patient should be returned slowly to supine position.

    c. **Physiologic effects**
      (1) **Cardiovascular system**
        (a) Diminished cardiac return resulting in decreased cardiac output.
        (b) Decrease in brainstem perfusion due to gravity.
        (c) Pooling of blood in lower extremities.
        (d) Possibility of circulatory overload if returned to supine position quickly.
      (2) **Respiratory system**
        (a) Unimpaired respiratory movement with minimal restrictions of ventral expansion of anterior chest wall.
        (b) Potential reduction in the diffusing capacity of oxygen owing to perfusion of upper regions of lungs.
        (c) Potential for respiratory insufficiency and respiratory acidosis.

6. **Lithotomy**
    a. **Procedures:** perineal, vaginal, rectal surgeries; combined abdominal-vaginal procedures.
    b. **Positioning techniques**
      (1) Exaggerated variation of supine position; can be dangerous and uncomfortable to patient.
      (2) Patient is placed in supine position with buttocks near lower break in the table (sacrum area should be well padded).
      (3) Feet are placed in stirrups or knee rests attached to operating table on both sides.
      (4) Stirrup height should not be excessively high or low, but even on both sides.
      (5) Padded stirrups (knee brace) must not compress vascular structures or nerves in the popliteal space.
      (6) Pressure from metal stirrups against upper inner aspect of thigh/calf should be avoided.
      (7) Legs should be raised and lowered slowly and simultaneously (may require two people).
    c. **Physiologic effects**
      (1) **Cardiovascular system**
        (a) Circulatory pooling in the lumbar region.
        (b) Rapid lowering of legs could cause sudden drop in blood pressure (500-800 mL of blood may shift from lumbar area to legs).
        (c) Compromise to circulatory system due to compression of abdominal contents on inferior vena cava and abdominal aorta.
      (2) **Respiratory system**
        (a) Reduction in respiratory efficiency due to pressure from thighs on abdomen and pressure from the diaphragm on abdominal viscera, restricting respirations.
        (b) Lung tissue becomes engorged with blood; vital capacity and tidal volume decreased.
      (3) In addition to circulatory and respiratory problems associated with this position, major concern is nerve damage to femoral, obturator, and perineal nerves; dislocation of hip; crushing of fingers if they are left too close to the lower table break when raising table to supine position.

7. **Modified Fowler (sitting)**
    a. **Procedures:** otorhinology (ear and nose), neurosurgery (posterior or occipital approach).
    b. **Positioning techniques**
      (1) Variation of reverse Trendelenburg position.
      (2) Patient is supine, positioned over the upper break in the table (footboard optional).
      (3) Backrest is elevated, knees flexed.
      (4) Arms rest on pillow placed in lap; safety strap 2 in. above the knees.
      (5) Pressure areas include the scapula, olecranon, sacrum, ischial tuberosities, and calcaneus.
      (6) Slow movement in and out of position must be used to prevent drastic changes in blood volume movement.
      (7) Antiembolic hose should be used to assist venous return.
      (8) When using special neurologic headrest, eyes must be protected.
    c. **Physiologic effects**
      (1) **Cardiovascular system**
        (a) Venous pooling in lower extremities.
        (b) Potential presence of air emboli due to negative pressure on the head and neck.

(c) Hypotension related to position and effect of anesthesia.
NOTE: Doppler and/or C.V.P. line may be used for detection and treatment should venous sinus be opened.

(2) Respiratory system
(a) Same as for reverse Trendelenburg.

8. **Kraske (jackknife)**
   a. **Procedures:** rectal procedures, sigmoidoscopy, colonoscopy.
   b. **Positioning techniques**
      (1) Variation of prone position.
      (2) Table is flexed at center break (90°).
      (3) All precautions taken with prone position are taken with Kraske position.
      (4) Table (safety) strap applied over thighs.
   c. **Physiologic effects:** Because of its adverse effects on both cardiovascular and respiratory systems, the Kraske is considered the most dangerous of all surgical positions. Physiologic responses are the same as with prone, only more exaggerated.

9. **Lateral recumbent**
   a. **Procedures:** chest and kidney surgeries.
   b. **Positioning techniques**
      (1) Special pad, "bean bag" or "Vac-Pac" is placed on operating table.
      (2) Initially, patient is positioned supine for induction.
      (3) Patient is then lifted and turned onto the non-operative side (usually requires four people during the move).
      (4) Head is supported and aligned with spinal column.
      (5) **For chest surgery**
         (a) Upper arm is flexed slightly at elbow and raised above head; padded overhead armboard may be used or padded Mayo stand.
         (b) Lower arm is brought forward slightly, flexed and placed on padded armboard.
         (c) The lower leg is flexed with a pillow placed between legs; feet are placed on pillow to maintain proper alignment.
         (d) Safety strap is applied at hip level.
      (6) **For kidney surgery**
         (a) Patient is positioned over kidney elevator of operative table (beneath bony iliac crest).
         (b) This position elevates operative area between the twelfth rib and iliac crest.
         (c) Upper extremities may be perpendicular to shoulder level; naturally flexed and supported with padded armboards (two lying side-by-side), or upper arm on overhead armboard.
         (d) Lower leg is flexed, and pillow placed between legs, with feet supported with pillow.
         (e) Safety strap across thigh (out of operative field).
      (7) Once in proper position, bean bag (Vac-Pac) is inflated; for kidney surgery, kidney elevator is raised and table is flexed.
   c. **Physiologic effects**
      (1) **Cardiovascular system**
         (a) Slight change in cardiac output may be evident.
         (b) Circulation may be impaired by pooling of blood in dependent limb.
         (c) If kidney rest is elevated, additional compromise may occur owing to pressure on abdominal vessels.
         (d) In left lateral position, mean arterial pressure drops 24 mm Hg; and in right lateral position it drops 33 mm Hg.
      (2) **Respiratory system**
         (a) Respiratory efficiency may be effected owing to pressure from weight of the body on the lower chest.
         (b) Restricted movement of chest results in possible compromise in gas exchange.
         (c) When anesthetized patient is breathing spontaneously, dependent lung has better ventilation at expense of lower lung.

(d) When patient is paralyzed, upper lung assumes greater compliance and ventilations increase.

(e) Simple lateral position reduces vital capacity 10 percent and tidal volume 8 percent; kidney position decreases vital capacity by 14.5 percent due to impairment of chest expansion in all directions.

IV. COMMON POSITIONING DEVICES AND CLINICAL IMPLICATIONS

1. Many devices are on the market today to aid in safely positioning the surgical patient. The perioperative nurse should have a working knowledge of these devices to provide optimum patient positioning, safety, and comfort.

2. Ideally, any materials used for positioning, especially padding, should accomplish four tasks: (1) absorb compressive force, (2) redistribute pressure, (3) prevent excessive stretching, and (4) provide support for optimum operative stability. All materials should be able to be cleaned adequately and disinfected.

A. TABLE ATTACHMENTS

1. The following are some of the more common table attachments that can be used during positioning:
   a. Safety table straps
   b. Armboards and wrist restraints
   c. Stirrup bars and popliteal knee supports
   d. Head rests (specialty) and attachments
   e. Kidney elevator and kidney rests
   f. Shoulder braces/supports and overhead arm rests
   g. Footboards

2. **Safety table straps**
   a. **The safety strap is the most important positioning device, since it is used the moment a patient is placed on the operating table and remains in place during the entire procedure, as a restraining tool.** It must be applied with specific principles in mind:
      (1) The strap is placed above the knees for supine position and below the knees for prone position.
      (2) It must be secure, yet not constricting, and must be positioned between the blanket (sheet) covering the patient and the patient to avoid any skin irritation.
      (3) The strap should be tightened enough to allow only a three-finger breadth beneath the strap, to avoid any possible pressure.
   b. Some straps are attached individually on each side of the operating table, with the ends brought together and secured with a Velcro closure device. Others attach on one side of the table frame and extend and attach to the opposite side.
   c. **When the safety strap cannot be used, some measure of safety restraint must be used to protect the patient from falling, moving, or turning.** Keep in mind that the operating table is very narrow, and remind the patient of this fact and the purpose of the safety restraint.

3. **Armboards and wrist restraints**
   a. **Armboards are used to support patients' arms and hands when they are not placed at their sides.** The armboards are attached to the metal frame of the O.R. table approximately at the axilla level, and once in place have a self-locking mechanism to prevent movement. The angle of the board, however, can be manipulated by a rod-like projection under the board to assist in a more natural placement of the extremities.
   b. An important concept to remember when positioning an extremity on a board is that *it should not exceed a 90-degree angle to the body, regardless of the position.*
   c. **Wrist restraints** come in a variety of materials and closures. They should be soft and nonconstricting, yet offer security for the arm when placed around an armboard.
   d. A modification of this armboard is the **adjustable extremity table,** which is either attached to the side of the table frame or slipped under the table mattress, extending the working

surface laterally to accommodate surgeries of the upper extremities. When this extension is used, the surgical team usually sits during the procedure.

4. **Stirrup bars and popliteal knee supports**
    a. Metal **stirrup posts** are placed inside holders that slide onto the table frame to support the legs and feet while in lithotomy position. The feet are placed in canvas or padded loops suspended from the stirrup, and usually cause the legs to be at right angle to the feet.
    b. For extensive surgery in the lithotomy position, padded **knee supports** can be used in which the popliteal space is supported in a padded "trough" like stirrup attached to the table. Careful positioning, and protecting the space behind the knee, can avoid pressure on the popliteal vessels and nerves.

5. **Head rests (specialty) and attachments**
    a. Commonly used for neurosurgical procedures, **head rests** attach to the head of the table after removing the pillow section of the table. The head rest supports and exposes areas of the head and cervical vertebrae.
    b. They can be used with the supine, prone, sitting, or lateral positions; some types use pin attachments, while others are horseshoe-shaped. The surgeon positions the head while the perioperative nurse stabilizes the head during final positioning and head rest attachment.

6. **Kidney elevator and kidney rests**
    a. The **kidney elevator** is part of the operating table, and can be elevated using the control panel (or crank) at the head of the table. It is used to elevate the mid torso area of the body when a patient is lying in the lateral position.
    b. The **kidney rest** is a concave padded metal attachment that is anchored to the table frame to stabilize the patient while he or she is in the lateral position. Kidney rests are place on both the anterior and posterior sides of the patient, and should be heavily padded to avoid pressure against the body.

7. **Shoulder braces/supports and overhead arm rests**
    a. The **shoulder braces** are attached to the head of the table and are used to prevent the patient slipping toward the head of the table when in the Trendelenburg position. They are metal, concave, and are covered with a foam slipcover.
    b. Shoulder braces should not be used when the arm is extended on a arm board, to avoid compression of the axillary nerve.
    c. Similar to a double armboard, this positioning device is attached to the table in line with the upper torso, with a flat, padded surface extending over the patient's head (face). A **Mayo stand**, padded and covered, can be used for the same purpose. Used in the lateral position, care must be used when positioning to avoid hyperextension of the axillary region, and the surface must be well padded to prevent pressure on vessels or nerves of the upper extremity.

8. **Footboards**: The footboard can serve two purposes:
    a. Left flat, as a horizontal surface extension of the table during vaginal or perineal surgeries performed in the lithotomy position.
    b. Raised perpendicular to the table and padded to support the feet, with the soles resting securely against it. This is used primarily in the Trendelenburg position.

B. ADDITIONAL POSITIONING AIDS

1. **Sandbags/pillows**: available in a variety of shapes and sizes to accommodate anatomic structures. This category includes doughnut-shaped head rests and foam rubber/gelled support pads for stabilization and immobilization of body sections.
2. **Flotation mattresses (gelled/egg crate)**: created in full table size or proportioned to fit specific devices. They are used to minimize pressure on bony prominences, peripheral blood vessels, and nerves during prolonged procedures (more than 2 hours), and for all cases in which the patient is awake or under conscious sedation.
3. **Chest rolls/commercial bolsters**: manufactured or can be created by the perioperative nurse using bath blankets; primarily used when the patient is in the prone position. They are placed longitudinally between the axilla and the hip bone, bilaterally in order to maintain adequate

respiratory exchange, and to prevent pressure on the chest (breasts), genitalia, and abdominal structures.

4. **Laminectomy frame:** a padded metal frame used to elevate the spinal area. The frame is positioned on the table and the patient placed on the frame, being supported from the acromioclavicular joint to the iliac crest. Extensive padding must be used with this frame, and the femoral artery and nerve must be protected.

5. **Towels, tape, ace bandages, soft roll, etc.:** can be used to stabilize a position, depending on the type of device being used. Additionally, the table draw sheet (lift sheet) can be used to assist in repositioning a patient or to secure the patient's arms when placed at the sides.

V. COMMON INJURIES RELATED TO POSITIONING

1. **Planning and preparation can avoid common injuries related to positioning the surgical patient. However, certain events increase the possibility of injury for all surgical patients.** For example, anesthesia prevents the body's normal defense against pain from warning the patient about exaggerated stretching, twisting, and compression of body parts. Peripheral nerve damage and ischemia caused by hyperextension or preexisting disease conditions are also common positioning injuries.

2. **Five areas are commonly susceptible to positioning complications and/or injury: (1) brachial plexus region, (2) ulnar/radial area, (3) saphenous and peroneal nerves, (4) the integumentary system, and (5) eye and facial injuries.** Crushing injuries to digits (upper and lower) can also occur whenever the Mayo tray or instrument table is repositioned or resting on or exerting pressure against the patient.

3. **Brachial plexus injury:** can result from improper positioning and/or hyperextension of the arm(s) or armboard(s), especially for patients in the supine position. To avoid this injury, the perioperative nurse should never allow the patient's arm to be extended to more than a 90-degree angle, and the patient's head should be turned toward the extended arm with the palm supinated or in a natural position. Brachial plexus injuries can also occur when a shoulder brace is used owing to improper positioning of the brace.

4. **Ulnar/radial nerve injury**
   a. The **ulnar nerve** is most commonly injured when an elbow slips off the mattress to the metal edge of the table, and the nerve is compressed between the table and the medial epicondyle.
   b. **Radial nerve** injury can occur either when the arm slips off the armboard and strikes the table or when it is placed at the side and is pressed between the patient and the table surface.
   c. To eliminate either of these possible injuries, position the hand downward along the patient's side, pad the elbow, and use the draw sheet to secure the arm and hand, and/or use wrist restraints placed loosely yet securely around the armboard and the patient's arm (especially an arm with an I.V. infusion catheter).

5. **Saphenous and peroneal nerve damage**
   a. **Saphenous and peroneal nerve injury are usually associated with the lithotomy position and the use of stirrups.** Special care must be used when placing a patient in and out of stirrups in order to avoid these injuries.
   b. Both legs should be raised together when placing a patient in the lithotomy position, first to the knee-chest position, then into the stirrups, to avoid strain on the hip joint and surrounding nerves. Injury to the peroneal nerve can also occur if the thigh is compressed against the stirrup bar (holder); therefore, the bar should be padded around the area of the fibula bone.
   c. Injury to the saphenous nerve can occur if the nerve is pressed between the metal popliteal knee support stirrup and the medial tibial condyle. This pressure could result in numbness in the calf and possible paralysis. Padding of the knee support can prevent this injury, especially between the stirrup and medial aspect of the knee.

6. **Integumentary damage**
   a. **Excessive pressure caused by any position can result in damage to the skin in the form of excoriation or actual bruises.** When planning positions for any procedure, certain factors to

protect the skin and soft tissue should be considered, including the patient's age, general health status, weight distribution, blood pressure, hydration status, and proposed length of immobility.

    b. To prevent these injuries, adequate padding must be used, especially on bony prominences and those anatomic areas requiring special consideration owing to the nature of the required position.

7. **Eye and facial injuries**

    a. The eyes should be closed and, if needed, an ointment used to maintain moisture and prevent scratching. Excessive pressure against the eye can cause thrombosis of the central retinal artery and can even result in blindness in some instances if the problem goes uncorrected.

    b. Compression of facial structures can be caused by position, equipment, or the surgical team leaning or pressing against the patient's face. This can be avoided by constant monitoring of the patient's head position, and if necessary, the use of a Mayo stand over the face to elevate the drapes, thus preventing possible injury.

8. **Preventive measures taken before positioning surgical patients can avoid undue harm and protect patients when they cannot protect themselves: one of the primary goals of perioperative nursing practice.**

VI. PREPARING THE INCISION SITE

1. **After the patient has been checked for proper positioning, the next phases of preparing the patient for surgery begin: (1) selection of the incision site based on the proposed surgical procedure, and (2) preparation of the skin by removing the resident flora, dirt, and oils.**

2. Even though nurses do not usually assist in the decision of what type of an incision to use for the surgical procedure, the knowledge of incisions in relationship to involved anatomy, positioning, instrumentation, suture choice, and skin preparation area is needed to plan for optimal patient outcomes.

A. IMPACT OF SITE SELECTION

1. **Two of the primary factors determining where the incision will be are the patient's diagnosis and the pathology the surgeon expects to encounter.** Other factors may affect the selection of sites: these include maximum exposure, ease and speed of entry or reentry (in an emergent state), the possibility of extending the incision, maximum postoperative wound strength with minimal postoperative discomfort, and finally, the general cosmetic effect.

2. *For the nurse technician* assisting at the sterile field, the knowledge of anatomic layers and structures as they relate to the incision site can assist in choosing the right instruments and suture/stapling choices. Knowledge of the incision site can also be used to help gauge the progress of the operation, thereby assisting in anticipating the needs of the surgeon/assistant during the procedure.

3. *For the circulating nurse,* knowledge of the incision site is of primary importance, since it will guide him or her in performing the surgical skin preparation. The prep should always begin at the site of the incision and work outward, toward the periphery. Additionally, gauging the progress of surgery assures the performance of counts at the proper interval and can help estimate the proper time for requesting the next patient to be premedicated.

4. *For the anesthesiologist/anesthesia clinician,* the choices of sites can directly or indirectly affect the method and/or technique for administration of anesthesia, depending on the anatomic structure involved.

B. INCISION SITE LOCATIONS

1. When discussing incisions and their locations, it is important to know anatomic directional terms, such as **median** and **horizontal** planes of the body, so that basic landmarks can be located when other directional terms are used, such as **upper quadrant, oblique,** or **paramedian.** For example, a **right paramedian** would be located just to the right of and perpendicular to the median

(middle) line. It is essential that the perioperative nurse become familiar with these areas/plans to prepare the incision site effectively.

2. Although it is not uncommon for surgeries to have several approaches, the perioperative nurse also should be familiar with the most common incision sites as they relate to anatomic structures and/or surgical procedures associated with the thoracic, abdominal, and pelvic cavities. Common incisions sites include the following:

    a. **Midline:** This is the simplest and most common abdominal incision, and is used primarily with general surgical procedures as it provides adequate exposure to nearly all the structures within the abdominal cavity. It usually extends in the upper region from the xiphoid process to the umbilicus and in the lower abdomen from the umbilicus to the symphysis pubis.

    b. **Subcostal (Kocher's):** This incision, either right or left, follows the lower costal margin in a semicurved shape. Because the rectus muscles are severed, this incision can be more painful postoperatively than the midline incision.

    c. **Obliques**

        (1) The term **oblique** refers to a slanting or inclined line which is usually associated with the inguinal regions or when performing an appendectomy (McBurney's). However, it can be used to denote any incision created on this angle.

        (2) **Inguinal:** The right/left oblique in the inguinal region gives excellent exposure of the structures located in the groin area.

        (3) **McBurney's:** Traditionally associated with an exploration of the appendix, this incision can be used for exploration of any other structure located in the right lower quadrant of the abdomen, although visibility is limited.

    d. **Transverse:** There are two commonly used transverse incisions: **lower (Pfannensteil)** and **midabdominal.**

        (1) **Pfannensteil:** This incision, nicknamed the "bikini-cut," is frequently used in gynecologic surgery. The incision is a curved line across the lower abdomen, above the symphysis pubis.

        (2) **Midabdominal:** This incision is used on the right or left side, or for a retroperitoneal approach. It begins slightly above or below the umbilicus and is extended to the lumbar region at an angle, between the ribs and the crest of the ilium.

    e. **Thoracoabdominal:** This incision is used when exposure to the thoracic and abdominal cavities may be required. The incision begins at a point mid-way between the xiphoid process and the umbilicus, extending across to the seventh or eighth intercostal space, and to the midscapular line superiorly.

VII. SURGICAL SKIN PREPARATION

A. GENERAL CONSIDERATIONS

1. **The majority of postoperative infections result from contamination acquired in the operating room.** Three factors seem to have a dominant role in the development of surgical infections:
    a. Microbial contamination of the wound.
    b. Condition of the wound at the end of the surgery.
    c. Patient susceptibility.

2. Since the interaction of these factors is complex, measures intended to prevent surgical wound infections are aimed at all three.

3. The actual surgical technique will ultimately determine the condition of the wound at the end of surgery. Measures taken by the perioperative nurse to prevent surgical wound infections can be directly related to the preparation of the incision site.

4. **The area to be prepped is determined by the site of the incision and the nature of the planned surgical intervention.** A wide area is usually preferable, since it allows the surgeon to extend the incision and/or strategically place tubes or drains as needed within an aseptically prepared area.

5. **Since the patient's skin cannot be sterilized, measures must be taken to reduce the resident and transient flora naturally present on the skin surface.** This can be accomplished by the application

of an **antimicrobial agent**, rendering the skin "surgically clean," and is performed prior to the draping procedure.

6. **Antimicrobial solutions**
   a. The antimicrobial agent(s) chosen for the skin preparation should be capable of removing superficial oils, dirt, and debris without causing undue tissue reaction to the agent. It should be able to decrease the microbial count while leaving a protective film or residue on the skin.
   b. Two generic groups of antimicrobial agents are capable of reducing both gram-positive and gram-negative bacteria to a minimum. These are **(1) povidone/iodine** and **(2) chlorhexidine gluconate**. Both these agents meet the criteria for selection of an effective antimicrobial agent since both: (1) are rapid acting, (2) are not dependent on cumulative action, (3) have a broad spectrum of activity in reducing transient/resident flora, (4) have minimal harsh effects on the skin, (5) inhibit rapid rebound growth of microbes, (6) have a contact time based on documentation in scientific literature, and (7) are economical to use.

B. **SEQUENCE OF THE SURGICAL SKIN PREP**

   1. **The surgical skin prep is performed by the circulating nurse (or designated person, e.g., intern) using strict aseptic technique. The area of the skin prep, the solutions used, and any undesirable patient reactions (e.g., allergenic) should be documented on the intraoperative record.**
   2. The following recommended practices are associated with the surgical skin prep, and should be used as a guide for effective practice:
      a. The area surrounding the operative site should be cleaned.
      b. The skin or the operative site and surrounding areas should be prepared with an antimicrobial agent(s) before incision.
      c. The preoperative skin preparation should be documented in the patient's record.
   3. The skin preparation is performed in three segments:
      a. Assessing and documenting skin condition and removing any hair directly interfering with the incision site.
      b. Cleansing (scrubbing) the skin with the antimicrobial scrub solution, removing the superficial dirt, oils, and debris.
      c. Applying the antimicrobial solution, which creates an antiseptic-like bacterial barrier.
   4. Today, there are a variety of prep solutions and prepping set-ups to choose from. Some require only one step, while others require both the scrubbing and the painting. Regardless of how the agent(s) is dispensed, the overall principles of performing an aseptic procedure remain the same: **the prep begins at the site of the incision and works outward toward the periphery, never going over an area already prepared.**

C. **PERIOPERATIVE NURSING CONSIDERATIONS**

   1. Prior to beginning the surgical skin prep, the perioperative nurse should be mindful of the following considerations:
      a. **The patient should have no known allergies to the planned solution.**
         (1) Review patient admission assessment for sensitivity or allergies to iodine or seafood.
         (2) For those patients who have demonstrated skin sensitivities to either agent, another broad-spectrum antimicrobial agent, parachlorometaxylenol, may be substituted after consultation with the surgeon.
      b. **Chlorohexidine gluconate should not be used for or near the eyes, ears, or mouth.**
      c. **Alcohol is *not* recommended for use as a primary prepping agent.** If it is used, the skin *must* be completely dried before using electrosurgery and/or laser.
      d. **Sponges need not be saturated (dripping) with the agent in order to be effective.** The combination of the chemical and mechanical friction create an acceptable mechanism for preparing the patient's skin.
   2. **Supplies and set-up**
      a. **The supplies needed to perform the surgical skin preparation should be arranged on a separate surface a safe distance from the sterile field.** Most prep trays are preassembled and

disposable, with contents varying according to manufacturer; some contain individual bottles of prep solution, while others are "dry," to add the solution of choice.

b. If additional procedures (e.g., insertion of a Foley catheter) are to be performed, they should be done prior to the prep, using a completely separate set-up to avoid accidental contamination of the aseptically prepared area.

3. **Special areas of consideration**

   a. **Eyes:** The eyes should be washed with cotton balls and a nonirritating solution (surgeon's preference). Prep should begin at the nose and continue outward toward the cheeks. Prep solution should be rinsed with warm sterile water.

   b. **Traumatic/open wounds:** Large amounts of detergent-irrigating solution combination may be used prior to the prep and/or in addition to the prep, to remove gross dirt from the wound, depending on the condition of the traumatized area. Once the wound has been initially cleansed, handle the prep as if it was a stoma or contaminated area prep.

   c. **Stomas:** The external stoma (orifice) of a colostomy or ileostomy may be (1) sealed off from the operative site with a detergent-soaked sponge, and the area surrounding it (considered clean) prepped first, or (2) cleaned from the outer boundary of the stoma area outward, then coming back to the stoma with a new sponge. Since the area has been aseptically prepared, the paint sequence is started from the incision site outward, including the stoma area.

   d. **Limb preparation:** A circumferential prep should be performed on all extremities, which usually will require an assistant to extend and hold up the extremity. Persons should have sterile gloves so as not to interfere with the aseptic area involved.

   e. **Tumors/aneurysms/ovarian cysts**

      (1) **Tumors/biopsy:** Carcinoma cells can become disseminated with vigorous scrubbing; therefore, use gentle yet comprehensive scrubbing technique.

      (2) **Aortic aneurysms:** Aneurysms could rupture during the prepping sequence; thus, work quickly yet gently.

      (3) **Ovarian cyst:** Large ones could rupture as a result of a vigorous scrub.

   f. **Fractures:** Fractures must be stabilized during the prep (e.g., with an additional person holding the affected extremity), and gentle scrubbing should be used to avoid further complications. A circumferential prep should be used. If the fracture is comminuted, solution may be poured over the area instead of painted.

   g. **Genitalia:** This area is considered dirty; therefore, it should be done last when incorporated with an abdominal prep. Internal vaginal preps should be performed with solution only, since detergent may cause a reaction (itching, burning, etc.).

   h. **Dirty/contaminated areas (colostomy, infections, etc.)**

      (1) **Umbilicus:** cleaned separately with cotton-tipped applicator.

      (2) **Perineal prep:** vagina and anus prepped last and with separate sponge.

      (3) **Shoulder:** axilla is prepped last.

      (4) **Draining sinuses, skin ulcers:** scrub last--*clean to dirty* principle applies to all aseptic skin preps, regardless of the area involved.

   i. **Grafts:** A separate set-up for donor and recipient site should be used. The donor site is prepped first. Two nurses may be required to do a simultaneous prep. The donor site should be prepped with a colorless antiseptic solution to allow postoperative visibility of the vascularity of the graft. The donor site is covered with a sterile towel if not dressed immediately.

   j. **Emergency preps:** There are occasions when the urgency to begin the surgery overrides the need for a full surgical prep (e.g., leaking aortic aneurysm, emergency cesarean section, traumatic hemorrhage). The surgical scrub may be omitted and the solution used alone.

D. SURGICAL PREP GUIDELINES

NOTE: For specific procedures, refer to the institutional reference manual or the Physician's Preference Card.

1. **Abdomen:** includes breastline to upper third of thighs; table-line to table-line, when in supine position.
2. **Chest/breast:** includes shoulders, upper arm to elbow, axilla, and chest wall to table-line and 2 in. beyond the sternum to the opposite shoulder (lateral or supine with surgical side slightly elevated).
3. **Lateral/thoracotomy:** includes axilla, chest, and abdomen from neck to crest of ilium. Area should extend beyond the midline, anteriorly and posteriorly.
4. **Rectoperineal/vaginal:** includes pubis, vulva, labia, perineum, anus, and adjacent areas, including inner aspects of upper third of thighs.
5. **Abdominal/vaginal:** abdomen to above the umbilicus to pubis area, including vaginal area as previously described.
6. **Knee/lower leg:** includes the entire circumference of affected leg and extends from the foot to the upper part of the thigh.
7. **Hip/lower extremity:** includes the abdomen on the affected side, thigh to knee, buttocks to table-line; groin, and pubis. Prep must be circumferential.

PRACTICE QUESTIONS

1. **The primary role of the circulating nurse during the intraoperative period can *best* be described as:**

   1. *transporting, positioning, and preparing the patient for surgery.*

   2. *maintaining a sterile field inside the surgical suite.*

   3. *managing patient care activities in the procedure room during surgery.*

   4. *serving as the assistant to the surgeon during the surgical procedure.*

2. **Of primary importance during the time the patient is being transported to the designated procedure room is:**

   1. *speed.*

   2. *patient safety.*

   3. *protection of surgical equipment.*

   4. *nursing accountability.*

3. **Which of the following is NOT an accepted guideline for assuring a safe transition for the patient from the holding area to the procedure room?**

   1. *Move the patient in a smooth, nonjerking motion, with feet to the rear.*

   2. *Maintain the side rails in an up position during transport.*

   3. *Transport the patient only after the preadmission procedure has been completed.*

   4. *Never leave a patient on the operating table without immediate supervision present.*

4. **At what point during the intraoperative period is the patient repositioned on the operating table?**

   1. *In the holding area, once the patient has been sedated and is about to be transported to the procedure room.*

   2. *Just prior to induction and after the patient record has been examined for accuracy and completeness.*

   3. *Just prior to induction and after all bony prominences have been padded and all I.V. lines, catheters, and breathing circuits have been protected.*

   4. *After induction and when the anesthesia clinician believes the patient is stable.*

5. **Which of the following is NOT an accepted guideline for moving and repositioning any patient who who has been anesthetized or whose protective reflexes have been impaired?**

   1. *Before moving the patient, always ask permission from the anesthesia clinician.*

   2. *To avoid injury to an extremity, avoid abducting a limb to an angle greater than 90 degrees.*

   3. *Maintain proper body alignment, regardless of the position required for the procedure.*

   4. *To avoid possible injury, move all necessary accessories for positioning the patient into the room after the move is completed.*

6. **Determination of the position for optimal exposure of the incision site is made by the:**

   1. *surgeon alone.*

   2. *surgeon in collaboration with the anesthesiologist.*

   3. *anesthesiologist in collaboration with the surgeon.*

   4. *entire surgical team.*

7. **Which of the following is generally not a *major* factor for the nurse to consider when planning the position of a patient for surgery?**

   1. *The type of anesthesia to be used.*

   2. *The anatomy involved with the procedure.*

   3. *The surgical approach and/or surgeon's preference.*

   4. *The comfort and safety of the patient and staff.*

8. **During surgery, the respiratory system may be affected in several ways by patient positioning. Which of the following is NOT one of these potential changes?**

   1. *The inspired air in the lungs may be redistributed, affecting the available air needed to oxygenate blood.*

   2. *Lung tissue compliance is increased, which increases the amount of air that can be taken in for rapid exchange.*

    3. *A change in position alters the pulmonary capillary blood flow volume, thereby affecting the amount of blood available for oxygenation.*

    4. *Expansion of the lungs is limited, either by mechanical restriction of the ribs or a reduced ability of the diaphragm to force the abdominal contents downward.*

9. **The most common and most natural surgical position, and one used in many abdominal, extremity, vascular, chest, neck, facial, ear, and breast procedures, is the:**

    1. *prone.*

    2. *Trendelenburg.*

    3. *supine.*

    4. *lithotomy.*

10. **Which of the following pairings of a surgical position with the type of procedures for which the position is commonly used is INCORRECT?**

    1. *Prone: surgeries involving the posterior surface of the body (e.g., buttocks).*

    2. *Trendelenburg: procedures involving the lower abdomen and pelvic organs.*

    3. *Modified Fowler: neurosurgery and ear and nose procedures.*

    4. *Lateral recumbent: combined abdominal-vaginal procedures.*

11. **Of the following surgical positions, the one associated with the highest incidence of respiratory problems is the:**

    1. *prone.*

    2. *modified Fowler.*

    3. *reverse Trendelenburg.*

    4. *lateral recumbent.*

12. **A surgical position in which the patient is supine with the head higher than the feet is the:**

    1. *Kraske.*

    2. *Trendelenburg.*

    3. *reverse Trendelenburg.*

    4. *modified Fowler.*

13. **The surgical position that requires the use of stirrups or knee rests attached to the operating table on both sides is the:**

    1. *Kraske.*

    2. *lateral recumbent.*

3. *Trendelenburg.*

4. *lithotomy.*

14. **The most dangerous of the various surgical positions is the:**

    1. *modified Fowler.*

    2. *reverse Trendelenburg.*

    3. *lateral recumbent.*

    4. *Kraske.*

15. **The most important of the common surgical positioning devices is the:**

    1. *safety table strap.*

    2. *head rest and attachments.*

    3. *footboard.*

    4. *stirrup bar.*

16. **An important concept to remember when positioning an extremity on an armboard is that it should:**

    1. *not exceed a 90-degree angle to the body, regardless of the position.*

    2. *always be used in conjunction with a shoulder brace to avoid compression of the axillary nerve.*

    3. *be placed as far away from the body as possible for maximum comfort and safety.*

    4. *be placed in an upright position, with the armboard extended vertically from the procedure table.*

17. **Padded knee supports are *most* likely to be used for which of the following procedures?**

    1. *Those in which the patient is in a lateral position.*

    2. *Those involving extensive surgery in the lithotomy position.*

    3. *Those in which the head of the operating table is elevated.*

    4. *Those in which the patient is in the reverse Trendelenburg position.*

18. **Shoulder braces are *most* likely to be used when the patient is in which of the following positions?**

    1. *Modified Fowler.*

    2. *Trendelenburg.*

    3. *Lithotomy.*

    4. *Lateral recumbent.*

19. For which of the following procedures is a flotation mattress *most* likely to be used?

1. *For a procedure in which the mid torso area of the body is elevated.*

2. *For a procedure involving deep surgery to the lower abdomen or pelvic region.*

3. *For a procedure in which the patient is in a prone position.*

4. *For a prolonged procedure in which the patient is awake.*

20. For procedures in which a laminectomy frame is used, the nurse should take special care to:

1. *secure the patient's arms when placed at the sides.*

2. *avoid compression of the axillary nerve.*

3. *use slow movement in and out of position to prevent drastic changes in blood volume movement.*

4. *protect the femoral artery and nerve with extensive padding.*

21. Injury to the ulnar and radial nerves during surgery can be avoided by following several guidelines. Which of the following is NOT one of these guidelines?

1. *Pad the elbow.*

2. *Use properly secured wrist restraints.*

3. *Position the hand upward.*

4. *Position the hand along the patients's side.*

22. Injury to saphenous and peroneal nerves is *most* likely to be associated with which of the following?

1. *Lithotomy position; use of stirrups.*

2. *Trendelenburg position; use of a Mayo stand.*

3. *Supine position; use of a shoulder brace.*

4. *Modified Fowler position: use of a head rest.*

23. Compression of facial structures during surgery, causing facial injury, can be avoided by constant monitoring of the patient's head position. Another step that can be taken if necessary is using a(n):

1. *"bean bag" or "Vac-Pac" for added protection.*

2. *adjustable extremity table to extend the operating surface laterally.*

3. *padded Mayo stand over the face to elevate the drapes.*

4. *chest roll placed longitudinally between the axilla and the hip bone.*

24. **Before deciding where the surgical incision will be, the surgeon takes into account several factors. Which of the following typically is NOT one of these factors?**

    1. *The patient's diagnosis.*

    2. *The pathology the surgeon expects to encounter.*

    3. *The type of anesthesia used.*

    4. *The possibility of extending the incision.*

25. **For the circulating nurse, knowledge of the incision site is of primary importance because it will guide him or her in:**

    1. *choosing the right instruments for the procedure.*

    2. *performing the surgical skin preparation for the procedure.*

    3. *making the right suture/stapling decisions for the procedure.*

    4. *anticipating the needs of the surgeon/assistant during the procedure.*

26. **A surgeon performing an exploration of the appendix is likely to use which of the following *general* types of incisions?**

    1. *Midline.*

    2. *Subcostal (Kocher's).*

    3. *Oblique (McBurney's).*

    4. *Transverse.*

27. **A surgeon begins an exploratory laparotomy of the abdomen by making an incision slightly below the umbilicus and extending it to the lumbar region at an angle, between the ribs and the crest of the ilium. This incision is known as a(n):**

    1. *oblique.*

    2. *Pfannensteil.*

    3. *subcostal.*

    4. *midabdominal.*

28. **Measures intended to prevent surgical wound infections during the intraoperative phase are aimed at three primary factors that play a dominant role in the development of these infections. Which of the following is NOT one of these factors?**

    1. *Microbial contamination of the wound.*

    2. *Condition of the wound at the end of surgery.*

3. *Poor postoperative aseptic technique.*

4. *Patient susceptibility to infection.*

29. **In determining the skin area to be prepped, the circulating nurse will want to know two *essential* facts: the site of the incision and the:**

1. *antimicrobial agent to be used.*

2. *anticipated length of surgery.*

3. *tubes or drains that will be needed.*

4. *nature of the planned procedure.*

30. **The primary purpose of the skin prep is to:**

1. *remove all hair from the area of the incision.*

2. *sterilize the patient's skin at the incision site.*

3. *kill all gram-positive bacteria surrounding the incision site.*

4. *reduce the resident/transient flora surrounding the incision site.*

31. **Besides decreasing the microbial count on the skin, an effective antimicrobial agent should have several other properties. Which of the following is NOT one of these desirable properties?**

1. *It should be capable of removing superficial oils, dirt, and debris from the skin.*

2. *It should not harm the skin.*

3. *It should leave a protective film or residue on the skin.*

4. *Its antimicrobial activity should be cumulative.*

32. **The following are all recommended practices associated with the surgical skin prep, and should be used as a guide for effective practice, EXCEPT:**

1. *The area surrounding the operative site should be cleaned.*

2. *The skin or the operative site and surrounding areas should be prepared with an antimicrobial agent(s) before incision.*

3. *The skin should be cleaned starting at the periphery and moving inward toward the incision site.*

4. *The preoperative skin preparation should be documented in the patient's record.*

33. **Surgical skin preparation is performed in three steps. Which of the following is NOT one of these steps?**

1. *Assessing and documenting skin condition.*

2. *Removing any hair within 12 inches of the incision area.*

3. *Cleansing (scrubbing) the skin with the antimicrobial scrub solution, removing the superficial dirt, oils, and debris.*

4. *Applying the antimicrobial solution, which creates an antiseptic-like bacterial barrier.*

34. **A surgical patient is found to be allergic to povidone/iodine. In performing the surgical skin prep, the circulating nurse should:**

   1. *check with the surgeon and plan to use or substitute with parachlorometaxylenol.*

   2. *use chlorohexidine gluconate alone if the procedure involves the eyes, ears, or mouth.*

   3. *substitute with alcohol.*

   4. *use chlorohexidine alone regardless of the location of the surgery.*

35. **A perioperative nurse will be inserting a Foley catheter prior to a patient's cholecystostomy. In planning the surgical skin prep, the nurse is aware that Foley insertion should be done:**

   1. *prior to the skin prep, using a completely separate set-up.*

   2. *prior to the skin prep, using the same set-up that will be used for the prep.*

   3. *after the skin prep, using a completely separate set-up.*

   4. *after the skin prep, using the same set-up that was used for the prep.*

36. **One common approach to surgical skin preparation involving an external stoma (orifice) of a colostomy or ileostomy is to:**

   1. *seal off the stoma from the operative site with a detergent-soaked sponge, then prep the area surrounding it first.*

   2. *clean from the inner boundary of the stoma area outward, then come back to the stoma with a new sponge.*

   3. *clean from the outer boundary of the stoma inward, using a single sponge.*

   4. *seal off the stoma from the operative site with a detergent-soaked sponge, then prep from the incision site outward toward the stoma.*

37. **An important principle for the nurse to remember during the prepping sequence for surgery on a tumor is to avoid using:**

   1. *a circumferential prep on the incision area.*

   2. *detergent on the incision area.*

   3. *a vigorous scrub on the incision area.*

   4. *antimicrobial solution on the incision area.*

38. **In performing a prep that incorporates an area such as the anus, external genitalia, or axilla, or a skin ulcer or draining sinus, the nurse should remember to:**

    1. *prep these areas last.*

    2. *perform the prep with solution only to avoid tissue reaction.*

    3. *perform the prep with detergent only to avoid contamination of the incision.*

    4. *prep these areas first.*

39. **In an emergency situation (e.g., emergency cesarean, traumatic hemorrhage), the nurse should approach the skin prep by:**

    1. *omitting both the solution and the surgical scrub.*

    2. *following the full prep sequence.*

    3. *omitting the surgical scrub and using the solution alone.*

    4. *omitting the solution and performing the surgical scrub alone.*

40. **When performing a surgical skin prep involving grafts, the nurse should remember to:**

    1. *use the same set-up for the donor and recipient sites.*

    2. *prep the donor site with a colorless antiseptic solution.*

    3. *prep the receptor site first.*

    4. *avoid prepping the donor and recipient sites simultaneously.*

ANSWER EXPLANATIONS

1. **The answer is 3.** As the only nonscrubbed member of the surgical team, besides anesthesia personnel, the circulating nurse represents the coordinating link between the scrub team and all other departments and personnel associated with the surgical patient and the procedure. The circulating nurse therefore is responsible for managing patient care activities in the procedure room during surgery. His or her duties begin long before the patient arrives in the procedure room and continue until the final dispensation of the patient, operating room records, and specimens is completed. These duties include: (1) assisting and preparing the procedure room; (2) supervising the transporting, moving, and lifting of the patient; (3) assisting anesthesia as requested during induction and reversal of anesthesia; (4) positioning the patient for surgery; (5) performing the surgical skin prep; (6) conducting and maintaining accurate records of counts; (7) maintaining accurate documentation of nursing activities during the procedure; (8) dispensing supplies and medications to the surgical field; (9) maintaining an aseptic and safe environment; (10) estimating fluid and blood loss; (11) handling special equipment, specimens, etc.; and (12) communicating special postoperative needs to appropriate persons at the conclusion of the case.

2. **The answer is 2.** When the preoperative admission procedures have been completed, and the operating room is prepared for the surgical procedure, the patient is transported to the designated procedure room. The process of transporting the patient to the procedure room is often viewed by the nurse as a chore, and is usually delegated to the aide or orderly assigned to the surgical suite. It is not unusual for this transition time to be neglected by nursing personnel, yet the patient may be vulnerable, helpless, and extremely

anxious during this time, and may need the support of a perioperative nurse. Of primary importance during this time is patient safety--maintenance of a safe, nonthreatening transition for the patient.

3. **The answer is 1.** The patient should be moved feet first. Other guidelines for maintaining a safe, nonthreatening transition for the patient include: (1) assure that upper extremities are well within the framework of the stretcher; (2) prior to moving the patient to the operating table, position the stretcher by the side of the operating table, lower the side rail nearest the operating table, lock the stretcher, and lower the other side rail; if the patient is alert, caution him or her to move slowly to the table, and provide assistance as necessary; if the patient is sedated, use a roller to assist in the moving process; (3) when transporting a child in a crib, raise all side rails of the crib to their highest point to prevent the child from crawling over the top; and (4) if the patient has special tubes, machines, and so on, a nurse should accompany the patient to the procedure room if the circulator is unable to assist in the transport process, and assist with moving the patient in order to manage the special equipment.

4. **The answer is 4.** The patient initially is moved to the OR table and made comfortable for induction. If repositioning is necessary to accommodate the procedure, it is not done until after induction and the patient is stabilized.

5. **The answer is 4.** All necessary accessories for positioning the patient should be in the room before the move is initiated. Additional repositioning guidelines include: (1) obtain enough help to move the patient smoothly and safely; (2) be gentle when manipulating joints into desired position; (3) support all joints and extremities during the move, since they will be vulnerable to injury; (4) respect the patient's dignity by avoiding any unnecessary exposure during the positioning; (5) move the patient slowly and deliberately, maintaining a total awareness of physiologic impairment that can occur related to positioning; (6) protect from tension I.V. lines, catheters, and breathing circuits; (7) provide padding for all bony prominences; (8) protect yourself by using proper body mechanics during the move; and (9) once in position, secure the patient with a safety strap, avoiding occlusion or pressure over an area. The safety strap should be placed on top of the blanket (sheet) covering the patient; if an electrocautery unit is to be used, place the ground pad in proper position at this time.

6. **The answer is 2.** The responsibility for safely positioning the surgical patient involves the entire surgical team. The surgeon, however, determines the position for optimal exposure of the surgical site, while the anesthesiologist, being concerned with airway maintenance, vascular access, and cardiovascular stability, will either agree or make an alternative suggestion, trying to accommodate the surgeon while assuring physiologic stability for the patient. The perioperative nurse, aware of this decision, coordinates the activities related to positioning, such as preparation of the positioning aids and equipment.

7. **The answer is 1.** Another important factor is respiratory and circulatory freedom. The chest should be relieved from external pressure, and an adequate airway should be maintained. To be avoided are pressure on extremities that could decrease venous blood flow; hyperextension of arms without proper support; and crossed ankles or legs in supine position. Anatomy involved with the procedure includes knowledge of the area in relation to organs and the site of disease/tumor; right or left-sided extremity; and an area to be grafted or repaired. Patient comfort includes support for head and extremities, proper body alignment, avoidance of pressure points by adequate padding, avoidance of overexposure (privacy, hypothermic complications), and proposed length of surgery. Patient and staff safety involves proper use of safety strap and placement of positioning devices, moving and lifting using proper body mechanics and adequate personnel, protecting neuromuscular and skeletal structures, proper placement of electrosurgical ground pad, and knowledge of one's own physical limitations. Finally, the area must be easily accessible and provide maximum exposure to expedite surgery. At times, the type of anesthesia used also may be a factor, e.g., in the prone or semi-Fowler positions.

8. **The answer is 2.** Lung tissue compliance is *decreased*, not increased, thereby *decreasing* the amount of air that can be taken in for rapid exchange. Patient positioning can also influence the cardiovascular and neurologic systems, and coupled with the respiratory changes and the effects of anesthesia, can become a potential danger for all surgical patients. With the cardiovascular system, anesthesia (general or regional) causes the peripheral blood vessels to dilate. Hypotension can occur related to positioning effects; pooling

can occur in dependent areas, caused by dilated vascular beds; and the amount of blood returned to the heart and lungs can be reduced, affecting oxygenation and redistribution of oxygenated blood. Usually, pressure and/or obstruction of a vessel causes the greatest amount of damage to the cardiovascular system. With the neurologic system, most of the problems related to positioning are seen during the postoperative phase. Peripheral and superficial nerves are vulnerable to damage from mechanical pressure. The majority of the problems are related to pressure, obstruction, and stretching due to faulty positioning, and are most commonly associated with nerve injury. Motor/sensory nerve loss can happen within minutes of improper positioning and tissue damage can have a long-term effect.

9. **The answer is 3.** In the supine position, the patient lies flat on back with arms either extended on arm boards or placed along side of body. A small padding is placed under the patient's head and neck and under the knees. Vulnerable pressure points are padded, e.g., heels, elbows, sacrum. If the procedure will be longer than 1 hour, or if the patient is particularly vulnerable to pressure, an egg crate or flotation mattress is used. A safety strap is applied 2 inches above the knees. If the head is turned to one side, a doughnut or special head rest is used to protect superficial facial nerves and blood vessels. Eyes are protected by using an eye patch, and ointment is used to prevent drying. The position results in a decrease of mean arterial pressure and heart rate, an increase in cardiac output and stroke volume, a decrease in diastolic blood pressure, and the potential for venous pooling in lower extremities. It also produces compromised respiratory function, a decrease in vital capacity and diaphragmatic excursion, and more even distribution of ventilation from apex to base of lung.

10. **The answer is 4.** The lateral recumbent position is used principally for chest and kidney surgeries. With this position, a special pad ("bean bag" or "Vac-Pac") is placed on the operating table. Initially, the patient is positioned supine for induction, then is lifted and turned onto the non- operative side (usually requires four people during the move). The head is supported and aligned with spinal column. Modifications in this position then are made for chest and kidney surgeries, respectively. In this position, respiratory efficiency may be affected owing to pressure from the weight of the body on the lower chest. The restricted movement of the chest results in possible compromise in gas exchange.

11. **The answer is 1.** With the prone position, induction of anesthesia is performed in a supine position either on the patient's bed or on the operating table. Once asleep, patient is "log rolled" onto stomach. Chest rolls or bolsters are placed on the operating table prior to positioning, lengthwise on both sides. A foam head rest or doughnut is used, and the head is turned to the side or facing downward. The patient's arms are rotated to the padded armboards that face the head, bringing them through their normal range of motion, elbows bent. Padding for knees and a pillow for the lower extremities prevent toes from touching the mattress. A safety strap is applied 2 inches below knees. This position makes patients most vulnerable to respiratory problems. Body weight against the abdominal wall limits diaphragmatic movement, resulting in increased airway pressure with difficulty in ventilation, as well as tidal volume.

12. **The answer is 3.** In the reverse Trendelenburg position, the patient is supine with the head higher than the feet. A small pillow is placed under the neck and knees, and a well-padded footboard is used to prevent slippage to the foot of the table. Antiembolic hose is used if the position is to be maintained for an extended period of time. The patient should be returned slowly to a supine position. The position causes diminished cardiac return resulting in decreased cardiac output, a decrease in brainstem perfusion due to gravity, pooling of blood in the lower extremities, and the possibility of circulatory overload if the patient is returned to a supine position quickly.

13. **The answer is 4.** The lithotomy position, used for perineal, vaginal, rectal, and combined abdominal-vaginal procedures, is an exaggerated variation of the supine position that can be dangerous and uncomfortable to the patient. With this position, the patient is placed in a supine position with buttocks near the lower break in the table (sacrum area should be well padded). Feet are placed in stirrups or knee rests attached to operating table on both sides. Legs should be raised and lowered slowly and simultaneously (may require two people). In addition to circulatory and respiratory problems associated with this position, a major concern is nerve damage to femoral, obturator, and perineal nerves; dislocation of the hip; and crushing of fingers if they are left too close to the lower table break when raising the table to a supine position.

14. **The answer is 4.** Because of its adverse effects on both cardiovascular and respiratory systems, the Kraske, used for rectal procedures, is considered the most dangerous of all surgical positions. Physiologic responses are the same as with prone, only more exaggerated. The table is flexed at the center break (90 degrees). All precautions taken with the prone position are taken with Kraske position.

15. **The answer is 1.** The safety strap is the most important positioning device, since it is used the moment a patient is placed on the operating table and remains in place during the entire procedure, as a restraining tool. It must be applied with specific principles in mind: (1) the strap is placed above the knees for supine position and below the knees for prone position; (2) it must be secure, yet not constricting, and must be positioned between the blanket (sheet) covering the patient and the patient to avoid any skin irritation; and (3) the strap should be tightened enough to allow only a three-finger breadth beneath the strap, to avoid any possible pressure. When the safety strap cannot be used, some measure of safety restraint must be used to protect the patient from falling, moving, or turning.

16. **The answer is 1.** Armboards are used to support patients' arms and hands when they are not placed at their sides. The armboards are attached to the metal frame of the O.R. table approximately at the axilla level, and once in place have a self-locking mechanism to prevent movement. The angle of the board, however, can be manipulated by a rod-like projection under the board to assist in a more natural placement of the extremities. An important concept to remember when positioning an extremity on an armboard is that brachial plexus injury can result from improper positioning and/or hyperextension of the arm(s) or armboard(s), especially for patients in the supine position. To avoid this injury, the perioperative nurse should never allow the patient's arm to be extended to more than a 90-degree angle, and the patient's head should be turned toward the extended arm with the palm supinated or in a natural position. Brachial plexus injuries can also occur when a shoulder brace is used owing to improper positioning of the brace.

17. **The answer is 2.** For extensive surgery in the lithotomy position, padded knee supports can be used in which the popliteal space is supported in a padded "trough"-like stirrup attached to the table. Careful positioning, and protecting the space behind the knee, can avoid pressure on the popliteal vessels and nerves.

18. **The answer is 2.** Shoulder braces are attached to the head of the table and are used to prevent the patient slipping toward the head of the table when in the Trendelenburg position (e.g., for surgery on the lower abdomen). They are metal, concave, and are covered with a foam slipcover. Shoulder braces should not be used when the arm is extended on a arm board, to avoid compression of the axillary nerve. Similar to a double armboard, this positioning device is attached to the table in line with the upper torso, with a flat, padded surface extending over the patient's head (face). A Mayo stand, padded and covered, can be used for the same purpose. Used in the lateral position, care must be used when positioning to avoid hyperextension of the axillary region, and the surface must be well padded to prevent pressure on vessels or nerves of the upper extremity.

19. **The answer is 4.** Flotation mattresses (gelled/egg crates) are created in full table size or proportioned to fit specific devices. They are used to minimize pressure on bony prominences, peripheral blood vessels, and nerves during prolonged procedures (more than 2 hours), and for all cases in which the patient is awake or under conscious sedation.

20. **The answer is 4.** The laminectomy frame is a padded metal frame used to elevate the spinal area (e.g., for a lumbar laminectomy for herniated disk). The frame is positioned on the table and the patient placed on the frame in a prone position, being supported from the acromioclavicular joint to the iliac crest. Extensive padding must be used with this frame, and the femoral artery and nerve must be protected, as well as female breasts and male genitalia.

21. **The answer is 3.** The ulnar nerve is most commonly injured when an elbow slips off the mattress to the metal edge of the table, and the nerve is compressed between the table and the medial epicondyle. Radial nerve injury can occur either when the arm slips off the armboard and strikes the table or when it is placed at the side and is pressed between the patient and the table surface. To eliminate either of these possible

injuries, position the hand *downward* along the patient's side, pad the elbow, and use the draw sheet to secure the arm and hand, and/or use wrist restraints placed loosely yet securely around the armboard and the patient's arm (especially an arm with an I.V. infusion catheter).

22. **The answer is 1.** Saphenous and peroneal nerve injury are usually associated with the lithotomy position and the use of stirrups (e.g, for perineal, rectal, or vaginal procedures). Special care must be used when placing a patient in and out of stirrups in order to avoid these injuries. Both legs should be raised together when placing a patient in the lithotomy position, first to the knee-chest position, then into the stirrups, to avoid strain on the hip joint and surrounding nerves. Injury to the peroneal nerve can also occur if the thigh is compressed against the stirrup bar (holder); therefore, the bar should be padded around the area of the fibula bone. Injury to the saphenous nerve can occur if the nerve is pressed between the metal popliteal knee support stirrup and the medial tibial condyle. This pressure could result in numbness in the calf and possible paralysis. Padding of the knee support can prevent this injury, especially between the stirrup and medial aspect of the knee.

23. **The answer is 3.** Compression of facial structures can be caused by position, equipment, or the surgical team leaning or pressing against the patient's face. This can be avoided by constant monitoring of the patient's head position, and if necessary, the use of a Mayo stand over the face to elevate the drapes, thus preventing possible injury.

24. **The answer is 3.** Two of the primary factors determining where the incision will be are the patient's diagnosis and the pathology the surgeon expects to encounter. Other factors may affect the selection of sites, including: maximum exposure, ease and speed of entry or reentry (in an emergent state), the possibility of extending the incision, maximum postoperative wound strength with minimal postoperative discomfort, and finally, the general cosmetic effect. Under some circumstances (for example, if the patient cannot be placed under general anesthesia and the surgeon wishes to minimize the pain the patient will experience), the type of anesthesia used might influence the surgeon's decision. Even though nurses do not usually assist in the decision of what type of an incision to use for the surgical procedure, the knowledge of incisions in relationship to involved anatomy, positioning, instrumentation, suture choice, and skin preparation area is needed to plan for optimal patient outcomes.

25. **The answer is 2.** Knowledge of the incision site guides the circulating nurse in performing the surgical skin preparation. The prep should always begin at the site of the incision and work outward, toward the periphery. Additionally, gauging the progress of surgery assures the performance of counts at the proper interval and can help the nurse estimate the proper time for requesting the next patient to be premedicated. For the nurse technician assisting at the sterile field, the knowledge of anatomic layers and structures as they relate to the incision site can assist in choosing the right instruments and suture/stapling choices. Knowledge of the incision site can also be used to help gauge the progress of the operation, thereby assisting in anticipating the needs of the surgeon/assistant during the procedure.

26. **The answer is 3.** The term oblique refers to a slanting or inclined line which is usually associated with the inguinal regions or when performing an appendectomy (McBurney's). However, it can be used to denote any incision created on this angle. The right/left oblique in the inguinal region (inguinal incision) gives excellent exposure of the structures located in the groin area, while a McBurney's incision can be used for exploration of the appendix or any other structure located in the right lower quadrant of the abdomen, although visibility is limited.

27. **The answer is 4.** There are two commonly used transverse incisions: lower (Pfannensteil) and midabdominal. The Pfannensteil ("bikini-cut") is frequently used in gynecologic surgery. The incision is a curved line across the lower abdomen, above the symphysis pubis. The midabdominal is used on the right or left side, or for a retroperitoneal approach. It begins slightly above or below the umbilicus and is extended to the lumbar region at an angle, between the ribs and the crest of the ilium. Although it is not uncommon for surgeries to have several approaches, the perioperative nurse should be familiar with the most common incision sites as they relate to anatomic structures and/or surgical procedures associated with the thoracic, abdominal, and

pelvic cavities. These include midline, subcostal (Kocher's), oblique, transverse, and thoracoabdominal incisions.

28. **The answer is 3.** The *majority* of postoperative infections result from contamination acquired in the operating room. Three factors seem to have a dominant role in the development of surgical infections: microbial contamination of the wound; the condition of the wound at the end of the surgery; and patient susceptibility to infection. Since the interaction of these factors is complex, measures intended to prevent surgical wound infections are aimed at all three. The actual surgical technique will ultimately determine the condition of the wound at the end of surgery. Measures taken by the perioperative nurse to prevent surgical wound infections can be directly related to the preparation of the incision site.

29. **The answer is 4.** The area to be prepped is determined by the site of the incision and the nature of the planned surgical intervention. A wide area is usually preferable, since it allows the surgeon to extend the incision and/or strategically place tubes or drains as needed within an aseptically prepared area.

30. **The answer is 4.** Since the patient's skin cannot be sterilized, measures must be taken to reduce the resident and transient flora naturally present on the skin surface. This can be accomplished by the application of an antimicrobial agent, rendering the skin "surgically clean," and is performed prior to the draping procedure.

31. **The answer is 4.** The antimicrobial agent(s) chosen for the skin preparation should be capable of removing superficial oils, dirt, and debris without causing undue tissue reaction to the agent. It also should be able to decrease the microbial count while leaving a protective film or residue on the skin. In addition, it should be *rapid acting* and not dependent on cumulative action, have a broad spectrum of activity in reducing transient/resident flora, inhibit rapid rebound growth of microbes, have a contact time based on documentation in scientific literature, and be economical to use. Two generic groups of antimicrobial agents that meet these criteria are povidone/iodine and chlorhexidine gluconate.

32. **The answer is 3.** The surgical skin prep is performed by the circulating nurse (or designated person, e.g., intern) using strict aseptic technique. The area of the skin prep, the solutions used, and any undesirable patient reactions (e.g., allergenic) should be documented on the intraoperative record. Regardless of how the antimicrobial agent(s) is dispensed, the overall principles of performing an aseptic procedure remain the same: the prep begins at the site of the incision and works outward toward the periphery, never going over an area already prepared.

33. **The answer is 2.** Only hair that is directly interfering with the incision site need be removed prior to scrubbing with the antimicrobial agent. Today, there are a variety of prep solutions and prepping set-ups to choose from. Some require only one step, while others require both scrubbing (3) and painting (4).

34. **The answer is 1.** Prior to beginning the surgical skin prep, the perioperative nurse should be mindful of the following considerations: (1) the patient should have no known allergies to the planned solution; this means reviewing patient admission assessment for sensitivity or allergies to iodine or seafood; for those patients who have demonstrated skin sensitivities to *either* agent, another broad-spectrum antimicrobial agent, parachlorometaxylenol, may be substituted after consultation with the surgeon; (2) chlorohexidine gluconate should *not* be used for or near the eyes, ears, or mouth; (3) alcohol is *not* recommended for use as a primary prepping agent; if it is used, the skin must be completely dried before using electrosurgery and/or laser; and (4) sponges need not be saturated (dripping) with the agent in order to be effective; the combination of the chemical and mechanical friction create an acceptable mechanism for preparing the patient's skin.

35. **The answer is 1.** If additional procedures (e.g., insertion of a Foley catheter) are to be performed, they should be done prior to the prep, using a completely separate set-up to avoid accidental contamination of the aseptically prepared area. The supplies needed to perform the surgical skin preparation should be arranged on a separate surface a safe distance from the sterile field.

36. **The answer is 1.** The external stoma (orifice) of a colostomy or ileostomy may be (1) sealed off from the operative site with a detergent-soaked sponge, and the area surrounding it (considered clean) prepped first, or (2) cleaned from the outer boundary of the stoma area outward, then coming back to the stoma with a new sponge. Since the area has been aseptically prepared, the paint sequence is started from the incision site outward, including the stoma area.

37. **The answer is 3.** Carcinoma cells can become disseminated with vigorous scrubbing; therefore, a gentle yet comprehensive scrubbing technique should be used. Gentle scrubs also should be used for aortic aneurysms, ovarian cysts, and fractures.

38. **The answer is 1.** These are considered dirty/contaminated areas and should be done last when incorporated with a prep involving clean areas. The clean to dirty principle applies to all aseptic skin preps, regardless of the area involved. Internal vaginal preps should be performed with solution only, since detergent may cause a reaction (itching, burning, etc.). The umbilicus should be cleaned separately with cotton-tipped applicator.

39. **The answer is 3.** In those occasions when the urgency to begin the surgery overrides the need for a full surgical prep (e.g., leaking aortic aneurysm, emergency cesarean section, traumatic hemorrhage), the surgical scrub may be omitted and the solution used alone.

40. **The answer is 2.** For grafts, a separate set-up for donor and recipient site should be used. The donor site is prepped first, or two nurses may be required to do a simultaneous prep. The donor site should be prepped with a colorless antiseptic solution to allow postoperative visibility of the vascularity of the graft. The donor site is covered with a sterile towel if not dressed immediately.

12 Intraoperative Patient Care Management: Maintaining a Safe Environment

STUDY OUTLINE

I. INTRAOPERATIVE EQUIPMENT AND ACCESSORY ITEMS

1. In addition to surgical instruments and specialty supplies, there are standard pieces of equipment that are used routinely during a variety of surgical procedures. In order to maintain a safe environment and protect the patient and/or staff from harm, the person handling the equipment must have a thorough knowledge and understanding of the how's and why's of each piece of equipment and accessory item. Additionally, he or she should be familiar with what to do should the equipment fail to function within acceptable guidelines and/or established safety criteria.

2. Power equipment ranges in type from electrosurgical units to high-technology laser units, and includes equipment such as power drills, saws, tourniquets, and specialized light sources. They all have one common factor, however technologically advanced they may seem: they need a source of power to operate. This power is derived from one of two sources: **electrical power** or **air/gas power**, either from a freestanding tank or a supply coming through a wall outlet in the procedure room.

3. According to A.O.R.N.'s Patient Outcome Standard IV: *The patient is free from injury related to . . . electrical and physical hazards....* This standard can be achieved only by applying safety measures associated with the equipment and thoroughly understanding the equipment to be used.

4. **General considerations for safety:** The proper handling of any piece of equipment used in surgery is the responsibility of every member of the surgical team. Some general safety guidelines, which can aid in protecting the patient and the staff from harm, include:

    a. All electrical equipment should be routinely inspected by qualified personnel.

    b. All power equipment should be inspected by the user prior to and after each use.

    c. Power cords should never be crimped or bent; any tears or breaks in the cord should negate the use of that cord until it is repaired.

    d. Extension cords should be avoided whenever possible, and power cords should lie flat on the floor or be suspended to prevent obstruction of traffic areas and/or entrances.

    e. Freestanding pressure tanks should be checked before and after each use, replaced immediately when the pressure in the tank is below a safe limit, and monitored during its use.

    f. Equipment must be maintained through proper cleaning, lubrication, and sterilization procedures, according to the manufacturer's written recommendations.

    g. Verification that the correct attachments for a piece of equipment are in fact being used should be performed by the person using the equipment, including confirmation that the attachments are seated properly before activating the unit.

    h. When not in use, equipment should be maintained in a neutral power state, and sharp tips protected to avoid accidental injury.

    i. All persons handling power equipment should be educated about their function and proper use.

II. ELECTRICAL EQUIPMENT USED IN SURGERY

A. ELECTROSURGICAL UNITS

1. **The purpose of the electrosurgical unit (E.S.U.) is to (1) control bleeding through the application of heat, and (2) to cut tissue.**
2. In the early 1970s, solid-state electrosurgical units were introduced to the surgical setting. These units, unlike their predecessors, were more compact, with new added safety features. Through the years, and with the help of advanced medical technology, changes have intensified the safety features and increased the versatility of the unit. Today, a variety of units are found in most surgical procedure rooms and in other settings where this technology is required.
3. **Electrosurgical unit and components:** To perform electrosurgery, three basic components are required: (1) the power unit, (2) the active electrode, and (3) the dispersive (return) electrode. These, along with the patient, are necessary to complete the electrical circuit.
4. **Monopolar versus bipolar:** The active electrode is available as monopolar or bipolar, and depending on the surgical procedure, one or the other may be used.
    a. **Monopolar:** With monopolar electrosurgery, only one pole is *active*, and it carries current to the operative site. The current flows from the monopolar connection to the electrode, which is applied to the tissue, is dispersed over the dispersive electrode (ground pad), and returned to the E.S.U. via the dispersive electrode cable.
    b. **Bipolar:** A bipolar active electrode has a forceps configuration. In the bipolar electrode, one tip acts as the active pole while the other tip acts as the return (dispersive) pole. With bipolar, a ground pad is not required, since the dispersive electrode is one of the bipolar tips. **By using a bipolar electrode, the power is distributed to a very limited area (between the tips only) and the actual wattage power required is reduced, making it safe for use on delicate tissue, such as the brain.**
5. Electrosurgical safety
    a. **Safety measures are intended to minimize the potential for electric hazards. The three most common hazards associated with electricity are fire, electric shock and burns.** These are hazards for both patient and personnel; therefore, the entire staff must make every attempt to maintain a safe environment.
    b. Although **fire hazards** have been greatly reduced, faulty wiring, poorly maintained equipment and a lack of regard for safety measures can cause a spark, resulting in a fire.
    c. Contact with 110/220 volt power (common household current) can cause **electric shock** and/or electrocution. Safety measures that can assist in preventing this hazard should include inspecting electric cords, plugs and connectors; operating the unit at its lowest acceptable setting; and never operating equipment with wet hands or when standing on a wet surface.
    d. **Burns** can occur from direct contact with hot electric wires or from items overheating by electric wires. Safety measures that can reduce the possibility of burns include:
        (1) Avoiding use of a power unit as an "extra" table surface.
        (2) Not allowing the patient ground cable to contact a hypothermia blanket.
        (3) Never activating the active electrode (hand piece) with wet gloves or gloves with a hole in them.
        (4) Maintaining an awareness of where the active electrode tip is located and/or storing it in an appropriate holder when not in use.
        (5) Checking the equipment before each use, including cords, connectors, and the alarm system.
        (6) Never turning down the volume of the alarm so that it cannot notify the team of a possible problem alert.
    e. The least understood hazard associated with the use of electrosurgery is patient burns. Patient burns usually result when too much current flows through an inadequate area for a too long a time; therefore, **the use, placement, and proper connection of the ground pad becomes one of the most important factors associated with safe use of the E.S.U.**
    f. If not properly placed, or if complete contact with the patient is not maintained throughout the procedure, or if the ground pad becomes wet from prepping solutions, the high-frequency

current could become concentrated or find an alternative path--the patient--and cause a severe burn. This injury has in fact necessitated plastic and/or reconstructive surgery (at the hospital's expense) in addition to traumatizing the patient.

g. To avoid this potential problem, the use of an E.S.U. and ground pad with a return electrode monitoring (R.E.M.) alarm system provides additional safety for the patient by deactivating the system should the dispersive electrode be faulty for whatever reason.

h. Additionally, electrosurgical burns may result when other electrical equipment is used during a procedure, such as ECG monitoring electrodes or temporary pacing wires. It is recommended that the ECG electrodes be placed on the posterior aspect of the shoulders, away from the dispersive electrode site thus avoiding any unnecessary hazards when both pieces of equipment are in use.

i. Since the E.S.U. can interfere with a pacemaker signal, it should not be used in patients with pacemakers if at all possible, to avoid an inadvertent reprogramming of the pacemaker, but if needed, special monitoring of the patient should be intensified.

6. **Electrosurgical safety list:** The creation of an electrosurgical safety checklist should be used for all patients and/or procedure rooms, and should be completed by the person using the electrosurgical unit.

B. FIBEROPTIC POWER SOURCES

1. The term **fiberoptic** describes a power source found in a variety of surgical instruments and used for both diagnostic and therapeutic procedures. A **fiberoptic cable** is composed of a flexible material, either glass or plastic, which is capable of transmitting light along its fibers by reflecting the light from the side or the wall of the fiber. To illuminate this cable, a **power source** is required as the source of light for the cable.

2. **Endoscopic equipment/instruments**
    a. **Fiberoptics are used in endoscopy procedures, performed either in surgery, the G.I. suite, or the physician's office, through a natural opening in the body (e.g., bronchoscopy, colonoscopy, or cystoscopy) or through an artificial opening created via an incision, such as an arthroscopy or laparoscopy.** Additional types of endoscopic procedures can be performed during a surgical procedure--for example, a choledochoscopy during a gallbladder procedure, or a nephroscopy during surgery on the kidney.

    b. Although each piece of equipment is unique and serves a specific purpose, all endoscopic equipment have similar working parts. The four common components associated with endoscopic equipment are (1) the **viewing instrument,** (2) a **light source,** (3) a **power source,** and (4) the **projection lamp housing/light cord.**

    c. A fiberoptic power cable (**light cord**) transmits the light from the projection lamp to the instrument. Both ends of the cable must have the correct fittings to attach to the lamp housing and the instrument.

    d. **Not all fiberoptic cables are interchangeable, and therefore in order to have maximum illumination, the perioperative nurse must make sure that all connections appropriately match prior to beginning the procedure.**

    e. To preserve the efficiency of the light source, the intensity of the light should be lowered before switching the unit on or off, and light cords should be coiled loosely to prevent damage to the fibers. *Never bend the light cord* or the fiberoptic bundles will break, decreasing the amount of projected light.

    f. Today, all surgical specialties benefit from a fiberoptic source of light. Additionally, the optical segment of the instrument may be attached to other pieces of equipment, including a teaching head attachment, laser, or video cameras. The accessory items needed will be determined by the type of endoscope and the purpose of the procedure.

3. **Care and handling of endoscopic equipment**
    a. The following recommendations have been created by the A.O.R.N. as a guide for the care and handling of endoscopic equipment/instruments: *Flexible and rigid endoscopes should be inspected, tested, and processed according to design/type and manufacturer's instructions.*
    b. As with any piece of equipment, proper cleaning and maintenance along with gentle handling will save the instrument and/or equipment from costly repairs. Recommendations regarding the sterilization, disinfection, and storage should be known to all persons working with the equipment, and should include, but not be limited to:
        (1) Sterilization rather than disinfection of endoscopes and accessories is preferred to increase patient safety.
        (2) Following cleaning and disinfection, endoscopes should be thoroughly rinsed with sterile water and completely dried before storage.
        (3) The use of damaged instruments could possibly increase the risk of tissue injury, infection, and length of the surgical procedure; therefore, all endoscopes should be inspected and tested prior to each use, along with power cords and accessory items used during the procedure.

C. **THE OPERATING MICROSCOPE**

1. In the early 1950s, using the principles of binocular magnification and stereoscopic vision, which enabled ophthalmologists to examine the eye in three dimensions, the operating microscope was developed by the Carl Zeiss Company, and the first of the present-day operating microscopes was developed in 1960.
2. With the advent of this new tool, instrumentation that could be used for this type of surgery followed close behind, and so began the development and clinical use of **microsurgery** techniques in all of the surgical specialties.
3. **Features of the operating microscope**
    a. The operating microscope has an interchangeable lens that allows for precise visualization of the surgical field. A variety of support systems are available for mounting the microscope, ranging from a floor base to ceiling-mounted brackets, allowing flexibility of use during a procedure.
    b. Autoclave attachments and/or special microscope drapes allow the surgeon total range of movement during surgery, yet under sterile conditions. The microscope uses an internal fiberoptic light source whose intensity can be adjusted depending on the area being viewed.
    c. Basically, all operating microscopes consist of the same basic components: (1) **an optical lens system** with controls for magnification, illumination, and focusing; (2) a **mounting system** for stability; (3) an **electrical system**; and (4) **accessory items/attachments**, including assistant's binoculars, a microscope drape, camera/video adapter, laser microadapter, and remote foot control.
    d. Like all electric equipment, safety and proper maintenance are essential to its optimum usage. Circuits, plugs, and connectors must be protected from overload by breaker relays and fuses. Light controls should be in the "off" position when turning the unit on and off to avoid short circuiting the unit or creating sparks.
4. **Special nursing considerations**
    a. **The circulating nurse's responsibility is to know how to care for and position the microscope.** This includes the following:
        (1) Check to see that all knobs are secured after the microscope has been placed in final position.
        (2) Assist the surgeon with attachments of accessory items.
        (3) Take special care of power cables to prevent accidental breakage; position them out of the path of the microscope; be sure they are properly coiled for storage.
        (4) Take special care of lenses to avoid breaking, scratching, or leaving fingerprints; tighten to fingertip tightness only, being careful not to cross-thread during attachment. When attaching the lens, perform the task over a padded surface to prevent accidental breakage if dropped. Cleaning process should follow manufacturer's recommendations.

(5) Keep extra lamp bulbs and fuses available and know where to find accessories and anticipate their usage depending on the proposed procedure and/or surgeon's preference.

(6) When moving microscope, position the viewing portion over the base to add stability; acquire adequate moving help to accommodate the move safely.

(7) When storing microscope, avoid using a plastic bag or cover; instead, use a cloth pillowcase.

(8) Cover foot pedal with clear bag to keep it clean and dry, and position it for easy access after surgeon has been seated or has determined desired position to perform the surgery.

b. **The scrub nurse's responsibility is to maintain a sterile field and know how to pass instruments when using a microscope.** This includes the following:

(1) Verify with the circulator the lens and binoculars for a specific surgeon/procedure.

(2) Make sure lens and oculars are clean.

(3) Have the proper drape to accommodate microscope accessory items; know how to apply the drape properly, maintaining sterile technique.

(4) Place Mayo tray and instrument table in convenient location (if assisting) so your eyes do not have to leave the field or look around the microscope.

(5) Maintain a calm atmosphere, knowing that dissection may be slow and tedious. Do not let attention stray; use video monitor to watch progress of procedure.

D. ADDITIONAL LIGHT SOURCES AND MAGNIFICATION AIDS

1. Besides the equipment mentioned above, other accessory aids can provide additional light or magnification during surgery. For example, **a fiberoptic headlight is used whenever the surgeon requires a highly intense light into a small area, such as the throat, ear, nose, or deep cavities.** The headlight has a cord attached to it, and is usually positioned on the surgeon's head prior to the scrub procedures. Once the gowning procedure is finished, the circulator will attach the headlight to the light source and increase the intensity as required.

2. **Magnifying loupes are worn much the same as eyeglasses, and are used to increase an area's size when the use of a microscope is not indicated.** Because they are less cumbersome, the loupes are used whenever the surgery does not require the magnification power of the microscope.

   a. Surgical magnifying loupes come in the form of glasses with the magnifying portion attached or in the shape of a visor with magnifying lenses built into the front portion of the unit.

   b. Placing the magnifying loupes in the solution warming cabinet prior to use can reduce the possibility of the glasses fogging.

   c. Before beginning any case requiring delicate surgery in a small area, refer to the Physician's Preference Card for the specific equipment preferred by the surgeon, and confirm its condition for use.

E. THERMAL BLANKETS: MAINTAINING BODY TEMPERATURE

1. The skin is the organ that maintains the body's normothermic state. As body temperature increases, superficial blood vessels dilate to allow more blood to circulate near the surface. If the body temperature decreases, owing to prolonged exposure, the body will attempt to self-regulate by decreasing the flow of blood to the surface, thus conserving heat internally. It is obvious, then, that heat loss or heat production can directly effect the patient's physiologic response to surgery.

2. **In the normal course of a surgical event, a loss of heat is primarily the result of exposure to the physical environment, the incision itself, the patient's immobility, and/or coexisting circulatory insufficiency.**

3. **The thermal control unit**

   a. **External control of the patient's body temperature can be accomplished through the use of a thermal blanket placed on the operating table.** When activated, the thermal blanket will heat or cool the patient through coils filled with water or gel, which circulates through channels in the blanket until the desired, preset temperature is reached.

b. In emergent situations, such as a malignant hyperthermia crisis, the thermal blanket can be placed on top of the patient to facilitate surface cooling.

4. Guidelines for nursing action

   a. **To ensure effective operation of the thermal blanket, safety guidelines should be followed, since thermal burns, pressure necrosis, or electric shock can occur as a result of incorrect usage.** The A.O.R.N.'s recommended practice suggests that potential hazards relating to controlling the patient's temperature *should be identified and safe practices established,* which should include preventive measures relating to the safe operational use of the equipment, and monitoring of the patient's response to this intervention.

      (1) **Thermal blankets are recommended for any surgical procedure lasting more than 2 hours, and for all pediatric procedures and procedures in patients with impaired circulatory status.**

      (2) Direct skin contact with the thermal blanket should be avoided by placing a sheet between the blanket and the patient.

      (3) Folds and/or creases should be avoided so that hot spots or pressure injuries do not occur during its use.

      (4) Observation and monitoring of both the unit and the patient should be constant throughout the procedure.

      (5) Skin integrity should be inspected before and after the procedure with corresponding documentation of assessment findings.

      (6) Power cords and connective lines to the blanket should be checked before and after each use for cracks, breaks, or holes in the cords or blanket that could increase the possibility of electric shock.

   b. When safely used, the thermal blanket can be a major assistance in preventing an adverse response to surgical intervention by maintaining the near-normal physiologic status, and can decrease the possibility of postoperative hypothermia.

5. **Besides the use of a thermal blanket, there are other interventions the perioperative nurse and surgical team can use to maintain body temperature during a surgical procedure.** Some of these include:

   a. **The use of warmed prep solutions and irrigating solutions.**

   b. **Providing warm blankets** upon arrival to the procedure room and before transferring to the postanesthesia area.

   c. **Administering warm blood** if transfusions are required.

   d. **Limiting exposure area** to the direct operative site.

   e. **Monitoring physiologic parameters,** such as skin color, texture, and external/internal temperature throughout the procedure.

   f. **Providing psychologic support,** thereby reducing anxiety and fear.

F. INTRAOPERATIVE AUTOTRANSFUSIONS

1. Occasionally a patient needs an immediate replacement of blood, or the surgical procedure planned necessitates replacement of several units of blood during the course of the procedure. **Autotransfusion** can be accomplished before elective surgery, using the patient as his or her own donor. One advantage to autotransfusions is having sufficient blood if there is a blood shortage; it also precludes the danger of receiving contaminated blood from a commercial blood bank, thus increasing the safety factors relating to transfusion therapy.

2. Autotransfusion is not always applicable; in fact, it is contraindicated if the patient has cancer, if gross contamination from the bowel or stomach contents have occurred, or, in the case of a trauma patient, if the wounds are more than 4 hours old. If these conditions are not present, autotransfusion can be the safest method for replacing lost blood cells.

3. **Cell saver (autologous transfusion system)**
    a. The **cell saver unit for autologous blood recovery** is the next best answer to safe blood replacement during a surgical procedure, since it returns washed packed cells to the patient via a filtered reinfusion bag. **This autotransfusion system provides intraoperative salvage of blood, without the threat of disease transmission, transfusion reactions, or incompatibility testing.**
    b. Although most units are designed to cycle automatically, a nurse or clinical perfusionist should be assigned to manage the unit while in use, to coordinate the delivery of blood to anesthesia personnel as needed. Full records of the amount of irrigant, numbers of units processed, and so on should be kept during the procedure, and be incorporated with the total amount of infusion solutions administered during the procedure.
    c. **The use of this system has created a positive outcome not only for emergency patients, but also for those whose surgery may require extensive replacement (more than 2-3 units) during the course of the procedure.**
    d. Examples of surgeries that may require extensive replacement include procedures involving the spleen, liver, chest wall, or heart/pulmonary vessels, or reconstructive orthopedic surgeries such as posterior spinal fusions (Harrington rod insertion) or total hip arthroplasty.
    e. Postoperatively, the autotransfusion system can continue to replace the patient's own blood via an A.T.S. transfusion bag (e.g., open heart procedures with chest drainage devices).

G. LASER EQUIPMENT

1. **The clinical application of lasers is rapidly gaining acceptance as a precision surgical tool primarily owing to its ability to reduce bleeding, reduce swelling, and minimize scar tissue formation.**
2. **Laser** is an acronym for *L*ight *A*mplification by *S*timulated *E*mission of *R*adiation. A laser beam is created by stimulating photons inside a resonating chamber. As the photons bounce back and forth they gain energy, which is emitted through the delivery system, producing a laser beam that can be used to cut or coagulate tissue.
3. **Types of lasers:** There are a variety of lasers, but three are commonly associated with surgery: the **carbon dioxide laser;** the **ND: Yag laser,** and the **argon laser.** Each has special characteristics, benefits, and disadvantages.
    a. **Carbon dioxide laser:** Molecules of carbon dioxide (CO_2) provides the active lasing medium for the CO_2 laser.
        (1) **The CO_2 laser is the most versatile laser, since it can perform both coagulation and cutting functions, and can be operated in continuous or pulsed modes.** By varying the length and frequency of each pulse, different tissue effects can be produced and thermal effects can be more precisely controlled.
        (2) The CO_2 laser wavelength is absorbed by water and since the body is 75 percent to 90 percent water, an extremely precise beam can vaporize even a single cell while avoiding surrounding tissue.
        (3) The CO_2 beam is regulated by the surgeon, and can be optically controlled to work in three focal positions: focus, defocus, and prefocus. In focus, the laser beam vaporizes tissue, and in defocus, the reaction on tissue is coagulation; prefocus has no practical application.
        (4) **The precision of the laser beam provides maximum impact on intended tissue with minimal damage to surrounding tissue.** In addition, the laser beam causes minimal immediate postoperative pain and allows faster recovery.
        (5) Surgical specialties that can benefit from a CO_2 laser include general, gynecology, E.N.T., neurosurgery, and plastic surgery.
    b. **ND:Yag laser**
        (1) A solid crystal **made of yttrium aluminum garnet (Yag)** covered with **neodymium (ND)** supplies the active medium for the ND:Yag laser. Electrons are excited, not by electric current as in the CO_2 or gas lasers, but by the bright flashing lamp striking the neodymium, causing a mini-explosion.

(2) **The primary function of this laser is coagulation, and although it provides great penetration depth, the energy is not highly focused.** Tissue is heated to a point of coagulation without vaporization, producing a homogenous coagulative effect.

(3) The special characteristics of this laser medium enables the surgeon to control its impact and judge tissue response during its use. In addition, the surgeon can use this laser through endoscopic instrumentation via a fiber, or by direct contact with the structure using a contact probe (a wand-like instrument). Applications of this laser include gastroenterology, pulmonary, urology, gynecology, and ophthalmology.

c. **Argon laser**

(1) The **argon laser** also uses gas as its medium; however, it functions at a different wavelength than the CO_2 laser. The argon beam is effectively absorbed by pigmented tissue, yet passes through clear structures with minimal effect.

(2) The primary clinical applications include ophthalmology, dermatology, gastro-enterology, gynecology, and otology. Since the argon beam is well suited for ophthalmic surgery, it is the most common form of treatment for diabetic retinopathy, and is well adapted to ambulatory surgery settings and use in an ophthalmologist's office.

4. **Potential hazards and safety guidelines**

a. As with any new technology, certain hazards are associated with this form of treatment, and the perioperative nurse, as a patient advocate, must ensure a safe environment during its usage.

b. In January 1989, the A.O.R.N. established recommended practices directly relating to laser safety, which include the following concepts:

(1) A warning sign stating the type of laser being used should be pasted on all doors leading in and out of the laser area, to alert all personnel that they must take certain precautionary measures:

(a) Application of special goggles/glasses which are applicable to the medium being used:

CO_2 laser	clear
ND:Yag laser	green tint
Argon laser	orange tint

(2) A smoke evaluator system should be used during all laser cases to absorb the pflume from the laser.

(3) Though the laser beam is invisible, it can ignite flammable materials and be reflected off shiny surfaces. Instruments should be brushed or ebonized and emergency equipment such as sterile water and a halon fire extinguisher should be readily available.

(4) Lasers should not be used with alcohol preps, or be kept near combustible solutions or substances.

(5) The patient's eyes should be protected, and all sponges used at the field should be damp (for CO_2 lasers) to prevent the laser beam from striking any other tissue and/or area or igniting a fire.

(6) One nurse who has been instructed in the medium and its safety factors should be assigned to use the laser and should not be involved with circulating duties while working with the laser.

(7) The laser should be placed in the stand-by mode when not in use.

(8) Continuous monitoring and observation of the environment and the patient must be practiced by all persons working with a laser, regardless of the medium.

(9) A Laser Committee, responsible for creating policies, procedures, and protocols, in addition to credentialing physicians wishing to use the laser, should be established within the institution.

(10) All personnel should be aware that although the laser is an asset to surgery, it can be a potentially dangerous piece of equipment if not used properly.

III.   AIR/GAS POWER EQUIPMENT IN SURGERY

A.   TYPES OF EQUIPMENT

1.   Many power-driven instruments, such as drills, saws, and dermatomes, are used during surgery. Some are electrically powered, as previously mentioned, but others use alternative sources derived from air power in the form of compressed nitrogen, CO_2, or oxygen. **The perioperative nurse should be familiar with the tanks, regulators, and power hoses associated with this source of power so that safe connections and usage can be achieved.**

2.   **The most common piece of equipment associated with air power is the pneumatic tourniquet.** Tourniquets are used during most operations on the extremities when a "bloodless" wound site is desired. They prevent venous oozing, yet do not totally obstruct the arterial blood supply, thereby preserving the circulation through the extremity.

3.   The nonsterile tourniquet is composed of an inner bladder covered with an outer layer of synthetic material, similar to a blood pressure cuff. The tourniquet is connected to a compressed source of air/gas via a regulator attached to a valve extending from near the end of the cuff. Depending on its intended use, the cuff can be single or double, each with its separate gauge.

B.   APPLICATION AND NURSING CONSIDERATIONS

1.   **The tourniquet cuff should be applied far enough away from the incision site so that it will not be in the way, and the area should be prepared with a thin soft cotton sheeting (soft roll), smoothly applied, to prevent the skin from becoming "pinched" during inflation.** The cuff chosen must be appropriate in size to the extremity (overlapping of ends by 2-3 in.), allowing for proper expansion of the cuff and constriction of the extremity. Following the application of the cuff, the position should be confirmed by the surgeon, prior to prepping and inflation.

2.   The extremity is prepared by elevating it, with the help of another person, and a circumferential prep is performed up to the tourniquet cuff. Upon completion of the prep, the surgeon will apply a sterile covering, called a **stockinette**, so that the extremity can be placed onto a sterile surface or held for sterile draping.

3.   To drain the venous blood from the extremity, the limb, still elevated, is wrapped with a wide sterile rubber bandage (*Esmarck* or *Martin*) from the distal to the proximal end, and the tourniquet is then inflated to the desired setting. It is recommended that the setting for an arm be between 250 and 300 mm Hg and for legs, 400 to 500 mm Hg. Once the setting has been reached, the rubber bandage is removed, and the extremity can be lowered onto the sterile field.

C.   IMPLICATIONS FOR SAFETY

1.   **Improperly used, the tourniquet can cause serious nerve and vascular damage; therefore, careful planning, application, and monitoring are essential to its safe usage.**

2.   Using the A.O.R.N. recommended practices as a reference guide for safe implementation, the following practices should be employed:

    a.   **Tourniquets should be tested regularly before use, monitored during use, and maintained in proper working order.** Tourniquet gauges should be checked for accuracy prior to each application to prevent tourniquet paralysis from occurring. All connectors, the tubing, and the bladder cuff should be checked for cracks and/or leaks, and replaced if not in acceptable working condition. During the procedure, the pressure should be checked and verified at least every 30 minutes to detect any pressure variation, with documentation of the time of inflation, deflation, and location of the cuff.

    b.   **Selection and placement of the cuff should be determined by the patient's age, anatomy, and medical condition.** The cuff should be applied to the extremity so that underlying skin and tissue are not unduly traumatized. *Its use is contraindicated in patients with vascular disease or poor peripheral circulation.* The cuff should be positioned at the point of maximum circumference of the extremity. Once inflated it should not be readjusted.

      c. **Although there is no actual time limit regarding the use of tourniquets, the recommended time limits range from 1 hour for an arm and 1 1/2 hours for a leg.** If more time is required, the cuff should be deflated for 10 minutes, then reinflated to the desired pressure.

      d. **Documentation of tourniquet time, position, and the person who applied the cuff should be part of the intraoperative nurse's notes.**

      e. **The tourniquet should be cleaned with an appropriate disinfection solution and stored properly after each use.** The remaining air in the tank should be checked, and if low, replaced prior to storage.

   3. Surgical power tools and equipment represent a major investment for any institution; therefore, proper care and handling can save costly repairs and extend the working life of the equipment, in addition to providing a safe environment for the patient and personnel working with the equipment.

IV. X-RAY EQUIPMENT IN SURGERY

   1. **During the course of a surgical procedures, X-rays may be needed to confirm a location and/or position or to perform diagnostic studies related to the surgical procedure.**

A. TYPES OF X-RAYS AND X-RAY EQUIPMENT

   1. **Types of intraoperative X-rays**

      a. The most common types of X-rays, performed during or just prior to the incision, include:

         (1) **X-rays for positioning**--KUB, pacemaker, reconstructive orthopedics, tube placement.

         (2) **Diagnostic studies**--operative cholangiograms, ureteral retrogrades, angiography.

         (3) **Emergent procedures**--X-ray for trauma presence of foreign objects (needles, bullets, sponges).

      b. An X-ray procedure can be invasive, in which a dye or radiopaque contrast material is injected into a vein, duct, or passageway within the body, or non-invasive, such as a confirmation X-ray of implantable devices.

   2. **Types of X-ray equipment:** There are three types of X-ray equipment commonly found in today's surgical suite--**fixed X-ray equipment, portable X-ray equipment,** and **image intensifiers.** Although each can be used separately, at times a combination of methods may be used. The **image intensifier** converts X-ray beams through the body into a fluoroscopic image, which is projected on a T.V. monitor screen.

   3. **Radiopaque contrast media**

      a. These agents, composed of nonmetallic compounds or heavy metal salts, permit the visualization of internal structures during an X-ray procedure. Some of the more commonly used substances for invasive studies are cardiographin, hypaque, renografin, and cysto-angio conray.

      b. **As with many of the contrast media, they contain iodine; therefore, if invasive X-rays are to be taken, it is vitally important that known sensitivities to iodine-related substances such as shellfish or previous problems with invasive studies using iodine be obtained through the preoperative assessment, and the information communicated to the surgeon.**

      c. If contrast media is used during the procedure, it must be dispensed under sterile conditions, and must be administered according to the surgeon's dilution request, using warm sterile saline (usually 50-60 dilution) in a labeled syringe (30-60 mL) with appropriate needle for injection.

B. RADIATION SAFETY GUIDELINES

1. Following the A.O.R.N.'s recommended practices for radiation safety will ensure an optimum environment for the patient and personnel. The following suggestions are based on those guidelines:

   a. Sterile technique involving the surgery must be maintained during an X-ray procedure.

   b. The X-ray machine or overhead unit should be damp dusted with cleaning solution before use.

   c. When using a cassette, the scrub nurse must enclose the cassette in a sterile cassette cover, maintaining aseptic technique, before it can be brought to the sterile field.

   d. The sterile members of the team should apply protective "lead aprons" prior to the scrub to facilitate sterile application of the gown while being protected against exposure to X-rays during the procedure.

   e. During filming, remove all unnecessary instruments from the field, unless otherwise directed by the surgeon, and cover the incision with sterile towel.

   f. An X-ray detector badge, indicating the amount of exposure received in a month, should be worn on the outside of the lead apron (under sterile gown) during all X-ray procedures, by all personnel in the room.

   g. Positioning of the equipment should be done prior to draping and confirmed by a "scout" film, to prevent having to replace the drapes if positioning is not correct.

   h. The circulating nurse should assist the X-ray technician in placing the cassette into the cassette table holder by lifting the drapes and sliding the cassette into the desired location.

   i. While the film is being developed, the surgical team should not contaminate their gowns/hands by folding arms across chest or under arms, or sit while in sterile attire.

   j. Unless absolutely necessary, all nonscrubbed personnel should leave the room during a single-series filming. Those persons who must remain should wear a lead apron or stand behind protective (lead-lined) screen in the procedure room.

   k. Female personnel who are pregnant should be excused from X-ray procedures.

   l. For optimum protection during fluoroscopy, persons within 2 meters of the unit should wear a thyroid shield, and leaded sterile gloves should be worn when hands are in direct exposure to fluoroscopy.

   m. Leaded protective devices should be routinely checked for cracks or tears, which can significantly reduce the effectiveness of the shield.

   n. A qualified radiologic technician (or radiologist) should be in attendance throughout the X-ray/fluoroscopy sequence, and should always be aware of the other members of the team, allowing them time to properly prepare for the X-ray exposure.

V. THE SEQUENCE OF SURGERY

1. **Although each surgical procedure contains its own special elements, essentially the same sequence of events occurs with each operation. Specific details, relating to a given procedure, involve only the choice of instrumentation, sutures, and other specialized accessory items.**

2. The *art* of intelligent assistance, regardless of the role assumed, requires a working knowledge of the sequential steps for a specific surgical procedure based on four concepts that should be considered for any surgical event. These concepts are the **approach**, the **procedure**, the **possible complications**, and the **closure**.

3. Effective implementation also depends on six components of knowledge, which include:

   a. Understanding the involved anatomy.

   b. Knowing the surgeon's approach (position and incision).

   c. Recognizing accepted techniques for a given institution (counts, usage of equipment, etc.).

   d. Knowing the capabilities of the nursing staff (scrub, circulator, assistant).

   e. Knowing the general condition of the patient (age, weight, preexisting conditions).

   f. Anticipating the possible complications related to the proposed surgery (intraoperative, postoperative).

4. As the professional nurse in the procedure room, it is up to the perioperative nurse to create an atmosphere of confidence to assure the procedure is performed using the highest possible quality of standards.

A. THE FIVE PHASES OF SURGERY

1. **To provide expert aid to the surgeon and the surgical team, the perioperative nurse should be familiar with the phases of surgery, in order to anticipate the needs of all those involved with the procedure.** Each procedure can be broken down into five phases, each phase representing a sequence of events that occurs during a surgical procedure. A laparotomy procedure will be used to review each of these phases:

Phase I: Preparation Sequence
(1) Selection and preparation of procedure room and supplies.
(2) Preincisional count--sponges, sharps, and instruments.

Phase II: Preincision Sequence
(3) Transference of patient to procedure room and positioning.
(4) Induction of anesthesia.
(5) Prepping and draping.
(6) Establishment and verification of suction and electrosurgical capabilities.

Phase III: Operative Sequence
(7) **Incision**--The skin and subcutaneous tissue are incised with the skin knife, which is then placed on the back table.
(8) **Hemostasis**--Subcutaneous bleeders are clamped with a curved hemostat and ligated/cauterized according to the surgeon's preference. The area is periodically sponged by the assistant to aid in visualization of further sources of bleeding.
(9) **Dissection and exposure**--A clean knife, curved cutting scissors (Metzenbaum), or cautery is used to incise the deep fascia and peritoneum. Toothed forceps are used to elevate the peritoneum prior to incising it, as this will prevent inadvertent damage to the underlying bowel.
(10) **Exploration and isolation**--Prior to definitive surgery, the entire abdomen is explored, and the pathology isolated for further action. Very often the operative site is obscured by surrounding viscera, making dissection of intended pathology dangerous. In this case, the surgeon will "pack" the abdomen using large moist lap sponges, and insert a self-retaining abdominal retractor to maximize exposure.
(11) **Surgical repair: excision or revision**
  (a) Depending on the purpose of the surgery and local anatomy, each surgical procedure will require a certain amount of dissection of surrounding tissue. For most abdominal cases, Metzenbaum scissors, smooth tissue forceps, and sponges are required.
  (b) As the depth increases the length of the instrument should also increase.
  (c) Each surgeon will have a preference as to which instrument, suture, etc. will be used. This choice will be anticipated by the scrub nurse only through experience and familiarity with the surgeon's routine.
  (d) The operation frequently focuses on the removal of an entire organ, resection of a part of an organ, reconstruction of an organ, or both resection and reconstruction. These acts often require specialized instruments designed to accomplish this task.
(12) **Hemostasis and irrigation**--In preparation for closing, the surgeon will survey the operative site for bleeders, control the bleeding via ligation/cauterization, and irrigate the wound with warmed normal saline (with or without antibiotic). If a drain will be needed, the site is prepared and a drain is inserted.
(13) **Collection and verification of specimen**--With permission from the surgeon, specimens for routine analysis are removed from the surgical field and passed off to the circulator for processing.

Phase IV: Closing Sequence
(14) Closing counts
  (a) The scrub nurse anticipates the closure and begins the first closing count with the circulating nurse. Sponges, sharps, and instruments are counted prior to closure of the peritoneal cavity.
  (b) In the case of a laparotomy, sponges and retaining instruments are removed, the wound is irrigated, and heavy holding clamps (e.g., Kocher) are used to grasp the edges of the peritoneum. The peritoneum and fascia will be closed serially. Then the second closing count is performed; sponges and sharps only, and the skin is closed using either sutures or skin staples.
(15) Anesthesia reversal and stabilization
(16) Application of dressing/tape--The dressing is applied by the surgeon and assistant following the surface cleaning of the incision and removal of dried surgical prep solution. The drape sheets are removed, and the tape is applied by the circulating nurse.

Phase V: Postoperative Sequence
(17) Preparation for transfer--The intraoperative records are completed; a warm blanket is placed on the patient; the circulator assists in transferring the patient from the operating table to the recovery bed only when anesthesia personnel are ready.
(18) Transference to postanesthesia area--The circulating nurse accompanies the patient and anesthesia personnel to the postanesthesia care area, and gives a verbal report to the nurse who will continue to care for the patient.
(19) Postprocedural routine--The postprocedural routine consists of delivery of specimen and records to designated location by the circulating nurse, and assistance in the clean-up and preparation for the next procedure performed in the room.

2. As outlined, each phase has specific tasks to be accomplished and specific duties and responsibilities for each member of the surgical team. It takes a great deal of practice and intelligent experience to become proficient in each task, but by understanding the sequence of events, the perioperative nurse can learn to anticipate and to make versatile judgments based on the needs of the patient and the surgical team.

VI. **CARE AND HANDLING OF SURGICAL SPECIMENS**

1. **The care and handling of surgical specimens is of vital importance to the outcome of the surgical procedure.**
2. **During the surgery, the surgeon will hand the specimen, either tissue or fluid, to the scrub person, who then either gives it directly to the circulating nurse for processing or safeguards it on the sterile field (e.g., in a basin) until the end of the procedure. The dispensation will be directly related to the nature of the specimen, and the pathologic examination required.**

A. **TYPES OF SURGICAL SPECIMENS**

1. Two types of specimens are commonly obtained during a surgical procedure:
   a. Those collected for routine examination.
   b. Those collected for diagnostic purposes: (1) **frozen section** and (2) **cultures.**
2. **Routine specimens**
   a. **These specimens do not require immediate attention by the Pathology department, and are collected and placed in a preservation fluid, labeled, and sent to Pathology following the conclusion of the procedure.**
   b. According to J.C.A.H.O. recommendations, all tissues removed from the patient should be sent to Pathology, with very few exceptions, and these exceptions should be specified in the department's policy and procedures manual, including their methods of collection.
   c. Once the pathologist has reviewed the specimen, a dictated report of the findings will appear on the patient's record to assist the surgeon with further treatment.

d. Foreign bodies required for forensic identification, such as bullets or a knife used in a homicide case, require additional handling and identification, and therefore an established protocol must be followed for transfer to a law-enforcement officer after Pathology has made the initial identification of the object.

e. Proper routine handling of specimens requires some basic guidelines, which should be modified to the institutional requirements:

(1) Routine specimens are covered with a preserving fluid, usually 10 percent formalin, unless otherwise directed by the surgeon and/or the Pathology department.

(2) Both the specimen container and its lid should be properly labeled, using a printed patient label. Additional information should include:
  • Specimen description and analysis to be performed
  • Surgeon's name
  • Date and O.R. room number

(3) A completed tissue requisition slip should accompany each specimen container.

(4) The scrub nurse should separate like specimens from different locations (e.g., right/left; anterior/posterior) by placing them on a glove wrapper until collected by the circulating nurse.

(5) Multiple specimens from the same location should be tagged, if not placed in separate containers, designating side (number) of the specimen (e.g., tonsillectomy--right tonsil tagged).

(6) Specimens not immediately passed off the field should be kept moist in saline unless contraindicated or specified by surgeon or pathologist.

(7) Calculi should not be placed in formalin, since the preservative could change the chemical composition of stone. They should be placed in a dry container, and labeled as to their course. (Foreign bodies should be sent dry, e.g., screws, plates, bullets, etc).

(8) **Specimens should never be passed off on a counted sponge.** The sponge may be taken out of the room, causing possible error during the closing counts.

(9) Amputated extremities are wrapped before sending them to the pathology lab/morgue, depending on the specific protocol established by the Pathology department.

(10) All specimens should be handled with gloved hands only.

3. **Diagnostic specimens**

a. **Frozen section**

(1) **This type of specimen requires special handling and immediate examination by the pathologist, with a verbal report of the findings communicated to the surgeon during the surgical procedure.** Examples include a breast biopsy, or biopsy of any organ, tumor, or lesion, for determination of tissue pathology.

(2) **The specimen is sent dry, in a container or on a towel (never on a counted sponge), properly labeled with a tissue requisition slip and immediately given to the pathologist for microscopic examination.** A fixed, or permanent, section will follow, reaffirming the preliminary findings.

b. **Cultures**

(1) **Wound cultures are taken on a patient who comes to the operating room with a known or suspected infection.** Drainage that is cultured may be frank pus or serous fluid.

(2) There are two types of cultures: **aerobic** and **anaerobic**; each is collected in a similar fashion, but may require a different medium for growth. Additionally, cultures may be used to determine the antibiotic that will specifically affect the organism (**sensitivity**).

(3) **Cultures are obtained under sterile conditions, using an appropriate collection tube consisting of cotton-tipped swab attached to the lid, or the fluid is drawn up into a sterile syringe.** The scrub person collects the specimen from the surgeon, and passes it off to the circulator. The exact procedure for collecting cultures for specific tests will vary from each institution, but generally cultures must be sent to the laboratory immediately. If cultures are placed on glass slides (smears), these too must be sent to the laboratory immediately for accurate processing. Each requires an appropriate label and tissue requisition.

(4)   The perioperative nurse must be aware of the proper collection procedure for surgical specimens, so that accuracy can be assured during the examination process. Remember, both the scrub person and the circulating nurse are legally responsible and accountable for proper handling of tissue specimens.

VII.   MANAGEMENT OF TUBES AND DRAINS

1.   **The perioperative nurse is responsible for the proper management of many types of drains, catheters, and other devices used by the surgeon during the course of the surgical procedure.** There are a wide variety of devices available, serving several purposes, and the choice will be determined by the surgeon based on the specific need required by the surgical procedure performed.

2.   As a general rule, the terms **tubes** and **catheters** are used interchangeably, but there is a slight difference in the type and materials used. The primary purpose of all catheters, tubes, and drains is to permit or encourage the escape of body fluids that could be detrimental to the patient's welfare if allowed to remain and/or accumulate within a given area.

A.   TYPES OF DRAINS

1.   Drains remove fluid or exudate by one of two mechanisms: either by gravity or by mechanical means.

2.   The **Foley catheter**, although usually associated with urinary drainage, can be used to serve as a gastrostomy tube in addition to draining the gallbladder when a cholecystostomy is indicated. The catheter's balloon acts to prevent accidental extrusion from the gallbladder or stomach. A "T"-tube serves as a drain for the common duct following a cholangiogram or cholecystectomy, when small fragments of stone may need to be evacuated.

3.   A **Salem sump catheter** is a double-lumen device that prevents adjacent structures from clogging the opening in the suction tube by means of an outer screen of perforated tubing. It is considered a mechanical drainage device, since it is usually attached to low suction (continuous or intermittent), and is particularly appropriate when a large volume of fluid is expected, such as with intestinal fistulae or pancreatitis.

4.   In addition to the drainage tubes mentioned above, there are portable self-contained close-wound mechanical devices that suction fluid or exudate from a wound. After the device is collapsed and closed, the fluid is forced into the collection chamber. Examples of these drains include the **Hemovac** and the **Jackston-Pratt.**

5.   Additional examples of drains commonly used in surgery include the **Pleuro-Vac** and **Atrium chest drainage** systems. These systems are used when the thoracic cavity has been entered and/or the possibility of a tension pneumothorax exists. The **nasogastric tube** (e.g., Levine) is used to decompress the stomach during abdominal surgery. The **Robinson catheter** us used to drain the bladder when an indwelling catheter is not needed, and a variety of urologic catheters used for diagnostic studies, such as a **ureteral olive tip catheter** or a **3-way Foley** are used for continuous irrigation following a transurethral resection of the prostate (T.U.R.P.).

6.   **There are many other catheters and drains, but the responsibility of the perioperative nurse for the management of these tubes, catheters, and drains is the same during the intraoperative phase:**
(a)   **To record the type and location of the drain(s) in addition to the type and amount of drainage.**
(b)   **To communicate this information to the nurses caring for the patient during the post-operative period.**

B. POSSIBLE COMPLICATIONS OF DRAINS

1. **Three basic complications can be associated with the use of drains: hemorrhage, sepsis, and loss of the drain/intraluminal catheter and bowel herniation (when a drain is placed in the abdomen).**
2. Although these complications are rare, any patient with a drainage device should be carefully monitored postoperatively and the surgeon notified immediately for corrective action should a complication develop. An understanding of the basic principles will aid the perioperative nurse in the management of the various drainage devices, regardless of the area of the body. The surgical staff should be properly instructed in the application/insertion techniques, to prepare for use during surgical insertion.

VIII. APPLICATION OF DRESSINGS AND TAPE

1. **The final step for any surgical procedure is the application of dressings and tape.** Dressings accomplish five basic functions, all of which are important to the final outcome of the surgical intervention:
   a. Protect the incision from contamination and/or trauma.
   b. Absorb drainage.
   c. Provide support, or splint or immobilize a body part and/or the incision.
   d. Facilitate hemostasis and minimize edema.
   e. Enhance the patient's physical, esthetic, and psychologic comfort.
2. **The choice of type of dressing used is based on the type of surgery performed, the condition of the wound at time of closure, and the area of the incision.** Under extreme circumstances, the wound may be packed prior to applying the dressing, to be closed at a later date once an infection has subsided, but most patients will leave the procedure room with a dressing in place.
3. Postoperative surgical dressings for abdominal procedures are usually applied in three layers, depending on the complexity of the surgery:
   a. **First layer (closest to the skin):** nonadherent dressing; most common is Telfa; will not stick to wound, thus decreasing trauma during dressing changes.
   b. **Second layer:** gauze 4 x 4 dressing sponges (Raytec sponges should never be used for dressings).
   c. **Third layer:** absorbent pad, usually an ABD; provides absorbency with protection.
4. Alternative surgical dressings range from an adhesive synthetic permeable membrane, such as OpSite, for use on a small area, to Montgomery straps, which are applied over a conventional dressing when frequent dressing changes may be required, thus eliminating removal and reapplication of tape.
5. **Application protocol**
   a. The wound and surrounding area is cleaned by the scrub person with a sterile sponge and dried with a sterile towel.
   b. The sterile dressing material is prepared (cut, fluffed, etc.) and applied in layers using sterile technique. Drain sites require a sterile dressing.
   c. The laparotomy drape is removed while the dressings are held in place with sterile gloves.
   d. The circulating nurse applies the appropriate tape, making sure that all edges are secured and the dressing is sealed.
   NOTE: Some patients may have sensitivities to a certain type of tape, and this factor must be taken into account during the application procedure.
6. Once the dressings are secure, and the patient is relatively stable from the anesthesia and beginning to awaken, the perioperative nurse finalizes the intraoperative paperwork, assists in moving the patient to the recovery bed, and proceeds to transport the patient, with an anesthesiologist/anesthesia clinician, to the Postanesthesia Care Unit (PACU), where the next phase of patient care begins.

PRACTICE QUESTIONS

1. **General considerations for safety in the handling of power equipment used in surgery include all of the following EXCEPT:**

   1. *All power equipment should be inspected by the user prior to and after each use.*

   2. *Extension cords should be avoided whenever possible, and power cords should lie flat on the floor or be suspended to prevent obstruction of traffic areas and/or entrances.*

   3. *Verification that the correct attachments for a piece of equipment are in fact being used should be performed by the supervising nurse.*

   4. *Freestanding pressure tanks should be replaced immediately when the pressure in the tank is below a safe limit.*

2. **To complete the electrical circuit of an electrosurgical unit (E.S.U.), and therefore to perform electrosurgery, four components are needed. One is the power unit itself. The other three are the:**

   1. *active and dispersive electrodes, and the patient.*

   2. *two poles of the active electrode, and the dispersive electrode.*

   3. *ground pad and active and dispersive electrodes.*

   4. *dispersive electrode, ground pad, and patient.*

3. **One advantage in using a bipolar active electrode rather than a monopolar active electrode is that it:**

   1. *is safer to use on delicate tissue, such as the brain.*

   2. *generates more power and is more effective on tough and fibrous tissues.*

   3. *can be used with a ground pad, which makes it more flexible and more effective.*

   4. *is spark-proof, and therefore can be used in a high-oxygen operating atmosphere.*

4. **Several guidelines should be followed by the perioperative nurse to minimize the risk of burns associated with use of the electrosurgical unit (E.S.U.). Which of the following activities is regarded as acceptable?**

   1. *Using a power unit as an "extra" table surface.*

   2. *Allowing the patient ground cable to contact a hypothermia blanket.*

   3. *Using a ground pad when a monopolar active electrode is being used.*

   4. *Activating the active electrode (hand piece) with wet gloves or gloves with a hole in them.*

5. **A patient is admitted for arthroscopic knee surgery. The type of power source used for this procedure is:**

   1. *electrosurgical.*

   2. *fiberoptic.*

3. *argon laser.*

4. *ND:Yag laser.*

6. **Recommendations regarding the maintenance and use of endoscopic equipment should be known to all persons working with the equipment, and should include all of the following EXCEPT:**

    1. *Disinfection rather than sterilization of endoscopes and accessories is preferred because of the difficulty of sterilizing this equipment.*

    2. *Following cleaning and disinfection, endoscopes should be thoroughly rinsed with sterile water and completely dried before storage.*

    3. *All endoscopes should be inspected and tested prior to each use, along with power cords and accessory items used during the procedure.*

    4. *Flexible and rigid endoscopes should be inspected, tested, and processed according to design/type and manufacturer's instructions.*

7. **When assisting in a procedure in which an operating microscope is being used, it is the circulating nurse's principal responsibility to:**

    1. *maintain a sterile field around the microscope.*

    2. *know how to pass instruments when using the microscope.*

    3. *make sure the microscope lens and oculars are clean.*

    4. *know how to take care of and position the microscope.*

8. **Nursing guidelines for the use of thermal blankets during surgery include all of the following EXCEPT:**

    1. *For safety reasons, thermal blankets are not recommended for any surgical procedure lasting more than 2 hours.*

    2. *Thermal blankets are recommended for all pediatric procedures and procedures in patients with impaired circulatory status.*

    3. *Direct skin contact with the thermal blanket should be avoided by placing a sheet between the blanket and the patient.*

    4. *Folds and/or creases should be avoided so that hot spots or pressure injuries do not occur during use of a thermal blanket.*

9. **Besides a thermal blanket, other interventions can be used by the perioperative nurse and surgical team to maintain body temperature during a surgical procedure. Which of the following is NOT one of these interventions?**

    1. *Using warmed prep solutions and irrigating solutions.*

    2. *Providing psychologic support, thereby reducing anxiety and fear.*

3. *Ensuring patient immobility to minimize heat loss through movement.*

4. *Providing warm blankets upon arrival to the procedure room and before transferring to the postanesthesia area.*

10. **Autotransfusion is contraindicated in which of the following cases?**

    1. *If wounds are fresh (less than 4 hours old).*

    2. *If the patient has cancer.*

    3. *If the surgery is elective.*

    4. *If there is danger of blood contamination.*

11. **For a surgical procedure in which extensive blood replacement is anticipated (e.g., splenectomy), without the threat of disease transmission, transfusion reactions, or incompatibility, the method of choice is likely to be:**

    1. *autotransfusion using the patient's own blood.*

    2. *transfusion of blood from a commercial blood bank.*

    3. *transfusion of packed blood cells from a commercial bank.*

    4. *use of the autologous transfusion (cell saver) system.*

12. **For delicate surgical procedures such as plastic surgery or neurosurgery, in which laser equipment will be used both for precise cutting and coagulation, the laser of choice is likely to be the:**

    1. *carbon dioxide laser.*

    2. *ND:Yag laser.*

    3. *argon laser.*

    4. *molybdenum crystal laser.*

13. **For an ophthalmologic procedure such as diabetic retinopathy, in which a laser beam must be effectively absorbed by pigmented tissue, yet pass through clear structures with minimal damage, the laser of choice is likely to be the:**

    1. *carbon dioxide laser.*

    2. *ND:Yag laser.*

    3. *argon laser.*

    4. *molybdenum crystal laser.*

14. **To ensure a safe environment during the use of laser equipment, the perioperative nurse should be certain that all of the following procedures are followed EXCEPT:**

    1. *A smoke evaluator system should be used to absorb the pflume from the laser.*

    2. *Lasers should not be used with alcohol preps, or be kept near combustible solutions or substances.*

    3. *All sponges used at the field should be dry (for CO_2 lasers) to prevent the laser beam from vaporizing water molecules and igniting a fire.*

    4. *Instruments should be brushed or ebonized to avoid reflecting the laser beam.*

15. **A tourniquet cuff applied to a leg is typically inflated to between:**

    1. *150 and 250 mm Hg.*

    2. *250 and 300 mm Hg.*

    3. *300 and 400 mm Hg.*

    4. *400 and 500 mm Hg.*

16. **In which of the following cases is use of a tourniquet contraindicated?**

    1. *When the incision site is on an extremity.*

    2. *When the patient has a vascular disease.*

    3. *When surgical power tools are to be used in the procedure.*

    4. *When laser equipment is to be used in the procedure.*

17. **A precaution to take before using a radiopaque contrast media for an X-ray procedure is:**

    1. *checking for patient sensitivity to iodine-related substances such as shellfish.*

    2. *removing any implanted device prior to administration of the contrast agent.*

    3. *standing behind a protective (lead-lined) screen or wearing a lead apron before the agent is administered.*

    4. *asking all nonscrubbed personnel to leave the procedure room before the agent is administered.*

18. **Which of the following is NOT a recommended practice for radiation safety in the use of X-ray equipment?**

    1. *The X-ray machine or overhead unit should be damp dusted with cleaning solution before use.*

    2. *During filming, all unnecessary instruments should be removed from the field unless otherwise directed by the surgeon..*

    3. *Female personnel who are pregnant should be excused from X-ray procedures.*

    4. *Positioning of the equipment should be done immediately after draping to avoid contamination.*

19. **Routine specimens are distinguished from diagnostic specimens in that they:**

    1. *are collected dry, in a container or on a towel.*

    2. *are given by the scrub nurse directly to the circulating nurse for processing.*

    3. *normally are not sent to the Pathology department for review.*

    4. *do not require immediate attention by the Pathology department.*

20. **Proper routine handling of surgical specimens requires some basic guidelines, which are modified to the requirements of the institution. Which of the following is NOT one of these guidelines?**

    1. *Multiple specimens from the same location should be tagged, if not placed in separate containers.*

    2. *Calculi should be placed in formalin immediately, since their chemical composition deteriorates rapidly outside the body.*

    3. *Specimens should never be passed off on a counted sponge.*

    4. *Specimens not immediately passed off the field should be kept moist in saline unless contraindicated or specified by surgeon or pathologist.*

21. **A biopsy is normally sent to the Pathology department in the form of a:**

    1. *culture.*

    2. *routine specimen.*

    3. *frozen section.*

    4. *formalin-preserved specimen.*

22. **Which of the following statements about culture specimens is correct?**

    1. *Aerobic and anaerobic cultures are collected differently but usually can be grown on the same medium.*

    2. *Generally cultures are not sent to the laboratory until the procedure is complete.*

    3. *Because of their nonsterile nature, cultures cannot be collected under sterile conditions.*

    4. *The scrub person collects the specimen from the surgeon, and passes it off the circulator.*

23. **Of the following types of drains, the one that would normally be used when a large volume of fluid is expected, such as with intestinal fistulae or pancreatitis, is the:**

    1. *Hemovac drain.*

    2. *Salem sump catheter.*

    3. *Pleuro-Vac.*

    4. *Foley catheter.*

24. **One of the primary responsibilities of the perioperative nurse for the management of tubes, catheters, and drains during the intraoperative period is to:**

    1. *choose the type of drainage device that will be used for the surgical procedure being performed.*

    2. *record the type and location of the drain(s) and the type and amount of drainage.*

    3. *attach the appropriate drainage device after the incision has been closed.*

    4. *instruct the surgical staff in the proper application/insertion of all drainage devices used in surgery.*

25. **Among the major factors that influence the choice of dressing used for a surgical wound are all of the following EXCEPT:**

    1. *the type of surgery performed.*

    2. *the area of the incision.*

    3. *the condition of the wound at the time of closure.*

    4. *the type of packing used for the wound.*

26. **Perioperative nursing protocols for the application of dressings and tapes include all of the following EXCEPT:**

    1. *The laparotomy drape is removed after the dressing is sealed.*

    2. *The wound and surrounding area is cleaned by the scrub person.*

    3. *Drain sites require a sterile dressing.*

    4. *The circulating nurse applies the appropriate tape.*

ANSWER EXPLANATIONS

1. **The answer is 3.** Verification that the correct attachments for a piece of equipment are in fact being used should be performed by the person using the equipment, including confirmation that the attachments are seated properly before activating the unit. Some additional general safety guidelines for protecting the patient and the staff from harm include: (1) all electrical equipment should be routinely inspected by qualified personnel; (2) power cords should never be crimped or bent; any tears or breaks in the cord should negate the use of that cord until it is repaired; (3) freestanding pressure tanks should be checked before and after each use, replaced immediately when the pressure in the tank is below a safe limit, and monitored during its use; (4) equipment must be maintained through proper cleaning, lubrication, and sterilization procedures, according to the manufacturer's written recommendations; (5) when not in use, equipment should be maintained in a neutral power state, and sharp tips protected to avoid accidental injury; and (6) all persons handling power equipment should be educated about the function and proper use of this equipment. The proper handling of any piece of equipment used in surgery is the responsibility of every member of the surgical team.

2. **The answer is 1.** The purpose of the electrosurgical unit (E.S.U.) is to (1) control bleeding through the application of heat, and (2) to cut tissue. To perform electrosurgery, three basic components are required: (1) the power unit, (2) the active electrode, and (3) the dispersive (return) electrode. These, along with the patient, are necessary to complete the electrical circuit.

3. **The answer is 1.** The active electrode of an E.S.U. is available as monopolar or bipolar, and depending on the surgical procedure, one or the other may be used. With monopolar electrosurgery, only one pole is active, and it carries current to the operative site. The current flows from the monopolar connection to the electrode, which is applied to the tissue, is dispersed over the dispersive electrode (ground pad), and returned to the E.S.U. via the dispersive electrode cable. A bipolar active electrode has a forceps configuration. In the bipolar electrode, one tip acts as the active pole while the other tip acts as the return (dispersive) pole. With bipolar, a ground pad is not required, since the dispersive electrode is one of the bipolar tips. By using a bipolar electrode, the power is distributed to a very limited area (between the tips only) and the actual wattage power required is reduced, making it safe for use on delicate tissue, such as the brain.

4. **The answer is 3.** Burns can occur from direct contact with hot electric wires or from items overheating by electric wires. Patient burns usually result when too much current flows through an inadequate area for a too long a time; therefore, the use, placement, and proper connection of the ground pad becomes one of the most important factors associated with safe use of the E.S.U. One measure that reduces risk is using a bipolar unit, since a ground pad is not needed when the active electrode is bipolar. Additional safety measures that can reduce the possibility of burns include: (1) maintaining an awareness of where the active electrode tip is located and/or storing it in an appropriate holder when not in use; (2) checking the equipment before each use, including cords, connectors, and the alarm system; (3) using an E.S.U. and ground pad with a return electrode monitoring (R.E.M.) alarm system, which deactivates the system should the dispersive electrode be faulty for whatever reason; (4) never turning down the volume of the alarm so that it cannot notify the team of a possible problem alert; and (5) placing ECG electrodes on the posterior aspect of the shoulders, away from the dispersive electrode site, thus avoiding any unnecessary hazards when both an E.S.U. and ECG monitoring equipment are in use.

5. **The answer is 2.** The term fiberoptic describes a power source found in a variety of surgical instruments and used for both diagnostic and therapeutic procedures. A fiberoptic cable is composed of a flexible material, either glass or plastic, which is capable of transmitting light along its fibers by reflecting the light from the side or the wall of the fiber. To illuminate this cable, a power source is required as the source of light for the cable. Fiberoptics are used in endoscopy procedures, performed either in surgery, the G.I. suite, or the physician's office, through a natural opening in the body (e.g., bronchoscopy, colonoscopy, or cystoscopy) or through an artificial opening created via an incision, such as an arthroscopy or laparoscopy. Additional types of endoscopic procedures can be performed during a surgical procedure--for example, a choledochoscopy during a gallbladder procedure, or a nephroscopy during surgery on the kidney.

6. **The answer is 1.** Recommendations regarding the sterilization, disinfection, and storage of endoscopic equipment should be known to all persons working with the equipment. Sterilization rather than disinfection of endoscopes and accessories is preferred to increase patient safety. As with any piece of equipment, proper cleaning and maintenance along with gentle handling will save the instrument and/or equipment from costly repairs. The use of damaged instruments could possibly increase the risk of tissue injury, infection, and length of the surgical procedure; therefore, all endoscopes should be inspected and tested prior to each use, along with power cords and accessory items used during the procedure. Because not all fiberoptic cables are interchangeable, in order to have maximum illumination the perioperative nurse must make sure that all connections appropriately match prior to beginning the procedure. Also, to preserve the efficiency of the light source, the intensity of the light should be lowered before switching the unit on or off, and light cords should be coiled loosely to prevent damage to the fibers. The light cord and fiberoptic bundles should never be bent or they will break, decreasing the amount of projected light.

7. **The answer is 4.** The other responsibilities are principally those of the scrub nurse. Specific responsibilities of the circulating nurse include: (1) checking to see that all knobs are secured after the microscope has been placed in final position; (2) assisting the surgeon with attachments of accessory items; (3) taking special care of power cables to prevent accidental breakage; (4) taking special care of lenses to avoid breaking, scratching, or leaving fingerprints; (5) keeping extra lamp bulbs and fuses available; knowing where to find accessories and anticipating their usage depending on the proposed procedure and/or surgeon's preference; (6) when moving the microscope, positioning the viewing portion over the base to add stability; acquiring adequate moving help to accommodate the move safely; (7) when storing the microscope, avoiding using

a plastic bag or cover; instead, use a cloth pillowcase; and (8) and covering the foot pedal with a clear bag to keep it clean and dry, and positioning it for easy access after the surgeon has been seated or has determined the desired position to perform the surgery.

8. **The answer is 1.** Thermal blankets are recommended for any surgical procedure lasting more than 2 hours. When safely used, the thermal blanket can be a major assistance in preventing an adverse response to surgical intervention by maintaining the near-normal physiologic status, and can decrease the possibility of postoperative hypothermia. Additional nursing guidelines include the following: (1) observation and monitoring of both the unit and the patient should be constant throughout the procedure; (2) skin integrity should be inspected before and after the procedure with corresponding documentation of assessment findings; and (3) power cords and connective lines to the blanket should be checked before and after each use for cracks, breaks, or holes in the cords or blanket that could increase the possibility of electric shock.

9. **The answer is 3.** In the normal course of a surgical event, a loss of heat is primarily the result of exposure to the physical environment, the incision itself, the patient's immobility, and/or coexisting circulatory insufficiency. Additional measures for maintaining body temperature address these sources of heat loss and include: (1) monitoring physiologic parameters, such as skin color, texture, and external/internal temperature throughout the procedure; (2) limiting exposure area to the direct operative site; and (3) administering warm blood if transfusions are required.

10. **The answer is 2.** Autotransfusion (using the patient as his or her own blood donor prior to elective surgery) is not always applicable and is contraindicated if the patient has cancer, if gross contamination from the bowel or stomach contents have occurred, or, in the case of a trauma patient, if the wounds are more than 4 hours old. If these conditions are not present, autotransfusion can be the safest method for replacing lost blood cells.

11. **The answer is 4.** The cell saver unit for autologous blood recovery returns washed packed cells to the patient via a filtered reinfusion bag. This autotransfusion system provides intraoperative salvage of blood, without the threat of disease transmission, transfusion reactions, or incompatibility testing. Although most units are designed to cycle automatically, a nurse or clinical perfusionist should be assigned to manage the unit while in use, to coordinate the delivery of blood to anesthesia personnel as needed. Full records of the amount of irrigant, numbers of units processed, and so on should be kept during the procedure, and be incorporated with the record of the total amount of infusion solutions administered during the procedure. The use of this system has created a positive outcome not only for emergency patients, but also for those whose surgery may require extensive replacement (more than 2-3 units) during the course of the procedure.

12. **The answer is 1.** The CO_2 laser is the most versatile laser, since it can perform both coagulation and cutting functions, and can be operated in continuous or pulsed modes. By varying the length and frequency of each pulse, different tissue effects can be produced and thermal effects can be more precisely controlled. The CO_2 laser wavelength is absorbed by water and since the body is 75 percent to 90 percent water, an extremely precise beam can vaporize even a single cell while avoiding surrounding tissue. The precision of the laser beam provides maximum impact on intended tissue with minimal damage to surrounding tissue. In addition, the laser beam causes minimal immediate postoperative pain and allows faster recovery. Surgical specialties that can benefit from a CO_2 laser include general, gynecology, E.N.T., neurosurgery, and plastic surgery.

13. **The answer is 3.** Like the CO_2 laser, the argon laser uses gas as its medium; however, it functions at a different wavelength than the CO_2 laser. The argon beam is effectively absorbed by pigmented tissue, yet passes through clear structures with minimal effect. The primary clinical applications include ophthalmology, dermatology, gastroenterology, gynecology, and otology. Since the argon beam is well suited for ophthalmic surgery, it is the most common form of treatment for diabetic retinopathy, and is well adapted to ambulatory surgery settings and use in an ophthalmologist's office.

14. **The answer is 3.** Sponges should be damp (for CO_2 lasers) to prevent the laser beam from striking any other tissue and/or area or igniting a fire. Other procedures to follow include: (1) pasting a warning sign

on all doors leading in and out of the laser area, stating the type of laser being used on all doors leading in and out of the laser area, to alert personnel that they must take certain precautionary measures, including application of special goggles/glasses which are applicable to the medium being used; (2) making sure that emergency equipment such as sterile water and a halon fire extinguisher are readily available; (3) protecting the patient's eyes; and (4) placing the laser in the stand-by mode when not in use. One nurse who has been instructed in the medium and its safety factors should be assigned to use the laser and should not be involved with circulating duties while working with the laser. However, continuous monitoring and observation of the environment and the patient must be practiced by all persons working with a laser, regardless of the medium.

15. **The answer is 4.** Tourniquets are used during most operations on the extremities when a "bloodless" wound site is desired. They prevent venous oozing, yet do not totally obstruct the arterial blood supply, thereby preserving the circulation through the extremity. To drain the venous blood from the extremity, the limb, still elevated, is wrapped with a wide sterile rubber bandage (Esmarck or Martin) from the distal to the proximal end, and the tourniquet is then inflated to the desired setting. It is recommended that the setting for an arm be between 250 and 300 mm Hg and for legs, 400 to 500 mm Hg. Once the setting has been reached, the rubber bandage is removed, and the extremity can be lowered onto the sterile field. During the procedure, the pressure should be checked and verified at least every 30 minutes to detect any pressure variation, with documentation of the time of inflation, deflation, and location of the cuff. Although there is no actual time limit regarding the use of tourniquets, the recommended time limits range from 1 hour for an arm and 1 1/2 hours for a leg. If more time is required, the cuff should be deflated for 10 minutes, then reinflated to the desired pressure.

16. **The answer is 2.** Improperly used, the tourniquet can cause serious nerve and vascular damage; therefore, careful planning, application, and monitoring are essential to its safe usage. Selection and placement of the cuff should be determined by the patient's age, anatomy, and medical condition. The cuff should be applied to the extremity so that underlying skin and tissue are not unduly traumatized. Its use is contraindicated in patients with vascular disease or poor peripheral circulation. The cuff should be positioned at the point of maximum circumference of the extremity. Once inflated it should not be readjusted.

17. **The answer is 1.** An X-ray procedure can be invasive, in which a dye or radiopaque contrast material is injected into a vein, duct, or passageway within the body, or non-invasive, such as a confirmation X-ray of implantable devices. Contrast agents, composed of nonmetallic compounds or heavy metal salts, permit the visualization of internal structures during an X-ray procedure. As with many of the contrast media, they contain iodine; therefore, if invasive X-rays are to be taken, it is vitally important that known sensitivities to iodine-related substances such as shellfish or previous problems with invasive studies using iodine be obtained through the preoperative assessment, and the information communicated to the surgeon. If contrast media is used during the procedure, it must be dispensed under sterile conditions, and must be administered according to the surgeon's dilution request, using warm sterile saline (usually 50-60 dilution) in a labeled syringe (30-60 mL) with appropriate needle for injection. The other precautions listed apply to the actual filming procedure.

18. **The answer is 4.** Positioning of the equipment should be done prior to draping and confirmed by a "scout" film, to prevent having to replace the drapes if positioning is not correct. Additional A.O.R.N. guidelines include: (1) sterile technique involving the surgery must be maintained during an X-ray procedure; (2) when using a cassette, the scrub nurse must enclose the cassette in a sterile cassette cover, maintaining aseptic technique, before it can be brought to the sterile field; (3) the sterile members of the team should apply protective "lead aprons" prior to the scrub to facilitate sterile application of the gown while being protected against exposure to X-rays during the procedure; (4) an X-ray detector badge, indicating the amount of exposure received in a month, should be worn on the outside of the lead apron (under sterile gown) during all X-ray procedures, by all personnel in the room; (5) the circulating nurse should assist the X-ray technician in placing the cassette into the cassette table holder by lifting the drapes and sliding the cassette into the desired location; (6) while the film is being developed, the surgical team should not contaminate their gowns/hands by folding arms across chest or under arms, or sit while in sterile attire; (7) unless absolutely necessary, all nonscrubbed personnel should leave the room during a single-series filming; those persons who must remain should wear a lead apron or stand behind protective (lead-lined) screen in the

procedure room; (8) for optimum protection during fluoroscopy, persons within 2 meters of the unit should wear a thyroid shield, and leaded sterile gloves should be worn when hands are in direct exposure to fluoroscopy; (9) leaded protective devices should be routinely checked for cracks or tears, which can significantly reduce the effectiveness of the shield; and (10) a qualified radiologic technician (or radiologist) should be in attendance throughout the X-ray/fluoroscopy sequence, and should always be aware of the other members of the team, allowing them time to properly prepare for the X-ray exposure.

19. **The answer is 4.** Two types of specimens are commonly obtained during a surgical procedure: those collected for routine examination, and those collected for diagnostic purposes (frozen section and cultures). Review specimens do not require immediate attention by the Pathology department, and are collected and placed in a preservation fluid, labeled, and sent to Pathology following the conclusion of the procedure. According to J.C.A.H.O. recommendations, all tissues removed from the patient should be sent to Pathology, with very few exceptions, and these exceptions should be specified in the department's policy and procedures manual, including their methods of collection. Once the pathologist has reviewed the specimen, a dictated report of the findings will appear on the patient's record to assist the surgeon with further treatment.

20. **The answer is 2.** Calculi should not be placed in formalin, since the preservative could change the chemical composition of stone. They should be placed in a dry container, and labeled as to their course. (Foreign bodies should be sent dry, e.g., screws, plates, bullets, etc). Additional guidelines include: (1) routine specimens are covered with a preserving fluid, usually 10 percent formalin, unless otherwise directed by the surgeon and/or the Pathology department; (2) both the specimen container and its lid should be properly labeled, using a printed patient label; (3) a completed tissue requisition slip should accompany each specimen container; (4) the scrub nurse should separate like specimens from different locations (e.g., right/left; anterior/posterior) by placing them on a glove wrapper until collected by the circulating nurse; (5) amputated extremities are wrapped before sending them to the pathology lab/morgue, depending on the specific protocol established by the Pathology department; and (6) all specimens should be handled with gloved hands.

21. **The answer is 3.** A frozen section requires special handling and immediate examination by the pathologist, with a verbal report of the findings communicated to the surgeon during the surgical procedure. Examples include a breast biopsy, or biopsy of any organ, tumor, or lesion, for determination of tissue pathology. The specimen is sent dry, in a container or on a towel (never on a counted sponge), properly labeled with a tissue requisition slip and immediately given to the pathologist for microscopic examination. A fixed, or permanent, section will follow, reaffirming the preliminary findings.

22. **The answer is 4.** The scrub person collects the specimen from the surgeon, and passes it off to the circulator. The exact procedure for collecting cultures for specific tests will vary from each institution, but generally cultures must be sent to the laboratory immediately. If cultures are placed on glass slides (smears), these too must be sent to the laboratory immediately for accurate processing. Each requires an appropriate label and tissue requisition.

23. **The answer is 2.** The primary purpose of all catheters, tubes, and drains is to permit or encourage the escape of body fluids that could be detrimental to the patient's welfare if allowed to remain and/or accumulate within a given area. Drains remove fluid or exudate by one of two mechanisms: either by gravity or by mechanical means. A Salem sump catheter is a double-lumen device that prevents adjacent structures from clogging the opening in the suction tube by means of an outer screen of perforated tubing. It is considered a mechanical drainage device, since it is usually attached to low suction (continuous or intermittent), and is particularly appropriate when a large volume of fluid is expected, such as with intestinal fistulae or pancreatitis.

24. **The answer is 2.** There are many types of catheters and drains, but the responsibility of the perioperative nurse for the management of these tubes, catheters, and drains is the same during the intraoperative phase: (1) to record the type and location of the drain(s) in addition to the type and amount of drainage; and (2) to communicate this information to the nurses caring for the patient during the postoperative period.

25. **The answer is 4.** The choice of type of dressing used is based on the type of surgery performed, the condition of the wound at time of closure and the area of the incision. Under extreme circumstances, the wound may be packed prior to applying the dressing, to be closed at a later date once an infection has subsided, but most patients will leave the procedure room with a dressing in place.

26. **The answer is 1.** Postoperative surgical dressings for abdominal procedures are usually applied in three layers, depending on the complexity of the surgery. Application protocols include the following: (1) the wound and surrounding area is cleaned by the scrub person with a sterile sponge and dried with a sterile towel; (2) the sterile dressing material is prepared (cut, fluffed, etc.) and applied in layers using sterile technique; drain sites require a sterile dressing; (3) the laparotomy drape is removed while the dressings are held in place with sterile gloves; and (4) the circulating nurse applies the appropriate tape, making sure that all edges are secured and the dressing is sealed.

13 Postoperative Patient Care Management

STUDY OUTLINE

I. POSTPROCEDURAL CHECKLIST

1. **The postoperative phase of the perioperative period begins with the transference of the patient to the designated postanesthesia area and ends with the resolution of the surgical experience.**
2. For the perioperative nurse, the care of the surgical patient does not end with the conclusion of the surgical procedure, but continues through to the immediate postoperative phase; that is, transfer of the patient to the Postanesthesia Care Unit (PACU) or designated postoperative area (e.g., ambulatory surgery unit, surgical nursing unit). Before this transfer is accomplished, however, the following activities should be completed by the perioperative nurse:
   a. **Intraoperative documentation and charges are completed and reviewed for accuracy.**
   b. **Specimens are properly identified, labeled, and placed in the appropriate container(s).**
   c. **Special equipment for the postanesthesia area, requested by the anesthesiologist or nurse anesthetist, has been communicated to appropriate personnel.**
   d. **Patient is moved to a recovery bed and transported to the PACU.**
   e. **Verbal/written reports are given to the appropriate PACU nurse upon arrival to the unit.**

II. EVALUATING PERIOPERATIVE NURSING CARE

1. **Ideally, the perioperative nurse's role does not end with the admission of the patient to the PACU, but extends to a Postoperative Evaluation and Reassessment Phase, in order to obtain information regarding the quality and effectiveness of perioperative nurse care.**
2. Evaluation of patient care may occur not only in the PACU, but in the case of an ambulatory surgery patient, may also be performed through a **telephone interview** following discharge, or, for the hospitalized patient, a **follow-up postoperative visit.**
3. **The postoperative evaluation is important for several reasons,** including these:
   a. It gives the nurse feedback about how successful the care plan was for a particular patient, and can help to determine the quality of care delivered, which is all part of the reassessment process.
   b. It helps the nurse determine what could have been done differently that would have improved the effectiveness of the nursing care. An introspective self-evaluation is sometimes the hardest to accomplish, but through it, the perioperative nurse can continue to develop her or his knowledge and skill levels, which can only strengthen the professional commitment: *to deliver quality patient care throughout the perioperative period.*

III. POSTANESTHESIA NURSING CARE

1. Most modern operating room suites are designed with a **Postanesthesia Care Unit (PACU) (recovery room),** which is specifically created to manage the postanesthesia patient during the immediate postoperative period.
2. Postanesthesia care was not always provided by a separate group of nurses; in fact, today in small hospitals and/or during off-shift hours or on-call situations, the perioperative nurse may be

responsible for the management of patient care during this phase. For this reason, and for a better understanding of the perioperative cycle, a brief overview of managing patient care during the immediate postoperative period will be discussed in this unit.

A. OBJECTIVES AND STANDARDS OF POSTANESTHESIA NURSING CARE

1. **There are four primary objectives of nursing care in the PACU:**
   a. **To recognize the major potential problems associated with a specific surgical procedure, and the appropriate corresponding actions.**
   b. **To identify and demonstrate the general procedures routinely carried out in the PACU area.**
   c. **To maintain accurate documentation of the patient's progress during the recovery phase.**
   d. **To recognize and use the criteria for discharging a patient from the PACU, using an established scoring guide.**
2. Each institution should have established policies for implementing patient care during the immediate postoperative period, including documentation guidelines and specific tasks and activities that will assist the patient during this critical transition.
3. **Standards of Practice: PACU:** In 1986, the American Society of Post Anesthesia Nurses (A.S.P.A.N.) developed their Standards of Practice to serve as guidelines for providing patient care during the immediate postanesthesia recovery period, and like the Perioperative Standards of Practice, they are based on the nursing process format: Assessment, Nursing Diagnoses, Planning, Implementation, and Evaluation.
   a. Health status data is collected. This data is recorded, retrievable, continuous, and communicated.
   b. The Nursing Diagnoses statements are derived from health status data.
   c. Goals for nursing care are formulated.
   d. The plan for nursing care prescribes nursing actions to achieve the goals.
   e. The plan for nursing care is implemented.
   f. The plan of care is evaluated.
   g. Reassessment of the patient, reconsideration of nursing diagnoses, resetting of goals, and modification and implementation of the care plan are a continuous process.

B. MANAGEMENT OF PATIENT CARE IN THE PACU

1. **To ensure the continuity of care from the intraoperative phase to the immediate postoperative phase, the surgical team, consisting of the anesthesiologist or nurse anesthetist and the circulating nurse, will give a report to the recovery nurse about the patient's status upon admission to the unit.**
2. This report should include, but not be limited to, the following information:
   a. Surgery performed.
   b. Type/agents of anesthesia administered; time and amount last dose was given.
   c. Presence and status of drains and dressings.
   d. Length of procedure/anesthesia.
   e. Setting for oxygen/administration preference.
   f. Hemodynamic monitoring lines; peripheral I.V. lines.
   g. Status of fluid and electrolyte balance; intraoperative intake and output, including blood and blood products, if used.
   h. Presence and status of catheters or tubes.
   i. Potential problems that may occur owing to the patient's physiologic status or surgical procedure.

C. INITIAL ASSESSMENT ACTIVITIES

1. **The primary goal of immediate postanesthesia nursing care is the safe recovery and arousal of the patient from the effects of anesthesia.** The recovery nurse works with the patient, performing

specific nursing activities to "stir-up" the patient from the effects of the anesthesia, while providing emotional support through orientation, teaching, and encouragement of specific activities to accomplish this goal.

2. **The patient's well-being is directly related to adequate ventilation and circulation; therefore, the patient's respiratory status, skin color, and cardiovascular status are the first to be evaluated during the initial assessment.**

3. When the recovery nurse is satisfied that the respiratory and cardiac status are adequate, the surgical team members can safely leave the area, and a total assessment of the patient's physiologic status is evaluated according to preestablished protocols and procedures.

4. **Specific nursing activities are based on the patient's individual needs.** These activities relate to seven major areas: (1) promoting adequate respiratory function, (2) promoting adequate circulatory function, (3) promoting normal reflex return, (4) promoting safety and comfort, (5) promoting wound healing, (6) promoting fluid and electrolyte balance, and (7) reducing anxiety and providing psychosocial support. These areas will be discussed in the Implementation segment of this unit.

5. Using the A.S.P.A.N. Standards of Practice as a guide, the initial assessment of the patient should include, but not be limited to, the following areas:
   a. Vital signs
      (1) Respiratory status
      (2) Circulatory status
      (3) Pulses
      (4) Temperature
      (5) O_2 saturation level
   b. Color and condition of skin and mucous membranes
   c. Hemodynamic values
   d. Position of the patient (comfort and safety)
   e. Type and patency of drainage tubes and catheters
   f. Condition of dressings; amount/type of drainage
   g. Activity status; extremity movement
   h. Level of consciousness; response to stimuli
   i. Level of comfort/safety
      (1) Pain
      (2) Status of protective reflexes
   j. I.V. therapy; patency of catheter

6. **Aldrette Scoring System (1970): This system is used to assess the postoperative patient's status by measuring five physiologic factors: respiration, circulation, skin color, activity, and level of consciousness. By using specific, predetermined criteria, values ranging from 0 to 2 are placed on each one of these factors. These assessment factors are usually measured upon arrival, then 15 minutes, 30 minutes, 60 minutes, and prior to discharge from the unit.**

D. NURSING DIAGNOSIS STATEMENTS

1. **The postoperative nursing diagnoses for the immediate postanesthesia patient should be incorporated into the overall patient care plan.**

E. PLANNING

1. **The use of standardized care plans for the postanesthesia area provides continuity of patient care, since more than one recovery nurse may be caring for the patient during the recovery period.** The care plan should incorporate all aspects of postanesthesia care, and be modified according to the individual needs of the patient.

F. IMPLEMENTATION

1. **Nursing interventions are based on continued systems monitoring that can assist in promoting and maintaining the physical and emotional needs of the patient.**
2. **Seven major areas of nursing intervention**
   a. **Promoting adequate respiratory function**
      (1) **Respirations are affected by anesthesia, blood loss, or preexisting cardiac or pulmonary disease.** The recovery nurse must be observant for changes in rate, rhythm, depth, and quality of respirations, through auscultation of breath sounds at least every 15 minutes, and grade the patient according to the Aldrette score for respiratory status. If supportive respiratory equipment is in place, such as an endotracheal tube or oral airway, it too should be assessed for position and function.
      (2) **The patient should be positioned so that a patent airway can be maintained, secretions can be suctioned, and oxygen can be administered, as per protocol/order.** Once the patient is breathing adequately and independently, the position can be changed to accommodate comfort. The recovery nurse should encourage the patient to breathe deeply and to move extremities, which will assist in "blowing-off" the inhalation agents and increase circulation. Coughing may or may not be appropriate, depending on the surgical procedure.
      (3) **Skin color and condition**
         (a) **Skin color should be assessed as an indicator of oxygenation, and graded according to the Aldrette Scoring System.**
         (b) **A pulse oximeter** is now considered the standard of care and should be used with every patient to assess oxygen saturation at tissue level. The condition of the skin should be assessed, especially areas that were subjected to constant pressure because of patient positioning or the use of electrosurgical equipment during surgery.
   b. **Promoting adequate circulatory function**
      (1) **Throughout the immediate postoperative period, circulatory function should be assessed, since it may continue to be compromised owing to the effects of anesthesia, surgical positioning, fluid and blood loss, and general immobility.**
      (2) The nurse should monitor the patient's vital signs and circulatory status according to protocol, and use the Aldrette score for documenting circulatory status, in addition to obtaining an initial rhythm strip, since all patients should be on a cardiac monitor during the stay in the unit.
      (3) **Vital signs: Temperature** may be affected by the operating room environment, the surgical procedure, or fluid replacement therapy. Lowering the body temperature decreases oxygen demand and therefore, in some surgeries, hypothermia may have been induced. Frequently, the patient's temperature may be lower than normal following surgery. **To prevent chill and shivering, which would increase oxygen demand, the nurse must be aware of the patient's temperature, and take appropriate steps to correct the condition.**
      (4) **Pulse rate and rhythm:** The pulse may be affected by anesthesia, blood loss, or preexisting cardiac disease. **The nurse should note the rate and character of the pulse, and be observant for tachycardia, bradycardia, and/or arrhythmias.**
      (5) **Blood pressure**
         (a) As with other vital signs, the blood pressure may also be affected by anesthesia, blood loss, and preexisting cardiovascular or pulmonary disease. **The nurse must be observant for hypotension, hypertension, or changes in pulse pressure.**
         (b) Surgery may produce a great deal of stress on the patient's heart, and even without preexisting disease the heart may not be able to cope with the increased work load, which may be induced by changes in pulse, blood pressure, and respirations.
   c. **Promoting normal reflex return**
      (1) **An indication of postoperative progress is the patient's level of consciousness.** As the patient recovers from anesthesia, he or she should progress from anesthesia-induced unconsciousness, where normal reflexes are absent and respirations must be supported,

through semiconsciousness, where normal reflexes are returning and the patient starts breathing on his or her own. Finally, the patient should be awake and oriented with the return of all normal reflexes. The assessment value is entered using the Aldrette score for consciousness.

    (2) **For the patient who has received spinal or epidural anesthesia, frequent assessment of the lower extremities must be done to determine the return of function.** Specific indicators of return of function are mobility, sensation, temperature, and color. The skin must be assessed for signs of pressure or other injuries.

  d. **Promoting safety and comfort**

    (1) **Safety factors that should be assessed during the postanesthesia recovery period should include the use of side rails, stretcher safety belts, and wheel locks on stretchers; patient positioning; proper maintenance and grounding of electrical equipment; and availability and proper functioning of emergency equipment (e.g., crash carts, suction devices, tracheostomy trays, etc.).**

    (2) Although the patient may feel alert and capable of moving, movement may be uncoordinated and residual drowsiness and sedation probably persist.

    (3) **Pain management**

      (a) **As the patient recovers from anesthesia, he or she should be assessed for intensity and location of pain or discomfort.** How the patient expresses pain (e.g., facial expressions, irritability, restlessness, or verbalization) should be documented.

      (b) Do not assume that *pain* refers only to incision pain. General muscular aches and pains may also occur as a consequence of prolonged surgical immobility and positioning, or a sore throat may be present as a residual effect of endotracheal intubation.

      (c) Nursing comfort measures to alleviate pain, such as turning, positioning, and distraction, may temporarily lessen the pain, but pain medication should be freely administered as per order, and the response of the patient evaluated and recorded.

    (4) **Pain management strategies**

      (a) **Pain management strategies, based on individual patient assessment criteria, should be adaptable to a variety of clinical situations.** Several different methods for managing postoperative pain are available today, including traditional nurse-administered analgesia, patient-controlled analgesia (P.C.A.), and epidural analgesia or local epidural analgesia (L.E.A.).

      (b) The last two strategies mentioned are fast becoming important alternatives to the traditional postoperative pain management techniques. The most common agents currently being used, via all three methods, include **morphine, fentanyl, and meperidine.**

    (5) **Monitoring for behavioral indications of pain**

      (a) **Inadequate analgesia during the immediate postoperative phase is usually the result of fluctuating plasma levels, significant individual variations in pain tolerance, and cultural characteristics.** For this reason, as well as others, I.M. administration is frequently ineffective, promoting the use of other pain management strategies.

      (b) Generally, small I.V. doses of a narcotic analgesic can be titrated to meet the individual patient's needs. The dosage should be determined by the patient's behavior, which includes such actions as:
- Verbalizations of pain
- Agitation (when not related to hypoxia)
- Crying or "fighting back" tears
- Changes in vital signs (increase in B/P, H.R.)
- Attempting to change positions to find one of comfort
- Facial expressions (nonverbal language)

      (c) Since demand dosing by nurses is not always convenient or effective, strategies that allow patients to medicate themselves under controlled supervision (e.g., the P.C.A. pump) are safe and effective for postoperative pain management.

e. **Promoting wound healing**
  (1) **In the immediate postoperative period, observing for hemorrhage is a major responsibility of the nurse caring for the surgical patient.** The recovery nurse should assess both the dressing and the drainage tubes.
  (2) **Incision dressings: Incision dressings should be assessed for signs of postoperative bleeding or other drainage.** The dressings should be dry and intact. If the wound can be directly observed, its condition should be assessed, including approximation of wound edges, amount of bleeding, location and function of indwelling drains, and color and amount of drainage.
  (3) **Dressing tubes**
    (a) Often during surgery, supportive drainage tubes such as urinary catheters and nasogastric tubes will be inserted to support biologic functions and prevent possible complications. **All drainage tubes should be assessed for patency and appropriate function.**
    (b) Color and amount of gastrointestinal drainage and thoracic drainage should be noted, in addition to listening for bowel sounds and moist rales in the chest.
f. **Promoting fluid and electrolyte balance**
  (1) The time it takes an anesthetic to wear off depends on several factors, including the amount of saturation of body tissues with the anesthetic. With inhalation anesthesia, recovery may be rapid; however, with intravenous adjuncts, the time may be longer. **If the patient is adequately hydrated, and if elimination is adequate (30mL/hr), the body will respond quickly to interventions designed to reverse the effects of the anesthesia agent.**
  (2) **Parenteral infusions: On admission to the postanesthesia area, all infusion lines, central and peripheral, should be assessed for patency.** The nurse should also note the type of solution, the prescribed flow rate, the gauge of the needle/catheter, and the type and amount of medication additives.
g. **Reducing anxiety and providing psychosocial support**
  (1) **The postoperative patient who is recovering from anesthesia experiences many anxieties related to the stress produced by the surgical event.** These include physiologic, psychologic, environmental, and psychosocial factors. Therefore, nursing interventions should be directed at reducing the patient's anxiety level.
  (2) **The emotional needs of the patient's family members and significant others must also be considered during this phase.** As soon as possible, the patient's family should be contacted and informed of the patient's progress and the anticipated time of arrival back to the surgical unit or designated intermediate postoperative area.

G. DOCUMENTATION OF POSTANESTHESIA CARE

1. **Accurate recording of the patient's progress usually involves the use of a flow sheet, progress note, and standard care plan.** Whatever the form, the content should include documentation of all assessment data during the immediate recovery period, in addition to the patient's response to the nursing care provided.
2. Implementation of the individualized care plan should be documented on the patient's record by denoting:

Standard Care Plan Followed?
Yes [ ] No [ ] If no, list exceptions:

H. EVALUATION AND DISCHARGE

1. **The recovery nurse must ensure that the patient to be discharged is stable and ready to return to the postoperative area by meeting preestablished criteria for discharge using the Aldrette Scoring System and institutional policies for patient discharge.**

2. Prior to discharge, the anesthesiologist will assess the patient and sign the Recovery Room Record, confirming the patient's readiness to leave the unit. **Postanesthesia discharge criteria should include the following:**
   a. **Patient is able to maintain a clear airway.**
   b. **Vital signs have been stable and/or consistent with preoperative vital signs for at least 30 minutes.**
   c. **Protective reflexes are active.**
   d. **Patient is conscious and oriented.**
   e. **Adequate I & O (urinary output 30mL/hr).**
   f. **Afebrile or condition attended to.**
   g. **Dressings are dry and intact; no overt drainage.**
3. **An Aldrette score of 8 or higher (out of a possible 10) usually indicates that the patient is ready for transfer to the designated postoperative area.** However, individual hospital policies for discharging a patient should be followed.
4. To provide continuity of care, the recovery nurse should accompany the patient to the designated postsurgical nursing unit, and give a verbal report of the patient's status to the next professional nurse responsible for the continuing postoperative management of the surgical patient.

PRACTICE QUESTIONS

1. **Before the patient is transferred to the designated postanesthesia area, the perioperative nurse completes a number of activities. Which of the following is NOT one of these activities?**

   1. *The postoperative evaluation is completed and is transmitted to the recovery nurse.*

   2. *Intraoperative documentation and charges are completed and reviewed for accuracy.*

   3 *Specimens are properly identified, labeled, and placed in the appropriate container(s).*

   4. *The patient is moved to a recovery bed and transported to the postanesthesia recovery area.*

2. **The perioperative nurse's postoperative evaluation of a patient may take place in one of several ways. One commonly used method is the:**

   1. *A.O.R.N. Postoperative Assessment Form.*

   2. *surgeon debriefment procedure.*

   3. *PACU audit.*

   4. *telephone interview.*

3. **The perioperative nurse's postoperative evaluation is important for several reasons, including its role in:**

   1. *establishing a physiologic baseline for postoperative care.*

   2. *assuring the patient's full recovery from anesthesia and other surgical medications.*

   3. *completing the nurse's initial assessment activities.*

   4. *helping the nurse and others determine the quality of care delivered.*

4. **One of the primary objectives of nursing care in PACU is to:**

   1. *attach any drainage devices called for by the surgeon following completion of the surgical procedure.*

   2. *recognize and use the criteria for discharging a patient from the PACU, using an established scoring guide.*

   3. *conduct a postoperative evaluation that is thorough, timely, and consistent with the institution's protocols.*

   4. *provide continuity of care as the recovery nurse hands over responsibility for patient care to the perioperative nurse.*

5. **Guidelines for providing patient care during the immediate postanesthesia recovery period derive principally from the:**

   1. *American Society of Post Anesthesia Nurses' Standards of Practice: PACU.*

   2. *American Nurses' Association Standards of Practice: Postoperative Phase.*

   3. *American Society of Anesthesiology's Standards of Practice: Postoperative Phase.*

   4. *A.O.R.N.'s Standards for Perioperative Nursing Practice.*

6. **The patient's status upon admission to the PACU is summarized in a report from the surgical team. Included in this report is all of the following information EXCEPT:**

   1. *the type and length of surgery performed.*

   2. *the type/agents of anesthesia administered, along with the time and amount of the last dose.*

   3. *the presence and status of drains, catheters, tubes, and dressings.*

   4. *the estimated time period until discharge.*

7. **During the initial assessment of the patient admitted to the PACU, the recovery nurse *first* checks the patient's:**

   1. *level of consciousness and response to stimuli.*

   2. *level of pain and status of protective reflexes.*

   3. *respiratory and cardiac status and skin color.*

   4. *drainage tubes and catheters for type and patency.*

8. **Which of the following is NOT directly incorporated into the Aldrette Scoring System used to assess patients' postoperative status?**

   1. *The patient's skin color.*

   2. *The status of the patient's wound.*

   3. *The patient's level of consciousness.*

   4. *The status of the patient's respiration and circulation.*

9. **In promoting adequate respiratory function in the postoperative patient, it is important that the nurse:**

    1. *auscultate breath sounds at least hourly.*

    2. *place primary emphasis on the patient's comfort.*

    3. *position the patient so that a patent airway can be maintained.*

    4. *keep the patient immobile.*

10. **In promoting adequate circulatory function in the postoperative patient, it is important that the nurse monitor all of the following EXCEPT:**

    1. *temperature.*

    2. *cardiac rhythm on a cardiac monitor.*

    3. *blood pressure.*

    4. *behavioral indications of pain.*

11. **Frequent assessment of the lower extremities must be done to determine the return of function in patients who:**

    1. *were under general anesthesia for more than 2 hours.*

    2. *received spinal or epidural anesthesia.*

    3. *had a tourniquet cuff installed during the procedure.*

    4. *lost more than 2 liters of blood in the procedure.*

12. **Pain experienced by the patient during the postoperative period may be the result of the incision, or more general pain may be due in large measure to the effects of:**

    1. *medications used in the procedure.*

    2. *fluid and electrolyte loss during the procedure.*

    3. *heat loss and accompanying increased oxygen demand.*

    4. *prolonged surgical immobility and positioning.*

13. **Because I.M. administration is frequently ineffective, other pain management strategies for the postoperative patient may be used, including:**

    1. *patient-controlled anesthesia (P.C.A.).*

    2. *small doses of inhalation anesthesia.*

    3. *topical anesthetics such as fentanyl or meperidine.*

    4. *electrolyte infiltration.*

14. **In the immediate postoperative period, observing for hemorrhage is a major responsibility of the nurse caring for the surgical patient. Of the following activities, the one that is *most* closely related to this responsibility is:**

    1. *assessing drainage tubes for patency, amount of drainage, and appropriate function.*

    2. *monitoring the patient's level of consciousness.*

    3. *observing for changes in respiratory rate, rhythm, depth, and quality.*

    4. *using nursing comfort measures such as turning, positioning, and distraction.*

15. **Several factors influence the speed at which a patient emerges from anesthesia in the PACU. One factor that facilitates rapid emergence is:**

    1. *lowered body temperature.*

    2. *use of a pulse oximeter intraoperatively.*

    3. *adequate hydration, oxygenation, and elimination.*

    4. *use of intravenous anesthetic agents.*

16. **Mr. B., a patient in the PACU, has an Aldrette score of 6. He is able to maintain a clear airway, is conscious and oriented, and has adequate I & O (urinary output 30 mL/hr.). His dressings are dry and intact. This patient should be discharged:**

    1. *as soon as his protective reflexes are active.*

    2. *as soon as his Aldrette score is 8 or higher.*

    3. *as soon as the recovery nurse signs the Recovery Room Record.*

    4. *immediately.*

ANSWER EXPLANATIONS

1. **The answer is 1.** For the perioperative nurse, the care of the surgical patient does not end with the conclusion of the surgical procedure, but continues through to the immediate postoperative phase; that is, transfer of the patient to the postanesthesia care unit (PACU) or designated postoperative area (e.g., ambulatory surgery unit, surgical nursing unit). Other activities that are part of this transfer are: (1) communicating to appropriate personnel the anesthesiologist's or nurse anesthetist's request for special equipment for the postanesthesia area; and (2) giving verbal/written reports to the appropriate professional nurse upon arrival to the unit. The postoperative evaluation takes place after transfer.

2. **The answer is 4.** The perioperative nurse's role usually does not end with the admission of the patient to the PACU, but extends to a Postoperative Evaluation and Reassessment Phase, in order to obtain information regarding the quality and effectiveness of perioperative nurse care. Evaluation of patient care may occur not only in the PACU, but in the case of an ambulatory surgery patient, may also be performed through a telephone interview following discharge, or, for the hospitalized patient, a follow-up postoperative visit.

3. **The answer is 4.** The postoperative evaluation is important because it gives the nurse feedback about how successful the care plan was for a particular patient, and can help to determine the quality of care delivered,

which is all part of the reassessment process. It also helps the nurse determine what could have been done differently that would have improved the effectiveness of the nursing care. An introspective self-evaluation is sometimes the hardest to accomplish, but through it, the perioperative nurse can continue to develop her or his knowledge and skill levels, which can only strengthen the professional commitment: to deliver quality patient care throughout the perioperative period.

4. **The answer is 2.** There are four primary objectives of nursing care during the immediate postoperative phase: (1) to recognize the major potential problems associated with a specific surgical procedure, and the appropriate corresponding actions; (2) to identify and demonstrate the general procedures routinely carried out in the PACU area; (3) to maintain accurate documentation of the patient's progress during the recovery phase; and (4) to recognize and use the criteria for discharging a patient from the PACU, using an established scoring guide. Each institution should have established policies for implementing patient care during the immediate postoperative period, including documentation guidelines and specific tasks and activities that will assist the patient during this critical transition.

5. **The answer is 1.** In 1986, the American Society of Post Anesthesia Nurses (A.S.P.A.N.) developed their *Standards of Practice: PACU* to serve as guidelines for providing patient care during the immediate postanesthesia recovery period, and like the A.O.R.N.'s *Standards for Practice*, they are based on the nursing process format: Assessment, Nursing Diagnoses, Planning, Implementation, and Evaluation.

6. **The answer is 4.** To ensure the continuity of care from the intraoperative phase to the immediate postoperative phase, the surgical team, consisting of the anesthesiologist or nurse anesthetist and the circulating nurse, will give a report to the recovery nurse about the patient's status upon admission to the unit. Other information in this report includes: (1) setting for oxygen/administration preference; (2) hemodynamic monitoring lines and peripheral I.V. lines; (3) status of fluid and electrolyte balance; intraoperative intake and output, including blood and blood products, if used; and (4) potential problems that may occur owing to the patient's physiologic status or surgical procedure.

7. **The answer is 3.** The primary goal of immediate postanesthesia nursing care is the safe recovery and arousal of the patient from the effects of anesthesia. The recovery nurse works with the patient, performing specific nursing activities to "stir-up" the patient from the effects of the anesthesia, while providing emotional support through orientation, teaching, and encouragement of specific activities to accomplish this goal. The patient's well-being is directly related to adequate ventilation and circulation; therefore, the patient's respiratory status, skin color, and cardiovascular status are the first to be evaluated during the initial assessment. When the recovery nurse is satisfied that the respiratory and cardiac status are adequate, the surgical team members can safely leave the area, and a total assessment of the patient's physiologic status is evaluated according to preestablished protocols and procedures.

8. **The answer is 2.** The Aldrette Scoring System is used to assess the postoperative patient's status by measuring five physiologic factors: respiration, circulation, skin color, activity, and level of consciousness. By using specific, predetermined criteria, values ranging from 0 to 2 are placed on each one of these factors. These assessment factors are usually measured upon arrival, then 15 minutes, 30 minutes, 60 minutes, and prior to discharge from the unit.

9. **The answer is 3.** Respirations are affected by anesthesia, blood loss, or preexisting cardiac or pulmonary disease. The recovery nurse must be observant for changes in rate, rhythm, depth, and quality of respirations, through auscultation of breath sounds at least *every 15 minutes*, and grade the patient according to the Aldrette score for respiratory status. If supportive respiratory equipment is in place, such as an endotracheal tube or oral airway, it too should be assessed for position and function. The patient should be positioned so that a patent airway can be maintained, secretions can be suctioned, and oxygen can be administered, as per protocol/order. Once the patient is breathing adequately and independently, the position can be changed to accommodate comfort. The recovery nurse should encourage the patient to breathe deeply and to move extremities, which will assist in "blowing-off" the inhalation agents and increase circulation. Coughing may or may not be appropriate, depending on the surgical procedure.

10. **The answer is 4.** Throughout the immediate postoperative period, circulatory function should be assessed, since it may continue to be compromised owing to the effects of anesthesia, surgical positioning, fluid and blood loss, and general immobility. The nurse should monitor the patient's vital signs and circulatory status according to protocol, and use the Aldrette score for documenting circulatory status, in addition to obtaining an initial rhythm strip. Along with temperature, blood pressure, and cardiac rhythm, the nurse should monitor pulse rate and rhythm, since the pulse may be affected by anesthesia, blood loss, or preexisting cardiac disease. The nurse should note the rate and character of the pulse, and be observant for tachycardia, bradycardia, and/or arrhythmias, and be observant for hypotension, hypertension, or changes in pulse pressure. Surgery may produce a great deal of stress on the patient's heart, and even without preexisting disease the heart may not be able to cope with the increased work load, which may be induced by changes in pulse, blood pressure, and respirations.

11. **The answer is 2.** An indication of postoperative progress is the patient's level of consciousness. As the patient recovers from anesthesia, he or she should progress from anesthesia-induced unconsciousness, where normal reflexes are absent and respirations must be supported, through semiconsciousness, where normal reflexes are returning and the patient starts breathing on his or her own. Finally, the patient should be awake and oriented with the return of all normal reflexes. The assessment value is entered using the Aldrette score for consciousness. For the patient who has received spinal or epidural anesthesia, frequent assessment of the lower extremities must be done to determine the return of function. Specific indicators of return of function are mobility, sensation, temperature, and color. The skin must be assessed for signs of pressure or other injuries.

12. **The answer is 4.** The nurse should not assume that pain refers only to incision pain. General muscular aches and pains may also occur as a consequence of prolonged surgical immobility and positioning, or a sore throat may be present as a residual effect of endotracheal intubation. Nursing comfort measures to alleviate pain, such as turning, positioning, and distraction, may temporarily lessen the pain, but pain medication should be freely administered as per order, and the response of the patient evaluated and recorded.

13. **The answer is 1.** Inadequate analgesia during the immediate postoperative phase is usually the result of fluctuating plasma levels, significant individual variations in pain tolerance, and cultural characteristics. For this reason, as well as others, I.M. administration is frequently ineffective, promoting the use of other pain management strategies. Generally, small I.V. doses of a narcotic analgesic can be titrated to meet the individual patient's needs, with the dosage determined by the patient's behavior (e.g., verbalizations of pain). However, since demand dosing by nurses is not always convenient or effective, strategies that allow patients to medicate themselves under controlled supervision (e.g., the P.C.A. pump) are safe and effective for postoperative pain management.

14. **The answer is 1.** The recovery nurse should assess both the dressing and the drainage tubes. Incision dressings should be assessed for signs of postoperative bleeding or other drainage. The dressings should be dry and intact. If the wound can be directly observed, its condition should be assessed, including approximation of wound edges, amount of bleeding, location and function of indwelling drains, and color and amount of drainage. Often during surgery, supportive drainage tubes such as urinary catheters and nasogastric tubes will be inserted to support biologic functions and prevent possible complications. All drainage tubes should be assessed for patency and appropriate function. Color and amount of gastrointestinal drainage and thoracic drainage should be noted, in addition to listening for bowel sounds and moist rales in the chest. Note that choices 2 and 3 are other, less critical activities related to observing for hemorrhage.

15. **The answer is 3.** The time it takes an anesthetic to wear off depends on several factors, including the amount of saturation of body tissues with the anesthetic. With inhalation anesthesia, recovery may be rapid; however, with intravenous adjuncts, the time may be longer. If the patient is adequately hydrated, and if elimination is adequate (30 mL/hr), the body will respond quickly to interventions designed to reverse the effects of the anesthesia agent.

16. **The answer is 2.** The recovery nurse must ensure that the patient to be discharged is stable and ready to return to the postoperative area by meeting preestablished criteria for discharge using the Aldrette Scoring System and institutional policies for patient discharge. Prior to discharge, the anesthesiologist will assess the patient and sign the Recovery Room Record, confirming the patient's readiness to leave the unit. Postanesthesia discharge criteria should include the following: (1) patient is able to maintain a clear airway; (2) vital signs have been stable and/or consistent with preoperative vital signs for at least 30 minutes; (3) protective reflexes are active; (4) patient is conscious and oriented; (5) adequate I & O (urinary output 30 mL/hr); (6) afebrile or condition attended to; and (7) dressings are dry and intact; no overt drainage. An Aldrette score of 8 or higher (out of a possible 10) usually indicates that the patient is ready for transfer to the designated postoperative area. However, individual hospital policies for discharging a patient should be followed.

14   Legal Aspects of Perioperative Nursing Practice

STUDY OUTLINE

I.   **AMERICAN NURSES ASSOCIATION CODE FOR NURSES**

   1. According to the American Nurses Association (A.N.A.) Code for Nurses, first established in 1976, professional nursing responsibility consists of the following elements:
      a. The professional nurse's obligation to protect the patient's right to safety.
      b. The professional nurse's role as the patient advocate, protecting the patient from incompetent, unethical, or illegal actions/practices.
      c. The professional nurse's qualifications relating to the administration of proficient patient care.
      d. The professional nurse's obligation to maintain the highest level of competency in nursing practice, through continuing education activities.
      e. The professional nurse's responsibility and obligation to the profession, to the society in general, and to those entrusted to her/his care.
   2. The professional nurse, by virtue of her/his educational preparation and license, is legally responsible for all her/his own actions, and although the Code for Nurses is not a legal document, many courts use it, along with professional standards of practice, as a basis for expected standards of conduct for the profession, since it is applicable to all nurses, regardless of in what area they practice nursing.

II.   **KEY CONCEPTS RELATED TO LEGAL ISSUES**

   1. General negligence principles demand that behavior be measured against an objective standard of care. The standard of care is based on **statutory law** and **common law**.

A.   **STATUTORY LAW**

   1. **Statutory laws** are those created by state legislatures. These laws are created through the police power of the state for the benefit of its citizens. The states' police power is used in order to guard the morals, safety, order, and welfare of its citizens.
   2. Statutory law defines who health care providers are and includes anyone licensed, registered, or certified by the state to practice in the field of health care. This includes the nurse practice act, the medical practice act, and the dental act, among others. Violating this act or any statute would be a criminal act, because it would be a crime against the people of the state. The state, representing its citizens, would then bring charges against the offender.

262

B. COMMON LAW

1. **Common laws** are those that are not created by the legislature, but are based on the principles and rules of action relating to the security of individuals and their property. The authority of these laws comes solely from the usage and customs of society or the judgments and decrees of the courts, which recognize, affirm, and enforce such usages and customs.

2. Under common law, the person injured who brings suit must offer evidence that:
    a. There was a duty to use reasonable care.
    b. There was a failure to conform to the required standard.
    c. He/she suffered harm.
    d. The harm caused was due to the breach of duty.

3. To determine whether there was a duty owed to the person bringing suit, the courts would use a reasonable prudent standard. **In the case of health care providers, the standard is in accordance with the standards of practice among members of the same health care profession, with similar training and experience, situated in the same or similar community at the time the alleged act occurred.**

3. This standard is fictitious, however, since it is based on conduct consistent with a reasonable, prudent person who possesses superior knowledge or skill, that is, conduct specifically tailored to the professional. Thus, when a professional is charged, the court will require an **expert witness** who would give testimony concerning the actions of the nurse. The expert witness is a person practicing the same profession (nursing), with the same or similar training and education. The expert witness is used because most jury members do not have the background necessary to understand nursing or the technical aspects of malpractice.

4. The standards used by the expert witness are those established by the professional group. The patient (the plaintiff) alleges, for example, that she/he has been injured by an injection with an unsterilized needle. Here, expert testimony would have to be given as to what constitutes an unsterilized needle, when is it considered to be sterilized, and whether the nurse, as the professional, used the proper technique when injecting the medication.

5. The nurse, as a professional, can also be held to the nonprofessional standard (in which no expert witness is needed), when the alleged act of negligence does not involve professional skill or judgment, for example, the wrong patient was operated on. In this case, the jury would understand without the use of the expert.

6. **An acceptable standard of care is documented by:**
    a. **Expert witnesses from the same profession with similar educational and experiential background.**
    b. **Written regulations and policies from a hospital's policy and procedure manual(s) for that time.**
    c. **Joint Commission Accreditation manuals.**
    d. **Published and nationally recognized standards from various organizations, such as the A.N.A. or the Association of Operating Room Nurses (A.O.R.N.).**

7. Whether the nurse has a specialized practice, such as perioperative nursing, or is a staff nurse on a medical floor or in a long-term facility, the legal duty to patients is the same--that is, **to deliver reasonable, prudent, and safe care so as not to cause injury to the patient.** But in the case of the perioperative nurse, there is an additional responsibility. In the operating room, patients are more prone to injury because of receiving anesthesia, being in a sedated state, and the intrusive nature of the surgical procedure. Thus, more prudent, safe, and reasonable care must be given.

III. LEGAL DOCTRINES: IMPLICATIONS FOR PRACTICE

1. Patients undergoing surgical intervention are unable to protect themselves; they must totally rely on others for their well-being. Thus, four legal doctrines come into play. These four doctrines are the **(1) captain of the ship, (2) borrowed servant, (3)** *respondeat superior,* and **(4)** *res ipsa loquitur* doctrines.

A. **CAPTAIN OF THE SHIP DOCTRINE**

1. The **captain of the ship doctrine** in medical malpractice first appeared in the Pennsylvania courts in 1949 in the case of *McConnel v Williams*. This phrase was used as an analogy of the responsibility of the surgeon to the responsibility of a navy captain. That is, the surgeon was in total command and had full responsibility for the care and efficiency of the procedure room (the ship) and the welfare of all persons present.

2. Under this doctrine, the minute the surgeon entered a procedure room, he/she was liable for any and every negligent act that might occur, no matter who committed the act and whether or not he/she was aware of the act.

3. The Texas Supreme Court, in 1977, in the case of *Sprager v Worley Hospital*, overturned this doctrine. This was a case of failure to remove a sponge from the abdomen. The jury found that the operating room nurse failed to take a sponge count, which was the cause of the injury. The court rejected the notion that the surgeon's mere presence in the operating room made him liable for the negligence of anyone in the operating room.

4. The court stated that **nurses remained liable for their own negligent acts**. The court further held that the surgeon was not the captain of the ship and that surgeons and hospitals were subject to the same rules of agency, including the borrowed servant doctrine, that applies to the general population.

B. **THE BORROWED SERVANT DOCTRINE**

1. The principle of the **borrowed servant doctrine** is simple. **It is used when an employee commits a negligent act while under the direction of control of another who is not the employer; then that "borrower" is liable for the employees' actions.**

2. The most common place that this doctrine comes into play is in the operating room. In surgery, the surgeon has complete control over the scrub nurse's actions; therefore, that nurse would be considered as having been "borrowed" from the hospital. Thus, instead of the hospital being held liable, the surgeon would be. (It is very similar to the captain of the ship doctrine, except that the surgeon is not controlling everyone in the operating room.)

3. In *Sprager*, the Texas Supreme Court held that the surgeon was not negligent. The nurses, however, were found to be negligent because the Supreme Court stated that nurses were not borrowed servants and the surgeon was not the captain of the ship. The court based their decision on the following facts:
   a. The nurses were hired and assigned by the hospital.
   b. The surgeon did not participate in their selection.
   c. The duties of scrub and circulating personnel were detailed in the hospital's policy and procedures manual.
   d. The procedures for sponge counts were intended for use regardless of the surgeon who performed the operation.
   e. The nurses counted sponges at specific intervals, including prior to the incision.
   f. The scrub nurse testified that the surgeon did not direct her and the circulating nurse to take the count.

4. There is still confusion over the captain of the ship and the borrowed servant doctrines, so this doctrine may change again in the near future. **However, most courts still hold that the borrowed servant doctrine is more correct than the captain of the ship doctrine in deciding who is liable.**

C. **THE *RESPONDEAT SUPERIOR* DOCTRINE**

1. According to the ***respondeat superior*** doctrine, a subordinate acts according to his/her superior's direction. Therefore, **the hospital is liable for the negligent actions of a nurse**, for example, a nurse who administers the wrong drug, which harms a patient. The hospital can be held liable for that nurse's action because the nurse was giving the drug as part of his or her duties as nurse.

D. *RES IPSA LOQUITUR* (THE THING SPEAKS FOR ITSELF)

1. **The *res ipsa loquitur* doctrine is applied to the perioperative nurse's practice much more frequently than to any other area of nursing practice. According to this doctrine, the nurse must show that the standard of care was not breached, rather than the usual requirement that the injured party show that the standard was breached.**

2. To invoke this doctrine successfully the person claiming he/she was harmed, must establish that:
    a. The injury does not ordinarily occur unless someone was negligent; in this case the operating room (O.R.) personnel.
    b. The instrumentality causing the injury was within the exclusive control of O.R. personnel.
    c. The plaintiff did not contribute to the injury in any way.

3. **These three elements are easier to establish when the injury occurs in the operating room because the patient is anesthetized or sedated;** the equipment that caused the injury is clearly controlled by the nurse, the surgeon, or other hospital personnel.

4. The California Supreme Court, in the 1984 case of *Ybarra v Spangard*, held that "where a plaintiff receives unusual injuries while unconscious and in the course of medical treatment, **all those defendants who had any control over his body or the instrumentalities which might have caused the injuries, may properly be called upon to meet the inference of negligence by giving an explanation of their conduct.**"

5. **The most common injuries occurring in the operating room are caused by iodine or other pooled solutions, electrosurgical devices, or improperly aerated equipment sterilized with ethylene oxide, or are ulnar or peroneal nerve injuries due to positioning or to foreign bodies being left in the patient.**

IV. POLICIES, PROCEDURES, AND PROTOCOLS

1. **In the surgical suite, where there is an increased potential for injury, there must be written policies.** These written policies protect the patient, the perioperative nurse, and other personnel in at least two distinct ways:
    a. **Consistent adherence to uniform policy, procedures, and protocols provides safe patient care, thus decreasing the likelihood that the patient will be injured.**
    b. **If an injury does occur and suit is filed, it will be easier to show that the nurse complied with the standard of care if the nurse followed the policy and procedures of the institution.**

2. **Maintaining standards of care**
    a. **In order to be successful in malpractice cases, the plaintiff's attorney must prove that the nurse failed to deliver or breached acceptable standards of care--what a "reasonable and prudent nurse of similar education and experience would have done under similar circumstances." This is the legal description of standards of care.**
    b. Standards of care, from professional nursing organizations such as the A.N.A. and A.O.R.N. and federal/state agencies such as the Joint Commission on the Accreditation of Healthcare Organizations and the Health & Rehabilitative Services, provide the guidelines that will be compared with the proficiency of the care provided by the nurse-defendant and/or the institution.
    c. **If the perioperative nurse is familiar with these standards, and she/he practices within the recommended guidelines, it is very difficult for the plaintiff's attorney to prove negligence: that is that the nurse/institution failed to meet the legal standards of care.**

V. INFORMED CONSENT

A. DEFINITION OF INFORMED CONSENT

1. Based on the U.S. Constitution, a person has a right to privacy. This includes the right of the person to himself, his body, and what happens to him. In the case of *Pratt v Davis* the court stated it best, that "this right necessarily forbids a physician or surgeon, however skilled or

eminent, who has been asked to examine, diagnose, advise, and prescribe, to violate without permission, the bodily integrity of his patient... without his consent or knowledge..."

2. Informed consent has two basic elements:
    a. **Informed** refers to information given to the patient about a proposed procedure or treatment.
    b. **Consent** refers to the patient's agreement to the procedure or treatment.
3. **To give informed consent, a patient must receive, in terms he/she understands, all the information that would affect a reasonable person's decision to consent to or refuse a treatment or procedure. This information should include:**
    a. **A description of the treatment or procedure.**
    b. **The name and qualifications of the person who will perform the treatment or procedure.**
    c. **An explanation of the potential for death or serious harm (such as brain damage, paralysis, or disfiguring scars) or for uncomfortable side effects during or after the treatment or procedure.**
    d. **An explanation of the possible effects of not having the treatment or procedure.**
    e. **An explanation that the patient has a right to refuse the treatment or procedure without having other care or support withdrawn, and that he/she can withdraw his/her consent after having given it.**
4. *Salgo v Leland Stanford, Jr. University Board of Trustees*, established the basic rule that a physician "violates a duty to his patient and subjects himself to liability, if he withholds any facts that are necessary to form the basis of an intelligent consent by the patient to the proposed treatment." **Since this ruling, a patient can sue for negligent nondisclosure if his/her doctor fails to give him/her enough information to make an informed decision.**
5. But how much information is enough? There are two standards used: the **reasonable patient standard** and the **reasonable physician standard.**
    a. **The reasonable patient standard determines that the amount of material that a patient has received is sufficient to make an informed consent.** A Washington State court defined *material*: "When a reasonable person in the patient's position would attach significance to the specific risk in deciding on treatment, the risk is material and must be disclosed" (*Smith v Shannon*).
    b. **The reasonable physician standard is used more often; it is based on what another physician would disclose to a similar patient under similar circumstances.** This standard has been upheld in court. Physicians face a variety of situations, which may differ from state to state, but can include:
        (1) A life-threatening situation.
        (2) Complete and candid disclosure would have caused a detrimental effect on the patient.
        (3) The risk is too obvious to justify.
        (4) The procedure is simple and risks too remote.
        (5) The patient decided he/she did not wish to be informed.
6. The doctrine of informed consent assumes that an informed patient can act in his/her own best interests. There are two types of consent: **implied** or **express.**
    a. **Express consent is the agreement between the persons involved.** A consent form, which is a contract, is a formal means of documenting express consent and, if the consent itself is valid, the form serves to validate that fact.
    b. **Implied consent occurs routinely in health care, when parents, by their conduct in cooperating with caregivers, provide the necessary authorization for caregivers' actions.**

B. THE PERIOPERATIVE NURSE'S RESPONSIBILITY

1. **The perioperative nurse's duty regarding informed consent is confined to ensuring that informed consent has been obtained, documented, and placed in the health record in accordance with the policy of the hospital.** The courts do not require that hospitals or nurses assume the surgeon's duty to inform the patient or to obtain the patient's consent.
2. To emphasize this point further, **the perioperative nurse's role does not include the undertaking of informing the patient of procedures, risks, benefits, or alternatives, or ascertaining the extent of the patient's understanding of the procedure.**

3. Although the legal responsibility to inform and obtain consent lies with the surgeon, the hospital may have a duty to ensure that the patient's consent has been obtained; however, courts have not recognized any independent nursing duty beyond that which is stated in the policies and procedures of that institution, as employees of the agency.

4. **Invalid/defective consent forms**

   a. What if the consent is defective? What then is the nurse's duty? **Defective** means that something is wrong with the consent form, for example, a specific area of a leg was noted on the consent form and another area was operated on, a relative has signed for the patient, or the patient is not able to make a reasonable decision because of his or her present condition.

   b. The courts may hold that in the case of the wrong area, for example, the consent for the specific operation was not obtained and the hospital would be liable. Additionally, the hospital, through its agent, the nurse, may be held liable for not preventing the surgery.

   c. **To date, the courts have refused to find the perioperative nurse negligent when a surgeon continues with a surgical procedure once the nurse has told the surgeon that there is no consent for the procedure being performed.** The courts suggest that the perioperative nurse has met her legal duty by directing the surgeon's attention to the lack of consent. However, the hospital will be held responsible because it has an independent duty to the patient and has given the surgeon permission to conduct surgery on its premises.

   d. **There is also a legal risk involved in doing nothing, and the nurse and the hospital can be held legally responsible.** Usually the courts will not hold the hospital responsible if the patient sues the doctor for battery for performing a procedure without the patient's consent. But the courts might hold the nurse responsible if the nurse took part in the battery by assisting with the treatment or knew the procedure was taking place without consent and did not try to stop it.

   e. **Also, the courts usually will not hold the hospital responsible if the patient sues the doctor for negligent nondisclosure for failing to provide adequate information for consent. But again, the court might hold the nurse responsible if, knowing the physician had not provided adequate information to the patient, the nurse allowed the procedure to continue.** The nurse was not performing her/his professional and legal duty to the patient unless he/she tried to stop the procedure by informing the supervisor. Usually, **the nurse can meet the legal obligation for informed consent by ensuring that the consent form has been signed and witnessed and that it has been attached to the patient's charge.**

   f. Another area of concern for the perioperative nurse involves not only a lack of consent, but also consent that has been signed under the influence of a medication, such as a narcotic. Survey respondents reported that most of the time the procedure is delayed for a designated period of time before the patient signs the correct form (varies for each institution) and/or the surgeon makes an entry in the patient's record that the patient had been informed and did consent to the correct procedure prior to the administration of the premedication.

   g. Regardless, the policy and procedures of the institution dictate the nurse's role in informed consent, and present law dictates that the **surgeon is the designated person to inform the patient and obtain the patient's consent to perform the surgery.**

   h. There are other aspects of perioperative nursing care that involve legal ramifications: documentation of perioperative nursing care and counts performed during the surgical procedure.

VI. DOCUMENTING PERIOPERATIVE NURSING CARE

1. **Documentation of nursing care is an essential and legal responsibility of the perioperative nurse.** In the courtroom, nurses can better meet the burden of proof that they were not negligent if the O.R. record reflects that the standard of care was met.

2. Documentation during the perioperative period should meet the A.O.R.N. Recommended Practices for Documentation, which states:

   a. The patient's record should reflect the preoperative assessment and planning carried out by the perioperative nurse.

    b. The patient's record should reflect care given by members of the surgical team and its outcomes. The care should be documented on the patient's chart.

    c. The patient record should reflect a continued evaluation of the perioperative nursing care and the patient responses to nursing interventions.

    d. The documentation of perioperative nursing care will be determined by policies and procedures of the practice setting.

A. IMPLEMENTATION OF RECOMMENDED PRACTICES

1. **The most important thing that nurses can do to protect themselves and the hospital is to document everything that is done or not done for the patient, even if it only involves filling out a check list. Doing a procedure routinely, however, will not protect the nurse unless it is documented.**

2. The **patient record** may serve as legal documentation of care provided to the patient and as such is admissible evidence in a court of law. Additionally, the record can be used as an indicator of the quality of nursing care by hospital quality assurance (surgical audit) committees or the medical records committee.

3. **It is the nurse's responsibility to ensure that charting takes place according to institutional policy.** The patient record then accompanies the patient throughout the perioperative period, conveying all information gathered regarding assessment, planning, and patient response to treatment and nursing intervention. While the majority of documentation relates specifically to the perioperative nurse, some of the preoperative assessment, planning, and intervention may be conducted and recorded by the office nurse or the nurse on the patient unit, and it needs to be accurately communicated to other members of the healthcare team.

4. **In order to be complete, documentation must not only provide the assessment data and planning, but also indicate the patient's response to the care provided and the subsequent modification of nursing care.**

5. By documenting assessments, interventions, and evaluation of nursing care provided in a precise manner, the perioperative nurse can show evidence that the standards of patient care have been met, since the court views documentation synonymous with actual care given.

B. GUIDELINES FOR EFFECTIVE DOCUMENTATION

1. **Legal standards require the perioperative nurse to record observations accurately and completely, and in a timely manner, reflecting the exact nursing interventions performed during the intraoperative period.** As patient care becomes more complex, as in the operating room, accurate documentation is likely to become an even greater legal and professional responsibility.

2. **The most common error made when charting, regardless of the area, is writing value judgments and opinions (subjective data) rather than factual information (objective data).** For example, during a preoperative assessment, the nurse may be listening to bowel sounds and may record the following: "Bowel sounds normal." (What is normal?) It would be better to chart "Bowel sounds present in all quadrants. Abdomen flat; N.P.O. since 1201."

3. According to surveys conducted by lawyers and consultants who review patient's charts, especially those involved with possible litigation, nine common errors seem to be prominent:

    a. **Omission of information:** could be misconstrued as a "coverup" or failure to provide care. *Suggestion:* Never leave blank spaces, especially on preprinted forms. If nonapplicable signify by N/A.

    b. **Personal opinion:** use of subjective data. *Suggestion:* Document only factual information and avoid paraphrasing.

    c. **Generalizations:** usage of broad terms, which may mean very little. *Suggestions:* Avoid meaningless phrases, such as "apparent absence of foreign bodies" or "skin appears to be intact." Definitive statements leave no room for doubt.

  d. **Late (retrospective) charting:** late entries due to unintentional omissions may be seen as a method to alter a record.

  Suggestion: Enter information at time of occurrence; take your time in completing the record. If necessary, consult the medical records department for proper protocol for late entries.

  e. **Improper use of abbreviations:** arbitrary use of abbreviations, which may not say the same thing you wish to state.

  Suggestions: Use only the abbreviations approved by the medical records department, and then only when absolutely necessary; use of abbreviations should be avoided on all consent forms.

  f. **Illegibility:** if the court/attorney is unable to read the notes recorded, it may place doubt as to the credibility of the information provided and the care giver.

  Suggestion: Take time when making entries; print if cursive handwriting is illegible.

  g. **Incorrect spelling:** can lead to confusion and/or misinterpretation of the facts.

  Suggestion: When in doubt, refer to a dictionary or other reference book.

  h. **Improper error correction:** could be interpreted as an altered record.

  Suggestion: Never use "white-out" or "liquid paper." Errors should be corrected according to hospital policy (single line through error, with initials).

  i. **Improper signature:** if signature is incomplete for example, status omitted, questions may arise as to who actually provided care.

  Suggestion: Signatures should be standardized within the institution: first initial, last name, and status (including specialty certification, if applicable).

4. Persons licensed or certified by the state hold a legal signature for charting. All others who are allowed to document, by institutional policy, must be cosigned by those legally responsible for documentation.

5. **Points to remember**

  a. The intraoperative record is generally in duplicate form that provides a second or third copy; therefore use ballpoint pen for entries (preferably black).

  b. There cannot be any erasures or white-out on a legal document. If an error is made, follow the acceptable method for correcting the document.

  c. Fill out the record as if you anticipated a court case, since this document can be used as evidence.

  d. The preoperative and postoperative diagnosis should be obtained by the surgeon for accuracy and verification with the surgical procedure performed. It is not a safe practice to use the surgery schedule for the operative procedure entry.

  e. The operative procedure should correspond with the specimen(s) obtained, and they should be listed on the record.

  f. Count status, times of events, and final dispensation of the patient (Post Anesthesia Care Unit, outpatient surgery) should be entered on the record.

6. **In addition to the intraoperative nurse's notes, the circulating nurse is responsible for recording the supplies and equipment used during surgery, since the patient is entitled to an itemized accounting of charges incurred during the hospitalization.** Since each institution has its own mechanism for charging and charting, it is the responsibility of the perioperative nurse to be familiar with this mechanism.

7. **As the patient advocate, it is the perioperative nurse's responsibility to safeguard the patient against inappropriate use of supplies and equipment.** Careful consideration when choosing specific items needed for a case will ensure a safe, cost-effective surgical procedure. If unsure, always consult with the surgeon before the procedure.

VII. SPONGE, SHARP, AND INSTRUMENT COUNTS

1. **Counting during a surgical procedure is another aspect of the perioperative nurse's legal responsibility.** This activity ensures a safe outcome according to the Standards of Care for Perioperative Nursing Practice.

2. **Counting is also a legal responsibility of the surgical team, with complete documentation of the count status entered on the intraoperative record by the circulating nurse.**

3. Counts are addressed in the Standards of Practice (Standard III), in the Outcome Standards for Patient Care (Standard IV), and as a Recommended Practice, stating, "Sponges, sharps, and instruments will be counted on all procedures." However, in some instances, a patient's emergency condition does not permit time for a count to be taken prior to surgery. When this occurs, it is recommended that the incident be documented, that intraoperative and closing counts be performed, and that an X-ray be performed immediately after surgery.

4. In the legal climate of today's malpractice arena, nearly 45 percent of all malpractice claims involve foreign objects left in patients during surgery. By adhering to the standards of care, as recommended by A.O.R.N., this potential high-risk area need no longer be a factor in malpractice cases brought against nurses and/or institutions.

5. According to the statements for sponge, sharp, and instrument counts in the A.O.R.N. Recommended Practices (1991), "It is the responsibility of each institution to develop a well delineated policy (protocol) and procedure for counts performed in the operating room, which should include (1) the delineation of materials to be counted, (2) the appropriate frequency (intervals) of the counts, (3) the mechanism for performing the count, and (4) the documentation of the count status."

A. COUNTING MECHANISM AND FREQUENCY

1. **Before surgery begins, during the preincision phase, the scrub person and the circulating nurse should count sponges, sharps, and instruments together (and out loud) as each item is separated and identified.**

2. **The circulating nurse records the specific amounts of each item counted by type and units per package, on the appropriate record sheet and/or on a counting board located in a visible spot in the procedure room.**

3. **During the operative phase of the procedure, sponges, sharps and instruments added to the sterile field are simultaneously counted by the scrub person and circulating nurse, and this number is added, per type, to the count record and counting board, maintaining a visible "running" numerical count throughout the procedure.**

4. **Sponges**
   a. **As soiled sponges are discarded from the sterile field, the circulating nurse gathers them according to type and number contained in the original package, and when the designated increment has been reached, the sponges are counted by both scrub and circulator, and then placed in clear plastic bags for future reference.**
      Example: 10 Lap Sponges (requires two plastic bags; 5 sponges in each bag)
      10 Ray-Tec Sponges (requires one plastic bag; 10 sponges in the bag)
   b. This mechanism not only provides for quick recounting but provides a technique that maintains the principle of contain and control, advocated by infection control practices.

5. **Surgical needles**
   a. **To ensure an accurate needle count, the needles should be passed, and received on a one-to-one basis, between the scrub person and the surgeon.** The used needle is placed in a designated and self-closing "needle box" located on the sterile field, and all foil wrappers from needle packages should be retained by the scrub person until the end of the procedure, until the final count is taken and verified.
   b. If multiple needles are contained in one package, the scrub person should show the circulating nurse each needle during the counting sequence.

6. **Instruments**
   a. **For instruments, a count sheet, contained inside the instrument tray, will act as the basic reference for the instrument count and is passed to the circulating nurse at the beginning of the procedure.** The count sheet can be created by the institution or commercially prepared, as part of a total inventory control system.
   b. **The circulating nurse should announce the instrument to be counted, the scrub person counts the specific type of instrument, and the amount is compared to the worksheet total for verification.** Should there be a discrepancy during the initial count, the circulator will

enter the actual amount next to the instrument type so as not to confuse the numbers during the final count.

c. **Extra instruments, given either at the beginning of the case, or during the case, should be added to the worksheet, specifying type and amount.** For example: (1) Gelpi; (2) 9-in. needle holders. The instrument count may or may not be added to the counting board, depending on how the board columns are arranged.

d. **Throughout the procedure, the scrub person keeps a silent count of all sponges, needles, and instruments, since this is her/his area of responsibility: the sterile field.**

e. **During the closing phase of the procedure, and prior to the closure of any body cavity and/or incision, the first closing count is taken and verified by both the scrub person and the circulator, starting at the sterile field, progressing to the instrument table/Mayo tray, and finally to the discarded sponges collected by the circulating nurse. The first closing count involves sponges, needles, and instruments. The status of the count is announced to the surgeon, who verbally confirms that the count has been taken and is correct. This number, per item, is recorded on the intraoperative nurse's notes under the first closing count (actual number of instruments may not be noted, only the status of the count, i.e., "correct").**

f. **The second closing count is taken prior to closure of skin/subcutaneous layer, and is taken by both the scrub person and circulator, out loud, and compared with the numbers entered for the first count. Should sponges and/or needles be added between the first and second counts, the numbers are added to the sheet. The count is verified by the circulator, reported to the surgeon, and entered on the intraoperative record under the appropriate column.**

g. **If the surgery involves a cavity-within-a-cavity, for example, uterus, lung, or heart, a cavity count must be taken, which becomes the first closing count, making the total number of closing counts three, instead of the routine two closing counts.**

B. **GUIDELINES FOR AN INCORRECT COUNT**

1. Although each institution should have its own policies and procedures for an incorrect count, the following guidelines should be incorporated into those documents:

   a. The circulator should notify the team of the findings and an immediate search for the item should be initiated; at the field, the nonsterile area surrounding the operating room table, within the discarded sponge packages, and the receptacles within the room.

   b. If the item is not found, the circulator should inform the core desk/supervisor, and make arrangements for an X-ray to be taken to confirm presence/absence of the missing item in the patient.

   c. An incident report/unusual occurrence report should be initiated, stating the factual events and activities that occurred, including corrective actions taken and the results.

   d. Incorrect count documentation should follow written policy and procedure regarding the intraoperative record.

   e. Should the item be found, a recount should be made to reconfirm the presence of the missing item. X-ray and incident reports are not necessary, since the item was found.

2. Because of the high level of risk to the patient related to foreign objects left in the wound, a detailed policy and procedure for counts should be known by all members of the surgical staff, including the surgeons, and any deviations from this procedure requires immediate corrective action, according to an established and written protocol.

PRACTICE QUESTIONS

1. **For which of the following would a nurse NOT be responsible, according to the American Nurses Association Code for Nurses?**

   1. *Keeping a patient safe from harm from electric shock.*

   2. *Protecting a patient from an incompetent surgeon.*

3. *Taking a continuing education course in nursing practice.*

4. *Participating in the hospital's "Walk for Hunger" fund raiser.*

2. **A perioperative nurse is being sued by a patient under common law. In order to prove negligence by the nurse, the patient must offer evidence of all following EXCEPT:**

   1. *the nurse violated the state's nurse practice act.*

   2. *the nurse had a duty to use reasonable care with the patient.*

   3. *the nurse failed to conform to the required standard.*

   4. *the patient suffered harm, and this harm was due to the nurse's breach of duty.*

3. **In the above suit, which of the following would the courts be *most* likely to use to determine if the nurse was negligent?**

   1. *Precedents set under statutory law, such as a nurse practice act.*

   2. *The A.O.R.N.'s Standards for Perioperative Nursing Practice.*

   3. *An expert witness with an M.D. or other non-nursing degree.*

   4. *The A.H.A.'s Patient's Bill of Rights.*

4. **In the above suit, under what circumstances would an expert witness NOT be called on to give testimony concerning the nurse's alleged act of negligence?**

   1. *If the act did not involve the nurse's professional skill or judgment.*

   2. *If jury members lack the background necessary to understand nursing.*

   3. *If the act involved a highly specialized or technical aspect of nursing.*

   4. *If the nurse could not reasonably be expected to adhere to a particular nursing standard.*

5. **One reason perioperative nurses generally have a greater responsibility to patients than do other nurses is that:**

   1. *the standards of perioperative nursing are much stricter.*

   2. *certification does not protect the perioperative nurse from legal responsibility.*

   3. *surgical patients are more prone to injury because they are often sedated.*

   4. *the nature of perioperative nursing places more responsibility on fewer nurses.*

6. **During a surgical procedure, a perioperative nurse knocks over a piece of electrical equipment, which falls on and severely burns the patient. Who is probably negligent in this situation, and under what legal doctrine?**

   1. *The nurse, under the res ipsa loquitor doctrine.*

   2. *The surgeon, under the captain of the ship doctrine.*

3. *The hospital, under the <u>respondeat superior</u> doctrine.*

4. *The surgeon, under the borrowed servant doctrine.*

7. **The most common injuries occurring in the operating room involving the perioperative nurse include all of the following EXCEPT:**

1. *injuries caused by iodine or other pooled solutions.*

2. *injuries caused by improperly administered anesthesia.*

3. *injuries caused by electrosurgical devices.*

4. *injuries caused by foreign bodies being left in the patient.*

8. **In what way do written policies covering the surgical suite protect the perioperative nurse in the event an injury does occur and a suit is filed?**

1. *Written policies of an institution normally take precedence over professional standards in court cases involving negligence.*

2. *It is usually easier to show that the nurse complied with the standard of care if the nurse followed written policies.*

3. *If written policies are in place, the doctrine of <u>res ipsa loquitor</u> places the burden of proof of negligence on the patient rather than on the nurse or hospital.*

4. *Written policies are often held as equivalent to waivers in court cases involving negligence.*

9. **In a malpractice suit against a nurse, the guidelines that will be compared with the proficiency of the care provided by the nurse-defendant are *most* likely to be:**

1. *standards of practice from nursing organizations.*

2. *written policies of the institution.*

3. *standards of care from nursing organizations.*

4. *standards supplied by an expert witness.*

10. **With informed consent, information must be given to the patient about a procedure or treatment. What else must be true?**

1. *The conversation must be witnessed or taped.*

2. *The information must be given both verbally and in writing.*

3. *The information also must be given to members of the patient's family.*

4. *The patient must agree to the procedure or treatment.*

11. **To give informed consent, a patient must receive, in terms he/she understands, all the information that would affect a reasonable person's decision to consent to or refuse a treatment or procedure. This information normally includes all of the following EXCEPT:**

    1. *a description of the procedure or treatment.*

    2. *an explanation of the potential for death or serious harm or for uncomfortable side effects during or after the treatment or procedure.*

    3. *an explanation of the possible effects of not having the treatment or procedure.*

    4. *an explanation of the outcome of other, similar treatments or procedures undertaken by that physician.*

12. **Depending on the state, a physician may legally withhold information from a patient undergoing a procedure or treatment under a variety of circumstances. These circumstances include all of the following EXCEPT:**

    1. *when the situation is life-threatening.*

    2. *when complete and candid disclosure would have a detrimental effect on the patient.*

    3. *when the physician is sharing treatment responsibility with other physicians.*

    4. *when the patient has decided he/she does not wish to be informed.*

13. **Implied consent refers to situations in which:**

    1. *informed consent is secured after the procedure or treatment has been completed.*

    2. *consent is validated by a contract or other formal document.*

    3. *the patient is unconscious and the procedure or treatment is undertaken without any formal consent by patient or family.*

    4. *parents provide the necessary authorization for caregivers' actions.*

14. **The perioperative nurse's duty regarding informed consent is *best* expressed as follows:**

    1. *To ensure that informed consent has been obtained, documented, and placed in the health record in accordance with hospital policy.*

    2. *When appropriate, to inform the surgeon that consent was granted by the patient while he/she was medicated.*

    3. *To inform the patient of procedures, risks, benefits, or alternatives, or ascertaining the extent of the patient's understanding of the procedure.*

    4. *When appropriate, to attempt to stop the surgeon from performing a procedure for which there is no consent.*

15. **Documentation of the patient's record during the perioperative period should reflect all of the following features of nursing care EXCEPT:**

    1. *the hospital's policies regarding specific procedures and treatments to be undertaken.*

    2. *preoperative assessment and planning carried out by the perioperative nurse.*

3. *care given by members of the surgical team and its outcomes.*

4. *a continued evaluation of the perioperative nursing care and the patient responses to nursing interventions.*

16. **Legal documentation of care provided to the patient is** *most* **likely to be provided by the:**

    1. *hospital's written policies.*

    2. *patient's record.*

    3. *nurse's patient care plan.*

    4. *nurse's outcome statements.*

17. **"The patient's breathing appears labored and the skin is hot to the touch." The problem with this charting entry is its:**

    1. *overspecificity.*

    2. *lack of psychosocial assessment.*

    3. *subjectivity.*

    4. *lack of physiologic assessment.*

18. **All of the following are guidelines for the perioperative nurse's preparation of patient records that will withstand scrutiny in court EXCEPT:**

    1. *Do not erase or white-out information on the record.*

    2. *Obtain the preoperative and postoperative diagnosis from the surgeon.*

    3. *Enter information at the time of its occurrence, not later.*

    4. *Leave blank spaces if information is not available.*

19. **Mrs. J. is admitted for surgery following a serious automobile accident. Her emergency condition does not permit time for a count of sponges, sharps, and instruments used in her surgery. In this situation, it is recommended that all of the following steps be taken EXCEPT:**

    1. *An X-ray should be performed immediately after surgery.*

    2. *The incident should be documented.*

    3. *Mrs J.'s family should be asked to sign a count waiver.*

    4. *Intraoperative and closing counts should be performed.*

20. **According to A.O.R.N. Recommended Practices, an institution's policy (protocol) and procedure for counts performed in the operating room must cover all of the following EXCEPT:**

    1. *the delineation of materials to be counted.*

    2. *the number of individuals to be involved in the count.*

3. *the appropriate frequency (intervals) of the count.*

4. *the documentation of the count status.*

21. **Responsibility for counts of sponges, sharps, and instruments before and during surgery rests with:**

    1. *both the scrub nurse and circulating nurse.*

    2. *the scrub nurse only.*

    3. *the circulating nurse only.*

    4. *the scrub nurse, circulating nurse, and assistant to the surgeon.*

22. **Soiled sponges discarded from the sterile field during surgery are handled in which way?**

    1. *As each individual sponge is discarded, it is counted and then placed in its own clear plastic bag.*

    2. *Soiled sponges and sharps are gathered together in incremental batches (e.g., 5 or 10) and then placed in clear plastic bags when the increment has been reached.*

    3. *Soiled sponges of mixed types are gathered together in incremental batches (e.g., 5 or 10) and then placed in clear plastic bags when the increment has been reached.*

    4. *Soiled sponges are gathered by type and number contained in the original package (e.g., 5 or 10) and then placed in clear plastic bags when the increment has been reached.*

23. **The first closing count of sponges, sharps, and instruments is taken:**

    1. *prior to the opening of any body cavity and/or incision, i.e., before surgery begins.*

    2. *prior to the closure of any body cavity and/or incision.*

    3. *subsequent to the closure of any body cavity and/or incision and prior to the closure of skin/subcutaneous layer.*

    4. *subsequent to the closure of skin/subcutaneous layer and prior to the final count.*

24. **Throughout the surgical procedure, a silent count of all sponges, needles, and instruments is kept by the:**

    1. *O.R. supervisor or assistant to the surgeon.*

    2. *circulating nurse.*

    3. *scrub nurse.*

    4. *circulating nurse and scrub nurse.*

25. **An incorrect count of needles used during a surgical procedure occurs after closure of the incision site. If the needle is not found in the operating room, and after the core desk/supervisor has been informed, the next step is to:**

    1. *make arrangements for an X-ray to be taken to confirm the presence or absence of the needle in the patient.*

    2. *reopen the incision site and examine the patient for the missing needle.*

3. *file an incident report/unusual occurrence report that includes the corrective actions taken and the results.*

4. *assume that the inaccurate count was an error and do nothing unless the patient develops complications.*

ANSWER EXPLANATIONS

1. **The answer is 4.** According to the A.N.A.'s Code for Nurses, first established in 1976, professional nursing responsibility consists of the following elements: (1) the professional nurse's obligation to protect the patient's right to safety; (2) the professional nurse's role as the patient advocate, protecting the patient from incompetent, unethical, or illegal actions/practices; (3) the professional nurse's qualifications relating to the administration of proficient patient care; (4) the professional nurse's obligation to maintain the highest level of competency in nursing practice, through continuing education activities; and (5) the professional nurse's responsibility and obligation to the profession, to the society in general, and to those entrusted to her/his care. Although the Code for Nurses is not a legal document, many courts use it, along with professional standards of practice, as a basis for expected standards of conduct for the profession, since it is applicable to all nurses, regardless of in what area they practice nursing.

2. **The answer is 1.** Common laws are those that are not created by the legislature (unlike statutory laws, such as a nurse practice act), but are based on the principles and rules of action relating to the security of individuals and their property. The authority of these laws comes solely from the usage and customs of society or the judgments and decrees of the courts, which recognize, affirm, and enforce such usages and customs. Under common law, the person injured who brings suit must offer evidence that: (1) there was a duty to use reasonable care; (2) there was a failure to conform to the required standard; (3) he/she suffered harm; and (4) the harm caused was due to the breach of duty.

3. **The answer is 2.** To determine whether there was a duty owed to the patient, the courts would use a reasonable prudent standard. In the case of health care providers, the standard is in accordance with the standards of practice among members of the same health care profession, with similar training and experience, situated in the same or similar community at the time the alleged act occurred. When a professional is charged, however, such as perioperative nurse, the court will require an expert witness who would give testimony concerning the actions of the nurse. The expert witness is a person practicing the same profession (nursing), with the same or similar training and education. The expert witness is used because most jury members do not have the background necessary to understand nursing or the technical aspects of malpractice. The standards used by the expert witness are those established by the professional group (e.g., the A.O.R.N's *Standards for Perioperative Nursing Practice*).

4. **The answer is 1.** The nurse, as a professional, can be held to the nonprofessional standard (in which no expert witness is needed), when the alleged act of negligence does not involve professional skill or judgment, for example, the wrong patient was operated on. In this case, the jury would understand without the use of the expert.

5. **The answer is 3.** Whether the nurse has a specialized practice, such as perioperative nursing, or is a staff nurse on a medical floor or in a long-term facility, the legal duty to patients is the same--that is, to deliver reasonable, prudent, and safe care so as not to cause injury to the patient. But in the case of the perioperative nurse, there is an additional responsibility: in the operating room, patients are more prone to injury because of receiving anesthesia, being in a sedated state, and the intrusive nature of the surgical procedure. Thus, more prudent, safe, and reasonable care must be given.

6. **The answer is 1.** In *Sprager v Worley Hospital,* in a case involving an O.R. nurse who failed to take a sponge count, resulting in injury to the patient, the Texas Supreme Court held the O.R. nurses negligent because nurses were not "borrowed servants" (under the control of the surgeon) and the surgeon was not "captain of the ship" (with full responsibility for the care of the patient). The court based their decision on several facts of the case, including: the nurses were hired and assigned by the hospital; the surgeon did not participate in their selection; the duties of scrub and circulating personnel were detailed in the hospital's

policy and procedures manual; the procedures for sponge counts were intended for use regardless of the surgeon who performed the operation; and the scrub nurse testified that the surgeon did not direct her and the circulating nurse to take the count. The doctrine often applied to such cases is that of *res ipsa loquitor*. According to this doctrine, the nurse must show that the standard of care was not breached, rather than the usual requirement that the injured party show that the standard was breached. To invoke this doctrine successfully, the person claiming he/she was harmed must establish that the injury does not ordinarily occur unless someone was negligent (in this case the O.R. nurse who knocked over the equipment); the instrumentality causing the injury was within the exclusive control of the nurse (which it appeared to be); and the plaintiff did not contribute to the injury in any way (which he/she did not). These three elements are easier to establish when the injury occurs in the operating room because the patient is anesthetized or sedated; the equipment that caused the injury is clearly controlled by the nurse, the surgeon, or other hospital personnel.

7. **The answer is 2.** The most common injuries occurring in the operating room are caused by iodine or other pooled solutions, electrosurgical devices, or improperly aerated equipment sterilized with ethylene oxide, or are ulnar or perineal nerve injuries due to positioning or to foreign bodies being left in the patient.

8. **The answer is 2.** In the surgical suite, where there is an increased potential for injury, there must be written policies. These written policies protect the patient, the perioperative nurse, and other personnel in at least two distinct ways: (1) consistent adherence to uniform policy, procedures, and protocols provides safe patient care, thus decreasing the likelihood that the patient will be injured; and (2) if an injury does occur and a suit is filed, it will be easier to show that the nurse complied with the standard of care if the nurse followed the policy and procedures of the institution.

9. **The answer is 3.** In order to be successful in malpractice cases, the plaintiff's attorney must prove that the nurse failed to deliver or breached **acceptable standards of care**--what a "reasonable and prudent nurse of similar education and experience would have done under similar circumstances." This is the legal description of standards of care. Standards of care, from professional nursing organizations such as the A.N.A. and A.O.R.N. and federal/state agencies such as the Joint Commission on the Accreditation of Healthcare Organizations and the Health & Rehabilitative Services, provide the guidelines that will be compared with the proficiency of the care provided by the nurse-defendant and/or the institution. If the perioperative nurse is familiar with these standards, and she/he practices within the recommended guidelines, it is very difficult for the plaintiff's attorney to prove negligence: that is that the nurse/institution failed to meet the legal standards of care.

10. **The answer is 4.** Informed consent has two basic elements: (1) **informed** refers to information given to the patient about a proposed procedure or treatment and (2) **consent** refers to the patient's agreement to the procedure or treatment. To give informed consent, a patient must receive, in terms he/she understands, all the information that would affect a reasonable person's decision to consent to or refuse a treatment or procedure.

11. **The answer is 4.** Informed consent information also should include the name and qualifications of the person who will perform the treatment or procedure; an explanation that the patient has a right to refuse the treatment or procedure without having other care or support withdrawn; and that he/she can withdraw his/her consent after having given it.

12. **The answer is 3.** *Salgo v Leland Stanford, Jr. University Board of Trustees*, established the basic rule that a physician "violates a duty to his patient and subjects himself to liability, if he withholds any facts that are necessary to form the basis of an intelligent consent by the patient to the proposed treatment." Since this ruling, a patient can sue for negligent nondisclosure if his/her doctor fails to give him/her enough information to make an informed decision. The **reasonable physician standard** is based on what another physician would disclose to a similar patient under similar circumstances. This standard has been upheld in court. Physicians face a variety of situations, which may differ from state to state, in which information can be withheld. These include choices 1, 2, and 4, and also situations when the risk is too obvious to justify, and when the procedure is simple and the risks too remote.

13. **The answer is 4.** The doctrine of informed consent assumes that an informed patient can act in his/her own best interests. There are, however, two types of consent: implied and express. **Express consent** is the agreement between the persons involved. A consent form, which is a contract, is a formal means of documenting express consent and, if the consent itself is valid, the form serves to validate that fact. **Implied consent** occurs routinely in health care, when parents, by their conduct in cooperating with caregivers, provide the necessary authorization for caregivers' actions.

14. **The answer is 1.** The perioperative nurse's duty regarding informed consent is confined to ensuring that informed consent has been obtained, documented, and placed in the health record in accordance with the policy of the hospital. The courts do not require that hospitals or nurses assume the surgeon's duty to inform the patient or to obtain the patient's consent, i.e., the perioperative nurse's role does not include the undertaking of informing the patient of procedures, risks, benefits, or alternatives, or ascertaining the extent of the patient's understanding of the procedure. Nor is the nurse responsible for trying to stop a surgeon from performing a procedure for which there is no consent, although the nurse should inform the surgeon if consent has not been issued.

15. **The answer is 1.** Documentation of nursing care is an essential and legal responsibility of the perioperative nurse. In the courtroom, nurses can better meet the burden of proof that they were not negligent if the O.R. record reflects that the standard of care was met. Documentation during the perioperative period should meet the A.O.R.N. *Recommended Practices for Documentation*, which states: (1) the patient's record should reflect the preoperative assessment and planning carried out by the perioperative nurse; (2) the patient's record should reflect care given by members of the surgical team and its outcomes; the care should be documented on the patient's chart; (3) the patient record should reflect a continued evaluation of the perioperative nursing care and the patient responses to nursing interventions; and (4) the documentation of perioperative nursing care will be determined by policies and procedures of the practice setting.

16. **The answer is 2.** The most important thing that nurses can do to protect themselves and the hospital is to document everything that is done or not done for the patient, even if it only involves filling out a check list. Doing a procedure routinely, however, will not protect the nurse unless it is documented. The patient record may serve as legal documentation of care provided to the patient and as such is admissible evidence in a court of law. Additionally, the record can be used as an indicator of the quality of nursing care by hospital quality assurance (surgical audit) committees or the medical records committee. It is the nurse's responsibility to ensure that charting takes place according to institutional policy. The patient record then accompanies the patient throughout the perioperative period, conveying all information gathered regarding assessment, planning, and patient response to treatment and nursing intervention.

17. **The answer is 3.** Legal standards require the perioperative nurse to record observations accurately and completely, and in a timely manner, reflecting the exact nursing interventions performed during the intraoperative period. The most common error made when charting, regardless of the area, is writing value judgments, generalizations ("breathing appears labored"), and opinions (subjective data) rather than factual information (objective data). This entry could be clarified by means of a specific rate of respiration, patient temperature, changes over time, etc.

18. **The answer is 4.** Some points to remember about documenting the patient record are: (1) the intraoperative record is generally in duplicate form that provides a second or third copy; therefore use ballpoint pen for entries (preferably black); (2) there cannot be any erasures or white-out on a legal document; if an error is made, follow the acceptable method for correcting the document; (3) fill out the record as if you anticipated a court case, since this document can be used as evidence; (4) the preoperative and postoperative diagnosis should be obtained by the surgeon for accuracy and verification with the surgical procedure performed; it is not a safe practice to use the surgery schedule for the operative procedure entry; (5) the operative procedure should correspond with the specimen(s) obtained, and they should be listed on the record; and (6) count status, times of events, and final dispensation of the patient (postanesthesia care unit, outpatient surgery) should be entered on the record.

19. **The answer is 3.** Counts are addressed in the *Standards of Practice* (Standard III), in the *Outcome Standards for Patient Care* (Standard IV), and as a *Recommended Practice*, stating, "Sponges, sharps, and instruments will be counted on all procedures." However, in some instances, a patient's emergency condition does not permit time for a count to be taken prior to surgery. When this occurs, it is recommended that the incident be documented, that intraoperative and closing counts be performed, and that an X-ray be performed immediately after surgery.

20. **The answer is 2.** According to the statements for sponge, sharp, and instrument counts in the A.O.R.N. Recommended Practices (1991), "It is the responsibility of each institution to develop a well delineated policy (protocol) and procedure for counts performed in the operating room, which should include (1) the delineation of materials to be counted, (2) the appropriate frequency (intervals) of the counts, (3) the mechanism for performing the count, and (4) the documentation of the count status."

21. **The answer is 1.** Before surgery begins, during the preincision phase, the scrub person and the circulating nurse should count sponges, sharps, and instruments together (and out loud) as each item is separated and identified. The circulating nurse records the specific amounts of each item counted by type and units per package, on the appropriate record sheet and/or on a counting board located in a visible spot in the procedure room. During the operative phase of the procedure, sponges, sharps and instruments added to the sterile field are simultaneously counted by the scrub person and circulating nurse, and this number is added, per type, to the count record and counting board, maintaining a visible "running" numerical count throughout the procedure.

22. **The answer is 4.** As soiled sponges are discarded from the sterile field, the circulating nurse gathers them according to type and number contained in the original package, and when the designated increment has been reached, the sponges are counted by both scrub person and circulator, and then placed in clear plastic bags for future reference. Example: 10 Lap Sponges (requires two plastic bags; 5 sponges in each bag). This mechanism not only provides for quick recounting but provides a technique that maintains the principle of contain and control, advocated by infection control practices.

23. **The answer is 2.** During the closing phase of the procedure, and prior to the closure of any body cavity and/or incision, the first closing count is taken and verified by both the scrub person and the circulator, starting at the sterile field, progressing to the instrument table/Mayo tray, and finally to the discarded sponges collected by the circulating nurse. The first closing count involves sponges, needles, and instruments. The status of the count is announced to the surgeon, who verbally confirms that the count has been taken and is correct. This number, per item, is recorded on the intraoperative nurse's notes under the first closing count (actual number of instruments may not be noted, only the status of the count, i.e., "correct"). The second closing count is taken prior to closure of skin/subcutaneous layer, and is taken by both the scrub person and circulator, out loud, and compared with the numbers entered for the first count. Should sponges and/or needles be added between the first and second counts, the numbers are added to the sheet. The count is verified by the circulator, reported to the surgeon, and entered on the intraoperative record under the appropriate column.

24. **The answer is 3.** Throughout the procedure, the scrub person keeps a silent count of all sponges, needles, and instruments, since this is her/his area of responsibility: the sterile field.

25. **The answer is 1.** Although each institution should have its own policies and procedures for an incorrect count, the following guidelines should be incorporated into those documents: (1) the circulator should notify the team of the findings and an immediate search for the item should be initiated at the field, the nonsterile area surrounding the operating room table, within the discarded sponge packages, and the receptacles within the room; (2) if the item is not found, the circulator should inform the core desk/supervisor, and make arrangements for an X-ray to be taken to confirm presence/absence of the missing item in the patient; and (3) an incident report/unusual occurrence report should be initiated, stating the factual events and activities that occurred, including corrective actions taken and the results. Incorrect count documentation should follow written policy and procedure regarding the intraoperative record. Should the item be found, a recount should be made to reconfirm the presence of the missing item. X-ray and incident reports are not necessary, since the item was found.

15 Additional Topics for Perioperative Nursing Practice

STUDY OUTLINE

I. AMBULATORY SURGERY CONCEPTS

1. During the 1980s, ambulatory health care and surgical procedures have undergone a veritable explosion in the range of services provided and the popularity of this mode of treatment. In fact, patient visits have increased in such numbers that freestanding Same Day SurgiCenters have been opening all across the country, and many hospitals/agencies now officer ambulatory surgery (outpatient surgery) for an increased number of procedures that once required inpatient hospitalization.

2. In 1986, an important milestone was reached regarding the ambulatory surgery unit/facility. Standards of care, specifically written for this area, were developed and monitored by accreditation agencies to evaluate and improve the quality of health care provided in this setting. To this end, a separate chapter, now a separate manual, was written by the Joint Commission Organization (J.C.A.H.O.), outlining the specific aspects of care to be provided, staffing, the physical plant, and the types of patients recommended for this service.

3. The 1990 *Ambulatory Health Care Standards Manual* consists of 14 chapters, including quality assurance (Q.A.); medical records; surgical and anesthesia services; teaching, education, research; and ancillary services associated with this unique service.

4. As with any health-care service, evaluation, education, and consultation are vital elements for improving the quality of care. These elements, coupled with the commitment of dedicated professionals, provide the foundation for a successful ambulatory care program for persons seeking this mode of treatment.

A. SETTINGS FOR AMBULATORY SURGERY

1. **There are four kinds of ambulatory surgery settings: (1) the integrated, or hospital-affiliated, model; (2) the separated facility; (3) the satellite facility; and (4) the freestanding facility.**

2. In the **integrated model,** a hospital develops a formal ambulatory surgery program that is incorporated into an existing inpatient surgery program. Approximately 80 percent of outpatient surgery is performed in this setting.

3. The second, the **separated model,** can either be within the hospital itself, or on the grounds of the hospital, with dedicated operating rooms for ambulatory surgery, rather than a dual purpose as in the integrated model.

4. The **satellite model** is a facility separated from the hospital, yet linked in name, and/or organizational structure. It may be close to the main facility, or in an area that requires medical/surgical services, yet be too small to merit a full hospital service.

5. The fourth kind is the **independent** or **freestanding model.** This facility is not affiliated with any hospital or health-care agency. It may have been started by a group of surgeons who deal in one specialty (e.g., plastic surgery, ophthalmology, etc.), and was brought to public attention in the 1970s when Wallace Reed and John Ford, both anesthesiologists, opened their SurgiCenter in

Phoenix, Arizona. It is this model that has been used to design and facilitate ambulatory surgery across the country.

B. ADVANTAGES OF AMBULATORY SURGERY

1. Ambulatory surgery has four advantages that have an impact on current health care and the patient population seeking the service, including (1) decreased cost to the patient and institution, (2) increased bed availability for seriously ill patients, (3) decreased risk of acquiring a nosocomial infection during the perioperative period, and (4) less disruption to the patient's personal life, resulting in decreased psychologic stress associated with the hospital experience.

C. RECOMMENDATIONS FOR PATIENT SELECTION AND SURGICAL PROCEDURES

1. Many members of the medical and surgical community suggest that the requirements for patient selection for ambulatory surgery procedures should include:
   a. Patients undergoing an operation of 60 to 90 minutes or less with minimal bleeding; procedures that are associated with minor psychologic derangements.
   b. Patients who are expected to have minimal postoperative complications.
   c. Patients who are in good health (e.g., A.S.A. Classification I or II).
   d. Reliable patients and those with support systems (e.g., family and significant others willing to follow pre- and postoperative instructions).
   e. Patients who psychologically accept the concept of ambulatory surgery.
   f. Cooperative surgeons, anesthesiologists, and nursing personnel.
2. In one survey, of the ten procedures most frequently performed in the United States, seven would be appropriate for ambulatory surgery: biopsies, dilation and curettage, excision of skin lesions, tubal ligations, cataract extraction, inguinal herniorrhaphy, and diagnostic urologic procedures (e.g., cystourethroscopy). Additionally, miscellaneous orthopedic; ear, nose, and throat; and plastic surgeries are frequently performed on an outpatient basis, along with a variety of surgeries performed on children.

D. PERIOPERATIVE NURSING CONSIDERATIONS

1. The perioperative nurse's role--that of caring for the patient during the preoperative, intraoperative, and postoperative phases of surgical intervention--can be optimally practiced in the ambulatory surgery setting. The A.O.R.N.'s Standards and Recommended Practices are the same, with slight differences during the preoperative and postoperative phases since the entire process takes place over a shorter period of time, but the nursing practice requires the same commitment to quality patient care as if the procedure were being performed in a traditional hospital setting.
2. Perioperative nursing practice--in whatever type or model or setting--is intense and varied, and includes all services and phases of surgical intervention. The nurse working in this setting must be flexible, capable of working in any setting, able to perform as a team member, and qualified to perform nursing activities with minimal direct supervision. All nurses working in this setting should be cross-trained for all areas, and continuing education and staff development programs should be on-going, since the quality of patient care is of primary importance, and changes in technology, methods and techniques present a constant challenge.
3. Ambulatory surgery can be safe and effective for the patient requiring surgery if it is performed properly and patient selection is carefully observed. As innovative ways to provide low-cost, high-quality care are explored, ambulatory surgery will increase in popularity.

II. A CLINICAL LADDER PROGRAM FOR PERIOPERATIVE NURSING

A. WHAT IS A CLINICAL LADDER PROGRAM?

1. Traditionally, nursing rewarded clinical competency by providing a means of moving upward on the continuum to management positions. However, with this move, nursing care was directed

away from patient care activities into the administrative circle, which emphasizes the managerial role of the nurse, not clinical practice. Since this role requires more time away from the bedside, clinical performance competency would fall, and some nurses, who were unprepared for their new position, became frustrated as they tried to "practice" effective bedside nursing. A newer, more palatable solution to this problem is the establishment of a **clinical ladder program**, designed to promote clinical competence rather than remove nurses from bedside nursing practice.

2. **A clinical ladder program is described as a hierarchy of criteria, intended to provide a means of evaluation and development of nurses providing direct patient care.** The objectives of such a program should be to:
   a. Provide recognition and placement of the highly skilled nurse practitioners performing direct patient care activities.
   b. Identify levels of nursing competence within the institution/area.
   c. Acknowledge the nurses' educational preparation and/or certification in a specialty area.
   d. Provide realistic and measurable expectations for practice that can serve as a guide toward advancement within the program and/or nursing area.
   e. Allow the practitioner to set his or her goals related to nursing practice.
   f. Assist in recruitment and retention programs within the institution, thus promoting highly qualified practitioners within the institution.

3. The implementation of a clinical ladder program may be lengthy and involved, or it may be simple and self-explanatory, but whatever the format, certain steps should be incorporated into its design including the depth of knowledge that forms the basis for clinical decisions, the scope of practice, and the degree of responsibility and accountability for patient care for each level created. By using the Basic Competency Statements for Perioperative Nursing Practice, a framework for the position descriptions for each level can be created, implemented, and evaluated realistically using preestablished criteria.

4. By incorporating this nontraditional approach to recognizing the competent clinical practitioner, nurses striving for excellence in clinical practice can see how their careers progress, and find the challenge of reaching the next level rewarding not only for themselves but for the patient, the institution, and their specialized nursing profession.

B. CERTIFICATION: THE FIRST STEP ON THE LADDER

1. **Certification** is described as a process by which a nongovernmental agency or association grants recognition to an individual who has met certain predetermined qualifications that have been specified by that agency or association.

2. In 1979 the first national certification examination for perioperative nursing practice was administered. In that year, 688 nurses became certified in perioperative nursing practice, and were entitled to add the initials CNOR to their credentials. By January of 1990, 13,317 perioperative nurses had become certified, which has helped to establish the first level of advanced clinical practice for a clinical ladder program.

3. Through this national certification program, perioperative nurse practitioners have been able to enhance the quality of patient care; identify nurses who have demonstrated professional achievement in perioperative nursing; provide a means for self-evaluation and self-satisfaction; and create a sense of awareness, both within and outside the nursing profession, of clinical competence in nursing practice during the perioperative period.

C. CLINICAL NURSE SPECIALIST ROLE

1. The perioperative **clinical nurse specialist (C.N.S.)** is the last step on the clinical ladder series, since the role not only signifies advanced clinical competence, but the candidate has, in addition to certification, attained an advanced degree in nursing as defined by the A.N.A. Position Paper for C.N.S.:

   *The CNS is a nurse prepared at the **graduate level**, with focus in a specific clinical area. The CNS role incorporates clinical, administrative and educational aspects of professional nursing practice,* *with a goal of coordinating and managing the specific needs of the patient and/or family.* A.N.A. (1978)

2. The interest in and need for the perioperative C.N.S. has been explored and requested by many institutions across the country. As it is a comparatively new role in relation to other clinical nurse specialties, support from other clinical nurse specialists and universities offering a **master's program with emphasis in perioperative nursing practice** can assist in achieving this goal: to advance clinical nursing through higher education within a chosen field. For the perioperative C.N.S., certification in perioperative nursing practice (CNOR) would become a requirement, since it signifies a mastery level in perioperative nursing practice as specified for the C.N.S. role.

3. The next logical step in the development of a perioperative C.N.S. role is to create a realistic position description that can evolve and develop as the specialty progresses. In this way, the perioperative C.N.S. role will become an innovative and vital component of the health-care system and the professional practice of nursing during the perioperative period.

III. **QUALITY ASSURANCE: MONITORING THE EFFECTIVENESS OF CARE**

A. **WHAT IS QUALITY ASSURANCE?**

1. **Quality** can be defined as a characteristic or attribute that states excellence or superior degree; related to a grade of excellence.
2. **Assurance** refers to acts or actions taken that guarantee the state of being assured or being certain; free of doubt; confidence.
3. **Quality assurance (Q.A.), therefore, is described as a process intended to guarantee a level of excellence by comparing current practices to an established standard(s) to assure quality patient care.**

B. **J.C.A.H.O. MONITORING CHARACTERISTICS**

1. In 1985, Q.A. officially became a separate component in the Joint Commission accreditation process, and in 1989, a revised and specific criteria for that process became the focus of all accreditation reviews. As stated in the 1990 *Accreditation Manual*:

    There shall be evidence of a well defined, organized program, designed to enhance patient care through ongoing assessment of the important aspects of care, and the correction of identified problems.

    J.C.A.H.O. Manual (1990)

2. Seven characteristics established by the Joint Commission formulated the initial investigation program, and are still applicable today when reviewing the Quality Assurance program and activities:
    a. The Q.A. activities are planned, systematic, and on-going.
    b. The Q.A. activities are comprehensive in scope.
    c. The Q.A. activities are based on **indicators** and **criteria** that the department, service, or staff agree on and that are acceptable to the organization/institution.
        (1) **Indicator**--signs, symptoms, events, or occurrences that may signal potential problems ("red flag").
        (2) **Criteria**--key elements of care which, if met, reflect compliance with a preestablished standard.
    d. The Q.A. activities are accomplished by routine collection and periodic evaluation of the collected data.
    e. The Q.A. activities result in appropriate actions to solve identified problems, or take other identified opportunities to improve patient care.
    f. The Q.A. activities are continual and concurrent in an effort to ensure that improvements in care and performance are maintained.

g. The Q.A. activities share within the institution on a routine basis the information delivered from the monitors and the evaluation data.

C. FOUR ESSENTIAL COMPONENTS FOR QUALITY ASSURANCE PROGRAMS

1. **For a Q.A. program to be effective, the design of the program should contain four essential elements or components: setting program objectives, promoting quality, activity monitoring, and performance assessment.**

2. **Setting and stating program objectives:** Quality assurance begins with the establishment of goals and objectives. These goals and objectives will form the foundation of the Q.A. program at all levels. The goals are usually derived from the desire to achieve standards.
   a. **Goal:** is written in futuristic terms; is broad in definition and gives direction for the program.
   b. **Standard:** defines how the goal will be attained; is stated in present tense.
   c. **Examples:**   Management Goals for the Department of Surgery Performance Standards: Circulating Nurse

3. **Continuing quality improvement--QCI:** The quality of a person's performance is related to his or her own standards of performance, skills in attaining them, and the support systems that reward acceptable performance. Examples include:
   a. Staff development/skills training programs.
   b. Continuing education--products, technology, personnel.
   c. Employee performance appraisals.
   d. Advanced education programs (specialty certification and advanced degrees).
   e. Product evaluation task force.
   f. Development of positions or programs that may lead to recruitment and retention (e.g., perioperative nursing internship program).

4. **Activity monitoring:** Performances should be monitored by **quality control** and **quality supervision**.
   a. **Quality control:** Quality control is a concurrent system of performance monitoring and remediation when needed. Examples include:
      (1) **Occurrence screening:** a concurrent review of the intraoperative record or chart to identify deviations from the required procedure of documentation.
      (2) **Nursing audits:** focus on current clinical practice to identify potential or actual problems. The audits should include solutions for correction and be concurrent, requiring a follow-up for comparison.
   b. **Quality supervision:** Supervisory rounds and incident tracking are two forms of current monitoring, conducted and reviewed by the supervisor (nurse manager).
      (1) **Supervisory rounds (inspection):** can encourage and maintain a high standard of performance through visibility.
      (2) **Incident tracking:** can determine whether there are any trends or recurrent problems and devise the necessary action(s) or recommendations to correct the identified problems. Follow-up audits maintain the concurrent format.

5. **Performance assessment:** Performance assessment is the periodic assessment and evaluation of nursing care, using the pre-established standards, with corrective counseling as needed. Three aspects should be considered: **(1) quality review, (2) quality evaluation, and (3) quality approval**.
   a. **Quality review:** analysis of performance of employee and system; retrospective audits that indicate the quality of care; review of previous performances; trend of actions (if any).
   b. **Quality evaluation:** audits (criteria-based measurements of performance based on objective data) conducted on a regular basis with follow-up as needed; can be based on outcome standards and/or include medical audits (e.g., physician survey).
   c. **Quality approval:** retrospective survey of performance of personnel and system from others (e.g., patients, hospital personnel, or outside agencies).

D. NURSING MANAGEMENT AND QUALITY ASSURANCE PROGRAMS

1. A successful Q.A. program needs the cooperation of all members of the surgical staff, including management. By participating in the selection of the person(s) who will aide in the program

design and selection of topics, the nurse-manager can demonstrate a commitment to quality assurance while establishing an environment conducive to quality patient care.

2. During the planning stage, certain tasks should be performed by all members selected (volunteered) to be part of the Q.A. Committee for Surgery:

   a. **Review the existing program:** Determine the strengths and weaknesses of the current activities and develop a plan that can correct the weaknesses while retaining the existing strengths.

   b. **Designate the time for development and implementation of program activities.**

   (1) Review the goals and objectives of the program.

   (2) Determine how the components fit into the three categories of nursing standards:

   (a) **Structure standards**
   - People, equipment, environment

   (b) **Process standards**
   - Protocols, procedures, standards of care

   (c) **Outcome standards**
   - Quality of results, productivity, patient/client satisfaction

   c. **Select and/or appoint responsible person(s) for Q.A. activities and unit-based Q.A. committee:** Members should include management staff (A.H.N., team leaders), staff nurses, clinical nurse specialist/educator.

   d. **Assess changes that need to be made to reflect actual or current activities:** As policies/protocols change, so too should the Q.A. monitors, criteria, and evaluation tools.

   e. **Plan activities to create acceptance and recognize achievement of Q.A. program:** Staff input is vital for a dynamic program. Report studies and findings at staff meetings; ask for ways of improving findings if needed. Meetings should involve all staff members, not just nurses.

3. Accountability is no longer a luxury, but a demand by consumers of all health-care services. It is required by federal legislation (e.g., H.R.S., J.C.A.H.O.) and is mandated by the profession. Self-regulation and accountability are the hallmarks of a mature profession. Quality assurance programs can assist in maintaining quality of care as the nursing profession expands its potential.

IV. PERIOPERATIVE NURSING EDUCATION

1. The operating room experience for student nurses was at one time an important part of the generic nursing education program. But as program needs changed and the ideologies of nursing education underwent modification, the operating room rotation, as a clinical learning experience, was eventually eliminated from the basic curriculum, leaving a deficit in entry level practitioners for this specialty area.

2. In an effort to ensure that qualified operating room nurses are providing this specialized nursing practice, several steps have been taken, including:

   a. The establishment, through A.O.R.N., of *Project Alpha,* created for the purpose of reinstituting a perioperative nursing component into curricula in nursing education at a variety of levels, both nationally and through local A.O.R.N. chapters.

   b. The creation of postgraduate courses in perioperative nursing, conducted in a variety of settings across the country.

3. A **perioperative nursing internship program**, conducted outside the hospital environment, has recently become more cost-effective than the previous one-on-one courses that were conducted in the hospital as staffing needs demanded, and through these extended programs, perioperative nursing as a specialty, has again become part of nursing education.

4. Since its inception, the A.O.R.N. has been directly involved with promoting perioperative nursing education. Since teaching has always been an integral part of the professional nurse's role, it was natural that perioperative nurses became involved with establishing methods to offer perioperative nursing practice to both entry level students and those wishing to expand their current knowledge through formal education. The Perioperative Nursing Internship Program, regardless of its setting, has become one of those methods.

5. **Prospective participants**

   a. There are several reasons why a nurse and/or students would want to participate in a Perioperative Nursing Internship Program:

(1) To work in an area they have always wanted to but could not owing to lack of knowledge or experience.

(2) To explore the role of the perioperative nurse in order to decide whether this is the area they wish to practice (entry level).

(3) To update skills and knowledge in order to reenter the workforce of operating room nurses.

(4) To provide a means for nurses to change their current area of practice.

(5) To provide existing practitioners a means to expand their existing knowledge and skills to a higher level of practice and/or review for the CNOR examination.

b. For whatever the reason, the Perioperative Nursing Internship Program provides both a recruitment and a retention tool for hospitals, especially during the current critical shortage of nurses, and as a means to further one's formal education when it is affiliated with a university as an elective.

V. PERIOPERATIVE NURSING RESEARCH

1. The ultimate goal of any profession is to improve the practice of its members so that the recipient of the service receives the greatest benefit. Since nursing is a learned, service-oriented profession, we must constantly seek scientific data not only to assist in expanding existing knowledge, but also to create safe, more efficient methods for delivery of this service. To this end, **perioperative nursing research** has become the tool for finding these answers and help guide current practices.

2. Traditionally, many of the nursing activities performed during the perioperative period have been "passed-down" from one nurse to another or have been accepted as a standard of care based on common consensus in the nursing community. This method, however, should no longer be considered acceptable, since many of these activities were founded not on scientific principles, but on a traditional approach to nursing.

3. It is only in the past 40 years that nursing has earnestly searched for a scientific base for practice. Many nursing actions have yet to be empirically tested for their effectiveness, including those related to perioperative nursing practice. Much of the research that does exist pertains to nurses rather than to the effects of nursing actions or how these actions have affected and/or changed client outcomes, and very little research has been specifically conducted relating to the practice of perioperative nursing.

4. If perioperative nursing is to continue to grow and mature into a profession and receive the professional recognition and status it seeks, priority must be given to conducting research studies during the perioperative period that relate to clinical issues and client problems. Traditional nursing actions need to be tested in order to determine their effect, thereby demonstrating that **perioperative nursing practice is a planned process founded upon scientific research results rather than upon assumptions, hunches, or the performance of skills based on previous success or inherited practice.**

5. Perioperative nursing, as a component of the discipline of nursing, has an obligation to the patients they serve; that is, to improve and *validate* the quality of practice through on-going clinical research. Perioperative nurses need to educate not only their peers, but also agency administrators and surgeons as to the professional benefits derived from clinical research, including economic gains, employee efficiency, and patient satisfaction.

6. But by far the most important benefit is the practitioner's feeling of self-satisfaction, as he or she realizes the accomplishment of his or her ultimate goal to *render to all quality patient care*. It is because of the desire to improve current practices that perioperative nurses will continue to be SPECIALISTS IN CARING.

PRACTICE QUESTIONS

1. **The most common setting for ambulatory surgery is one in which the facility is:**

    1. *separated from and yet linked to a hospital in name and/or organizational structure.*

    2. *on the grounds of a hospital, with dedicated operating rooms for ambulatory surgery.*

    3. *incorporated into an existing inpatient surgery program.*

    4. *not affiliated with any hospital or health-care agency.*

2. **One of the major advantages of ambulatory surgery compared with inpatient surgery is:**

    1. *decreased cost to the patient and institution.*

    2. *overall better access to modern surgical equipment.*

    3. *more effective use of operating room personnel.*

    4. *greater attention to postoperative complications.*

3. **Which of the following patients is the *best* candidate for ambulatory surgery?**

    1. *Mr. R., whose surgery may involve postoperative complications.*

    2. *Ms. G., whose physical status is A.S.A. Class 2.*

    3. *Mr. V., whose surgery may require blood transfusions.*

    4. *Ms. B., whose surgery is expected to last 2 to 3 hours.*

4. **The primary purpose of a clinical ladder program is to:**

    1. *train nurses to become better managers.*

    2. *prepare nurses for certification.*

    3. *provide a structure for nurses to achieve excellence in clinical administration.*

    4. *promote clinical competence in nurses.*

5. **A perioperative clinical nurse specialist is a nurse who has achieved all of the following EXCEPT:**

    1. *CNOR certification.*

    2. *an MBA or equivalent business degree.*

    3. *advanced clinical competence.*

    4. *advanced educational preparation in nursing (MSN).*

6. **Quality assurance (Q.A.) in nursing is implemented by:**

   1. *comparing current practices to established practices to assure quality patient care.*

   2. *demonstrating professional achievement in nursing as a means for self-satisfaction and self-evaluation.*

   3. *advancing clinical nursing through higher education in a chosen field.*

   4. *cross-training nurses for all areas of nursing, to achieve maximum flexibility and quality of care.*

7. **Which of the following would be *least* likely to be part of a hospital's quality assurance (Q.A.) program in perioperative nursing?**

   1. *Setting performance standards for scrub nurses.*

   2. *Reimbursing circulating nurses for their continuing education courses.*

   3. *Reviewing program activities on an annual rather than on a continual basis.*

   4. *Developing a perioperative nursing internship program.*

8. **Which of the following would be *least* likely to be part of a hospital's quality assurance (Q.A.) program in perioperative nursing?**

   1. *A review of intraoperative charts to identify deviations from required documentation.*

   2. *A program of incident tracking to determine recurrent problems and devise solutions.*

   3. *A nursing audit that focuses on outcome standards for perioperative nursing.*

   4. *A program for reducing supervisory rounds and placing more responsibility on O.R. nurses.*

9. **A cost-effective approach being used by many hospitals, in conjunction with universities, to recruit and retain quality nurses, as well as to upgrade the overall quality of perioperative nursing within the hospital, is the:**

   1. *A.O.R.N.'s Project Alpha.*

   2. *perioperative nursing internship program.*

   3. *hospital-based perioperative nursing graduate degree program.*

   4. *hospital-based postgraduate residency in perioperative nursing.*

10. **Which of the following is true of most perioperative nursing research done to date?**

    1. *It primarily has dealt with problems of patient care.*

    2. *It pertains to nursing activities rather than to patient care responses.*

    3. *Its objectives have been to change client outcomes.*

    4. *It has focused on clinical rather than on professional issues.*

ANSWER EXPLANATIONS

1. **The answer is 3.** There are four kinds of ambulatory surgery settings: (1) the integrated, or hospital-affiliated, model; (2) the separated facility; (3) the satellite facility; and (4) the freestanding facility. In the **integrated model,** a hospital develops a formal ambulatory surgery program that is incorporated into an existing inpatient surgery program. Approximately 80 percent of outpatient surgery is performed in this setting. The second, the **separated model,** can either be within the hospital itself, or on the grounds of the hospital, with dedicated operating rooms for ambulatory surgery, rather than a dual purpose as in the integrated model. The **satellite model** is a facility separated from the hospital, yet linked in name, and/or organizational structure. It may be close to the main facility, or in an area that requires medical/surgical services, yet be too small to merit a full hospital service. The fourth kind is the **independent or freestanding model.** This facility is not affiliated with any hospital or health-care agency. It is this model that has been used to design and facilitate ambulatory surgery across the country.

2. **The answer is 1.** Ambulatory surgery has four advantages that have an impact on current health care and the patient population seeking the service, including (1) decreased cost to the patient and institution, (2) increased bed availability for seriously ill patients, (3) decreased risk of acquiring a nosocomial infection during the perioperative period, and (4) less disruption to the patient's personal life, resulting in decreased psychologic stress associated with the hospital experience.

3. **The answer is 2.** Many members of the medical and surgical community suggest that the requirements for patient selection for ambulatory surgery procedures should include: (1) patients undergoing an operation of 60 to 90 minutes or less with minimal bleeding, including procedures that are associated with minor psychologic derangements; (2) patients who are expected to have minimal postoperative complications; (3) patients who are in good health (e.g., A.S.A. Class 1 or 2); (4) reliable patients and those with support systems (e.g., family and significant others willing to follow pre- and postoperative instructions); (5) patients who psychologically accept the concept of ambulatory surgery; and (6) cooperative surgeons, anesthesiologists, and nursing personnel.

4. **The answer is 4.** Traditionally, nursing care has been directed away from patient care activities into the administrative circle, which emphasizes the managerial role of the nurse, not clinical practice. Since this role requires more time away from the bedside, clinical performance competency would fall, and some nurses, who were unprepared for their new position, became frustrated as they tried to "practice" effective bedside nursing. A newer, more palatable solution to this problem is the establishment of a clinical ladder program, designed to promote clinical competence rather than remove nurses from bedside nursing practice. A clinical ladder program is described as a hierarchy of criteria, intended to provide a means of evaluation and development of nurses providing direct patient care. By incorporating this nontraditional approach to recognizing the competent clinical practitioner, nurses striving for excellence in clinical practice can see how their careers progress, and find the challenge of reaching the next level rewarding not only for themselves but for the patient, the institution, and their specialized nursing profession.

5. **The answer is 2.** The perioperative clinical nurse specialist (CNS) is the last step on the clinical ladder series, since the role not only signifies advanced clinical competence, but the candidate has, in addition to certification, attained an advanced degree in nursing as defined by the A.N.A. Position Paper for CNS: "The CNS is a nurse prepared at the graduate level, with focus in a specific clinical area. The CNS role incorporates clinical, administrative and educational aspects of professional nursing practice, with a goal of coordinating and managing the specific needs of the patient and/or family." A.N.A. (1978)

6. **The answer is 1.** Quality assurance (Q.A.) is described as a process intended to guarantee a level of excellence by comparing current practices to an established standard(s) to assure quality patient care. Seven characteristics established by the J.C.A.H.O. are applicable when reviewing a Quality Assurance program in nursing and its activities: (1) the Q.A. activities are planned, systematic, and on-going; (2) the Q.A. activities are comprehensive in scope; (3) the Q.A. activities are based on indicators and criteria that the department, service, or staff agree on and that are acceptable to the organization/institution; (4) the Q.A. activities are accomplished by routine collection and periodic evaluation of the collected data; (5) the Q.A.

activities result in appropriate actions to solve identified problems, or take other identified opportunities to improve patient care; (6) the Q.A. activities are continual and concurrent in an effort to ensure that improvements in care and performance are maintained; and (7) the Q.A. activities share within the institution on a routine basis the information delivered from the monitors and the evaluation data.

7. **The answer is 3.** For a Q.A. program to be effective, the design of the program should contain four essential elements or components: setting program objectives, promoting quality, activity monitoring, and performance assessment. The activities stated in choices 1, 2, and 4 relate to the first two of these elements: (1) Quality assurance begins with the establishment of goals and objectives, which form the foundation of the Q.A. program at all levels. The goals are usually derived from the desire to achieve standards. (2) The quality of a person's performance is related to his or her own standards of performance, skills in attaining them, and the support systems that reward acceptable performance. Examples include: staff development/skills training programs; continuing education--products, technology, personnel; employee performance appraisals; advanced education programs (specialty certification and advanced degrees); product evaluation task force; and development of positions or programs that may lead to recruitment and retention (e.g., perioperative nursing internship program).

8. **The answer is 4.** Choices 1 through 3 focus on the third and fourth element of an effective Q.A. program in perioperative nursing: activity monitoring and performance assessment. With **activity monitoring**, performances should be monitored by quality control and quality supervision. Examples of quality control include: (1) occurrence screening--a concurrent review of the intraoperative record or chart to identify deviations from the required procedure of documentation; and (2) nursing audits--with a focus on current clinical practice to identify potential or actual problems; the audits should include solutions for correction and be concurrent, requiring a follow-up for comparison. Examples of quality supervision/current monitoring include: (1) supervisory rounds, which can encourage and maintain a high standard of performance through visibility; and (2) incident tracking, which can determine whether there are any trends or recurrent problems and devise the necessary action(s) or recommendations to correct the identified problems. **Performance assessment** is the periodic assessment and evaluation of nursing care, using the pre-established standards, with corrective counseling as needed. Three aspects should be considered: (1) quality review--analysis of performance of employee and system; retrospective audits that indicate the quality of care; review of previous performances; trend of actions (if any); (2) quality evaluation--audits (criteria-based measurements of performance based on objective data) conducted on a regular basis with follow-up as needed; can be based on outcome standards and/or include medical audits (e.g., physician survey); and (3) quality approval --retrospective survey of performance of personnel and system from others (e.g., patients, hospital personnel, or outside agencies).

9. **The answer is 2.** A perioperative nursing internship program, conducted outside the hospital environment, has recently become more cost-effective than the previous one-on-one courses that were conducted in the hospital as staffing needs demanded, and through these extended programs, perioperative nursing as a specialty has again become part of nursing education. Since teaching has always been an integral part of the professional nurse's role, it was natural that perioperative nurses became involved with establishing methods to offer perioperative nursing practice to both entry level students and those wishing to expand their current knowledge through formal education. The perioperative nursing internship program, regardless of its setting, has become one of those methods, providing both a recruitment and a retention tool for hospitals, especially during the current critical shortage of nurses, and a means for nurses to further their formal education when the hospital is affiliated with a university.

10. **The answer is 2.** Many nursing actions have yet to be empirically tested for their effectiveness, including those related to perioperative nursing practice. Much of the research that does exist pertains to nurses rather than to the effects of nursing actions or how these actions have affected and/or changed client outcomes, and very little research has been specifically conducted relating to the practice of perioperative nursing. If perioperative nursing is to continue to grow and mature into a profession and receive the professional recognition and status it seeks, priority must be given to conducting research studies during the perioperative period that relate to clinical issues and client problems. Traditional nursing actions need to be tested in order to determine their effect, thereby demonstrating that perioperative nursing practice

is a planned process founded upon scientific research results rather than upon assumptions, hunches, or the performance of skills based on previous success or inherited practice.

Appendix A

Common Anesthetic Agents

STUDY OUTLINE

I. PREOPERATIVE MEDICATIONS

1. **Sedative-hypnotics**
   a. **Medication:** Nembutal (pentobarbital sodium)
      (1) **Desired effects:** reduces anxiety and promotes sleep.
      (2) **Adverse effects:** may cause confusion in the elderly; no analgesia actions.
2. **Anticholinergics**
   a. **Medication:** Atropine (atropine sulfate)
      (1) **Desired effects:** decreases secretions; prevents laryngospasms; prevents anesthesia-induced bradycardia.
      (2) **Adverse effects:** excessive dry mouth; tachycardia; blurred vision; restlessness; confusion; possible urinary retention.
   b. **Medication:** Robinul (glycopyrrolate)
      (1) **Desired effects:** Same as atropine (secretions decrease rapidly)--five to six times more potent than atropine.
      (2) **Adverse effects:** same as atropine: does not cross the blood-brain barrier, so C.N.S. effects are usually absent; longlasting dry mouth (good for outpatient surgery).
   c. **Medication:** Hyoscine (scopolamine)
      (1) **Desired effects:** same as atropine with additional sedative and tranquilizer effect.
      (2) **Adverse effects:** same as atropine; can produce C.N.S. depression and bradycardia. (More profound C.N.S. effects are due to ease of agent crossing blood-brain barrier).
3. **Narcotics**
   a. **Medication:** Demerol (meperidine HCI, synthetic)
      (1) **Desired effects:** analgesia with sedation and mild euphoria; rapid onset with short duration.
      (2) **Adverse effects:** C.N.S. disturbances; potent myocardial depressant; hypotension; syncope; bradycardia; nausea/vomiting; pupillary constriction.
   b. **Medication:** Morphine sulfate (generic)
      (1) **Desired effects:** analgesia with sedation; (peak analgesia within 50 to 90 minutes with intramuscular [I.M.] pain management up to 4 hours).
      (2) **Adverse effects:** C.N.S. disturbances, bradycardia; orthostatic hypotension; syncope; gastrointestinal (G.I.) disturbances.
   c. **Medication:** Sublimaze (fentanyl)
      (1) **Desired effects:** Same as morphine sulfate, but action is faster and less prolonged.
      (2) **Adverse effects:** 80 times more potent than morphine sulfate; if given rapid I.V. push, it can produce "frozen chest," circulatory depression, and cardiac arrest. (When given with other analgesics or C.N.S. depressants on board, use 1/4 to 1/2 usual dose.)
   d. **Medication:** Innovar (fentanyl and droperidol)

(1) **Desired effects**: General calmness with euphoria; analgesia (fentanyl); antiemetic/tranquilizer (droperidol).

(2) **Adverse effects**: Respiratory depression; hypotension; muscle rigidity; occasional dysphoria (outer tranquility with inner anxiety).

4. **Antianxiety/antiemetics**

    a. **Medication**: Vistaril (hydroxyzine)

       (1) **Desired effects**: reduces anxiety, with antiemetic property; mild skeletal muscle effect.

       (2) **Adverse effects**: drowsiness; dry mouth; headache; dizziness.

    b. **Medication**: Inapsine (droperidol)

       (1) **Desired effects**: reduces anxiety with antiemetic effects.

       (2) **Adverse effects**: orthostatic hypotension; tachycardia; drowsiness; mental depression; elevation of blood pressure following administration with parenteral analgesics, and despite the appearance of tranquility, calmness with severe inner irritability can occur.

    c. **Medication**: Valium (diazepam)

       (1) **Desired effects**: provides sedation and amnesia in 40 to 50 percent of patients; reduces anxiety and apprehension.

       (2) **Adverse effects**: respiratory depression; excessive drowsiness (long-acting effect postinjection can last up to 2 to 4 hours, with half-life remaining in the system 3 to 8 days); no analgesic effect.

    d. **Medication**: Versed (midazolam HCl)

       (1) **Desired effects**: short-acting depressant with clinical action similar to Valium with fewer adverse effects.

       (2) **Adverse effects**: three times more potent than Valium; decreased respiratory rate; laryngospasm; cardiac changes (ventricular).

5. **Antiemetics**

    a. **Medication**: Reglan (metoclopramide)

       (1) **Desired effects**: increases gastric motility with increase in lower esophageal sphincter tone; prevents nausea and vomiting.

       (2) **Adverse effects**: restlessness; headache; dizziness; sedation (use cautiously with anticholinergics and narcotics--can antagonize effects of these agents).

II. INHALATION AGENTS

A. PIONEER AGENTS

1. Chloroform (trichloromethane)
2. Ether (diethyl ether)

B. MODERN INHALATION AGENTS

1. **Halothane (fluothane)**

    a. **Characteristics**: safe to use over short term; produces a rapid, smooth induction; nonflammable and nonexplosive; very potent; used with nitrous oxide and muscle relaxants as its speed of emergence is intermediate; seldom causes nausea and vomiting; nonirritating to mucous membranes; excellent bronchodilator.

    b. **Risks and contraindications**: "shivering" is common during recovery; can cause cardiopulmonary depression and, when used with epinephrine, ventricular fibrillation; may cause decreased blood pressure by depressing the myocardium and dilating the peripheral blood vessels; **suspected of being hepatotoxic and therefore contraindicated in patients with liver disease; considered one of the "trigger" agents associated with malignant hyperthermia.**

2. **Penthrane (methoxyflurane)**

    a. **Characteristics**: potent; slow induction and emergence with some nausea and vomiting; effective in low doses; has muscle relaxant properties.

    b. **Risks and contraindications**: nephrotoxic and may have adverse renal effects, especially when used with certain antibiotics (e.g., tetracycline); effects potentiated by C.N.S depressants such as alcohol, which also prolong postoperative drowsiness and analgesia; contraindicated in patients with renal or liver disease.

3. **Ethrane (enflurane)**
    a. **Characteristics:** colorless, nonflammable; produces pleasant and rapid induction and emergence; good muscle relaxant and analgesic with little nausea and vomiting; excellent blockade to surgical stress related to adrenal hormone release; free of hepatic or renal toxicity; often used with intraabdominal surgery.
    b. **Risks and contraindications:** depresses respiration and lowers blood pressure, although with minimal alteration in cardiac rate or rhythm; can produce postoperative shivering; contraindicated in patients with seizures, head injuries, and certain obstetrical conditions.

4. **Forane (isoflurane)**
    a. **Characteristics:** newest and last of the hydrocarbon series to be released for general use; nonflammable and nonexplosive clear liquid; produces rapid induction and emergence with low incidence of nausea and vomiting; does not stimulate excessive secretions; no apparent renal or hepatic toxicity owing to minimal metabolism of the agent; excellent choice for neurosurgical procedures.
    b. **Risks and contraindications:** can produce respiratory irritation and therefore not recommended for children under 2 years of age; potent respiratory depressant; causes mild sinus tachycardia; shivering may be seen.

III. INTRAVENOUS AGENTS

A. BARBITURATES

1. **Pentothal (thiopental sodium--NSP)**
    a. **Characteristics:** ultra-short-acting; usually administered via bolus injection, with dose matched to kilogram weight of patient; produces rapid induction and emergence with decreased emergence delirium.
    b. **Risks and contraindications:** may produce respiratory and cardiac depression, so all preparation for ventilator support must be completed prior to administration; must be used with caution in patients with severe cardiac disease, myxedema, and neuromuscular disorders; **absolutely contraindicated in patients with porphyria,** a rare metabolic disorder; can produce shivering, prolonged somnolence, arrhythmias, and laryngospasm and bronchospasms; effects are irreversible.

2. **Brevital (methohexital sodium) and Surital (thiamylal sodium)**
    a. **Characteristics:** short acting; administered by bolus injection, with dose matched to kilogram weight of patient; Brevital is frequently used prior to electroconvulsive therapy (E.C.T.), oral surgery, gynecologic and urologic examinations, and closed reductions of fractures; Surital is mainly used with general anesthesia.
    b. **Risks and contraindications:** side effects are similar to Pentothal; may also cause muscular twitching, headache, excessive salivation, and acute allergic reactions; effects are irreversible.

B. NARCOTIC ANALGESICS

1. **Demerol (meperidine HCl)**
    a. Reversal agent = naloxone (narcan).
    b. Demerol acts within 10 to 15 minutes of injection, and is therefore slower than the other agents.
    c. When given I.V., Demerol should be diluted and given slowly; it can cause hypotension, bradycardia, and respiratory depression.

2. **Morphine sulfate (generic)**
    a. Reversal agent = naloxone (narcan).
    b. Morphine sulfate has little adverse effects on blood pressure, cardiac rate, or cardiac output; it acts within 5 to 7 minutes of injection and is usually the drug of choice when dealing with cardiac patients due to its cardiovascular stability.

   c. The pharmacology of morphine sulfate provides a reference base for narcotics.

3. Sublimaze (fentanyl)

   a. Sublimaze is 80 times more potent than morphine sulfate, and more rapid in action (1- to 2-minute onset); therefore, smaller dosages are recommended to achieve the same effect.

   b. Rapid injection of Sublimaze can result in a "frozen chest" syndrome, which can be reversed with a muscle relaxant such as Anectine.

   c. Sublimaze is shorter in duration than morphine sulfate (20-40 minutes), and is therefore an ideal agent for patients undergoing ambulatory surgery.

   d. Nonanesthesia personnel who administer Sublimaze, such as during a local procedure with I.V. sedation, should refer to hospital policy for administration guidelines, since it can produce cardiorespiratory complications.

   e. Reversal agent = naloxone (narcan).

4. Alfenta (alfentanil hydrochloride) and Sufenta (sufentanil citrate)

   a. Alfenta and Sufenta are derivatives of fentanyl. Both are similar to Sublimaze in action, yet differ in potency and duration of action.

   b. Like fentanyl, both can be used alone for short-duration procedures in bolus dosages, or for procedures lasting over 45 minutes via the continuous infusion method.

   c. Sufenta is 10 times more potent than Sublimaze, while Alfenta is one third to one quarter as potent and, unlike fentanyl, can produce nausea and vomiting (although the incidence is slight).

   d. When these agents are administered, respiratory maintenance should be constantly available; therefore, these modern synthetic narcotics can be administered only by qualified anesthesia personnel familiar with artificial ventilation and maintenance techniques.

   e. Reversal agent = naloxone (narcan).

5. Tranquilizers

   a. Valium, Versed, and Inapsine were previously mentioned as preoperative agents, but they too can be used as adjunct agents for general, regional, or local anesthesia.

   b. **Inapsine (droperidol)**

     (1) Inapsine potentiates both narcotics and barbiturates, with an onset of 10 minutes and a duration of 2 to 4 hours, to a maximum of 12 hours depending on the dosage and patient reaction.

     (2) It possesses strong antiemetic and antipsychotic properties, and can be mixed with fentanyl, producing Innovar, or given separately with other narcotics. Inapsine can produce hypotension and tachycardia.

   c. **Valium (diazepam)**

     (1) Valium can produce antegrade amnesia in 40 to 50 percent of patients, with good relaxation effects that last 8 to 12 hours after injection.

     (2) **Valium cannot be mixed with other agents**, but can be given at the same time. Respirations must be monitored, since it is a potent respiratory depressant.

     (3) Reversal agent = flumazenil (mazicon).

   d. **Versed (midazolam HCl)**

     (1) Versed is the newest of the tranquilizers. It has a minimal residual effect, yet in smaller doses provides potent antegrade amnesia in 70 to 80 percent of patients, without the adverse side effects of diazepam. It is three times more potent than Valium.

     (2) Versed is water soluble: therefore, it is easily diluted in the circulation and excreted.

     (3) Reversal agent = flumazenil (mazicon).

C. MUSCLE RELAXANTS (ANESTHESIA ADJUNCTS)

1. Depolarizing muscle relaxants

   a. **Succinylcholine (Anectine; Quelicin)**

     (1) Succinylcholine is a rapid acting agent (within 1 minute) with a short duration of action (3 to 10 minutes) depending on the amount given. It is frequently administered prior to intubation, and can be given either by bolus injection or continuous drip infusion when longer periods of muscle relaxation are required.

(2) Succinylcholine is slow to metabolize, and is the drug of choice to reverse "frozen chest syndrome," which can occur if fentanyl (Sublimaze) is given too quickly, or as an antidote for toxic reactions caused by local anesthetic agents.

(3) The **disadvantages** of succinylcholine include bradycardia, a transient rise in intraocular pressure, increased fasciculations, and postoperative myalgia. Drug requires refrigeration.

(4) Succinylcholine is contraindicated in patients with recent burns, muscle trauma, or neuromuscular disorders, and **is thought to be the major I.V. triggering agent for malignant hyperthermia.**

(5) NOTE: Since Anectine and Quelicin are clear, I.V. solutions should be colored to differentiate them from a standard I.V., thus avoiding accidental administration during a procedure.

2. **Nondepolarizing muscle relaxants**
   a. **Curare (d-Tubocurarine; tubocurarine; dTc)**
      (1) **Characteristics:** not widely used today; onset time is 3-5 minutes, with peak action occurring within 30 minutes and duration lasting up to 60 minutes.
      (2) **Risks and contraindications:** may cause a histamine release, with symptoms of tachycardia, hypotension, and bronchospasms, leading to cardiac arrhythmias; action is potentiated by several anesthetic agents (e.g., fluothane) and by some antibiotics; contraindicated in patients with crush injuries or fresh spinal cord injuries.
      (3) **Reversal agents** include neostigmine, pyridostigmine (Regonol), or edrophonium (Tensilon).
   b. **Pavulon (pancuronium bromide)**
      (1) **Characteristics:** longer acting and more potent than curare; administered by bolus injection; excellent for procedures of long duration.
      (2) **Risks and contraindications:** can increase heart rate and arterial pressure and therefore not recommended for patients with cardiac or hypertensive disorders; can cause residual muscle weakness and should be used cautiously in elderly or debilitated patients and in the presence of renal or hepatic impairment or neuromuscular disorders.
      (3) **Reversal agents** include neostigmine, Regonol, and Tensilon.
   c. **Flaxedil (gallamine triethiodide):** rarely used in today's anesthesia practice.
   d. **Norcuron (vercuronium bromide)**
      (1) **Characteristics:** intermediate duration muscle relaxant; more potent than Pavulon, with a shorter neuromuscular blocking effect; no known contraindications.
      (2) **Risks and contraindications:** prolonged recovery has been seen in patients with hepatic disease and conditions associated with acute circulatory disorders; must be reconstituted and protected from light; needs refrigeration after reconstitution and should be used within 8 hours.
      (3) **Reversal agents** include Regonol and neostigmine.
   e. **Tracrium (atracurium besylate)**
      (1) **Characteristics:** one of the newer muscle relaxants; faster recovery time than most other relaxants (8-10 minutes); unique in being broken down (physically) and spontaneously as long as patient maintains normal temperature and pH.
      (2) **Risks and contraindications:** can produce a histamine-like reaction when administered too fast; requires refrigeration; solution should be made fresh.
      (3) **Reversal agents** include neostigmine and atropine.
3. **Diprivan (propofol):** a total intravenous anesthetic agent and not specifically a muscle relaxant.
   a. **Characteristics:** used for induction and maintenance; rapid onset and emergence (5-10 minutes); usually administered via a control syringe; quickly eliminated from the system (half-life 30-60 minutes).
   b. **Risks and contraindications:** may cause pain if injected into a small vein.

Appendix B

Drugs Used in Surgery and Their Nursing Considerations

STUDY OUTLINE

I. **PREPARATION AND ADMINISTRATION GUIDELINES**

    1. **Reconstituted powders or liquid medications are delivered to the scrub nurse/technician by the circulating nurse.** The contents may be transferred via a sterile syringe or by pouring vial contents into an appropriate receptacle according to acceptable institutional policy. In either case, the procedure for accepting or preparing a drug requires the use of strict aseptic technique.

    2. As with any drug, the nurse must:

        a. Know the proper reconstitution and preparation procedures, using the manufacturer's recommendations and/or the institutional policies.

        b. Know the proper dosage, routes of administration, and possible complications and side effects of each drug administered.

        c. Check with the manufacturer's recommendations for storing a drug to maintain the drug's maximum effectiveness.

        d. Confirm the drug type and dosage requested prior to administration to the sterile field (both the scrub and circulator must do this). The drug should be checked for color and consistency, and if a change has been noticed, the product should not be used.

        e. Label each agent or agent in solution with the name and amount on the container/syringe after administration to the sterile field.

        f. Use a sterile decanting spout when mixing a drug in an I.V. bag (e.g., heparin solution) for delivery to the sterile field, to avoid contamination of the field.

        g. Document on the intraoperative record all drugs administered to the sterile field.

    3. As an added precaution, neither the circulating nurse nor the scrub nurse/technician can permit familiarity with a bottle shape or size, label, or color to interfere with the proper checking procedures. Poor technique and disregard for safety may result in injury to or adverse reaction by the patient.

II. **CATEGORIES OF DRUGS**

    1. **Drugs used in surgery include those that are administered parenterally; administered topically; administered in irrigation solution; or introduced into a hollow organ or duct for diagnostic purposes.**

    2. Pharmacologic agents are commonly placed into categories according to their similarities in action and/or their physiologic effect when introduced into the system.

    3. As with any medication, the nurse should have knowledge of the actions, methods of administration and nursing considerations associated with each drug. Unlike other medications administered by the nurse, administration of these agents does not require a written physician's order, since it is considered standard protocol during the intraoperative period, based on the physician preference card and/or a verbal order from the surgeon during surgery.

4. The following monograph describes the ten categories of drugs commonly administered in the operating room: antimicrobial agents (antiinfective; antibiotic); anticoagulants; hemostatic agents; oxytocics; steroids (antiinflammmatory); diagnostic imaging agents; dyes; diuretics; central nervous system agents; and emergency protocol drugs.

A. ANTIMICROBIAL (ANTIINFECTIVE; ANTIBIOTIC)

1. **General description:** Chemical agents that eliminate living organisms pathogenic to the host (patient). The methods for classifying these agents include:
   a. Mechanism of action--inhibition of protein synthesis, activity on the cell membrane, alteration of the nucleic acid metabolism.
   b. Spectrum of activity--gram positive or gram negative.
   c. Similarity in chemical structure--penicillins; cephalosporins; aminoglycosides; sulfonamides.
   d. Source--living organisms; chemical synthesis.
2. Selection is based on the organism's sensitivity, patient variations, and relative toxicity of the proposed agent.
3. Examples include, but are not limited to:
   - penicillins (e.g., ampicillin)
   - cephalosporins (e.g., cefazolin [Ancef])
   - aminoglycosides (e.g., neomycin sulfate; gentamycin sulfate [Garramycin])
   - sulfonamides (e.g., gantrisin)
   - others (e.g., bacitracin, choloromycetin, vancomycin, tetracycline)
4. **Administration method:** in saline irrigation solution.
5. **Nursing considerations in surgery**
   a. Although cephalosporins may be used for patients allergic to penicillin, some patients may show sensitivity and subsequently develop allergies to this group.
   b. All drugs in irrigation solution in the sterile field must be labeled to avoid confusion with plain solutions.
   c. All agents used in irrigation must be documented on the intraoperative record.

B. ANTICOAGULANTS

1. **General description:** Anticoagulants are given to prolong the time it takes blood to clot by preventing the conversion of fibrinogen to fibrin. In addition, they are used prevent the occurrence of clot enlargement or fragmentation (thromboembolism). Example: heparin.
2. **Administration method:** I.V. (administered by anesthesiologist); in irrigation solution (sterile field).
3. **Nursing considerations for surgery**
   a. It is clinically safer and far more accurate to measure the dose in units than in milligrams.
   b. Intravenous heparin must be administered via an infusion pump.
   c. Heparin should be administered in an isotonic sodium chloride solution (I.V.), not a sodium chloride irrigation solution.
   d. Heparin is available in U/mL as Beef Lung, Calciparine, and Lipo-Heparin. Check with physician as to preference.
   e. Document irrigation solution on intraoperative record.

C. HEMOSTATIC AGENTS

1. **General description:** Hemostatic agents reduce capillary bleeding and arrest blood flow, thereby assisting in blood clotting during surgery.
2. **Examples**
   - absorbable gelatin sponge (e.g., Gelfoam)
   - microfibrillar collagen (e.g., Avetine)
   - oxidized cellulose (e.g., Surgicel; Oxycel)
   - Topical Thrombin
   - systemic hemostatic (e.g., Amicar)

3. **Administration method:** placed topically on the bleeding surface to absorb blood and reduce bleeding.
4. **Nursing considerations for surgery**
   a. Topical Thrombin must be reconstituted before use, and is generally used with Gelfoam for greater absorbency.
   b. Amicar must be reconstituted, and is given I.V.
   c. Gelfoam does not have to be removed; however, the oxidized cellulose should be removed after hemostasis has been accomplished.
   d. Avitine is applied directly to the bleeding area in dry-powered form, but will adhere to wet gloves, instruments, or tissue surfaces. Handle with smooth, dry forceps.

D. OXYTOCICS

1. **General description:** Oxytocics are normally found in the posterior pituitary gland and stimulate smooth muscle of the uterus during childbirth, thereby forcing the uterus to contract and thus decreasing bleeding after a cesarean section. Examples: oxytocin (Pitocin) and methergine.
2. **Administration method:** added to I.V. (by anesthesiologist).
3. **Nursing considerations for surgery**
   a. Store at temperatures below 25° C (77° F); avoid freezing.
   b. Oxytocics can have an antidiuretic effect; monitor intake and output.
   c. They are usually administered after delivery of the placenta.
   d. Use cautiously in patients with a history of cervical or uterine surgery and in primigravida women over 35 years of age.
   e. Rotate bottle gently to distribute drug solution.
   f. Do not use ampules with discolored solution.
   g. I.V. methergine is used for emergencies only.

E. STEROIDS (ANTIINFLAMMATORY)

1. **General description:** Corticosteroids are hormones produced naturally by the adrenal cortex. They are used in surgery to reduce inflammation and possible postoperative swelling.
2. Examples include, but are not limited to:
   - decadron
   - hexadrol
   - Solu-Cortef
   - Solu-Medrol
   - Depo-Medrol
   - Aristocor
   - Kenalog
3. **Administration method:** administered parenterally to the affected site by the surgeon.
4. **Nursing considerations for surgery**
   a. Reconstitute according to manufacturer's recommendations.
   b. Agitate to dissolve particles prior to delivery.
   c. Label syringe on back table to avoid accidental usage.
   d. Provide scrub nurse/technician with a 19g needle for withdrawal and a 23g to 27g needle for injection (surgeon's preference).
   e. Hydrocortisone (Solu-Cortef) should be given deep I.M.
   f. Carefully check label for recommended route of administration.
   g. Document medication on intraoperative record.

F. DIAGNOSTIC IMAGING AGENTS

1. **General description:** Contrast imaging agents, also known as radiopaque media, are impenetrable by X-rays. They allow radiologic visualization of internal structures during operative procedures, such as intraoperative cholangiograms, cystoretrogrades, and so on. Depending on its structure,

the contrast media may be instilled directly into a duct or organ and may or may not be diluted with normal saline. Therefore, check with the surgeon for administration preferences.

2. Examples include, but are not limited to:
   - Renografin (cholangiography, hysterosalpingography)
   - Cystografin, Cysto-Conray (cystourethrography)
   - Hypaque
   - Hyskon
3. **Administration method:** direct instillation into duct or organ via tube or special catheter.
4. **Nursing considerations for surgery**
   a. Although the incidence of iodine hypersensitivity related to contrast media is low, preoperative assessment of problems associated with previous X-ray procedures should be reported immediately.
   b. Be prepared to treat any adverse reactions (usually with Benadryl) when using contrast media.
   c. The surgeon is responsible for instillation of the agent during the X-ray procedure.
   d. Label all syringes and check with surgeon as to dilution strength if requested or required.
   e. Document agent on intraoperative record.

G. DYES

1. **General description:** Solutions used to stain or mark a specific surface or area. Most solutions for skin marking have been replaced by sterile "marking pens"; however, dyes can also be used to color solutions or to test the patency of specific organs.
2. Examples include but are not limited to: methylene blue and indigo carmine.
3. **Administration methods:** added to solution; administered into structure; or used as a topical marker on skin.
4. **Nursing considerations for surgery**
   a. No adverse effects have been reported.
   b. May be diluted per surgeon's preference.
   c. Rinse container immediately after use as it may cause permanent discoloration.
   d. If instilled internally, document use on intraoperative record.

H. DIURETICS

1. **General description:** Diuretics reduce the body's total volume of water and salt by increasing their urinary excretion. This occurs mainly because diuretics impair sodium chloride reabsorption in the renal tubules. Additionally, diuretics can increase the osmotic pressure, inhibiting tubular reabsorption of water and electrolytes, thus reducing retention of water and possible reduction of swelling in traumatized areas, for example, the brain.
2. Examples include but are not limited to: furosemide (Lasix) and mannitol (Osmitrol).
3. **Administration method:** I.V. (by anesthesiologist).
4. **Nursing considerations for surgery**
   a. Lasix should be given over 1 to 2 minutes.
   b. Monitor serum potassium levels. Make note of patients on digitalis.
   c. Mannitol solution often crystalizes, especially at low temperatures. Therefore store it in a solution-warming cabinet.
   d. Do not use solution with dissolved crystals.
   e. Hemodynamic monitoring equipment should be available (e.g., central venous pressure catheter, Foley catheter with urimeter).

I. CENTRAL NERVOUS SYSTEM AGENTS

1. **General description:** Central nervous system (CNS) agents are those that affect the body's response to stimuli, coordination of activity, and level of consciousness. This category includes agents such as analgesics, tranquilizers, anticonvulsants, and anesthetic agents (see Chapter 4 and Appendix A). All these agents can alter the patient's perception of pain or well being, and must

be used with extreme caution since unfavorable interactions and/or reactions are often ncountered.

2. **Examples**
   a. **Analgesics:** bind with opiate receptors at many sites in the central nervous system, altering both pain and emotional response to pain. Example include but are not limited to:
      - fentanyl and fentanyl derivatives (Sublimaze; Alfenta; Sufenta)
      - morphine sulfate
      - meperidine HCl (Demerol)
      - codeine
      - hydromorphone (Dilaudid)

      NOTE: In high doses, narcotic analgesics can be further classified as anesthetic agents, and are administered by the anesthesiologist and/or C.R.N.A., not the perioperative nurse.

   b. **Tranquilizers:** reduce anxiety without inducing sleep. Most tranquilizers have muscle-relaxant and anticonvulsive properties, and closely resemble sedative-hypnotics in pharmacologic properties. Examples include, but are not limited to:
      - diazepam (Valium)
      - midazolam (Versed)
      - droperidol (Inapsine)

3. **Administration method:** I.V.

4. **Nursing considerations for surgery**
   a. Know the institutional policies for administration protocols before administering these agents.
   b. During a local procedure, document all patient response every 15 minutes or more often as needed.
   c. Keep antagonist agents available when administering these agents.

5. Chapter 4 and Appendix A contain further discussion specific to anesthetic agents, narcotics, and tranquilizers.

J. EMERGENCY PROTOCOL DRUGS

1. **General description:** This category includes: cardiac stimulants (e.g., epinephrine); vasoconstrictors (e.g., levophed); vasodilators (e.g., nipride); cardiotonics (e.g., digitalis); antiarrhythmics (e.g., lidocaine).

2. **Nursing considerations for surgery**
   a. The perioperative nurse should be prepared through annual Basic Life Support review, to correctly handle the common drugs used during emergency situations, including dosages, administration routes, and indications for use.
   b. By following the current American Heart Association protocol for Advanced Cardiac Life Support (A.C.L.S.), the perioperative nurse can deliver comprehensive emergency care and assist as necessary in the preparation and administration of emergency drugs and solutions.

K. SUPPLEMENTAL DRUGS AND SOLUTIONS

1. In addition to the previous categories, the surgical patient may receive additional drugs and solutions to maintain hemostasis during the perioperative period. These agents include:
   a. **Volume expanders,** to increase circulating fluid volume. (Examples include hespan, albumin, and hetastarch.)
   b. **Blood and blood components,** to restore cell volume. (Examples include fresh-frozen plasma, washed packed cells, whole blood, cryoprecipitate, and factor VIII.)
   c. **Intravenous solutions,** with or without electrolytes. (Examples include D_5W, D_5LR, Lactate Ringer's.)

Appendix C

Surgical Procedures and Nursing Considerations

- **CATEGORIES OF SURGICAL PROCEDURES**

- **GENERAL SURGERY AND NURSING IMPLICATIONS**

- **THE PEDIATRIC PATIENT IN SURGERY**

STUDY OUTLINE

For a complete survey of surgical procedures and their nursing considerations, review Chapter 14 of the text, *Perioperative Nursing: Principles and Practice*, by Susan S. Fairchild.

I. **CATEGORIES OF SURGICAL PROCEDURES**

1. Surgical procedures, for descriptive purposes, are traditionally classified in groups according to their related anatomic structure or physical system, and/or to the specialist performing the procedure (e.g., general, gynecologist, etc.).

2. **With the incorporation of the Nursing Process, however, procedures have been reclassified for ease of recognition, according to the reason or reasons for the planned surgical intervention, allowing the perioperative nurse and the surgical team to create a more realistic and effective plan for individualizing patient care.** While the traditional descriptions still exist, the redefining of surgical procedures produced six general categories, which can overlap the traditional descriptions depending on the specific anatomic area(s) involved.

3. Knowledge of these categories, and the specific nursing considerations associated with each procedure, can assist the team in preparing and selecting the appropriate equipment and supplies requested by the surgeon, but more important, they can enhance the ability to anticipate the need for special equipment and supplies that may not be specifically requested but by the nature of the surgery may be needed.

4. **The most important factors, regardless of the proposed surgical intervention, are team work and the ability to provide a safe and therapeutic environment for both the patient and the team.**

A. **CATEGORY I: SURGERY INVOLVING THE LOSS OF A BODY PART, ORGAN, OR FUNCTION**

1. Examples include, but are not limited to, hysterectomy; limb amputation; enucleation of an eye; mastectomy.

2. **Perioperative nursing considerations**
   a. **Patient/family/significant others**
   (1) Recognition of psychic stress, related to:
   - Grieving process
   - Loss of positive body image/self-esteem
   - Family/significant other response

      (2)   Support systems/outside agencies to assist with adjustment.

      (3)   Patient preparation and education.

  b. Procedure

      (1)   Selection and preparation of specialty instrumentation, supplies, equipment.

      (2)   Positioning, prepping, draping, sequence of surgery.

B. CATEGORY II: SURGERY INVOLVING THE REMOVAL OF A TUMOR, CYST, OR FOREIGN BODY

1.   Examples include, but are not limited to, ovarian cystectomy; craniotomy (for tumor); extraction of a bullet; removal of painful hardware.

2.   **Perioperative nursing considerations**

  a. Patient/family/significant others

      (1)   Recognition of psychic stress, related to:
- Fear of the unknown
- Outcome/diagnosis
- Disfiguration, death
- Dysfunction of body part

  b. Procedure

      (1)   Type of procedure, e.g., curative, palliative, emergent, elective.

      (2)   Trauma/triage activation (personnel).

      (3)   Procedural guidelines/law enforcement protocol:
- Chain of command (bullet, etc.)
- Selection and preparation of specialty instrumentation
- Positioning, prepping, draping, sequence of surgery

C. CATEGORY III: SURGERY PERFORMED FOR DIAGNOSTIC PURPOSES

1.   Examples include, but are not limited to, mediastinoscopy, frozen section specimens, cystoscopy; cardiac catheterization; endoscopic procedures (colon, stomach, biliary, etc.).

2.   **Perioperative nursing considerations**

  a. Patient/family/significant others

      (1)   Recognition of psychic stress, related to:
- Changes in lifestyle, self-esteem, independence
- Fear of unknown diagnosis

      (2)   Patient preparation.

      (3)   Discharge planning and follow-up care.

  b. Procedure

      (1)   Additional procedures required.

      (2)   Additional procedure set-ups as needed.

      (3)   Selection and preparation of specialty instrumentation.

      (4)   Positioning, prepping, draping, sequence of surgery.

D. CATEGORY IV: SURGERY FOR INSERTION, REMOVAL, OR APPLICATION OF A PROSTHESIS, GRAFT, TRANSPLANTED ORGAN, OR THERAPEUTIC DEVICE

1.   Examples include, but are not limited to, pacemaker insertion; venous-access graft; kidney transplant; insertion of total hip arthroplasty.

2.   **Perioperative nursing considerations**

  a. Patient/family/significant others

      (1)   Recognition of psychic stress, related to:
- Acceptance of reconstructed/replaced organ
- Postoperative effect on current lifestyle

      (2)   Patient preparation and education: physical imitations, if any, and for what period of time (dependence).

    (3) Prophylactic antibiotic therapy.
    (4) Discharge planning and follow-up care; teaching.
  b. Procedure
    (1) Preparation of implantable devices.
    (2) Special set-ups, additional personnel, instrumentation, etc.
    (3) Positioning, prepping, draping, sequence of surgery.
    (4) Prevention of postoperative infections.

E. CATEGORY V: SURGERY FOR RECONSTRUCTION OR COSMETIC REVISION

1. Examples include, but are not limited to, rhinoplasty; repair of cleft lip; breast reconstruction; skin grafting (post-burn); otoplasty.
2. **Perioperative nursing considerations**
  a. Patient/family/significant others
    (1) Recognition of psychic stress, related to:
      • Self-image (need for seeking help)
      • Postoperative acceptance (posttrauma)
      • Acceptance (change in image)
    (2) Patient preparation and education.
    (3) Discharge planning and follow-up care (sequential surgeries required).
  b. Procedure
    (1) Management of patient under local anesthesia.
    (2) Alloplastic/autogenous materials (grafting).
    (3) Selection and preparation of instrumentation and specialty supplies.
    (4) Positioning, prepping, draping, sequence of surgery.

F. CATEGORY VI: SURGERY TO ESTABLISH DRAINAGE OR REESTABLISH A PASSAGEWAY

1. Examples include, but are not limited to, colostomy; insertion of chest tubes; V-P shunt; colostomy closure; colon resection (with anastomosis); tuboplasty (reestablishment of fallopian tubes).
2. **Perioperative nursing considerations**
  a. Patient/family/significant others
    (1) Recognition of psychic stress, related to:
      • Changes in lifestyle, body image
      • Acceptance by family, coworkers, etc.
      • Management of artificial apparatus (e.g., colostomy, ileostomy, etc.)
      • Patient expectations (tuboplasty)
    (2) Patient preparation and education.
    (3) Activation of support systems/discharge planning.
  b. Procedure
    (1) Specialty supplies required.
    (2) Special set-ups as required.
    (3) Positioning, prepping, draping, sequence of surgery.

II. GENERAL SURGERY AND NURSING IMPLICATIONS

1. **General surgery** encompasses operations of the digestive system structures, including the gastrointestinal tract, biliary system (spleen, pancreas, and liver), hernias of the abdominal wall, and procedures of the rectum and the breast. Included also in this category are surgeries involving the thyroid gland and associated structures, and the esophagus.
2. **General surgery provides the foundation for all surgical procedures.** Inherent in all general surgical procedures is:
  a. Most procedures require similar instrumentation, as well as special items for rectal, breast, and thyroid procedures. The gastrointestinal instruments can be used interchangeably for

various procedures involving the stomach and intestines.
b. **A central core of knowledge and skills is common to all surgical specialties,** based on similar instrumentation, positioning, prepping and so on.
c. Diagnosis, preoperative, intraoperative, and postoperative care of the patient with diseases involving organs of the alimentary tract, abdomen and its contents, breast, neck, and immediately adjacent structures of the endocrine system are involved with general surgical procedures.
d. Employment and knowledge of endoscopic techniques for diagnosis and treatment may also be required, in addition to an understanding of general principles of anesthesiology and pathophysiology.

A. PERIOPERATIVE NURSING IMPLICATIONS

1. Frequently, the surgery performed depends on the results of the biopsy and frozen section obtained at the time of surgery, while the patient is under anesthesia.
2. **Although the patient has been informed preoperatively of an anticipated procedure, the fear of the unknown is cause for apprehension and anxiety. The perioperative nurse must convey support and concern for the patient, both physiologically and psychologically.**
3. Operability of malignant tumors may be determined only after a thorough exploration during surgery, and alternative therapy may be decided at this time. The perioperative nurse must be flexible to these situations, and be ready to assist the surgical team should a change in supplies be required.
4. Frequently, **two set-ups must be prepared,** depending on the diagnosis and/or anticipated procedures. Two special techniques used with specific procedures, which require special handling, include:
   a. **Bowel technique:** used when the anatomy involves the jejunum or structures below the jejunum, in which instruments coming in contact with this area are isolated from other instruments, and a separate, clean closing set-up is used (new instruments, change of gown and gloves, and reinforcement of drapes around the incision).
   b. **No-touch technique:** not as severe as bowel technique, yet requires isolation of the instruments contacting a contaminated structure (e.g., appendix, gallbladder, lung, cervix).
5. Positioning and draping for general surgery areas are as varied as the procedure itself, although **a general laparotomy pack, with a fenestrated sheet (transverse or horizontal), will usually be appropriate for most procedures.** Extra pillows, padding, and positional aides should be available.
6. Instrumentation is varied and is selected for a specific need, in addition to a generic tray (major laparotomy tray), which can accomplish the initial exploration and closure of the abdomen.
7. A variety of anesthesia techniques are used during general surgery, depending on the condition of the patient and the type of surgery anticipated.
8. A number of general surgical procedures are adaptable to an ambulatory setting, while others are extremely extensive and require the patient to be hospitalized following the procedure.

B. SPECIAL NURSING CONSIDERATIONS

For procedures performed in the abdominopelvic cavity, the following considerations should be reviewed and applied as necessary, depending on the surgical procedure being performed:

1. **The electrosurgical unit (ESU) is frequently used, but in some cases, a laser may be used, with or without the ESU.** The ESU pencil tips may vary, depending on the specific structure/area involved.
2. A **nosogastric tube (NG tube)** is frequently inserted during abdominal surgery by the anesthesiologist, to decompress the stomach during surgery.
3. **Following entry into the abdominal cavity, Ray-Tec (4 x 4) sponges should be replaced by laparotomy sponges.** Ray-Tecs should only be used on a sponge stick for hemostasis or blunt dissection in deep areas.

4. **Suction should always be available, even on simple cases.** The Poole abdominal tip or the Yankauer tip may be used, depending on the circumstances; therefore, both should be available.
5. **Drains can be used as either retractors (e.g., Penrose) or for wound drainage.** They are either placed along the incision line or used through a stab wound incision. The drain should be moistened first with saline, then passed to the surgeon or placed on an instrument (Kelly clamp) and passed.
6. **Prior to closure, the wound is often irrigated with saline solution.** This solution should be warm (not hot) to prevent systemic shock to the system, and may contain antibiotics as per surgeon's preference card. The amount of irrigation must be subtracted from the suction canister, in order to measure accurately the blood loss during surgery.
7. **The insertion of an indwelling Foley catheter is not unusual for involved abdominal procedures, to maintain an accurate record of intake and output during the surgery.** Consult with the surgeon and the anesthesiologist prior to beginning the skin prep for possible insertion.
8. **All dyes, medications, and solutions on the back table *must* be labeled with the name and amount of medication.** Sterile water should not be on the back table, unless specifically requested by the surgeon (for cancer tumors) and labeled appropriately.

III. THE PEDIATRIC PATIENT IN SURGERY

1. **It is important for the surgical team members to realize that children respond very differently to their fears and anxieties than adults:** they are not "little adults." In most cases, children cannot understand the surgical environment or the reason for the planned surgical intervention, and the perioperative nurse and surgical team members must approach children with an awareness of these fears, to protect the child from an experience that may be emotionally damaging.
2. **Anxiety related to separation from the family is the child's most overwhelming feeling.** They can feel abandoned, alone, and afraid while awaiting surgery, or worse, they can feel that the separation is a form of punishment for something he or she has done that was "bad." To help overcome these fears, the perioperative nurse who cares for the child during the surgical experience needs to be near the child and provide reassurance that he or she will be reunited with the family after surgery, and that the family is waiting for the child in the child's room or outpatient surgery area.
3. **Classification of pediatric patients:** Pediatric patients are generally grouped according to the following age groups (biologic grouping):
   a. Neonate   Birth to 1 month
   b. Infant   Up to 1 year
   c. Toddler   1 to 3 years
   d. Preschooler 3 to 6 years
   e. School age   6 to 11 years
   f. Adolescent   11 to 18 years

A. PEDIATRIC SURGICAL PROCEDURES

1. Pediatric surgery involves all specialty areas and is usually classified into three major divisions:
   a. **Surgery involving congenital anomalies:** A congenital anomaly involves any deviation from normal anatomy and/or location of an organ or any part of the body. Mortality rates in the neonate are influenced by three uncontrollable factors usually associated with congenital anomalies: (1) multiplicity of anomalies, (2) premature birth, and (3) low birth weight (failure to thrive).
   b. **Surgery associated with an acquired disease process:** Systemic and/or specific organ infections or disease, malignant tumors, or benign lesions can occur in children as they do in the adult, and like the adult, the condition may be treated surgically, usually without further difficulty to the child, depending on the pathophysiologic cause and location.
   c. **Surgery performed for repair of traumatic injuries:** Accidental injury is the leading cause of death or disfigurement in children. Injury can occur during the birth process or any time thereafter, to any part of the body. It is imperative that diagnosis be made quickly to minimize

long-term effects of the injury, since the margin for error in diagnosis and treatment of a child is less than that in an adult with a similar injury.
2. Technical advancements and a greater understanding of the special needs of the child in surgery have advanced pediatric surgery so that the anomalies and injuries that may not have been treated in previous years can now be treated with a successful outcome for the patient.
3. Pediatric surgery is a specialty within the field of surgery, and the surgeons who perform pediatric procedures have an expanded understanding of not only the technical aspects of the procedures, but also the unique psychologic and pathophysiologic problems involving the child from birth through adolescence.

B. PERIOPERATIVE NURSING CONSIDERATIONS

1. **Because of the uniqueness of the child, the perioperative nurse should be aware of several crucial factors affecting the outcome of the surgical event. These include, but are not limited to, metabolism, fluid and electrolyte balance, temperature regulation, cardiovascular and pulmonary responses, infection, safety, and pain management during the preoperative and postoperative phases.**
2. General nursing considerations for pediatric surgical care should include the following areas:
   a. **Maintenance of body temperature and/or prevention of heat loss considerations**
      (1) Transport neonates and infants in a heated isolette.
      (2) Adjust operating room temperature at least 10 minutes before the start of the procedure.
      (3) Use thermal blankets (e.g., K-Pad), head covering, radiant heat lamps, or a combination of these for all pediatric procedures.
      (4) Use a soft roll or other means to cover the extremities to assist in preserving body heat.
      (5) Warm all I.V., irrigation, and skin prep solutions prior to administration and/or use.
      (6) Continuously monitor external and/or internal body temperature throughout the procedure.
   b. **Monitoring of fluid and electrolyte status**
      (1) Accurately measure all irrigation solutions used.
      (2) Weigh sponges if significant blood loss is anticipated. Immediate weighing of sponges reduces the evaporation factor.
      (3) Report all fluid and blood loss to anesthesiologist for prompt intervention.
   c. **Proper use of restraints to aid in position and provide immobility**
      (1) Use a mummy-like wrap for newborns and small infants.
      (2) Use soft, well-padded, nonconstricting extremity restraints.
      (3) Prevent cardiovascular compromise or respiratory embarrassment while restrained.
   d. **Adherence to skin care precautions to avoid chemical burns or skin breakdown**
      (1) Avoid pooling of solutions in or under the patient.
      (2) Avoid the use of direct application of adhesive tape whenever possible. Use hypoallergenic tape (e.g., Durapore; Micropore), or create a double-sided tape.
      (3) Pad pressure points (e.g., sacrum, elbows, heels, and knees) to avoid skin breakdown and nerve injuries.
   e. **Avoidance of injury related to positioning and safety**
      (1) For small infants and neonates, drop the foot and/or head of the operating table to facilitate easier access to the patient.
      (2) Avoid hyperextension and/or hyperflexion of jointed areas.
      (3) *Never leave a child unattended on the operating table*, even if he or she is restrained.
      (4) Restrain the child with your body, covering the patient during induction of anesthesia if necessary.
      (5) Remain with the anesthesiologist until the child is stable and all monitoring and I.V. lines are secure.
      (6) For small children and infants, carry the child to the operating room instead of transporting him or her in a crib.
      (7) When transporting a child in a crib, keep the side-rails up at all times.

3. **Preoperative preparation**
   a. **Preoperative teaching is most important for pediatric patients and their families.** A formal program should be designed to meet the unique needs of the patient through "Show and Tell" with objects from surgery (e.g., masks for the child to play with and/or tour of the holding area). If possible, a tour or view of an operating room accompanied by the parent and the perioperative nurse, in addition to seeing and talking with the team members in O.R. attire, can reduce the anxiety of seeing strange people in strange clothing.
   b. The child should be allowed to bring his or her favorite toy or stuffed animal with them to surgery, and whenever possible let the parents remain with the child in the holding area prior to surgery.
   c. The shave prep should not be needed except for cranial surgery or surgery in the adolescent, and because of skin sensitivity, a depilatory is not recommended.

C. **SPECIAL EQUIPMENT/SUPPLIES**

1. **Instrumentation**
   a. Specific instruments, designed to accommodate the size of a child, include those normally found on an adult tray. Size and weight are more critical factors; very small and delicate instruments must be used to protect and preserve anatomic structures. For example, hemostats with fine points, noncrushing vascular clamps that permit occlusion of major vessels, and lightweight instruments that will not inhibit respirations should be part of a basic pediatric tray. In addition, instruments should never be laid on top of the patient when they are not in use (which is often done with adults), since it could restrict circulation to that area or cause a bruise.
   b. **Surgery performed on adolescents usually requires the use of an adult instrument tray.** However, discussion by surgical team members to determine the appropriate tray for the age and weight of the patient will provide an effective surgical outcome.
2. **Supplies/equipment**
   a. **Disposable drape sheets without a fenestration are often advantageous,** since the surgeon can create the opening to fit the proposed surgical approach, especially for neonates and small infants. Towels with small towel clips and a pediatric drape sheet may be used for most surgical procedures involving children, while adult drape sheets are usually preferred for adolescents.
   b. **Ray-Tec (4 x 4) sponges are frequently used with small Laps or "tapes" (4 x 18) in place of the large laparotomy sponges.** Dissector sponges (e.g., Kittners) are frequently used for blunt dissection, preserving surrounding structures.
   c. **The electrosurgical unit may be replaced by a handheld battery-operated cautery unit for neonatal and infant surgery, or a fine-tipped bipolar cautery forceps may be used.** Should the electrosurgical unit be preferred, a pediatric ground pad (dispersive electrode) is chosen based on the size of the patient. An adult ground pad should *never* be used unless the size of the patient is comparable to the size of the dispersive electrode surface area.
   d. **Sutures, ranging from size 0-0-0 to 5-0, are most common for delicate, fragile tissue.** The material can be either absorbable or nonabsorbable depending on the wound need, wedged to a 1/2-in. or 3/8-in. circle needle. A subcuticular closure is usually performed with small Steri Strips used to help approximate the skin edges, while small skin staples may be preferred for the adolescent patient.
   e. **Catheters as small as size 8 French are available if needed for neonates and infants.** For urinary retention, a Foley catheter with a 3-mL balloon is preferred, and a pediatric urometer will provide a more accurate measurement of urinary output. If a stomach tube is needed a plain or whistle-tipped catheter may be used, depending on the surgeon's preference.
   f. Since adhesive tape is often abrasive to young, tender skin, **an adhesive spray, or collodion, is frequently used with Steri Strips over a small incision** (especially when a subcuticular closure has been used). A stockinette, placed over the dressing of an extremity, can protect it from soiling and help keep the dressing in place, yet facilitate an easy dressing change when needed.

D. AMBULATORY SURGERY AND THE PEDIATRIC PATIENT

1. Since separation can produce the greatest anxiety for the child, many pediatric patients are now being safely managed as either ambulatory (same-day) or short stay (23-hour) surgery patients, depending on the type of surgery, the individual need of the patient, and the set-up of the institution.

2. Procedures such as hernia repair, circumcision, cystoscopy, and corrective eye muscle surgery are just a few of the procedures that can be accommodated by ambulatory surgery, while tonsillectomies or open/closed reduction of fractures may require additional monitoring and therefore a short-stay procedure may be the safest method. Either way, the child is less traumatized since separation is shortened, eliminating a traumatic hospitalization.

3. During the preoperative period, the child should undergo the routine preoperative laboratory studies, a medical history, and a physical examination either as an outpatient or in the physician's office, and receive an explanation of the proposed surgical procedure by the surgeon. The nursing assessment and preoperative teaching program should include home care instructions, with specific emphasis related to diet, activity restrictions, and adverse signs and symptoms related to the procedure to be alert for during the recovery phase.

4. Postoperatively, the child should be taken to the PACU for close monitoring until physiologic signs and symptoms are stable. The child can then be transported to the respective second-stage recovery area for observation, and any additional teaching or discharge instructions for the parent(s) can be discussed during this time. The child is usually ready for discharge 1 to 2 hours postoperatively. For infants and younger children, the criteria for discharge should usually include the ability to drink fluids and/or to urinate, assuring the full recovery of the swallowing reflex and adequate kidney function. If short-stay is recommended, a rooming-in arrangement may be available for the parent to avoid any trauma or fear during the postoperative period.

Comprehensive Practice Examination

Allow a maximum of three hours for this test. Answers and explanations begin on page 346.

1. **Mr. J., 52 years old, is scheduled for a coronary artery bypass graft procedure. During the admission interview, the patient seems anxious and tells the perioperative nurse that he "didn't really understand a lot of the things the doctor said" about his surgery. The *best* action for the nurse to take is to:**

   1. *explain the surgery in words that the patient can understand, then have the patient sign the consent form.*

   2. *have the patient sign the consent form, but attach a note to the chart informing the patient's physician that the patient needs more information before surgery.*

   3. *call the patient's physician to report the patient's need for additional information, and notify the charge nurse of a potential schedule delay.*

   4. *assure the patient that anxiety sometimes changes one's ability to hear what is being said; go over available teaching materials; and ask the patient to sign the consent form.*

2. **Mrs. S. is a 68-year-old woman scheduled for a left nephrectomy related to chronic pyelonephritis. In anticipation of the need to replace up to several units of blood during the course of the procedure, the perioperative nurse plans for use of the cell saver unit for autologous blood recovery. In reviewing Mrs. S.'s chart, the perioperative nurse would be *most* concerned about which of the following factors?**

   1. *A history of cancer.*

   2. *A hemoglobin value of 11 gm/100 mL.*

   3. *$PCO_2 = 48$; $pH = 7.30$.*

   4. *The absence of a family member to sign the consent form.*

Questions 3-11 refer to the following patient information:

Mr. T., 76 years old, is scheduled for surgical removal of a cataract and an intraocular lens implant in his right eye. While he has known about his cataracts for about three years, Mr. T.'s vision suddenly became vary blurry in his "good eye". His physician was not hopeful that another prescription change in his eyeglasses would significantly improve his vision. Mr. T. is identified as a "heavy cigarette smoker" and has had emphysema for several years. He is scheduled to have the procedure under local anesthesia in the Day Surgery Unit.

3. **In a preoperative telephone interview with Mr. T., the perioperative nurse should encourage Mr. T. to:**

    1. *come to the hospital for pulmonary function studies before surgery.*

    2. *complete one period of exercise each day until surgery.*

    3. *abstain from smoking until healing from surgery is complete.*

    4. *drink eight glasses of water each day until the day prior to surgery, to help liquefy secretions.*

4. **One goal the perioperative nurse has for Mr. T. is for safety to be maintained. In addition to the diagnosis of *Potential for injury*, what other safety-related nursing diagnosis should the nurse be prioritizing in her care of this patient?**

    1. *Impaired gas exchange.*

    2. *Anxiety.*

    3. *Potential for impaired skin integrity.*

    4. *Sensory/perceptual alterations.*

5. **The perioperative nurse is ready to begin the preoperative instillation of eye drops to Mr. T's right eye as indicated in the surgeon's orders. Prior to administering this medication, the *best* way for the perioperative nurse to verify that the right eye is the "correct" eye is to:**

    1. *verbally verify this information with the patient.*

    2. *review the history and physical in the chart.*

    3. *verify the procedure with the surgery schedule.*

    4. *check the informed consent form for agreement.*

6. **In preparing for Mr. T's surgical skin prep, the perioperative nurse should be aware that:**

    1. *chlorhexidine gluconate is the prep solution of choice.*

    2. *the prep solution should be rinsed off with warm, sterile water.*

    3. *light, mechanical friction with the scrub sponge will be most effective in preparing the skin.*

    4. *the prep should begin at the forehead and proceed in a circular motion around the eye.*

7. **In order to effectively monitor Mr. T. during the procedure, the perioperative nurse should obtain baseline information regarding:**

    1. *blood pressure, temperature, and EKG reading.*

    2. *pulse, respirations, and potassium value.*

    3. *blood pressure, respirations, and oxygen saturation.*

    4. *pulse, oxygen saturation, and potassium value.*

8. During the procedure, Mr. T. complains of an increasing headache. His heart rate increases from 80 to 120 beats per minute, and he shows visible signs of apprehension and sweating. In this situation, the perioperative nurse should first:

   1. *start an I.V. line.*

   2. *administer oxygen.*

   3. *run an EKG strip.*

   4. *report the observations to the surgeon.*

9. Preoperative teaching for Mr. T. should include which of the following?

   1. *Mr. T. will be asked to deep breathe and cough every 15 minutes postoperatively.*

   2. *Mr. T. should expect his eyesight to be almost normal after surgery; he should bring some light reading material to help him endure the recovery period.*

   3. *Mr. T. should expect to wear an eye patch and metal shield for the next month.*

   4. *Mr. T. should understand that the eye drops he receives before surgery may make him sensitive to light and may blur his vision.*

10. The intervention of asking Mr. T. to repeat verbally the discharge instructions to the perioperative nurse, including a description of which physical signs and symptoms should prompt him to call his physician after he is home, is directed at achieving which desired outcome?

    1. *The patient participates in the rehabilitation process.*

    2. *The patient is free from infection.*

    3. *The patient is free from harm.*

    4. *The patient's skin integrity is maintained.*

11. In reviewing discharge instructions with Mr. T., the perioperative nurse is *most* concerned that he understand:

    1. *the recommended activity limitations to be observed.*

    2. *the anticoagulant action of aspirin.*

    3. *that drainage from the right eye is to be expected.*

    4. *that the eye patch should be removed every two hours to check for bleeding.*

12. Mr. W. is a 68-year-old man who has just undergone a cholecystectomy. PACU labwork results are Hct. = 32, Hgb. = 10, K = 3.6, WBC = 7,500, Na = 138. Based on this information, the nurse's *primary* concern for Mr. W. postoperatively is related to:

    1. *cardiac arrhythmias.*

    2. *muscle weakness.*

3. *wound healing.*

4. *infection.*

13. **The circulating nurse involved in microsurgery must know how to care for and position the operating microscope. When caring for microscope lenses, it is important** *always* **to:**

    1. *firmly tighten the lens into the scope.*

    2. *clean the lens before each case with a 0.5% alcohol solution.*

    3. *attach the lens to the microscope over a padded surface.*

    4. *change the light bulb between each patient use.*

14. **Mr. P., a 27-year-old male, is brought to the emergency room unresponsive following a fall off of his roof while shoveling snow. After evaluation by the emergency room, Mr. P. is rushed to the operating room with a diagnosis of intracranial bleeding and an A.S.A. classification of Class 4E. In the preoperative assessment, the perioperative nurse finds no evidence of a history, physical, or informed consent on the chart. Because Mr. P. has been identified as Class 4E, the perioperative nurse knows that:**

    1. *it is imperative to have a thorough history on the chart before surgery begins.*

    2. *Mr. P. has been declared legally dead, and family members must be found to inquire about donor possibilities.*

    3. *surgery must be initiated immediately without the history and physical or signed consent form.*

    4. *anesthesia should be called immediately to perform a "mini" assessment before surgery proceeds.*

Questions 15-22 refer to the following patient information:

Mr. R., a 68-year-old retired executive, is admitted for treatment of benign prostatic hypertrophy. During the preoperative history and physical, Mr. R. reports frequent urination, including several trips to the bathroom at night, and a decrease in the size of his urinary stream. Upon physical examination by his physician, he was diagnosed with an enlarged prostate. As his symptoms seem to be getting worse, Mr. R. has been scheduled for a transurethral resection of the prostate gland (T.U.R.P.) with a spinal block. Mr. R. had a cystoscopy several years ago and feels fairly comfortable with the idea of surgery. He has some concerns about being conscious during surgery, however.

15. **Information that is** *most* **important for the perioperative nurse to include in preoperative preparation for Mr. R. includes a(n):**

    1. *explanation of the risks and possible complications of general anesthesia.*

    2. *explanation that Mr. R. should anticipate seeing blood-tinged urine following surgery.*

    3. *exploration of Mr. R's feelings of becoming impotent after the surgery.*

    4. *description of postoperative management of neurogenic bladder syndrome.*

16. **In assembling supplies for this procedure, the nurse should select an isotonic, non-hemolytic irrigation solution. The *best* solution to use in this procedure is:**

    1. *warm, sterile water.*

    2. *glycine solution at body temperature.*

    3. *normal saline at body temperature.*

    4. *cool, sterile water.*

17. **An important nursing diagnosis that reflects the *individualized* plan of care for Mr. R. during the intraoperative period is:**

    1. *Sensory/perceptual alteration.*

    2. *Altered urinary elimination.*

    3. *Functional incontinence.*

    4. *Altered sexuality patterns.*

18. **In preparing for Mr. R.'s procedure, the nurse chemically disinfects the cystoscope that will be used for the procedure. Which of the following *most* accurately represents the actions the perioperative nurse should take?**

    1. *Refuse to use anything but a sterile cystoscope.*

    2. *Clean and rinse cystoscope, submerge in quaternary ammonium compound for 10 minutes, rinse in sterile water, and dry.*

    3. *Clean, rinse, and dry cystoscope, soak in 2% glutaraldehyde for 10 minutes, and rinse with copious amounts of sterile water.*

    4. *Clean and rinse cystoscope, soak in 2% glutaraldehyde for 5 minutes, rinse with copious amounts of sterile water.*

19. **During the procedure, the *most* appropriate position for the dispersive electrode (ground pad) would be:**

    1. *beneath the buttocks on the side away from the irrigation fluid.*

    2. *beneath the scapula.*

    3. *on the lateral abdomen after shaving hair, if needed.*

    4. *on the lateral aspect of the thigh after positioning.*

20. **During the immediate postoperative care for Mr. R., the perioperative nurse is *most* concerned with which of the following patient outcome standards?**

    1. *The patient will be free from infection.*

    2. *The patient will express his understanding of the surgery.*

3. *The patient will be free from injury.*

4. *The patient's fluid and electrolyte balance will be maintained.*

21. **On entering the PACU, Mr. R. begins shivering and states that he is very cold. The recovery nurse quickly takes measures to correct this condition. Her *primary* concern is that chills and shivering may:**

    1. *slow the metabolism of drugs used by anesthesia.*

    2. *increase oxygen demand.*

    3. *enhance the patient's perception of pain.*

    4. *lead to cardiac arrhythmias.*

22. **Before leaving the PACU, Mr. R. complains of a "pounding headache". Nursing measures to assist Mr. R. include:**

    1. *quickly elevating the head of his bed.*

    2. *increasing Mr. R.'s fluid intake.*

    3. *informing the surgeon to be on standby for emergency surgery.*

    4. *stopping the continuous flow irrigation of his bladder.*

23. **Mr. I. is admitted with a diagnosis of non-union malrotation of a right tibial fracture. The procedure scheduled is an *open reduction tibia, right tibial rodding.* In interviewing the patient and reviewing the chart, the perioperative nurse finds that the patient currently has a tibial rod in place and was being admitted for removal of an intermedullar tibial nail, and for re-rodding. The informed consent is signed and states: *Removal of intermedullar tibial nail and renailing osteotomy right fibula.* The *best* step for the perioperative nurse to take next is to:**

    1. *contact the patient's surgeon to validate the correct surgical procedure.*

    2. *communicate the findings to the appropriate nurse manager in the operating room.*

    3. *change the operative permit to match the operating room schedule and then have the patient sign the permit.*

    4. *arrange for the cast cart to be available postoperatively.*

24. **During induction/intubation, the anesthesiologist asks the perioperative nurse to assist in the Sellick maneuver. The perioperative nurse understands that she is being asked to:**

    1. *apply cricoid pressure.*

    2. *pass the endotracheal tube.*

    3. *obtain the emergency malignant hyperthermia cart.*

    4. *apply diaphragmatic pressure.*

25. During the induction and reversal stages of anesthesia, the perioperative nurse is available to assist anesthesia personnel. This is because she is *most* concerned about which of the following nursing diagnoses?

    1. *Potential for suffocation.*

    2. *Potential for aspiration.*

    3. *Potential for injury.*

    4. *Dysreflexia.*

Questions 26-33 refer to the following patient information:

Mrs. E., a 58-year-old mother of three children, is being admitted on the morning of surgery for a vaginal hysterectomy with a diagnosis of benign myoma of the uterus. She has a history of diabetes, which has been regulated by oral hypoglycemic drugs and diet. In addition, during review of the history and physical the perioperative nurse finds that Mrs. E. underwent a bilateral total hip replacement for osteoarthritis two years earlier. She claims to have had pain-free mobility since then.

26. Which of the following questions would be the *most* appropriate to ask next as the nurse continues the assessment interview?

    1. *"How do you feel about your surgery?"*

    2. *"Have you talked to your doctor about the need for insulin?"*

    3. *"Are you experiencing depression at the thought of having your uterus removed?"*

    4. *"Do you take any additional medications for pain?"*

27. Risk assessment for Mrs. E. includes identification and documentation of the correct wound classification for her specific type of surgery. The perioperative nurse would classify Mrs. E.'s wound as:

    1. *Class I.*

    2. *Class II.*

    3. *Class III.*

    4. *Class IV.*

28. Of the following preoperative assessment data for Mrs. E., which will be *most* important for the circulating nurse assigned to Mrs. E.'s care?

    1. *Description of skin integrity.*

    2. *Blood glucose.*

    3. *Patient's response to preoperative teaching.*

    4. *Family members available.*

29. **To optimize wound healing for Mrs. E., the circulating nurse knows that the *most* important action to take is to:**

    1. *select synthetic monofilament suture for wound closure.*

    2. *notify the surgeon of the risk of infection and ask the surgical team to handle tissue with minimal trauma.*

    3. *notify team members of any breaks in technique and facilitate corrective action.*

    4. *damp-dust all horizontal surfaces prior to the patient entering the operating room.*

30. **Which of the following nursing diagnoses *most* accurately reflects individualization of the standard perioperative nursing care plan for Mrs. E.?**

    1. *Altered nutrition: less than body requirement related to n.p.o. status since midnight.*

    2. *Potential for impaired skin integrity related to lithotomy position.*

    3. *Impaired physical mobility related to anesthesia.*

    4. *Potential for injury related to position during surgery.*

31. **The *most* important consideration in positioning Mrs. E. for surgery will be to:**

    1. *provide adequate padding of the coccyx to prevent tissue ischemia.*

    2. *place the stirrups in a high position.*

    3. *consult with the surgeon and anesthesiologist for alteration in routine position.*

    4. *abduct stirrups to avoid pressure against the upper inner aspect of thigh.*

32. **During the immediate postoperative period, the recovery nurse would take several measures to promote wound healing in Mrs. E. These measures include:**

    1. *Assess for signs of postoperative bleeding.*

    2. *Assess the condition of the wound every 15 minutes.*

    3. *Change the dressing when soiled.*

    4. *Assess catheter for patency.*

33. **Mrs. E. is given Valium preoperatively according to the physician's orders. Thirty minutes after administration of the medication, Mrs. E. appears agitated and anxious and asks why she is not asleep yet. She states that she just wants to go to sleep and "forget all this business." The perioperative nurse is *most* concerned that:**

    1. *Mrs. E. is showing signs of denial and grief.*

    2. *the dose of Valium was not large enough to have its intended effect.*

3. *Mrs. E.'s misconceptions about the purpose of Valium and her resulting anxiety may hamper administration of the actual anesthetic drugs.*

4. *Mrs. E. must see her surgeon before going to sleep.*

Questions 34-36 refer to the following patient information:

Mrs. Q. is a 54-year-old married homemaker undergoing a hysteroscopy for resection of a polyp for dysfunctional uterine bleeding. During the procedure, it is noted that there is a 3000 cc discrepancy between the amount of solution administered and that returned to suction. Upon inspection, it becomes clear that the resectoscope is leaking. The case is ended, and upon removing the drapes it is noted that the patient's abdomen is distended.

34. **The patient is sent to the PACU for physiologic monitoring with a nursing diagnosis of:**

    1. *Altered protection.*

    2. *Fluid volume excess.*

    3. *Potential for injury.*

    4. *Unilateral neglect.*

35. **This situation could *best* have been prevented if the perioperative nurse had:**

    1. *inspected the resectoscope prior to use.*

    2. *more closely monitored the amount of fluid being returned.*

    3. *checked the patient's abdomen for distention during the procedure.*

    4. *asked the surgeon to test the resectoscope before she used it.*

36. **In reviewing this case, the Quality Assurance Committee is *most* concerned with which set of standards?**

    1. *Structure standards.*

    2. *Process standards.*

    3. *Outcome standards.*

    4. *Discipline standards.*

Questions 37-39 refer to the following patient information:

Mr. M. is to be positioned, prepped, and draped for a left nephrectomy.

37. **Important considerations in positioning Mr. M. include:**

    1. *flexing the left leg, placing a pillow between the knees, and placing a foot board at the foot of the bed.*

    2. *flexing the right leg, placing a pillow between the legs, supporting the feet with a pillow, and placing a safety strap across the thigh.*

3. *flexing the right leg, placing a pillow between the legs, placing a footboard at the foot of the bed, and placing a safety strap across the calves.*

4. *flexing the left leg, placing a pillow between the legs, supporting the feet with a pillow, and placing a safety strap across the calves.*

38. **Preoperative blood gas values are documented as within normal limits. As the surgeon makes the incision on Mr. M., the anesthesiologist draws blood gases once again. The results are reported as pH = 7.34; paO_2 = 75; pCO_2 = 48; HCO_3 = 25. The perioperative nurse knows these values may be evidence of:**

1. *respiratory acidosis.*

2. *metabolic acidosis.*

3. *respiratory alkalosis.*

4. *metabolic alkalosis.*

39. **The perioperative nurse also knows that a primary reason for this recent change in blood gas values is that:**

1. *the infection in Mr. M.'s kidney interferes with its role in maintaining acid-base balance.*

2. *chest rolls may be inhibiting lung expansion.*

3. *the vital capacity is reduced since Mr. M.'s position impairs chest expansion.*

4. *the physiologic and psychologic effects of stress have caused a temporary shift in blood gas values.*

Questions 40-44 refer to the following patient information:

During the preoperative assessment of Mr. D., the perioperative nurse discovers that the patient has complaints of muscle cramping and fatigue. In addition, during the patient interview the patient relates that "my father almost died in surgery". He is observably restless and nervously taps his finger on the desk as he speaks.

40. **The nurse's *first* response is to:**

1. *call the anesthesiologist for further evaluation.*

2. *explore the patient's feelings related to the threat of surgery.*

3. *assure the patient that every individual responds differently to surgery.*

4. *collect additional information about the father's response to surgery.*

41. **Based on this information, the nurse's *individualized* patient care plan would emphasize a nursing diagnosis of:**

1. *Anxiety.*

2. *Potential altered body temperature.*

3. *Potential activity intolerance.*

4. *Ineffective individual coping.*

42. **The patient care plan for this patient will include which of the following activities?**

    1. *Assure, the availability of sufficient amounts of warm saline solution.*

    2. *Gather extra pillows and foam pads for supporting extremities during positioning.*

    3. *Place the operating room bed in a Trendelenburg position.*

    4. *Assure the availability of sufficient amounts of Dantrium and diluent for reconstitution.*

43. **A realistic patient outcome goal for this patient would be:**

    1. *Patient tolerance for physical activity will be at preoperative level by discharge.*

    2. *Preoperative anxiety will be at a manageable level as measured by patient statement, vital signs at documented preadmission baseline, and relaxed posture prior to induction.*

    3. *Patient will work with nurse to identify three steps to improve coping during perioperative period.*

    4. *Patient body temperature will remain at patient normal during perioperative period.*

44. **Postoperative nursing management for this patient *must* include:**

    1. *close monitoring for 72 hours.*

    2. *discharge planning for home care.*

    3. *range of motion exercises q.i.d.*

    4. *a physical therapy consult.*

45. **Shortly after administration of Demerol for pain control, the PACU nurse recognizes that Mrs. B. appears restless and pale. He notices cyanosis around the lips. Respirations are slow and shallow while breath sounds are diminished. The PACU nurse knows that the drug of choice for these symptoms is:**

    1. *neostigmine.*

    2. *atropine.*

    3. *Tensilon.*

    4. *naloxone.*

46. During the preoperative assessment interview, the perioperative nurse recognizes that the patient is extremely anxious. The nurse's attempts to discuss the anxiety and to assist the patient in reducing his anxiety appear to be ineffective. The nurse checks the preoperative orders to see if an antianxiety medication was ordered preoperatively by the anesthesiologist. Which of the following medications would *most* likely have been ordered?

   1. *Versed.*

   2. *Reglan.*

   3. *atropine.*

   4. *Sublimaze.*

47. During the preoperative assessment in the preoperative holding room, the circulating nurse discovers that Mr. C. is HIV positive. The *first* thing the perioperative nurse does in response to this information is:

   1. *place a label on the front of the patient's chart identifying him as HIV positive.*

   2. *proceed to the operating room and communicate this information to the surgical team.*

   3. *obtain red disposal bags and signage for use during the procedure.*

   4. *continue the preoperative interview and proceed as for any other patient.*

48. As the scrub nurse is nearing completion of setting up the sterile field for a procedure, the operating room team receives a message that the patient has been delayed in X-ray and that the procedure has been postponed for one hour. The scrub nurse must make an important phone call and sees this delay as an opportunity to break scrub and make the call. The *most* appropriate action for the scrub nurse to take next is to:

   1. *tear down the sterile field and gather supplies needed for setting up a new field when the patient is through in X-ray.*

   2. *completely cover the sterile field with a large sterile drape until notified that the patient is on the way to the operating room, then use aseptic technique to uncover the field.*

   3. *break scrub and place tape across the operating room door(s), identifying the field as "Sterile" before leaving to make the phone call.*

   4. *note the time the delay began, ask the circulating nurse to stay in the room to observe and monitor the sterile field, and break scrub.*

49. Upon learning about a significant patient delay after the sterile field has been set up, the perioperative nurse is *most* concerned about the patient's potential for infection related to:

   1. *contamination of the sterile field by air currents that carry potential pathogens.*

   2. *the increased time lapsed between the preoperative antimicrobial preparation of the skin and making the incision.*

   3. *contamination of the sterile field by contact with an unsterile team member.*

   4. *direct contact contamination by the scrubbed surgical team.*

50. **During the surgical procedure, the scrub nurse requests 1000 cc of warm 0.9% normal saline for irrigation. As the circulating nurse pours the solution into the 1000 cc graduate, several cc's splash out of the graduate onto the back table, which is covered by a sterile linen drape. The *most* appropriate corrective action for the surgical team to take is to:**

    1. *stop the procedure, consider the back table setup contaminated, tear down the setup, and set up a new, sterile back table.*

    2. *remove all instruments and supplies that are near the splash from the sterile field, and continue with the surgical procedure.*

    3. *remove all instruments and supplies in contact with the moisture-permeated drapes, place a folded sterile towel to cover the moistened area, and continue with the surgical procedure.*

    4. *create a mental barrier around the contaminated area and use only instruments and supplies outside the area of possible contamination.*

Questions 51-61 refer to the following patient information:

Mr. S., a 46-year-old male, is scheduled for an open reduction and internal fixation of an intertrochanteric fracture of the right hip with spinal anesthesia.

51. **The perioperative nurse's plan for the transfer of Mr. S. to the Preoperative Room *must* include:**

    1. *provisions for Buck's traction and weights.*

    2. *avoidance of the use of a transfer gurney.*

    3. *instructions for his family.*

    4. *early notification of his unit.*

During the preoperative assessment, the perioperative nurse notes that Mr. S. has a history of alcohol abuse, his skin is warm and dry with decreased turgor, and his vital signs are: T = 39.5° C, P = 112, BP = 172/120, Hgb. = 16.8, Hct. = 57%.

52. **Based on these findings, the nurse will design an *individualized* patient care plan that incorporates which of the following nursing diagnoses?**

    1. *Impaired tissue integrity.*

    2. *Decreased cardiac output.*

    3. *Fluid volume deficit.*

    4. *Ineffective thermoregulation.*

53. **The plan for this nursing diagnosis should include:**

    1. *Protect all bony prominence.*

    2. *Notify Cardiac Services.*

3. *Monitor I & O.*

4. *Place the malignant hyperthermia cart outside the patient's room.*

54. **Based on these readings for vital signs, the nurse knows that Mr. S. is at additional risk relative to which of the following nursing diagnoses for this category of patient?**

    1. *Potential altered body temperature.*

    2. *Knowledge deficit.*

    3. *Altered nutrition: less than body requirements.*

    4. *Potential for impaired skin integrity.*

Mr. S. is scheduled for an ORIF of the right hip with spinal anesthesia. He will be positioned on the fracture table.

55. **A critical adverse effect of spinal anesthesia is:**

    1. *total spinal anesthesia.*

    2. *hypotension.*

    3. *nausea and vomiting.*

    4. *spinal headache.*

56. **In such an event, the perioperative nurse should be prepared to:**

    1. *raise the head of the bed.*

    2. *administer oxygen and antiemetics.*

    3. *administer oxygen and vasopressors.*

    4. *provide respiratory assistance and cardiovascular support.*

57. **Mr. S. is at risk for decreased urine output due to:**

    1. *substance abuse and spinal anesthesia.*

    2. *immobilization and spinal anesthesia.*

    3. *decreased fluid volume and spinal anesthesia.*

    4. *substance abuse and immobility.*

58. **Of the following interventions, the one *most* likely to treat Mr. S.'s decreased urine output, which might reduce his hemoglobin, is:**

    1. *Increase fluid volume.*

    2. *Monitor urine output.*

3. *ROM.*

4. *Early ambulation.*

59. **Mr. S.'s individualized patient care plan includes a nursing diagnosis of** *Potential for injury related to* _____**; the appropriate nursing intervention is** _____**.**

    1. *retained foreign body; Complete all sponge, needle, blade and instrument counts*

    2. *fluoroscopy; Provide gonadal protection*

    3. *electrical hazard; Check functioning of all equipment*

    4. *chemicals; Protect skin from pooled solutions*

60. **To determine the effectiveness of nursing interventions directed toward the goal of** *Absence of injury related to positioning***, the perioperative nurse will assess the status of Mr. S.'s soft tissue at the:**

    1. *sacrum, scapulae, and left trochanter.*

    2. *occiput, scapulae, and sacrum.*

    3. *occiput, elbows, and heels.*

    4. *elbows, sacrum, and heels.*

61. **During the assessment described above, the perioperative nurse notes an area of non-blanchable erythema 1 cm x 1 cm on the right heel. The nurse would note the assessment in the chart and:**

    1. *follow-up with a verbal report to the PACU nurses.*

    2. *describe in the NCP the nursing plan for massage and reassessment.*

    3. *formulate a nursing diagnosis, describe an outcome, and plan for a nursing intervention.*

    4. *contact the QA coordinator.*

62. **Ms. S., 26 years old, is scheduled for an emergency appendectomy. Upon assessing the laboratory values, the nurse sees some discrepancies. Which lab value would indicate a risk for surgery?**

    1. *K = 3.3 mEq/L; Na = 158 mEq/L.*

    2. *WBC = 12.5.*

    3. *Hgb. = 13.5 gm/L; Hct. = 42%.*

    4. *Serum glucose = 100 mg/dL.*

Questions 63-71 refer to the following patient information:

Vanessa, a 10-year-old African-American female, is scheduled for bilateral ureteral reimplantations (BUR). She recently suffered an acute episode of pyelonephritis after discontinuing the long-term antibiotic prophylaxis she had been taking for her ureteral reflux. When told of the necessity for surgery, Vanessa chose to have her surgery as soon as possible because she was planning to be traveling, out of the country, with a school group during summer vacation.

63. **The hospital at which Vanessa's surgery is scheduled offers preoperative tours for young children and their families on Saturday afternoons and for adolescents on Tuesday evenings. What should the perioperative nurse plan for Vanessa?**

    1. *Schedule her for the Saturday tour so that Vanessa can enjoy the fun activities.*

    2. *Ask the patient educators to organize a pre-teen group.*

    3. *Contact Vanessa's mother and allow Vanessa to choose the tour she would like to attend.*

    4. *Postpone Vanessa's tour until the day of her surgery so that it can be individualized.*

64. **The perioperative nurse's action in planning for Vanessa's preoperative teaching and tour is an example of which type of nursing action?**

    1. *Independent.*

    2. *Interdependent.*

    3. *Dependent.*

    4. *Collateral.*

65. **While attending the Preoperative Family Tour, Vanessa's mother tells the perioperative nurse that Vanessa is coping quite well except for the prospect of awakening with a catheter. The perioperative nurse should:**

    1. *talk to Vanessa about the catheter, being certain to emphasize that it will not hurt.*

    2. *reassure Vanessa's mother that all BUR patients feel that way.*

    3. *tell Vanessa that she may not need a catheter and therefore not to worry.*

    4. *give Vanessa a catheter to examine and take home, encouraging her to share her feelings with her mother.*

66. **Incorporating developmental considerations into the patient care plan for Vanessa, the perioperative nurse will be sure to:**

    1. *maintain frequent communication with the family intraoperatively.*

    2. *determine how much teaching is needed.*

    3. *monitor all safety factors.*

    4. *provide a wagon for Vanessa's transport.*

67. The desired patient outcome for this nursing action is:

1. *Patient will effectively cope with separation from parents.*

2. *Patient will demonstrate understanding of the environment.*

3. *Patient will be free from injury.*

4. *Family will effectively employ coping strategies.*

Vanessa's surgery goes well. Following department protocols, the perioperative nurse applies an impermeable, transparent sealing dressing and ensures that Vanessa's catheter and drainage system are securely connected and taped to Vanessa's right thigh.

During a review of Vanessa's chart on the second post-op day, the perioperative nurse notes that Vanessa has had severe nausea and vomiting as a reaction to the epidural fentanyl, which was discontinued at 1430. She is also c/o incisional pain as well as localized pain in her right thigh. Vanessa's Foley catheter is still in, and her I & O is good.

68. The perioperative nurse will include which of the following in her postoperative evaluation?

1. *I & O, N/V.*

2. *Incisional and leg pain.*

3. *Incisional pain and I & O.*

4. *I & O and leg pain.*

69. The nurse determines that the dressing is pulling on the incision. Her *next* action should be to:

1. *contact the surgeon.*

2. *contact the Perioperative CNS.*

3. *reapply the dressing.*

4. *activate the nurse-call light.*

70. The nurse's *most* appropriate next action is:

1. *contact the QA committee.*

2. *share information with perioperative colleagues.*

3. *make notation in the chart.*

4. *continue with postoperative evaluation.*

71. Vanessa describes very sharp and localized discomfort under the connection of the catheter and drainage tube, where they are taped to her thigh. When the perioperative nurse removes the tape, she discovers a depressed, darkened area ~ 1 cm x 2.5 cm with a blister ~ 0.3 cm x 0.7 cm. Release of the tape immediately relieves Vanessa's discomfort. After completing her postoperative rounds, the nurse's *most* appropriate quality-oriented follow-up regarding her findings would be to:

    1. *contact the QA committee regarding further action.*

    2. *ensure that review of appropriate indicators occurs.*

    3. *contact the Perioperative CNS for follow-up with the QA Coordinator.*

    4. *notify the OR supervisor.*

72. The standard patient care plan for a pediatric patient *must* include additional, specific nursing interventions to:

    1. *prevent infection.*

    2. *address knowledge deficit.*

    3. *maintain normothermic status.*

    4. *prevent injury related to positioning.*

Questions 73-82 refer to the following patient information:

Mr. H., a 42-year-old carpenter, is admitted to the Ambulatory Surgery Unit for a bilateral carpal tunnel release under local anesthesia. Upon admission his vital signs are T = 38.5° C, P = 68, strong, regular; BP = 116/64, R = 12, regular. Mr. H. weighs 76 kilograms and is 5" 11" in height. He is alert and oriented but visibly anxious.

73. During administration of the first dose of bupivicaine 0.25% with epinephrine 1:200,000, the perioperative nurse notices that Mr. H.'s facial muscles are tense and that his skin is pale, cool, and moist. Pulse is 102; BP is 132/78. Teeth are clenched, and he appears to be holding his breath. While continuing physiologic monitoring, the nurse should:

    1. *encourage Mr. H. to take several slow, deep breaths.*

    2. *ask Mr. H. how he is feeling.*

    3. *provide oxygen per nasal cannula.*

    4. *ask the surgeon to stop.*

74. Mr. H. begins to hyperventilate. If allowed to continue, this could lead to:

    1. *respiratory acidosis.*

    2. *metabolic acidosis.*

    3. *respiratory alkalosis.*

    4. *metabolic alkalosis.*

75. In such a state, Mr. H. would complain of:

    1. *tingling of the hands and face.*

    2. *nausea.*

    3. *muscle weakness.*

    4. *headache.*

76. To curtail Mr. H.s' hyperventilating, the *most* appropriate intervention for the perioperative nurse is to:

    1. *administer oxygen.*

    2. *instruct the patient to close one nostril and breathe normally, with his mouth closed.*

    3. *increase the IV rate.*

    4. *raise the head of the bed.*

    Surgery on Mr. H.'s right hand is uneventful and requires 24 cc of bupivicaine 0.25% with epinephrine 1:200,000. Dressings are applied, the tourniquet is released, and the hand is elevated slightly.

77. Tourniquet time on the left side is 45 minutes; amount of bupivicaine 0.25% with epinephrine 1:200,000 is 16 cc. Mr. H. has become restless. He is alert and oriented. He denies any discomfort from the surgery but does complain of a headache. His VS for the last three readings are: P = 132, BP = 152/114, R = 16. His skin is moist. The perioperative nurse should notify the surgeon that Mr. H. is manifesting a/an:

    1. *toxic overdose of local anesthesia.*

    2. *allergic reaction.*

    3. *reaction to epinephrine.*

    4. *acute anxiety reaction.*

78. In addition to notifying the surgeon, ensuring airway patency, and administering oxygen, the perioperative nurse should:

    1. *increase IV fluids.*

    2. *continue to monitor for CV problems.*

    3. *administer diazepam.*

    4. *administer diphenhydramine.*

79. At the conclusion of Mr. H.'s surgery, the perioperative nurse should:

    1. *accompany him to the discharge area to meet his wife and return home.*

    2. *arrange for him to be admitted.*

3. *transfer him to the Ambulatory Surgery Unit PACU for cardiac evaluation and possible transfer to the hospital.*

4. *transfer him to the Ambulatory Surgery Unit PACU for monitoring and discharge teaching.*

80. **Due to child care complications, Mr. H.'s wife has been delayed in picking him up from the Ambulatory Surgery Unit. The perioperative nurse is ready to proceed with his discharge instructions. The perioperative nurse should:**

1. *complete his instructions and have him ready to leave when his wife arrives.*

2. *wait until his wife arrives to allow her to be included in the discharge process.*

3. *start his teaching and then repeat everything when his wife arrives.*

4. *begin his teaching and establish his goals.*

81. **Essential postoperative assessments of any patient having a carpal tunnel release are:**

1. *neurovascular.*

2. *cardiovascular.*

3. *cardiorespiratory.*

4. *musculoskeletal.*

82. **Had Mr. H. undergone a Bier block, it would have been critical for the perioperative nurse to make an assessment of which of his functions?**

1. *Sensory.*

2. *Vascular.*

3. *Motor.*

4. *Skeletal.*

83. **During the use of power saws and drills, the perioperative nurse provides irrigation to:**

1. *extend the life of the bit/blade.*

2. *ensure a clear field of vision.*

3. *prevent cell damage.*

4. *ensure a precise cut.*

84. **Kussmaul respirations are associated with:**

1. *respiratory alkalosis.*

2. *metabolic alkalosis.*

3. *respiratory acidosis.*

4. *metabolic acidosis.*

85. **Obese patients are at risk for impaired wound healing due to:**

1. *poor nutrition.*

2. *avascularity.*

3. *pressure.*

4. *friability.*

Questions 86-90 refer to the following patient information:

Mr. R., a 51-year-old investment banker, is diagnosed with severe coronary artery disease. He has been scheduled for a three vessel CABG. Mr. R.'s father and older brother both died from "heart attacks". He smokes 1-2 packs of cigarettes per day and describes himself as a social drinker. Both Mr. and Mrs. R. appear anxious. He is fidgeting with a pen; she says very little.

86. **During Mr. R.'s preoperative preparation, the perioperative nurse should:**

1. *review the nature of his disease, the reasons for surgery, and the surgical procedure.*

2. *reassure Mrs. R. that she will be reunited with her husband as soon as surgery is complete, and that she will be able to spend as much time as she wishes with him.*

3. *explain the risks involved in the procedure before having Mr. R. sign the operative permit.*

4. *reassure Mr. R. that he should be back at his office within three weeks.*

87. **The perioperative nurse will begin Mr. R.'s preoperative teaching by:**

1. *explaining TCH.*

2. *demonstrating leg exercises.*

3. *finding out what he knows about the procedure.*

4. *asking him if he is having any chest pain.*

88. **On the day of his surgery, Mr. R. arrives in the Preoperative Room 25 minutes late. He is very pale, appears tense, and his eyes are red and moist. He tells the perioperative nurse that he is "not going to wake up from anesthesia". The perioperative nurse should:**

1. *hold his hand and reassure him that he will be fine.*

2. *notify the anesthesiologist.*

3. *ask the supervisor to call Pastoral Services.*

4. *encourage him to tell her more about his feelings.*

89. To complete the skin prep following induction, the perioperative nurse will elevate Mr. R.'s legs and abduct and support them on leg holders. A towel will be placed over his scrotum and anus. The perioperative nurse should ask the student observer to leave during this procedure and to return after the completion of the draping. The goal of this nursing intervention is to:

    1. *maintain patient privacy.*

    2. *minimize traffic.*

    3. *reduce potential sources of contamination.*

    4. *reduce extraneous activity in the room.*

90. Due to his history of smoking and cardiovascular disease, Mr. R. is at increased risk for:

    1. *decreased cardiac output.*

    2. *impaired wound healing.*

    3. *decreased mobility.*

    4. *altered self-concept.*

91. In planning for the preoperative preparation of this patient, the nurse includes measures to minimize noise, maintain the patient's privacy, provide support, and provide instructions regarding the events and procedures. The theory of human needs that underlies this planning is that of:

    1. *Carl Jung.*

    2. *A.H. Maslow.*

    3. *Emmanuel Kant.*

    4. *Carl Rogers.*

92. The level of human needs addressed by these actions is:

    1. *biologic.*

    2. *social acceptance.*

    3. *self-esteem.*

    4. *safety and security.*

Questions 93 and 94 refer to the following patient information:

Mr. H. is 78 years old and wears both glasses and a hearing aid. He has had bilateral ectropion repairs in an area ASU.

93. **During discharge planning, Mr. H. indicates that he intends to have his prescription filled at an area discount pharmacy. By incorporating this action into Mr. H.'s discharge plan, the perioperative nurse is:**

    1. *encouraging the patient to make health-care decisions.*

    2. *following generally recognized protocols for patient discharge.*

    3. *making an inappropriate entry into the discharge plan.*

    4. *meeting AORN Patient Outcome Standard V.*

94. **While waiting for his son to pick up the prescription, Mr. H. looks at himself in the car mirror and begins to prod his cheeks, just below the incisions. Pooled blood is expressed through the suture lines and begins to run down his face. The perioperative nurse's *most* appropriate strategy for preventing this would have been to:**

    1. *insist that the prescription be filled at the center so that a stop at the pharmacy would not be necessary.*

    2. *admonish Mr. H. not to touch his face, and to use gauze dressings rather than the usual ointment to cover the incisions.*

    3. *instruct the family always to have someone with Mr. H.*

    4. *provide the patient with a mirror in the PACU, and inquire about any questions or concerns he may have.*

95. **During the preoperative interview, Ms. K. relates a history of porphyria. This condition:**

    1. *is a rare disorder of metabolism.*

    2. *results in the formation of poromas.*

    3. *can lead to a precipitous rise in temperature.*

    4. *requires the use of psychotherapy.*

96. **A history of porphyria absolutely contraindicates the use of:**

    1. *halothane.*

    2. *Mannitol.*

    3. *Anectine.*

    4. *pentothal.*

97. Ms. N., a married, 31-year-old elementary school teacher, is admitted to the Ambulatory Surgery Unit for a right breast biopsy under general anesthesia. She indicates that her surgeon has reassured her that, due to her age and family history, "everything will be fine." During wound closure, the pathologist's report arrives and indicates a malignancy. The permit has not been signed for any additional surgery. To proceed with Ms. N.'s care, what should happen next?

    1. *The perioperative nurse should have the husband sign the permit for a modified radical mastectomy.*

    2. *Ms. N. should be transferred to the Ambulatory Surgery Unit PACU, and this information should be incorporated into her discharge plan.*

    3. *The surgeon should have Ms. N.'s husband sign the permit for a modified radical mastectomy.*

    4. *Ms. N. should be transferred to PACU for recovery, and should sign the permit when she is awake.*

98. A patient whose greater trochanter will be removed during total hip arthroplasty will need additional instruction regarding:

    1. *partial weight bearing.*

    2. *an abduction pillow.*

    3. *drains.*

    4. *postoperative infections.*

99. During the preoperative telephone call to a patient scheduled for a total knee arthroplasty, the perioperative nurse should instruct the patient to:

    1. *shave the operative leg from toes to groin in the privacy of his own home.*

    2. *shower with Ivory soap during the 48 hours before the scheduled time of surgery.*

    3. *use a depilatory from toes to groin on the operative leg, and then rinse with alcohol.*

    4. *shower or bathe with an antimicrobial soap the night before surgery.*

100. Which of the following instructions regarding postoperative routines *must* be included in the teaching plan for a total hip arthroplasty patient?

    1. *Sleep on the operative side.*

    2. *Sleep with toes pointed in.*

    3. *Never cross one leg over another.*

    4. *Do not be concerned about bowel function until after ambulation begins.*

101. Ms. S. is a 43-year-old woman admitted for an emergency cholecystectomy. She has been on steroid therapy for 9 months. In planning her care, the perioperative nurse should realize that the patient is at *greatest* risk for:

    1. *cardiac arrhythmias.*

    2. *poor wound healing.*

3. *anaphylactic shock.*

4. *postoperative psychosis.*

102. **Mrs. J. has been admitted for a right breast biopsy, possible mastectomy. According to Maslow's hierarchy of needs, which level of need would be the patient's *primary* motivating factor at this time?**

1. *Self-esteem.*

2. *Biologic.*

3. *Safety.*

4. *Self-actualization.*

103. **Mr. H., an 87-year-old male, is admitted to ambulatory surgery for removal of a cataract. When doing the preoperative teaching, the perioperative nurse should give *greatest* emphasis to:**

1. *assessing Mr. H.'s present level of knowledge.*

2. *discussing all aspects of the surgery in detail.*

3. *discussing postoperative pain management.*

4. *including all members of the surgical team.*

104. **During preoperative assessment, the perioperative nurse discovers that her patient has been taking a diuretic for hypertension. Which lab value is *most* important for the nurse to check?**

1. *Blood urea nitrogen.*

2. *Serum sodium.*

3. *Hemoglobin and hematocrit.*

4. *Serum potassium.*

105. **It is important for the perioperative nurse to understand that attaining informed consent from the patient is:**

1. *the physician's responsibility.*

2. *the primary nurse's responsibility.*

3. *the function of any licensed RN.*

4. *variable, depending on the policies of the institution.*

106. **The A.O.R.N. recommends that the preoperative shave prep be done:**

1. *on all surgical procedures.*

2. *the evening before surgery.*

3. *not longer than 2 hours before surgery.*

4. *in the operating room suite, immediately before surgery.*

107. **Mr. T. is sent to the operating room after suffering severe injuries in a car accident. Blood pressure is 80/50 mm Hg; pulse is 140/minute and thready; the patient is unconscious. His right leg is lacerated from knee to ankle; his jaw is fractured; and his Foley is draining bloody urine. He has been intubated, and a central line has been inserted. Which surgical procedure would have *first* priority?**

1. *Tracheotomy to insure a patent airway.*

2. *Exploratory laparotomy to control internal bleeding.*

3. *Wound debridement to prevent infection.*

4. *Intercranial monitor insertion to assess intercranial pressure.*

108. **Mr. C.'s liver resection is complete. Which of the following is *not* a recommended guideline when moving the patient from the O.R. table to the stretcher?**

1. *Move Mr. C. as swiftly as a possible to prevent delay in reaching the postanesthesia care unit (PACU).*

2. *Wait until the anesthesia clinician gives permission to move Mr. C.*

3. *Support all joints and extremities since they will be vulnerable to injury.*

4. *Respect Mr. C.'s dignity by preventing unnecessary exposure.*

109. **Which of the following body systems is *most* vulnerable when the body is placed in the prone position?**

1. *The cardiovascular system.*

2. *The respiratory system.*

3. *The integumentary system.*

4. *The genitourinary system.*

110. **Mrs. J. is having a vaginal hysterectomy in the lithotomy position. She is 5'3" tall and weighs 200 pounds. She has suffered from back problems for many years. In developing Mrs. J.'s care plan, one of the *most* important nursing interventions for the nurse to write is, *At the completion of surgery*:**

1. *lower the legs quickly and simultaneously to decrease pressure on the back.*

2. *lower the legs slowly, one at a time, to prevent a rush of blood to the lower extremities and stress on the hip and back.*

3. *lower the legs slowly and simultaneously to prevent a rush of blood to the lower extremities and stress on the hip and back.*

4. *have four people available to help lower legs, due to the patient's obesity.*

111. The surgeon asks that the patient be placed in the Trendelenburg position. The circulating nurse realizes that this position can produce all of the following physiological changes *except:*

    1. *a drop in blood pressure when the patient is returned to the supine position.*

    2. *interference with respiratory exchange.*

    3. *diaphragmatic expansion.*

    4. *pulmonary congestion and edema.*

112. Mr. P. had surgery yesterday morning and is now experiencing numbness in his right calf. The perioperative nurse suspects that he may have suffered saphenous and peroneal nerve damage during surgery. This injury is *most* likely to have occurred if Mr. P. was in which position?

    1. *Kraske.*

    2. *Lateral recumbent.*

    3. *Reverse Trendelenburg.*

    4. *Lithotomy.*

113. While doing the preoperative assessment, the perioperative nurse discovers that her patient is allergic to seafood. The nurse realizes that:

    1. *povidone/iodine should not be used as a skin prep solution.*

    2. *the patient will probably experience nausea and vomiting after surgery.*

    3. *allergies to seafood are often associated with allergies to certain narcotics.*

    4. *this particular allergy poses no threat to the surgical patient.*

114. A perioperative nurse has been assigned to the cysto room for the day. She checks the electrosurgical unit and finds that it is bipolar. She understand that bipolar units:

    1. *distribute current over a large tissue area.*

    2. *are not recommended for delicate tissue.*

    3. *are not as safe as monopolar units.*

    4. *do not require the use of a grounding pad.*

115. A 29-year-old male is admitted for an emergency exploratory laparotomy following injuries suffered in a car accident. He ate a chicken sandwich for lunch at 12:00 pm and is scheduled for surgery at 3:00 pm. During induction, the anesthetist asks the perioperative nurse to provide cricoid pressure (Sellick maneuver). The *most* beneficial effect from this action is that it:

    1. *obstructs the esophagus.*

    2. *prevents vomiting.*

3. *aids in intubation.*

4. *prevents fasciculation.*

116. **A patient has been given atropine, an anticholinergic medication, preoperatively. The perioperative nurse realizes that the patient may complain of:**

    1. *nausea.*

    2. *urinary frequency.*

    3. *a dry mouth.*

    4. *drowsiness.*

117. **Mr. T., 85 years old, is scheduled to have a left inguinal hernia repair with spinal anesthesia. He has been given a sedative-hypnotic preoperatively due to his rising anxiety level. The perioperative nurse should be alert for which of the following symptoms?**

    1. *Hypertension.*

    2. *Numbness and tingling.*

    3. *Hyperventilation.*

    4. *Confusion.*

118. **Mrs. J. tells the perioperative nurse that after her three previous surgeries, she was nauseated and vomited for hours. The perioperative nurse alerts the anesthetist, who is *most* likely to administer which of the following drugs preoperatively?**

    1. *Vistaril (hydroxyzine).*

    2. *Morphine sulfate (generic)*

    3. *Sublimaze (fentanyl).*

    4. *Robinul (glycopyrrolate).*

119. **In the preoperative holding room, Mrs. L. tells the perioperative nurse that she is feeling anxious about her surgery. One of the *most* important actions the perioperative nurse can take to reduce Mrs. L.'s anxiety is to:**

    1. *get an order for Valium 10 mg I.M. stat.*

    2. *reassure her that anxiety is normal.*

    3. *instruct her to take slow, deep breaths.*

    4. *maintain a caring attitude toward her.*

120. Ms. K. comes to the holding room wide awake and anxious. She was given Nembutal 100 mg I.M. 45 minutes ago. She states, "I thought I would be asleep when I went to surgery." The *best* response by the perioperative nurse would be:

    1. *"The purpose of the shot you were given was to help you relax. Perhaps it might help if I went over the teaching you had earlier today."*

    2. *"Don't worry. The doctors will put you to sleep before your surgery."*

    3. *"You seem very anxious about your surgery. I will get an order for another medication."*

    4. *"If you lie back, close your eyes, and take a few deep breaths, you will begin to feel drowsy."*

121. The induction-intubation phase of anesthesia is considered the most dangerous for the patient. The circulating nurse's *most* important function during this period is to:

    1. *make sure that anesthesia's suction is working properly.*

    2. *keep noise levels at a minimum.*

    3. *remain beside the patient to assist the anesthetist.*

    4. *apply the safety strap over the patient's leg.*

122. Ms. J. developed a paralytic ileus postoperatively. Decreased intestinal peristalsis may occur postoperatively as a result of:

    1. *handling of the bowel during surgery.*

    2. *air swallowing associated with apprehension.*

    3. *early resumption of oral intake after surgery.*

    4. *irritation by a nasogastric tube.*

123. Ms. F. is scheduled for gastrointestinal surgery. When is the *best* time to teach her how to cough and deep breathe?

    1. *When she first discusses the surgery.*

    2. *One week prior to the procedure.*

    3. *The afternoon before the surgery.*

    4. *Immediate preoperatively.*

124. A patient emerges from anesthesia with wild, uncontrolled movements. The perioperative nurse should be aware that the:

    1. *patient is suffering from post-operative psychosis.*

    2. *patient is having a seizure.*

3. *patient's behavior is not abnormal.*

4. *patient should have neuro-checks done every 15 minutes.*

125. In the PACU, Mr. I is restless, his blood pressure is elevated, and he is crying out in pain. The perioperative nurse administers Demerol (meperidine) 100 mg I.M. On her next 15-minute check, the nurse notices that Mr. I.'s respirations have gotten very slow. She should be aware that:

1. *the Demerol is taking effect, and the patient's pain has diminished.*

2. *the patient's airway is probably obstructed as a result of the medication.*

3. *Demerol depresses respirations, and a reversal agent may be needed.*

4. *the patient should not be disturbed at this time.*

126. Before intubation, Ms. C. is given Anectine (succinylcholine). During the induction phase of anesthesia, the perioperative nurse is *most* likely to observe:

1. *muscle twitching.*

2. *flushing of the face.*

3. *fluttering eyelids.*

4. *increased respirations.*

127. During the preoperative assessment, the patient mentions that "my two sisters have had surgery and developed high fevers; the surgery had to be stopped." The perioperative nurse's *first* action should be to:

1. *gather cooling blankets and ice.*

2. *contact the family members for further information.*

3. *notify the anesthetist.*

4. *check the supply of Dantrium (dantroline sodium).*

128. Mr. P. is undergoing arthroscopic surgery of the knee with local infiltration anesthesia combined with epinephrine. The epinephrine is used because it:

1. *promotes faster healing.*

2. *has a calming effect when combined with an anesthetic agent.*

3. *keeps blood pressure stable.*

4. *aids in the control of bleeding.*

129. Mrs. T. is scheduled for a breast biopsy, possible lumpectomy. In working with this patient, the perioperative nurse should be *most* aware of the need to:

1. *use Universal Precautions.*

2. *prep the area gently.*

3. *wear gloves at all times.*

4. *personally carry any specimen to the lab.*

130. **A new nurse is orienting to the operating room. Her preceptor notices that the nurse has contaminated her glove while performing the skin prep. What is the *best* course of action for the preceptor to take?**

1. *Let the nurse continue, and discuss the mistake after the case.*

2. *Point out the mistake and take over the prep.*

3. *Point out the mistake and have the nurse change gloves and continue with the prep.*

4. *Point out the mistake and tell the nurse to review the skin prep procedure manual.*

131. **The scrub person hands off the specimen to the circulating nurse. The physician asks that it be sent for a frozen section. What is the *most* appropriate action for the circulating nurse to take next?**

1. *Cover the specimen with a preservative and send it to the lab after surgery.*

2. *Cover the specimen with preservative and send it to the lab immediately.*

3. *Place the specimen in a dry container and send it to the lab after surgery.*

4. *Place the specimen in a dry container and send it to the lab immediately.*

132. **A perioperative nurse is preparing the operating room for a patient scheduled for an arthroscopic knee procedure. The patient is 55 years old and obese. The surgeon's preference card states that a pneumatic tourniquet be applied to the operative extremity. The perioperative nurse should know that:**

1. *a pneumatic tourniquet should not be used on patients over the age of 50, or on obese patients.*

2. *a tourniquet applied to a leg should not be inflated for more than 2 hours.*

3. *the tourniquet cuff should be placed at the point of minimum circumference of the extremity.*

4. *the tourniquet cuff should be applied far enough away from the incision site so that it will not be in the surgeon's way.*

133. **A patient is brought to the postanesthesia care unit (PACU) breathing effectively, but is somewhat unresponsive. In this situation, the *primary* activity of the PACU nurse is to:**

1. *arouse the patient from the effects of anesthesia.*

2. *provide comfort through the use of warm blankets.*

3. *document patient progress using the Aldrette scoring system.*

4. *provide emotional support.*

134. **While in the PACU, Mr. R. exhibits restlessness, increased blood pressure, and increased heart rate. The PACU nurse's *first* action should be to:**

    1. *check for bleeding at the incision site.*

    2. *notify the anesthetist.*

    3. *ask Mr. R. if he is experiencing pain.*

    4. *check for a patent airway.*

135. **Mrs. W. is brought to the PACU after neurosurgery. The perioperative nurse should give *highest* periority to documenting the patient's preoperative:**

    1. *apical pulse.*

    2. *cranial nerve status.*

    3. *mental status and motor activity.*

    4. *medication and allergies.*

136. **In preparing to open supplies for the first case of the day, the perioperative nurse discovers that the room's humidity is 45 percent. What is the *first* action the nurse should take?**

    1. *Begin opening supplies, since this humidity is within normal range.*

    2. *Notify the environmental safety department that the humidity is low, and wait to open the supplies.*

    3. *Notify the environmental safety department that the humidity is high, and wait to open the supplies.*

    4. *Ask to have the case assigned to another procedure room.*

137. **A perioperative nurse is developing a care plan for a 16-month-old female child who will be having surgery for an intestinal obstruction. Which of the following interventions is *most* important to include in this patient's care plan?**

    1. *Carry the child to the operating room to decrease her anxiety.*

    2. *Increase the room temperature 15 minutes before surgery.*

    3. *Allow the parents to join the child in the holding area.*

    4. *Allow the child to bring her favorite toy to the operating room.*

138. **The *primary* purpose of Standards of Perioperative Nursing is to:**

    1. *assist the perioperative nurse in writing care plans.*

    2. *comply with the rules of the Joint Commission of Accreditation of Healthcare Organizations (J.C.A.H.O.).*

    3. *provide quality patient care to those undergoing surgical intervention.*

    4. *provide increased communication with other health professionals.*

139. **The perioperative nurse is assisting in the transfer of an elderly patient from the operating room table to the stretcher. The nurse's *main* objective should be to:**

    1. *maintain the integrity of the IV lines and catheter.*

    2. *provide a sufficient number of people to help with the transfer.*

    3. *offer emotional support to the patient.*

    4. *protect the patient from falling off the table.*

140. **During the preoperative assessment, the patient tells the nurse he is very nervous and feels somewhat nauseated. This information is an example of:**

    1. *a sign.*

    2. *a symptom.*

    3. *measurable data.*

    4. *objective data.*

141. **While scanning the patient's lab values during the preoperative visit, the perioperative nurse discovers that the patient's white blood cell (WBC) count is markedly elevated. The nurse should know that:**

    1. *the patient will be placed on antibiotics for 24 hours before surgery.*

    2. *surgery may be delayed or cancelled.*

    3. *the patient is at risk for hemorrhage during surgery.*

    4. *the patient's skin integrity may be compromised.*

142. **Which of the following factors is *not* essential for the perioperative nurse to assess when performing a preoperative psychologic assessment?**

    1. *The cause of any anxiety or fear.*

    2. *The patient's knowledge of relaxation techniques.*

    3. *The patient's support systems.*

    4. *The patient's past coping mechanisms.*

143. **Which of the following statements related to nursing diagnoses is *not* true?**

    1. *They are similar to medical diagnoses but use different terminology.*

    2. *They focus on the patient and not the disease.*

    3. *They describe actual or potential health problems that nurses are licensed to treat.*

    4. *They change as the patient's condition changes.*

144. **Nursing diagnoses are prioritized according to the relative importance of their being solved. Which of the following diagnoses would get *first* priority?**

    1. *Alteration in comfort.*

    2. *Impaired gas exchange.*

    3. *Potential for infection.*

    4. *Impaired skin integrity.*

145. **Which of the following patients would *not* be an acceptable candidate for intraoperative autotransfusion?**

    1. *A young child scheduled for reconstructive surgery.*

    2. *An adolescent female scheduled for a kidney transplant.*

    3. *A middle-aged male scheduled for the removal of a cancerous tumor.*

    4. *An elderly female scheduled for a coronary artery bypass.*

146. **Mrs. Z. is brought to the operating room for an emergency cesarean section. In such an emergency, the *best* approach to counting is to count:**

    1. *all sponges, sharps, and instruments before the incision is made.*

    2. *only what is possible without delaying the case.*

    3. *only the sponges, and begin the case.*

    4. *as soon as there is time after the case has begun.*

147. **Which of the following actions is of *primary* importance in preventing transmission of a blood-borne pathogen to the perioperative team?**

    1. *Routinely recap all needles and immediately dispose of them in the appropriate container.*

    2. *Always wear gloves if there is evidence of cuts or weeping lesions on the hands.*

    3. *Always wear gloves when in contact with blood or other body fluids.*

    4. *Always wear gloves while providing direct patient contact.*

148. **Ms. W. is scheduled to have a cesarean section under spinal anesthesia. While the anesthesia is being administered, the perioperative nurse's role is to:**

    1. *assist the anesthetist in preparing solutions.*

    2. *prepare the skin prep tray.*

    3. *check with the obstetric and pediatric personnel to see if needed equipment is available.*

    4. *assist anesthesia in positioning the patient during and after induction of anesthesia.*

149. The perioperative nurse is preparing the operating room for a pediatric patient. In her care plan for the child, one of the nurse's interventions is *Use thermal blanket to maintain body temperature.* When using a thermal blanket, the nurse should remember to:

    1. *place a sheet between the blanket and the patient.*

    2. *check the patient's preoperative temperature.*

    3. *check the previous preventive maintenance record.*

    4. *document postoperative skin integrity.*

150. Mrs. N. is undergoing an abdominal hysterectomy. The surgeon states that he is also going to perform a bilateral salpingectomy/oophorectomy. The perioperative nurse's legal responsibility in this situation is:

    1. *nonexistent; the surgeon has complete legal responsibility for the care of the patient.*

    2. *to inform the surgeon if consent has not been granted for this procedure.*

    3. *to call the supervisor and ask him or her to intervene before the procedure is initiated.*

    4. *to refuse to continue with the case.*

Answer Explanations for Comprehensive Practice Examination

The number in parentheses following each answer explanation refers to the chapter of this guide in which the concept is discussed. For those answers marked "SurgRef," you may turn to Chapter 14 of Susan Fairchild's text, *Perioperative Nursing: Principles and Practice*, or to some other source of information on specific surgical procedures and their nursing implications, for elaboration.

1.   **The answer is 3.** The nurse should assess the patient's understanding of the surgical procedure. If problems or concerns have not been addressed adequately, the surgeon and/or anesthesiologist should be notified immediately for further explanation and/or clarification of concepts for the patient. Attaining an informed consent is the responsibility of the operating surgeon. An explanation should contain information regarding the proposed surgical procedure, the possible risks involved, expected benefits, available alternatives, and so on. (10, 14)

2.   **The answer is 1.** Autotransfusion is contraindicated if the patient has cancer, if gross contamination from the bowel or stomach contents has occurred, or, in the case of a trauma patient, if the wounds are more than 4 hours old. (12)

3.   **The answer is 3.** Drugs can affect the production of collagen and protein synthesis, directly affecting the total healing process. In addition, smoking has an impact on wound healing, since it can reduce the amount of functional hemoglobin by 10-15 percent. The result is a prolonged or abnormal healing process. (5)

4.   **The answer is 4.** Mr. T. will experience visual alterations related to the preoperative instillation of eye medications. The perioperative nurse must plan interventions specific to maintaining safety for Mr. T. after the administration of medication. (10)

5.   **The answer is 1.** If not premedicated, the patient is the most accurate source of information. If patient information is not consistent with the physician's orders, informed consent, or surgery schedule, the surgeon should be notified immediately for clarification. (14, 11)

6.   **The answer is 2.** The eyes should be washed with cotton balls and a nonirritating solution (surgeon's preference). Prep should begin at the nose and continue outward toward the cheeks. Prep solution should be rinsed with warm sterile water. Chlorhexidine gluconate should not be used for or near the eyes, ears, or mouth. (11)

7.   **The answer is 3.** Physiologic monitoring consists of continual observation of the patient's vital signs, oxygen saturation, skin condition and color, and any changes in the patient's physical or behavioral status. (4, 12)

8.   **The answer is 4.** Any significant changes, either in vital signs, cardiac rhythm, or sensorium, should be reported to the surgeon immediately for appropriate corrective action. (4)

9. **The answer is 4.** Correct information will contribute to the desired outcome: *Patient will demonstrate knowledge of the physiological and psychological responses to surgical intervention.* Coughing is not recommended after surgery, since this activity may increase intraocular pressure. The physician will determine when Mr. T. may remove the eye patch and shield. Providing Mr. T. with information about what to expect will increase his ability to cope with and participate in his plan of care. (11)

10. **The answer is 1.** Ongoing evaluation of the patient's status is continued after discharge as the patient participates in his own care. Achieving this outcome is enhanced as the perioperative nurse validates the patient's understanding of the discharge plan and instructions. Asking the patient to repeat verbally his or her understanding of the discharge instructions is one method for evaluating the patient's understanding. (13)

11. **The answer is 1.** Patient teaching should be individualized and should include content related to postoperative activities and limitations. Certain types of activities may increase intraocular pressure to a dangerous level. The other options represent information that is either inaccurate or unnecessary. (10)

12. **The answer is 3.** Adequate oxygen is critical for wound healing. Mr. W's hemoglobin is low, which suggests an alteration in the oxygen carrying capacity of the blood from the lungs to the tissues. (5)

13. **The answer is 3.** The circulating nurse must know how to care for and position the microscope, and must take special care of lenses to avoid breaking, scratching, or leaving fingerprints. This includes tightening to fingertip tightness only, being careful not to cross-thread during attachment; when attaching the lens, performing the task over a padded surface to prevent accidental breakage if dropped; and following the manufacturer's recommendations during the cleaning process. (12)

14. **The answer is 3.** The patient classified by the American Society of Anesthesiology (A.S.A.) as Class 4 demonstrates severe systemic disorders that are already life-threatening and that are not always correctable by surgery planned. The letter "E" is placed beside the numerical class to indicate that this patient is operated on as an emergency and is considered a poor risk and/or in poor physical condition, with no evaluation performed owing to the acuteness of the situation. (4)

15. **The answer is 2.** A preoperative teaching program should include a general orientation to the surgical experience and instructions in anticipated postoperative activities. It is important to let patients know what they can expect postoperatively, particularly when an occurrence may cause the uninformed patient significant alarm. Blood-tinged urine is a common occurrence after surgery for T.U.R.P. If not informed, the patient may be alarmed by the site of blood in the urine postoperatively. (13, SurgRef)

16. **The answer is 2.** The irrigation solution of choice for a T.U.R.P. is 1.5% glycine solution. Irrigation solutions should be used at body temperature. (SurgRef)

17. **The answer is 1.** Regional anesthesia works to compromise the sensory system. The perioperative nurse who is planning care for such patients must include interventions focused on provision of comfort measures and maintenance of patient safety in light of the patient's altered sensorium. (6)

18. **The answer is 3.** All items to be chemically disinfected should be thoroughly cleaned, rinsed, and dried prior to beginning the process. Following the recommended immersion time, the item should be aseptically removed and rinsed with copious amounts of sterile water. The recommended immersion time for high-level disinfection with 2% glutaraldehyde is 10 minutes. (6)

19. **The answer is 4.** To maximize the efficiency and safety of the dispersive electrode, certain general placement/handling guidelines should be followed. For a patient having a T.U.R.P., the dispersive electrode (ground pad) should be positioned on the lateral aspect of the thigh after the patient has been positioned. (12, SurgRef)

20. **The answer is 4.** Hemorrhage is one postoperative complication associated with T.U.R.P. After resection of the hypertrophied prostate, fragments of tissue and blood clots are washed out of the bladder. Total removal of all fragments of tissue is required to prevent postoperative bleeding and/or complications. (SurgRef)

21. **The answer is 2.** To prevent chills and shivering, which would increase the oxygen demand, the nurse must be aware of the patient's temperature and take appropriate steps to correct the condition. (13)

22. **The answer is 2.** Mr. E. had spinal anesthesia. Cerebrospinal fluid pressure causes stress on the nerves between the cranium and the brain. Postspinal headaches, not seen with epidural techniques, can occur immediately or within 24 to 48 hours after injection. The treatment usually consists of bedrest, increased fluid intake, sedation, and, in severe cases, a blood patch graft to seal the hole (5-10 mL of the patient's blood via an epidural injection). (4)

23. **The answer is 2.** The O.R. schedule for an open reduction tibia, right tibial rodding does not suggest to the surgical team the presence of a rod in place that must be removed. Knowing that removal of an intermedular tibial nail may require special instrumentation, the perioperative nurse who discovers the discrepancy between the O.R. schedule and the history and physical/informed consent should inform the O.R. team of the planned procedure as soon as possible. This will allow the team to make any additional necessary preparations for the patient, thereby avoiding any unnecessary patient delays. (9)

24. **The answer is 1.** The Sellick maneuver is the application of cricoid pressure. (4)

25. **The answer is 3.** The induction and reversal stages of anesthesia are dangerous times for the patient, since physiologic changes could trigger unexpected events. The perioperative nurse must constantly be aware of the patient's status and be prepared to assist anesthesia personnel to prevent unnecessary injury. (4)

26. **The answer is 1.** It is important to assess Mrs. E.'s feelings about her surgery; it can be a devastating blow psychologically, since women may feel they have lost their primary sexual characteristic and therefore can no longer function as sexual women. (SurgRef)

27. **The answer is 2.** The definition of Class II (Clean-contaminated wounds) is "operative wounds in which the respiratory, alimentary, genital or urinary tract is entered under controlled conditions and without unusual contamination." Specifically, operations involving the biliary tract, appendix, vagina, and oropharynx are included, provided there is no evidence of infection or no major break in aseptic technique. (5)

28. **The answer is 1.** When planning positions for any procedure, certain factors to protect the skin and soft tissue should be considered, including the patient's age, general health status, weight distribution, blood pressure, hydration status, and proposed length of immobility. Vascular changes that accompany a diagnosis of diabetes increase Mrs. E.'s risk of developing skin breakdown related to potential excessive pressure of positioning. In making intraoperative and postoperative evaluations of skin integrity, the perioperative nurse should know the preoperative baseline established in the nursing assessment. (11)

29. **The answer is 3.** Patients with preexisting or coexisting diseases are more prone to wound infections due to a compromise in the body's immune response. Maintaining an aseptic environment is paramount in preventing exogenous contamination of the surgical wound. The perioperative nurse must ensure the sterility of all instruments and supplies and the proper preparation of the surgical site, and must monitor all activities and personnel involved with the procedure in order to maintain a safe, therapeutic environment. (5)

30. **The answer is 4.** While each of these nursing diagnoses represents standardized nursing care for the perioperative patient, Mrs. E. has an added risk for injury related to her bilateral hip prostheses. (9)

31. **The answer is 3.** For an individual with a history of bilateral total hip replacement, the lithotomy position would increase the risk of hip dislocation. The perioperative nurse should consult with the surgeon and anesthesiologist to determine the position for optimal patient safety and exposure of the surgical site. (11)

32. **The answer is 1.** In promoting wound healing during the immediate postoperative period, the perioperative nurse must observe carefully for hemorrhage in the surgical patient. (13)

33. **The answer is 3.** Most patients do not understand the purpose of the preoperative medication and tend to think the shot will "put them out". Therefore, they may arrive in the preoperative holding area anxious because they are still awake, thinking the medication is not working properly. With proper education concerning the purpose of the medication, the patient will arrive relaxed, which will assist in the administration of the actual anesthetic agents and adjunctive agents used during surgery. (4)

34. **The answer is 2.** The identification of a malfunctioning scope and a 3000 cc fluid deficit would suggest that fluid was leaking. The distended abdomen would suggest the nursing diagnosis of fluid volume excess. (7)

35. **The answer is 1.** The proper handling of any piece of equipment used in surgery is the responsibility of every member of the surgical team. Equipment should be inspected by the user prior to and after each use. (12)

36. **The answer is 3.** Outcome standards are concerned with the quality of results. The outcome in this case was not expected. Quality assurance activities will want to look at problems or circumstances that contributed to the undesired outcome, and identify changes that may be implemented to prevent the occurrence from happening again. (15)

37. **The answer is 4.** For a left nephrectomy, the patient will be in a lateral recumbent position. In this position, the lower leg is flexed and a pillow is placed between the legs, with feet supported with the pillow. A safety strap is placed across the thigh (out of the operative field). (11, SurgRef)

38. **The answer is 1.** In analyzing arterial blood gas values, the following values are considered to be within normal range: pO_2 = 80-100 mm Hg; pCO_2 = 35-45 mm Hg (dissolved CO_2 in blood); pH = 7.40 (7.35-7.45); HCO_3 = 22-26 mEq/L ; B.E. = -2 to +2; O_2 sat = 95% or greater. Arterial blood gas values are reported to the surgical team. In order to prescribe the correct therapy for acid-base imbalance, knowing how to interpret arterial blood gas reports is essential. (4)

39. **The answer is 3.** The patient in a lateral recumbent position may demonstrate physiologic effects on the respiratory system. The simple lateral position reduces vital capacity 10 percent and tidal volume 8 percent; the kidney position decreases vital capacity by 14.5 percent due to impairment of chest expansion in all directions. (11)

40. **The answer is 4.** Malignant hyperthermia syndrome (M.H.S.) is a dominantly inherited trait, but it remains dormant until one of the triggering agents or circumstances is activated. Since the patient has referred to an occurrence during surgery of another family member, it is important for the nurse to collect more data about the nature and type of that occurrence. If the information shared is consistent with a malignant hyperthermia crisis, the anesthesiologist should be contacted immediately. (4)

41. **The answer is 2.** One symptom of malignant hyperthermia is a sudden rise in temperature (1° F every 15 minutes) to as high as 108° F or higher. Nursing measures for treating a malignant hyperthermia crisis include those directed at cooling the patient. (4)

42. **The answer is 4.** From information gathered during the preoperative assessment, the perioperative nurse may determine that the patient is at risk for malignant hyperthermia syndrome. The nursing care plan for this patient must include preoperative preparation for the potential of a malignant hyperthermia syndrome

crisis. Precautions include assuring the availability of iced saline solution, Dantrium (unmixed), and additional drugs and supplies as directed by protocol. (4)

43. **The answer is 4.** Having been alerted to the potential for a malignant hyperthermia crisis, the perioperative team should prepare for such an occurrence to avoid wasting precious time during a crisis. Desired outcomes for this patient reflect actions taken to avoid or effectively manage such a crisis should it occur. (4)

44. **The answer is 1.** Although 80 percent of M.H.S. crises occur in surgery, the patient should be closely monitored for the next 72 hours, since the mortality rate from latent crisis is still high. (4)

45. **The answer is 4.** Naloxone (Narcan) is the reversal agent of choice for Demerol and most other narcotic analgesics. (AppA)

46. **The answer is 1.** As an antianxiety medication commonly used preoperatively, Versed is a short-acting depressant with clinical action similar to Valium but with fewer adverse effects. (AppA)

47. **The answer is 4.** In 1987, in response to the needs of persons working in "high-risk" areas, the C.D.C. established the Universal Precautions concept for health-care workers, designed to protect personnel from unknown exposure from the patient or the environment. Through the implementation of the Universal Precautions, the need for isolation of specific cases, and the special cleaning procedures associated with these cases, is no longer applicable. All procedures and/or patients are potentially contaminated; therefore, they are treated alike. (5)

48. **The answer is 4.** Recommended Practice V of the A.O.R.N. Recommended Practices for Basic Aseptic Technique states that *a sterile field should be constantly monitored and maintained.* Under no circumstances should a sterile field be covered for use at a later time, since covering and removal of the cover can cause contamination of the field. To monitor the field and maintain its integrity, the field should be in constant view. (5)

49. **The answer is 3.** Contamination can occur accidentally through movement around the sterile field by any member of the team. Contamination from the surgical team usually is related to direct contact contamination. The risk of infection related to the physical environment (i.e., air) is not as great as the human factor. (5)

50. **The answer is 3.** If the drapes become permeated or moist, they must be considered contaminated, and corrective action must be initiated to cover the area in question or to change the drapes. In this instance, a few cc's is not enough to justify completely tearing down and redoing the setup. (5)

51. **The answer is 2.** A patient with a fracture is at risk for additional injury and pain when moved. By transferring Mr. S. in his bed, his traction will be maintained. Unnecessary pain and movement will be avoided. (SurgRef)

52. **The answer is 3.** Elevated temperature, tachycardia, decreased skin turgor, and elevated hematocrit are all indicative of dehydration. This nursing diagnosis reflects unique aspects of Mr. S.'s condition. (9, 10)

53. **The answer is 3.** Only choice 3 addresses maintaining fluid volume. (4)

54. **The answer is 4.** Due to his substance abuse and dehydration, Mr. S.'s risk for impaired wound healing is increased. This nursing diagnosis would be *Potential for impaired skin integrity related to dehydration and substance abuse.* (5, 9, 11)

55. **The answer is 1.** This more critical adverse effect occurs when the anesthetic level is too high, thereby depressing the cardiac and respiratory systems. (4)

56. **The answer is 4.** Due to depression of the respiratory and cardiac systems, it is necessary to provide support until the condition passes. The agent is absorbed and detoxified in the body. (4)

57. **The answer is 3.** Spinal anesthesia can result in urinary retention due to an anesthetic-induced decrease in bladder tone; oliguria is a symptom of dehydration. (4)

58. **The answer is 1.** Treatment is to monitor urinary output, increase fluid volume, and administer appropriate diuretics. Increased intravascular fluid volume will decrease Mr. S.'s hemoglobin and hematocrit. (4)

59. **The answer is 2.** Radiologic procedures are used during the surgical procedure. As with any potential hazard, the perioperative nurse ensures protection. Only choice 2 is unique to Mr. S's condition. (13)

60. **The answer is 4.** In the supine position, the heels, elbows, and sacrum are the pressure points. (11)

61. **The answer is 3.** Only choice 3 describes a complete and cyclical nursing process. (9)

62. **The answer is 1.** Normal serum potassium values are in the range of 3.5-5 mEq/L; those of sodium are in the range of 136-145 mEq/L. A deficit state of these electrolytes could produce potential intraoperative and postoperative complications. (9)

63. **The answer is 3.** As a pre-teen, Vanessa may be comfortable in either group. Preoperative instruction must begin with the needs of the individual. Although choice 4 appears to be a good answer, postponement will not allow Vanessa to process what she learns, and her anxiety on the day of surgery may preclude learning. (10, AppC)

64. **The answer is 1.** Preoperative patient teaching is an independent domain of nursing. (9)

65. **The answer is 4.** It will help Vanessa to handle the objects that will be used in her care. The perioperative nurse's teaching plan should begin with the learning needs that Vanessa identifies. (SurgRef, AppC)

66. **The answer is 1.** Choices 2 and 3 apply to all patients. Choice 4 is inappropriate for a 10-year old who has demonstrated Vanessa's level of maturity. (AppC)

67. **The answer is 4.** Surgery on a child is a stressful event for a family system. (AppC)

68. **The answer is 2.** Perioperative patient goals include maintaining skin integrity and comfort levels. Intraoperative nursing interventions included application of dressing and tape as well as catheter insertion. Determination of the outcomes of these interventions must include the above. (13)

69. **The answer is 3.** The perioperative nurse applied the dressing and is knowledgeable regarding aseptic technique. (5)

70. **The answer is 4.** Because the postoperative evaluation is incomplete, it is premature to digress from these activities. (13)

71. **The answer is 2.** These may be isolated incidents. Given the frequency of use of Foley catheters and this type of dressing, however, there is potential for these types of occurrences in many services. It would be necessary to use the appropriate indicators to determine incidence and possible trends regarding these types of occurrences. (15)

72. **The answer is 3.** All other choices are standard for all surgical patients. Only choice 3 acknowledges the vulnerability of pediatric patients to loss of body heat. (2, AppC)

73. **The answer is 2.** Mr. H.'s anxiety has increased with the start of surgery. He will benefit from relaxation techniques and normal breathing. Physiologic monitoring must be maintained and the surgeon notified of any changes. (4)

74. **The answer is 4.** Mr. H. has a decreased level of CO_2 (4)

75. **The answer is 1.** This state is characterized by tachypnea, sensorium changes, and numbness and tingling of the hands and face. (4)

76. **The answer is 2.** Because this condition is usually accompanied by anxiety, the patient needs emotional support, as well as measures to assist in the restoration of a normal level of CO_2. (4)

77. **The answer is 3.** Epinephrine is a vasoconstrictor and a cardiac stimulant. (4)

78. **The answer is 2.** Measures are required to monitor and support the cardiac stimulation and vasoconstriction characteristics of epinephrine. (4)

79. **The answer is 4.** Mr. H.'s reaction is probably transient but does require further monitoring. (4)

80. **The answer is 4.** His family can be included when they arrive. Their inclusion in the process can take many forms other than repeating everything to them. (10)

81. **The answer is 1.** Most complications of this procedure are neurological in nature. (SurgRef)

82. **The answer is 3.** In regional anesthesia, motor function may be affected. (4)

83. **The answer is 3.** Cell damage occurs at temperatures above 120° F. (2)

84. **The answer is 3.** This is a deep, gasping type of respiration associated with acidosis. (4)

85. **The answer is 2.** Fatty tissue is relatively avascular and therefore can lack an adequate oxygen supply to support good wound healing. (5)

86. **The answer is 1.** A preoperative teaching program should include a general orientation to the surgical experience. (10)

87. **The answer is 3.** This is the starting point for all patient teaching. What the nurse teaches the patient (the patient's learning needs) is dictated by both the patient's perceived needs and those determined by the nurse. It is especially important with adults to acknowledge their prior learning and to employ that learning as the baseline for subsequent teaching. (10)

88. **The answer is 4.** Mr. R. needs support at this time. It would not be comforting to him to have the nurse walk away and begin paging other staff. (4)

89. **The answer is 1.** As a patient advocate, the perioperative nurse respects the patient's dignity by avoiding unnecessary exposure of the patient. (11)

90. **The answer is 2.** Adequate cell oxygenation is essential for wound healing. Smoking can reduce the functional hemoglobin by 10-15 percent. In addition, CV disease further impairs tissue perfusion. (5)

91. **The answer is 2.** In his theory, Maslow maintained that higher-level needs (e.g., self-esteem, self-actualization) cannot be met until lower-level needs (e.g., physical comfort) are satisfied. (10)

92. **The answer is 4.** These needs focus on feelings of being safe in a non-threatening environment that is comfortable and familiar. (10)

93. **The answer is 1.** Efforts to assist the patient to attain an optimal level of independence must respect, and incorporate into the patient care plan, the patient's autonomy. (10)

94. **The answer is 4.** Patient education is important in preparation for home self-care. A variety of methods and media can be used to address the needs of patients. (SurgRef)

95. **The answer is 1.** This is a rare metabolic disorder. (4, 10)

96. **The answer is 4.** The use of the ultra-short-acting barbiturate, pentothal, is absolutely contraindicated in patients with porphyria. (4)

97. **The answer is 4.** There are several treatment choices. Ms. N. first will need to recover from anesthesia to be able to consider these options fully. Choice 2 would not allow this. Choice 1 (informed consent) is not the role of the perioperative nurse; it is the responsibility of the surgeon. (SurgRef, 14)

98. **The answer is 1.** Only partial weight-bearing is allowed for patients when the greater trochanter has been removed. To facilitate recovery, the patient should be taught techniques for specific postoperative exercises, assisted ambulation, and any other postoperative activities recommended by the surgeon. (11, SurgRef)

99. **The answer is 4.** The patient's skin cannot be sterilized. Therefore, measures must be taken to reduce both the resident and transient flora. This should be done with povidone/iodine or chlorhexidine gluconate beginning the night before surgery. Shaving should be done within two hours of surgery. (10, 11)

100. **The answer is 3.** It is important for the T.H.A. patient to remember to maintain a degree of abduction. Crossing one leg over the other requires adduction. Laying on the operative side will also adduct the operative leg. Sleeping with the toes pointed in is unacceptable since external rotation is desirable in the operative leg. (SurgRef)

101. **The answer is 2.** A side-effect of steroids is poor wound healing. (SurgRef)

102. **The answer is 3.** Safety and security focus on feelings of being safe in a non-threatening environment. Surgery promotes fear of the unknown and possible loss of a body part, which threatens safety and security. (10)

103. **The answer is 1.** Patients may not want all the details of their surgery; it is therefore important to assess their level of knowledge before the teaching is implemented. (10)

104. **The answer is 4.** Diuretics are prescribed to promote the excretion of sodium and water. Many diuretics, however, also deplete potassium. A danger of hypokalemia (decreased potassium) in surgery is the increased likelihood of dangerous dyshymias. (AppB)

105. **The answer is 1.** Attaining informed consent is the responsibility of the physician. Nurses and other persons are responsible only for witnessing the consent, which means that the patient has signed it. (10)

106. **The answer is 3.** Hair should be removed as close to the surgical time as possible, but not in the operating room suite. Hair removal is not required for all surgical procedures. (10)

107. **The answer is 2.** An exploratory laparotomy can be performed following trauma to the abdomen, or when a patient has undetermined abdominal pain. Once the abdomen is opened and explored, the specific corrective procedure related to Mr. T.'s injuries can be performed. (SurgRef)

108. **The answer is 1.** Move the patient slowly and deliberately, maintaining total awareness of physiological impairment that can occur related to positioning. (11)

109. **The answer is 2.** Body weight against the abdominal wall limits diaphragmatic movement, resulting in increased airway pressure with difficulty in ventilation and limiting tidal volume. (11)

110. **The answer is 3.** Rapid lowering of legs could cause a sudden drop in blood pressure (500-800 mL of blood may shift from lumbar area to legs). Legs should be raised and lowered together to avoid strain on the hip joint and surrounding nerves. (11)

111. **The answer is 3.** In the Trendelenburg position, abdominal contents are shifted upward and press on the diagram, thus decreasing diaphragmatic expansion. (11)

112. **The answer is 4.** Saphenous and peroneal nerve injuries are usually associated with the lithotomy position and with the use of stirrups. Injury to the peroneal nerve may occur if the thigh is compressed against the stirrup and if legs are not raised simultaneously. Saphenous nerve damage can occur if the nerve is pressed between the metal popliteal knee support stirrup and the medial tibial condyle. These injuries result in numbness of the calf and possible paralysis. (11)

113. **The answer is 1.** Patients who are allergic to seafood may also be allergic to iodine; therefore, povidone/iodine should not be used as a skin prep. (11)

114. **The answer is 4.** A bipolar active electrode has a forceps configuration. In the bipolar electrode, one tip acts as the active pole while the other tip acts as the return (dispersive pole). With bipolar, a ground pad is not required, since the dispersive electrode is one of the tips. Power is distributed to a very limited area, making it safe for use on delicate tissues. (12)

115. **The answer is 1.** Since the patient has food in his stomach and may vomit and aspirate the contents, a precautionary measure is to press on the cricoid to close off the esophagus in the event the patient does vomit. (4)

116. **The answer is 3.** Atropine dries up secretions so that the patient will not choke or aspirate on secretions during surgery. Other side effects are restlessness and possible urinary retention. (4)

117. **The answer is 4.** Sedative/hypnotics may cause confusion in the elderly. Desired effects are reduced anxiety and promotion of sleep. (4, AppA)

118. **The answer is 1.** Vistaril reduces anxiety but also has an antiemetic effect. Morphine sulfate and sublimaze are narcotics; Robinul is an anticholinergic. (AppA)

119. **The answer is 4.** An extremely effective method that nurses can use to reduce anxiety is to maintain an attitude of caring. Valium and slow deep breaths will help but are not as important as the nurse's attitude. Reassurance by itself often is not therapeutic. (4)

120. **The answer is 1.** Many patients do not understand the purpose of the preoperative medication. This is a time for the nurse to clarify and provide further education as needed. (4)

121. **The answer is 3.** The circulating nurse should stay with the patient during induction to assist anesthesia as needed. The safety strap should be applied pre-induction. Patent suction equipment and low noise levels are also important. (4)

122. **The answer is 1.** Handling of the bowel is most likely to cause a decrease in intestinal peristalsis. (SurgRef)

123. **The answer is 3.** Instruction close to the time of surgery will be most effective. (10)

124. **The answer is 3.** Some patients emerge with wild, uncontrolled movements, while other emerge smoothly. It is important to handle patients gently so that they do not harm themselves. (4)

125. **The answer is 3.** Narcotics depress respirations; it is essential to assess respirations to determine if a reversal agent is needed. (AppA)

126. **The answer is 1.** Muscle twitching or fasculations are often seen when Anectine is administered. Anectine can also produce flushing, but not as commonly. (AppA)

127. **The answer is 3.** When patients or their families have an unusual anesthesia history, it is imperative that the perioperative nurse notify the anesthetist immediately so that the patient can be evaluated. One sign of malignant hyperthermia is a sudden rise in temperature after administration of certain anesthetic agents (e.g., halothane). (4)

128. **The answer is 4.** Epinephrine is a vasoconstrictor, and is often administered to control bleeding. Side effects may include tachycardia and restlessness. (4)

129. **The answer is 2.** Carcinoma cells can become disseminated with vigorous scrubbing. Therefore, it is important to use gentle yet comprehensive strokes. (12)

130. **The answer is 3.** Aseptic techniques must be maintained at all times; gloves must therefore be changed if contaminated. (11)

131. **The answer is 4.** Frozen sections are sent dry, in a container or on a towel, properly labeled, and immediately given to the pathologist for microscopic examination. Routine specimens are covered with a preservative and usually do not need immediate attention. (12)

132. **The answer is 4.** It is recommended that tourniquets applied to a leg be inflated for no more than 1 1/2 hours. The cuff should be placed at the point of maximum circumference of the extremity. Tourniquet use is not contraindicated in persons over 50 years, or in obese patients, but is contraindicated in persons with vascular disease or poor peripheral circulation. Selection and placement should be determined by age, anatomy, and medical condition. (12)

133. **The answer is 1.** The primary goal of the postanesthesia nursing care is the safe recovery and arousal of the patient from the effects of anesthesia. The other three activities also are important, but are not primary. (13)

134. **The answer is 3.** If a patient is experiencing postoperative pain, vital signs are often elevated and the patient is restless. After effective pain management is obtained and vital signs are stabilized, the patient should be able to rest more comfortably. (13)

135. **The answer is 3.** It is essential that the nurse assess and document preoperative mental and motor status of a neurosurgical patient, so that postoperative deficit can be determined. (13)

136. **The answer is 2.** Humidity levels should be kept between 50 and 55 percent to prevent static electricity. (2)

137. **The answer is 2.** Room temperature should be increased 10-15 minutes before pediatric surgery, since children rapidly lose body heat. (2, AppC)

138. **The answer is 3.** The goal and purpose of the Perioperative Standards is quality care for the surgical patient. Communication and accreditation are important, but are not the primary purpose of the standards. (3)

139. **The answer is 4.** When transporting or moving a patient, the nurse's primary objective is to provide for patient safety. (11)

140. **The answer is 2.** Patient complaints that are not measurable or observable are examples of subjective data, also called symptoms. (10)

141. **The answer is 2.** If a patient's WBC count is elevated, it usually indicates a pre-existing infection, and surgery may be delayed or cancelled. (10)

142. **The answer is 2.** In performing a preoperative psychologic assessment, the nurse should be sure to verify the patient's reasons for anxiety or fear and identify his or her support systems and methods of coping. Relaxation techniques are a method of coping. (10)

143. **The answer is 1.** Medical diagnoses identify specific disease processes and usually remain the same during the course of treatment. Nursing diagnoses identify the patient's response to the disease, injury, or situation, and focus on problems that nurses are capable and licensed to treat. Nursing diagnoses change as the patient progresses through treatment. (10)

144. **The answer is 2.** Gas exchange problems can be life-threatening, thus should receive priority over the other responses. (10)

145. **The answer is 3.** Autotransfusion is contraindicated in persons with cancer, since cancer cells could be circulating in the blood. It is also contraindicated if gross contamination from the bowel or stomach contents has occurred, or, in the case of a trauma patient, if the wounds are more than 4 hours old. (12)

146. **The answer is 2.** If the patient's condition is critical, there may not be time for a complete preincision count, or perhaps any preincision count at all. It is recommended that the incident be documented, that the intraoperative and closing counts be performed, and that an X-ray be performed immediately after surgery. (14)

147. **The answer is 3.** It is of primary importance that Universal Precautions be used on all patients. This means that gloves should be worn at all times when in contact with, or when there is the potential for contact with, blood or other body fluids. Health care workers with exudate lesions or weeping dermatitis should refrain from all direct patient care and from handling patient care equipment. Needles should not be recapped. Gloves are not necessary at *all* times while engaging in direct patient contact. (5)

148. **The answer is 4.** The circulating nurse should stay with the patient and help with positioning while providing ongoing emotional support to the patient. (4)

149. **The answer is 1.** Patients can suffer harm if their skin is exposed directly to the thermal unit. Always place a sheet between the blanket and patient for protection. (12)

150. **The answer is 2.** To date, courts have refused to find the perioperative nurse negligent when a surgeon continues with a surgical procedure after the nurse has informed the surgeon that there is no consent for the procedure. The courts suggest that the perioperative nurse has met her legal duty by directing the surgeon's attention to the lack of consent. (14)

Page 3:   II.A.1, Footnote: *Standards and Recommended Practices*, 1991, I:1-2

                       II.A.4, Footnote: *Standards and Recommended Practices*, 1991, I:1-3

Page 10/11:   Traffic patterns: Controlling the Environment

                       Supplies and Equipment

                       Environmental Safety

AORN *Standards and Recommended Practices* states that the "practice setting should be designed to facilitate movement of patients and personnel through defined areas within the surgical suite. Environmental and dress controls increase as progression is made from unrestricted to restricted areas." The "movement of clean and sterile supplies and equipment should be separated as much as possible from soiled equipment and waste by space, time, or traffic patterns." These recommended practices have been interpreted as follows:

Page 13:   V.A.1. All persons who enter the semi-restricted and restricted areas of the surgical suite should be in surgical attire intended for use only within the surgical suite (AORN, 1991). Footnote: *Standards and Recommended Practices*, 1991, III:18-2. This recommended practice has been interpreted as follows:

Page 13:   V.A.3a—In accordance with AORN recommended practices (1991), the scrub suit should be made of fabric that meets or exceeds the National Fire Prevention Association (NFPA) standards for proper fabric construction. Footnote: *Standards and Recommended Practices*, 1991, III:18-2.

Page 14:   B.1. Patients should be provided with a safe, clean environment free from dust and organic debris (AORN, 1991). Footnote: Standards *and Recommended Practices*, 1991, III:9-1. This AORN recommended practice has been interpreted as follows:

Page 32:   III. Standards of Perioperative Nursing Practice (1992) The following AORN *Standards of Perioperative Nursing Practice* have been interpreted as follows:

Page 35:   V.4. To assist the nurse in determining whether this level has been achieved, the AORN has researched and developed the *Competency Statements for Perioperative Nursing Practice* applicable to nurses working in surgery for 6 months or longer (AORN, 1991). Footnote: *Standards and Recommended Practices*, 1991, I:2-1-I:2-12.

Page 35:   V.5 Using the nursing process format and the *Standards of Perioperative Nursing Practice* as the framework, the competency statements can be directly correlated with current technology implementation of patient care activities. The statements are written in measurable terms, clearly redefining the need for qualified registered nurses performing specialized tasks for the patient undergoing surgical intervention.

Page 56:   XI.A.1: According to AORN, the following recommended practices are considered the minimum standards of care for the patient undergoing surgery with local anesthesia (AORN, 1991) Footnote: *Standards and Recommended Practices*, 1991, III:8 1-3.

Page 74:   II. According to the AORN *Patient Outcome Standards for Perioperative Nursing*, protecting the patient from infection is a primary goal (AORN, 1991). Footnote: *Standards and Recommended Practices*, 1991, II:5-1. Therefore, it becomes the responsibility of all persons rendering care to the patient during the perioperative period.

Page 75:   II.C.3...This can be accomplished through the implementation of strict traffic control procedures and policies, as suggested by the AORN *Recommended Practices for Traffic Patterns in the Surgical Suite* (AORN, 1991). Footnote: *Standards and Recommended Practices*, 1991, III:21-2.

Page 84:   D.1. As a means of preventing infection during any invasive procedure, the AORN established *Recommended Practices for Basic Aseptic Technique, Recommended Practices for Surgical Hand Scrubs,* and *Recommended Practices for Evaluating Aseptic Barrier Materials for Surgical Gowns and Drapes*, as a guide for anyone who is present during the procedure, either directly or indirectly involved with patient care (AORN, 1991). Footnote: *Standards and Recommended Practices*, 1991, III:1-1-III:1-4; III:6-1-6-3; III:19-1-19-5. This recommended practice has been interpreted as follows:

Page 107:   C. Recommended Practices for Sterilization: AORN has developed *Recommended Practices for Sterilization and Disinfection*. The recommended practices have been interpreted as follows:

Page 107:   C.3.a. All wrapped articles to be sterilized should be packaged in materials that meet the criteria given in the AORN *Recommended Practices for Selection and Use of Packaging Materials*.

page 108:   C.5.c,d,e. These highlighted areas are author interpretations. They are not actual recommended practices as is 5.a.

Page 109:   7--EO sterilization should be used for processing heat and moisture sensitive items. EO sterilizers and aerators should be used and vented according to the manufacturer's written instructions.

Page 110:   9.b,c,d,e. These highlighted areas are author interpretation. They are not actual recommended practices as is 9.a.

Page 111:   10.a Performance records for all sterilizers should be maintained for each cycle and retained for the period of time indicated by individual policy and/or the state's statute of limitations.

Page 111:   10.c. This highlighted area is author interpretation. It is not an actual recommended practice as is 10.a.

Page 112:   12.a. Preventive maintenance of all sterilizers should be performed according to individual policy on a scheduled basis by qualified personnel, using the sterilizer manufacturer's service manual as a reference.

Page 160:   II.1. The Association of Operating Room Nurses (AORN) has developed (1975) and reaffirmed (1990) the *Standards of Perioperative Nursing Practice* to ensure that guidelines are available for delivering quality patient care during the perioperative period. The standards are interpreted as:

Page 225:   3.a. Footnote: *Perioperative Nursing: Principles and Practice*, 1993, pg 29.

*all references to AORN material are from the 1991 *Standards and Recommended Practices*.